Access 2000 Client/Server Solutions

Lars Klander

President, CEO
Keith Weiskamp

Publisher
Steve Sayre

Acquisitions Editor
Stephanie Wall

Marketing Specialist
Tracy Schofield

Project Editor
Toni Zuccarini Ackley

Technical Reviewer
Mark Linsenbardt

Production Coordinator
Laura Wellander

Cover Design
Jody Winkler

Layout Design
April Nielsen

CD-ROM Developer
Robert Clarfield

The Coriolis Group, LLC
14455 North Hayden Road
Suite 220
Scottsdale, Arizona 85260

480/483-0192
FAX 480/483-0193
http://www.coriolis.com

Library of Congress Cataloging-in-Publication Data
Klander, Lars.
    Access 2000 client/server solutions/ by Lars Klander
        p.   cm.
    Includes index.
    ISBN 1-57610-417-6
    1. Microsoft Access   2. Client/server computing.
3. Application software—Development.   I. Title.

QA76.9.D3 K5697   2000
005.75'85 — dc21   99-051342

CIP

Printed in the United States of America
10 9 8 7 6 5 4 3 2 1

14455 North Hayden Road • Suite 220 • Scottsdale, Arizona 85260

Dear Reader:

Coriolis Technology Press was founded to create a very elite group of books: the ones you keep closest to your machine. Sure, everyone would like to have the Library of Congress at arm's reach, but in the real world, you have to choose the books you rely on every day *very* carefully.

To win a place for our books on that coveted shelf beside your PC, we guarantee several important qualities in every book we publish. These qualities are:

- *Technical accuracy*—It's no good if it doesn't work. Every Coriolis Technology Press book is reviewed by technical experts in the topic field, and is sent through several editing and proofreading passes in order to create the piece of work you now hold in your hands.

- *Innovative editorial design*—We've put years of research and refinement into the ways we present information in our books. Our books' editorial approach is uniquely designed to reflect the way people learn new technologies and search for solutions to technology problems.

- *Practical focus*—We put only pertinent information into our books and avoid any fluff. Every fact included between these two covers must serve the mission of the book as a whole.

- *Accessibility*—The information in a book is worthless unless you can find it quickly when you need it. We put a lot of effort into our indexes, and heavily cross-reference our chapters, to make it easy for you to move right to the information you need.

Here at The Coriolis Group we have been publishing and packaging books, technical journals, and training materials since 1989. We're programmers and authors ourselves, and we take an ongoing active role in defining what we publish and how we publish it. We have put a lot of thought into our books; please write to us at **ctp@coriolis.com** and let us know what you think. We hope that you're happy with the book in your hands, and that in the future, when you reach for software development and networking information, you'll turn to one of our books first.

Keith Weiskamp
President and CEO

Jeff Duntemann
VP and Editorial Director

Look For These Other Books From The Coriolis Group

Access 2000 Developer's Black Book
by Lars Klander and Dave Mercer

Access 2000 Programming Blue Book
by Wayne Brooks and Lars Klander

To Brett: My wife, my love, my inspiration

&

About The Author

Lars Klander, MCSE, MCSD, MCDBA, MCT, is the author or co-author of over a dozen books, including *Access 2000 Developer's Black Book* and *Access 2000 Programming Blue Book* for The Coriolis Group. As Vice President of Technology for KLS Enterprises, an international consulting firm, he is actively involved in the design and implementation of complex, multi-tier solutions—both with Internet front ends and Visual Basic and Access-based Win32 front ends. An experienced developer with current projects using most major development platforms and running on a variety of different operating systems, he recently won a *Visual Basic Programmer's Journal* Reader's Choice Award for his book *1001 Visual Basic Programmer's Tips*.

Klander lives in Las Vegas with his wife and brood of animals, including two large dogs and five cats, though he can more often be found in the field managing development teams and writing the (occasional) bit of program code. You can reach him at **lklander@lvcm.com**.

Acknowledgments

In publishing, like any other business, you learn quickly that the people around you can make you look good or they can make you look bad. Although my name is the only one that appears on the front of the book, it takes a lot of people to put together all the text that makes up something of this size. The number of contributors is too great to mention, but I would like to thank several people who played key roles in the finishing of this book. First and foremost, Toni Zuccarini Ackley, my good friend that I have never met, the Project Editor for the book, who always managed to cheer me up when I needed it, and was indulgent enough to laugh at my bad jokes when she needed cheering. You are always a pleasure to work with, Toni, and I look forward to our next endeavor.

Many thanks, as always, to my good friend and occasional business associate, Hal Ross of Michada Computers here in Las Vegas, who provided me with the equipment I needed to test all of the different client/server configurations discussed in this book. Couldn't have done it without you, Hal.

Laura Wellander, the Production Coordinator, and her team of layout professionals managed to take my chicken-scratch drawings and make them look good (no mean task) while still laying out a beautiful book. Robert Clarfield, the CD-ROM Developer, and Tracy Schofield, the Marketing Specialist, helped put together crucial add-ons for the book, including all the CD-ROM contents and the back cover (courtesy of Cover Designer Jody Winkler).

In addition to Toni, I have to send out real thanks and appreciation to my editors. The Copy Editor, Jennifer Mario, who slaved over chapter after chapter to help ensure that every sentence in every paragraph made sense and was readable, did a top-notch job. Just as marvelous was the Technical Editor, Mark A. Linsenbardt, who saved me many instances of "egg-on-the-face" in making sure that all the code in the book was perfect, and worked as advertised—and didn't hesitate to suggest an alternate method where appropriate.

Finally, thanks as always to Stephanie Wall, the Acquisitions Editor for the project (our third together) and David Fugate, my Agent (our who-knows-how-manyieth project together), who put this all together, and helped keep me moving through to deliver the book (mostly) on time.

Contents At A Glance

Table Of Contents

Part II   Access MDB As Front End

Chapter 7   Using Access 2000 As A Front End To SQL Server 193

Chapter 8   Using Oracle And Access For Client/Server 231

Part III   Access Data Project As Front End

Chapter 9   Introduction To Access Data Projects 271

Part VI   Appendixes

Introduction

When Microsoft released Access 1.0 for Windows 3.1, it was a significant step forward, in some ways, for database development (though there are those who would undoubtedly argue it was also a step backward). However, the simplicity of local database design that Access provided, combined with its (for the time), substantial scalability, made it a very interesting and useful addition to the Windows design universe. I remember working with the product when it first came out (in early 1991), and thinking that Microsoft was really on to something.

And they were. Since then, Access has been through many revisions, and has become one of the most commonly used database products in the world. Thankfully, Microsoft has continued to improve it substantially over the years, making the product able to handle the constantly increasing needs for database storage of most companies. Unfortunately, in modern times, data is growing too fast (in the most part) for the Jet engine (the underlying technology that drives Access) to continue to be the core of Access's processing.

At the same time as it's been making all these improvements to Access, Microsoft has also been consistently improving their server-based database product, Microsoft SQL Server. The end result of all this? SQL Server has become a powerful, flexible product—so flexible, in fact, that Microsoft has announced that, after Office 2000, the Jet engine will be retired, and Access will use a local, desktop version of SQL Server—or Access can be used to program directly against a SQL Server back end.

But don't mourn the retirement of the Jet engine—Access's loss is, in this case, your gain. The inclusion of SQL Server technology within Access at all levels, combined with new support for programming against the SQL Servers built into the Access product, has, as you might expect, resulted in a situation where developing client/server applications with Access is easier than ever before.

In addition, for experienced Access developers, transitioning to the substantially more robust SQL Server is easy because of the new Access interface to the SQL Server back end.

Hey, there's that buzzword (client/server)—and I actually managed to make it to the fourth paragraph in the Introduction before I used it. That's right—the focus in this book is on client/server design, primarily using Access as the client and either Access, Oracle, or (most commonly) SQL Server as the server.

I've been programming with Access for about as long as Access has been around, so I have tried to take my knowledge of what most commonly confronts the Access programmer when updating to a more distributed environment, and have constructed this book accordingly. You'll see things inside this Access book you probably never thought you would see in an Access book (for example, programming with Visual InterDev)—but these are concepts that are crucial to the scalability of your Access applications. So, I have struck out in a somewhat nonstandard fashion, in hopes of providing truly valuable assistance to you on the road to effective distributed development with Access and/or SQL Server.

Out of courtesy, however, I haven't leaped right into the development of COM objects, but rather have started at a point (somewhere) close to the beginning, a point that most Access programmers should be mostly familiar with by now—Data Access Objects (DAO), which I discuss in Chapter 1. In Chapter 2, I continue with DAO, this time considering the variations in the model that result from using ODBCDirect programming techniques. In Chapter 3, I look at exporting and linking tables with Access built-in support—both from the development environment and through code—with an eye toward setting the stage for Chapter 4, which in turn sets the stage (for the most part) for the rest of the book.

In Chapter 4, I introduce you to ActiveX Data Objects (ADO) and OLE DB, Microsoft's preferred modern-day solutions for programming with database products of all types—from Access to Oracle, SQL Server to DB2. Chapter 5 moves on to a consideration of converting from DAO to ADO. Chapter 6 follows up with a discussion of some advanced ADO programming techniques.

In Chapters 7 and 8, I consider using Access as a front-end product with SQL Server and Oracle at the back end. Both chapters focus on some of the issues involved with development with both products, and the architectures and engines that both products implement.

Part III, which begins with Chapter 9, looks in more detail at using Access as a front end to a SQL Server back end—particularly, using the new Access Data Project (ADP) file type as a way to communicate with and manage SQL Server databases. In Chapter 9, I overview ADPs and look at the Microsoft Development Engine (MSDE), the desktop version of SQL Server 7. In Chapter 10, I discuss the issues involved in the design of SQL Server databases, including an extensive discussion of the differences between SQL Server objects and Access objects, as well as the introduction and exploration of some new objects such as constraints. Chapter 11 concerns itself with the design and implementation of stored procedures and triggers, two special types of objects that reside at the SQL Server and execute previously compiled sequences of SQL statements.

In Chapter 12, I look at some of the other issues associated with any type of client/server development, but consider them directly from the ADP perspective, looking at transaction processing and how it works with ADPs, advanced stored procedure design, and the specifics of a new type of object for SQL Server 7 known as a database diagram. Chapter 13 considers SQL Server and ADP security issues, and how security is implemented completely differently with ADPs than it is with Access MDBs. The last chapter in the section, Chapter 14, looks at some more advanced programming issues with ADPs, integrating the knowledge of ADO that you gathered earlier in the book with the ADP technology, and also considering other specific issues, such as the design of forms and reports within the ADP environment.

Part IV looks at using Access 2000 as your primary development tool for Internet front ends. Chapter 15 considers the Data Access Page (DAP), a new Access 2000 object that lets you create HTML-based pages directly from your Access 2000 objects. It also lets you use related Microsoft technologies—such as the PivotTable control—to manage the display of data within your pages. Chapter 16 moves on with a consideration of Access 2000 and the Internet, looking at some of your other alternatives for Internet design before returning once again to DAPs and looking a bit more closely at the construction of some more complex DAP objects.

The last section, Part V, strikes out into new areas, considering how you might use different Microsoft technologies to deliver content over the Internet from your Access-built back end (whether Jet or SQL Server-based). Chapter 17 introduces Microsoft's recommended product for Internet development, Visual InterDev 6, part of Visual Studio. Chapter 18 looks at using VBScript to develop Active Server Pages (ASP) applications, a technique that lets you create browser-independent code that is still closely tied to your SQL Server or other back end.

Chapter 19 looks briefly at using Visual Basic to create Component Object Model (COM) objects, and then discusses somewhat how to integrate the COM objects with your Web applications, as well as a few of the unique issues involved in building COM objects using the Office Developer's COM Add-Ins Manager. Chapter 20 moves on to a brief discussion of programming client-side applications inside of the browser using VBScript and Dynamic HTML.

Chapter 21 returns to Active Server Pages with a discussion of database back-end programming from inside the ASP interface, including a discussion of the Data Environment and the use of ADO from inside Web server programs. Chapter 22 finishes it all off with a brief look at several types of Visual Basic projects that you can use for writing Internet-based solutions with VB, including Dynamic HTML objects, Active Documents, and Internet Information Server (IIS) objects (also known as WebClasses).

And that about covers it. Although this book is comprehensive in many ways, and will lead you down many of the paths you will need to travel, the nature of database design makes it, generally, unique to each developer's environment—meaning that you will frequently find yourself taking the code to the next level. For my part, I would love to see what you accomplish with it.

Coriolis likes to hear about what you have accomplished, as well—and also likes to hear what you liked and or didn't like about this book. On top of all that, despite my best efforts, I will be the first to admit that I am not perfect, and occasionally errors will creep into the CD-ROM or the text itself. If you find an error, or if something just doesn't seem right, don't hesitate to contact me at **lklander@lvcm.com**. Additionally, you can submit bug reports to **www.coriolis.com**, and they will make sure that I am notified. Should the error be a substantial one, we will post an errata page detailing the corrections at **www.coriolis.com**—so you may want to check there, too, to see if I have already posted the answer.

Good luck, and I hope you enjoy the book—I spent a lot of time putting it together, and hope that it brings you real value in whatever way you end up using it.

Thank you,
Lars Klander (**lklander@lvcm.com**)

Part I

Client/Server Development With DAO And ADO

Chapter 1
Working With DAO

As you hopefully already know, you can use the VBA programming language to perform advanced processing in your Access 2000 applications. When you perform such processing, you'll commonly find a need to manipulate database objects from code. Early versions of Microsoft Access, through Microsoft Access 97, supported Data Access Objects (DAO), an object model that was directly tied to the Microsoft Jet engine, as the means of accessing Access databases. Understanding how to use DAO is crucial for working with Access databases developed in any of these earlier versions.

However, Microsoft introduced ActiveX Data Objects (ADO), a part of the OLE DB object model, with the Visual Studio 5 revision early in 1997. Since that time, ADO has been extensively improved and expanded upon. Microsoft has indicated that it will release no new versions of the DAO standard, and that developers should use ADO for all new applications they design within Access 2000.

In this chapter, you'll learn about DAO, how the model is formed, and how to use it. In later chapters, you'll learn about ADO, the nature of its model, and how to use it as well. Over the course of this chapter, you'll learn how to perform common tasks with DAO. We'll start with DAO because it's simpler, and you're more likely to be familiar with it.

Introduction To Data Access Objects

Data Access Objects are used to create, modify, and remove Jet engine objects through program code. They provide you with the flexibility to move beyond the user interface to manipulate data and Jet engine objects. They can be used to perform the following tasks:

♦ Analyze the structure of an existing database

♦ Add or modify tables and queries

♦ Create new databases

♦ Change the underlying definitions for queries by modifying the Structured Query Language (SQL) on which the query is based

♦ Traverse through sets of records

♦ Modify table data

The DAO Object Model

Figure 1.1 shows an overview of the DAO Object Model for the Jet database engine—in Access 2000, the DAO 3.6 Object Library. At the top of the hierarchy is the Microsoft Jet database engine, referred to as the **DBEngine** object. The **DBEngine** object contains all the other objects that are part of the hierarchy. It's the only object that doesn't have an associated collection.

Each object within the DAO Object Model is important to you because you'll manipulate the various objects at runtime using code to accomplish the tasks required by your application. The following sections contain a description of each major object and how it affects you when you are working with DAO; more or less, the sections begin at the top of the Object Model and work their way down through the various trees and branches within the model.

Warning
Because Microsoft is gradually phasing out DAO as a development platform, you'll find that you must add the DAO 3.6 Object Library to your projects from the Tools menu References option within the VBA IDE. By default, Access 2000 will only load the ADO 2.0 library when you start a VBA project.

Understanding The Workspace Object And Workspaces Collection

The **Workspaces** collection contains **Workspace** objects. Each **Workspace** object defines the area within which a particular user operates. All security and transaction processing for a given user takes place within a particular **Workspace**. You can create multiple **Workspaces** within your programs. Moreover, you can create connections to the same database within the different **Workspaces**.

This is of great value because, using this technique, you can log in as another user behind the scenes and accomplish tasks not allowed by the security level of the current user. For

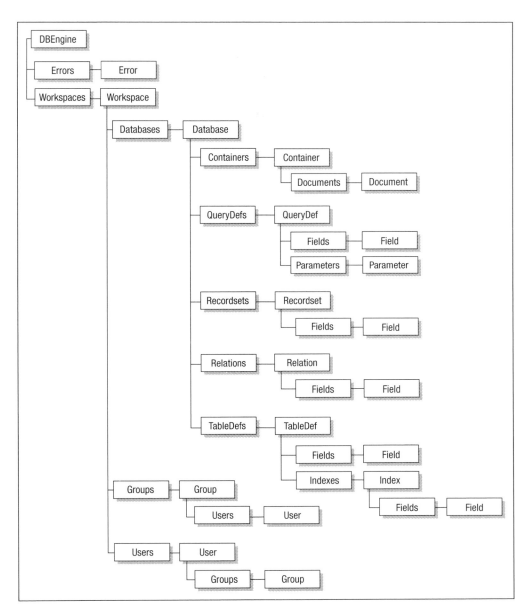

Figure 1.1
An overview of the DAO Object Model.

example, you can log in as a member of the Admins group, change the structure of a table that the current user doesn't have rights to, and log back out without the user of the system ever knowing that anything happened. The goal of such processing is to address a very common issue in client programs—the need for the program to have a higher level of access to the database than the user has.

Understanding The User Object And Users Collection

The **Users** collection contains the **User** objects for a particular **Workspace**. Each **User** object is a user account defined by a workgroup database. Because each user is a member of one or more groups, each **User** object contains a **Groups** collection that includes each group that a particular user is a member of. **User** objects can be easily added and manipulated at runtime.

It's worth considering the fact that a **User** (and, for that matter, a **Group**) within Access does not map cleanly to any of the other users- and groups-based models in the Microsoft environment. For example, when you look at security on SQL Server, it is implemented through *logins* and *roles*. Those concepts, as implemented in SQL Server, map quite closely to the users and groups maintained by Windows NT as part of its security model. Understanding **Users** and **Groups** in Access is important for programming in Access—but, in my experience, it can often create confusion for developers "moving up" to SQL Server or some other full-fledged database management system.

Understanding The Group Object And Groups Collection

The **Groups** collection contains all **Group** objects for a particular **Workspace**. Each **Group** object is a group defined by a workgroup database. Because each group contains users, the **Group** object contains a **Users** collection that consists of each user who's a member of the group. Like **User** objects, **Group** objects can be added and manipulated at runtime.

Because the last two sections seem to say different things, it is important to take a closer look: The **User** object contains a **Groups** collection—a collection that corresponds to the groups to which a given user belongs—which you would then reference as **Workspaces(**n**).Users(**n**).Groups(**n**).***property*. On the other hand, the generalized **Group** object contains a **Users** collection of its own—one that corresponds to all the members of that group. You would reference that collection as **Workspaces(**n**).Groups(**n**).Users(**n**).***property*.

Understanding The Database Object And Databases Collection

The **Databases** collection contains all the databases that are currently open within a particular **Workspace**. Multiple databases (and, therefore, multiple database objects) can be open at the same time. These open databases can be either Jet databases or external databases. A **Database** object refers to a particular database within the **Databases** collection. It's easy to loop through the **Databases** collection, printing the name of each **Database** object contained within the collection. The code to do so might look similar to the following:

```
Sub EnumerateDBs()
  Dim wksLocal As Workspace
```

```
  Dim dbsLocal As Database
  Dim dbsLocal1 As Database
  Dim dbsLocal2 As Database

  Set wksLocal = DBEngine(0)
  Set dbsLocal1 = CurrentDb
  Set dbsLocal2 = wksLocal.OpenDatabase("Northwind.mdb")
  For Each dbsLocal In wksLocal.Databases
    Debug.Print dbsLocal.Name
  Next dbsLocal
End Sub
```

This code loops through each open database within the current **Workspace**, printing the name of each open database. It's also easy to perform all the other tasks required to build, modify, and manipulate database objects at runtime.

Tip

*The **CurrentDb** function returns the currently selected database, which in the case of VBA applications will be the database with which the VBA program code is associated. You'll learn more about the **CurrentDb** function later in this chapter.*

Understanding The TableDef Object And TableDefs Collection

The **TableDefs** collection consists of all the tables contained within a particular database, whether they're open or not. The **TableDefs** collection also includes linked tables and contains detailed information about each table. It's easy to loop through the **TableDefs** collection, printing various properties (for instance, the **Name**) of each **TableDef** object contained within the collection. The code to do so might look similar to the following:

```
Sub EnumerateTables()
  Dim dbsLocal As Database
  Dim tblLocal As TableDef

  Set dbsLocal = CurrentDb
  For Each tblLocal In dbsLocal.TableDefs
    Debug.Print tblLocal.Name
  Next tblLocal
End Sub
```

This code loops through each **TableDef** in the current database, printing the name of each table. It's easy to write code that adds, deletes, modifies, and otherwise manipulates tables at runtime.

*As you work with **TableDefs**, you'll find that there are certain system-level tables in every Jet database, which the database engine will create for you automatically. You'll be able to enumerate these tables and even print out their names within your programs, but you won't be able to modify these tables directly.*

Understanding The QueryDef Object And QueryDefs Collection

The **QueryDefs** collection contains all the queries contained within a particular database, as well as information about each query. It's easy to loop through the **QueryDefs** collection, printing various pieces of information about each query. The code for doing so would look like the following:

```
Sub EnumerateQueries()
  Dim dbsLocal As Database
  Dim qryLocal As QueryDef

  Set dbsLocal = CurrentDb
  For Each qryLocal In dbsLocal.QueryDefs
    Debug.Print qryLocal.Name
    Debug.Print qryLocal.SQL
  Next qryLocal
End Sub
```

This code loops through each **QueryDef** in the current database and prints the name and SQL statement associated with each. It's easy to write code that adds, deletes, modifies, and otherwise manipulates queries at runtime. For example, the following code creates a pair of **QueryDef** objects—one temporary and one permanent:

```
Sub CreateQueryDefX()
  Dim dbsTemp As Database
  Dim qdfTemp As QueryDef
  Dim qdfNew As QueryDef

  Set dbsTemp = OpenDatabase("Northwind.mdb")
  With dbsTemp
    ' Create temporary QueryDef.
    Set qdfTemp = .CreateQueryDef("", "SELECT * FROM Employees")
    ' Open Recordset and print report.
    GetrstTemp qdfTemp
    ' Create permanent QueryDef.
    Set qdfNew = .CreateQueryDef("NewQueryDef", "SELECT * FROM Categories")
    ' Open Recordset and print report.
```

```
    GetrstTemp qdfNew
    ' Delete new QueryDef because this is a demonstration.
    .QueryDefs.Delete qdfNew.Name
    .Close
  End With
End Sub

Function GetrstTemp(qdfTemp As QueryDef)
  Dim rstTemp As Recordset

  With qdfTemp
    Debug.Print .Name
    Debug.Print "    " & .SQL
    ' Open Recordset from QueryDef.
    Set rstTemp = .OpenRecordset(dbOpenSnapshot)
    With rstTemp
      ' Populate Recordset and print number of records.
      .MoveLast
      Debug.Print "    Number of records = " & .RecordCount
      Debug.Print
      .Close
    End With
  End With
End Function
```

As you can see, the code has two calls to the **CreateQueryDef** method—one that passes in a name for the new **QueryDef** object, and one that does not. Creating a new **QueryDef** without a name results in that object being temporary—that is, the engine will delete it automatically as soon as it goes out of scope. On the other hand, specifying a name will add the object in question to the database permanently, unless you delete it from the **QueryDefs** collection, as shown in the last emphasized line in the code fragment.

Understanding The Field Object And Fields Collection

Fields collections are contained within the **TableDef**, **QueryDef**, **Index**, **Relation**, and **Recordset** objects. The **Fields** collection of an object is the collection of **Field** objects within the parent object. For example, a **TableDef** object contains **Field** objects that are contained within the specific table. Using the parent object, you can obtain information about its **Fields** collection. You might implement this technique as shown here:

```
Sub EnumFields()
  Dim dbsLocal As Database
  Dim tblLocal As TableDef
  Dim fldLocal As Field
  Set dbsLocal = CurrentDb
```

```
   For Each tblLocal In dbsLocal.TableDefs
     For Each fldLocal In tblLocal.Fields
       Debug.Print fldLocal.Name
       Debug.Print fldLocal.Type
     Next fldLocal
   Next tblLocal
End Sub
```

This code loops through each **TableDef** in the current database, printing the name and type of each field contained within the **Fields** collection of the **TableDef**. Code can also be used to add, delete, or change the attributes of fields at runtime.

Understanding The Parameter Object And Parameters Collection

As you know, Access queries can contain parameters created so the user can supply information required by the query at runtime. Each **QueryDef** object has a **Parameters** collection consisting of **Parameter** objects. You can write code to manipulate these parameters at runtime. The code looks similar to the following:

```
Sub EnumerateParameters()
  Dim dbsLocal As Database
  Dim qryLocal As QueryDef
  Dim prmLocal As Parameter

  Set dbsLocal = CurrentDb
  For Each qryLocal In dbsLocal.QueryDefs
    Debug.Print "*****" & qryLocal.Name & "*****"
    For Each prmLocal In qryLocal.Parameters
      Debug.Print prmLocal.Name
    Next prmLocal
  Next qryLocal
End Sub
```

This code loops through each **QueryDef** object within the current database. It prints the name of the **QueryDef** object, then loops through its **Parameters** collection, printing the name of each parameter. You can add, delete, and manipulate **Parameter** objects at runtime.

Understanding The Recordset Object And Recordsets Collection

Recordset objects exist only at runtime and are used to reference a set of records coming from one or more tables. The **Recordsets** collection contains all the **Recordset** objects currently open within the current **Database** object. **Recordset** objects are covered extensively later in this chapter.

Understanding The Relation Object And Relations Collection

The **Relations** collection contains all the **Relation** objects that describe the relationships established within a **Database** object. The following code loops through the current database, printing the **Table** and **Foreign Table** properties of each **Relation** object:

```
Sub EnumRelations()
  Dim dbsLocal As Database
  Dim relLocal As Relation

  Set dbsLocal = CurrentDb
  For Each relLocal In dbsLocal.Relations
    Debug.Print relLocal.Table & " Related To: " & relLocal.ForeignTable
  Next relLocal
End Sub
```

You can create, delete, and modify relationships at runtime using VBA code. However, you can only use DAO to do so.

Understanding The Properties Collection

Each Data Access Object has a **Properties** collection, which is a list of properties associated with that particular object. You can view or modify the properties of an object using its **Properties** collection. The code looks like this:

```
Sub EnumerateProperties()
  Dim dbsLocal As Database
  Dim cntLocal As Container
  Dim docLocal As Document
  Dim prpLocal As Property
  Set dbsLocal = CurrentDb
  Set cntLocal = dbsLocal.Containers!Forms
  For Each docLocal In cntLocal.Documents
    Debug.Print docLocal.Name
    For Each prpLocal In docLocal.Properties
      Debug.Print prpLocal.Name & " = " & prpLocal.Value
    Next prpLocal
  Next docLocal
End Sub
```

This code loops through each form in the current database, printing all the properties of each **Form** object.

Understanding The Error Object And Errors Collection

The **Errors** collection consists of **Error** objects containing information about the most recent error that occurred. Each time an operation generates an error, the **Errors** collection is cleared of any previous errors. Sometimes a single operation can cause more than one error. For this reason, one or more **Error** objects might be added to the **Errors** collection when a single data access error occurs.

The Containers Collection

A **Container** object maintains information about saved **Database** objects. The types of objects within the **Containers** collection are **Databases**, **Tables** (including **Queries**), **Relationships**, **SysRel**, **Forms**, **Reports**, **Scripts** (macros), and **Modules**. The **Container** object is responsible for letting Jet know about the user interface objects. **Databases**, **Tables**, **Relationships**, and **SysRel** all have Jet as their parent object. **Forms**, **Reports**, **Scripts**, and **Modules** all have the Access application itself as their parent object.

Each **Container** object possesses a collection of **Document** objects. These are the actual forms, reports, and other objects that are part of your database. The **Document** objects contain only summary information about each object (date created, owner, and so on); they don't contain the actual data of the objects. To refer to a particular document within a container, you must use one of two techniques, as shown here:

```
Containers("Name")
Containers!Name
```

To list each **Container** object and its associated **Document** objects, you need to use code similar to the following:

```
Sub ListAllDBObjects()
  Dim dbsLocal As Database
  Dim conLocal As Container
  Dim docLocal As Document

  Set dbsLocal = CurrentDb
  For Each conLocal In dbsLocal.Containers
    Debug.Print "*** " & conLocal.Name & " ***"
    For Each docLocal In conLocal.Documents
      Debug.Print docLocal.Name
    Next docLocal
  Next conLocal
End Sub
```

This code loops through all the **Containers** and all of the documents within each **Container**, listing each one.

Manipulating Objects From The Containers Collection

As you saw in the last section, the **Containers** collection contains information about each saved **Database** object. Using the **Containers** collection, you can manipulate all the objects contained within the current database. Consider the following code, which does just that:

```
Sub EnumContainers()
  Dim dbsLocal As Database
  Dim cntLocal As Container

  Set dbsLocal = CurrentDb
  For Each cntLocal In dbsLocal.Containers
    Debug.Print cntLocal.Name
  Next cntLocal
End Sub
```

This code loops through the **Containers** collection, printing the name of each **Container** object. The results are **Databases**, **Forms**, **Modules**, **Relationships**, **Reports**, **Scripts**, **Data Access Pages**, **SysRel**, and **Tables**.

Understanding The Document Object And Documents Collection

As discussed previously, a **Document** object represents a specific object in the **Documents** collection. You can loop through the **Documents** collection of a **Container** object. The code to do so might look similar to the following:

```
Sub EnumerateForms()
  Dim dbsLocal As Database
  Dim cntLocal As Container
  Dim docLocal As Document

  Set dbsLocal = CurrentDb
  Set cntLocal = dbsLocal.Containers!Forms
  For Each docLocal In cntLocal.Documents
    Debug.Print docLocal.Name
  Next docLocal
End Sub
```

This code sets a **Container** object to point to the forms within the current database. It then loops through each document in the **Container** object, printing the name of each **Document** object (in this case, the name of each form).

It's important to understand the difference between the **Forms** *container* and the **Forms** *collection*. The **Forms** container is part of the **Containers** collection, containing all the forms that are part of the database. The **Forms** collection contains all the forms open at runtime. The properties of each form in the **Forms** container differ from the properties of a form in the **Forms** collection.

Understanding And Using The DBEngine Object

As mentioned, the **DBEngine** object refers to the Jet database engine, which is at the top of the Data Access Object hierarchy. The **DBEngine** object contains only two collections—**Workspaces** (the top-level DAO object) and **Errors** (a collection which, for the most part, exists outside any type of context, but instead simply gathers information from the engine directly). When referring to the current database, you can use the **CurrentDB** function discussed in the next section, but when referring to any database other than the current database, you must refer to the **DBEngine** object, as in the following example:

```
Sub ReferToCurrentDB()
  Dim wksLocal As Workspace
  Dim dbsLocal As Database

  Set wksLocal = DBEngine(0)
  Set dbsLocal = wksLocal.OpenDatabase("Northwind.mdb")
  Debug.Print dbsLocal.Version
End Sub
```

This code creates a **Workspace** object variable that points at the current **Workspace**. The **OpenDatabase** method of the **Workspace** object is then used to open another database. The version of the database is printed by the routine.

Using The CurrentDB Function

DAO offers a shortcut you can use when creating an object variable that points to the current database. Using the **CurrentDB** function, you don't need to point at the **Workspace**, and you don't need to invoke the **OpenDatabase** method. Instead, set the **Database** object variable equal to the result from the **CurrentDB** function. The code looks similar to the following (which you've seen throughout this chapter):

```
Sub UseCurrentDBFunc()
  Dim dbsLocal As Database

  Set dbsLocal = CurrentDb()
  Debug.Print dbsLocal.Version
End Sub
```

This code declares the **Database** object variable and then points it at the current database object. It's important to note that the **CurrentDB** function can't be used to refer to objects that aren't part of the current database.

Creating And Modifying Database Objects Using Code

When you're developing an Access application, it might be useful to add tables or queries, define or modify relationships, change security, or perform other data definition techniques at runtime. You can accomplish all of this by manipulating the various DAOs or ADOs. In this chapter, we will consider how to do this with DAO—in Chapter 5, you will look at each of the examples in this chapter again, this time from the perspective of how to implement them in ADO.

Adding A Table Using Code

Many properties and methods are available for adding and modifying Jet engine objects. The following code uses DAO to create a table, to add some fields, and to add a primary key index:

```
Sub CreateTable()                    'DAO Version
  Dim dbsLocal As Database
  Dim tdfLocal As TableDef
  Dim fldLocal As Field
  Dim idxLocal As Index

  Set dbsLocal = CurrentDb()                    ' Create new TableDef.
  ' Add field to Table Definition
  Set tdfLocal = dbsLocal.CreateTableDef("tblBooks")
  Set fldLocal = tdfLocal.CreateField("BookID", DB_TEXT, 5)
  tdfLocal.Fields.Append fldLocal

  Set fldLocal = tdfLocal.CreateField("Title", DB_TEXT, 25)
  tdfLocal.Fields.Append fldLocal

  Set fldLocal = tdfLocal.CreateField("Author", DB_INTEGER)
  tdfLocal.Fields.Append fldLocal
  dbsLocal.TableDefs.Append tdfLocal

  ' Designate the BookID field as the Primary Key Index
  Set idxLocal = tdfLocal.CreateIndex("PrimaryKey")
  Set fldLocal = idxLocal.CreateField("BookID")
  idxLocal.Primary = True
  idxLocal.Unique = True
  idxLocal.Fields.Append fldLocal
```

```
' Add the index to the Indexes collection
tdfLocal.Indexes.Append idxLocal
End Sub
```

This code first creates a table definition called **tblBooks**. Before it can add the table definition to the **TableDefs** collection, it must add three fields to the table. Notice that the field name, type, and length are specified. After the table definition has been added to the database, indexes can be added to the table. The index added in the example is a primary key index.

Removing A Table Using Code

Just as you can add a table using code, you can also remove a table using code. The DAO code looks like this:

```
Sub DeleteTable()                ' DAO Version
  Dim dbsLocal As Database

  Set dbsLocal = CurrentDb
  dbsLocal.TableDefs.Delete "tblBooks"
End Sub
```

The **Delete** method is issued on the **TableDefs** collection. The table you want to delete is passed to the **Delete** method as an argument.

Establishing Relationships Using Code

If you're creating tables using code, you'll want to establish relationships between these tables using code. Here's how:

```
Sub CreateRelation()
  Dim dbsLocal As Database
  Dim relLocal As Relation
  Dim fldLocal As Field

  Set dbsLocal = CurrentDb
  Set relLocal = dbsLocal.CreateRelation()
  With relLocal
    .Name = "MembersBooks"
    .Table = "tblBooks"
    .ForeignTable = "tblMembers"
    .Attributes = dbRelationDeleteCascade
  End With
  Set fldLocal = relLocal.CreateField("BookID")
  fldLocal.ForeignName = "BookID"
  relLocal.Fields.Append fldLocal
```

```
    dbsLocal.Relations.Append relLocal
End Sub
```

This code begins by setting a **Relation** object to a new relationship. It then populates the **Name**, **Table**, **Foreign Table**, and **Attributes** properties of the relationship. After the properties of the relationship have been set, the field on which the relation applies is added to the **Relation** object. Finally, the **Relation** object is appended to the **Relations** collection.

Tip

You can't create relationships with ADO. Instead, you will use joins, in conjunction with primary key and foreign key definitions within your database's tables, to control the relationships of your data. If you are working within Access, you can also set the relationships from the Relationship window. If you are working within SQL Server (or against a SQL Server from the Access Data Project [ADP] window, explained in later chapters), you can use a database designer to specify the relationships between the tables in a database. As always, you can also use SQL Data Definition Language (DDL) statements to define primary and foreign keys (the two fields in the two tables which, together, define a relation).

Creating A Query Using Code

You might want to build your own query designer into your application and allow the users to save the queries they build. This requires that you build the queries yourself, using code, after the user has designed them. As you saw previously, the code needed to build a query from DAO looks like this—the only difference in this example is that you are receiving the necessary strings from the user, rather than hard-coding them into the application:

```
Sub CreateQuery(ByVal UserEnteredName As String, ByVal SQLString As String)
   Dim dbsLocal As Database
   Dim qdfLocal As QueryDef

   Set dbsLocal = CurrentDb
   Set qdfLocal = dbsLocal.CreateQueryDef ("UserEnteredName")
   qdfLocal.SQL = SQLString
End Sub
```

This code uses the **CreateQueryDef** method of the **Database** object to create a new query definition. It then sets the SQL statement associated with the query definition. This two-step process builds and stores the query.

It's important to understand that unlike the **CreateQueryDef** method of the database object, which immediately adds the query definition to the database, the **CreateTableDef** method doesn't immediately add the table definition to the database. You must use the **Append** method of the **TableDefs** collection to actually add the table definition to the database.

Tip
*As you saw earlier in this chapter, you can create a temporary query definition by using a zero-length string for the **Name** argument of the **CreateQueryDef** method.*

With ADO, you'll generally either work with stored procedures on the server, or you'll use the **Recordset** object's **Save** method to persist a recordset.

Understanding Recordset Types

A **Recordset** object is used to represent the records in a table or the records returned by a query. A **Recordset** object can be a direct link to the table, a dynamic set of records, or a snapshot of the data at a certain time. Recordset objects are used to directly manipulate data in a database. They let you add, edit, delete, and move through data as required by your application. Access 2000 supports three types of **Recordset** objects: Table, Dynaset, and Snapshot.

Understanding The Use Of Dynaset-Type Recordsets

A **Recordset** object of the Dynaset type can be used to manipulate local or linked tables or the results of queries. A Dynaset is actually a set of references to table data that allows you to extract and update data from multiple tables, even tables from other databases. In fact, the tables in which data is included in a Dynaset can even come from databases that aren't of the same type (for example, Microsoft SQL Server, Oracle, Paradox, and Sybase SQL Server).

True to its name, a Dynaset is a dynamic set of records. This means that changes made to the Dynaset are reflected in the underlying tables, and changes made to the underlying tables by other users of the system are reflected in the Dynaset. Although a Dynaset isn't the fastest type of **Recordset** object, it's definitely the most flexible.

Understanding The Use Of Snapshot-Type Recordsets

A **Recordset** object of the Snapshot type is similar to a Dynaset. The major difference is that the data included in the Snapshot is fixed at the time that it's created. The data within the Snapshot, therefore, can't be modified and isn't updated when other users make changes to the underlying tables. This trait can be either an advantage or a disadvantage. It's a disadvantage, of course, if it's necessary for the data in the recordset to be updateable. It's an advantage if you're running a report and want to ensure that the data doesn't change during the time in which the report is being run. You can, therefore, create a Snapshot and build the report from the Snapshot-type **Recordset** object.

Snapshots are more efficient with small resultsets than Dynasets because, by nature, a Snapshot object creates less processing overhead. But regardless of their reduced overhead, Snapshots are actually less efficient than Dynasets when returning a resultset with a large volume of data (generally more than 500 records). This is because when you create a Snapshot object, all fields are returned to the user as each record is accessed. On the other hand, a Dynaset object contains a set of primary keys for the records in the resultset. The other fields are returned to the user only when they're required for editing or display.

Understanding The Use Of Table-Type Recordsets

A **Recordset** object of the Table type is often used to manipulate local or linked tables created using Microsoft Access or the Jet database engine. When you open a Table type **Recordset** object, all operations are performed directly on the table.

Certain operations, such as a **Seek**, can be performed only on a Table type of recordset. You get the best performance for sorting and filtering records when using a Table type of recordset.

The downside of the Table type is that it can contain the data from only one table. It can't be opened using a **Join** or **Union** query. It also can't be used with tables created with engines other than Jet (for example, open database connectivity [ODBC] data sources or other indexed sequential access method [ISAM] data sources).

Selecting Among The Recordset Objects

Deciding which type of recordset to use involves looking at the task to determine which type of recordset is most appropriate. When fast searching is most important and retrieving all the records isn't a problem, a Table is the best choice. If you must retrieve the results of a query and your resultset needs to be editable, a Dynaset is the best choice. And when there's no need for the results to be updated, but the results must consist of a relatively small subset of the data, a Snapshot is most appropriate.

Working With Recordset Properties And Methods

Like other objects, **Recordset** objects have properties and methods. Properties are the attributes of the **Recordset** objects, and methods are the actions you can take on the **Recordset** objects. Some properties are read-only at runtime; others can be read from and written to at runtime.

Creating A Recordset Variable

When working with a recordset, you must first create a **Recordset** variable. The **OpenRecordset** method is used to create a **Recordset** object variable. You must first declare a generic **Recordset** variable, then point a specific recordset at the variable using a **Set** statement. The code to do so will generally look similar to the following:

```
Sub OpenTable()
  Dim dbsInfo As Database
  Dim rstClients As Recordset
```

```
      Set dbsInfo = CurrentDb()
      Set rstClients = dbsInfo.OpenRecordset("tblClients")
      Debug.Print rstClients.Updatable
   End Sub
```

This code creates a **Database** object variable and a **Recordset** object variable. It then uses the **CurrentDb** function to point the **Database** object variable to the current database. Next, it uses the **OpenRecordset** method to assign the resultset based on **tblClients** to the object variable **rstClients**.

The type of recordset created is determined by the default type for the object or by a second parameter of the **OpenRecordset** method. If the **OpenRecordset** method is executed on a table and no second parameter is specified, the recordset is opened as the Table type. When the **OpenRecordset** method is performed on a query and no second parameter is specified, the recordset is opened as the Dynaset type. You can override this default behavior by passing a second parameter to the **OpenRecordset** method. The code to override the default behavior of **OpenRecordset** might look similar to the following:

```
Sub OpenDynaSet()
   Dim dbsInfo As Database
   Dim rstClients As Recordset

   Set dbsInfo = CurrentDb()
   Set rstClients = dbsInfo.OpenRecordset("tblClients", dbOpenDynaset)
   Debug.Print rstClients.Updatable
End Sub
```

This code opens the recordset as a Dynaset. The DAO library defines **dbOpenTable**, **dbOpenDynaset**, and **dbOpenSnapshot** as intrinsic constants you can use to open a **Recordset** object. A query can be opened only as a Dynaset or Snapshot **Recordset** object. The code to open a recordset based on a query (or a **QueryDef** object) appears as follows:

```
Sub OpenQuery()
   Dim dbsInfo As Database
   Dim rstClients As Recordset

   Set dbsInfo = CurrentDb()
   Set rstClients = dbsInfo.OpenRecordset("qryHoursByProject", dbOpenSnapshot)
   Debug.Print rstClients.Updatable
End Sub
```

Finally, you can also open a **Recordset** object by passing in a SQL string. The **Recordset** object will return the results of the query as if you entered it within the SQL window of the

Query Designer. For example, you might use code similar to the following to create a recordset based on an incoming variable:

```
Sub OpenQuery(strQryParam as String)
  Dim dbsInfo As Database
  Dim rstEmployees As Recordset

  Set dbsInfo = CurrentDb()
  Set rstEmployees = _
      dbsInfo.OpenRecordset("Select * From tblStaff " & _
      "Where [Employee] Like '" & _
      strQryParam & "'", dbOpenSnapshot)
  Debug.Print rstEmployees.Updatable
End Sub
```

This code creates a **Database** object variable and a **Recordset** object variable. It then uses the **CurrentDb** function to point the **Database** object variable to the current database. Next, it uses the **OpenRecordset** method to assign the recordset based on the SQL statement and the incoming parameter to the object variable **rstEmployees**.

Understanding The Arguments That OpenRecordset Accepts

The DAO Object Model's definition provides for several arguments that control the way in which a recordset is opened. Table 1.1 details the arguments and their uses.

You can use the arguments described in Table 1.1 in combination to accomplish the desired objectives. The following example shows the use of the **OpenRecordset** method with arguments to override its default behavior:

```
Sub OpenRecordsetArgs()
  Dim dbsLocal As Database
  Dim rstLocal As Recordset

  Set dbsLocal = CurrentDb
  Set rstLocal = _
      dbsLocal.OpenRecordset("tblBooks", dbOpenDynaset, dbReadOnly)
  Debug.Print rstLocal.Updatable
End Sub
```

This code opens a Dynaset-type recordset as read-only. It then prints the value of the **Updatable** property in the Immediate Window.

Record Movement Methods

When you have a **Recordset** object variable set, you probably want to manipulate the data in the recordset. You can use several methods to traverse through the records in a recordset:

Table 1.1   The constant arguments you can use with the OpenRecordset method.

Constant	Usage
dbAppendOnly	When this option is used, records can be added to the recordset only. Existing data can't be displayed or modified. This option is useful when you want to ensure that existing data isn't affected by the processing. This option applies to Dynasets only.
dbConsistent	This argument applies to Dynasets. It allows consistent updates only. This is the default argument for Dynasets.
dbDenyRead	Using this constant prevents other users from even reading the data contained within the recordset as long as the recordset remains open. This option can be used only on Table recordsets.
dbDenyWrite	When you're creating a Dynaset or Snapshot, this option prevents all other users from modifying the records contained with the recordset until the recordset is closed. Other users are still able to view the data contained within the recordset. When this option is applied to a Table type of recordset, other users are prevented from opening the underlying table.
dbForwardOnly	This argument creates a forward-scrolling Snapshot. This type of recordset is fast but limited in that you can use only the **Move** and **MoveNext** methods to move directly through the Snapshot.
dbInconsistent	This argument allows for inconsistent updates, meaning that in a one-to-many join, you can update all columns in the recordset.
dbReadOnly	This option prevents your recordset from modifying data. If you don't want the data within the recordset to be updateable, but you expect a large number of records to be returned and you want to take advantage of the record paging offered by Dynasets, you might want to open the recordset as a Dynaset.
dbSeeChanges	This option ensures that a user receives an error if the code issues an **Edit** method and another user modifies the data before an **Update** method is used. It is useful in a high-traffic environment when it's likely that two users will modify the same record at the same time. You can apply this option to Dynaset and Table recordsets only.
dbSQLPassThrough	When the source of the recordset is a SQL statement, this argument passes the SQL statement to an ODBC database for processing. This option doesn't completely eliminate Jet; it simply prevents Jet from making any changes to the SQL statement before passing it on to the ODBC Drive Manager. The **dbSQLPassThrough** argument can be used only with Snapshots and read-only Dynasets.

♦ **MoveFirst** moves to the first record in a recordset.

♦ **MoveLast** moves to the last record in a recordset.

♦ **MovePrevious** moves to the previous record in a recordset.

♦ **MoveNext** moves to the next record in a recordset.

♦ **Move[n]** moves forward or backward a specified number of records.

The following code contained within the Chap01.mdb database shows some examples of how you can use the **Move** methods:

```
Sub RecordsetMovements()
  Dim dbsLocal As Database
  Dim rstLocal As Recordset

  Set dbsLocal = CurrentDb
  Set rstLocal = dbsLocal.OpenRecordset("tblBooks", dbOpenDynaset)
  Debug.Print rstLocal!BookID
  rstLocal.MoveNext
  Debug.Print rstLocal!BookID
  rstLocal.MoveLast
  Debug.Print rstLocal!BookID
  rstLocal.MovePrevious
  Debug.Print rstLocal!BookID
  rstLocal.MoveFirst
  Debug.Print rstLocal!BookID
  rstLocal.Close
End Sub
```

This code opens a Dynaset. The record pointer is automatically placed on the first record of the Dynaset when the recordset is opened. The routine prints the contents of the **BookID** field, then moves to the next record, printing its **BookID**. It then moves to the last record of the Dynaset, printing its **BookID**; moves to the previous record, printing its **BookID**; then moves to the first record, again printing its **BookID**. Finally, the **Close** method is applied to the **Recordset** object, properly closing the recordset and ensuring that all changes are written to disk.

Detecting The Limits Of A Recordset

Before you begin to traverse through recordsets, you need to understand two crucial **Recordset** properties: **BOF** and **EOF**. These properties are used to determine whether you've reached the limits of your recordset. The **BOF** property is **True** when the record pointer is before the first record, and the **EOF** property is **True** when the record pointer is after the last record. Here's a code sample that shows the use of the **EOF** property:

```
Sub FindRstLimits()
  Dim dbsLocal As Database
  Dim rstClients As Recordset

  Set dbsLocal = CurrentDb()
  Set rstClients = dbsLocal.OpenRecordset("tblClients", dbOpenSnapshot)
  Do While Not rstClients.EOF
    Debug.Print rstClients![ClientID]
```

```
        rstClients.MoveNext
    Loop
    rstClients.Close
End Sub
```

This code traverses through a Snapshot recordset, printing the value of the **ClientID** field for each record until it reaches the position after the last record in the recordset. It then exits the loop and closes the recordset.

You need to keep in mind some important characteristics of the **BOF** and **EOF** properties when you use them within your program code:

♦ If a recordset contains no records, both the **BOF** and **EOF** properties evaluate to **True**.

♦ The moment you open a recordset containing at least one record, the **BOF** and **EOF** properties are set to **False**.

♦ If the record pointer is on the first record in the recordset and the **MovePrevious** method is issued, the **BOF** property is set to **True**. When you attempt to use **MovePrevious** again, a trappable runtime error occurs.

♦ If the record pointer is on the last record in the recordset and the **MoveNext** method is issued, the **EOF** property is set to **True**. If you attempt to **MoveNext** again, a trappable runtime error occurs.

♦ When the **BOF** and **EOF** properties are set to **True**, they remain **True** until you move to a valid record.

♦ When the only record in a recordset is deleted, the **BOF** and **EOF** properties remain **False** until you attempt to move to another record—in which case they're set to **True**, and a trappable runtime error occurs.

Counting The Number Of Records In A Recordset

The **RecordCount** property of a recordset returns the number of records in a recordset that have been accessed. The problem with this is evident if you open a recordset and view the **RecordCount** property. You'll discover that the count is equal to 0 if there are no records in the recordset, or equal to 1 if there are records in the recordset. The record count becomes accurate only if you visit all the records in the recordset. This can be done using the **MoveLast** method. In other words, if you want to gain an accurate count of all the records in a recordset, you should immediately move to the last record in the recordset and then back to the current position in the recordset, as shown here:

```
Sub CountRecords()
  Dim dbsLocal As Database
  Dim rstBooks As Recordset

  Set dbsLocal = CurrentDb()
  Set rstBooks = dbsLocal.OpenRecordset("tblBooks", dbOpenSnapshot)
```

```
      Debug.Print rstBooks.RecordCount        ' Prints 0 or 1
      rstBooks.MoveLast
      Debug.Print rstBooks.RecordCount        ' Prints an accurate record count
      rstBooks.Close
End Sub
```

The **MoveLast** method has its own problems, however. It's slow and inefficient, especially in a client/server environment. Furthermore, in a network environment, the **RecordCount** property becomes inaccurate as people add and remove records from the table. This means that if determining the record count isn't absolutely necessary, you should avoid it. The **RecordCount** property has one good use, though: It can be used to see whether there are any records in a recordset. When you're performing an operation that might return an empty recordset, you can easily use the **RecordCount** property to determine whether records were returned—if its value is 0, no records were returned; otherwise, the recordset contains records.

Using The AbsolutePosition Property

The **AbsolutePosition** property returns the position of the current record. It's a zero-based value and can be used to specify where in a recordset a specific record was found. The following code shows how you might use the **AbsolutePosition** property:

```
Sub FindPosition(lngValue As Long)
   Dim dbsLocal As Database
   Dim rstBooks As Recordset
   Dim strSQL As String

   Set dbsLocal = CurrentDb()
   Set rstBooks = dbsLocal.OpenRecordset("tblBooks", dbOpenDynaset)
   strSQL = "[BookID] = " & lngValue
   rstBooks.FindFirst strSQL
   If rstBooks.NoMatch Then
     MsgBox lngValue & " Not Found"
   Else
     Debug.Print rstBooks.AbsolutePosition
   End If
End Sub
```

This code finds the first record with a **BookID** equal to the long integer received as a parameter. If the **BookID** is found, the value in the **AbsolutePosition** property of the record is printed.

Warning

*Don't rely on the presumption that the **AbsolutePosition** of a particular record will stay the same. The **AbsolutePosition** of a record changes as records are added or deleted or their order within the database is changed as the records are modified.*

Using The Bookmark Property

A **Bookmark** is a system-generated byte array that uniquely identifies each record in a recordset. The **Bookmark** property of a recordset changes as you move to each record in the recordset. It's often used when you need to store the current position in the recordset so you can perform some operation, then return to the position after the operation is completed. Three steps are involved in this process:

1. Store the current **Bookmark** of the recordset to a **Variant** variable.

2. Perform the desired operation.

3. Set the **Bookmark** property of the recordset to the value contained within the **Variant** variable.

The operation looks similar to the following when you use it within your program code:

```
Sub UseBookMark()
  Dim dbsLocal As Database
  Dim rstBooks As Recordset
  Dim strSQL As String
  Dim vntPosition As Variant

  Set dbsLocal = CurrentDb()
  Set rstBooks = dbsLocal.OpenRecordset("tblBooks", dbOpenDynaset)
  vntPosition = rstBooks.Bookmark
  Do Until rstBooks.EOF
    Debug.Print rstBooks!BookID
    rstBooks.MoveNext
  Loop
  rstBooks.Bookmark = vntPosition
  Debug.Print rstBooks!BookID
End Sub
```

This code begins by opening a recordset and storing the **Bookmark** of the first record into a **Variant** variable. It then loops through each record in the recordset, printing the value within the **BookID**. After the loop is completed, the **Bookmark** property of the recordset is set equal to the **Variant** variable, setting the current position of the recordset back to where it was before the loop began processing.

Using The RecordsetClone Property

The **RecordsetClone** property of a form is used to refer to the recordset underlying the form. This property is useful when you want to perform an operation, then synchronize the form with its underlying recordset. The following code provides an example:

```
Private Sub cmdFindClient_Click()
  Me.RecordsetClone.FindFirst "ClientID = " & Me!txtClientID
```

```
   If Me.RecordsetClone.NoMatch Then
     MsgBox Me!txtClientID & " Not Found"
   Else
     Me.Bookmark = Me.RecordsetClone.Bookmark
   End If
End Sub
```

This routine performs the **FindFirst** method on the **RecordsetClone** of the current form. If the record is found, the **Bookmark** property of the form is set equal to the **Bookmark** of the recordset. This matches the form's position to the underlying recordset's position.

Modifying Table Data Using Code

So far, you've learned how to loop through and work with **Recordset** objects. Now you'll learn how to change the data contained in a recordset.

Changing Record Data One Record At A Time

You'll often want to loop through a recordset, modifying all the records that meet a specific set of criteria. The code required to accomplish this task looks like this:

```
Sub IncreaseEstimate()                    ' DAO Version
  Dim dbsLocal As Database
  Dim rstBooks As Recordset
  Dim strSQL As String
  Dim intUpdated As Integer

  Set dbsLocal = CurrentDb()
  Set rstBooks = dbsLocal.OpenRecordset("tblBooksChange", dbOpenDynaset)
  strSQL = "BookTotalCopies < 5"
  intUpdated = 0
  rstBooks.FindFirst strSQL
  Do While Not rstBooks.NoMatch
    intUpdated = intUpdated + 1
    rstBooks.Edit
      rstBooks.Fields("BookTotalCopies") = _
          rstBooks.Fields("BookTotalCopies") + 5
    rstBooks.Update
    rstBooks.FindNext strSQL
  Loop
  Debug.Print intUpdated & " Records Updated"
  rstBooks.Close
End Sub
```

This code finds the first record with a **BookTotalCopies** value of less than five. The code uses the **Edit** method to ready the current record in the Dynaset for editing and replaces the **BookTotalCopies** with **BookTotalCopies** plus five. It then issues the **Update** method to write the changes to disk. Finally, the program uses the **FindNext** method to locate the next occurrence of the criteria.

Making Bulk Changes

Many of the tasks that you can perform by looping through a recordset can also be accomplished with an update query. Executing an update query is often more efficient than the process of looping through a recordset. If nothing else, it takes much less code. Therefore, it's important to understand how to execute an update query through code.

Let's assume that you have a query called **qryChangeBookCopies** that increases the **BookTotalCopies** for all projects in which the **BookTotalCopies** value is less than six. The query defines an update query. The following code executes the stored query definition:

```
Sub RunUpdateQuery()                    ' DAO Version
  Dim dbsLocal As Database
  Dim qdfLocal As QueryDef

  Set dbsLocal = CurrentDb
  Set qdfLocal = dbsLocal.QueryDefs("qryChangeBookCopies")
  qdfLocal.Execute
End Sub
```

Notice that the **Execute** method operates on the query definition, executing the action query that the definition contains—that is, the **Update** query.

Deleting An Existing Record

The **Delete** method enables you to programmatically delete records from a recordset. It works like this:

```
Sub DeleteCusts(lngNumberOfCopies As Long)
  Dim dbsLocal As Database
  Dim rstBooks As Recordset
  Dim intCounter As Integer

  Set dbsLocal = CurrentDb
  Set rstBooks = dbsLocal.OpenRecordset("tblBooksChange", dbOpenDynaset)
  intCounter = 0
  Do While Not rstBooks.EOF
    If rstBooks.Fields("BookTotalCopies") < lngNumberOfCopies Then
      rstBooks.Delete
```

```
      intCounter = intCounter + 1
    End If
    rstBooks.MoveNext
  Loop
  Debug.Print intCounter & " Customer Records Deleted"
End Sub
```

This code loops through the **rstBooks** recordset. If the **BookTotalCopies** value is less than the value passed in as a parameter, the record is deleted. This task could also be accomplished with a delete query.

Adding A New Record

The **AddNew** method enables you to programmatically add records to a recordset. Here's an example:

```
Private Sub cmdAddRecord_Click()          ' DAO Recordset
  Dim dbsLocal As Database
  Dim rstBooks As Recordset

  Set dbsLocal = CurrentDb()
  Set rstBooks = dbsLocal.OpenRecordset("tblBooksChange", DB_OPEN_DYNASET)
  With rstBooks
    .AddNew
      .Fields("Author") = Me!txtAuthor
      .Fields("Title") = Me!txtTitle
      .Fields("BookID") = Me!cboBookID
    .Update
  End With
  Me!txtBookID = rstBooks!BookID
End Sub
```

This code is used with an unbound form called **frmUnbound**. The code issues an **AddNew** method, which creates a buffer ready to accept data. Each field in the recordset is then populated with the values from the controls on the form. The **Update** method writes the data to disk, and if you forget to include the **Update** method, the record is never written to disk. The last line of code is there to illustrate a problem: When an **AddNew** method is issued, the record pointer is never moved within the Dynaset. Even after the **Update** method is issued, the record pointer remains at the record it was on prior to the **AddNew**. You must explicitly move to the new record before populating the **txtBookID** text box with the **BookID** from the recordset, if that is the record you wish to display. This can easily be accomplished using the **LastModified** property, covered in the next section.

Using The LastModified Property

The **LastModified** property contains a **Bookmark** of the most recently added or modified record. By setting the **Bookmark** of the recordset to the **LastModified** property, the record pointer is moved to the most recently added record. The code looks like this:

```
Private Sub cmdLastModified_Click()
  Dim dbsLocal As Database
  Dim rstBooks As Recordset
  Set dbsLocal = CurrentDb()
  Set rstBooks = dbsLocal.OpenRecordset("tblBooksChange", DB_OPEN_DYNASET)
  With rstBooks
    .AddNew
      .Fields("Title") = Me!txtTitle
      .Fields("Author") = Me!txtAuthor
      .Fields("BookID") = Me!cboBookID
    .Update
    .Bookmark = rstBooks.LastModified
  End With
  Me!txtBookID = rstBooks!BookID
End Sub
```

Notice that the **Bookmark** of the recordset is set to the **LastModified** property of the recordset.

Warning

*ADO doesn't support the **LastModified** property.*

Sorting, Filtering, And Finding Records

Sometimes you might need to sort or filter an existing recordset. You also might want to locate each record in the recordset that meets some specified criteria. The following techniques allow you to sort, filter, and find records within a **Recordset** object.

Sorting A Recordset

You can't actually change the sort order of an existing Dynaset or Snapshot. Instead, you create a second recordset based on the first recordset. The second recordset is sorted in the desired order. It works like this:

```
Sub SortRecordset()                      ' DAO Version
  Dim dbsLocal As Database
  Dim rstTimeCardHours As Recordset

  Set dbsLocal = CurrentDb
```

```
     Set rstTimeCardHours = _
         dbsLocal.OpenRecordset("tblTimeCardHours", dbOpenDynaset)
     Debug.Print "NOT Sorted!!!"
     Do While Not rstTimeCardHours.EOF
       Debug.Print rstTimeCardHours![DateWorked]
       rstTimeCardHours.MoveNext
     Loop
     Debug.Print "Now Sorted!!!"
     rstTimeCardHours.Sort = "[DateWorked]"
     Set rstTimeCardHours = rstTimeCardHours.OpenRecordset
       Do While Not rstTimeCardHours.EOF
       Debug.Print rstTimeCardHours.Fields("DateWorked")
       rstTimeCardHours.MoveNext
     Loop
End Sub
```

In this case, you're sorting a Dynaset that's based on the table **tblTimeCardHours**. The first
time you loop through the recordset and print each date worked, the dates are in the default
order (usually the primary key order). After you've used the **Sort** method to sort the recordset,
the records appear in order by the date worked.

Filtering A Recordset

Filtering an existing recordset is similar to sorting one. The following example is a variation
of the previous one. Instead of sorting an existing recordset, it filters it:

```
Sub FilterRecordSet()
  Dim dbsLocal As Database
  Dim rstTimeCardHours As Recordset

  Set dbsLocal = CurrentDb
  Set rstTimeCardHours = _
      dbsLocal.OpenRecordset("tblTimeCardHours", dbOpenDynaset)
  Debug.Print "Without Filter"
  Do While Not rstTimeCardHours.EOF
    Debug.Print rstTimeCardHours![DateWorked]
    rstTimeCardHours.MoveNext
  Loop
  rstTimeCardHours.Filter = "[DateWorked] Between #1/1/95# and #1/5/95#"
  Debug.Print "With Filter"
  Set rstTimeCardHours = rstTimeCardHours.OpenRecordset
    Do While Not rstTimeCardHours.EOF
    Debug.Print rstTimeCardHours.Fields("DateWorked")
    rstTimeCardHours.MoveNext
  Loop
End Sub
```

The first time the code loops through the recordset, no filter is set. The program code then sets the filter and the remaining code loops through the recordset again. The second time, only the records meeting the filter criteria are displayed.

Finding A Specific Record Within A Recordset

The **Seek** method enables you to find records in a **Table** recordset. It's usually the quickest method of locating data, because it uses the current index to locate the requested data. It works like this:

```
Sub SeekProject(lngProjectID As Long)
  Dim dbsLocal As Database
  Dim rstProjects As Recordset

  Set dbsLocal = CurrentDb()
  Set rstProjects = dbsLocal.OpenRecordset("tblProjects", dbOpenTable)
  rstProjects.Index = "PrimaryKey"
  rstProjects.Seek "=", lngProjectID
  If rstProjects.NoMatch Then
    MsgBox lngProjectID & " Not Found"
  Else
    MsgBox lngProjectID & " Found"
  End If
End Sub
```

This code uses the primary key index to locate the first project with the project number that was passed to the function. It then displays a message box to indicate whether the value was found.

The **Seek** method can't be used to locate data in a Dynaset or Snapshot. Furthermore, it can't be used to search for records in an attached table, regardless of whether the attached table is an Access table or a client/server table. In this case, you must use the **FindFirst**, **FindLast**, **FindNext**, and **FindPrevious** methods. The **FindFirst** method finds the first occurrence of data that meets the criteria, and **FindLast** finds the last occurrence of such data. The **FindNext** and **FindPrevious** methods enable you to find additional data, as shown here:

```
Sub FindProject(lngValue As Long)
  Dim dbsLocal As Database
  Dim rstProjects As Recordset
  Dim strSQL As String

  Set dbsLocal = CurrentDb()
  Set rstProjects = dbsLocal.OpenRecordset("tblProjects", dbOpenDynaset)
  strSQL = "[ProjectID] = " & lngValue
```

```
    rstProjects.FindFirst strSQL
    If rstProjects.NoMatch Then
      MsgBox lngValue & " Not Found"
    Else
      MsgBox lngValue & " Found"
    End If
End Sub
```

This code uses the **FindFirst** method to find the first occurrence of the parameter that was passed in. Again, it displays an appropriate message box.

Tip

You can use another trick to search a linked table: You can open the database that contains the linked table and seek directly on the table data.

Running Parameter Queries

Access parameter queries are very powerful. They enable the user to specify criteria at runtime. This ability is often helpful if your user wants to fill out a form at runtime and have the values on that form fed to the query. Consider the following code:

```
Sub RunParameterQuery(datStart As Date, datEnd As Date)  ' DAO Version
  Dim dbsLocal As Database
  Dim qdfLocal As QueryDef
  Dim rstLocal As Recordset

  Set dbsLocal = CurrentDb
  Set qdfLocal = dbsLocal.QueryDefs("qryBillAmountByClient")
  qdfLocal.Parameters("Please Enter Start Date") = datStart
  qdfLocal.Parameters("Please Enter End Date") = datEnd
  Set rstLocal = qdfLocal.OpenRecordset
  Do While Not rstLocal.EOF
    Debug.Print rstLocal.Fields("CompanyName"), _
        rstLocal.Fields("[BillAmount")
    rs.MoveNext
  Loop
End Sub
```

This subroutine receives two **Date** variables as parameters, but it could just as easily receive form controls as parameters. It opens a query definition called **qryBillAmountByClient** and sets the values of the parameters called **Please Enter Start Date** and **Please Enter End Date** to the **Date** variables passed into the subroutine as parameters. The query is then executed by issuing the **OpenRecordset** method on the **Recordset** object.

Where To Go From Here

In this chapter, we have focused on a brief discussion of the DAO Object Model, and the use of the components of the DAO library. As we have discussed, DAO is the historic technology that is used with the Jet engine, and was originally introduced with Access.

We looked at the many different ways in which you could use DAO to control databases from your VBA code—including how to reference the current database, how to use workspace information to provide applications with a higher level of access than their users, and so on. We have also explored how you can use DAO code to create new databases and database objects.

In Chapter 2, we will consider a variant on the DAO object model discussed here—the use of DAO and ODBCDirect for client/server. We will consider some of the benefits and implications of that model, before moving on to the use of linked tables for client/server support in Chapter 3.

Chapter 2

A Brief Introduction To Client/Server With Access

In Chapter 1, you read a brief refresher on the Data Access Objects (DAO) Object Model. You reviewed its use in a handful of situations, and considered the power that you now had at your disposal with the addition of programming code to your Access applications. However, the discussion that we had about DAO in Chapter 1 was limited in one very important way, particularly given the purpose of this book: We didn't discuss client/server issues *at all*. In fact, I focused on how to do things in a simpler manner, ensuring that we were reading from the same page as we moved into the discussion, analysis, and implementation of client/server solutions. In this chapter, we will begin this process with a discussion of several of the issues that surround the transition to client/server, including differences in the way you will design your application. We will also look at two issues that are *very* important in a client/server environment, but have either no corollary at all in a single-user environment, or, at best, no useful corollary: locks and transactions.

Designing Your Application With Multiuser Issues In Mind

When you develop applications that will be accessed over the network by multiple users, you must ensure that your applications effectively handle the sharing of data and other application objects. Developers have many options available when they design multiuser applications. This chapter covers the pros and cons of these options.

Multiuser issues are the issues surrounding the locking of data, including deciding where to store database objects, when to lock data, and how much data to lock. In a multiuser environment, having several users simultaneously attempting to modify the same data can generate conflicts. As a developer, you need to design your database to handle these conflicts; otherwise, your users will experience unexplainable errors.

Multiuser Design Strategies

Numerous methodologies exist for handling concurrent access to data and other application objects by multiple users. Each of these methodologies introduces solutions as well as problems. It's important to select the best solution for your particular environment.

Strategies For Installing Access

You can choose between two strategies for installing Access:

♦ Running Access from a file server

♦ Running a separate copy of Access on each workstation

Each of these strategies has associated pros and cons. Running Access from a file server has the following advantages:

♦ It allows for central administration of the Access software.

♦ It potentially reduces the licensing requirements. This is true because when Access is installed on a file server, the licensing requirements deal with concurrent users. When Access is installed locally, each user must have her own license, even if she rarely uses any Access applications. If all users won't be working with Access applications at the same time, it might be more cost-effective to purchase a local area network (LAN) license and install Access on the file server.

♦ It reduces hard disk requirements. The Access software takes up between 14MB and 42MB of hard disk space, depending on the type of installation. Although using the Access runtime engine can reduce this, local hard disk space can definitely be a problem. Installing Access on the file server at least partially eliminates this problem. It can totally eliminate the problem when dynamic link libraries are also installed on the file server.

♦ Access applications can be installed on diskless workstations.

Although these advantages might seem compelling, installing Access on a file server has serious drawbacks, including the following:

♦ Every time the user launches an Access application, the Access EXE, DLL, and any other files required to run Access are *all* sent over the network wire to the local machine. Obviously, this generates a significant volume of network traffic.

♦ Performance is generally degraded to unacceptable levels.

Because the disadvantages of running Access from a file server are so pronounced, it's generally more appropriate, in most networks, for you to install Access, or at least the Access runtime, on each user's machine.

Strategies For Installing Your Application

Just as you can use different strategies for installing Access, you can also employ various strategies for installing your application, such as the following:

♦ Install both the application and data on a file server.

♦ Install the data on the file server and the application on each workstation.

In other words, after you've created an application, you can place the entire application on the network, which means that all of the tables, queries, forms, reports, macros, and modules that make up the system reside on the file server. Although this method of shared access keeps everything in the same place, you'll see many advantages to placing only the data tables in a database on the file server. The remainder of the objects are placed in a database on each user's machine. Each local application database is linked to the tables on the network. In this way, users share the data in the application, but not the rest of the application objects.

The advantages of installing one database containing data tables on the file server and installing another database containing other application objects locally are as follows:

♦ Because each user has a copy of the local database objects (queries, forms, reports, macros, and modules), both load time and network traffic are reduced.

♦ It's very easy to back up data without having to back up the rest of the application objects.

♦ When redistributing new versions of the application, it's not necessary to be concerned with overwriting the application's data.

♦ Multiple applications can all be designed to use the same centrally located data.

♦ Users can add their own objects (such as their own queries) to their local copies of the database.

In addition to storing the queries, forms, reports, macros, and modules that make up the application in a local database, most developers also recommend that you store the following objects within each local database:

♦ *Temporary tables*—Temporary tables should be stored in the database that's located on each workstation, because when two users are performing operations that build the same temporary tables, you don't want one user's process to interfere with the other's. You can eliminate the potential conflict of one user's temporary tables overwriting the other's by storing all temporary tables in each user's local copy of the database.

♦ *Static tables*—Static lookup tables, such as a **State** table, should also be placed on each workstation. Because the data does not change, maintenance isn't an issue. The benefit is that Access doesn't need to pull that data over the network each time it's needed.

♦ *Semistatic tables*—Semistatic tables can also be placed on the local machine. These tables are rarely updated. As with static tables, the major benefit of having these tables reside in a local database is that reduced network traffic means better performance, not only for the user requiring the data, but also for anyone sharing the same network wire. Changes made to the semistatic tables can be transported to each workstation using Access replication.

Now that we have looked at some of the considerations surrounding your move to Access, let's consider one of the most important issues in effective management of distributed databases—the use of locking mechanisms by the database management system (DBMS). All database products that support even a minimal client/server deployment include a built-in locking mechanism. Access is no exception, and locks can cause substantial performance drops. In the next section, we will consider the locking mechanisms Access uses, and how to manage locking issues most effectively.

Understanding Access's Locking Mechanisms

Although the preceding tips for designing network applications reduce network traffic, they in no way reduce locking conflicts, which, with the ever-increasing amounts of network bandwidth, may be a more significant consideration by far for your application.

To protect shared data, Access locks a page of data as the user edits a record. When a page of records is locked, multiple users can read the data, but only one user can make changes to the data. Data can be locked through a form and also through a recordset that isn't bound to a form. Access offers three methods of locking an application:

♦ Page locking

♦ Table and recordset locking

♦ Opening an entire database with exclusive access (the most common type of database locking)

With *page locking*, only the page containing the record that's being edited is locked. On the other hand, with *table* and *recordset locking*, the entire table or recordset containing the record that's being edited is locked. With *database locking*, the entire database is locked, unless the user opening the database has opened it for read-only access. When the user opens the database for read-only access, other users can also open the database for read-only access. The ability to obtain exclusive use of a database can be restricted through security.

It's important to note that the locking scheme to which you must adhere depends on the source of the data that you're accessing. When you're accessing data on a database server using open database connectivity (ODBC), you'll inherit the locking scheme of the particular back end that you're using. When you're accessing indexed sequential access method (ISAM) data over a network, you'll get any record locking that the particular ISAM database supports. For example, if you're accessing FoxPro data, you have the capability to utilize record locking or any other locking scheme that FoxPro supports.

Locking And Refreshing Strategies

Access provides several tools for controlling locking methods in datasheets, forms, and reports. To configure the global multiuser settings, select Tools I Options. Access will display the Options dialog box. Within the Options dialog box, click on the Advanced tab. The dialog box pictured in Figure 2.1 appears.

The following multiuser settings can be configured from this dialog:

◆ Default Open Mode

◆ Default Record Locking

◆ Number of Update Retries

◆ ODBC Refresh Interval

◆ Refresh Interval

◆ Update Retry Interval

Default Record Locking

The Default Record Locking option enables you to specify the default record locking as No Locks (Optimistic), All Records (locks entire table or Dynaset), or Edited Record (Pessimistic). This is where you can affect settings for all objects in your database. Modifying this option won't affect any existing queries, forms, and reports, but it'll affect any new queries, forms, and reports. These options are discussed later in this chapter as they apply to forms and recordsets.

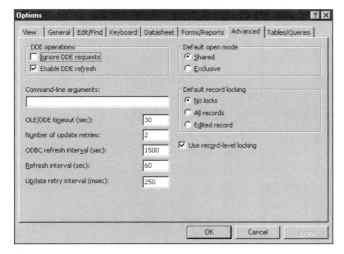

Figure 2.1
The Advanced tab of the Options dialog box.

Determining The Locking Mechanism For A Query

When you want to determine the locking method for a particular query, you can do so by modifying the Record Locks query property. Once again, the options are No Locks, All Records, and Edited Record. You can set this information within the Query Properties dialog box.

Determining The Locking Mechanism For A Form Or Report

Just as you can configure the locking mechanism for a query, you can also configure the locking mechanism for each form and report. Forms and reports have Record Locks properties, just as queries do. Changing these properties modifies the locking mechanism for that particular form or report.

Tip

Reports don't provide the Edited Records choice for locking. The Edited Records option isn't necessary, because report data can't be modified.

Default Open Mode

The Default Open Mode of the Advanced Options dialog enables you to configure the Default Open Mode for databases. By encouraging users to set this option within their own copies of Access, you prevent people from inadvertently opening up a database exclusively. Take a good look at the Access Open dialog, shown in Figure 2.2.

As you can see in the bottom-right corner of the Open dialog box, you can choose the open mode. The dialog box defaults to the Default Open Mode setting in the Advanced Options dialog.

Number Of Update Retries

The Number Of Update Retries option allows you to specify how many times Access will reattempt to save data to a locked record. The higher this number, the larger the chance that the update will succeed. The down side is that the user has to wait while Access continues attempting to update the data, even when there is no hope that the update will complete successfully. The default for this setting is 2. The value can range from 0 to 10.

ODBC Refresh Interval

The ODBC Refresh Interval option determines how often your form or datasheet is updated with changes made to data stored in ODBC data sources. For example, assume that two users are viewing the same data stored in a back-end Microsoft SQL Server database. User 1 makes a change to the data. The ODBC Refresh Interval determines how long it'll be before User 2 sees the change. The higher this number, the less likely it is that User 2 will

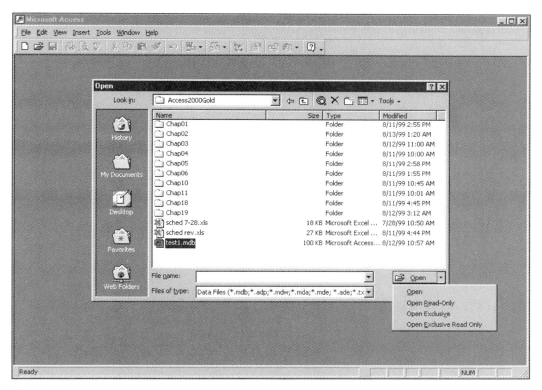

Figure 2.2
The Open dialog box.

see the current data. The lower this number, the more network traffic. The default for this setting is 1,500 seconds; the value can range from 1 to 3,600 seconds.

Refresh Interval

The Refresh Interval option allows you to specify how long it takes for a form or datasheet to be updated with changed data from an Access database. This is very similar to the ODBC Refresh Interval option, but the ODBC Refresh Interval applies only to ODBC data sources, and the Refresh Interval applies only to Access data sources. As with the ODBC Refresh Interval, the higher this number, the lower the chance that the data viewed by the user is current. The lower this number, the more network traffic. The default for this setting is 60 seconds; the value can range from 1 to 32,766 seconds.

Tip

Access automatically refreshes the data in a record whenever the user attempts to edit the record. The benefit of a shorter refresh interval is that the user sees that the record has been changed or locked by another user before attempting to edit it.

Refreshing Vs. Requerying Data

It's important that you understand the difference between refreshing and requerying a recordset. The process of refreshing a recordset updates changed data and indicates any deleted records. The refresh process doesn't attempt to bring a new recordset over the network wire. Instead, it *refreshes* the data in the existing recordset. This means that records aren't reordered, new records don't appear, and deleted records aren't removed from the display. The record pointer remains on the same record.

In contrast, the requery process obtains a new set of records. This means that the query is run again and all of the resulting data is sent over the network wire. The data is reordered, new records appear, and deleted records are no longer displayed. The record pointer is moved to the first record in the recordset.

Update Retry Interval

The Update Retry Interval option allows you to determine how many seconds Access waits before once again attempting to update a locked record. The default for this setting is 250 milliseconds; the value can range from 0 to 1,000 milliseconds.

Form Locking Strategies

Earlier in the chapter, you learned about the locking strategies for forms—No Locks, All Records, and Edited Record. Utilizing the three locking strategies as appropriate, you can develop a multiuser application with little or no multiuser-specific programming. You won't gain the same power, flexibility, and control that you get out of recordsets, but you can quickly and easily implement multiuser techniques. In this section, you'll see how all three of these strategies impact the bound forms within your application.

Using The No Locks Option

The No Locks option means that the page of data containing the edited record won't be locked until Access attempts to write the changed data to disk. This occurs when there's movement to a different record or the data within the record is explicitly saved. The No Locks locking option is the least restrictive of the three locking options for forms. Multiple users can be editing data within the same 2K page of data at the same time. The conflict occurs when two users attempt to modify the same record. Consider the following example:

User 1 attempts to modify data within the record for customer ABCDE. User 2 attempts to modify the *same* record. No error occurs because the No Locks option is specified for the form both users are accessing. User 1 makes a change to the address. User 2 makes a change to the Contact Title. User 1 moves off the record, saving her changes. No error occurs because Access has no way of knowing that User 2 is modifying the record. Now User 2 attempts to move off the record. The Write Conflict dialog box appears. User 2 has three choices: He can save his changes, thereby overwriting the changes that User 1 made; he can copy User 1's changes to the clipboard so that he can make an educated decision as to what to do; or he can drop his own changes and accept the changes that User 1 made.

Using The All Records Option

The All Records locking option is the most restrictive. When All Records is in effect, other users can only view the data in the tables underlying the form. They can't make any changes to the data, regardless of their own locking options. When opening the form, they receive a quick status bar message that the data isn't updateable. If they attempt to modify data within the form, the computer beeps and a message displays in the status bar.

Using The Edited Record Option

The Edited Record option allows you to prevent the conflicts that occur when the No Locks option is in place. Instead of getting potential conflicts regarding changed data, the users are much more likely to experience locking conflicts because every time a user begins editing a record, the entire 2K page of data surrounding the record will be locked. Consider this scenario:

User 1 begins editing a record. User 2 attempts to modify the same record. The computer beeps and a lock symbol appears in the form's record selector. Now User 2 moves to another record. If the other record is in the same 2K page as the record User 1 has locked, the locking symbol appears and User 2 is unable to edit that record as well until User 1 has saved the record that she was working on, thereby releasing the lock.

When you want to override any of the default locking error dialogs that appear in a form, you must code the **Error** event of the form. Although you can use this method to replace any error message that appears, you can't trap for the situation with Pessimistic locking when another user has the record locked. Users are only cued that the record is locked by viewing the locking symbol and hearing the beep that occurs when they attempt to edit the record. If you want to inform users that the record is locked before they attempt to edit it, you need to place code in the timer event of the form that checks to see whether the record is locked. Checking to see whether a record is locked is covered in the "Testing A Record For Locking Status" section of this chapter.

Recordset Locking

Recordset locking is the process of locking pages of data contained within a recordset. Using recordset locking, you can determine when and for how long the data is locked. This is different from locking data via bound forms, because with bound forms, you have little control over the specifics of the locking process.

When you're traversing through a recordset, editing and updating data, locking occurs regardless of whether you intervene. It's important for you to understand when the locking occurs and whether you need to step in to intercept the default behavior.

If you do nothing, an entire page of records will be locked each time you issue an **Edit** method from within your Visual Basic for Applications (VBA) code. This page is 2,048 bytes (2K) in size (4K with Unicode Support enabled) and surrounds the record being edited. When an object linking and embedding (OLE) object is contained within the record being edited, it's not locked with the record because the object occupies its own space; only a reference to the object exists within the record itself.

Using Pessimistic Locking

VBA enables you to determine when and for how long a page is locked. The default behavior is called *Pessimistic locking*. This means that the page is locked when the **Edit** method is issued. Here is some sample code (using DAO) that illustrates this process:

```
Sub PessimisticLock(strCustID As String)
  Dim db As Database
  Dim rst As Recordset
  Dim strCriteria As String

  Set db = CurrentDb()
  Set rst = db.OpenRecordSet("tblCustomers", dbOpenDynaset)
  rst.Lockedits = True  'Invoke Pessimistic Locking
  strCriteria = "[CustomerID] = '" & strCustID & "'"
  rst.FindFirst strCriteria
  rst.Edit                     ' Lock Occurs Here
    rst.Fields("City") = "Las Vegas"
  rst.Update                   ' Lock Released Here
End Sub
```

In this scenario, although the lock occurs for a very short period of time, it's actually being issued at the edit. It's then released upon update.

This method of locking is advantageous because you can ensure that no changes are made to the data between the time that the **Edit** method is issued and the time that the **Update** method is issued. Furthermore, when the **Edit** method succeeds, you're ensured write access to the record. The disadvantage is that the time between the edit and the update might force the lock to persist for a significant period of time, locking other users out of not only that record, but the entire page of records within which the edited record is contained. This phenomenon is exacerbated when transaction processing is invoked. Basically, transaction processing ensures that when you make multiple changes to data, all changes complete successfully or no changes occur (you'll learn more about transaction processing in later chapters).

Using Pessimistic Code With Transaction Processing

The following code provides an example of how to perform transaction processing from code with Pessimistic record locking:

```
Sub PessimisticTrans(strOldCity As String, strNewCity As String)
  Dim wrk As Workspace
```

```
    Dim db As Database
    Dim rst As Recordset
    Dim strCriteria As String

    Set wrk = DBEngine(0)
    Set db = CurrentDb()
    Set rst = db.OpenRecordSet("tblCustomers", dbOpenDynaset)
    rst.Lockedits = True    'Pessimistic Locking
    strCriteria = "[City] = '" & strOldCity & "'"
    rst.FindFirst strCriteria
    wrk.BeginTrans
    Do Until rst.NoMatch
      rst.Edit                          ' Lock Occurs Here
      rst.Fields("City") = strNewCity
      rst.Update
      rst.FindNext strCriteria
    Loop
    wrk.CommitTrans                     ' Lock Released Here
End Sub
```

Here you can see that the lock is in place from the very first edit that occurs until the **CommitTrans** is issued. This means no one can update any pages of data involving the edited records until the **CommitTrans** is issued. This can be prohibitive during a long process.

Understanding The LDB File

Every database that's opened for shared use has a corresponding LDB file. This is a locking file that's created to store computer and security names and to place byte range locks on the recordset. The LDB file always has the same name and location as the database whose locks it's tracking, and it's automatically deleted when the last user exits the database file. The LDB file isn't deleted in the following two situations:

• When the database is marked as damaged (politically correct term)

• When the last user out doesn't have delete rights in the folder containing the database and LDB files

The Jet database engine writes an entry to the LDB file for every user who opens the database. The size of the entry is 64 bytes. The first 32 bytes contain the user's computer name, and the last 32 bytes contain the user's security name. Because the maximum number of users for an Access database is 255, the LDB file can get only as large as 16K. The LDB file information is used to prevent users from writing data to pages that other users have locked and to determine who has the pages locked.

When a user exits an Access database, the user's entry in the LDB file isn't removed. Instead, the entry is overwritten by the next person accessing the database. For this reason, the LDB file doesn't necessarily provide an accurate picture of who is currently accessing the database.

Coding Around Pessimistic Locking Conflicts

It's fairly simple to write code to handle Pessimistic locking conflicts. Here is an example of what your code should look like:

```
Sub PessimisticRS(strCustID As String)
   Dim db As Database
   Dim rst As Recordset
   Dim strCriteria As String
   Dim intChoice As Integer

   On Error GoTo PessimisticRS_Err
   Set db = CurrentDb()
   Set rst = db.OpenRecordSet("tblCustomers", dbOpenDynaset)
   rst.LockEdits = True   'Invoke Pessimistic Locking
   strCriteria = "[CustomerID] = '" & strCustID & "'"
   rst.FindFirst strCriteria
   rst.Edit                                 ' Lock Occurs Here
   rst.Fields("City") = "Las Vegas"
   rst.Update                               ' Lock Released Here
   Exit Sub

PessimisticRS_Err:
   Select Case Err.Number
     Case 3197
       rst.Move 0
       Resume
     Case 3260
       intChoice = MsgBox(Err.Description, vbRetryCancel + vbCritical)
       Select Case intChoice
         Case vbRetry
           Resume
         Case Else
           MsgBox "Couldn't Lock"
       End Select
     Case 3167
       MsgBox "Record Has Been Deleted"
     Case Else
       MsgBox Err.Number & ": " & Err.Decription
   End Select
End Sub
```

The error-handling code for this routine handles all of the errors that can occur with Pessimistic locking. If a Data Has Changed error occurs, the data is refreshed by the **rst.Move 0** invocation, and the code resumes on the line causing the error, forcing the **Edit** to be reissued. If a 3260 error occurs, the user is asked whether he wants to try again. If he responds affirmatively, the **Edit** is reissued; otherwise, the user is informed that the lock failed. If the record being edited has been deleted, an error 3167 occurs, and the user is informed that the record has been deleted. Here's what your code should look like when transaction processing is involved:

```
Sub PessimisticRSTrans()
  Dim wrk As Workspace
  Dim db As Database
  Dim rst As Recordset
  Dim intCounter As Integer
  Dim intTry As Integer
  Dim intChoice As Integer

  On Error GoTo PessimisticRSTrans_Err
  Set wrk = DBEngine(0)
  Set db = CurrentDb
  Set rst = db.OpenRecordSet("tblCustomers", dbOpenDynaset)
  rst.LockEdits = True
  wrk.BeginTrans
  Do While Not rst.EOF
    rst.Edit
    rst.Fields("CompanyName") = rst.Fields("CompanyName") & "1"
    rst.Update
    rst.MoveNext
  Loop
  wrk.CommitTrans
  Exit Sub

PessimisticRSTrans_Err:
  Select Case Err.Number
    Case 3197
      rst.Move 0
      Resume
    Case 3260
      intCounter = intCounter + 1
      If intCounter > 2 Then
        intChoice = MsgBox(Err.Description, vbRetryCancel + vbCritical)
        Select Case intChoice
          Case vbRetry
            intCounter = 1
          Case vbCancel
            Resume CantLock
        End Select
      End If
      DoEvents
```

```
        For intTry = 1 To 100: Next intTry
        Resume
      Case Else
        MsgBox "Error: " & Err.Number & ": " & Err.Description
      End Select
CantLock:
  wrk.Rollback
  Exit Sub
End Sub
```

This code attempts to lock the record. If it's unsuccessful (that is, an error 3260 is gener-ated), it tries three times before prompting the user for a response. When the user selects Retry, the process repeats. Otherwise, a **Rollback** occurs and the subroutine is exited. When a Data Has Been Changed error occurs, the subroutine refreshes the data and tries again. When any other error occurs, the **Rollback** is issued and none of the updates are accepted.

Using Optimistic Locking

Optimistic locking delays the time at which the record is locked. The lock is issued upon update of the record, rather than at the start of the edit. The code to use Optimistic locking will often look similar to the following:

```
Sub OptimisticLock(strCustID As String)
  Dim db As Database
  Dim rst As Recordset
  Dim strCriteria As String

  Set db = CurrentDb()
  Set rst = db.OpenRecordSet("tblCustomers", dbOpenDynaset)
  rst.Lockedits = False 'Optimistic Locking
  strCriteria = "[CustomerID] = '" & strCustID & "'"
  rst.FindFirst strCriteria
  rst.Edit
    rst.Fields("City") = "Las Vegas"
  rst.Update 'Lock Occurs and Is Released Here
End Sub
```

As you can see, in this case, the lock doesn't happen until the **Update** method is issued. The advantage of this method is that the page is locked very briefly. The disadvantage of this method occurs when two users grab the record for editing at the same time. When one user attempts to update, no error occurs. When the other user attempts to update, she receives an error indicating that the data has changed since her edit was first issued. The handling of this error message is covered later in this chapter.

Using Optimistic Locking With Transaction Processing

Optimistic locking with transaction handling isn't much different from Pessimistic locking. As the code reaches the **Update** method for each record, that record is locked. The code appears as follows:

```
Sub OptimisticTrans(strOldCity As String, strNewCity As String)
  Dim wrk As Workspace
  Dim db As Database
  Dim rst As Recordset
  Dim strCriteria As String

  Set wrk = DBEngine(0)
  Set db = CurrentDb()
  Set rst = db.OpenRecordSet("tblCustomers", dbOpenDynaset)
  rst.Lockedits = False  'Optimistic Locking
  strCriteria = "[City] = '" & strOldCity & "'"
  rst.FindFirst strCriteria
  wrk.BeginTrans
  Do Until rst.NoMatch
    rst.Edit
    rst.Fields("City") = strNewCity
    rst.Update                          ' Lock Occurs Here
    rst.FindNext strCriteria
  Loop
  wrk.CommitTrans                       ' Lock Released Here
End Sub
```

Coding Around Optimistic Locking Conflicts

Remember that with Optimistic locking, VBA attempts to lock the page when the **Update** method is issued. A strong chance exists that a 3197 (data has changed) error could, therefore, occur. This possibility needs to be handled within your code. Let's modify the preceding subroutine for Optimistic locking:

```
Sub OptimisticRS(strCustID)
  Dim db As Database
  Dim rst As Recordset
  Dim strCriteria As String
  Dim intChoice As Integer
  Set db = CurrentDb()

  On Error GoTo OptimisticRS_Err
  Set rst = db.OpenRecordSet("tblCustomers", dbOpenDynaset)
  rst.Lockedits = False 'Optimistic Locking
```

```
      strCriteria = "[CustomerID] = '" & strCustID & "'"
      rst.FindFirst strCriteria
      rst.Edit
      rst.Fields("City") = "Las Vegas"
      rst.Update                        ' Lock Occurs and Is Released Here
      Exit Sub

OptimisticRS_Err:
   Select Case Err.Number
     Case 3197
       If rst.EditMode = dbEditInProgress Then
         intChoice = MsgBox("Overwrite Other User's Changes?", _
         vbYesNoCancel + vbQuestion)
         Select Case intChoice
           Case vbCancel, vbNo
             MsgBox "Update Cancelled"
           Case vbYes
             rst.Update
             Resume
         End Select
       End If
     Case 3186, 3260  'Locked or Can't Be Saved
       intChoice = MsgBox(Err.Description, vbRetryCancel + vbCritical)
         Select Case intChoice
           Case vbRetry
             Resume
           Case vbCancel
             MsgBox "Update Cancelled"
         End Select
     Case Else
       MsgBox "Error: " & Err.Number & ": " & Err.Description
     End Select
End Sub
```

As with Pessimistic error handling, this routine traps for all potential errors that can occur with Optimistic locking. In the case of a Data Has Changed conflict, the user is warned of the problem and asked whether she wants to overwrite the other user's changes or cancel her own changes. In the case of a locking conflict, the user is asked whether she wants to try again. Here's what it looks like with transaction processing involved:

```
Sub OptimisticRSTrans()
  Dim db As Database
  Dim rs As Recordset
  Dim iCounter As Integer
  Dim iTry As Integer
  Dim iChoice As Integer
```

```
On Error GoTo OptimisticRSTrans_Err
Set db = CurrentDb
Set rs = db.OpenRecordSet("tblCustBackup", dbOpenDynaset)
rs.Lockedits = False
BeginTrans
Do While Not rs.EOF
  rs.Edit
  rs.Fields("CompanyName") = rs.Fields("CompanyName") & "1"
  rs.Update
  rs.MoveNext
Loop
CommitTrans
Exit Sub

OptimisticRSTrans_Err:
  Select Case Err.Number
    Case 3197
      If rs.EditMode = dbEditInProgress Then
        iChoice = MsgBox("Overwrite Other User's Changes?", _
        vbYesNoCancel + vbQuestion)
        Select Case iChoice
          Case vbCancel, vbNo
            Resume RollItBack
          Case vbYes
            'rs.Update
            Resume
        End Select
      End If
    Case 3186, 3260   'Locked or Can't Be Saved
      iCounter = iCounter + 1
      If iCounter > 2 Then
        iChoice = MsgBox(Err.Description, vbRetryCancel + vbCritical)
        Select Case iChoice
          Case vbRetry
            iCounter = 1
          Case vbCancel
            Resume RollItBack
        End Select
      End If
      DoEvents
      For iTry = 1 To 100: Next iTry
      Resume
    Case Else
      MsgBox "Error: " & Err.Number & ": " & Err.Description
    End Select
```

```
RollItBack:
  Rollback
  Exit Sub
End Sub
```

When a Data Has Changed conflict occurs and the user opts not to overwrite the other user's changes, the entire processing loop is canceled (a **Rollback** occurs). When a locking error occurs, the lock is retried several times. If it's still unsuccessful, the entire transaction is rolled back.

Effectively Handling Locking Conflicts

When a user has a page locked and another user tries to view data on that page, no conflict occurs. On the other hand, when other users attempt to edit data on that same page, they experience an error.

You won't always want Access's own error handling to take over when a locking conflict occurs. For example, rather than having Access display its generic error message indicating that a record is locked, you might want to display your own message and attempt to lock the record a couple of additional times. To do something like this, it's necessary that you learn to interpret each locking error that's generated by VBA, so you can make a decision about how to respond.

Locking conflicts occur when:

♦ A user tries to edit or update a record that's already locked.

♦ A record has changed or been deleted since the user first started to edit it.

These errors can occur whether you're editing bound data via a form or accessing the records via VBA code.

Errors With Pessimistic Locking

To begin the discussion of locking conflicts, let's take a look at the types of errors that occur when Pessimistic locking is in place. With Pessimistic locking, you generally need to code for the errors detailed in Table 2.1.

Table 2.1   The errors you should generally trap for with Pessimistic locking.

Error Number	Description
3167	This error occurs when the record has been deleted since the user last accessed it. It's best to refresh the data.
3197	This error occurs when a record has been changed since the user last accessed it. It's best to refresh the data, and then attempt the **Edit** method again.
3260	This error occurs when the current record is locked by another user. It's generally sufficient to wait a short period of time and then try the lock again.

Unbound Forms

One solution to locking conflicts is to use unbound forms. They allow you to greatly limit the amount of time that a record is locked, and you can fully control when Access attempts to secure the lock. Unbound forms require significantly more coding than bound forms, so make sure that the benefits you receive from using unbound forms outweigh the coding and maintenance involved. With improvements to both forms and the Jet engine, the reasons to use unbound forms with Access data are less compelling, when writing to Access databases in any location on the network. We'll cover unbound forms in more detail later in this chapter; however, unbound forms will be substantially more useful thant bound forms for most client/server programming, simply because they allow you to manage implementation programmatically—a more powerful, yet simpler, way of accomplishing the task.

Errors With Optimistic Locking Or New Records

Now that you've seen what happens when a conflict occurs with Pessimistic locking, let's see what happens when Optimistic locking is in place or when users are adding new records. Table 2.2 details the three most common error codes generated by locking conflicts when Optimistic locking is in place.

Testing A Record For Locking Status

Often, you want to determine the locking status of a record *before* you attempt an operation with it. By setting the **LockEdits** property of the recordset to **True** and attempting to modify the record, you can determine whether the current row is locked. The code looks like this:

```
Sub TestLocking()
  Dim db As Database
  Dim rst As Recordset
  Dim fLocked As Boolean
```

Table 2.2   The errors you should generally trap for with Optimistic locking.

Error Number	Description
3186	This error occurs when the **Update** method is used to save a record on a locked page. It generally occurs when a user tries to move off of a record that she is adding onto a locked page. It also can occur when Optimistic locking is used and a user tries to update a record on the same page as a record that's locked by another machine. It's generally sufficient to wait a short period of time, and then try the lock again.
3197	This error occurs with Optimistic locking when User 1 has updated a record in the time since User 2 first started viewing it. It can also occur when User 2 is viewing data that isn't current; the data has changed, but the changes haven't yet been reflected on User 2's screen. You have two options: You can requery the recordset, losing User 2's changes, or you can resume and issue the **Update** method again, overwriting User 1's changes.
3260	This error usually occurs when the **Edit** method is issued and the page containing the current record is locked. It's best to wait a short period of time, and then try the lock again.

```
      Set db = CurrentDb
      Set rst = db.OpenRecordset("tblCustomers", dbOpenDynaset)
      fLocked = IsItLocked(rst)
      MsgBox fLocked
End Sub

Function IsItLocked(rstAny As Recordset) As Boolean
   On Error GoTo IsItLocked_Err
   IsItLocked = False
   With rstAny
     .LockEdits = True
     .Edit
     .MoveNext
     .MovePrevious
   End With
   Exit Function
IsItLocked_Err:
   If Err = 3260 Then
     IsItLocked = True
     Exit Function
   End If
End Function
```

The **TestLocking** routine sends its recordset to the **IsItLocked** function. The **IsItLocked** function receives the recordset as a parameter and sets its **LockEdits** property to **True**. It then issues an **Edit** method on the recordset. When an error occurs, the record is locked. The error handler sets the return value for the function to **True**.

Verifying that a record is locked is valuable, but sometimes it is also helpful to know who has locked the record. In the next section, you will see how you can verify who has a record locked.

Testing To See Who Has A Record Locked

Regardless of what type of error occurs with record locking, it's often useful to find out who has locked a particular record. You can easily accomplish this using VBA code. It's simply a matter of parsing the **Description** property of the **Err** object, as shown in the following code:

```
Sub WhoLockedIt()
   Dim db As Database
   Dim rst As Recordset

   On Error GoTo WhoLockedIt_Err
   Set db = CurrentDb
```

```
    Set rst = db.OpenRecordset("tblCustomers", dbOpenDynaset)
    rst.Edit
      rst.Fields("CompanyName") = "Hello"
    rst.Update
    Exit Sub

WhoLockedIt_Err:
  Dim strName As String
  Dim strMachine As String
  Dim intMachineStart As Integer

  intMachineStart = InStr(43, Err.Description, " on machine ") + 13
  If Err = 3260 Then
    strName = Mid(Err.Description, 44, _
        InStr(44, Err.Description, "'") - 44)
    strMachine = Mid(Err.Description, intMachineStart, _
        Len(Err.Description) - intMachineStart - 1)
  End If
  MsgBox strName & " on " & strMachine & " is the culprit!"
End Sub
```

The preceding routine simply parses the standard error description, pulling out the user name and machine name, and displays the information within a custom error message box.

Using Code To Refresh Or Requery

Throughout the chapter, we've referred to the need to requery a recordset. In this section, you'll see how to accomplish the requery process using code.

The **Requery** method ensures that the user gets to see any changes to existing records, as well as any records that have been added. It also ensures that deleted records are removed from the recordset. It's easiest to understand the requery process by looking at the data underlying a form. Consider the following code:

```
Private Sub cmdRequery_Click()
  If Me.RecordsetClone.Restartable Then
    Me.RecordsetClone.Requery
  Else
    MsgBox "Requery Method Not Supported On This Recordset"
  End If
End Sub
```

This code first tests the **Restartable** property of the recordset underlying the form. When the **Restartable** property is **True**, the recordset supports the **Requery** method. The **Requery** method is performed on the form's recordset. Of course, the **Restartable** property and

Requery method work on any recordset, not just the recordset underlying a form. The only reason that a recordset might not be restartable is because some back-end queries can't be restarted (you will learn more about this later).

Before this code is run, new records don't appear in the recordset and deleted records appear with **#Deleted**. After the **Requery** method is issued, all new records appear, and deleted records are removed.

Creating Custom Counters

Access provides an **AutoNumber** field type. The **AutoNumber** field can be set to automatically generate sequential or random values. Although the **AutoNumber** field type is sufficient for most situations, you might want to home-grow your own **AutoNumber** fields for any of the following reasons:

♦ You want an increment value other than 1.

♦ You don't like the fact that the **AutoNumber** field discards values from canceled records.

♦ The primary key value needs to be some algorithm of the other fields in the table (for example, the first few characters from a couple of fields).

♦ The primary key value needs to contain an alphanumeric string.

To generate your own automatically numbered sequential value, you should probably build a system table. This table contains the next available value for your custom **AutoNumber** field. It's important that you lock this table while a user is grabbing the next available sequential value. Otherwise, it's possible that two users will be assigned the same value.

Moving On To Specific Client/Server Techniques

Client/server refers to distributed processing of information. It involves storing data on database servers that are dedicated to the tasks of processing data as well as storing it. These database servers are referred to as *back ends*. The data is presented by a front-end tool such as Microsoft Access. Microsoft Access, with its tools that assist in the rapid development of queries, forms, and reports, provides an excellent front end for the presentation of back-end data. As more and more applications are downsized from mainframes and upsized from personal computers, it's becoming necessary for us to understand the details of client/server technology.

For years, most information professionals have worked with traditional programming languages. These languages are responsible for both processing and maintaining data integrity within the application. This means that data-validation rules must be embedded within the programming code. Furthermore, these types of applications are record-oriented. All records are read into memory and processed. This scenario has several drawbacks:

♦ If the underlying data structure changes, every application that uses the data structure has to be changed.

♦ Data-validation rules must be placed in *every* application that accesses a data table.

♦ Presentation, processing, and storage are all handled by one program.

♦ Record-oriented processing results in an extraordinary amount of unnecessary network traffic.

The client/server model introduces a separation of functionality. The client, or front end, is responsible for presenting the data and doing some processing. The server, or back end, is responsible for storing, protecting, and performing the bulk of processing on the data.

Determining When Client/Server Is Appropriate

Client/server was not as necessary when a clear delineation existed between mainframe applications and personal computer applications. Today, the line of demarcation is becoming blurry. Personal computer applications are beginning to take over many applications that had been relegated to mainframe computers in the past. The problem is that we're still very limited by the bandwidth of network communications. This is one place where client/server can really help.

Many developers are confused about what client/server really is. Access is a front-end application that can process data stored on a back end. In this scenario, the Access application runs on the client machine, accessing data stored on a database server that's running software such as Microsoft SQL Server. Access does an excellent job acting as the client-side, front-end software in this scenario. The confusion lies in Access's capability to act as a database server.

Many people mistakenly believe that an Access MDB database file stored on a file server acts as a database server. This isn't the case. The difference lies in the way in which data is retrieved when Access is acting as the front end to a database server versus when the data is stored in an Access MDB file. Imagine the following scenario:

Assume that you have a table with 500,000 records. A user runs a query that's based on the 500,000-record table stored in an Access database on a file server. The user wants to see a list of all the Nevadans who make more than $75,000 per year. With the data stored on the file server in the Access MDB file format, all records are sent over the network to the workstation, and the query is performed on the workstation. This results in significant network traffic, as shown in Figure 2.3.

On the other hand, assume that these 500,000 records are stored on a database server such as Microsoft SQL Server. The user runs the same query. In this case, only the names of the Nevadans who make more than $75,000 per year are sent over the network. In fact, if you request only specific fields, only the fields you request are retrieved, as shown in Figure 2.4.

Considering the implications of this for your development, why you should become concerned with client/server technology, and what doing so can offer you are difficult—but

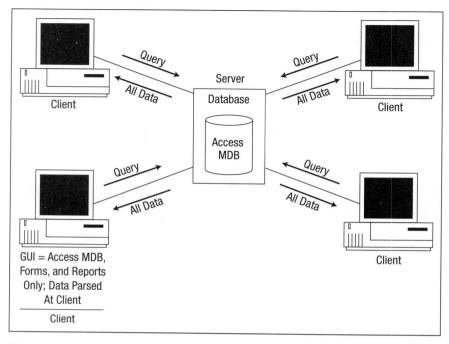

Figure 2.3
Network traffic resulting from Access running on a file server.

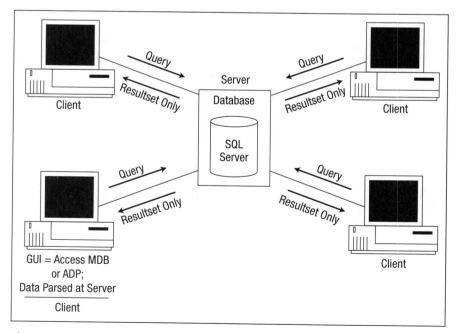

Figure 2.4
Access as a front end using a true server back end.

important—questions. The following sections are meant to provide guidelines for why you might want to upsize.

Large Volume Of Data

As the volume of data within an Access database increases, you'll probably notice a degradation in performance. Many people say that 100MB is the magic number for the maximum size of an Access database, whereas many back-end database servers can handle databases containing multiple gigabytes (and even terabytes) of data. Although a maximum size of 100MB for an Access database is a good general guideline, it's *not* a hard-and-fast rule. You might find that the need to upsize occurs when your database is significantly larger or smaller than 100MB. The magic number for you depends on all the factors discussed in the following sections, as well as on how many tables are included in the database. Generally, Access performs better with large volumes of data stored in a single table rather than in multiple tables.

Large Number Of Concurrent Users

Just as a large volume of data can be a problem, so can a large number of concurrent users. In fact, more than 10 users concurrently accessing an Access database can really degrade performance. As with the amount of data, this isn't a magic number. As a developer, you may have seen applications with less than 10 users where performance is awful, and you may have seen applications with significantly more than 10 users where performance is acceptable. It often depends on how the application is designed, as well as what tasks the users are performing.

Demand For Faster Performance

Certain applications, by nature, demand better performance than other applications. An online transaction processing system (OLTP) generally requires significantly better performance than a decision support system (DSS). Imagine 100 users simultaneously taking phone orders. It would not be appropriate for the users of the system to ask their customers to wait 15 seconds between entering each item that's ordered. On the other hand, asking a user to wait 60 seconds to process a management report the user runs once each month isn't a lot to ask (although many users will still complain about the minute). Not only does the client/server architecture itself lead to better performance, but most back-end database servers can utilize multithreaded operating systems with multiple processors. Access can't.

Problems With Increased Network Traffic

As a file server within an organization experiences increasing demands, the Access application might simply exacerbate an already growing problem. By moving the application data to a database server, the reduced demands on the network overall might provide all users on the network with better performance regardless of whether they're utilizing the Access application.

Probably one of the most exaggerated situations where this might be true is one in which all the workstations are diskless. Windows and all application software would be installed on a file server. The users might all concurrently load Microsoft Word, Microsoft Excel, and

Microsoft PowerPoint over the network. In addition, they might have large Access applications with many database objects and large volumes of data, which would all be stored on the file server as well. In such a situation, needless to say, performance would be terrible. You can't expect an already overloaded file server to be able to handle sending large volumes of data over a small bandwidth. The benefits offered by client/server technology can help alleviate this problem.

Importance Of Backup And Recovery

The backup and recovery options offered with an Access MDB database stored on a file server simply don't rival the options for backup and recovery on a database server. Any database server worth its salt sports very powerful uninterruptable power supplies (UPSs). Many have hot swapping disk drives with disk mirroring, disk duplexing, or disk striping with parity (redundant array of independent [or inexpensive] disks [RAID] Level 5 protection). Disk mirroring and duplexing mean that data can be written to multiple drives at one time, providing instantaneous backups.

Furthermore, some database server tape backup software enables backups to be completed while users are accessing the system. Many offer automatic transaction logging. All these mean less chance of data loss or downtime. With certain applications, this type of backup and recovery is overkill. With other applications, it's imperative.

Tip

Some of what back ends have to offer in terms of backup and recovery can be mimicked by using code and replication. However, it's nearly impossible to get the same level of protection from an Access database stored on a file server that you can get from a true back-end database stored on a database server.

Importance Of Security

Access offers what can be considered the best security for a desktop database. Although this is the case, the security offered by an Access database can't compare with that provided by most database servers. Database server security often works in conjunction with the network operating system. This is the case, for example, with Microsoft SQL Server and Windows NT Server. Remember that no matter how much security you place on an Access database, this doesn't prevent a user from deleting the entire MDB file from the network disk. It's very easy to offer protection from this potential problem, and others, on a database server. Furthermore, many back-end application database server products offer field-level security not offered within an Access MDB file. Finally, many back ends offer integrated security with one logon for both the network and the database.

Need To Share Data Among Multiple Front-End Tools

The Access MDB file format is proprietary. Very few other products can read data stored in the Access database format. With a back-end database server that supports ODBC, front-end applications can be written in a variety of front-end application software, all concurrently utilizing the same back-end data.

Applying The Guidelines

Well, everything in the previous sections is important and useful. Nevertheless, you need to make a determination for your application in your environment. To do so, you need to evaluate the specific environment in which your application will run, including the following considerations:

- How many users are there?
- How much data is there?
- What is the network traffic like already?
- What type of performance is required?
- How disastrous is downtime?
- How sensitive is the data?
- What other applications will utilize the data?

After you answer all these questions, and additional ones, you can begin to make decisions as to whether the benefits of the client/server architecture outweigh the costs involved. The good news is that it's not an all-or-none decision. Various options are available for client/server applications that utilize Access as a front end. Furthermore, when you design your application with upsizing in mind, moving to client/server won't require you to throw out what you've done and start again.

Client/Server Strategies

As you might have inferred from the previous sections, it's very easy to implement client/server ineffectively. This can result in worse, rather than better, performance. The developer's task is to intelligently apply appropriate techniques that deploy client/server systems effectively. The following sections discuss strategies to help you develop smart client/server applications. One of the most important issues for you to consider when developing for client/server is the type of recordset that you use to maintain record information returned from the database. As with most considerations in a distributed environment, this is not a simple issue—there are many possible variations of what you might do with the data, and each of those variations will have implications for the recordset type that you choose.

Selecting The Best Recordset Type

When making choices about recordsets, sometimes it's best to create a Dynaset, and at other times it's more efficient to create a Snapshot. It's very important that you understand under what circumstances each choice is the most appropriate.

In essence, a *Dynaset* is a collection of bookmarks that enables each record on the server to be identified uniquely. Each bookmark corresponds to one record on the server and is generally equivalent to the primary key of the record. Because the bookmark is a direct pointer back to the original data, a Dynaset is an updateable set of records. When you create a

Dynaset, you create a set of bookmarks of all rows that meet the query criteria. When you open a recordset using code, only the first bookmark is returned to the user PC's memory. The remaining columns from the record are brought into memory only when they're directly referenced using code. This means that large fields, such as OLE and Memo, aren't retrieved from the server unless they're explicitly accessed using code. Access uses the primary key to fetch the remainder of the columns. As the code moves from record to record in the Dynaset, additional bookmarks and columns are retrieved from the server.

> ### Warning
>
> *All the bookmarks aren't retrieved (just as all records in the recordset aren't retrieved) unless a **MoveLast** method is issued or each record in the recordset is visited using code.*

Although this keyset method of data retrieval is relatively efficient at the client side, Dynasets carry significant overhead associated with their ability to be edited. This is why Snapshots are often more efficient.

When you open a *Snapshot* type of recordset, all columns from the first row are retrieved into memory. As you move to each row, all columns within that new row are retrieved. When a **MoveLast** method is issued, all rows and all columns meeting the query criteria are immediately retrieved into the client machine's memory. Because a Snapshot isn't editable and maintains no link back to the server, it can be more efficient. This is generally true only for relatively small recordsets. The caveat lies in the fact that, when you invoke **MoveLast** with a Snapshot, all rows and all columns in the resultset are returned to the user's computer memory whether they're accessed or not. With a resultset containing more than 500 records, the fact that all columns are returned to the user's computer memory outweighs the benefits provided by a Snapshot. In these cases, you may want to create a read-only Dynaset.

Forward-Scrolling Snapshots

When your data doesn't need to be updated and moving forward through a recordset is sufficient, you may want to use a forward-scrolling Snapshot. Forward-scrolling Snapshots are extremely fast and efficient. You create a forward-scrolling Snapshot by using the **dbForwardOnly** option of the **OpenRecordset** method. This means that you can't issue a **MovePrevious** or **MoveFirst** method. You also can't use a **MoveLast**. This is because only one record is retrieved at a time. There is no concept of a set of records, so Access can't move to the last record. This method of data retrieval provides significantly better performance than regular Snapshots with large recordsets.

Keyset Fetching

The fact that Dynasets return a set of primary keys causes problems with forms. With a very large set of records and a large primary key, sending just the primary keys over the network wire can generate a huge volume of network traffic. When you open a form, Access retrieves just enough data to display on the form. It then continues to fetch the remainder of the primary keys that satisfy the query criteria. Whenever keyboard input is sensed, the fetching process stops until idle time is available. It then continues to fetch the remainder of the primary keys. To prevent the huge volume of network traffic associated with this process, you must carefully limit the size of the Dynasets that are returned. Methods of accomplishing this are covered in the section titled "Optimizing Forms."

Utilizing Pass-Through Queries And Stored Procedures

It's important to remember that executing pass-through queries and stored procedures is much more efficient than returning a recordset to be processed by Access. The difference lies in where the processing occurs. With pass-through queries and stored procedures, all the processing is completed on the server. When operations are performed using VBA code, all the records that will be affected by the process must be returned to the user's memory, modified, then returned to the server. This generates a significant amount of network traffic and slows down processing immensely.

Reducing The Number Of Connections To The Server

Some database servers are capable of running multiple queries on one connection. Other servers, such as Microsoft SQL Server, are capable of processing only one query per connection. You should try to limit the number of connections required by your application. Here are some ways that you can reduce the number of connections your application requires.

Dynasets containing more than 100 records require two connections—one to fetch the key values from the server, and the other to fetch the data associated with the first 100 records. Therefore, try to limit query results to fewer than 100 records wherever possible.

When connections are at a premium, close connections that you're no longer using. You can accomplish this by moving to the last record in the resultset or by running a Top 100 Percent query. Both of these techniques have dramatic negative effects on performance because all the records in the resultset are fetched. Therefore, you should use these techniques only when reducing connections is more important than optimizing performance.

Finally, you might want to set a connection timeout. This means that if no action has been taken for a specified period of time, the connection will be closed. The default value for the connection timeout is 10 minutes. You can modify this value in the HKEY_ LOCAL_MACHINE\SOFTWARE\Microsoft\Jet\4.0\Engines\ODBC key of the Windows Registry by changing the **ConnectionTimeout** setting. The timeout occurs even if a form is open. Fortunately, Access automatically reestablishes the connection when it's needed.

Optimizing Data Handling Activities

One of the best things that you can do to optimize data handling—such as edits, inserts, and deletes—is to add a version field (timestamp) to each remote table. This version field is used when users update the data on the remote table to avoid overwrite conflicts. When this field doesn't exist, the server compares every field to see whether it's changed since the user first began editing the record. This is quite inefficient and is much slower than evaluating a timestamp.

The use of transactions is another way to improve performance significantly, because transactions enable multiple updates to be written as a single batch. As an added benefit, they protect your data by ensuring that everything has executed successfully before changes are committed to disk.

Optimizing Queries And Forms

On the whole, the movement to client/server improves performance. If you aren't careful when designing your queries, forms, and reports, however, the movement to client/server can actually degrade performance. You can do several things to ensure that the movement to client/server is beneficial. These techniques are broken down into query optimization techniques, form optimization techniques, and report optimization techniques. Report optimization is outside the scope of what we are looking at in this chapter; however, it is worth taking some time to consider both query and form optimizations. The next two sections consider each type of optimization in turn.

Optimizing Queries

Servers can't perform many of the functions offered by the Access query builder. The functions that can't be processed on the server are performed on the workstation. This often results in a large amount of data being sent over the network wire. This extra traffic can be eliminated if your queries are designed so they can be processed solely by the server.

The following are examples of problem queries that can't be performed on the server:

♦ Top N percent queries

♦ Queries containing user-defined or Access functions

♦ Queries that involve tables from two different data sources—for example, a query that joins tables from two different servers or from an Access table and a server table

Optimizing Forms

The following techniques can help you design forms that capitalize on the benefits of the client/server architecture. The idea is to design your forms so they request the minimal amount of data from the server and they obtain additional data only when requested by the user. This means that you request as few records and fields as possible from the server. You can accomplish this by basing forms on queries rather than directly on the tables. You can further refine your forms by designing them specifically with data retrieval in mind. For example, a form can initially be opened with no **RecordSource**. The form can require that users limit the criteria before any records are displayed.

You should store static tables, such as a **State** table, locally. This reduces network traffic and requests to the server. Furthermore, combo boxes and list boxes shouldn't be based on server data. Whenever possible, the row source for combo boxes and list boxes should be based on local static tables. If this isn't possible, you can use a text box in conjunction with a combo box. The **Row Source** property of the combo box is initially left blank. The user must enter the first few characters into the text box. The **Row Source** of the combo box is based on a SQL **SELECT** statement using the characters entered into the text box.

Furthermore, **OLE Object** and **Memo** fields are large and, therefore, significantly increase network traffic. It's best not to display the contents of these fields unless they're specifically requested by the user. This can be accomplished by setting the **Visible** property of **OLE** and **Memo** fields to **False**, or by placing these fields on another page of the form. You can add a command button that enables the user to display the additional data when required.

Finally, you may want to use unbound forms. This involves creating a form and removing its **RecordSource**. Users are provided with a combo box that enables them to select one record. A recordset is built from the client/server data with the one row the user selected. With this method of form design, everything needs to be coded. Your form code needs to handle all adds, edits, and deletes. None of the controls on the form should have their **Control Source** property filled in. The name of each control will then correspond with a field in the database server table. The **Open** event of such a form might look similar to the following:

```
Private Sub Form_Open(Cancel As Integer)
   Set mdb = CurrentDb
   Me.txtTitle.SetFocus
End Sub
```

The event code sets a module-level database variable to the current database and sets focus to the **txtTitle** text box. The **AfterUpdate** event of the text box would then look similar to the following:

```
Private Sub txtTitle_AfterUpdate()
   Me!cboTitle.RowSource = "SELECT DISTINCTROW " _
       & " [dbo_titles].[title_id] FROM [dbo_titles] " _
       & "WHERE [dbo_titles].[title_id] Like '" & Me!txtTitle.Text & "*';"
End Sub
```

The code in the **AfterUpdate** event sets the **RowSource** property of the combo box to a SQL **SELECT** statement that selects all records from the **Titles** table where the **title_id** field begins with the first few characters that the user typed. In this way, the combo box isn't populated with all the titles from the server. The **AfterUpdate** event of the combo box would look similar to the following:

```
Private Sub cboTitle_AfterUpdate()
   Dim fSuccess As Boolean
```

```
    Set mrst = mdb.OpenRecordset("Select * From dbo_Titles " _
        & "Where title_id = '" & Me!cboTitle.Value & "';")
    fSuccess = PopulateForm(Me, mrst)
    If Not fSuccess Then
      MsgBox "Record Not Found"
    End If
End Sub
```

The **OpenRecordset** method is used to open a recordset based on the linked table called **dbo_Titles**. Notice that only the records with the matching **title_id** are retrieved. Because the **title_id** is the primary key, only one record is returned. The **PopulateForm** function is then called, which you might implement as shown here:

```
Function PopulateForm(frmAny As Form, rstAny As Recordset)
  If rstAny.EOF Then
    PopulateForm = False
  Else
    Dim fld As Field
    For Each fld In rstAny.Fields
      frmAny(fld.Name) = fld
    Next fld
    PopulateForm = True
  End If
End Function
```

The **PopulateForm** function checks to ensure that the recordset that was passed has records. It then loops through each field on the form, matching field names with controls on the form. It sets the value of each control on the form to the value of the field in the recordset with the same name as the control name.

Note that these changes to the data within the form don't update the data on the database server. Furthermore, the form doesn't provide for inserts or deletes. You need to write code to issue updates, inserts, and deletes, and you have to provide command buttons to give your users access to that functionality.

Briefly Considering The Use Of DAO With ODBCDirect

The ODBCDirect **Workspace** provides an alternative when you only need to execute queries or stored procedures against a back-end server, such as Microsoft SQL Server, or when your client application needs the specific capabilities of ODBC, such as batch updates or asynchronous query execution. The DAO Object Model when working with ODBCDirect connections is slightly different than the DAO Object Model when working against Jet databases, as shown in Figure 2.5.

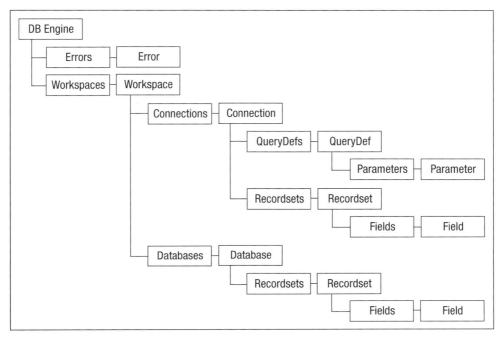

Figure 2.5
The ODBCDirect DAO Object Model.

Connecting To A Database Through ODBCDirect

A **Connection** object is similar to a **Database** object. In fact, a **Connection** object and a **Database** object represent different references to the same object. Properties of each of these two object types allow you to obtain a reference to the other corresponding object, which simplifies the task of converting ODBC client applications that use Microsoft Jet to use ODBCDirect instead. Use the **OpenConnection** method to connect to an ODBC data source. The resulting **Connection** object contains information about the connection, such as the server name, the data source name, and so on.

Using Queries With ODBCDirect

Although DAO doesn't support stored queries in an ODBCDirect workspace, you can create a compiled query as a **QueryDef** object and use it to execute action queries as well as to execute stored procedures on the server. The **Prepare** property lets you decide whether to create a private, temporary stored procedure on the server from a **QueryDef** before actually executing the query.

Parameter queries can also be passed to the server, using **Parameter** objects in the **Parameters** collection of the **QueryDef**. The **Direction** property lets you specify a **Parameter** as input, output, or both, or lets you accept a return value from a stored procedure.

Data Manipulation With ODBCDirect

Creating a **Recordset** object is a convenient way to query a database and manipulate the resulting set of records. The **OpenRecordset** method accepts a SQL string or a **QueryDef** object (stored query) as a data source argument. The resulting **Recordset** object features an extremely rich set of properties and methods with which to browse and modify data.

The **Recordset** object is available in four different types: Dynamic, Dynaset, Forward-Only, and Snapshot, which correspond to ODBC cursor types: Dynamic, Keyset, Forward-Only, and Static.

A batch update cursor library is available for client applications that need to work with a cursor without holding locks on the server or without issuing update requests one record at a time. Instead, the client stores update information on many records in a local buffer (or *batch*) and issues a batch update.

Asynchronous Method Execution

The **Execute**, **MoveLast**, **OpenConnection**, and **OpenRecordset** methods feature the **dbRunAsync** option. This allows your client application to perform other tasks (such as loading forms, for example) while the method is executing. You can check the **StillExecuting** property to see whether the task is complete and terminate an asynchronous task with the **Cancel** method.

Where To Go From Here

In this chapter, we have identified some of the key differences between client/server solutions with Access and local, desktop-based solutions with Access. We have also looked at many of the issues that surround true client/server computing—whether implemented with Access on the back-end or a more scalable solution, such as Microsoft SQL Server.

Most notably, we have dedicated a substantial amount of consideration to locking and transactions, and discussed the significance of such issues when working with databases in a client/server environment. Although we focused on addressing such issues from within the Access model, clearly these issues will arise no matter what database product you use.

We looked as well at the DAO ODBCDirect Object Model, which is slightly different in implementation from the standard DAO Object Model, and at some of the ways in which you could use ODBCDirect for more efficient processing in the client/server environment.

In Chapter 3, we will move on to a consideration of some of the other, simpler ways you can use Access to connect with remote databases for a client/server environment. Most notably, we will focus on linking to the data stored within those locations, both from the Access IDE and from the program code within your applications.

Building Client/Server Applications By Exporting And Linking Tables

As you've probably seen quite clearly from the previous chapters in this book, programming for a multiuser environment—whether one that runs pure client/server, distributed workgroup, or some other multiuser configuration—has substantial issues of its own. When you consider the fact that client/server today can also include Internet front ends, as well as connection to a wide variety of back ends, from SQL Server to Oracle, the innate complexity of client/server programming only increases. This chapter will guide you through some of the primary issues of exported and linked data within client/server development.

Roles That Access Can Play In The Application Design Model

Before you move on to learn more about linking and exporting and the role they play in client/server implementations, let's take a look at the different roles that Access can take in an application's design. Several options are available.

Access As Both The Front End And Back End

In previous chapters of this book, you've focused on using Access as the front end; in some situations—particularly if you have used the Database Splitter Wizard or a similar technique—it's possible to use Access as both the front end and the back end. In such deployments, however, the Access database isn't acting as a true back end in that it's not doing any processing. The architecture in

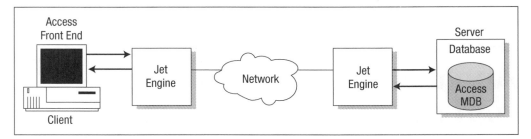

Figure 3.1
Access as a front end using an MDB file for data storage.

this scenario is shown in Figure 3.1. The Access application resides on the workstation. Using the Microsoft Jet engine, it communicates with data stored in an Access MDB database file stored on the file server.

Access As The Front End Using Links To Communicate To A Back End

In the second scenario, back-end tables can be linked to the front-end application database. The process of linking to back-end tables is almost identical to that of linking to tables in other Access databases or to external tables stored in FoxPro, Paradox, dBASE, or some other desktop database product. After the back-end tables have been linked to the front-end application database, they can be treated like any other linked tables. Access utilizes open database connectivity (ODBC) to communicate with the back-end tables.

In use, your application sends an Access SQL statement to the Access Jet engine. Jet translates the Access SQL statement into ODBC SQL. The ODBC SQL statement is then sent to the ODBC manager. The ODBC manager locates the correct ODBC driver and passes it the ODBC SQL statement. The ODBC driver, supplied by the back-end vendor, translates the ODBC SQL statement into the back end's specific dialect. The back-end–specific query is sent to the SQL Server and to the appropriate database. As you might imagine, all this translation takes quite a bit of time. That's why one of the two alternatives that follow might present a better solution.

Access As The Front End Using SQL Pass-Through To Communicate To A Back End

One of the bottlenecks of linked tables is the translation of the Access SQL statement by Jet to ODBC SQL, which is translated by the ODBC driver to a generic SQL statement. Not only is the translation slow, but there might be other reasons why you'd want to bypass the translation process:

♦ Access SQL might not support some operation that's supported by the native query language of the back end.

◆ Either the Jet engine or the ODBC driver produces a SQL statement that isn't optimized for the back end.

◆ You want a process performed in its entirety on the back end.

We covered pass-through queries in Chapter 2 in some detail, and we'll discuss them in more detail in the "Pass-Through Queries" section later in this chapter. For now, let's look at what happens when a pass-through query is executed. The pass-through query is written in the syntax specific to the back-end database server. Although the query does pass through the Jet engine, Jet does not perform any translation on the query. Neither does ODBC. The ODBC manager sends the query to the ODBC driver. The ODBC driver passes the query on to the back end without performing any translation. In other words, exactly what was sent from Access is what is received by the SQL database. This scenario is illustrated in Figure 3.2.

Notice that the Jet engine, the ODBC manager, and the ODBC driver aren't eliminated entirely. They're still there, but they have much less impact on the process than they do with attached tables. As you'll see in the section on pass-through queries, pass-through queries aren't a complete solution, although they're very useful. For example, the results of a pass-through query aren't updateable. Furthermore, because pass-through queries are written in the back end's specific SQL dialect, you will need to rewrite them if you swap out your back end. For these reasons, and others, pass-through queries are usually used in combination with other solutions.

Note

The ODBCDirect Object Model was explored in detail in Chapter 2.

Access As The Front End Using ActiveX Data Objects To Communicate To A Back End

One additional scenario is available when you're working with a back-end database server. This involves using ActiveX Data Objects (ADO), which you've seen mentioned several

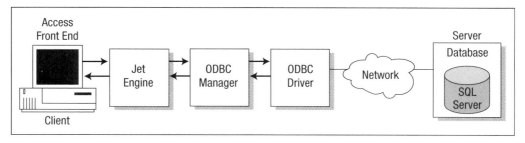

Figure 3.2
Access sending a pass-through query to a back-end database.

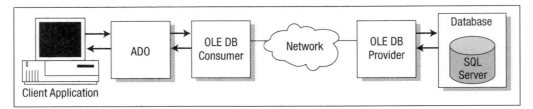

Figure 3.3
Access using ADO to communicate to a back end.

times but which you will not explore in depth until the next chapter. Using ADO, you bypass the Jet engine entirely. SQL statements are written in ODBC SQL. Figure 3.3 illustrates this scenario.

As you've learned previously, ADO is a very thin wrapper on the OLE DB COM interfaces—which are themselves a wrapper of the ODBC application programming interface (API) calls. The SQL statement travels quickly through all the layers to the back-end database. From a performance standpoint, this solution puts Jet to shame. The major advantage of ADO over pass-through queries is that you write the SQL statements in ODBC SQL rather than the back-end–specific SQL. This means your application is easily portable to other back-end database servers. You can swap out your back end with little modification to your application.

The major disadvantage of ADO is that it can't be used with bound forms or reports—meaning more coding for you in many cases. As with pass-through queries, you can use this option in combination with the other solutions to gain required performance benefits in mission-critical parts of the application.

The Basics Of Linking To External Data

Linking to external data, including data that isn't stored within another Access database, is covered extensively throughout this chapter. However, at this point it's valuable to understand the three options available to you when linking to external data. You can:

◆ Design the databases separately from the start (which is almost always the case when linking to non-Access-based back ends or databases running on other platforms).

◆ Include all objects in one database and split them manually when you're ready to distribute your application.

◆ Include all objects in one database and split them using the Database Splitter Wizard.

Be aware that when you're distributing an application using linked tables, it's necessary to write code to ensure that the data tables can be located from each application database on the network. When each user has the same path to the file server, this isn't a problem. If the path to the file server varies, you need to write a routine that ensures the tables can be located. If they can't be located, the routine should prompt the user for the location of the data. The following sections detail how to use data in each of the manners detailed previously.

Using The Database Splitter Wizard

To use the Database Splitter Wizard to split the objects within a database into two separate MDB files, perform the following steps:

1. Open the database whose objects you want to split.

2. Select Tools | Database Utilities | Database Splitter. The Database Splitter dialog box will appear, as shown in Figure 3.4.

3. Click on Split Database. The Create Back-End Database dialog box will appear.

4. Enter the name for the database that will contain all of the tables and click on Split. The Database Splitter Wizard creates a new database that contains all of the tables. Links are created between the current database and the database containing the tables. When it finishes, the wizard will display a message indicating that the split was successful and then return you to the Database window. Although this technique is useful when working with a single database, often you will work with other databases. The next section details how to manually create a link to another Access database using the Access IDE.

Creating Links To Access Tables

To create a link to an Access table, perform the following steps:

1. Right-click on any tab of the Database window.

2. Select Link Tables. The Link dialog box will appear.

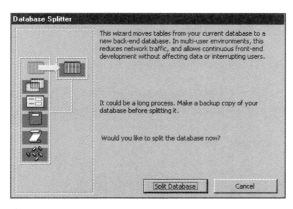

Figure 3.4
The Database Splitter dialog box.

3. Within the Link dialog box, select the name of the database containing the table you want to link to.

4. Click on Link. The Link Tables dialog box will appear.

5. Within the Link Tables dialog box, select the tables to which you want to establish a link.

6. Click on OK. The link process finishes. Notice the arrow indicating that the tables are linked tables rather than tables whose data is stored within the current database.

Although linking to Access tables is straightforward, often you will want to link to non-Access tables from your Access front end. In the next section, I will detail how you create links to non-Access databases from the IDE.

Creating Links To Other Types Of Tables

The process of creating links to other types of database files is a little different. To create a link to another type of database file, perform the following steps:

1. Right-click on any tab of the Database window.

2. Select Link Tables. The Link dialog box will appear.

3. Within the Link dialog box, use the Files Of Type drop-down list to indicate the type of table you're linking to.

4. Select the external file whose data you'll be linking to.

5. Click on Link. The Select Index Files dialog will appear. It's important that you select any index files associated with the data file. These indexes are automatically updated by Access as you add, change, and delete table data from within Access.

6. You'll receive a message indicating that the index was added successfully and that you can add other indexes if you choose. Click on OK.

7. Add any additional indexes and click on Close when you're done.

8. Access will display the Select Unique Record Identifier dialog box. This dialog box enables you to select a unique identifier for each record in the table. Select a unique field and click on OK. Notice the icon indicating the type of file you linked to.

Now that you have seen some of the different techniques at your disposal for accessing external data from within your database applications, let's take a little different look at this issue—when and why you will use each of these techniques, and the considerations you should keep in mind when making your decisions.

When And Why To Use Importing, Linking, And Opening

The process of importing data into an Access table makes a copy of the data, placing the copy within an Access table. After data is imported, it's treated like any other native Access table. In fact, neither you nor Access has any way of knowing where the data came from. As a result, imported data offers the same performance and flexibility as any other Access table.

The process of linking to external data is quite different from the process of importing data. Linked data remains in its native format. By establishing a link to the external data, you're able to build queries, forms, and reports that use or display the data. After you've created a link to external data, the link remains permanently established unless you explicitly remove it. The linked table appears in the database window just like any other Access table. The only difference is you can't modify its structure from within Access. In fact, if the data source permits multiuser access, the users of your application can be modifying the data along with users of the applications written in its native database format (such as FoxPro, dBASE, or Paradox).

The process of opening an external table is similar to linking to the table, except that a permanent relationship isn't created. When you link to an external table, connection information is maintained from session to session. When you open the table, you create a temporary recordset referencing the remote table, and no permanent link is established.

Knowing Which Option To Select

It's important that you understand when to import external data, when to link to external data, and when to open an external table directly. Import external data under the following circumstances:

♦ When you're migrating an existing system into Access.

♦ When you want to take advantage of and access external data that you will then use to run a large volume of queries and reports, but you won't be updating the data. In such cases, you will often want the added performance that native Access data provides without converting the data between formats.

When you're migrating an existing system to Access and you're ready to permanently migrate either test or production data into your application, you should then import the tables into Access. Another good reason to import external data is because data is downloaded from a mainframe into ASCII format on a regular basis, and you want to utilize the data for reports. Rather than attempting to link to the data and suffer the performance hits associated with such a link, you can import the data each time it's downloaded from the mainframe. You should link to external data under the following circumstances:

♦ The data is used by a legacy application requiring the native file format.

♦ The data resides on an ODBC-compliant database server.

♦ You'll access the data on a regular basis.

Often, you won't have the time or resources needed to rewrite an application in FoxPro, Paradox, or some other language. You might be developing additional applications that will share data with the legacy application, or you might want to utilize the strong querying and reporting capabilities of Access rather than developing queries and reports in the native environment. By linking to the external data, users of existing applications can continue to work with the applications and their data. Your Access applications can retrieve and modify data without concern for corrupting, or in any other way harming, the data.

When the data resides in an ODBC database such as Microsoft SQL Server, you will likely want to reap the data-retrieval benefits provided by a database server. By linking to the ODBC data source, you can take advantage of Access's ease of use as a front-end tool, while taking advantage of client/server technology at the same time. Finally, if you intend to access data on a regular basis, linking to the external table, rather than temporarily opening the table directly, provides you with ease of use and performance benefits. When you've created the link, Access treats the table just like any other Access table.

Warning

Access can corrupt linked data when it rewrites data to the linked file.

Open an external table directly under the following circumstances:

♦ When you rarely need to establish a connection to the external data source

♦ When you've determined that performance actually improves by opening the data source directly

If you rarely need to access the external data, it might be appropriate to open it directly. Links increase the size of your MDB file. This size increase isn't necessary if you'll rarely access the data. Furthermore, in certain situations, when accessing indexed sequential access method (ISAM) data, you might find that opening the table directly provides better performance than linking to it.

Although this chapter does cover the process of importing external data, it focuses on linking to or directly opening external data tables rather than importing them. We focus on linking to external data because the import process is a one-time process. When data is imported into an Access table, it's no longer accessed by the application in its native format. Microsoft Access enables you to import, link to, and open files in the following formats:

♦ Microsoft Jet databases (including versions prior to the Jet 4 engine that ships with Office)

♦ Microsoft FoxPro versions 2, 2.5, 2.6, 3, and DBC (Visual FoxPro)

♦ dBASE versions III, IV, and V

♦ Paradox versions 3.x, 4.x, and 5.x

♦ Microsoft Excel spreadsheets versions 3, 4, 5, 6, 7, 97, and 2000

♦ Lotus WKS, WK1, WK3, and WK4 spreadsheets

♦ ASCII text files stored in a tabular format

Using External Data

Microsoft Access is very capable of interfacing with data from other sources. It can utilize data from any ODBC data source, as well as data from FoxPro, dBASE, Paradox, Lotus, Excel, and many other sources. External data is data stored outside the current database. It can refer to data stored in another Microsoft Access database as well as to data stored in a multitude of other file formats including ODBC, ISAM, spreadsheet, ASCII, and more.

Access is an excellent front-end product, providing a powerful and effective means of presenting data—even data from external sources. Data is stored in places besides Access for many reasons. For instance, large databases can be more effectively managed on a back-end database server such as Microsoft SQL Server. Data is often stored in a FoxPro, dBASE, or Paradox file format because the data is being used by a legacy application written in one of these environments. Text data has often been downloaded from a mainframe. Regardless of the reason why data is stored in another format, it's necessary that you understand how to manipulate this external data within your VBA modules. When you're able to access data from other sources, you can create queries, forms, and reports that utilize the data.

When accessing external data, you have three choices: You can import the data into an Access database, access the data by linking to it from within your Access database, or open a data source directly. As you'll learn in the next section, importing the data is optimal (except with ODBC data sources), but not always possible. Short of importing external data, you should link to external files because Microsoft Access maintains a lot of information about these linked files. This optimizes performance when you're manipulating the external files. Sometimes a particular situation warrants accessing the data directly. Therefore, you should know how to work with linked files, as well as how to open and manipulate files directly.

Tip

Many of the examples in this chapter use data stored in the ISAM file format, which includes files created in FoxPro, dBASE, and Paradox. If you performed a standard installation of Access 2000, you probably didn't install the drivers necessary to communicate with an ISAM file. You need to rerun setup and select the ISAM's checkbox if you want to perform many of the exercises covered in this chapter.

Importing External Data

The process of importing external data is quite simple. You can import external data by using either the user interface or VBA code. When you're planning to import the data only once or twice, utilize the user interface. When you're importing data on a regular basis—for example, from a downloaded mainframe file—write code that accomplishes the task transparently to the user.

Importing External Data Using The User Interface

To import an external data file using the user interface, perform the following steps:

1. Right-click on any tab of the database window.

2. Within the pop-up menu, select the Import option. The Import dialog box will appear.

3. Use the Files Of Type drop-down list to select the type of file you're importing.

4. Select the file you want to import and click on Import.

Depending on the type of file you select, the import process might finish, or you might be provided with additional dialogs. For example, when you select Excel Spreadsheet, Access invokes the Import Spreadsheet Wizard, as shown in Figure 3.5. The Import Spreadsheet Wizard then walks you through the process of importing spreadsheet data.

> **Tip**
>
> *Although this procedure is correct and will work in most situations, you will occasionally discover that you can't bring a text file directly into a large (40MB to 50MB) Access database. In such cases, change the text file into an Excel spreadsheet first, then import that file.*

Importing External Data Using Code

The **DoCmd** object has three methods that assist you with importing external data: **TransferDatabase**, **TransferText**, and **TransferSpreadsheet**. The following sections show implementations of each of these methods.

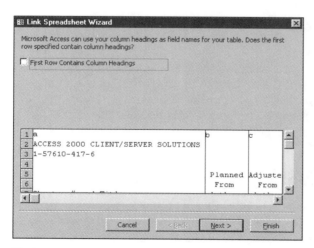

Figure 3.5
The Import Spreadsheet Wizard.

Importing Database Data Using Code

The **TransferDatabase** method of the **DoCmd** object is used to import data from a database such as FoxPro, dBASE, Paradox, or another Access database. The code to do so looks similar to the following:

```
Sub ImportDatabase()
  DoCmd.TransferDatabase _
      TransferType:=acImport, _
      DatabaseType:="FoxPro 3.0", _
      DatabaseName:="c:\Databases", _
      ObjectType:=acTable, _
      Source:="Customers", _
      Destination:="tblCustomers", _
      StructureOnly:=False
End Sub
```

Table 3.1 details the arguments to the **TransferDatabase** method.

Importing Text Data Using Code

The **TransferText** method of the **DoCmd** object is used to import text from a text file. The following code provides an example of how you might use this method:

```
Sub ImportText()
  DoCmd.TransferText _
      TransferType:=acImportDelim, _
      TableName:="tblCustomerText", _
      FileName:="c:\Databases\Customer.txt"
End Sub
```

Table 3.2 lists the arguments for the **TransferText** method.

Table 3.1   The arguments for the TransferDatabase method.

Argument	Description
TransferType	The type of transfer being performed.
DatabaseType	The type of database being imported.
DatabaseName	The name of the database. When the table is a separate file—as is the case with dBASE, Paradox, and earlier versions of FoxPro—the database name is the name of the directory containing the table file. Do *not* include a backslash after the name of the directory.
ObjectType	The type of object you want to import. This argument is ignored for all but Access objects.
Source	The name of the object you're importing. Do *not* include the file extension.
Destination	The name of the imported object.
StructureOnly	Specifies whether you want the structure of the table only or the structure and data.

Table 3.2   The arguments for the TransferText method.

Argument	Description
TransferType	Type of transfer you want to make.
SpecificationName	Specification name for the set of options that determines how the file is imported.
TableName	Name of the Access table that will receive the imported data.
FileName	Name of the text file to import from.
HasFieldHeadings	Specifies whether the first row of the text file contains field headings.

Importing Spreadsheet Data Using Code

The **TransferSpreadsheet** method of the **DoCmd** object is used to import data from a spreadsheet file. The following code provides an example:

```
Sub ImportSpreadsheet()
  DoCmd.TransferSpreadsheet _
      TransferType:=acImport, _
      SpreadsheetType:=9, _
      TableName:="tblCustomerSpread", _
      FileName:="c:\Databases\Customer.xls", _
      HasFieldNames:=True
End Sub
```

Table 3.3 explains the arguments to the **TransferSpreadsheet** method.

Warning

You can import from and link (read-only) to Lotus WK4 files, but you can't export Access data to this spreadsheet format. Access also no longer supports importing, exporting, or linking data from Lotus WKS or Excel version 2 spreadsheets with this action. If you want to import from or link to spreadsheet data in Excel version 2 or Lotus WKS format, convert the spreadsheet data to a later version of Excel or Lotus 1-2-3 before importing or linking the data into Access.

Table 3.3   The arguments for the TransferSpreadsheet method.

Argument	Description
TransferType	Type of transfer you want to make.
SpreadsheetType	Type of spreadsheet to import from. The default is Excel 3.
TableName	Name of the Access table that will receive the imported data.
FileName	Name of the spreadsheet file to import from.
HasFieldNames	Specifies whether the first row of the spreadsheet contains field headings.
Range	The range of cells to import.

Creating A Link To External Data

When you need to keep the data in its original format but want to treat the data just like any other Access table, linking is the best solution. All of the information required to establish and maintain the connection to the remote data source is stored within the linked table definition. You can create links through the user interface and by using code. Both alternatives are covered in this section.

Probably one of the most common types of links is a link to another Access table. This type of link is created so the application objects (queries, forms, reports, macros, and modules) can be placed in a local database and the tables can be stored in another database on a file server. Such a configuration offers numerous benefits, including easier redistribution of program interfaces, easier upsizing to larger database products with growth, and so on. The following sections detail how to work with such links.

Creating A Link Using The User Interface

It's very common to create a link using the user interface. When you know what links you want to establish at design time, this is probably the easiest way to establish links to external data. You can establish links using the Database Splitter or manually. You learned about the Database Splitter previously in this chapter.

To link to a remote table through the user interface, right-click on the Tables tab of the Database window. Select Link Tables. Select ODBC Databases from the Files Of Type drop-down list. The Select Data Source dialog box shown in Figure 3.6 will appear.

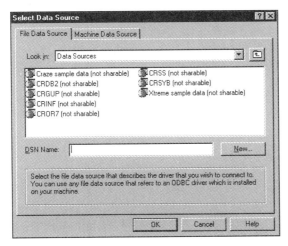

Figure 3.6
The Select Data Source dialog box.

You can select an existing data source or define a new data source directly from the Select Data Source dialog. After selecting a data source, you're prompted for a password. You can't obtain access to the server data unless you have a valid login ID and password.

When you successfully log onto the server, you're presented with a list of tables contained within the database that the data source is referencing. Here, you must select the table to which you want to link.

After you select one or more tables and click on OK, you might be prompted with the Select Unique Record Identifier dialog box. Selecting a unique identifier for the table enables you to update records on the back-end data source. Select a unique identifier and click on OK. The linked tables will appear in the Database window. You can treat these linked tables just as you would any other table (with a few exceptions detailed throughout this chapter).

Linking To External Tables Using Code

You've just learned how you can link to a remote table by using Access's user interface. Now let's take a look at how you can link to the same table by using code. The following subroutine accepts six parameters: the names for the Access table, the server database, the server table, the dataset, the user ID, and the password:

```
Sub LinkToSQL(strAccessTable, strDBName, strTableName, _
    strDataSetName, strUserID, strPassWord)
  Dim db As DATABASE
  Dim tdf As TableDef

  Set db = CurrentDb
  Set tdf = db.CreateTableDef(strAccessTable)
  tdf.Connect = "ODBC;Database=" & strDBName _
      & ";DSN=" & strDataSetName & ";UID=" & strUserID _
      & ";PWD=" & strPassWord
  tdf.SourceTableName = strTableName
  db.TableDefs.Append tdf
End Sub
```

Note

You must set a reference to the DAO 3.6 Object Library before you try to compile your code.

Presume for the moment that the Access table you're creating is called **tblStores**. The database name on the server is **Pubs**. The table to which you're linking is called **dbo.Stores**, and the dataset name is **PublisherData**. You're logging in as database system administrator (SA) without a password. The user ID and password could have been supplied as the user logged into your application and could have been stored in variables until needed for logging into the server. The following code, then, will invoke a routine that accepts all of those parameters and uses them to create a link from the program code:

```
LinkToSQL "tblStores", "Pubs", "dbo.Stores", _
    "PublisherData", "sa", ""
```

Creating a link to an external table using code, then, is a five-step process. Here are the steps involved in establishing the link:

1. Open the Microsoft Access database that will contain the link to the external file.

2. Create a new table definition using the external data source.

3. Set connection information for the external database and table.

4. Provide a name for the new table.

5. Link the table by appending the table definition to the database. The code to do so looks similar to the following:

```
Sub LinkToAccessTableProps()
    Dim db As DATABASE
    Dim tdf As TableDef

    Set db = CurrentDb
    Set tdf = db.CreateTableDef("tblLinkedTable")
    tdf.Connect = ";Database=c:\Databases\Chap03Data.mdb"
    tdf.SourceTableName = "tblClients"
    db.TableDefs.Append tdf
End Sub
```

Following the preceding steps, the database does not need to be opened because you're adding a table definition to the current database. The **CreateTableDef** method is used to create the new table definition. The **Connect** property is set and the **SourceTableName** is defined. Finally, the table definition is appended to the **TableDefs** collection of the database.

Creating An External Table From Code

Creating a foreign table from code isn't particularly difficult. Here's how it works:

```
Sub CreateSQLServTable()
    Dim db As Database
    Dim rst As Recordset
    Dim fld As Field
    Dim dbSQLServ As Database
    Dim tdfSQLServ As TableDef
```

```
    Set dbSQLServ = DBEngine.Workspaces(0).OpenDatabase_
        ("Provider=SQLOLEDB;User ID=sa;Password=;" & _
        "Data Source=SQLSERVER;Initial Catalog=Chap03")
    Set tdfSQLServ = dbSQLServ.CreateTableDef("PayMeth")
    Set db = CurrentDb
    Set rst = db.OpenRecordset("tblPaymentMethods", dbOpenSnapshot)
    For Each fld In rst.Fields
      Set fld = tdfSQLServ.CreateField(fld.Name, fld.Type, fld.Size)
      tdfSQLServ.Fields.Append fld
    Next fld
    dbSQLServ.TableDefs.Append tdfSQLServ
End Sub
```

This example reads an Access table and writes its structure out to a SQL Server table. It utilizes two database object variables, one recordset object variable, a table definition object variable, and a field object variable. It opens up a table called **tblPaymentMethods** as a Snapshot. This is the table whose structure you'll send out to SQL Server. Looking at each field in the table, it grabs that field's name, type, and size properties. It uses these properties as parameters to the **CreateField** method of the SQL Server table definition, appends each SQL Server field as it loops through each field in the Access table definition, and appends the table definition to create the SQL Server table.

Linking To Views Rather Than To Tables

Views on a database server are like Access queries: They provide a form of security by limiting what rows and columns a user can see. Users are granted access to the view rather than directly to the underlying table. By default, views aren't updateable. You can make a view updateable by including all the fields that comprise the primary key in the view and building a unique index on the primary key. Views can be created in one of three ways:

♦ Using the SQL Server Enterprise Manager for SQL Server 7 (or the equivalent option for your back-end database server)

♦ Using the **Create View** statement in Access

♦ Using an Access Data Project (ADP) to directly manipulate the SQL Server using the DaVinci toolset.

I will consider the first and third bullet points in later chapters. The next section details how to use the **Create View** statement in Access.

Creating A Remote View From Access

To create a remote view from Access, perform the following steps:

1. Create a new query.

2. When you're prompted with the Show Table dialog box, click on Close *without* selecting a table.

3. Select Query I SQL Specific I Pass-Through.

4. Type the **Create View** statement.

5. Click on Run.

6. Select a SQL Data Source. Click on OK.

7. Supply the Login Information and click on OK.

Once you create a remote view, you can link to it like any other table. When you link to the view, you're prompted with the Select Unique Record Identifier dialog box. It's very important to supply Access with a unique index. Otherwise, the results of the view won't be updateable. You can then treat the view as if it were a link to a table.

Providing Connection Information

When you link to an external table, you must provide information about the type, name, and location of the external database. You can accomplish this in one of two ways:

♦ Set the **SourceTableName** and **Connect** properties of the **TableDef** object.

♦ Include the **Source** and **Connect** values as arguments to the **CreateTableDef** method.

The process of setting the **SourceTableName** and **Connect** properties is illustrated by the following three lines of code:

```
Set tdf = db.CreateTableDef("tblLinkedTable")
tdf.Connect = ";Database=c:\Databases\Chap03Data.MDB"
tdf.SourceTableName = "tblClients"
```

Including the **Source** and **Connect** values as arguments to the **CreateTableDef** method looks like this:

```
Set tdf = db.CreateTableDef("tblLinkedTable", 0, "tblClients", _
    ";Database=c:\Databases\Chap03Data")
```

As you can see from the example, both the **Source (tblClients)** and the **Connect** value are included as arguments to the **CreateTableDef** method.

The connect string is actually composed of several pieces. These include the source database type, database name, password, and Data Source Name (DSN). The database name is used for tables that aren't ODBC-compliant, and the DSN is used for ODBC tables.

The source database type is the ISAM format that'll be used for the link. Each source database type is a different key in the Windows Registry. The source database type must be entered exactly as it appears in the Registry. Valid source database types include the following:

♦ *dBASE*—dBASE III, dBASE IV, dBASE V, dBASE 6, and dBASE 7, as well as Visual dBASE databases and subsequent InterBase products, up to and including InterBase 5.5

♦ *Excel*—Excel 3, Excel 4, Excel 5, Excel 7, Excel 8, Excel 9 (Excel 2000)

- *FoxPro*—FoxPro 2, FoxPro 2.5, FoxPro 2.6, FoxPro 3, FoxPro DBC
- *Lotus*—Lotus WK1, Lotus WK3, Lotus WK4
- *ODBC*—ODBC
- *Paradox*—Paradox 3.x, Paradox 4.x, Paradox 5.x
- *Text*

> **Warning**
>
> *If you don't use the exact spaces and punctuation, Access will be unable to communicate with the database engine to correctly convert or link to the file.*

The database name must include a fully qualified path to the file. The path can be specified with a drive letter and directory path or by using Uniform Naming Conventions (UNCs). For a local database, the path must be specified in this fashion:

```
Database=c:\Databases\Chap03Data
```

For a file server, either the UNC path or the drive letter path (if you've mapped a drive to the directory) can be specified. The UNC path looks like this:

```
\\FILESERVERNAME\Databases\Chap03Data
```

In this case, the database called Chap03Data is stored on the Databases share of a particular file server.

Password is used to supply a password to a database (Access or other) that has been secured. It's best to fill in this part of the connection string from a variable at runtime rather than hard coding it into the VBA code. The completed connection string, then, looks like this:

```
tdf.Connect = "Provider=SQLOLEDB;Database=SQLSERVER;" & _
    "Catalog=Chap03DB;login=sa;PWD="
```

In this example, the connection string is set up to link to a SQL Server 7 database named Chap03DB residing on the SQLSERVER server. The login is sa, the system administrator login, and no password is specified.

Further Considering Connection Strings

The connection string comprises the source database type, database name, user ID, password, and DSN. Each part of the connection string must be separated by a semicolon.

Each source database type has a valid name. This is the name that you must use when accessing that type of data. These database types are listed in Help under the Connect Property item. They can also be found in the Windows Registry under HKEY_ LOCAL_MACHINE\Software\Microsoft\Jet\4.0\ISAM Formats. The source database type must be specified accurately, or you won't be able to access the external data.

The source database name is the name of the database to which you're linking. In the case of ISAM files, this is the name of the directory in which the file is contained. The **Database** keyword is used to specify the database name.

The user ID is used whenever a username must be specified to successfully log onto the data source. This is most common when dealing with back-end databases such as Oracle, Sybase, or Microsoft SQL Server. This part of the parameter string can be required to successfully log the user onto the system where the source data resides. The **UID** keyword is used to refer to the user ID.

As with the user ID, the password is most often included in dealing with back-end data. It can also be used on other database types that support passwords, such as Paradox, or when linking to an external Access table. The **PWD** keyword is used when specifying the password.

Finally, the dataset name is used to refer to a defined ODBC data source. Communicating with an ODBC data source is covered in detail later in this chapter. The **DSN** keyword is used when referring to the dataset name in the connection string.

Tip

ActiveX Data Objects (ADO) let you connect to databases without DSNs.

Creating The Link

So, after all that, here's how you put it all together to establish a link to an external table:

```
Sub LinkToSQLServ(strServName As String, strDatabaseName As String, _
    strTableName As String, strAccessTable)
  Dim db As Database
  Dim tdf As TableDef

  Set db = CurrentDb
  Set tdf = db.CreateTableDef(strAccessTable)
  tdf.Connect = "Provider=SQLOLEDB;User ID=sa;Password=;" & _
      "Data Source=" & strServName & ";Initial Catalog=" & _
      strTableName & ";"
  tdf.SourceTableName = strTableName
  db.TableDefs.Append tdf
End Sub
```

Here is an example of how this subroutine would be called:

```
Call LinkToSQLServ("SQLSERVER","Customer","tblCustomers", "ltblCustomers")
```

The **LinkToSQLServ** subroutine receives four parameters. The first parameter is the name of the SQL Server to connect to. The second parameter is the name of the database on the server to which you want to connect. The third parameter is the name of the table or view on the SQL Server from which you are reading. The fourth parameter is the name of the Access table that you're creating. The subroutine creates two object variables: a database object variable and a table definition object variable. It points the database object variable at the current database. Next, it creates a table definition called **ltblCustomers**. It establishes a connection string for that table definition. The connection string specified in the subroutine indicates that you'll link to a SQL Server 7 database and component table. The directory name acts as the database to which you're linked. After you've set the **Connect** property of the database definition, you're ready to indicate the name of the table with which you're establishing the link. Finally, you're ready to append the table definition to the database.

Tip

*Alternatively, you could pass all the information into the function and use the values as parameters to the **CreateTableDef** method.*

You've seen how you can link to a SQL Server 7 table. Putting everything that you've learned together, let's review how you can create a link to an Access table stored in another database. The following code shows an example:

```
Sub LinkToAccess(strDBName As String, strTableName As String, _
    strAccessTable)
  Dim db As DATABASE
  Dim tdf As TableDef

  Set db = CurrentDb
  Set tdf = db.CreateTableDef(strAccessTable)
  tdf.Connect = ";DATABASE=" & strDBName
  tdf.SourceTableName = strTableName
  db.TableDefs.Append tdf
End Sub
```

Notice that the connection string no longer specifies the type of database to which you're connecting. Everything else in this routine is the same as the routine that connected to SQL Server earlier in the chapter. Also, looking at the parameters passed to the routine (listed next), the database passed to the routine is an actual Access database (as opposed to a directory), and the table name is the name of the Access table in the other database:

```
Call LinkToAccess("C:\databases\northwind","Customers","tblCustomers")
```

Refreshing And Removing Links

Refreshing links refers to the updating of the link to an external table. It's done when the location of an external table has changed. *Removing* links refers to the process of permanently removing a link to an external table.

Access can't find external tables if their location has been moved. You need to take this into consideration when writing your VBA code. Furthermore, there might be times when you want to remove a link to external data. This occurs when it's no longer necessary to use the data or when the data has been permanently imported into Access.

Updating Links That Have Moved

To refresh a link using VBA code, redefine the connection string and then perform a **RefreshLink** method on the table definition. The code to perform such an operational pair looks similar to the following:

```
Sub RefreshLink()
  Dim db As Database

  Set db = CurrentDb
  db.TableDefs!FoxCusts.Connect = "FoxPro 2.6;DATABASE=d:\newdir"
  db.TableDefs!FoxCusts.RefreshLink
End Sub
```

This routine can be modified to prompt the user for the directory containing the data tables. The modified routine looks like this:

```
Sub RefreshLink()
  Dim db As Database
  Dim tdf As TableDef
  Dim strNewLocation As String

  On Error GoTo RefreshLink_Err
  Set db = CurrentDb
  Set tdf = db.TableDefs("tblClients")
  tdf.RefreshLink
  Exit Sub

RefreshLink_Err:
  strNewLocation = InputBox("Please Enter Database Path and Name")
  db.TableDefs!tblClients.Connect = ";DATABASE=" & strNewLocation
  Resume
End Sub
```

This routine points a **TableDef** object (referenced by the variable **tdf**) to the **tblClients** table. It then issues a **RefreshLink** method on the table definition object. The **RefreshLink** method attempts to refresh the link for the table. When an error occurs, an input box prompts the user for the new location of the database. The **Connect** property for the database is modified to incorporate the new location. The code then resumes on the offending line of code (the **RefreshLink**). This routine should be modified to allow the user a way out, because the **Resume** routine in this code throws the user into an endless loop when the database isn't available. Modifying the code is left as an exercise for you.

Deleting Links From Code

To remove a link using VBA code, simply execute a **Delete** method on the table definition collection of the database, like this:

```
Sub RemoveLink()
  Dim db As Database

  Set db = CurrentDb
  db.TableDefs.Delete "FOXCUSTS"
End Sub
```

Opening An External Table

As mentioned earlier in the chapter, it's generally preferable to link to, rather than open, an external table because of the additional performance that linking provides and the ease of use in dealing with a linked table. After you link to a table, it's treated just like any other Access table. But on some occasions, it's necessary to open an external table without creating a link to it. Opening an external table is a two-step process:

1. Open the database using the **OpenDatabase** method.
2. Create a recordset object based upon the external table.

Providing Connection Information

The connection information you provide when you open an external table is similar to the information you provide when you link to the table. The connection information is provided as arguments of the **OpenDatabase** method. Here's an example:

```
OpenDatabase("c:\customer\data", False, False, "FoxPro 3.0")
```

Here, the connection string is to the c:\customer\data database file using the FoxPro 3.0 ISAM.

Opening The Table

The **OpenDatabase** method receives the following arguments:

```
OpenDatabase(DBname, Exclusive, Read-Only, Source)
```

The **DBname** is the name of the database you're opening. The **Exclusive** and **Read-Only** parameters are used to specify whether you're opening the database exclusively or as read-only.

The **Source** argument is used to specify the database type and connection string. When you put it all together, it'll look similar to the following code:

```
Sub OpenExternalFox(strDBName As String, strTableName As String)
  Dim db As Database
  Dim rst As Recordset

  Set db = DBEngine.Workspaces(0).OpenDatabase(strDBName, False, _
      False, "FoxPro 3.0")
  Set rst = db.OpenRecordset(strTableName)
  Do While Not rst.EOF
    Debug.Print rst.Fields(0).Value
    rst.MoveNext
  Loop
End Sub
```

This code is called as follows:

```
Call OpenExternalFox("c:\customer\data","Customer")
```

Notice that, here, you aren't appending a table definition. Instead, you're creating a temporary recordset that refers to the external data. After the external table is opened as a recordset, the code traverses through each record of the table, printing out the value of the first field. Of course, after the recordset is opened, you can manipulate it in any way you like. The table won't show up as a linked table in the database window. In fact, when the routine has completed and the local variable has gone out of scope, the recordset no longer exists.

Creating An External Table

Not only can you link to existing tables, you can even create new external tables. This means you can actually design a FoxPro, Paradox, or other type of table using VBA code. The table will reside on disk as an independent entity and can be used by the application for which it was created.

It's sometimes necessary for your application to provide a data file to another application. That other application might not be capable of reading an Access table. In such cases, it's necessary for you to create the file in a format native to the application that needs to read it.

Creating a "foreign" table isn't as difficult as you might think. It's actually not very different from creating an Access table using VBA code.

Now that you've seen how you can link to external tables as well as open and create them, you're ready to take a look at how you can refine both of these processes. This involves learning about the Windows Registry settings that affect the linking process, the parameters that are available to you in specifying connection information, how to specify passwords, how to refresh and remove links, and how to create an external table using VBA code.

Understanding Windows Registry Settings

Each ISAM driver has a separate key in the Windows Registry. These keys are used to configure the driver upon initialization. As you can see in Figure 3.7, the setup program for Access 2000 has created entries for each of the available data sources. Looking at a specific data source (in this case Paradox 7.X), you can see all of the settings that exist for the Paradox 7.X driver. For example, the ExportFilter is set to Paradox 7 (*.db). At times, you'll need to modify one of the Registry settings to customize the behavior of the ISAM driver. This is covered in the following "Special Considerations" section. You can find this entry under HKEY_LOCAL_MACHINE\Software\Microsoft\Jet\4.0\ISAM Formats.

Special Considerations

When you're dealing with different types of external files, different problems and issues arise. If you understand these stumbling blocks before they affect you, you'll get a great head start in dealing with these potential obstacles.

dBASE Considerations

The major concerns you'll have in dealing with dBASE files have to do with deleted records, indexes, data types, and memo fields. When you delete a record from a dBASE table, it's not actually removed from the table. Instead, it's just marked for deletion. A **Pack** process must be completed for the records to actually be removed from the table. When records are deleted from a dBASE table using an Access application, the records aren't removed. Because you can't pack a dBASE database from within an Access application, the records still

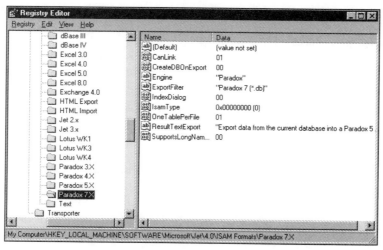

Figure 3.7
The Windows Registry Editor with keys for ISAM drivers.

remain in the table. In fact, they aren't automatically filtered from the Access table. To filter deleted records so they can't be seen within the Access application, the Deleted value in the \Jet\3.0\Engines\Xbase section of the Registry must be set to 01 (true).

The dBASE indexes can be utilized by Access to improve performance. When you link to a dBASE table and select an index, an INF file is created. This file has the same name as your dBASE database with an .inf extension. It contains information about all of the indexes being used. Here's an example of an INF:

```
[dBASE IV]
NDX1=CUSTID.NDX
UNDX1=CUSTID.NDX
```

dBASE IV is the database type identifier. NDX1 is an index number for the first index. The UNDX1 entry is used to specify a unique index.

The data types available in dBASE files are different than those available in Access files. It's important to understand how the field types map. Table 3.4 shows how each dBASE data type is mapped to a Jet data type.

Finally, it's important to ensure that the dBASE memo files are stored in the same directory as the table. Otherwise, Access is unable to read the data in the memo file.

FoxPro Considerations

Like dBASE files, the major issues you'll have with FoxPro files concern deleted records, indexes, data types, and memo fields. Deleted records are handled in the same way as dBASE files. By setting the Deleted value in the \Jet\4.0\Engines\Xbase section of the Registry to 01, you filter deleted records.

As with dBASE indexes, the Access Jet engine can take advantage of FoxPro indexes. The format of an INF file for a FoxPro file is identical to that of a dBASE file.

FoxPro field types are mapped to Jet field types in the same way that dBASE fields are mapped. The only difference is that FoxPro 3 supports **Double**, **Currency**, **Integer**, and

Table 3.4　Mapping of dBASE data types to Jet data types.

dBASE Data Type	Jet Data Type
Character	Text
Numeric, Float	Double
Logical	Boolean
Date	Date/Time
Memo	Memo
OLE	OLE Object

DateTime field types. These map to the corresponding Jet field types. As with dBASE, make sure the Memo files are stored in the same directory as the data tables.

Text Data Considerations

When linking to an ASCII text file, Jet can determine the format of the file directly, or it can use a schema information file. The schema information file resides in the same directory as the text file. It's always named SCHEMA.INI and contains information about the format of the file, column names, and data types. The schema information file is optional for delimited files, but it's required for fixed-length files. It's important to understand that ASCII files can never be opened for shared use.

Troubleshooting With External Data

Unfortunately, the process of working with external data isn't always a smooth one. Many things can go wrong, including connection problems and a lack of temporary disk space. Both of these are discussed in this section.

Connection Problems

Difficulties with accessing external data can be caused by any of the following:

♦ The server on which the external data is stored is down.

♦ The user doesn't have rights to the directory in which the external data is stored.

♦ The user doesn't have rights to the external data source.

♦ The external data source was moved.

♦ The UNC path or network share name was modified.

♦ The connection string is incorrect.

♦ The installable ISAM driver has not been installed.

Temporary Disk Space

Access requires a significant amount of disk space to run complex queries on large tables. This disk space is required whether the tables are linked tables stored remotely in another format or whether they reside on the local machine. When enough disk space isn't available to run a query, the application will behave unpredictably. Therefore, it's necessary to ensure that all users have enough disk space to meet the requirements of the queries that are run.

Links And Performance Considerations

Because your application has to go through an extra translation layer, the installable ISAM, performance is nowhere near as good with ISAM files as it is with native Jet data. It's always best to import ISAM data whenever possible. When it's not possible to import the data, you need to either accept the performance that linking offers or consider linking to be the best solution to an otherwise unsolvable problem. Opening the recordset using the **OpenDatabase** method might alleviate the problem, but remember that this option can't be used with bound forms.

Working With The Database Server

After you define a data source, you're ready to connect to it. You can use one of four methods to access server data:

◆ Link to tables residing on the server.

◆ Link to views residing on the server.

◆ Use pass-through queries to send SQL statements directly to the server.

◆ Use VBA code to open the server tables directly.

The easiest method of accessing data on the server is to link to the external tables. These linked tables act almost exactly like native Access tables. When you link to remote tables, Access analyzes the fields and indexes contained within the tables so it can achieve optimal performance. It's important to relink the tables when the structures of the remote tables change. The following sections discuss how you can link to remote tables both through the user interface and through code.

Pass-Through Queries

Ordinarily, when you store and execute a query in Access, even if it's running on remote data, Access compiles and optimizes the query. In many cases, this is exactly what you want. On certain other occasions, however, it might be preferable for you to execute a pass-through query because they aren't analyzed by Access's Jet engine. They're passed directly to the server, and this reduces the time Jet spends analyzing the query and enables you to pass server-specific syntax to the back end. Furthermore, pass-through queries can log informational messages returned by the server. Finally, bulk update, delete, and append queries are faster using pass-through queries than they are using Access action queries based on remote tables.

Pass-through queries do have their down side. They always return a Snapshot, rendering them nonupdateable. You also must know the exact syntax that the server requires, and you must type the statement into the query window rather than painting it graphically. Finally, you can't parameterize a query so it prompts the user for a value.

Creating A Pass-Through Query Using The User Interface

To create a pass-through query, you can build the query in the Access query builder. To do this, select Query | SQL Specific | Pass-Through. Access will present you with a text-editing window in which you can enter the query statement. The SQL statement that you enter must be in the SQL flavor specific to your back end.

Defining An ODBC Data Source

Before you can use Microsoft Access with a database server, you need to load the ODBC drivers. These drivers come with Access, but—depending on which version of Office you are using—they may not be installed automatically when you select the standard installation of the product. Depending on how you ran the setup, if you need to subsequently install the ODBC drivers, the Windows Installer may prompt you for a CD-ROM, or you may need to rerun Setup and choose the Custom installation option.

In addition to installing the ODBC Driver Manager and the default drivers, you will also need to load drivers for the specific back-end database servers to which you want to connect. These drivers are usually purchased from the back-end database vendor and often come with a per-seat charge. This means you must purchase a client license for each user who will connect to the remote data.

An ODBC data source is a user-defined name that points to a remote source of data. It contains all the properties of the data source necessary to communicate to data stored on a database server.

Before you can access a remote table from Access, you must define it using the ODBC administrator. If you don't define that data source, or if it's not defined correctly, you'll be unable to obtain access to the data.

ODBC data sources are set up in the ODBC administrator. Depending on your installation, the ODBC administrator could be a standalone application, or it could appear as a Control Panel icon. It enables you to create, modify, and delete data sources, and to obtain information about existing drivers. Remember that a data source is simply a user-definable name that stores settings that can be used to access a back end located on a particular server using a specified driver. Figure 3.8 shows the User DSN tab within the ODBC administrator.

When you've entered the ODBC administrator, you should probably set up a new data source. To define a new data source, click on the Add button in the ODBC Data Source Administrator dialog. The Create New Data Source dialog box, where you must select the name of the driver that the data source will use, will appear, as shown in Figure 3.9.

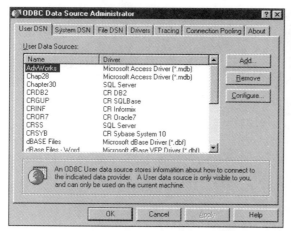

Figure 3.8
The User DSN tab within the ODBC administrator.

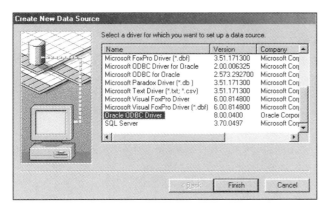

Figure 3.9
The Create New Data Source dialog box.

The list of available drivers varies depending on which client drivers have been installed on the machine. After you select a data source and click on Finish, you're shown another dialog, which varies depending on the driver you've selected. This dialog enables you to define specific information about the data source you're creating. An example is the Oracle8 ODBC Drive Setup dialog box shown in Figure 3.10.

As you can see, the Oracle8 ODBC Driver Setup dialog enables you to specify information, such as the data source name, a description of the data source, and the network name of the SQL Server to connect to.

At this point, you might be wondering how you can possibly go through the process of defining data sources on thousands of user machines in a large installation. Fortunately, you can automate the process of defining data sources by using dynamic-linked library (DLL) functions. It's a matter of using the ODBC Administrator DLL function calls to set up the data source by using code. However, explaining the process is beyond the scope of this book.

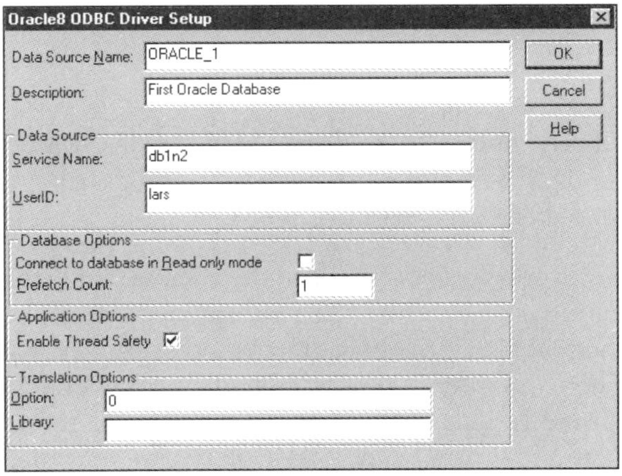

Figure 3.10
The Oracle8 ODBC Driver Setup dialog box.

Executing A Pass-Through Query Using Code

You can also perform a pass-through query using VBA code. In fact, you must create the pass-through query by using VBA code if you want the query to contain parameters that you'll pass to the server. Here's one way you can create a pass-through query using VBA code:

1. Use the **OpenDatabase** method of the workspace object to open the SQL Server database. You must supply the connect string as the fourth parameter to the **OpenDatabase** function.

2. Use the **Execute** method to execute the SQL statement on the back-end database server. As with a SQL statement created by using the Query menu, the statement you create must be in the syntax specific to your particular back end. The code to perform such processing looks similar to the following:

```
Sub PassThroughQuery(strDBName As String, strDataSetName As String, _
    strUserID As String, strPassWord As String)
  Dim ws As Workspace
  Dim db As Database
  Dim strConnectString As String

  strConnectString = "ODBC;DATABASE=" & strDBName & _
      ";DSN=" & strDataSetName & ";UID=" & strUserID & _
      ";PWD=" & strPassWord
  Set ws = DBEngine(0)
  Set db = ws.OpenDatabase( "", False, False, strConnectString)
  db.Execute "Update dbo.Sales Set Qty = Qty + 1", _
      dbSQLPassThrough
End Sub
```

You would then call this routine from elsewhere in your program with the following statement:

```
Call PassThroughQuery("Pubs", "PublisherData", "SA","" )
```

This subroutine uses a connect string that connects to a database called **Pubs**, with a datasource named **PublisherData**, a user ID of **SA**, and no password. It then executes a pass-through query that updates the **Qty** field of each record to **Qty+1**.

As you saw, one method of executing a pass-through query is to open the database using the **OpenDatabase** method, and then execute the query using the **Execute** method on the database object. The limitation of this method is that the **Execute** method doesn't enable you to execute queries that return data. There's another method of executing a pass-through query you can use when you want to return records. It involves creating a query definition within the local database and opening a recordset using a pass-through query or a stored procedure as the SQL property for the query definition. This method is covered in the next section.

Executing A Stored Procedure

As the previous section details, you have several different options when executing a stored procedure on a back-end database server. In addition to the specific examples therein, you can also execute a stored procedure on a back-end database server. A stored procedure is like a query or program stored on the back end, and it performs some action. An example is the SQL Server 7 stored procedure called **sp_columns**, which returns information on the fields in a particular table. Figure 3.11 illustrates how you would execute the **sp_columns** stored procedure from the Query Design window.

As you can see from the figure, you simply type the name of the stored procedure and any parameters that it must receive. Take a good look at the Query Properties window shown in Figure 3.11. If you enter a valid ODBC connect string, the user won't be prompted to log in at runtime. The **Return Records** property is another important property. In this case, you want to set the value of the property to **Yes** so that you can see the results of the stored procedure. When the stored procedure doesn't return records, as is the case with the Create View pass-through query we created in the section titled "Linking To Views Rather Than To Tables," it's important to set this property to **No**. Otherwise, you receive an error message indicating that no rows were returned.

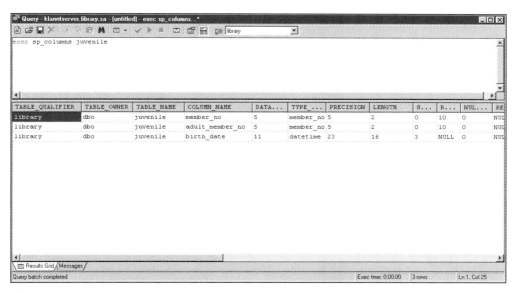

Figure 3.11
Executing the **sp_columns** stored procedure from the Query Design window.

Executing A Stored Procedure With VBA Code

The following procedure executes the **sp_columns** stored procedure using code:

```
Sub StoredProcedure()
  Dim ws As Workspace
  Dim db As Database
  Dim dbAccess As Database
  Dim qdf As QueryDef
  Dim rst As Recordset

  Set dbAccess = CurrentDb
  Set ws = DBEngine(0)
  Set db = ws.OpenDatabase("", False, False, _
      "ODBC;DATABASE=Pubs;DSN=PublisherData;UID=SA;PWD=")
  Set qdf = dbAccess.CreateQueryDef("")
  qdf.Connect = "ODBC;DATABASE=Pubs;DSN=PublisherData;UID=SA;PWD="
  qdf.SQL = "sp_columns 'sales'"
  qdf.ReturnsRecords = True
  Set rst = qdf.OpenRecordset(dbOpenSnapshot)
  Do While Not rst.EOF
    Debug.Print rst.Fields("Column_Name")
    rst.MoveNext
  Loop
End Sub
```

Here's how it works. Because you want to return records, you can't use the **Execute** method. Another way to execute a pass-through query is to first create a Data Access Object (DAO) **QueryDef** object. In this case, the **QueryDef** object is temporary (notice the quotation marks). The **Connect** property is set for the **QueryDef** object. Rather than specifying a back-end–specific SQL statement, the **SQL** property of the **QueryDef** object is set to the name of the stored procedure and any parameters it expects to receive. The **ReturnsRecords** property of the **QueryDef** object is set to **True**. The **OpenRecordset** method is then issued on the **QueryDef** object. This returns the **Snapshot** from the stored procedure. The **Do-While** loop loops through the resulting recordset, printing the **Column_Name** column of each row returned from the **sp_columns** stored procedure.

Opening A Server Table Directly

As you saw in Chapter 2, the **OpenDatabase** method of the **Workspace** object can be used to execute pass-through queries. This is a valid use of the **OpenDatabase** method. This method can also be used in place of linking to tables to access server data directly. This is generally extremely inefficient because the data structure isn't analyzed and maintained in the Access database engine. With linked tables, the fields, indexes, and server capabilities are all cached in memory so they'll be readily available when needed.

Regardless, there are times when you might want to open a database directly. One reason is to preconnect to a server so you'll already be connected when you need access to the data.

Using OpenDatabase To Connect To A Remote Server Database

The following subroutine shows how you can use the **OpenDatabase** method of the **Workspace** object to connect to a remote server database:

```
Sub OpenRemoteDB(strDBName As String, strDataSetName As String, _
    strUserID As String, strPassWord As String)
  Dim ws As Workspace
  Dim db As Database
  Dim tdf As TableDef
  Dim intCounter As Integer
  Dim strConnectString As String

  Set ws = DBEngine(0)
  strConnectString = "ODBC;DATABASE=" & strDBName & _
      ";DSN=" & strDataSetName & ";UID=" & strUserID & _
      ";PWD=" & strPassWord
  Set db = ws.OpenDatabase( "", False, False, strConnectString)
  For Each tdf In db.TableDefs
    Debug.Print tdf.Name
  Next tdf
End Sub
```

The routine is called like this:

```
Call OpenRemoteDB("Pubs", "PublisherData", "SA", "")
```

The routine uses the **OpenDatabase** method of the **Workspace** object to open the database called **Pubs** with the connect string specified. It then loops through the collection of table definitions, listing all the tables found within the remote server database.

Preconnecting To A Server

The following code preconnects to the server. It would generally be placed in the startup form for your application:

```
Sub PreConnect(strDBName As String, strDataSetName As String, _
    strUserID As String, strPassWord As String)
  Dim db As Database
  Dim strConnectString As String
  strConnectString = "ODBC;DATABASE=" & strDBName & _
      ";DSN=" & strDataSetName & ";UID=" & strUserID & _
      ";PWD=" & strPassWord
```

```
    Set db = OpenDatabase("", False, False, strConnectString)
    db.Close    ' Closes the database but maintains the connection
End Sub
```

The trick here is that the connection and authentication information will be maintained even when the database is closed.

Using Replication To Improve Performance

Replication can be used to improve performance in a multiuser application. You can place multiple copies of the database containing the tables out on the network, each on a different file server. Different users can be set up to access data from the different file servers, thereby better distributing network traffic. Using the Replication Manager, the databases can be synchronized at regular intervals. Although this isn't a viable solution when the data that users are viewing needs to be fully current, there are many situations in which this type of solution might be adequate. It's often the only solution when limited resources don't allow the migration of an application's data to a client/server database. That being said, the focus of this book *is* on migration to, and programming for, a client/server environment, so we will not discuss replication in any detail—it's only offered as a possible choice, depending on your needs.

Upsizing: What To Worry About

Suppose your database is using Microsoft Access as both the front end and back end. Although an Access database on a file server might have been sufficient for a while, the need for better performance, enhanced security, or one of the other benefits that a back-end database provides is compelling your company (or your client's company) to upsize to a client/server architecture. The Access tables have already been created and even contain volumes of data. In this scenario, it might make sense to upsize.

Because all the tables have been designed as Access tables, they need to be upsized to the back-end database server. Upsizing means moving tables from a local Access database (or from any PC database) to a back-end database server that usually runs on Unix, Windows NT Server, OS/2 LAN Server, or as a Novell NetWare NLM.

Another reason that tables are upsized from Access to a back-end server is that many developers prefer to design their tables from within the Access environment. Access offers a more user-friendly environment for table creation than do most server applications.

Regardless of your reasons for upsizing, you need to understand several issues regarding the movement, or upsizing, of Access tables to a database server. Indeed, because of the many caveats in moving tables from Access to a back end, many people opt to design the tables directly on the back end. If you do design your tables in Access, you should export them to the back end, then link them to your local database. As you export your tables to the database server, you need to be aware of the issues covered in the sections that follow.

Index Considerations

When exporting a table to a server, no indexes are created. All indexes need to be re-created on the back-end database server.

Exporting AutoNumber Fields

AutoNumber fields are exported as **Long** integers. Because most database servers don't support autonumbering, you have to create an insert trigger on the server that provides the next key value. Autonumbering can also be achieved using form-level events, but this isn't desirable because the numbering won't be enforced when other applications access the data.

Using Default Values

Default values aren't automatically moved to the server, even when the server supports default values. You can set up default values directly on the server, but these values do *not* automatically appear when new records are added to the table unless the record is saved without data being added to the field containing the default value. As with autonumbering, default values can be implemented at the form level, with the same drawbacks.

Exporting Validation Rules

Validation rules aren't exported to the server—they must be re-created using triggers on the server. No Access-defined error messages are displayed when a server validation rule is violated; your application should be coded to provide the appropriate error messages. Validation rules can also be performed at the form level, but they're enforced if the data is accessed by other means.

Exporting Relationships

Relationships need to be enforced using server-based triggers. Access's default error messages don't appear when referential integrity is violated. You need to respond to, and code for, these error messages within your application. Relationships can be enforced at the form level, but as with other form-level validations, this method of validation doesn't adequately protect your data.

Applying Security To The New Database

Security features that you've set up in Access don't carry forward to the server. You need to reestablish table security on the server. When security has been set up on the server, Access becomes unaware that the security exists until the Access application attempts to violate the server's security. Then, error codes are returned to the application. You must handle these errors by using code and display the appropriate error message to the user.

Exporting Table And Field Names

Servers often have much more stringent rules regarding the naming of fields than Access does. When you export a table, all characters that aren't alphanumeric are converted to underscores. Most back ends don't allow spaces in field names. Furthermore, most back ends limit the length of object names to 30 characters or less. If you've already created queries, forms, reports, macros, and modules that utilize spaces and very long field and table names, these database objects might become unusable when you move your tables to a back-end database server.

Considerations With Reserved Words

Most back ends have many reserved words. It's important that you're aware of the reserved words of your specific back end. It's quite shocking when you upsize a table to find that field names that you've been using are reserved words on your database server. When this is the case, you need to rename all the fields in which a conflict occurs. Once again, this means modifying all the queries, forms, reports, macros, and modules that reference the original field names.

Understanding Case Sensitivity

Many back-end databases are case sensitive. When this is the case with your back end, you might find that your queries and application code don't process as expected. Queries or code that refer to the field or table name by using the wrong case aren't recognized by the back-end database and don't process correctly.

Using Properties With Remote Tables

Most properties can't be modified on remote tables. Any properties that can be modified are lost upon export, so you need to set them up again when the table is exported.

Proactively Preparing For Upsizing

When you set up your tables and code modules with upsizing in mind, you can eliminate many of the preceding pitfalls. Despite many of the problems that upsizing can bring, the scalability of Access is one of its stronger points. Sometimes resources aren't available to implement client/server technology in the early stages of an application. If you think through the design of the project with the possibility of upsizing in mind, you'll be pleased at how relatively easy it is to move to client/server when the time is right.

In fact, Microsoft provides an Access upsizing tool, specifically designed to take an Access application and upsize it to Microsoft SQL Server. The Access 2000 version of this tool ships with the Microsoft Office CD-ROM.

Where To Go From Here

In this chapter, we have considered many of the issues surrounding the simplest type of client/server program with Microsoft Access—the linking of the Access database with remote (usually back-end) data sources. We have discussed how you can link to remote data, how you can export remote data into your applications, and even how you can embed remote data within your applications.

But even with all this discussion, it should have been relatively clear that this is not necessarily the best solution for the problem of accessing remote data—for any number of reasons. Throughout this book, we will consider several additional solutions that you have at your disposal for addressing the issues surrounding connecting to back-end data sources. However, in Chapter 4, we will open our discussion of ActiveX Data Objects (ADO). ADO is both Microsoft's recommended solution and the developer-preferred solution to the complex issues that the DAO model mostly avoids, handles in an inappropriate manner, or, in some cases, flat-out ignores.

Chapter 4

Introduction To ActiveX Data Objects And OLE DB

As we discussed Chapter 1, DAO is the tried-and-true model for working with Jet databases. However, as Microsoft has continued to improve Access technology (and the underlying technology of both the Jet engine and other database engines in their product stable) and as people have begun to use Access databases more and more as a desktop-based gateway to remote, client/server databases, developers have been requesting for some time that Microsoft make significant improvements to the DAO technology. Rather than investing significant time and energy improving DAO technology, Microsoft has, instead, rapidly improved the ActiveX Data Objects (ADO), making them a viable alternative to DAO. In fact, Microsoft intends to replace DAO entirely with ADO implementations in the next several years.

You, however, may be asking what the difference is between ADO and DAO—is there really a difference, and if so, what's the benefit to using ADO instead of DAO? To understand this issue, you must take a step back for a moment from ADO and consider OLE DB, a Windows Open Services Architecture (WOSA)-based model that implements dual-sided Component Object Model (COM) interfaces as the means for data access. In fact, OLE DB is the underlying technology on which ADO is based.

When most developers and users think of data stores, they generally consider databases—both relational and hierarchical—as the most likely places to store data. If you think about it, however, volumes of data are stored on most computers that are nowhere near a database. For example, disk directories and email folders contain significant levels of important, useful information. In general, however, it has historically been very difficult, if not

107

impossible, to take advantage of the data stored in such locations. Moreover, although you may need to access such data, your typical data source is likely to remain a relational database that supports the Open Database Connectivity (ODBC) standard that you can manipulate with commands written in SQL.

The general solution Microsoft offers to this problem is OLE DB, a set of COM interfaces that provides uniform access to data stored in diverse information sources. However, the OLE DB application programming interface is designed to provide optimal functionality in a wide variety of applications—meaning it isn't particularly simple. In fact, because OLE DB is COM-based, it requires extensive manipulation of interfaces—making it somewhat more complex to work with than many other solutions.

To effectively use OLE DB from Access, you need an application programming interface (API) that's a bridge between your Access/VBA application and OLE DB. ADO provides that bridge. ADO defines a programming model—the sequence of activities necessary to gain access to and update a data source. The programming model summarizes the entire functionality of ADO. Before we move on to the consideration of ADO, however, let's take a brief look at how OLE DB works—basically, enough of a look to realize why we *want* to use ADO from our Access/VBA applications.

Analyzing OLE DB

OLE DB, a set of interfaces for data access, is Microsoft's component database architecture that provides universal data integration over an enterprise's network—from mainframe to desktop—regardless of the data type. Microsoft's ODBC industry-standard data access interface provides the underlying engine and a unified way to access relational data as part of the OLE DB specification.

OLE DB provides a flexible and efficient database architecture that offers applications, compilers, and other database components efficient access to Microsoft and third-party data stores. OLE DB is the fundamental COM building block for storing and retrieving records and unifies Microsoft's strategy for database connectivity. It will be used throughout Microsoft's line of applications and data stores.

OLE DB defines interfaces for accessing and manipulating all types of data. These interfaces are used not just by data-consuming applications, but also by database providers. By splitting databases apart, you can use the resulting components in an efficient manner. For example, components called *service providers* can be invoked to expose more sophisticated data manipulation and navigation interfaces on behalf of simple *data providers*.

Note

OLE DB is a specification, not a library or program.

OLE DB As A Component Technology

To meet its goal of providing data access to all types of data in a COM environment, OLE DB is designed as a component technology. In OLE DB, data stores expose the interfaces that reflect their native functionality. Common components can be built on top of those interfaces to expose more robust data models. To define its component architecture, OLE DB identifies common characteristics between different data providers and services, and defines common interfaces to expose those characteristics. So, for example, although a rowset may be obtained through a number of very different mechanisms, the end result is still a rowset, with well-defined interfaces, methods, and characteristics. With OLE DB, navigating the result of a complex multitable join is no different than navigating the result of a text file containing tabular data. Defining common interfaces in this manner allows components to augment the individual data provider's native functionality more efficiently.

Once the base functionality is defined, the next step is to view the additional functionality as incremental additions to this base functionality. Thus, the more sophisticated providers can expose these advanced features *in addition to* the base level interfaces. Furthermore, individual service components can be built to implement these features on top of the simpler providers.

Understanding Consumers

Developers writing OLE DB consumers can choose their level of interoperability with OLE DB providers. Consumers may be written to consume a specific provider, in which case they are designed to be aware of the functionality of the provider. Or they may be written to consume generic providers. To consume generic providers, the consumer may do one of the following:

◆ Consume a minimum set of functionality and work with all OLE DB providers

◆ Consume a higher level of functionality and query the provider for support of extended functionality

◆ Consume a higher level of functionality and invoke service components to implement missing functionality, where such service components are available

Base Consumer Functionality

A consumer can expect a minimum level of functionality to be supported by a provider whenever it talks to any OLE DB provider. This functionality will vary by object. Every object, however, provides certain base interfaces. If the provider supports updating data, it will implement another set of interfaces for doing so. Providers not supporting update functionality are considered read-only providers. The root enumerator interfaces, the data link interfaces, and the row position interface are always supported by common components in the SDK. They are never implemented directly by providers.

Consumers are guaranteed the functionality required by the specification in one of three ways:

♦ Data providers written in Visual Basic, Visual J++, C, or C++ by using the OLE DB Simple Provider (OSP) Toolkit automatically support all of the required functionality and more.

♦ Data providers natively written in C or C++ can expose the full set of interfaces required for full functionality.

♦ Data providers natively written in C or C++ can implement the minimal provider functionality required by the OLE DB specification. They rely upon service components to implement the additional functionality required for the base consumer functionality.

Understanding Providers

OLE DB providers can be classified broadly into two classes. A *data provider* is any OLE DB provider that owns data and exposes its data in a tabular form as a rowset, which is defined later in this chapter. Examples of data providers include relational DBMSs, storage managers, spreadsheets, indexed sequential access method (ISAMs), and email.

A *service provider* is any OLE DB component that does not own its own data, but encapsulates some service by producing and consuming data through OLE DB interfaces. A service provider is both a consumer and a provider. For example, a query processor is a service provider. Suppose a consumer asks to join data from tables in two different data sources. In its role as a consumer, the query processor retrieves rows from rowsets created over each of the base tables. In its role as a provider, the query processor creates a rowset from these rows and returns it to the consumer.

An OLE DB provider exposes OLE DB interfaces over some type of data. OLE DB providers include everything from a full SQL DBMS to a text file or data stream. Obviously these data providers have different functionality, and it's important not to limit that functionality. But at the same time it's not reasonable to expect all providers that expose simple tabular data to implement a full-blown query engine as well.

Providers support the native functionality of the data that they expose. This always includes at least the functionality described later in this chapter. Additional interfaces should be implemented as appropriate. If the provider natively supports all of the base functionality detailed in the OLE DB specification, then service components won't be needed to provide the minimal consumer functionality. In addition, providers may expose interfaces for extended functionality. All providers, however, must support one of the three standard COM component models: apartment, rental, or free-threaded.

Base Provider Functionality

It is important for provider writers to implement the full set of interfaces that apply to their particular type of data. At a minimum, the provider must implement the interfaces and

COM's Threading Architecture

In general, the simplest way to view COM's threading architecture is to think of all the COM objects in the process as divided into groups called *apartments*. A COM object lives in exactly one apartment, in the sense that its methods can legally be called directly only by a thread that belongs to that apartment. Any other thread that wants to call the object must go through a proxy. There are two types of apartments: single-threaded apartments and multithreaded apartments.

- *Single-threaded apartment*—Each thread that uses OLE is in a separate "apartment," and COM synchronizes all incoming calls with the Windows message queue. A process with a single thread of execution is simply a special case of this model. Single-threaded apartments consist of exactly one thread, so all COM objects that live in a single-threaded apartment can receive method calls only from the one thread that belongs to that apartment. All method calls to a COM object in a single-threaded apartment are synchronized with the Windows message queue for the single-threaded apartment's thread.

- *Multithreaded apartment*—Multiple threads in a single free-threaded apartment use COM, and calls made to COM objects are thus synchronized by the objects themselves. Multithreaded apartments consist of one or more threads, so all COM objects that live in a multithreaded apartment can receive method calls directly from any of the threads that belong to the multithreaded apartment. Threads in a multithreaded apartment use a model called *free-threading*. OLE does not provide any synchronization of method calls to COM objects in a multithreaded apartment. In particular, this means that the COM object must provide its own synchronization if needed.

A process can have zero or more single-threaded apartments, and zero or one multithreaded apartment. One way of looking at this is the following:

- A process that consists of just one single-threaded apartment is referred to as a *single-threaded process*.

- A process that has two or more single-threaded apartments and no multithreaded apartments is called an *apartment model process*.

- A process that has a multithreaded apartment and no single-threaded apartments is referred to as a *free-threaded process*.

- A process that has a multithreaded apartment and one or more single-threaded apartments is a *mixed model process*.

In reality, however, all processes are apartment model. The threading model really applies to an apartment, not to a process. It can also apply to a class of objects, but it doesn't really apply to a component, such as a DLL, but to the object classes within the DLL. Different classes in a DLL can have different threading models.

In a process, the main apartment is the first to be initialized. In a single-threaded process, this remains the only apartment. Call parameters are marshaled between apartments, and COM handles the synchronization through messaging. If you designate multiple threads in a process to be free-threaded, all free threads reside in a single apartment, parameters are passed directly to any thread in the apartment, and you must handle all synchronization. In a process with both free-threading and apartment threading, all free threads reside in a single apartment, and all other apartments are single-threaded apartments. A process that does COM work is a collection of apartments with, at most, one multithreaded apartment, but any number of single-threaded apartments.

The threading models in COM provide the mechanism for clients and servers that use different threading architectures to work together. Calls among objects with different threading models in different processes are naturally supported. From the perspective of the calling object, all calls to objects outside a process behave identically, no matter how the object being called is threaded. Likewise, from the perspective of the object being called, arriving calls behave identically, regardless of the threading model of the caller.

Interaction between a client and an out-of-process object is straightforward even when they use different threading models, because the client and object are in different processes and COM is involved in remoting calls from the client to the object. COM, interposed between the client and the server, can provide the code for the threading models to interoperate, with standard marshaling and the remote procedure call (RPC) protocol. For example, if a single-threaded object is called simultaneously by multiple free-threaded clients, the calls will be synchronized by COM—a task COM accomplishes by placing corresponding window messages in the server's message queue. The object's apartment will receive one call each time it retrieves and dispatches messages.

---

behavior described in the OLE DB specification as qualifications for a generic OLE DB provider. Providers implementing the minimum provider functionality can rely on common service components available in the SDK to implement the base consumer functionality.

Understanding Commands

In OLE DB, data definition language (DDL) and data manipulation language (DML) statements are referred to as *text commands*. A command object contains a text command and encapsulates the query processing services available in today's DBMSs. Commands expose various interfaces representing different areas of functionality of a query processor including query formulation, preparation, and execution. Figure 4.1 illustrates a typical OLE DB query processor.

The main purpose of a command object is to execute a text command. Executing a command such as a SQL **SELECT** statement creates a rowset, whereas executing a command such as a SQL **UPDATE** or **CREATE TABLE** statement does not create a rowset. Text commands are expressed in a provider-specific language, although this is typically ANSI SQL 92.

An OLE DB consumer that wants to use a command typically performs the following steps:

1. Obtains an interface on the command.

2. Builds a text string representing the command text.

3. Passes the text string to the command.

4. Requests properties to be supported by the resulting rowset, if any, including the interfaces it will expose.

5. Executes the command. If the command text specified the creation of a rowset, the command returns the rowset to the consumer.

Notice that because providers can both consume and produce rowsets, it is possible to compose query processors to process distributed, heterogeneous, or parallel queries. It is also

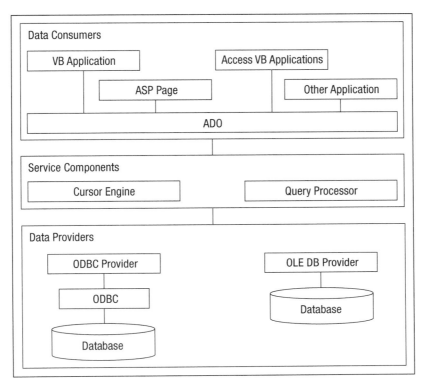

Figure 4.1
A typical OLE DB query processor.

possible to compose specialized query processors, such as SQL query processors, text-search query processors, and geographical or image query processors.

A command is used to execute a provider-specific text command, such as a SQL statement. It is important not to confuse a command, which is an OLE COM object, and its command text, which is a string. Commands are generally used for data definition, such as creating a table or granting privileges, and data manipulation, such as updating or deleting rows. A special case of data manipulation is creating a rowset—for example, a SQL **SELECT** statement.

Providers are not required to support commands. In general, providers built on top of a DBMS, such as a SQL DBMS, support commands, and providers built on top of a simple data structure, such as a file or an array of data in an application, do not support commands.

Understanding Rowsets

Rowsets are the central objects that enable all OLE DB data providers to expose data in tabular form. Conceptually, a rowset is a set of rows in which each row has columns of data. Base table providers present their data in the form of rowsets. Query processors present the result of queries in the form of rowsets. This makes it possible to layer components that consume or produce data through the same object. The most basic rowset object exposes four interfaces. Other rowset interfaces expose additional rowset capabilities. For example, there is an interface to insert, delete, and update rows and interfaces that expose richer row navigation models, such as direct access and scrollability.

Rowsets are created in one of two ways: as the result of a query or directly as the result of calling interfaces in the OLE DB specification. All providers support the latter method, whereas simple providers, such as those built over a base table, index, file, or in-memory structure, generally do not support the former.

Index rowsets are rowsets whose rows are formed from index entries. Index rowsets have the additional property of allowing efficient access to contiguous rows within a range of keys. They are used primarily by query processor components. Indexes abstract the functionality of balanced-trees (B-trees) and indexed-sequential files.

Understanding OLE DB Error Objects

OLE DB error objects extend the capabilities of automation error objects with the capabilities to return multiple error records and to return provider-specific errors. An error object is accessed by calling the **GetErrorInfo** function exposed by the Automation DLL and retrieving an **IErrorInfo** interface on the objects. Providers can also create error objects using **CoCreateInstance**.

Records in OLE DB error objects are numbered starting from zero. The methods in **IErrorRecords** allow consumers to specify the record from which to retrieve error information. As error records are added, they are added to the top of the list (that is, the number of the existing error records is increased by one and a new record zero is added), so consumers can start with the highest level of error information and then retrieve increasingly more detailed information.

Each error record is composed of five parts: an **ERRORINFO** structure, error parameters, a pointer to a custom error object, a dynamic error ID, and a lookup ID.

Error Parameters

The error parameters are provider-specific values that are incorporated into error messages. For example, the provider might associate the following error message with a **dwMinor** value of 10:

```
Cannot open table <param1>.
```

In such a case, you would use the error parameters to supply the name of the table that could not be opened. Error parameters are substituted into error messages by a provider-specific error lookup service. Thus, the format of error parameters and how they are substituted into error messages is completely provider specific. The error lookup service is called by the code in **IErrorInfo**.

Custom Error Objects

Associated with each error record is a custom error object; an interface pointer to the object is stored in the record. If no custom error object exists, this pointer is **NULL**. The custom error object is the mechanism by which OLE DB error objects are extensible.

When an error record is added, the error object calls **AddRef** to add a reference to the custom error object. The provider that created the custom error object calls **Release** to release its hold on the custom error object. Thus, ownership of the custom error object is effectively transferred from the provider to the error object. The error object releases all custom error objects when it is released.

For example, ODBC-related providers can expose **ISQLErrorInfo** on a custom error object to return the **SQLSTATE**.

Dynamic Error ID

The dynamic error ID is the ID of an error message created at runtime by the error lookup service, as opposed to an error message hard-coded in the lookup service. The dynamic error ID is used by the error object to release the dynamic error message when the error object is released. Generally, all error messages associated with a single error object have the same dynamic error ID.

Lookup ID

The lookup ID is used by the error lookup service in conjunction with the return code to identify the error description, help file, and context ID for a specific error. It can also be a special value, **IDENTIFIER_SDK_ERROR**. This special value tells the default implementation of **IErrorInfo** (the interface version shipped with the OLE DB SDK) to ignore the provider's lookup service and use the description supplied in the error resource DLL (also shipped with the OLE DB SDK).

Using OLE DB From Within Applications

Clearly, as you can see, OLE DB exposes a great number of interfaces that your applications can take advantage of to access data sources. Despite the power of OLE DB, Microsoft suggests that developers use the ADO wrappers to access the underlying COM interfaces.

The CD-ROM that accompanies this book includes a simple implementation of an OLE DB program (written in C++) that accesses a simple Jet engine-based database. The consumer application accesses the database through the Microsoft OLE DB provider for ODBC and dumps the database's contents to a text file in tab-delimited format. To keep the code simple, the code presumes that all fields in the databases are text fields. The code is too long to reprint here, but is explained in comments as it goes.

So, clearly, the upshot of all this is just as we discussed at the beginning of the chapter: Working with the OLE DB interfaces through the ADO Object Model is the best way to get at the functionality of OLE DB. In fact, from within Access, it is really the *only* way to get at that functionality. However, we took the time to discuss the concepts of OLE DB because they provide important groundwork for understanding ADO—a goal that we will accomplish in the next section.

Understanding The ActiveX Data Object (ADO) Object Model

Figure 4.2 shows an overview of the ADO Object Model. At the top of the hierarchy is the **Connection** object that contains all the other objects and collections that are part of the hierarchy. It's the only object that doesn't have an associated collection.

Each object within the ADO Object Model is important to you, because you'll manipulate the various objects at runtime using code, so you can accomplish the tasks required by your application. The following is a description of each major object and how you'll use it when programming with ADO.

Understanding The Connection Object

A **Connection** object represents a unique session with a data source. It's akin to the DAO **Workspace** object, but doesn't have a parent engine object. Instead, the parent engine is

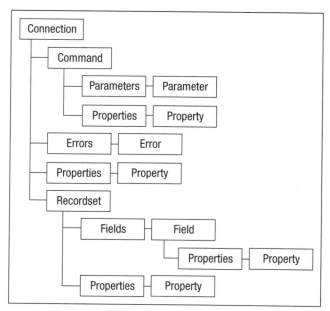

Figure 4.2
An overview of the ADO Object Model.

specified within the connection string you use when initiating the **Connection** object. In the case of a client/server database system, the **Connection** will generally be equivalent to an actual network connection to the server. Depending on the functionality the database provider supports, some collections, methods, or properties of a **Connection** object may not be available. You can create **Connection** objects independently of any other previously defined object.

When using the collections, methods, and properties of a **Connection** object, you can do the following:

♦ Configure the connection before opening it with the **ConnectionString, Connection-Timeout**, and **Mode** properties

♦ Set the **CursorLocation** property to invoke the Client Cursor Provider, which supports batch updates

♦ Set the default database for the connection with the **DefaultDatabase** property

♦ Set the level of isolation for the transactions opened on the connection with the **IsolationLevel** property

♦ Specify an OLE DB provider with the **Provider** property

♦ Establish, and later break, the physical connection to the data source with the **Open** and **Close** methods

♦ Execute a command on the connection with the **Execute** method and configure the execution with the **CommandTimeout** property

♦ Manage transactions on the open connection, including nested transactions if the provider supports them, with the **BeginTrans, CommitTrans**, and **RollbackTrans** methods and the **Attributes** property

♦ Examine errors returned from the data source with the **Errors** collection

♦ Obtain schema information about your database with the **OpenSchema** method

You can execute a query against a data source without using a **Command** object. Instead, you can pass a query string to the **Execute** method of a **Connection** object. However, a **Command** object is required when you want to persist the command text and re-execute it or use query parameters.

Understanding The Command Object And Commands Collection

When using ADO, you'll use a **Command** object to query a database and return records in a **Recordset** object, to execute a bulk operation, or to manipulate the structure of a database. Depending on the functionality the provider supports, some **Command** methods or properties may generate an error when referenced.

In general, the **Command** object replaces DAO **QueryDefs**, **TableDefs**, the **OpenRecordset** method, and more. With the collections, methods, and properties of a **Command** object, you can perform the following actions, among others:

♦ Define the executable text of the command—which will, in general, be a SQL statement—with the **CommandText** property.

♦ Define parameterized queries or stored-procedure arguments with **Parameter** objects and the **Parameters** collection (both of which are children of the **Command** object, as you can see in Figure 4.2).

♦ Execute a command and return a **Recordset** object if appropriate with the **Execute** method.

♦ Set the number of seconds a provider will wait for a command to execute with the **CommandTimeout** property—an especially useful technique when you're working with remote databases.

♦ Associate an open connection with a **Command** object by setting its **ActiveConnection** property. In other words, you can create a **Command** object, use it within one connection (that is, one database), and immediately thereafter associate it with another connection simply by changing this property.

♦ Pass a **Command** object to the **Source** property of a **Recordset** to obtain data.

To create a **Command** object independently of a previously defined **Connection** object, set the **Command** object's **ActiveConnection** property to a valid connection string. ADO still creates a **Connection** object, but it doesn't assign that object to an object variable. However, if you're associating multiple **Command** objects with the same connection, you should explicitly create and open a **Connection** object. If you don't set the **Command** object's **ActiveConnection** property to this object variable, ADO creates a new **Connection** object for each **Command** object, even if you use the same connection string, which can slow performance.

To execute a **Command**, simply call it by its **Name** property on the associated **Connection** object. The **Command** must have its **ActiveConnection** property set to the **Connection** object. If the **Command** has parameters, pass values for them as arguments to the method.

Understanding The Error Object And Errors Collection

The **Errors** collection contains all **Error** objects for a particular **Connection**. Any operation involving ADO objects can generate one or more provider errors. As each error occurs, the provider will place one or more **Error** objects into the **Errors** collection of the **Connection** object. When another ADO operation generates an error, ADO will clear the **Errors** collection, and the provider will then place the new set of **Error** objects into the **Errors** collection.

Each **Error** object represents a specific provider error, not an ADO error. ADO errors are exposed to the runtime exception-handling mechanism. In other words, the occurrence of an ADO-specific error will trigger an **On Error** event and appear in the **Err** object. However, because provider errors don't trigger the **On Error** event, test the **Errors** collection to ensure proper performance after each task.

The set of **Error** objects in the **Errors** collection describes all errors that occurred in response to a single statement. Enumerating the specific errors in the **Errors** collection enables your error-handling routines to more precisely determine the cause and origin of an error and take appropriate steps to recover.

In addition to pure errors, some properties and methods will return warnings that appear as **Error** objects in the **Errors** collection but don't halt a program's execution. Such methods include the **Resync**, **UpdateBatch**, and **CancelBatch** methods for the **Recordset** object.

Understanding The ADO Recordset Object And Recordsets Collection

As you saw earlier in this chapter, the DAO **Recordset** object is one of the most important objects in data-access management. If anything, the ADO **Recordset** object is even more important, as it fills more roles in the ADO structure.

A **Recordset** object represents the entire set of records from a base table or the results of an executed command. At any time, the **Recordset** object refers to only a single record within the set as the current record.

Just as with DAO, you'll use **Recordset** objects to manipulate data from a provider. When you use ADO, you manipulate data almost entirely using **Recordset** objects. All **Recordset** objects are constructed using records (rows) and fields (columns). Depending on the functionality supported by the provider, some **Recordset** methods or properties may not be available.

Tip

ADOR.Recordset and ADODB.Recordset are ProgIDs that you can use to create a Recordset object. The Recordset objects that result behave identically, regardless of the ProgID. The ADOR.Recordset is installed only with Microsoft Internet Explorer, whereas the ADODB.Recordset is installed with ADO. The behavior of a Recordset object is affected by its environment (that is, client, server, Internet Explorer, and so on). Recognizing that the object will perform differently in different situations is important because ADO supports Visual Basic, Scripting Edition (VBScript) and may, in fact, be invoked directly from a Web page.

As you learned earlier, four different cursor types are defined in ADO. A *cursor type* corresponds loosely to a recordset type as defined by DAO. The four ADO cursor types are as follows:

♦ *Dynamic cursor*—Allows you to view additions, changes, and deletions by other users, and allows all types of movement through the **Recordset** that don't rely on bookmarks. Furthermore, dynamic cursors allow bookmarks if the provider supports them. The Dynamic cursor is very similar to a Dynaset-type DAO **Recordset**.

♦ *Keyset cursor*—Behaves like a Dynamic cursor, except that it prevents you from seeing records that other users add and prevents access to records that other users delete. Data changes by other users will still be visible. It always supports bookmarks and, therefore, allows all types of movement through the ADO **Recordset**. As you can see, the Keyset cursor is also very similar to a Dynaset-type DAO **Recordset**.

♦ *Static cursor*—Provides a static copy of a set of records for you to use to find data or generate reports; it always allows bookmarks and, therefore, allows all types of movement through the **Recordset**. Additions, changes, or deletions by other users won't be visible. This is the only type of cursor allowed when you open a client-side (that is, from the Internet Explorer ActiveX Data Objects Recordset-support [ADOR] library) **Recordset** object. The Static cursor performs similarly to the DAO Snapshot-type **Recordset**.

♦ *Forward-Only cursor*—Behaves identically to a dynamic cursor except that it allows you to scroll only forward through records. This improves performance in situations where you need to make only a single pass through a **Recordset**. The Forward-Only cursor is consistent with the ODBCDirect DAO implementation of a Forward-Only **Recordset**.

Set the **CursorType** property before opening the **Recordset** to choose the cursor type, or pass a **CursorType** argument with the **Open** method. If you don't specify a cursor type, ADO will open a Forward-Only cursor by default.

Recordset objects can support two types of updating—immediate and batched. In immediate updating, all changes to data are written immediately to the underlying data source once you call the **Update** method. You can also pass arrays of values as parameters with the **AddNew** and **Update** methods and simultaneously update several fields in a record. If a provider supports batch updating, you can have the provider cache changes to more than one record, and then transmit them in a single call to the database with the **UpdateBatch** method. This applies to changes made with the **AddNew**, **Update**, and **Delete** methods. After you call the **UpdateBatch** method, you can use the **Status** property to check for any data conflicts to resolve them.

Understanding The Parameter Object And Parameters Collection

A **Parameters** collection contains all the **Parameter** objects of a **Command** object. As you learned earlier, a **Command** object has a **Parameters** collection made up of **Parameter** objects. Using the **Refresh** method on a **Command** object's **Parameters** collection retrieves provider parameter information for the stored procedure or parameterized query specified in the **Command** object. Some providers don't support stored procedure calls or parameterized queries; calling the **Refresh** method on the **Parameters** collection when using such a provider will return an error.

You can minimize calls to the provider to improve performance if you know the properties of the parameters associated with the stored procedure or parameterized query you wish to call. Use the **CreateParameter** method to create **Parameter** objects with the appropriate property settings and use the **Append** method to add them to the **Parameters** collection. This lets you set and return parameter values without having to call the provider for the parameter information. If you're writing to a provider that doesn't supply parameter information, you must manually populate the **Parameters** collection using this method to be able to use parameters at all. Use the **Delete** method to remove **Parameter** objects from the **Parameters** collection if necessary.

ADO **Parameter** objects perform functions consistent with DAO **Parameter** objects. The primary difference is that, in ADO, you can only use **Parameter** objects with **Command** objects.

Understanding The Properties Collection

Each ActiveX Data Object has a **Properties** collection, which is a list of properties associated with that particular object. Some ADO objects have a **Properties** collection made up of **Property** objects. Each **Property** object corresponds to a characteristic of the ADO object specific to the provider. ADO objects have two types of properties:

♦ *Built-in properties*—These properties are implemented in ADO and are immediately available to any new object, using the **ADOObject.Property** syntax. They don't appear as **Property** objects in an object's **Properties** collection, so although you can change their values, you can't modify their characteristics.

♦ *Dynamic properties*—Defined by the underlying data provider, they appear in the **Properties** collection for the appropriate ADO object. For example, a property specific to the provider may indicate whether a **Recordset** object supports transactions or updating. These additional properties will appear as **Property** objects in that **Recordset** object's **Properties** collection. Dynamic properties can be referenced only through the collection, using the **ADOObject.Properties(0)** or **ADOObject.Properties("Name")** syntax. In addition, a dynamic **Property** object has four built-in properties of its own, which you can use when enumerating through the **Properties** collection. The **Name** property is a **String** that identifies the property, whereas the **Type** property is an **Integer** that specifies the property data type. The **Value** property is a **Variant** that contains the property setting, and the **Attributes** property is a **Long** value that indicates characteristics of the property specific to the provider.

You can't delete either kind of property. However, you can view or modify the properties of an object using its **Properties** collection, just as you could in DAO. The code to do so looks similar to the following:

```
Public Sub PropsAndAttribs
   Dim cnn1 As New  ADODB.Connection
   Dim rstBooks As ADODB.Recordset
   Dim fldLoop As ADODB.Field
   Dim proLoop As ADODB.Property
   Dim strCnn As String
```

```
' Open connection and recordset.
strCnn = "driver={SQL Server};" & _
    "server=HomeServ;uid=lmk;pwd=pwd;database=ServSamp"

cnn1.Open strCnn
Set rstBooks = New ADODB.Recordset
rstBooks.Open "books", cnn1, , , adCmdTable

' Display the attributes of the Books table's properties.
Debug.Print "Property attributes:"
For Each proLoop In rstBooks.Properties
  Debug.Print "    " & proLoop.Name & " = " & _
      proLoop.Attributes
Next proLoop
rstBooks.Close
cnn1.Close
End Sub
```

This code creates a connection to a SQL Server database, then opens a table called **books** on the database. Next, the program code loops through each **Property** object for the table, printing each object's name and attributes.

Working With ADO Recordset Properties And Methods

Like other objects, **Recordset** objects have properties and methods. The properties are the attributes of the **Recordset** objects, and the methods are the actions that you can take on the **Recordset** objects. Some properties are read-only at runtime; others can be read from and written to at runtime.

Creating A Recordset Variable

When you're working with a recordset, you must first create a **Recordset** variable. The **Open** method is used to fill a **Recordset** object variable with returned values from the data source. To use a **Recordset** variable, begin by declaring a generic **Recordset** variable, then point the variable at a specific recordset using a **Set** statement. The code for this will generally look similar to the following:

```
Public Sub OpenRecordset()
  Dim cnn1 As Connection
  Dim rstBooks As Recordset
  Dim strCnn As String

  ' Open connection.
  strCnn = "driver={SQL Server};" & _
```

```
        "server=HomeServ;uid=lmk;pwd=pwd;database=ServSamp"
    Set cnn1 = New Connection
    cnn1.Open strCnn

    ' Open book table.
    Set rstBooks = New Recordset
    rstBooks.CursorType = adOpenKeyset
    rstBooks.LockType = adLockOptimistic
    rstBooks.Open "usp_all_books", cnn1, , , adCmdTable
End Sub
```

As you can see, the code creates a **Connection** object variable and a **Recordset** object variable. It then connects to a database on a SQL Server. Next, it assigns value to properties of the **Recordset** object, setting both the cursor type (to a Keyset cursor) and the locking to use on the recordset. Finally, it uses the **Open** method to assign the recordset based on the **usp_all_books** stored procedure to the object variable **rstBooks**.

Understanding The Arguments That The Open Method Accepts

You can see that the **Open** method accepts five parameters, each of which contains crucial information about the way ADO will open the recordset—parameters that ADO interprets in addition to the properties you set for the **Recordset** object. Much as it was worthwhile to examine the arguments to the **OpenRecordset** method, so too is it worthwhile to examine the parameters for the ADO **Open** method. The most substantial difference between the two methods, arguably, is that, unlike the **OpenRecordset** method, all the parameters for the **Open** method are optional, provided you've set valid values in the **Recordset**'s properties. The prototype for the **Open** method is shown here:

```
recordset.Open Source, ActiveConnection, CursorType, LockType, Options
```

The **Source** parameter is a **Variant** that evaluates to a valid **Command** object variable name, a SQL statement, a table name, a stored procedure call, or the file name of a persisted **Recordset**. The **ActiveConnection** parameter is also either a **Variant** or a **String**. When a **Variant**, it must evaluate to a valid **Connection** object variable name; if a string, it must contain valid **ConnectionString** parameters.

The third parameter, **CursorType**, is a **CursorTypeEnum** value that determines the type of cursor that the provider should use when opening the **Recordset**. As you saw in the previous example, you can also set the cursor type in the **CursorType** property, and then ignore this parameter. Valid values for the **CursorType** property or parameter appear in Table 4.1.

The fourth parameter, **LockType**, is a **LockTypeEnum** value that determines what type of locking (concurrency) the provider should use when opening the **Recordset**. As you saw in the previous example, you can also set the lock type in the **LockType** property, and then ignore this parameter. Valid values for the **LockType** property or parameter appear in Table 4.2.

Table 4.1 Valid values for the CursorType property or parameter (as defined in the ADO object library).

Constant	Description
adOpenForwardOnly	(Default) Opens a Forward-Only–type cursor.
adOpenKeyset	Opens a Keyset-type cursor.
adOpenDynamic	Opens a Dynamic-type cursor.
adOpenStatic	Opens a Static-type cursor.

Table 4.2 Valid values for the LockType property or parameter (as defined in the ADO object library).

Constant	Description
adLockReadOnly	(Default) Read-only; you can't alter the data.
adLockPessimistic	Pessimistic locking, record by record. The provider does what's necessary to ensure successful editing of the records, usually by locking records at the data source immediately upon editing.
adLockOptimistic	Optimistic locking, record by record. The provider uses Optimistic locking, locking records only when you call the **Update** method.
adLockBatchOptimistic	Optimistic batch updates. Required for batch update mode, as opposed to immediate update mode.

The fifth and final parameter is the **Options** parameter, a **Long** value that specifies how the provider should evaluate the **Source** argument if it represents something other than a **Command** object, or how the **Recordset** should be restored from a file where it was previously saved. Valid values for the **Options** parameter appear in Table 4.3 (note that the first five constants listed will also apply to the **CommandType** property).

Table 4.3 Valid values for the CommandType property or Options parameter (as defined in the ADO object library).

Constant	Description
adCmdText	Indicates that the provider should evaluate **Source** as a textual definition of a command.
adCmdTable	Indicates that ADO should generate a SQL query to return all rows from the table named in **Source**.
adCmdTableDirect	Indicates that the provider should return all rows from the table named in **Source**.
adCmdStoredProc	Indicates that the provider should evaluate **Source** as a stored procedure.
adCmdUnknown	Indicates that the type of command in the **Source** argument isn't known.
adCommandFile	Indicates that the persisted (saved) **Recordset** should be restored from the file named in **Source**.
adExecuteAsync	Indicates that the **Source** should be executed asynchronously.
adFetchAsync	Indicates that after the initial quantity specified in the **CacheSize** property is fetched, any remaining rows should be fetched asynchronously.

Record Movement Methods With ADO

Once you have created a **Recordset** variable, and pointed the variable at a resultset from the server, you will probably want to manipulate the data in the recordset—that is the whole point of accessing the data, after all. You can use several methods to traverse through the records in a recordset:

♦ **MoveFirst** moves to the first record in a recordset. (You can't use this method with a Forward-Only cursor or with any **Recordset** object that doesn't support bookmarks.)

♦ **MoveLast** moves to the last record in a recordset.

♦ **MovePrevious** moves to the previous record in a recordset. (You can't use this method with a Forward-Only cursor or with any **Recordset** object that doesn't support bookmarks.)

♦ **MoveNext** moves to the next record in a recordset.

♦ **Move [N]** moves forward or backward a specified number of records. (You can't use this method to move backward with a Forward-Only cursor or with any **Recordset** object that doesn't support bookmarks.)

You'll invoke the ADO **Move** methods against a **Recordset** object just as you did in DAO programming, as shown here:

```
' rstLocal is an ADO DB Recordset
rstLocal.MoveNext
rstLocal.MoveLast
rstLocal.MovePrevious        ' Causes ADO error if bookmarks not supported
rstLocal.MoveFirst           ' Causes ADO error if bookmarks not supported
```

Detecting The Limits Of A Recordset

Just as with DAO **Recordsets**, ADO **Recordsets** contain two crucial **Recordset** properties, **BOF** and **EOF**. These properties are used to determine whether you've reached the limits of your recordset. The **BOF** property is **True** when the record pointer is before the first record, and the **EOF** property is **True** when the record pointer is after the last record.

You need to keep in mind some important characteristics of the **BOF** and **EOF** properties as they apply to ADO **Recordsets**:

♦ If a recordset contains no records, both the **BOF** and **EOF** properties evaluate to **True**.

♦ The moment you open a recordset containing at least one record, the **BOF** and **EOF** properties are set to **False**.

♦ When the record pointer is on the first record in the recordset and the **MovePrevious** method is issued, the **BOF** property is set to **True**. Attempting to use **MovePrevious** again creates a trappable runtime error.

♦ If the record pointer is on the last record in the recordset and the **MoveNext** method is issued, the **EOF** property is set to **True**. If you attempt to **MoveNext** again a trappable runtime error will occur.

- When the **BOF** and **EOF** properties are set to **True**, they remain **True** until you move to a valid record.

- Deleting the only record in a recordset causes the **BOF** and **EOF** properties to remain **False** until you attempt to move to another record, in which case they're both set to **True** simultaneously, and a trappable runtime error occurs.

Counting The Number Of Records In A Recordset

The **RecordCount** property of a recordset returns the number of records in a recordset that have been accessed. If the **Recordset** object supports approximate positioning or book-marks—that is, if invoking **Supports (adApproxPosition)** or **Supports (adBookmark)**, respectively, against the **Recordset** returns **True**—this value will be the exact number of records in the **Recordset** regardless of whether it has been fully populated. If the **Recordset** object doesn't support approximate positioning, this property may be a significant drain on resources, because all records will have to be retrieved and counted to return an accurate **RecordCount** value, just as they would with DAO objects.

Using The AbsolutePosition Property

The **AbsolutePosition** property returns the position of the current record. It's a one-based value in ADO—as opposed to a zero-based value in DAO. Use the property to specify where in a recordset a specific record was found. Additionally, the property might contain one of the following values:

- The **adPosUnknown** constant means that either the **Recordset** is empty, the current position is unknown, or the provider doesn't support the **AbsolutePosition** property.

- The **adPosBOF** constant means that the current record pointer is at BOF (that is, the **BOF** property is **True**).

- The **adPosEOF** constant means that the current record pointer is at EOF (that is, the **EOF** property is **True**).

Using The Bookmark Property

Just as with DAO, an ADO **Bookmark** is a system-generated byte array that uniquely identifies each record in a recordset. The **Bookmark** property of a recordset changes as you move to each record in the recordset. It's often used when you need to store the current position in the recordset so you can perform some operation and return to the position after the operation is completed. However, some ADO recordsets won't support bookmarks. Check the **Supports (adBookmark)** method before trying to use bookmarks on a database.

Using The Clone Method

The **Clone** method of a **Recordset** object lets you create multiple, duplicate **Recordset** objects, which you'll use particularly if you want to maintain more than one current record in a given set of records. Using the **Clone** method is more efficient than creating and opening a new **Recordset** object with the same definition as the original.

Note that changes you make to one **Recordset** object are visible in all of its clones, regardless of cursor type. However, once you execute the **Requery** method on the original **Recordset**, the clones will no longer be synchronized to the original. Furthermore, closing the original **Recordset** doesn't close any of its copies, and the reverse is also true; closing a copy doesn't close the original or any of the other copies.

Warning

*In ADO, you can only clone a **Recordset** object that supports bookmarks. Bookmark values are interchangeable—that is, a bookmark reference from one **Recordset** object refers to the same record in any of its clones.*

Considering The ADO Event Model And Asynchronous Operations

The ADO Event Model supports certain synchronous and asynchronous ADO operations that issue events before the operation starts or after it completes. An *event* is actually a call to an event handler routine.

Event handlers that are called *before* the operation starts allow you to examine or modify the operation parameters, and then either cancel the operation or allow it to complete. On the other hand, event handlers called *after* an operation completes are especially important because ADO 2 supports asynchronous operations. For instance, an application that starts an asynchronous **Recordset.Open** operation is notified by an **ExecutionComplete** event when the operation concludes. There are two families of events:

♦ **ConnectionEvents** are issued when a transaction on a connection begins, is committed, or is rolled back; when a **Command** executes; and when a **Connection** starts or ends. Table 4.4 lists the **ConnectionEvents**.

Table 4.4   The ConnectionEvents that ADO supports.

ConnectionEvents	Description
BeginTransComplete, **CommitTransComplete**, **RollbackTransComplete**	These transaction management events provide notification that the current transaction on the connection has started, committed, or rolled back.
WillConnect, **ConnectComplete**, **Disconnect**	These connection management events provide notification that the current connection will start, has started, or has ended.
WillExecute, **ExecuteComplete**	These command execution management events provide notification that the execution of the current command on the connection will start or has ended.
InfoMessage	This informational event provides notification that there is additional information about the current operation (which you should then process within the event).

♦ **RecordsetEvents** are issued when you navigate through the rows of a **Recordset** object, change a field in a row of a **Recordset**, change a row in a **Recordset**, or make any change whatsoever in the **Recordset**. Table 4.5 lists the **RecordsetEvents**.

Understanding The Importance Of ADO's Events

Right about now you're probably asking yourself why you should care about ADO events. Most of the work you've been doing throughout this book has been with local databases—and DAO programming will halt the program's execution until, for example, the **Recordset** is filled, the update is complete, and so on. Although that *feature* makes writing programs easier—you always know that one thing is finished before you move on to the next—it isn't necessarily the most efficient way to access databases, *particularly* if the database is at a remote location.

Simply put, asynchronous processes (implementation through events in ADO) let your program send a request to the data source (over a **Connection** object), and then go about its business until the data source responds. In other words, you can write programs that let users perform other tasks while waiting for a **Recordset** to fill. With the **FetchProgress** event, you can even display a progress bar on screen that lets the user know how far along in the **Recordset** retrieval the database is. The possibilities for database programming are significant, and the level of functionality is far beyond what you could ever do in Access 2000 before.

Tip

To use events (particularly for asynchronous processing) with ADO objects, you must first place the objects within a class module, and then expose the events from the class module. The ADO_asynch_Exam.mdb database contained on the companion CD-ROM and its program modules show how to use these events within your own programs.

Table 4.5   The RecordsetEvents supported by ADO.

RecordsetEvents	Description
FetchProgress, **FetchComplete**	These retrieval status events provide notification of the progress of a data retrieval operation or notification that the retrieval operation has completed.
WillChangeField, **FieldChangeComplete**	These field change management events provide notification that the value of the current field will change or has changed.
WillMove, **MoveComplete**, **EndOfRecordset**	These navigation management events provide notification that the current row position in a **Recordset** will change, has changed, or has reached the end of the **Recordset**.
WillChangeRecord, **RecordChangeComplete**	These row change management events provide notification that something in the current row of the **Recordset** will change or has changed.
WillChangeRecordset, **RecordsetChangeComplete**	These recordset change management events provide notification that something in the current **Recordset** will change or has changed.

Where To Go From Here

In this chapter you learned about OLE DB, a set of interfaces for data access. OLE DB is Microsoft's component database architecture that provides universal data integration over an enterprise's network—from mainframe to desktop—regardless of the data type. Microsoft's ODBC industry-standard data access interface is the underlying technology on which the OLE DB specification is built.

Although you can write applications that access OLE DB directly, and may choose to do so in some very rare cases (particularly if there is a need for the consumer to be extremely thin), Microsoft generally recommends that you use the ActiveX Data Objects (ADO) wrapper of the OLE DB interfaces for your applications.

ADO enables you to write a client application to access and manipulate data in a data source through a provider. ADO is ideally suited to consume data exposed by OLE DB providers. ADO's primary benefits are ease of use, high speed, low memory overhead, and a small disk footprint. Working with ActiveX Data Objects, more than any other consideration, simply requires an understanding of how to work with standard COM objects. Throughout this chapter, you learned specific examples of how you can use ADO within your applications, and you also learned about potential problems to watch for within your application when working with ADO.

In Chapter 5, we will take the knowledge that you gathered in this chapter by analyzing the ADO Object Model and the nature of OLE DB processing to consider how to rewrite the DAO code that you saw in Chapters 1 and 2 using the ADO model. Then, in Chapter 6, we will move on to a consideration of some of the advanced programming techniques at your disposal with ADO.

Chapter 5
Converting From DAO To ADO

In Chapter 4, you spent time learning about how OLE DB works, and then focused on the use of ActiveX Data Objects (ADO) within your programming code. However, for many Access programmers with a history of using the product, it is not enough to understand that ADO exists, and can be used; it is also worthwhile to see how ADO works differently from your existing Data Access Objects (DAO) code, and what types of changes you need to watch out for when converting from one to the other.

In this chapter, we will look at each of the database examples that we used in Chapter 1 to explore DAO, and convert the example for use with ADO. In the interest of space, the examples from Chapter 1 will not be reprinted here; however, we will present the ADO code examples in more or less the same order as the DAO code examples were.

Using ADO Instead Of DAO

In developing an Access application, it might be useful to add tables or queries, define or modify relationships, change security, or perform other data definition techniques at runtime. You can accomplish this by manipulating the various Data Access Objects or ActiveX Data Objects. You saw how to do it with DAO in Chapter 1; in this chapter, we will look at how to do it with ADO.

To use the ADO code examples, you must first install the Microsoft Access Open Database Connectivity (ODBC) driver and create a Data Source Name (DSN) called Chap05 for the Access database file (Chap05.mdb) that is provided on the companion CD-ROM. To create a DSN, use the ODBC Data Source Administrator in Control Panel.

Adding A Table Using Code

In Chapter 1, you saw how to add a table using code from DAO—you created a table definition called **tblBooks**. It defined a matching **TableDef** object, and then added the new table definition to the **TableDefs** collection. After the table definition was added to the database, you used the DAO **Index** type to add a primary key index to the table.

Performing the same tasks is a bit different using ADO. In fact, because ADO's design lets you access many different types of databases, you'll actually use SQL statements and the **Execute** method of the **Command** object to perform similar processing, as shown here:

```
Sub CreateTable()          ' ADO Version
   Dim cnnLocal As ADODB.Connection
   Dim cmdLocal As ADODB.Command

   ' Create Connection object and open it on CHAP05.MDB
   Set cnnLocal = New ADODB.Connection
   cnnLocal.ConnectionString = "dsn=Chap05;UID=admin;PWD=;"
   cnnLocal.Open

   Set cmdLocal = New ADODB.Command
   Set cmdLocal.ActiveConnection = cnnLocal
   cmdLocal.CommandText = "CREATE TABLE tblBooks " _
       & "(BookID INTEGER, Title TEXT (25), Author TEXT (25));"
   cmdLocal.Execute

   cmdLocal.CommandText = "CREATE UNIQUE INDEX PrimaryKey " _
     & "ON tblBooks(BookID) " _
     & "WITH PRIMARY DISALLOW NULL;"
   cmdLocal.Execute
End Sub
```

Removing A Table Using Code

Just as you can add a table using code, you can also remove a table using code. The exact syntax involved in deleting tables with ADO depends on the underlying database product that you use—some databases may not let you delete tables or indexes from SQL code and may require that you use a separate management product to perform such processing. However, for databases (such as Access 2000) that do support table deletions from SQL, you can use code similar to the following to delete a table with ADO:

```
Public Sub DeleteTable()                ' ADO Version
   Dim cnnLocal As ADODB.Connection
   Dim cmdLocal As ADODB.Command
```

```
   ' Create Connection object and open it on CHAP05.MDB
   Set cnnLocal = New ADODB.Connection

   cnnLocal.ConnectionString = "dsn=Chap05;UID=admin;PWD=;"
   cnnLocal.Open

   Set cmdLocal = New ADODB.Command
   Set cmdLocal.ActiveConnection = cnnLocal
   cmdLocal.CommandText = "DROP TABLE tblBooks"
   cmdLocal.Execute
End Sub
```

Creating A Query Using Code

You might want to build your own query designer into your application and allow the users
to save the queries they build. This requires that you build the queries yourself, using code,
after the user has designed them. With ADO, you'll generally work with either stored procedures on the server, or you'll use the **Recordset** object's **Save** method to persist a recordset.
The following code, for example, uses a **Command** object together with a SQL Server
Transact-SQL statement to create a new stored procedure on the SQL Server:

```
Public Sub Create_SP()                    ' ADO Version
  Dim CRLF As String
  Dim cnnLocal As ADODB.Connection
  Dim cmdLocal As ADODB.Command

  ' Create Connection object and open it on CHAP05.MDB
  Set cnnLocal = New ADODB.Connection

  cnnLocal.ConnectionString = "dsn=Chap05;UID=admin;PWD=;"
  cnnLocal.Open

  CRLF = Chr(10) & Chr(13)
  Set cmdLocal = New ADODB.Command
  Set cmdLocal.ActiveConnection = cnnLocal
  cmdLocal.CommandText = "CREATE PROCEDURE Customer_Remove " & CRLF & _
      "@vEmail varchar(30), @vCount int OUTPUT " & CRLF & _
      "AS DECLARE @vCustomerID int " & CRLF & _
      "SELECT @vCustomerID = CustomerID FROM Customers " & CRLF & _
      "WHERE Email= @vEmail " & CRLF & _
      "IF @vCustomerID IS NULL " & CRLF & _
      "return (0)" & CRLF & _
      "ELSE" & CRLF & _
      "begin" & CRLF & _
      "DELETE FROM CustomerPasswords WHERE CustomerID = @vCustomerID" & _
          CRLF & _
      "DELETE FROM Customers WHERE CustomerID = @vCustomerID" & CRLF & _
```

```
            "SELECT @vCount = COUNT(*) FROM Customers" & CRLF & _
            "return (1)" & CRLF & _
            "end"  & CRLF
      cmdLocal.Execute
End Sub
```

We will work with stored procedures and other SQL Server objects in Chapter 11. For now, simply recognize that the stored procedure created here makes sure that there are customer(s) that match the ID value passed in—in this case, an email address. Then, if there are customers that match that criteria, it deletes them.

Creating A Recordset Variable

Just as in DAO, when you're working with a recordset from within ADO, you must first create a **Recordset** variable. You will do this by executing or calling a command of some type, either against a connection or using a command object. The code to create an ADO recordset will generally look similar to the following (when invoked against a SQL Server):

```
Sub OpenTable()
  Dim cnnBooksDB As Database
  Dim rstBooks As Recordset

  With cnnBooksDB
    .Provider = "SQLOLEDB"
    .ConnectionString = "User ID=sa;Password=;Data Source=SQLSERVER;" & _
        "Initial Catalog=BooksDB"
    .Open
  End With
  Set rstBooks = cnnBooksDB.Execute ("Select * From tblBooks")
End Sub
```

This code creates a **Connection** object variable and a **Recordset** object variable. It then sets properties on the **Connection** to point the connection at the **BooksDB** database on the SQL Server named SQLSERVER. Next, it uses the **Execute** method against the **Connection** object to construct a resultset and then assign it to the **rstBooks Recordset** variable.

Changing Record Data One Record At A Time

You'll often want to loop through a recordset, modifying all the records that meet a specific set of criteria. The code required to accomplish this task looks like the following:

```
Sub IncreaseCopies()                   ' ADO Version
  Dim cnnLocal As ADODB.Connection
  Dim cmdLocal As ADODB.Command
  Dim rstLocal As ADODB.Recordset
  Dim intUpdated As Integer
```

```
   ' Create Connection object and open it on CHAP05.MDB
   Set cnnLocal = New ADODB.Connection

   cnnLocal.ConnectionString = "dsn=Chap05;UID=admin;PWD=;"
   cnnLocal.Open

   Set cmdLocal = New ADODB.Command
   Set cmdLocal.ActiveConnection = cnnLocal
   cmdLocal.CommandText = "SELECT * FROM tblBooksChange " _
       & "WHERE BookTotalCopies < 5"
   Set rstLocal = New ADODB.Recordset
   rstLocal.CursorType = adOpenForwardOnly
   rstLocal.Open cmdLocal

   intUpdated = 0
   Do While Not rstLocal.EOF
     intUpdated = intUpdated + 1
     rstLocal.Fields("BookTotalCopies") = _
         rstLocal.Fields("BookTotalCopies") + 1
     rstLocal.Update
     rstLocal.MoveNext
   Loop
   Debug.Print intUpdated & " Records Updated"
   rstLocal.Close
End Sub
```

This code finds the first record with a **BookTotalCopies** value of less than 5. The code does not need to issue an **Edit** method, unlike with DAO—the recordset presumes that records are editable unless the recordset is specified as read-only. The code then replaces the **BookTotalCopies** with **BookTotalCopies** plus 1. It next issues the **Update** method to write the changes to the server. Finally, the program uses the **MoveNext** method to locate the next occurrence of the criteria.

Because most databases don't support the Jet engine **Find** methods, when you're working with ADO objects, you must create the recordset to update with a SQL **SELECT** statement, then move through the records in order.

Making Bulk Changes

Many of the tasks that you can perform by looping through a recordset can also be accomplished with an update query. Executing an update query is often more efficient than the process of looping through a recordset. If nothing else, it takes much less code. Therefore, it's important to understand how to execute an update query through code. Let's take a look at how to accomplish our goal from the previous section using an update query instead of iterating through the recordset:

```
Sub RunUpdateQuery()                    ' ADO Version
  Dim cnnLocal As ADODB.Connection
  Dim cmdLocal As ADODB.Command

  ' Create Connection object and open it on CHAP05.MDB
  Set cnnLocal = New ADODB.Connection
  cnnLocal.ConnectionString = "dsn=Chap05;UID=admin;PWD=;"
  cnnLocal.Open

  Set cmdLocal = New ADODB.Command
  Set cmdLocal.ActiveConnection = cnnLocal
  cmdLocal.CommandText = "UPDATE tblBooksChange " _
    & "SET BookTotalCopies = BookTotalCopies + 1 " _
    & "WHERE BookTotalCopies < 5;"
  cmdLocal.Execute
End Sub
```

As you can see, the program code simply assigns the update query to the **Command** object and executes the command. Note that, particularly in client/server environments, performing the update in this manner is far more attractive than doing the update in the manner discussed in the previous section.

The biggest reason why such a broad statement is acceptable can be summarized by the exploration of a concept called *round trips*. Any time you work against an object that is not local, you end up in a situation that can be generically referred to as a *proxy-and-stub architecture*. The proxy-and-stub architecture has a considerable amount of overhead associated with it. Much of this overhead is a function of the fact that the client's calling thread blocks (that is, stops executing) when the calling thread calls a method, and the calling thread does not regain control (resume execution) until after the call returns from the object.

Programmers refer to the method call and the execution return from the remote object as a *round trip*. You can imagine that the time to make a round trip to an object and back (in the context of our current discussion, the round trip to the database server and then back to the client computer) increases by an order of magnitude as you move the object out-of-process and onto another machine. In other words, no matter how powerful your SQL Server or how fast your network, it will always be slightly slower to access a SQL Server—even on a local network—than it is to access a local database on the calling machine.

Distance impacts performance significantly. Even if you could communicate between two machines 5,000 miles apart at the speed of light, the time of a method call would increase by a factor of 10. The actual transmission speed, of course, is much slower than the speed of light. Figure 5.1 shows the impact that round trips and distance have on communication speeds.

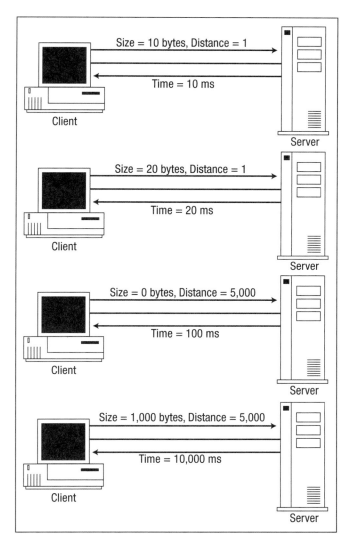

Figure 5.1
As distance and transmission size increase, so too does round-trip time.

Understanding How To Reduce Round Trips

As you learned in the previous section, the impact of round trips on your program performance is significant. When you design your interfaces, make sure that you design them to reduce round trips as much as possible. Never create multiple methods or properties when a single method can do the job just as well.

For example, using the code in the first of the two previous sections, you will have to access the server some unknown number of times—perhaps running even into the thousands—

one time for each record. On the other hand, using the second example, you only have to communicate with the server once—to send the **Update** statement—and then wait for the execution to occur locally. The entirety of the ADO model is built around this concept of reduced round trips and simplified database communications, the goal being to reduce network traffic and speed performance of applications.

Marshaling (that is, transferring) a lot of data in a single round trip is far better than marshaling smaller amounts of data in multiple round trips, as Figure 5.1 shows. Although you should optimize round trips first, you should also be conscientious about the packets of data that you move back and forth. You must push some data from the client to the server, and you must pull other data from the server back to the client. Some data must move in both directions.

In other words, in certain situations, certain types of recordsets will be appropriate, whereas in other situations, other types of recordsets will be appropriate. The biggest issue to keep in mind when transiting from DAO to ADO is that Dynasets are no longer the default **Recordset** type—nor would we want them to be. The concepts and applications that work well in the local model do *not* work well in the distributed model, and using the distributed model will require you to rethink some of the ways you do things.

Deleting An Existing Record

The **Delete** method enables you to programmatically delete records from a recordset. It works like this:

```
Sub DeleteCusts(lngNumberOfCopies As Long)          ' ADO Version
    Dim cnnLocal As ADODB.Connection
    Dim cmdLocal As ADODB.Command
    Dim rstBooks As ADODB.Recordset
    Dim intCounter As Integer

    ' Create Connection object and open it on CHAP05.MDB
    Set cnnLocal = New ADODB.Connection
    cnnLocal.ConnectionString = "dsn=Chap05;UID=admin;PWD=;"
    cnnLocal.Open

    Set cmdLocal = New ADODB.Command
    Set cmdLocal.ActiveConnection = cnnLocal
    cmdLocal.CommandText = "Select * From tblBooksChange"
    Set rstBooks = cmdLocal.Execute

    intCounter = 0
    Do While Not rstBooks.EOF
      If rstBooks.Fields("BookTotalCopies") < lngNumberOfCopies Then
        rstBooks.Delete
        intCounter = intCounter + 1
```

```
      End If
      rstBooks.MoveNext
   Loop
   Debug.Print intCounter & " Customer Records Deleted"
End Sub
```

This code loops through the **rstBooks** recordset. If the **BookTotalCopies** amount is less than the value passed in as a parameter, the record is deleted. This task could also be accomplished with a **Delete** query, as shown in the following fragment:

```
Sub RunDeleteQuery()                     ' ADO Version
   Dim cnnLocal As ADODB.Connection
   Dim cmdLocal As ADODB.Command

   ' Create Connection object and open it on CHAP05.MDB
   Set cnnLocal = New ADODB.Connection
   cnnLocal.ConnectionString = "dsn=Chap05;UID=admin;PWD=;"
   cnnLocal.Open

   Set cmdLocal = New ADODB.Command
   Set cmdLocal.ActiveConnection = cnnLocal
   cmdLocal.CommandText = "DELETE FROM tblBooksChange " _
      & "WHERE BookTotalCopies < 5;"
   cmdLocal.Execute
End Sub
```

Adding A New Record

The **AddNew** method enables you to programmatically add records to a recordset. The code in the following example shows how you can take advantage of this capability. The code to perform the **AddNew** action from ADO would look similar to the following:

```
Private Sub cmdAddRecord_Click()         ' ADO Version
   Dim cnnLocal As ADODB.Connection
   Dim cmdLocal As ADODB.Command
   Dim rstLocal As ADODB.Recordset

   ' Create Connection object and open it on CHAP05.MDB
   Set cnnLocal = New ADODB.Connection

   cnnLocal.ConnectionString = "dsn=Chap05;UID=admin;PWD=;"
   cnnLocal.Open

   Set cmdLocal = New ADODB.Command
   Set cmdLocal.ActiveConnection = cnnLocal
   cmdLocal.CommandText = "SELECT * FROM tblProjectsChange"
```

```
    Set rstLocal = New ADODB.Recordset
    rstLocal.CursorType = adOpenDynamic
    rstLocal.Open cmdLocal

    With rstLocal
      .AddNew
        .Fields("ProjectName") = Me!txtProjectName
        .Fields("ProjectDescription") = Me!txtProjectDescription
        .Fields("ClientID") = Me!cboClientID
      .Update
    End With
    Me!txtProjectID = rstLocal.Fields("ProjectID")
End Sub
```

The code resides in an unbound form called **frmUnbound** in the Chap05.mdb database file. The code issues an **AddNew** method, which creates a buffer ready to accept data. Each field in the recordset is then populated with the values from the controls on the form. The **Update** method writes the data to the database, and, just as with DAO, if you forget to include the **Update** method, the record is never written to disk.

The last line of code is there to illustrate a problem: When an **AddNew** method is issued, the record pointer is never moved within the Dynaset. Even after the **Update** method is issued, the record pointer remains at the record it was on prior to the **AddNew**. You must explicitly move to the new record before populating the **txtProjectID** text box with the **ProjectID** from the recordset. Again, you can use the ADO **Recordset** object's **AddNew** and **Update** methods to add records to a table or recordset.

Sorting, Filtering, And Finding Records

Sometimes you might need to sort or filter an existing recordset. You also might want to locate each record in the recordset that meets some specified criteria. The following techniques allow you to sort, filter, and find records within a **Recordset** object.

Sorting A Recordset

You can't actually change the sort order of an existing Dynaset or Snapshot. Instead, you create a second recordset based on the first recordset. The second recordset is sorted in the desired order. In this case, you're sorting a Dynaset that's based on the table **tblTimeCardHours**. The first time you loop through the recordset and print each date worked, the dates are in the default order (usually the primary key order). After using the **Sort** method to sort the recordset, the records appear in order by the date worked.

Unlike DAO, ADO doesn't support the **Sort** method; instead, you must sort the recordset before you assign it to the object. The following code shows how to create sorted and unsorted recordsets with ADO:

```
Sub SortRecordset()                    ' ADO Version
  Dim cnnLocal As ADODB.Connection
  Dim cmdLocal As ADODB.Command
  Dim rstLocal As ADODB.Recordset

  ' Create Connection object and open it on CHAP05.MDB
  Set cnnLocal = New ADODB.Connection
  cnnLocal.ConnectionString = "dsn=Chap05;UID=admin;PWD=;"
  cnnLocal.Open

  Set cmdLocal = New ADODB.Command
  Set cmdLocal.ActiveConnection = cnnLocal

  cmdLocal.CommandText = "SELECT * FROM tblTimeCardHours"
  cmdLocal.Execute
  Set rstLocal = New ADODB.Recordset
  rstLocal.CursorType = adOpenForwardOnly
  rstLocal.Open cmdLocal
  Debug.Print "NOT Sorted!!!"
  Do While Not rstLocal.EOF
    Debug.Print rstLocal.Fields("DateWorked")
    rstLocal.MoveNext
  Loop

  cmdLocal.CommandText = "SELECT * FROM tblTimeCardHours " & _
      "ORDER BY DateWorked"
  cmdLocal.Execute
  Set rstLocal = New ADODB.Recordset
  rstLocal.CursorType = adOpenForwardOnly
  rstLocal.Open cmdLocal
  Debug.Print "Now Sorted!!!"
  Do While Not rstLocal.EOF
    Debug.Print rstLocal.Fields("DateWorked")
    rstLocal.MoveNext
  Loop
End Sub
```

Finding A Specific Record Within A Recordset

As you have learned previously, the DAO **Seek** method enables you to find records in a **Table** recordset. It's usually the quickest method of locating data, because it uses the current index to locate the requested data.

As you learned earlier, ADO doesn't support the **Find** methods. As you might expect, because ADO doesn't support Table-Only cursors, ADO doesn't support the **Seek** method either.

However, effective manipulation of Transact-SQL (for example) or whatever SQL implementation exists on your data source will allow you to accomplish these, and other, tasks quite easily with ADO. We will explore how to accomplish more advanced tasks with ADO in Chapter 6—though we will use Transact-SQL as our primary tool of choice when we do so.

Running Parameter Queries

Access parameter queries are very powerful. They enable the user to specify criteria at runtime. This ability is often helpful if your user wants to fill out a form at runtime and have the values on that form fed to the query. Using ADO to perform such processing is similar to doing so with DAO; you simply append the parameters to the command object before opening the recordset. The following code implements the process in ADO:

```
Sub RunParameterQuery(datStart As Date, datEnd As Date)    'ADO Version
  Dim cnnLocal As ADODB.Connection
  Dim cmdLocal As ADODB.Command
  Dim rstLocal As ADODB.Recordset
  Dim prsLocal As ADODB.Parameters
  Dim prmLocal As ADODB.Parameter

  ' Create Connection object and open it on CHAP05.MDB
  Set cnnLocal = New ADODB.Connection
  cnnLocal.ConnectionString = "dsn=Chap05;UID=admin;PWD=;"
  cnnLocal.Open

  Set cmdLocal = New ADODB.Command
  Set cmdLocal.ActiveConnection = cnnLocal

  cmdLocal.CommandText = "SELECT * FROM tblBillAmountByClient " & _
      "ORDER BY StartDate Where StartDate > ? And EndDate < ?"

  Set prmLocal = cmdLocal.CreateParameter("StartDate", adDate, adParamInput)
  prmLocal.Value = datStart
  cmdLocal.Parameters.Append prmLocal
  Set prmLocal = cmdLocal.CreateParameter("EndDate", adDate, adParamInput)
  prmLocal.Value = datEnd
  cmdLocal.Parameters.Append prmLocal
  Set prmLocal = Nothing

  Set rstLocal = New ADODB.Recordset
  rstLocal.CursorType = adOpenForwardOnly
  rstLocal.Open cmdLocal
  Do While Not rstLocal.EOF
    Debug.Print rstLocal.Fields("CompanyName"), rstLocal.Fields("BillAmount")
    rstLocal.MoveNext
  Loop
End Sub
```

Unlike in DAO, you will work extensively with **Parameter** objects in ADO. As you can see from the code fragment, you will create **Parameter** objects and append them to a **Command** object when you need to pass parameters into a query. Note, however, that this particular example is trivial—you wouldn't generally construct it in this manner. Rather, you are more likely to call a stored procedure, and pass parameters into the stored procedure in accordance with its requirements through use of the **Parameters** collection. We will explore both this concept and the accompanying technique in Chapter 6.

Where To Go From Here

In this chapter, we compared the DAO code that you wrote in Chapter 1 with more advanced, powerful ADO code, all of which performs the same or similar processing. The goal for this chapter was to help make more clear both the differences and the similarities between DAO and ADO, and to ease your transition into ADO programming.

In Chapter 6, you will move on to a consideration of more advanced programming with ADO. In that chapter, I will discuss topics ranging from the design and implementation of complex activities against a remote SQL Server from your Access client, to a brief discussion of such tools as the SQL Server Distributed Management Objects (SQL-DMOs), a related set of technologies that let you perform all types of administration tasks—not just database-related tasks—against a SQL Server.

It is important to recognize the fact that the uses of ADO detailed in this chapter will form the root for much of the advanced programming that you will do with Access or any other development tool—such as Visual Basic, VBA, VBScript, and so on. In fact, throughout the rest of the book, we will focus substantially more on ADO than on its predecessor technology, DAO.

Chapter 6
Advanced ADO Issues

As you learned in the previous chapter, the ADO object model opens up a variety of new programming alternatives to you, most of which are centered on an improved ability to perform client/server database programming from within your VBA modules in Access, and, as you will see in more detail later on, most other programming platforms that Microsoft provides. In this chapter, we will cover in detail some of the programming issues involved in more advanced programming with ADO, including a brief discussion of the use of a special type of module, a *class module*, as an effective tool for creating object wrappers around database access code.

Understanding Cursors

When a **Recordset** object is created, specific records based on a SQL query are returned. This grouping of records is called a *cursor*, because it indicates the current position in the resultset, just as the cursor on a computer display indicates the current position on the screen. You can specify four types of cursors and two different locations. In this section and the following subsections, I will focus on the different cursor features, and how to implement the appropriate cursor for your application's needs.

Cursors are created in a computer's memory. Using ADO and certain databases, such as Microsoft SQL Server, you can specify on which computer the cursor is created. You can implement four types of cursors: Forward-Only, Static, Dynamic, and Keyset. Depending on their functionality, certain cursors use more system resources than others.

Selecting where the cursor should be built (its location) and the functionality of the cursor (its type) occurs when the recordset is first opened. The cursor type affects the performance and overhead of the cursor. The location and type of the cursor cannot be changed unless the recordset is first closed and then reopened.

Introduction To Cursors

A *cursor* is a database mechanism that allows a user to navigate and access data from a recordset. A cursor maintains the position of the current record and determines how you can move through the recordset. It also controls whether you can update data or see updates created by other users. Different types of cursors exist and each type consumes resources differently. You can avoid expending unnecessary resources by choosing the correct type of cursor for your application—whether the application is going to be running in a single tier, two tiers, or any further number of tiers. We will discuss tiers in some depth in Chapter 17.

Updateable Vs. Nonupdateable Cursors

Updateable cursors give the user the capability to make changes to the data in a recordset and have those changes propagate back to the data provider of the cursor. You can think of this as having write privileges on the original data. However, updateable cursors require that additional metadata be downloaded by the cursor engine, which can be expensive to retrieve.

In a nonupdateable (read-only) cursor, the user cannot make changes to the recordset. Nonupdateable cursors offer better performance, because they allow the data provider to offload the data to the cursor once and then essentially forget about it. The data provider can then continue servicing other requests, free from concerns about concurrency problems.

Scrollable Cursors

Cursors in all forms use the concept of a *current record*. The current record is the record in the recordset that is currently being pointed at by the cursor. When the user retrieves a field value from the recordset, the value is returned from the current record.

A cursor is scrollable if the user can change the current record, such as through the ADO **MoveNext** or **MovePrevious** methods. Nonscrollable cursors can only provide data in a first-in, first-out (FIFO) format as data is requested. Nonscrollable cursors are more efficient, because they do not require additional resources to support backwards scrolling. In many situations, a nonscrollable cursor (also known as a Forward-Only scrolling cursor) is useful because often data is simply read from the beginning of the recordset to the end.

Cursor Types

You can create four different types of cursors using ADO and SQL Server: Forward-Only, Static, Keyset, and Dynamic. Each type has a different effect on the memory and network resources of your server. To select the cursor type for a **Recordset** object, set the **CursorType** property to **adOpenForwardOnly**, **adOpenStatic**, **adOpenKeyset**, or **adOpenDynamic**. Table 6.1 describes each cursor type and its impact on performance.

Table 6.1 Cursor types supported by ADO and their performance implications.

Cursor Type	Description
Forward-Only	Forward-Only cursors require the least amount of overhead and are generally the fastest type of cursor. They retrieve each record one at a time from the beginning to the end of the recordset. They also allow updates to the data, although only one row at a time. Data changes by other users are not visible.
Static	Static cursors retrieve a copy of all the records requested in the query. They are fully scrollable and therefore consume more memory than Forward-Only cursors, because the data for the entire recordset must be stored. Data changes by other users are not visible.
Keyset	Keyset cursors build keys for each record in the query. When you read records from the recordset, the keys are used to retrieve the actual record values. This results in less overhead than Static or Dynamic cursors, because keys are being stored rather than the full record values. These cursors are scrollable. Deletions and updates to data by other users are visible; however, insertions by other users are not visible.
Dynamic	Dynamic cursors offer the most flexibility and functionality; however, they also consume the most memory and network resources. They are scrollable, and all insertions, deletions, and changes to the data by other users are visible in the recordset.

Cursor Location

When using ADO and SQL Server, you can choose to have the cursor exist on either the SQL Server computer or the client computer. The client computer of the database in a three-tier scenario is the server running MTS, and the clients are the MTS objects. SQL Server has built-in cursor functionality. By using SQL Server cursors, you can increase performance in several areas, mainly because the server is doing the caching required of a cursor instead of downloading records to be cached at the client.

Using a server-side cursor is useful when working with large recordsets in which you only update or read a few records. By caching the records on the server, you avoid sending them across the network. However, running many queries that build server-side cursors can quickly overload the server. In general, try to avoid server-side cursors unless they offer a real performance benefit. To specify the cursor location for a **Recordset** or **Connection** object, set the **CursorLocation** property to one of the following values:

♦ **adUseClient**—Uses client-side cursors supplied by a local cursor library. Local cursor engines often allow many features that server-supplied cursors may not, so using this setting may provide an advantage with respect to features that are enabled. For backward-compatibility, the synonym **adUseClientBatch** is also supported. ADO's client cursor engine only supports Static cursors.

♦ **adUseServer**—Default. Uses data provider- or server-supplied cursors. These cursors are sometimes very flexible and allow for some additional sensitivity to reflect changes that others make to the actual data source. However, some features of the Microsoft Client Cursor Provider (such as disconnected recordsets) cannot be used with server-side cursors; these features are unavailable with this setting.

As I have already noted, by default, the cursor location is at the server. To change the cursor location, modify the **CursorLocation** property of the **Connection** or **Recordset** object before calling the **Open** method.

Server-Side Cursors

If the data source you are connecting to does not support server-side cursors, a client-side cursor must be created. To explicitly specify the creation of a server-side cursor, set the **CursorLocation** property of the **Recordset** object to **adUseServer**. If a server-side cursor is created, the values of the records contained in the recordset are stored on the server. Using a server-side cursor can increase an application's performance, because the overhead on the client is limited and the amount of network traffic is reduced.

Creating A Server-Side Cursor

Server-side cursors are specified in the **CursorLocation** property. The following sample code opens a server-side cursor, presuming once again that the **cnBooks** connection object has been defined previously and remains in scope:

```
Sub cmdOpenRecordset_Click()
  Dim rsStudents As Recordset
  Set rsStudents = New Recordset
  With rsStudents
    .CursorLocation = adUseServer
    .Open "SELECT StudentID FROM Students", cnBooks
  End With
End Sub
```

Client-Side Cursors

You build client-side cursors by setting the **CursorLocation** property of the **Recordset** object to **adUseClient**. If a client-side cursor is created, the values of the records contained in the recordset are stored on the client's computer. This allows for the creation and management of disconnected recordsets and can be used to move the overhead of cursor management off the server.

Note

*When you set the **CursorLocation** property to **adUseClient**, the client cursor engine supports only "static" cursor types, no matter what's reported by the **CursorType** property.*

If the size of the recordset is too large, using a client-side cursor can slow an application's performance. Because most client machines have strict limitations on resources, use of client-side cursors should be restricted to small recordsets. Client-side cursors are specified in the **CursorLocation** property. The following code opens a client-side cursor called **rsStudents**:

```
Sub cmdOpenRecordset_Click()
  Dim rsStudents As Recordset
  Set rsStudents = New Recordset
  With rsStudents
    .CursorLocation = adUseClient
    .Open "SELECT StudentID FROM Students", cnBooks
  End With
End Sub
```

Understanding Forward-Only Cursors

The default recordset cursor type is Forward-Only. A Forward-Only cursor provides support exclusively for the **MoveNext** navigation method. Any other navigation method generates a runtime error. Due to the limited capabilities of a Forward-Only cursor, it is very efficient and uses the least amount of overhead.

Because Forward-Only is the default, you do not need to specify a cursor type when opening a recordset; however, it is recommended. To explicitly create a Forward-Only cursor, set the **CursorType** property of the recordset to **adOpenForwardOnly**. The following code creates a Forward-Only cursor:

```
Sub cmdOpenRecordset_Click()
  Dim rsPublishers As Recordset
  Set rsPublishers = New Recordset
  With rsPublishers
    .Open "SELECT pub_id FROM Publishers", cnBooks, adOpenForwardOnly
  End With
End Sub
```

Working With Static Cursors

A Static cursor does not detect changes made to the recordset, the order in which the records are returned by the cursor, or the changes made to the values in each record in the recordset after the cursor is opened. For example, suppose a Static cursor fetches a record and then another application updates that record. If the Static cursor uses the record again, the values seen by the Static cursor are unchanged, in spite of the changes that the other application made. For a Static cursor to reflect changes made to its records, it must be closed and reopened.

You can use a Static cursor when you need more flexible navigation, but do not need to see changes to the data. To create a Static cursor, set the **CursorType** property of a recordset to **adOpenStatic**. The following procedure code opens a Static cursor:

```
Sub cmdOpenRecordset_Click()
  Dim rsPublishers As Recordset
  Set rsPublishers = New Recordset
  With rsPublishers
```

```
      .Open "SELECT pub_id FROM Publishers", cnBooks, adOpenStatic
   End With
End Sub
```

Using Dynamic Cursors From Applications

Dynamic cursors are the most functional of the cursor types, but use the most overhead. A Dynamic cursor can detect changes made to records in the recordset and their order. For example, suppose a Dynamic cursor fetches two records, and then another application updates one of the records, deletes the other, and adds a new record that satisfies the query criteria. If the Dynamic cursor attempts to fetch these records again, it will return the updated value of the first record, it will not return the deleted record, and it will return the new record.

You can use a Dynamic cursor when you need a cursor that will always provide live data. To create a Dynamic cursor, set the **CursorType** property of the recordset to **adOpenDynamic**. The following sample code opens a dynamic recordset:

```
Sub cmdOpenRecordset_Click()
   Dim rsPublishers As Recordset
   Set rsPublishers = New Recordset
   With rsPublishers
      .Open "SELECT pub_id FROM Publishers", cnBooks, adOpenDynamic
   End With
End Sub
```

Using The Powerful Keyset Cursor

A Keyset cursor lies between a Static and Dynamic cursor in its ability to detect changes. Like a Static cursor, it does not always detect changes to its records and order of the recordset. For example, if the cursor is fully populated, new records are not included without refreshing the recordset. Like a Dynamic cursor, however, it does detect changes to the values of records in the recordset.

You should use a Keyset cursor when you need to be able to see changes to the data in the recordset, but do not need to see additions or deletions of records. To create a Keyset cursor, set the **CursorType** property of the recordset to **adOpenKeyset**. The following sample code opens a Keyset cursor:

```
Sub cmdOpenRecordset_Click()
   Dim rsPublishers As Recordset
   Set rsPublishers = New Recordset
   With rsPublishers
      .Open "SELECT pub_id FROM Publishers", cnBooks, adOpenKeyset
   End With
End Sub
```

Lock Types With ADO

The **LockType** property of the **Recordset** object determines the type of lock placed on the data of the underlying database during editing. By default, an ADO recordset is set to a read-only lock, allowing no modification to the data. To change the lock type, modify the **LockType** property before opening the recordset. Table 6.2 details the different lock types supported by the ADO model.

If you are not going to update the data, opening the recordset as read-only reduces the overhead consumed by the recordset. The following example code opens a read-only Keyset cursor recordset:

```
Private Sub ReadOnlyKeyset()
  Dim rs As ADODB.Recordset

  Set rs = New ADODB.Recordset
  rs.LockType = adLockReadOnly
  rs.CursorType = adOpenKeyset
  rs.Open "Select * from Categories", "DSN=Chap06DSN;User ID=sa;Password=;"
  ' Next statement causes error
  rs.Fields("CategoryID") = 10
End Sub
```

> **Note**
>
> *Pessimistic and Optimistic locking have the same effect inside MTS transactions. This is because MTS transactions communicate to resource managers such as SQL Server through the Distributed Transaction Coordinator (DTC). MTS declares DTC transactions as serializable, which is similar to Pessimistic locking.*

Choosing Cursor Types

In an enterprise solution, you need to choose the right kind of cursor for the task at hand. The cursor type, location, and lock type have implications on how network and memory resources are consumed. Following are some guidelines for using cursors in your applications. Ultimately, you need to apply performance testing to your applications to see which

Table 6.2 The different lock types you can select from within ADO.

Lock Type	Description
adLockReadOnly	The default lock type. Read-only—data cannot be altered.
adLockPessimistic	Pessimistic locking—the data is locked immediately upon editing.
adLockOptimistic	Optimistic locking—the data is locked when the **Update** method is called.
adLockBatchOptimistic	Optimistic batch update—this locking mode is required when using the **UpdateBatch** method.

cursors work best given the workload handled by your applications. In the following sections, however, I will consider some of the most common types of data that you will likely be accessing and/or manipulating, and make some suggestions for what types of cursors might be most appropriate.

Retrieving Read-Only Data

When you need to retrieve data and simply read it from beginning to end, consider using a server-side, read-only, Forward-Only cursor. This is the most efficient cursor to use in terms of network bandwidth and memory utilization when retrieving data. It is often the fastest cursor as well. This cursor is useful when populating Web pages with data, performing calculations based on data, or making business-rule decisions based on data.

If you need a snapshot of the data that does not change, consider using a client-side, read-only, Static cursor. These cursors are useful when you need an unchanging view of the data at a specific point in time. For example, a business object that retrieves all account balances to create a financial report must have all balances remain constant. Any balances that change while it is processing the recordset would cause the report to be inaccurate.

Also, if you need a snapshot, but don't need to scroll through the recordset, you can use a server-side, read-only, Forward-Only cursor. Changes to the data by other users are not seen by this cursor.

Retrieving Updateable Data

When you need to update data, consider using direct SQL statements through either the **Connection** object's **Execute** command or a **Command** object. This avoids the need to create cursors at all, and offers considerable savings in resources.

If you need to create an updateable recordset, use a client-side, Static cursor. In general, however, avoid using server-side cursors for updating data. In an enterprise application with many users, they can quickly overload a server. Also, avoid using Dynamic cursors. Although they offer the most up-to-date view of the data, they are by far the most costly cursor to create in terms of network and memory resources consumed.

Enforcing Data Integrity

Ensuring data integrity is a critical element of developing professional applications. Techniques such as record locking, transaction management, implementing data source features, and handling referential integrity errors help maintain data consistency. In the following sections, I will consider some of the useful techniques at your disposal for ensuring data integrity.

Using Record Locking

When you build a recordset, select a locking option to manage the user's access to records in a data source. In a multiuser environment, locking ensures that no two users can change the same record at the same time. Note that the combination of the cursor location, cursor type, and locking option affects the updateability of a recordset.

Note
Specifying a Forward-Only cursor that uses read-only locking is the most efficient implementation of a cursor and should be used whenever possible. This type of cursor is sometimes called a firehose cursor.

You specify a locking option when you open a recordset. As discussed previously in this chapter, you will set the **LockType** property of the recordset to one of the locking constants to control how the data source locks the records. The following sample code opens a new recordset and uses Pessimistic locking to control it:

```
Sub cmdOpenRecordset_Click()
   Dim cnBooks As Connection
   Dim rsStudents As Recordset
   Set cnBooks = New Connection
   With cnBooks
     .Provider = "SQLOLEDB"
     .ConnectionString = "User ID=sa;" &
         "Data Source=SQLSERVER;" & _
         "Initial Catalog=Books"
     .Open
   End With
   Set rsStudents = New Recordset
   rsStudents.Open "SELECT StudentID FROM Students", cnBooks, _
       adOpenKeyset, adLockPessimistic
End Sub
```

Using Database Transactions

Transactions help ensure data integrity by grouping one or more SQL statements together. A transaction is an "all or nothing" proposition; either all of the statements are committed, or none of them are. If any command in the statement set fails, you can roll back all of the commands, returning the data source to its original state. If all of the commands are successful, you can commit the changes and make them permanent. Transactions fall under two categories: implicit and explicit. I will consider each in turn in the following sections.

Implicit Transactions

Implicit transactions do not allow you to group multiple commands together. Instead, a transaction is built around each individual command. Using implicit transactions, you cannot programmatically roll back or commit the changes. However, you can trap for a runtime error if the command were to fail. Your program can then resubmit the individual change.

If you do not explicitly turn on a transaction, implicit transactions are used automatically. SQL Server will use auto-commit mode and build a transaction around each individual command.

Explicit Transactions

Explicit transactions allow your application to manage multiple SQL statements as if they were a single command. When you use an explicit transaction, your application groups commands into a single action.

For example, you can use an explicit transaction if your application transfers money between bank accounts. The act of transferring money consists of two operations: removing money from one account (a debit) and then adding it to another account (a credit). If any network problems or other errors prevent the credit from occurring, and you *do not* use a transaction, the money might be removed from the first account without being added to the second.

Your application can manage explicit transactions by using one of three transaction methods: **BeginTrans**, **RollbackTrans**, or **CommitTrans**. When you create an explicit transaction with the **BeginTrans** method, all statements that follow are automatically a part of that transaction. When you use the **RollbackTrans** or **CommitTrans** method, the transaction is closed and a new one can be created.

Transactions are managed at the level of the **Connection** object. Any **Recordset** objects or **Command** objects created when a transaction is enabled automatically share the transaction. The following example code creates a new transaction and closes it appropriately:

```
Sub cmdMakeChanges_Click()
  Dim cnBooks As Connection
  Dim sqlString As String

  Set cnBooks = New Connection
  With cnBooks
    .Provider = "SQLOLEDB"
    .ConnectionString = "User ID=sa;" & _
        "Data Source=SQLSERVER;" & _
        "Initial Catalog=Pubs"
    .Open
  End With

  ' A Transaction space is created
  cnBooks.BeginTrans
```

```
' Turn on the error handler
On Error Goto Error_Handler

' SQL Commands are executed in the transaction
sqlString = "INSERT INTO Authors " & _
    "VALUES ('999-99-9999', 'Klander', 'Lars', '702-555-1212'," & _
    "'Sample Street', "Sample Town', 'NV', '99999', 1)"
cnBooks.Execute sqlString
cnBooks.Execute "DELETE FROM Publishers WHERE state = 'MA'"

' If all commands are successful, commit them
cnBooks.CommitTrans

Exit Sub

Error_Handler:
  ' If an error occured, roll back the changes
  cnBooks.RollbackTrans
  MsgBox "An error occured changing the records.", vbExclamation
End Sub
```

SQL Server Data Integrity Features

SQL Server provides a number of features that help ensure data integrity in the database. From Visual Basic, ADO can automatically take advantage of these features. Depending on the feature, a trappable runtime error will occur if data integrity is violated, prompting the user for corrective action without terminating the program. Developers typically must work with the SQL Server database administrators at their sites to identify how specific data integrity issues should be handled in their applications.

> **Note**
>
> *It is usually more efficient for a client application to validate input data before sending it to the database.*

Referential Integrity Constraints

Constraints are the preferred way to restrict data being sent to a SQL Server. A constraint applies to a table's field or fields. Constraints provide the following advantages:

♦ Multiple constraints can be associated with a field, and a constraint can be associated with multiple fields.

♦ Constraints are created by using the SQL Server **CREATE TABLE** or **ALTER TABLE** statement and reside with the table definition.

♦ Constraints can be used to enforce referential integrity.

The five types of constraints are:

♦ **PRIMARY**

♦ **UNIQUE**

♦ **FOREIGN KEY**

♦ **DEFAULT**

♦ **CHECK**

Validation Rules

Rules are database objects that specify the acceptable values for a specific field based on simple criteria. Rules support only the individual fields being tested. They do not support references to other tables. A rule can specify one of the following:

♦ A set of values

♦ A range of values

♦ A format

You must first create a rule and then bind it to a field to use it. When bound to a field, the rule specifies the acceptable values that can be applied to that field. You can bind only one rule per field.

Field Defaults

Defaults provide a convenient way to ensure that a field has a reasonable value for every record, even when you insert a new record without a specified value for the field. In a SQL Server database, each field in a record must contain a value, even if that value is a null value. You determine whether a field can accept null values by the specified data type, default, or constraint on that field.

Defaults specify the value that SQL Server inserts when the user does not enter a value. For example, in a table with a field named "price," you can instruct SQL Server to enter a null value if the user does not know the price of an item. You must first create a default and then bind it to a field to use it.

An alternate, and preferred, method to creating a default is to create a default constraint. Constraints are the preferred method of restricting field data because the constraint definition is stored with the table and is deleted (dropped) automatically when the table is deleted. However, it is more efficient to use defaults when the default will be used repeatedly for multiple fields.

Handling Referential Integrity Errors

Referential integrity preserves defined relationships among tables when you enter and delete records in those tables. For example, assume your database contains two tables, **Customers** and **Orders**. Each customer in the **Customers** table can have multiple records in the **Orders** table. In the event that a customer record is deleted, all matching records in the **Orders** table will be left with an invalid Customer ID. This is an example of a referential integrity violation, because the integrity of the database has been violated.

If a referential integrity violation occurs, your application will receive a runtime error. Depending on the data source, the command that violates the integrity will fail. Therefore, if this type of error occurs, the data source will retain its original state and your application must respond accordingly.

> **Note**
>
> *Referential integrity error codes are specific to the data source your application is using. The errors are also specific to the kind of referential integrity error encountered, such as foreign key violation, duplicate key, and so forth.*

To verify the error code a given referential integrity error will generate in your application, force a situation that will generate the error you want to trap for and then check the error value returned by the data source. The following example code attempts to delete a record in a transaction that would result in a referential integrity violation:

```
Sub cmdDeleteRecords_Click()
   Dim cnBooks As Connection
   Dim errCodeError As Errors

   Set cnBooks = New Connection

   With cnBooks
     .Provider = "SQLOLEDB"
     .ConnectionString = "User ID=sa;" & _
         "Data Source=SQLSERVER;" & _
         "Initial Catalog=Pubs"
     .Open
   End With

   On Error Goto Error_Handler

   cnBooks.BeginTrans
   ' this command will generate a foreign key violation error
   cnBooks.Execute "DELETE FROM titles WHERE title_id = 14"
   cnBooks.CommitTrans
Exit Sub

Error_Handler:
      ' trap for the foreign key violation from SQL Server using the
      '  OLE DB Provider for SQL Server.
```

```
      If errCodeError.Number = -2147217900 Then
        ' the transaction will be rolled back
        cnBooks.RollbackTrans
      End If
  End Sub
```

Executing Statements On A Database

You can execute a statement on a Microsoft SQL Server directly, or by using a stored procedure. In this section, you will learn how to execute statements directly against a data source.

When your application runs SQL commands by executing them directly, these commands either return records, in the form of a recordset, or they affect the value of records. To execute commands that affect the value of records, such as updating current data and adding or deleting new records, use the appropriate SQL command and the **Execute** method of either the **Connection** object or the **Command** object.

Executing Directly Using The Connection Object

If the SQL command being executed will be called only once from your application, you can use the **Execute** method of the active connection. This is the most efficient technique for one-time execution of SQL commands. If your application will call the same command more than once, consider using a **Command** object. The following sample code creates a **Connection** object that updates records in the **Authors** table:

```
Sub cmdUpdateRecords_Click()
  Dim cnBooks As Connection
  Dim sSQL As String

  Set cnBooks = New Connection
  With cnBooks
    .Provider = "SQLOLEDB"
    .ConnectionString = "User ID=sa;" & _
                        "Data Source=SQLSERVER;" & _
                        "Initial Catalog=library"
    .Open
  End With
  sSQL = "INSERT INTO Authors(First_Name, Last_Name) " & _
      "VALUES ('Brett', 'Axelrod')"
  cnBooks.Execute sSQL
End Sub
```

Executing Directly Using The Command Object

For SQL commands that will be called more than once from the same application, use the **Command** object to build the query. Set the **Prepared** property to **True**. This technique improves the performance of your application, because the command is prepared and then saved in memory. Initially, this is slower than using the **Connection** object, but it will improve performance for subsequent calls. The following code creates a **Command** object and executes a SQL statement:

```
Sub cmdUpdateRecords_Click()
  Dim cnBooks As Connection
  Dim comBooks As Command
  Set cnBooks = New Connection
  With cnBooks
    .Provider = "SQLOLEDB"
    .ConnectionString = "User ID=sa;Data Source=SQLSERVER;" & _
        "Initial Catalog=Library"
    .Open
  End With

  Set comBooks = New Command
  With comBooks
    .Prepared = True
    .ActiveConnection = cnBooks
    .CommandType = adCmdText
    .CommandText = "UPDATE Books SET Price = Price * 1.1"
  End With
  comBooks.Execute
End Sub
```

Note

*If the **Prepared** property of a **Command** object has been set to **True**, you can re-execute the statement using the **Execute** method.*

Overview Of Stored Procedures And ADO

Stored procedures are compiled collections of SQL statements and control-of-flow language that execute quickly. Executing a stored procedure is similar to executing a SQL command, except that the stored procedure exists in the database as an object, even after execution has finished. Stored procedures hide potentially complex SQL statements from the components that use them. Also, the database compiles and stores stored procedures, which makes them run much faster than submitting the SQL statements as separate SQL queries.

To use a stored procedure, set the **CommandType** property of the **Command** object to the constant **adCmdStoredProc**, the **CommandText** to the name of the stored procedure, and then invoke the **Execute** method. You can see how this works in the following example code, which retrieves a recordset by invoking the **Customer_GetByEmail** stored procedure along the connection defined by the **cnnBackEnd Connection** object:

```
Public Sub CallStoredProc()
  Dim cmdBackEnd As ADODB.Command
  Dim rsBackEnd As ADODB.Recordset

  Set cmdBackEnd = New ADODB.Command
  'Use a previously created connection
  Set cmdBackEnd.ActiveConnection = cnnBackEnd
  cmdBackEnd.CommandType = adCmdStoredProc
  cmdBackEnd.CommandText = "Customer_GetByEmail " & "someone@kls.com"
  Set rsBackEnd = cmdBackEnd.Execute
End Sub
```

Calling A Stored Procedure With The Command Object

Stored procedures may require that one or more parameters be passed to them. For each required parameter, a **Parameter** object should be created and appended to the **Parameters** collection of the **Command** object.

There are two approaches to populating the **Parameters** collection. For situations where access to the data source is fast, or for rapid development purposes, you can have the data source automatically populate the parameters by calling the **Refresh** method of the collection. The command must have an active connection for this to succeed. Once completed, you can assign values to the parameters and then run the stored procedure. The following code calls the stored procedure **Customer_GetByEmail** using the **Refresh** method to fill the **Parameters** collection:

```
Public Sub AutoObtainParams()
  Dim cnnParam As ADODB.Connection
  Dim cmdParam As ADODB.Command
  Dim rsParam As ADODB.Recordset

  Set cnnParam = New ADODB.Connection
  Set cmdParam = New ADODB.Command
  cnnParam.ConnectionString = "DSN=Chap06DSN;User ID=sa;Password="
  cnnParam.Open

  Set cmdParam.ActiveConnection = cnnParam
  cmdParam.CommandType = adCmdStoredProc
  cmdParam.CommandText = "Customer_GetByEmail"
  cmdParam.Parameters.Refresh
  cmdParam.Parameters(1) = "someone@kls.com"
  Set rsParam = cmdParam.Execute
End Sub
```

Using the **Refresh** method causes ADO to make an extra trip to SQL Server to collect the parameter information. You can increase the performance of your components by creating the parameters in the collection yourself, and avoid the extra network trip. To fill the **Parameters** collection, create separate **Parameter** objects, fill in the correct parameter information for the stored procedure call, and then append them to the collection using the **Append** method. For multiple parameters, you must append the parameters in the order in which they are defined in the stored procedure. To understand better how this works, consider the following code example:

```
Public Sub UseParams()
  Dim cnnParam As ADODB.Connection
  Dim cmdParam As ADODB.Command
  Dim rsParam As ADODB.Recordset
  Dim prmParam As ADODB.Parameter

  Set cnnParam = New ADODB.Connection
  Set cmdParam = New ADODB.Command
  cnnParam.ConnectionString = "DSN=Chap06DSN;User ID=sa;Password="
  cnnParam.Open

  Set cmdParam.ActiveConnection = cnnParam
  cmdParam.CommandType = adCmdStoredProc
  cmdParam.CommandText = "Customer_GetByEmail"
  Set prmParam = cmdParam.CreateParameter("vEmail", adVarChar, _
    adParamInput, 50, "someone@kls.com")
  cmdParam.Parameters.Append prmParam
  Set rsParam = cmdParam.Execute
End Sub
```

When it's all said and done, this code accomplishes exactly the same goal as the program code in the previous section. However, for the most part, this code is clearer to read—even with only a single parameter. When you begin to call very complex stored procedures—taking 5 or 10 parameters or more—you will find that using parameters is, generally, an even better idea, as much for clarity as anything else.

So far, I have looked at input parameters—however, I have not discussed output parameters or return values. I will get to those in the next section.

Return Codes And Output Parameters

Stored procedures may contain input and output parameters and return values. For example, the **Customer_Remove** stored procedure contains the **@vCount** output parameter, which is assigned the number of records in the customer table after a customer is removed. Also, if **Customer_Remove** can successfully find and remove the desired record, it returns a code of 1. Otherwise, it returns a code of 0.

Because customer information is in both the **CustomerPasswords** and **Customers** tables, **Customer_Remove** must delete the information from both tables to completely remove the customer. The following sample code shows the SQL definition for the **Customer_Remove** stored procedure (you will learn more about how these types of statements are constructed in Chapters 10 and 11):

```
CREATE PROCEDURE Customer_Remove
  @vEmail varchar(30),
  @vCount int OUTPUT
AS
  DECLARE @vCustomerID int
  SELECT @vCustomerID = CustomerID FROM Customers
      WHERE Email= @vEmail
  IF @vCustomerID IS NULL
    return (0)
  ELSE
    begin
      DELETE FROM CustomerPasswords
          WHERE CustomerID = @vCustomerID
      DELETE FROM Customers
          WHERE CustomerID = @vCustomerID
      SELECT @vCount = COUNT(*) FROM Customers
      return (1)
    end
```

You can specify an input parameter for a stored procedure through the **Parameter** object. You must append the return parameter to the **Parameters** collection first. Then you can obtain any output parameters by reading their values from the **Parameters** collection. You can read the return code just like any other parameter, because it is the first parameter in the **Parameters** collection. Be aware that the return code parameter is at index 0, instead of 1.

Note

*If you execute a stored procedure that returns a recordset and you assign the returned recordset to a **Recordset** object, you must close the **Recordset** object before you can read any return or output parameters. You can find more information about this particular issue on the Microsoft Knowledge Base.*

The following code example shows how to call the **Customer_Remove** stored procedure and access both the return code and the **@vCount** output parameter after the call:

```
Public Sub UseOutputParam()
  Dim cnnParam As ADODB.Connection
  Dim cmdParam As ADODB.Command
  Dim prmParam As ADODB.Parameter
```

```
    Set cnnParam = New ADODB.Connection
    Set cmdParam = New ADODB.Command
    cnnParam.ConnectionString = "DSN=Chap06DSN; User ID=sa;"
    cnnParam.Open

    Set cmdParam.ActiveConnection = cnnParam
    cmdParam.CommandText = "Customer_Remove"
    Set prmParam = cmdParam.CreateParameter("Return", adInteger, _
        adParamReturnValue, , 0)
    cmdParam.Parameters.Append prmParam
    Set prmParam = cmdParam.CreateParameter("@vEmail", adVarChar, _
        adParamInput, 30, "test@kls.com")
    cmdParam.Parameters.Append prmParam
    Set prmParam = cmdParam.CreateParameter("@vCount", adInteger, _
        adParamOutput, , 0)
    cmdParam.Parameters.Append prmParam
    cmdParam.Execute
    Debug.Print cmdParam ("Return") 'Return Code
    Debug.Print cmdParam ("@vCount") 'Count
End Sub
```

Stored procedures can return an integer value called a *return status*. This status indicates that the procedure completed successfully, or it indicates the reason for failure. SQL Server has a defined set of return values, as detailed in Table 6.3.

Table 6.3 Return status values natively supported by SQL Server.

Value	Meaning
0	Procedure was executed successfully
-1	Object missing
-2	Data type error occurred
-3	Process was chosen as deadlock victim
-4	Permission error occurred
-5	Syntax error occurred
-6	Miscellaneous user error occurred
-7	Resource error, such as out of space, occurred
-8	Nonfatal internal problem encountered
-9	System limit was reached
-10	Fatal internal inconsistency occurred
-11	Fatal internal inconsistency occurred
-12	Table or index is corrupt
-13	Database is corrupt
-14	Hardware error occurred

Working With Disconnected Recordsets

An advanced feature of ADO is the disconnected recordset. A disconnected recordset contains a recordset that can be viewed and updated, but it does not carry with it the overhead of a live connection to the database. This is a useful way to return data to the client that is going to be used for a long time. While the client works on the data, the database server (and any middle-tier servers) are not tied up with any open connections.

The client can make changes to the disconnected recordset by editing the records directly, or by adding or deleting them using ADO methods such as **AddNew** and **Delete**. All of the changes are stored in the disconnected recordset until it is reconnected to the database.

Using Disconnected Recordsets In Three-Tier Applications

In a three-tier scenario, the middle tier creates disconnected recordsets and returns them to the client. For example, a client may request a listing of all furniture inventory for a specific store. The user on the client computer may wish to compare the inventory against a physical inventory list and correct any inaccuracies. This process may take a substantial amount of time.

A disconnected recordset is ideal for this scenario. A good approach is to have the middle tier create the disconnected recordset and return it to the client. A **Furniture** MTS object can be created that exposes a **GetFurnitureList** method. When this method is called, it creates a recordset, populates it with the furniture records, and returns it to the client. When the recordset is returned to the client, it is disconnected from the database. Now the client can work with the records as long as necessary without tying up an open connection to the database.

Later, when the user is ready to submit the changes, the client computer calls a **SubmitChanges** method on the **Furniture** object. The disconnected recordset is passed in as a parameter, and the **SubmitChanges** method reconnects the recordset to the database. Then **SubmitChanges** calls the recordset's **UpdateBatch** method. If there are any conflicts, **SubmitChanges** uses the existing business rules to determine the proper action.

Optionally, **SubmitChanges** could return the conflicting records to the client computer to let the user decide how to handle the conflicts. However, this scenario is more complicated. A separate recordset that contains the conflicting values from the database must be created and returned to the client.

Creating And Using Disconnected Recordsets

To create a disconnected recordset, you must create a **Recordset** object that uses a client-side, Static cursor with a lock type of **adLockBatchOptimistic**. The **ActiveConnection** property determines if the recordset is disconnected. If you explicitly set it to **Nothing**, you disconnect the recordset.

You can still access the data in the recordset, but there is no live connection to the database. Later, you can explicitly set **ActiveConnection** to a valid **Connection** object to reconnect the recordset to the database. The following code fragment shows how to create a disconnected recordset (note that **rsDisc** must be defined elsewhere and maintain its scope until after you reconnect the recordset):

```
Private Sub CreateDisconnected()
  Set rsDisc = New ADODB.Recordset
  rsDisc.CursorLocation = adUseClient
  rsDisc.CursorType = adOpenStatic
  rsDisc.LockType = adLockBatchOptimistic
  rsDisc.Open "Select * From Authors", "DSN=Pubs"
  Set rsDisc.ActiveConnection = Nothing
End Sub
```

If you return the disconnected recordset from a function, either as the return value or as an output parameter, the recordset copies its data to the caller. If the caller is a client in a separate process, or on another computer, the recordset marshals its data to the client's process.

When the recordset marshals itself across the network, it compresses the data to use less network bandwidth. This makes disconnected recordsets ideal for returning large amounts of data to a client.

Tip

*You can make a disconnected recordset marshal just the modified records across the network by setting the **MarshalOptions** property to **adMarshalModifiedOnly**. This is useful when you are submitting a recordset from the client to an MTS object for updating changes. It avoids copying records that won't be used by the MTS object.*

Submitting Changes From A Disconnected Recordset

While a recordset is disconnected, you can make changes to it by editing, adding, or deleting records. The recordset stores these changes so that you can eventually update the database. When you are ready to submit the changes to the database, you reconnect the recordset with a live connection to the database and call **UpdateBatch**, which updates the database to reflect the changes made in the disconnected recordset. The following example code shows how to reconnect a disconnected recordset to the database and update the database with the changes:

```
Private Sub ReconnectRs()
  Dim cnnDisc As ADODB.Connection
```

```
    Set cnnDisc = New ADODB.Connection
    cnnDisc.Open "DSN=Pubs"
    Set rsDisc.ActiveConnection = cnnDisc
    rsDisc.UpdateBatch
End Sub
```

Note

If the recordset is generated from a stored procedure, then you cannot call **UpdateBatch**. **UpdateBatch** *only works for recordsets created from SQL statements.*

Resolving Conflicts In Disconnected Recordsets

Before you call **UpdateBatch**, other users may have already changed records in the database. Depending on the business rules, you may not want to overwrite changes in the database with changes in the disconnected recordset. To guard against unwanted changes, the disconnected recordset contains three views of the data: original value, value, and underlying value. You can access these views by using the **Original**, **Value**, and **Underlying** properties of the **Recordset** object, as discussed in the following list:

♦ **Original**—Accesses the original values in the recordset when it was first created.

♦ **Value**—Accesses the current values in the recordset. These values reflect any changes you have made to the recordset.

♦ **Underlying**—Accesses the underlying values in the recordset. These values reflect the values stored in the database. These are the same as the original values when you first create the recordset and are only updated to match the database when you call the **ReSync** method.

When **UpdateBatch** is called, it creates a separate SQL query for each changed record to modify in the database. Part of the SQL query checks to see if the record has changed since the recordset was first created. It does this by comparing the underlying value against the database value. If they are the same, then the database has not changed, and the update can proceed. If they are different, then someone has recently changed the database, and the update fails.

When a record fails to update because of a conflict with the database, **UpdateBatch** flags it by changing its **Status** property. After **UpdateBatch** returns, you can check to see if there were any conflicts by setting the recordset's **Filter** property to **adFilterConflictingRecords**. This forces the recordset to navigate only through conflicting records. If there are conflicting records, you can check the **Status** property to determine why the update failed.

If there are conflicts, you must decide how best to resolve them. You can overwrite the conflicting records in the database, you can decide not to change the conflicting records, or you can take other action depending on the business rules. To help make this decision, you can update the underlying values in the disconnected recordset to examine the conflicting values in the database. To update the underlying values, call the **Resync** method with the **adAffectGroup** and **adResyncUnderlyingValues** parameters. You will resynchronize using code similar to the following:

```
rsDisc.Filter = adFilterConflictingRecords
rsDisc.Resync adAffectGroup, adResyncUnderlyingValues
```

Once the underlying values are synchronized with the database, you can see the changes other users have made through the **Underlying** property, and decide if you want to over-write them or not. If you decide to overwrite the conflicting records, simply call **UpdateBatch** again. Once the underlying values match the database, there are no conflicts, and the up-dates occur.

Note

When the disconnected recordset is passed from one process to another, it does not marshal the underlying values. Thus, if you return a disconnected recordset to a client for conflict resolution, you must pass the underlying values via another mechanism, such as a separate disconnected recordset containing just the underly-ing values. For more information about how to return conflicting records to a client, see the Microsoft Knowledge Base.

Brief Discussion Of ADO Good Programming Principles

Issues involving performance and scaling need to be considered when you're using ADO or any database access technology in a three-tier architecture. Here are some best practices that can help you write better code for working with databases:

♦ If your code retrieves field values repeatedly, consider binding object variables to the **Fields** collection. This improves performance, because you do not incur the overhead of looking up fields in the **Recordset.Fields** collection for each record in the recordset. You can bind object variables to fields using code similar to the following:

```
Public Sub CheckFields()
  Dim rsSamp As ADODB.Recordset

  Set rsSamp = New Recordset
  Dim fldId As ADODB.Field
  Dim fldFName As ADODB.Field
  Dim fldLName As ADODB.Field

  rsSamp.ActiveConnection = "Provider=SQLOLEDB;" & _
      Data Source=SQLSERVER;Database=pubs;" & _
```

```
        User Id=sa;Password=;"
    rsSamp.Source = "select au_id, au_fname, au_lname from authors"
    rsSamp.Open

    Set fldId = rsSamp.Fields(0)
    Set fldFName = rsSamp.Fields(1)
    Set fldLName = rsSamp.Fields(2)

    Do Until rsSamp.EOF
      Debug.Print fldId.Value, fldFName.Value, fldLName.Value
      rsSamp.MoveNext
    Loop
End Sub
```

♦ ADO uses the **Recordset** object's **CacheSize** property to determine the number of rows to fetch and cache. While you are within the range of cached rows, ADO returns data from the cache. When you scroll out of the range of cached rows, ADO releases the cache and fetches the next **CacheSize** number of rows. By monitoring how your application uses data, you can tune the **CacheSize** property to reduce the number of network trips for data.

♦ Microsoft Data Access Components (MDAC) 2.0 ships with native providers for three SQL data sources: SQL Server, Oracle, and Jet (.mdb). In earlier versions, you had to go through the OLE DB provider for ODBC data, which in turn used the appropriate ODBC driver to access these data sources. With MDAC 2.0, you can use these native OLE DB providers to access your data faster and with lower disk and memory footprints.

♦ ADO 2.0 includes a new execution option called **adExecuteNoRecords**, which you should use for commands that do not return rows. When you specify this option, ADO does not create a **Recordset** object, and does not set any cursor properties. Also, the provider can optimize for this case by not verifying any rowset properties. The following sample code uses the **adExecuteNoRecords** constant together with an ad hoc query:

```
Private Sub AdHoc()
  Dim cnnAdHoc As Connection
  Set cnnAdHoc = New Connection

  cnnAdHoc.Open "Provider=SQLOLEDB;" & _
      Data Source=SQLSERVER;Database=pubs;User Id=sa;Password=;"
  cnnAdHoc.Execute "INSERT INTO AddressBook values(5, 'Chewie', " & _
      "'Black Lab')", , adExecuteNoRecords
End Sub
```

♦ ADO 2.0 optimizes one-time command executions when they're done through **Connection.Execute**. This is a common scenario in Internet Information Server (IIS),

Active Server Pages (ASPs), and MTS environments where the code typically opens a connection, executes a row- or nonrow-returning command, processes results, and closes the connection. For such scenarios, use **Connection.Execute** instead of **Recordset.Open** or **Command.Execute**. When you use **Connection.Execute**, ADO does not preserve any command state information, which improves performance. Note that you may still need to use **Recordset.Open** or **Command.Execute** if you need a more functional cursor, or if you need to use the **Command.Parameters** collection.

♦ In general, acquire database resources such as connections and recordsets as late as possible, and release them as soon as possible. This means that connections and recordsets have a lifetime limited to the scope of the business or data object in which they were created.

♦ Be aware when using server-side cursors. Opening them in transactions can have locking implications such as blocking other users. They also consume server system resources. When possible, use a client-side cursor, or a disconnected recordset.

♦ Avoid transferring unnecessary data. For example, to insert a record into a table, you can execute a SQL **INSERT** command rather than create a recordset and use the **AddNew** and **Update** methods. When you use the SQL **INSERT** command, you do not create a recordset.

♦ Specify only those fields that you actually use when generating a **Recordset** object. Avoid **Select *** if you do not need all of the fields, as this returns unnecessary data over the network.

♦ Use the **MaxRecords** property of the **Recordset** object if you know how many records you are going to use. For example, set the property to 10 if you only want the first 10 records of a given recordset.

Manipulating ADO objects in and of themselves is a useful and beneficial technique; however, there is another, related concept that it is important to achieve mastery of, particularly in the context of middle-tier objects and similar topics that often arise when working with ADO. Specifically, you should be able to design class modules and, as a result, create objects. In the remainder of this chapter, I will focus on the use of class modules for object design.

Creating Objects With Class Modules

In previous chapters, you've learned about the different ways you can use Visual Basic for Applications (VBA) to add program code to your Access applications. As you've seen, you can use Form modules and Program Code modules to store and maintain program code. However, you'll often find that you want to manipulate custom program code in a fashion that allows you to encapsulate programs within a single related area. This concept is generally known as *object-oriented programming*. In this section, we'll look at some of the issues surrounding the use of VBA class modules in your Access applications. You'll learn more about classes and objects and how to create your own classes and objects in VBA.

Understanding Objects

In the simplest sense, an *object* is a thing or a real-world entity. When programmers create programs, they write instructions that work with different objects (things), like variables or files. Different objects have different operations that your programs perform on them. For example, given a file object, your program might perform such operations as reading, writing, or printing the file. As you'll learn, VBA programs can define objects in terms of a class. An object class defines the data the object will store and the functions that operate on the data. VBA programs often refer to the functions that manipulate the class data as *methods*. Some of your VBA programs, for example, might include the **Debug** and **RichTextBox** objects. In the case of these objects, methods, such as **Debug.Print** and **RichTextBox.SelRTF**, are the operations on the objects. Within VBA, every form and control your program uses is an object. You'll more clearly understand much of what you'll learn in this section if you think about what you're learning in the context of forms and controls. All that being said, the purpose of visualizing each of these items as objects is to simplify programming with them—a process known, as mentioned previously, as object-oriented programming, which I will discuss in the next section.

Understanding Object-Oriented Programming

Object-oriented programming is a way of looking at programs in terms of the objects (things) that make up a system. After you've identified the objects, you can determine the operations you or the user will usually perform on the object. If you have a document object, for example, common operations might include printing, spell checking, faxing, or even discarding. Object-oriented programming doesn't require a special programming language. You can write object-oriented programs in such languages as C++, Java, COBOL, and FORTRAN—though, in all fairness, it is much easier to do so in a language designed for such a purpose, like C++ or Java.

However, as you'll learn, languages described as object-oriented usually provide class data structures that let your programs group the data and methods into one central storage location. As you'll also learn, object-oriented programming has many advantages. The two primary advantages of object-oriented programming are object reuse and ease of understanding. Fortunately, objects that you write for one program can often be used in another. Rather than building a collection of function libraries, object-oriented programmers build *class libraries*. Likewise, by grouping an object's data and methods, object-oriented programs are often more readily understood than their non–object-based counterparts (at least after you learn the syntax of the programming language used). The best-known object-oriented languages are C++ and Java. In VBA 4, however, Microsoft started migrating VBA toward an object-oriented language. Now, VBA 6 is much more object-capable than VBA 4 or 5—in fact, in the Office 2000 model, VBA 6 implements almost all of the object-oriented features of VB 6.

VBA And Object-Oriented Design

You can write object-oriented programs in almost any language, including VBA. However, you should recognize that VBA isn't considered a true object-oriented language. The two main reasons why programmers don't consider VBA an object-oriented language are its roots in Basic and the number of predefined objects most programmers employ when they use VBA. The original Basic language was a procedure-based language. In other words, every program started at point A and finished at point B, and the sequence of execution was in a relatively straight line. Later, Basic gained the ability to call subroutines to perform branching activities. With the introduction of early versions of Visual Basic, and later VBA, Basic became an event-driven language.

Nevertheless, even with all of the advances made in the Basic language over the years, Basic is still fundamentally a language that manages program flow with subroutines. Therefore, you can't refer to it solely as an object-oriented language. Additionally, as you'll learn in later sections, one of the primary benefits of classes in a true object-oriented language is the ability to inherit other classes' characteristics. Because you can't inherit characteristics from the controls the majority of VBA programmers use, these objects aren't sufficient to qualify VBA as an object-oriented language.

Despite the fact that VBA is lacking a few of the characteristics that are generally used to define object-oriented programming, it nevertheless provides you with several tools that you can use to implement objects within your programs. The most common—and applicable—of these tools is the VBA class module. You will learn more about class modules in the following sections.

Understanding VBA Classes

As you write VBA programs, you'll often use *structures* (a program-defined type of value), also known as user-defined types (UDTs), to group related data. You can best view a VBA class as a responsive structure. A class stores data, manipulates data, and is capable of returning values to the invoking procedure. Consider, for example, the following structure definition:

```
Type Employee
  Name As String * 64
  Age As Integer
  SSN As String * 11                    ' Social security number
  Pay_Grade As Integer
  Salary As Single
  LastPayDay As Date
  Employee_Number As String * 11
End Type
```

If you use a class instead of a structure, you can actually process a **Last_Date_Paid** function within the class and automatically return the **LastPayDay** value whenever the user views an instance of the object. In fact, the **Last_Date_Paid** function will be a method of the class. A class, like a structure, describes a template for future variable declarations—it doesn't allocate memory for a variable. A class has a name, member variables, and member procedures. The following definition illustrates a simple class named **Employee**:

```
Private mvarEmpName As String              'local copy
Private mvarAge As Integer                 'local copy
Private mvarSSN As String                  'local copy
Private mvarPay_Grade As Integer           'local copy
Private mvarSalary As Single               'local copy
Private mvarEmployee_Number As String      'local copy

Public Function Last_Date_Paid(Name As String) As String
```

As you can see, the class definition is very similar to a structure. The only new items are the **Public** and **Private** labels, and the function definition. A section later in this chapter, "Understanding The Public Label," explains the **Public** label in detail. However, now that we have seen some of the basics of the implementation of classes in VBA, let's take a moment to step back and consider some of the underlying logic behind the creation of classes. In the following section, we will think about classes as they relate to some real-world objects—a technique that is often very successful in making some sense out of the complexity of the object-oriented world.

Conceptualizing Classes

Classes and objects are some of the most difficult programming constructs for both beginning and advanced programmers to master. As you've learned, the best way to visualize classes and objects is by thinking about real-world objects. For example, my pet Chewie is a dog—a Black Labrador, to be specific. In this case, the class would be either **Dogs** or **Labs**, depending on how you construct your object model, and **Chewie** is the object. **Dogs** share many characteristics—they have eyes, legs, a tail, a nose, and different types of ears. However, each dog also has unique characteristics, such as name, sex, eye color, length of tail, and so on. The shared characteristics are items consistent throughout the class. In VBA, for example, one of these characteristics might be the **Click** event for any **Button** class. The unique characteristics, on the other hand, would be properties: the name of the object, the length of the object, and other properties that would make the object unique.

The goal of any object-oriented program is to make generalizations about every object you use within your program—whether it be a visual object, data object, or mathematical object, to name just a few—and to group these generalized objects together in their own classes. In true object-oriented languages, you'll actually derive many classes from other, more general classes. For example, you might derive the class **Labs** from **Dogs**. Similarly, within Windows, you'll derive every visible object from the Windows-defined **CWin** class. In

VBA, because it doesn't fully support inheritance, your classes probably won't separate as efficiently as you might prefer, but the classes you can create support much of the power of object-oriented programming.

Tip

As you read other books and articles on object-oriented programming, you'll often encounter the term polymorphism. *Polymorphism lets programs apply the same operation to objects of different types. Because of this ability, polymorphism lets programmers use the same interface to access different objects. In C++, for example, virtual functions provide access to polymorphism. In the simplest sense, a virtual function is a pointer to a function the compiler resolves at runtime. Depending on the function to which a virtual function points, the operation the program performs will differ. As a result, a single interface (the virtual function) can provide access to different operations. Unfortunately, VBA doesn't support true polymorphism—you can simulate polymorphism with variant and optional parameters, and the* **Implements** *keyword comes close, but it's still generally a cumbersome and often difficult process.*

When you take a step back from classes and think about them in terms of how they relate to the rest of the world, it is much easier to see how classes can be useful and beneficial within your own programs. Now that you feel a little more comfortable with the theory behind classes, let's go ahead and design one, so that you can feel more comfortable with the implementation.

Creating Classes

As you begin to create classes within VBA, you'll insert class modules into the VBA Interactive Development Environment (IDE). To better understand how classes work, we'll create a basic class in this section, and then discuss some of the issues about it in the rest of this chapter. To build your first class, perform the following steps:

1. From within the VBA IDE, select the Insert menu's Class Module option. VBA will add a new class module, Class1, to the project.

2. Within the Properties window, change the **Name** property for the class to **Employees**.

3. Although we'll expose information about each instance of the **Employees** class through properties, doing so is a two-step process. First, you must add local variable definitions to the General Declaration section of the project, as shown in the following code listing:

```
Private mvarEmpName As String              'local copy
Private mvarAge As Integer                 'local copy
Private mvarSSN As String                  'local copy
Private mvarPay_Grade As Integer           'local copy
Private mvarSalary As Single               'local copy
Private mvarEmployee_Number As String      'local copy
```

4. After you add the variable definitions to the class, you need to add two functions for each property to the class—one to return the property to the calling function, and one to set the property when the instancing location attempts to set its value. The functions should look similar to the following—with, of course, variable name changes for each of the functions. This code sets and returns the **EmpName** property:

```
Public Property Let EmpName(ByVal vData As String)
  mvarEmpName = vData
End Property

Public Property Get EmpName() As String
  EmpName = mvarEmpName
End Property
```

You can see the entirety of the class file if you load it from the companion CD-ROM—it's in the Chapter 6 directory. The program code for the class is very similar to what you've already seen as to the programming of the class file.

Creating Classes Using The Class Builder Utility

If you have the Developer edition of Office 2000, you know that Microsoft has provided the Class Builder utility, an add-in to the VBA IDE, that you can use to create classes. To use the Class Builder utility to create another instance of the **Employees** class, perform the following steps:

1. After you add the Class Module to the project, use the Add-Ins menu to add the Class Builder Utility to the project, as shown in Figure 6.1.

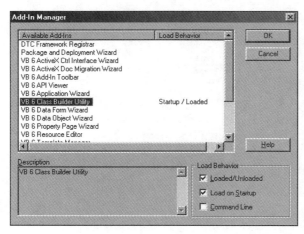

Figure 6.1
The Add-In Manager dialog box.

2. Within the Add-In Manager, select the VB 6 Class Builder Utility, then click on the Loaded/Unloaded checkbox and the Load On Startup checkbox. Click on OK to close the dialog box. The IDE will add the Class Builder utility to the Add-Ins menu.

3. From the Add-Ins menu, select the Class Builder utility. The VBA IDE will display the Class Builder dialog box.

4. Within the Class Builder dialog box, select File | New | Class. The VBA IDE will display the Class Module Builder dialog box.

5. Within the Class Module Builder dialog box, change the Name field to **Employees**. Click on the OK button. VBA will add the **CEmployee** class to the Class tree.

6. Select the Properties tab on the right side of the Class Builder window. Select File | New | Property. Visual Basic will display the Property Builder dialog box.

7. Within the Property Builder dialog box, enter "Age" into the Name field. Press the Tab key to move to the Data Type field and select the **Integer** type. Click on the OK button. Visual Basic will add the **Age** property to the **CEmployee** class.

8. Select the Properties tab on the right side of the Class Builder window. Select File | New | Property. Visual Basic will display the Property Builder dialog box.

9. Within the Property Builder dialog box, enter "SSN" into the Name field. Press the Tab key to move to the Data Type field and select the **String** type. Click on the OK button. Visual Basic will add the **SSN** property to the **CEmployee** class.

10. Select the Properties tab on the right side of the Class Builder window. Select File | New | Property. Visual Basic will display the Property Builder dialog box.

11. Within the Property Builder dialog box, enter "Pay_Grade" into the Name field. Press the Tab key to move to the Data Type field and select the **Integer** type. Click on the OK button. Visual Basic will add the **Pay_Grade** property to the **CEmployee** class.

12. Select the Properties tab on the right side of the Class Builder window, then select File | New | Property. Visual Basic will display the Property Builder dialog box.

13. Within the Property Builder dialog box, enter "EmpName" into the Name field. Press the Tab key to move to the Data Type field and select the **String** type. Click on the OK button. Visual Basic will add the **EmpName** property to the **CEmployee** class.

14. Select the Properties tab on the right side of the Class Builder window. Select File | New | Property. Visual Basic will display the Property Builder dialog box.

15. Within the Property Builder dialog box, enter "Salary" into the Name field. Press the Tab key to move to the Data Type field and select the **Single** type. Click on the OK button. Visual Basic will add the **Salary** property to the **CEmployee** class.

16. Select the Properties tab on the right side of the Class Builder window. Select File | New | Property. Visual Basic will display the Property Builder dialog box.

17. Within the Property Builder dialog box, enter "Employee_Number" into the Name field. Press the Tab key to move to the Data Type field and select the **String** type. Click on the OK button. Visual Basic will add the **Employee_Number** property to the **CEmployee** class.

Figure 6.2 depicts the Class Builder window after you add properties to the **CEmployee** class.

18. Click on the Methods tab within the Class Builder window. Select File | New | Method. Visual Basic will display the Method Builder dialog box.

19. Within the Name field, enter "Last_Date_Paid". Click on the + sign to the right of the Arguments field. Visual Basic will display the Add Argument dialog box.

20. Enter the name of the argument as "Name". Select String from within the Data Type dialog box. Click on OK. Visual Basic will return to the Method Builder dialog box. Notice Visual Basic added the **Name As String** argument to the **Arguments** field.

21. Within the Return Type combo box, select String. Click on the OK button to exit the Method Builder dialog box. Visual Basic will add the **Last_Date_Paid** method to the list of methods the **CEmployee** class recognizes.

22. Select File | Update Project to add the new class descriptors to your project. Select File | Exit to exit the VB Class Builder utility. Note that Visual Basic has added the **CEmployee** class file to your project.

If you open the **CEmployee** class file, you'll notice the declarations within the listing that appeared earlier in this section. As you proceed through this book, you'll learn what the definitions mean and how you'll use them within your programs.

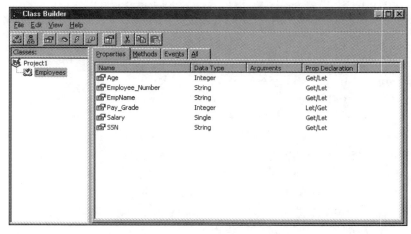

Figure 6.2
The CEmployee class and its properties.

Understanding The Public Label

In the previous section, you created a simple class, named **CEmployee**, which contained the **Public** label, as shown here:

```
Public Function Last_Date_Paid(Name As String) As String
```

Unlike a structure, with members that are all accessible to a program, a class can have members that the program can directly access using the dot operator (**.**), and other members (called private members) that the program can't access directly. The **Public** label identifies the class members the program can access using the dot operator. If you want the program to access a member directly, you must declare the member using the **Public** keyword.

Note that in this example, all the variables you declared in the previous section with the Class Builder utility appear to be private. Actually, the Class Builder utility has created a series of **Public Property Get** and **Property Let** functions to let your programs access the internal variables. In other words, if you have an object **JCohn**, which is an instance of the class **CEmployee**, and you want to assign the **Name** property, you'll assign the **Name** property using the dot operator, as shown here:

```
JCohn.Name = "Jeff Cohn"
```

The concept of using interface functions to control properties is an important one, because of the control that doing so provides in terms of managing errant or inappropriate values. This concept is known, generally, as creating interfaces or information hiding. You will learn more about information hiding in the next section.

Understanding Information Hiding

Information hiding is the process of hiding underlying implementation details of a function, program, or even a class. Information hiding lets programmers treat functions and classes as *black boxes*. In other words, if a programmer passes a value to a function, the programmer knows a specific result will occur. The programmer doesn't have to know how a function calculates a result but, instead, that the function works. For example, most programmers don't know the mathematics behind the **Atn** function, which returns an angle's arctangent. However, programmers know that if they pass a specific value to the function, a known result will occur. To use the function, the programmer must know only the input parameters and the values the **Atn** function returns.

In object-oriented programming, an object may have underlying implementation details. For example, a program may store a document's data in Word, Excel, or some other format. To use the document object, however, the program shouldn't have to know the format. Instead, the program should be able to perform read, write, print, and even fax operations without knowing the object details. To help programmers hide an object's underlying details, VBA lets you use the **Public** and **Private** keywords to divide class definitions. The program can directly access public data and methods, although it can't access the private data methods.

Tip

As you read articles and books about object-oriented programming, you might encounter the term encapsulation. *In the simplest sense, encapsulation is the combination of data and methods into a single data structure. Encapsulation groups together all the components of an object. In the "object-oriented" sense, encapsulation also defines how both the object itself and the rest of the program can reference an object's data. As you've learned, VBA classes let you divide your data into public and private sections. Programs can only access an object's private data using defined public methods. Grouping together an object's data and dividing your data into public and private sections protects the data from program misuses. In VBA, the class module is the fundamental tool for encapsulation.*

Using The Private Keyword Within A Class

As you've learned, VBA lets you divide a class definition into public and private parts. The program can access directly the public data and methods with the dot operator. The program can't access the private data and methods. The following class definition shows the **Employees** class again, with private and public parts:

```
Private mvarEmpName As String             'local copy
Private mvarAge As Integer                'local copy
Private mvarSSN As String                 'local copy
Private mvarPay_Grade As Integer          'local copy
Private mvarSalary As Single              'local copy
Private mvarEmployee_Number As String     'local copy

Public Function Last_Date_Paid(Name As String) As String
```

The client program accessing objects of that class type can access directly the data and methods that reside in the public section with the dot operator. The only way the program can access the private data and methods, however, is through public methods. For example, the next section presents a program that manipulates both the public and private data.

Using Public And Private Data

As you've learned, VBA lets you divide a class definition into public and private data and methods. Programs can access the public data and methods using the dot operator. To access the private data and methods, however, the program must call the public methods (also known as interface methods). The program can't directly manipulate or invoke private data and methods. Before you create the client, however, you must add code to the **Last_Date_Paid** method. Double-click your mouse on the CEmployee class icon within the Project Explorer. VBA will open a code window. Locate the **Last_Date_Paid** method and enter the following code:

```
Public Function Last_Date_Paid(Name As String) As String
  If UCase(Left(Name, 1)) < "L" Then
    Last_Date_Paid = ReturnDate(1)
  Else
    Last_Date_Paid = ReturnDate(2)
  End If
End Function
```

The **Last_Date_Paid** function (which the program code that invokes it will treat as a method) uses the function **ReturnDate**, which you haven't defined yet. To define the **ReturnDate** function, select Add-Ins | Class Builder. To add the **ReturnDate** function, perform the following steps:

1. Make sure that you've selected the **CEmployee** class within the Class Builder. If you haven't selected the **CEmployee** class, click on the CEmployee icon to select it.

2. Select File | New | Method. VBA will display the Method Builder dialog box.

3. Within the Name field, name the new method "ReturnDate". Click on the + symbol to the right of the Argument field. VBA will display the Add Argument dialog box.

4. Within the Name field, type "WhichHalf". Select the DataType As Integer option. Click on OK. VBA will add the **WhichHalf As Integer** argument to the Method Builder dialog box.

5. Within the Method Builder dialog box, select the ReturnType As String option. Click on the OK button. VBA will add the **ReturnDate** method to the **CEmployee** class.

6. Select File | Update Project. VBA will update the **CEmployee** class. Click on the X located in the top right-hand corner of the Class Builder window to exit the Class Builder.

7. If the **CEmployee** class code window isn't open, open it by double-clicking on the CEmployee icon within the Project Explorer. VBA will display a code window. Note that VBA has added the **ReturnDate** function just below the variable declarations. Click within the code window and change the **Public** keyword preceding the ReturnDate header to **Private**. Add the following code to the **ReturnDate** function:

```
Private Function ReturnDate(WhichDate As Integer) As String
  Dim DateValue As Integer

  DateValue = CInt(Format(Date, "d"))
  Select Case WhichDate
    Case 1
```

```
        If DateValue < 15 Then
          ReturnDate = "First of the month"
        Else
          ReturnDate = "Fifteenth of the month."
        End If
      Case 2
        If DateValue > 7 And DateValue < 22 Then
          ReturnDate = "Seventh of the month."
        Else
          ReturnDate = "Twenty-second of the month."
        End If
    End Select
  End Function
```

The **ReturnDate** function returns a string that indicates the last date paid to the calling function, **Last_Paid_Date**. However, because **ReturnDate** is a **Private** function, your programs can't access **ReturnDate** from anywhere outside of the class. To create a program to access the **CEmployee** class, perform the following steps:

1. Switch back to the Access window and add a new form to the project. Add a command button to the form.

2. Next, switch back to the VBA IDE and write the following code within the button's **Click** event:

```
Private Sub Command1_Click()
  Dim ThisEmployee As New CEmployee

  ThisEmployee.EmpName = "Jeff"
  ThisEmployee.Age = "29"
  ThisEmployee.SSN = "999-99-9999"
  ThisEmployee.Pay_Grade = 100
  ThisEmployee.Salary = ThisEmployee.Pay_Grade * 100
  ThisEmployee.Employee_Number = "1"
  Debug.Print ThisEmployee.Last_Date_Paid(ThisEmployee.Name)
  Debug.Print ThisEmployee.ReturnDate
End Sub
```

When you've finished entering the code, save the project, then try to execute the code by clicking on the command button. When you try to execute the program, VBA will display a "Method or data member not found" error message.

VBA won't execute the private method **ReturnDate** if you try to invoke it from within the program. Delete the offending line, and press F5 to continue execution. When you execute the program, VBA will display a message within the Immediate window, depending upon what day of the month it is when you execute the program. **Last_Date_Paid** can execute the **ReturnDate** method without difficulty, because **ReturnDate** is inaccessible only from the main program.

One of the most difficult tasks that programmers who are new to object-oriented programming face is trying to determine what they should hide and what they should make public. As a general rule, the less a programmer knows about a class, the better. Therefore, you should try to use private data and methods as often as possible. In this way, programs have to use the object's public methods to access the object data. As you'll learn, if you force programs to manipulate object data with only public methods, you can decrease programming errors. In other words, you don't usually want a program to directly manipulate an object's data using only the dot operator. If you force users to use public methods to access private data, it will improve information hiding and make objects of your classes more stable.

Tip

You've created several simple classes that defined both public and private function members. As the number of methods provided with each class and the complexity of each method increases, so too will the number of functions you'll eventually define as public and private to handle the processing of the class.

*Remember that when you define methods (functions) within a class, you should only declare those methods that the class must expose (that is, make available to procedures outside the class) using the **Public** keyword. You should declare all other functions internal to the class using the **Private** keyword.*

Clearly, if what I have said so far is true, you should make the vast majority of your variables within the class **Private**, and provide the user with the means to access those variables. VBA, in fact, provides an easy set of tools that you can use to access private variables. In the next section, we will learn about these function types, and how you will use them.

Using The Property Let And Property Get Methods

As you've learned, you can use the VBA Class Builder to design a series of **Property Get** and **Property Let** functions within the **CEmployee** class module. You also learned that the **Property Get** and **Property Let** functions are interface functions, which you'll use to control the values the program tries to set for properties, among other things. You'll implement the **Property Get** and **Property Let** functions within your class modules, as shown here:

```
[Public | Private | Friend] [Static] Property Let name _
    ([arglist,] value)
  [statements]
  [Exit Property]
  [statements]
End Property

[Public | Private | Friend] [Static] Property Get name _
    [(arglist)] _
```

```
    [As type]
    [statements]
    [name = expression]
    [Exit Property]
    [statements]
    [name = expression]
End Property
```

The **Property Get** and **Property Let** functions have the components Table 6.4 describes.

Table 6.4   The components of the Property Get and Property Let procedures.

Component	Description
Public	An optional keyword that indicates the **Property Get** or **Property Let** procedure is accessible to all other procedures in all modules. If you don't use it in a module that contains an **Option Private** statement, the procedure isn't available outside the project.
Private	An optional keyword that indicates the **Property Get** or **Property Let** procedure is accessible only to other procedures in the class.
Friend	An optional keyword that indicates that the **Property Get** or **Property Let** procedure is visible throughout the project, but not visible to a controller of an instance of an object.
Static	An optional keyword that indicates that VBA preserves the **Property Get** or **Property Let** procedure's local variables between calls.
Name	The name of the **Property Get** or **Property Let** procedure. It follows standard variable naming conventions, except that the name can be the same as a corresponding **Property Get** or **Property Let** procedure in the same module.
Arglist	A required list of variables that represent arguments passed to the **Property Get** or **Property Let** procedure when the program calls it. The name and data type of each argument in a **Property Let** procedure must be the same as the corresponding argument in a **Property Get** procedure, and vice versa.
Value	A variable that contains the value the procedure is to assign to the property. When your program calls the procedure, the **Value** argument must appear on the right side of the calling expression. The data type of **Value** must be the same as the return type of the corresponding **Property Get** procedure. VBA requires the **Value** argument for the **Property Let** procedure only. Attempts to set a **Value** argument in a **Property Get** procedure will cause a runtime error.
Statements	Any group of statements for VBA to execute within the **Property Get** or **Property Let** procedure. The statements typically check the assigned value or the returned value for validity.
Type	An optional argument that determines the data type of the value the **Property Get** procedure returns. Type may be **Byte**, **Boolean**, **Integer**, **Long**, **Currency**, **Single**, **Double**, **Date**, **String** (except fixed length), **Object**, **Variant**, or user-defined type. The procedure can't return arrays of any type, but a **Variant** that contains an array can. The return type of a **Property Get** procedure must be the same data type as the last (or sometimes the only) argument in a corresponding **Property Let** procedure (if one exists) that defines the value assigned to the property on the right side of an expression.

Tip

*Every **Property Let** function must define at least one argument for the procedure it defines. That argument (or the last argument if there's more than one) contains the actual value for you to assign to the property when the program invokes the procedure the **Property Let** statement defines. Table 6.4 refers to that argument as **Value**.*

If you don't explicitly specify the scope of a **Property** procedure using either the **Public**, **Private**, or **Friend** keyword, **Property** procedures are public. If you don't use the **Static** keyword, your program won't preserve the value of local variables between calls. You can use the **Friend** keyword only in class modules. However, procedures in any module of a project can access **Friend** procedures. A **Friend** procedure doesn't appear in the type library of its parent class.

Like a **Function** or **Property Get** procedure, a **Property Let** procedure is a separate procedure that takes arguments, performs a series of statements, and changes the value of its arguments. However, unlike a **Function** or **Property Get** procedure, both of which return a value, you can only use a **Property Let** procedure on the left side of a property assignment expression or **Let** statement. Conversely, you can only use a **Property Get** procedure on the right side of an expression in the same way you use a function or a property name when you want to return the value of a property. As a general rule, you should design your class modules using **Property** procedures to ensure that bad input doesn't corrupt the data within the object.

Once you have started working with class modules, it is only normal to be curious about the instancing of objects—that is, how the class module becomes an object. The next section discusses the process, and provides some examples, too.

Understanding Object Instances

Many books and articles about object-oriented programming refer to *object instances*. In short, an object instance is an object variable. As you've learned, a class defines a template for future variable declarations. When you later declare an object, you create an object instance. In other words, when VBA allocates memory for a variable, it creates an object instance. All instances of the same class have the same characteristics. For the purposes of this book, an instance is a variable of a specific class.

Creating Object Instances

As you've learned, VBA doesn't allocate memory for classes until you create an instance of a class. You've also learned that VBA creates an instance, or object instance, when you create a variable of the class type. Within VBA, you'll create variables having class type using one of the following three methods. The first looks like this:

```
Dim VariableName As New ClassName
Dim Variable2 As ClassName
Set Variable2 = New ClassName
```

Alternately, you can use a slightly different construction technique—this second technique is increasingly popular because it works in Visual Basic, VBA, VBScript, and with the Microsoft Transaction Server (MTS) product:

```
Dim VariableName As ClassName
Set VariableName = CreateObject("Class.ClassName")
```

Or, you can construct it with late binding:

```
Dim VariableName As Object
' Statements
Set VariableName = New ClassName
```

Any of these methods is valid. However, just as when working with **Object** and **Control** variables, if you assign the **VariableName** to a specific type, it forces VBA to perform early binding. If instead you create an **Object** variable, and later assign the class type to that **Object** variable, VBA will perform late binding. Additionally, if you use the **Dim** statement with the **New** keyword, VBA will reserve that variable space at the beginning of the program (or whenever you declare **VariableName**). If you use the **Set** statement, VBA won't reserve the variable space for that class variable until the program reaches the assignment statement.

Now that you have seen how you develop a class, and also how you instance that class into a single object, it is worthwhile to consider a little more closely the implications of how you define components of your class. Observe the suggestions carefully—they may save you a considerable amount of grief.

More On Private And Public Procedures And Functions

As you've learned, a private procedure or function is one that has limited scope. In other words, programs can only access a private procedure or function from within the area where the program defines the procedure or function. For example, only procedures within the same form can access a procedure within a form you declare as private. Similarly, procedures or functions that you declare as private within a module are visible or accessible only to other procedures or functions within the module. To let other programs (clients) access procedures or functions, you must make these procedures and functions public. Programmers refer to the process of letting other programs outside the class module access public functions within the class module as *exposing* these functions.

Visualizing Inheritance And Its Real-World Corollaries

As you visualize how you might derive classes using inheritance, drawing pictures might help you to understand the relationships between classes. You'll find that a class you derive from one or more base classes might well become the base class for other classes. As you begin to define your classes, start with general characteristics and work toward specifics as you derive new classes.

For example, if you're deriving classes for types of automotive vehicles, your first base class might simply be **Autos**. **Autos** would contain characteristics common to all automotives, such as color, number of doors, tire size, engine size, number of passengers, and so on. Your next level might become more refined when you create the classes. The second-level class types, **Cars** and **Trucks**, for example, would inherit the common characteristics that you defined in the **Autos** base class. As you further refine model types (for example, between a sedan and station wagon), however, you can use these second-level classes as base classes for other class definitions. Your base class levels will grow, conceptually similar to a family tree's growth, as shown in Figure 6.3.

Unfortunately, VBA doesn't support true inheritance. Although you can use some methods to avoid VBA's built-in constraints on inheritance, in general, you can't fully inherit classes, nor can you control how you inherit classes, as you can in C++. This book will design classes without inheritance.

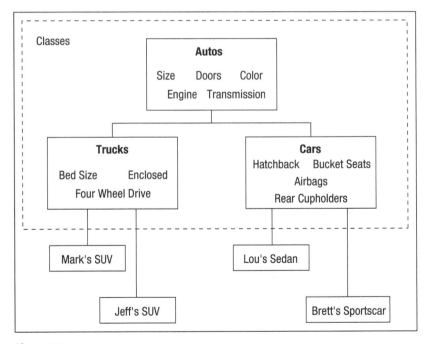

Figure 6.3
The **Autos** inheritance tree.

Private functions or procedures let you protect data from outside sources. The only way to retrieve and manipulate data in a private function or procedure is to call the routine from another public or private function or procedure within the same class module. Such indirect access to private functions or procedures lets the class (in this case, the ActiveX EXE) protect sensitive data. For example, imagine you have a private library of rare books in your house. A friend wants to read two of the books. However, you don't want anyone physically touching the books, because they're simply too valuable. If you let the friend physically touch the books, he may spill water on one, or worse, lose it. You must find a way to let your friend read the books without touching them. So, you make a digital copy of each page and transfer the contents to a computer program. Now your friend can read the books at his leisure without destroying anything. (Luckily, because the books are so old and rare, the copyright has expired, and you can make as many copies as you like.) In the same way, a private function would store the rare books, and a public function would read them on a computer screen without touching them.

Creating The Time-Based Class Module

The class modules described in the following sections show you how to create a **DateStamp** class that contains a **DateStamp** property, a **TimeStamp** property, and a **DateTimeStamp** property. Begin to build the **DateStamp** class by performing the following steps:

1. Open the Chap06Class.mdb database.

2. Select the Objects | Modules button from the Access 2000 database window, then select Insert | Class Module from the Access 2000 menu bar. Access will open the Visual Basic Editor and create a new class module.

3. Select File | Save Chap06Class from the Visual Basic Editor menu bar, then replace the name "Class1" with "DateStamp" in the Save As dialog box.

4. In the Declarations section of the class module window, create a private string variable with the name **mvarDateStamp**, as shown here:

```
Private mvarDateStamp As String
```

5. Select Class from the module window's Object drop-down menu, and enter the code for the **Class_Initialize** procedure:

```
Private Sub Class_Initialize()
  mvarDateStamp = Date
End Sub
```

6. Create a **Property Get** procedure by entering the following code into the code window:

```
Public Property Get DateStamp() As String
  DateStamp = mvarDateStamp
End Property
```

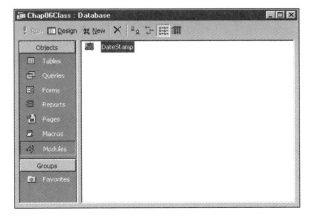

Figure 6.4
The new class module is represented by the DateStamp icon.

7. Select File | Save Chap06Class, then select File | Close And Return To Microsoft Access. Access will close the VBA IDE and return to the Database window. An icon will appear in the Access 2000 database window for the **DateStamp** class, as shown in Figure 6.4.

8. Select the Objects | Modules button from the Access 2000 database window, then select New from the window's toolbar to launch the VB Editor.

9. In the new module window, enter the following lines of code:

```
Sub ShowDateStamp()
  Dim Latest As New DateStamp

  MsgBox Latest.DateStamp
  Set Latest = Nothing
End Sub
```

10. Select File | Save Chap06Class, and save the new module as "ShowDateStamp".

11. Select Run | Run Sub/UserForm from the VBA Editor menu bar to run the **Show-DateStamp** procedure. A successful run results in a message box.

Creating A TimeStamp Property

Now that you've grasped the mechanics of how to build and run a class module, let's add the **TimeStamp** property to the **DateStamp** class. To do so, perform the following steps:

1. From within the VBA IDE, open the **DateStamp** class module.

2. In the Declarations section of the class module window, create a private string variable with the name **mvarTimeStamp**, as shown here:

```
Private mvarTimeStamp As String
```

3. Select Class from the module window's Object drop-down menu, then change the code for the **Class_Initialize** procedure so it looks like the following:

```
Private Sub Class_Initialize()
  mvarDateStamp = Date
  mvarTimeStamp = Time
End Sub
```

4. Create a **Property Get** procedure for the new property by entering the following code into the code window:

```
Public Property Get TimeStamp() As String
  TimeStamp = mvarTimeStamp
End Property
```

To test your code, modify the **ShowDateStamp** procedure to display the value of the **TimeStamp** property—the reference will look like the following:

```
MsgBox Latest.TimeStamp
```

Creating A DateTimeStamp Property

To complete the design of the **DateStamp** class module, you should add the **DateTimeStamp** property to the module. To do so, perform the following steps:

1. From the VBA IDE, open the **DateStamp** class module.

2. In the Declarations section of the class module window, create a private string variable with the name **mvarDateTimeStamp**, as shown here:

```
Private mvarDateTimeStamp As String
```

3. Select Class from the module window's Object drop-down menu, then change the code for the **Class_Initialize** procedure so it looks like the following:

```
Private Sub Class_Initialize()
  mvarDateStamp = Date
  mvarTimeStamp = Time
  mvarDateTimeStamp = Now
End Sub
```

4. Create a **Property Get** procedure for the new property by entering the following code into the code window:

```
Public Property Get DateTimeStamp() As String
```

```
    DateTimeStamp = mvarDateTimeStamp
  End Property
```

To test your code, modify the **ShowDateStamp** procedure to display the value of the **TimeStamp** property—the reference will look like the following:

```
MsgBox Latest.DateTimeStamp
```

Using Property Let With Class Modules

Now that you've seen how to create class modules that use programmatic functions and predefined defaults, let's look at how to customize an object property using the **Property Let** statement. In the case of this particular example, we're going to read some information from a text file. The code we'll write in the next two sections will let the user set a property corresponding to the file name; then we'll use the custom **ReadFile** method together with the property to read information into memory from a file. To do this, create a new class module in the project, called **FileClass**. Then, add the necessary code for the **FileName** property to the class, as shown here:

```
Private mvarFileName As String

Property Let FileName(NewName As String)
  mvarFileName = NewName
End Property

Property Get FileName() As String
  FileName = mvarFileName
End Property
```

Now let's look at how to set a method that can be invoked from outside the class module. To do so, create a **Public** function inside the class module. The **ReadFile** method will open the file and read the text into a private variable of the class—and return a success value, as shown here:

```
Private mvarFileString As String

Public Function ReadFile() As Boolean
  Dim lstrLocal As String

  On Error Goto File_Error
  Open mvarFileName For Input As # 1
  Do While Not EOF(1)
    Line Input #1, lstrLocal
    MvarFileString = mvarFileString & lstrLocal
  Loop
```

```
      ReadFile = True
      Exit Function


File_Error:
   ' Didn't work
   ReadFile = False
End Function
```

Instantiating A Class Module

Module instantiation is a process of resource allocation and object re-creation. We'll examine this more closely in the next chapter. For now, let's instantiate a copy of **FileClass**. To do so, within the **ShowDateStamp** module, create a new procedure with the name **NewObject**, as shown here:

```
Sub NewObject()
  Dim FileObject As New FileClass

  FileObject.FileName = "sample.txt"
  If FileObject.ReadFile Then
    MsgBox "File Read Successfully!"
  Else
    MsgBox "File Not Read Succesfully!"
  End If
End Sub
```

The **Dim** statement functions in the same way as if you were declaring a variable. In other words, it allocates space to create the new object. **FileObject** identifies what the object will be called, and **As New FileClass** tells you that, when created, the new object will have the characteristics of the existing **FileClass** object. Notice, however, that the object itself hasn't been created. Actual object creation occurs when a property or method of the identified object is referenced in your procedure.

Where To Go From Here

In this chapter, we looked at some advanced uses for ADO—including manipulating stored procedures, executing statements directly, and more. We also discussed good programming principles for you to keep in mind when using ADO, and closed with a discussion in the last third of the chapter on programming with class modules, an important technique.

In Chapter 7, I will discuss using Access as a front end to SQL Server, and some of the implications of that usage. I will focus, to some extent, on the nature of SQL Server, and then introduce some of the different techniques at your disposal for connecting to SQL Server from Access 2000. Later in the book, I will devote several chapters to the use of Active Data Projects (ADPs) as a SQL Server front end; we'll cover several other techniques available to you for connecting with SQL Server databases as well.

Part II

Access MDB As Front End

Using Access 2000 As A Front End To SQL Server

Throughout this book, we will focus on different client/server solutions with Access 2000. However, most of these solutions will be centered on the use of Microsoft's SQL Server 7 as the back end for the client/server solution. To that end, in this chapter I will examine what makes up the SQL Server engine and how it works, as well as some of the different options you have for connecting to the engine and the connecting points to the Jet engine and how it works. I will also point out system behavior that might affect application development and suggest ways to deal with it.

Additionally, an understanding of SQL Server database structure will help you develop and implement your client/server databases effectively. In addition to architecture explanations, this chapter discusses the types of databases found in SQL Server and also describes two types of structural elements: database objects and system tables.

The SQL Server Engine

Figure 7.1 shows the general architecture of SQL Server. For the sake of simplicity, I've made some minor omissions and simplifications and ignored certain "helper" modules.

Now let's look in detail at the major modules that make up the SQL Server engine, which are depicted in the figure.

The Net-Library

The *Net-Library* abstraction layer (often called Net-Lib; in this book, I will use the two terms interchangeably) enables SQL Server

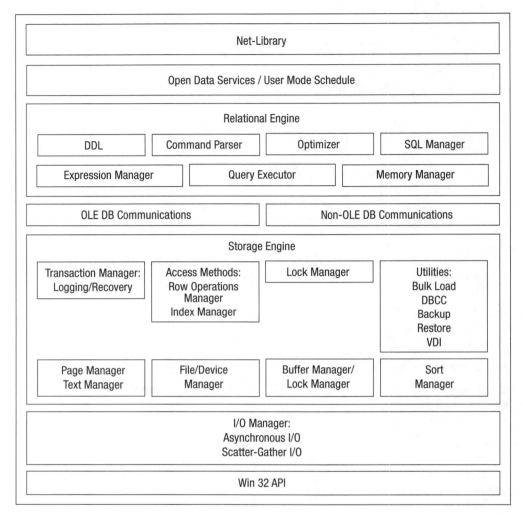

Figure 7.1
A simplified representation of the general architecture of SQL Server.

to read from and write to many different network protocols, and each such protocol (such as TCP/IP sockets) can have a specific driver. The Net-Library layer makes it relatively easy to support many different network protocols without having to change the core server code.

A Net-Library is basically a driver that is specific to a particular network interprocess communication (IPC) mechanism. (Be careful not to confuse *driver* with *device driver*.) All code in SQL Server, including Net-Library code, makes calls only to the Microsoft Win32 subsystem. SQL Server uses a common internal interface between Microsoft Open Data Services (ODS), which manages its use of the network, and each Net-Library. If your development project needs to support a new and different network protocol, all network-specific issues can be handled by simply writing a new Net-Library. In addition, you can load multiple Net-Libraries simultaneously, one for each network IPC mechanism in use.

SQL Server uses the Net-Library abstraction layer on both the server and client machines, making it possible to support several clients simultaneously on different networks. Microsoft Windows NT, Windows 95, and Windows 98 allow multiple protocol stacks to be used simultaneously on one system. Net-Libraries, on the other hand, are paired. For example, if a client application is using a Named Pipes Net-Library, SQL Server must also be listening on a Named Pipes Net-Library. (You can easily configure multiple Net-Libraries using the SQL Server Server Network Utility, which is available under Start | Programs | Microsoft SQL Server 7.0.)

It is important to distinguish between the IPC mechanisms and the underlying network protocols. IPC mechanisms used by SQL Server include named pipes, RPC, SPX, and Windows Sockets. Network protocols used include TCP/IP, NetBEUI, NWLink (IPX/SPX), Banyan VINES SPP, and Appletalk ADSP. Two Net-Libraries, Multiprotocol and Named Pipes, can be used simultaneously over multiple network protocols (NetBEUI, NWLink IPX/SPX, and TCP/IP). You can have multiple network protocols in your environment and still use only one Net-Library.

On machines running Windows 95 or Windows 98, you can also use Shared Memory as an IPC mechanism. This is considered both the IPC and the network protocol and is available only for local connections in which the client is running on the same machine as SQL Server. In addition, SQL Server running on Windows 95 or Windows 98 machines does not support named pipes as an IPC.

The Multiprotocol Net-Library uses the RPC services of Windows NT, Windows 95, or Windows 98. It could just as well have been called the *RPC Net-Library*, but *Multiprotocol* better conveys its key benefit: Because the Multiprotocol Net-Library uses the RPC services of the operating system, it can encrypt all traffic (including requests, data, and passwords) between the client application and the SQL Server engine.

Both named pipes and RPC services in Windows NT support impersonation of security contexts to provide an integrated logon capability (also known as Windows NT Authentication). Instead of requiring a separate user ID/password logon each time a connection to SQL Server is requested, SQL Server can impersonate the security context of the user running the application that requests the connection. If that user has sufficient privileges (or is part of a Windows NT domain group that does), the connection is established. Note that Windows NT Authentication is not available when SQL Server is running on Windows 95 or Windows 98. When you connect to SQL Server running on those platforms, you must specify a SQL Server logon ID and password.

Determining Which Net-Library Is Fastest
Strictly speaking, the TCP/IP Sockets Net-Library is the fastest. In a pure network test that does nothing except throw packets back and forth between Net-Library pairs, it is perhaps

---

Understanding Net-Library's Existence

If RPCs had been available years ago, Net-Library might never have been invented. When SQL Server ran only on OS/2, it supported only named pipes. The developers wanted to broaden this support to SPX and TCP/IP and potentially other protocols, so they developed Net-Library as an abstraction layer. Now RPC services are available with so many network protocols that RPC alone might have met the need.

---

30 percent faster than the slowest Net-Library. But for LAN environments and applications, the speed of the Net-Library probably makes little difference, because the network interface is generally not a limiting factor in a well-designed application.

On a LAN, however, turning on encryption with the Multiprotocol Net-Library will cause a performance hit—it's the slowest Net-Library option when encryption is turned on. But again, most applications probably wouldn't notice the difference. Your best bet is to choose the Net-Library that matches your network protocols and provides the services you need in terms of unified logon, encryption, and dynamic name resolution.

Open Data Services

Open Data Services (ODS) functions as the client manager for SQL Server; it is basically an interface between server Net-Libraries and server-based applications, including SQL Server. ODS manages the network: It listens for new connections, cleans up failed connections, acknowledges "attentions" (cancellations of commands), coordinates threading services to SQL Server, and returns resultsets, messages, and status back to the client.

SQL Server clients and the server speak a private protocol known as *tabular data stream (TDS)*. TDS is a self-describing data stream. In other words, it contains tokens that describe column names, data types, events (such as cancellations), and status values in the "conversation" between client and server. The server notifies the client that it is sending a resultset, indicates the number of columns and data types of the resultset, and so on—all encoded in TDS. Neither clients nor servers write directly to TDS. Instead, the open interfaces of DB-Library and ODBC at the client emit TDS. Both use a client implementation of the Net-Library.

ODS accepts new connections, and if a client unexpectedly disconnects (for example, if a user reboots the client computer instead of cleanly terminating the application), resources such as locks held by that client are automatically freed.

You can use the ODS open interface to help you write a server application such as a gateway. Such applications are called *ODS server applications*. SQL Server is an ODS server application, and it uses the same DLL (OPENDS70.DLL) as all other ODS applications.

ODS Read And Write Buffers

After SQL Server puts resultsets into a network output buffer that's equal in size to the configured packet size, the Net-Library dispatches the buffer to the client. The first packet is sent as soon as the network output buffer (the write buffer) is full or, if an entire resultset fits in one packet, when the batch is completed. In some exceptional operations (such as one that provides progress information for database dumping or provides DBCC messages), the output buffer is flushed and sent even before it is full or before the batch completes.

SQL Server has two input buffers (read buffers) and one output buffer per client. Double-buffering is needed for the reads, because while SQL Server reads a stream of data from the client connection, it must also look for a possible attention. (This allows that "Query That Keeps Going, And Going..." to be canceled directly from the issuer. Although the ability to cancel a request is extremely important, it's relatively unusual among client/server products.) Attentions can be thought of as "out-of-band" data, although they can be sent with network protocols that do not explicitly have an out-of-band channel. The SQL Server development team experimented with double-buffering and asynchronous techniques for the write buffers, but these didn't improve performance substantially. The single network output buffer works very nicely. Even though the writes are not posted asynchronously, SQL Server doesn't need to write through the operating system caching for these as it does for writes to disk.

Because the operating system provides caching of network writes, write operations appear to complete immediately, with no significant latency. But if several writes are issued to the same client and the client is not currently reading data from the network, the network cache eventually becomes full and the write operation blocks. This is essentially a throttle. As long as the client application is processing results, SQL Server has a few buffers queued up and ready for the client connection to process. But if the client's queue is already stacked up with results and is not processing them, SQL Server delays sending them and the network write operation to that connection has to wait. Because the server has only one output buffer per client, data cannot be sent to that client connection until it reads information off the network to free up room for the write to complete. (Writes to other client connections are not held up, however; only those for the laggard client are affected.)

SQL Server adds rows to the output buffer as it retrieves them. Often, SQL Server can still gather additional rows that meet the query's criteria while rows already retrieved are being sent to the client.

Stalled network writes can also affect locks. For example, if **READ COMMITTED** isolation is in effect (the default), a share lock can normally be released after SQL Server has completed its scan of that page of data. (Exclusive locks used for changing data must always be held until the end of the transaction to ensure that the changes can be rolled back.) However, if the scan finds more qualifying data and the output buffer is not free, the scan stalls. When the previous network write completes, the output buffer becomes available and the scan resumes. But, as stated above, that write won't complete until the client connection "drains" (reads) some data to free up some room in the pipe (the virtual circuit between the SQL Server and client connection).

If a client connection delays processing results that are sent to it, concurrency issues can result, because locks are held longer than they otherwise would be. A sort of chain reaction occurs: If the client connection has not read several outstanding network packets, further writing of the output buffer at the SQL Server side must wait, because the pipe is full. Because the output buffer is not available, the scan for data might also be suspended, because no space is available to add qualifying rows. Because the scan is held up, any lock on the data cannot be released. In short, if a client application does not process results in a timely manner, database concurrency can suffer.

The size of the network buffer can also affect the speed at which the client receives the first resultset. As mentioned earlier, the output buffer is sent when the batch, not simply the command, is done, even if the buffer is not full. (A *batch* is one or more commands sent to SQL Server to be parsed and executed together. For example, if you are using Query Analyzer, a batch is the collection of all the commands that appear before a specific **GO** command.) If two queries exist in the same batch and the first query has only a small amount of data, its results are not sent back to the client until the second query is done or has supplied enough data to fill the output buffer. If both queries are fast, this is not a problem. But suppose the first query is fast and the second is slow. And suppose the first query returns 1,000 bytes of data. If the network packet size is 4,096 bytes, the first resultset must wait in the output buffer for the second query to fill it. The obvious solution here is either to make the first command its own batch or to make the network packet size smaller. The first solution is probably the best one in this case, because it is typically difficult to fine-tune your application to determine the best buffer size for each command. But this doesn't mean that each command should be its own batch. Quite the contrary. In fact, under normal circumstances, grouping multiple commands into a single batch is most efficient and recommended, because it reduces the amount of handshaking that must occur between client and server.

ODS Default Net-Libraries

By default, SQL Server on Windows NT always listens on named pipes as well as on TCP/IP and Multiprotocol. SQL Server on Windows 95 and Windows 98 listens on the Shared Memory library instead of on named pipes, but it also has TCP/IP and Multiprotocol available. You can add other Net-Library interfaces. On Windows NT, you can also remove any of the Net-Libraries, but it's best not to remove named pipes. All the other Net-Libraries on Windows NT require an actual network. Because named pipe services exist in Windows NT even when no network is present, using named pipes leaves you a back door into SQL Server even if your network becomes totally nonfunctional. Similarly, SQL Server on Windows 95 and Windows 98 always listens over the Shared Memory IPC by default, so you should avoid removing this option. Even with no network, which is a more likely scenario in Windows 95 and Windows 98 than in Windows NT, Shared Memory is still available for interprocess communication.

Figure 7.2 shows the path from the SQL Server client application to the SQL Server engine and shows where the Net-Library interface fits in. On the server side, ODS provides functionality that mirrors that of ODBC, OLE DB, or DB-Library at the client. Calls exist for an

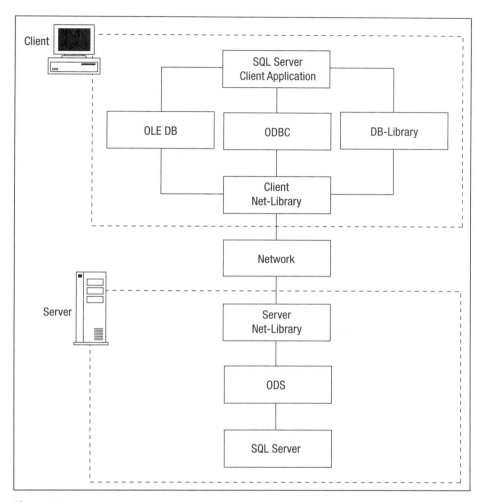

Figure 7.2
The path from a SQL Server client application to the SQL Server engine.

ODS server application to describe and send resultsets, to convert values between data types, to assume the security context associated with the specific connection being managed, and to raise errors and messages to the client application.

ODS uses an event-driven programming model. Requests from servers and clients trigger events to which your server application must respond. Using the ODS API, you create a custom routine, called an *event handler*, for each possible type of event. Essentially, the ODS library drives a server application by calling its custom event handlers in response to incoming requests.

ODS server applications respond to the following events:

♦ *Connect events*—When a connect event occurs, SQL Server initiates a security check to determine whether a connection is allowed. Other ODS applications, such as a gateway to DB/2, have their own logon handlers that determine whether connections are allowed. Events also exist that close a connection, allowing the proper connection cleanup to occur.

♦ *Language events*—When a client sends a command string, such as a SQL statement, SQL Server passes this command along to the command parser. A different ODS application, such as a gateway, would install its own handler that accepts and is responsible for execution of the command.

♦ *Remote stored procedure events*—These events occur each time a client or SQL Server directs a remote stored procedure request to ODS for processing.

ODS also generates events based on certain client and application activities. These events allow an ODS server application to respond to changes to the status of the client connection or of the ODS server application.

In addition to handling connections, ODS manages threads (and fibers) for SQL Server. It takes care of thread creation and termination and makes the threads available to the User Mode Scheduler (UMS). Because ODS is an open interface with a full programming API and toolkit, anyone writing server applications with ODS—from large-scale accounting programs like Great Plains to small development done by you or I—get the same benefits that SQL Server derives from this component, including SMP-capable thread management and pooling, as well as network handling for multiple simultaneous networks. This multithreaded operation enables ODS server applications to maintain a high level of performance and availability and to transparently use multiple processors under Windows NT, because the operating system can schedule any thread on any available processor.

The Relational Engine And The Storage Engine

The SQL Server database engine is made up of two main components, the relational engine and the storage engine. Unlike in earlier versions of SQL Server, these two pieces are clearly separated, and their primary method of communication with each other is through OLE DB. The relational engine comprises all the components necessary to parse and optimize any query. It requests data from the storage engine in terms of OLE DB rowsets and then processes the rowsets returned. The storage engine comprises the components needed to actually access and modify data on disk.

The Command Parser

The *command parser* handles language events raised by ODS. It checks for proper syntax and translates Transact-SQL commands into an internal format that can be operated on. This internal format is known as a *query tree*. If the parser does not recognize the syntax, a syntax error is immediately raised. Starting with SQL Server 6, syntax error messages identify where the error occurred. However, non-syntax error messages cannot be explicit about the exact source line that caused the error. Because only the parser can access the source of the statement, the statement is no longer available in source format when the command is actually executed. Exceptions to the calling sequence for the command parser are **EXECUTE(*"string"*)** and cursor operations. Both of these operations can recursively call the parser.

The Optimizer

The optimizer takes the query tree from the command parser and prepares it for execution. This module compiles an entire command batch, optimizes queries, and checks security. The query optimization and compilation result in an execution plan.

The first step in producing such a plan is to *normalize* the query, which potentially breaks down a single query into multiple, fine-grained queries. After the optimizer normalizes the query, it *optimizes* it, which means that the optimizer determines a plan for executing that query. Query optimization is cost-based; the optimizer chooses the plan that it determines would cost the least based on internal metrics that include estimated memory requirements, estimated CPU utilization, and the estimated number of required I/Os. It considers the type of statement requested, checks the amount of data in the various tables affected, looks at the indexes available for each table, and then looks at a sampling of the data values kept for each index or column referenced in the query. The sampling of the data values is called *statistics*. Based on the available information, the optimizer considers the various access methods and join strategies it could use to resolve a query and chooses the most cost-effective plan. The optimizer also decides which indexes, if any, should be used for each table in the query, and, in the case of a multitable query, the order in which the tables should be accessed and the join strategy to be used.

The optimizer also uses pruning heuristics to ensure that more time isn't spent optimizing a query than it would take to simply choose a plan and execute it. The optimizer does not necessarily perform exhaustive optimization. Some products consider every possible plan and then choose the most cost-effective one. The advantage of this exhaustive optimization is that the syntax chosen for a query would theoretically never cause a performance difference, no matter what syntax the user employed. But if you deal with an involved query, it could take much longer to estimate the cost of every conceivable plan than it would to accept a good plan, even if not the best one, and execute it. For example, in one product review, SQL Server (and some other products) consistently executed one complex eight-table join faster than a product whose optimizer produced the same "ideal" execution plan each time, even though SQL Server's execution plan varied somewhat. This was a case in which a pruning technique produced faster results than pure exhaustive optimization. In general, though, you typically get the same execution plan no matter what equivalent syntax you use to specify the query.

Some products have no cost-based optimizer and rely purely on rules to determine the query execution plan. In such cases, the syntax of the query is vitally important. (For example, the execution would start with the first table in the **FROM** clause.) Such products sometimes claim to have a "rule-based optimizer." This might simply be a euphemism for "no optimizer"—any optimization was done by the person who wrote the query.

The SQL Server optimizer is cost-based, and with every release it has become "smarter," to handle more special cases and to add more query processing and access method choices. However, by definition, the optimizer relies on probability in choosing its query plan, so sometimes it will be wrong. (Even a 99 percent chance of choosing correctly means that something will be wrong 1 in 100 times.) Recognizing that the optimizer will never be perfect, you can use SQL Server's *query hints* to direct the optimizer to use a certain index— for example, to force the optimizer to follow a specific sequence while working with the tables involved, or to use a particular join strategy.

After normalization and optimization are completed, the normalized tree produced by those processes is compiled into the execution plan, which is actually a data structure. Each command included in it specifies exactly which table will be affected, which indexes will be used (if any), which security checks must be made, and which criteria (such as equality to a specified value) must evaluate to true for selection. This execution plan might be considerably more complex than is immediately apparent. In addition to the actual commands, the execution plan includes all the steps necessary to ensure that constraints are checked. (Steps for calling a trigger are a bit different than those for verifying constraints. If a trigger is included for the action being taken, a call to the procedure that comprises the trigger is appended. A trigger has its own plan that is branched to just before the commit. The specific steps for the trigger are not compiled into the execution plan, like those for constraint verification.)

A simple request to insert one row into a table with multiple constraints can result in an execution plan that requires many other tables to also be accessed or expressions to be evaluated. The existence of a trigger can also cause many additional steps to be executed. The step that carries out the actual **INSERT** statement might be just a small part of the total execution plan necessary to ensure that all actions and constraints associated with adding a row are carried out.

The SQL Manager

The SQL manager is responsible for everything having to do with managing stored procedures and their plans. It determines when a stored procedure needs recompilation based on changes in the underlying objects' schemas, and it manages the caching of procedure plans so that they can be reused by other processes.

The SQL manager also handles autoparameterization of queries. In SQL Server 7, certain kinds of ad hoc queries are treated as if they were parameterized stored procedures, and query plans are generated and saved for them. This can happen if a query uses a simple equality comparison against a constant, as in the following statement:

```
SELECT * FROM pubs.dbo.titles
WHERE type = 'business'
```

This query can be parameterized as if it were a stored procedure with a parameter for the value of **type**:

```
SELECT * FROM pubs.dbo.titles
WHERE type = @param
```

A subsequent query, differing only in the actual value used for the value of **type**, can use the same query plan that was generated for the original query.

The Expression Manager

The expression manager handles computation, comparison, and data movement. Suppose your query contains an expression like this one:

```
SELECT @myqty = qty * 10 FROM mytable V
```

The expression service copies the value of **qty** from the rowset returned by the storage engine, multiplies it by 10, and stores the result in **@myqty**.

The Query Executor

The query executor runs the execution plan that was produced by the optimizer, acting as a dispatcher for all the commands in the execution plan. This module loops through each command step of the execution plan until the batch is complete. Most of the commands require interaction with the storage engine to modify or retrieve data and to manage transactions and locking.

The Access Methods Manager

When SQL Server needs to locate data, it calls the access methods manager. The access methods manager sets up and requests scans of data pages and index pages and prepares the OLE DB rowsets to return to the relational engine. It contains services to open a table, retrieve qualified data, and update data. The access methods manager doesn't actually retrieve the pages; it makes the request of the buffer manager, which ultimately serves up the page already in its cache or reads it to cache from disk. When the scan is started, a look-ahead mechanism qualifies the rows or index entries on a page. Retrieving rows that meet specified criteria is known as a *qualified retrieval*. The access methods manager is employed not only for queries (selects) but also for qualified updates and deletes (for example, **UP-DATE** with a **WHERE** clause).

Communication Between The Relational Engine And The Storage Engine

The relational engine uses OLE DB for most of its communication with the storage engine. This section describes how a **SELECT** statement that processes data from local tables uses only OLE DB to perform its processing.

First, the relational engine compiles the **SELECT** statement into an optimized execution plan. The execution plan defines a series of operations against simple rowsets from the individual tables or indexes referenced in the **SELECT** statement. (*Rowset* is the OLE DB term for a resultset.) The rowsets requested by the relational engine return the amount of data needed from a table or index to perform one of the operations used to build the **SELECT** resultset. For example, this **SELECT** statement requires a table scan if it references a table with no indexes:

```
SELECT * FROM ScanTable
```

The relational engine implements the table scan by requesting one rowset containing all the rows from **ScanTable**. This next **SELECT** statement needs only information available in an index:

```
SELECT DISTINCT LastName
FROM Northwind.dbo.Employees
```

The relational engine implements the index scan by requesting one rowset containing the leaf rows from the index that was built on the **LastName** column. The following **SELECT** statement needs information from two indexes:

```
SELECT CompanyName, OrderID, ShippedDate
FROM Northwind.dbo.Customers AS Cst
JOIN Northwind.dbo.Orders AS Ord
ON (Cst.CustomerID = Ord.CustomerID)
```

The relational engine requests two rowsets: one for the clustered index on **Customers** and the other for one of the nonclustered indexes on **Orders**. The relational engine then uses the OLE DB API to request that the storage engine open the rowsets.

As the relational engine works through the steps of the execution plan and needs data, it uses OLE DB to fetch the individual rows from the rowsets it requested the storage engine to open. The storage engine transfers the data from the data buffers to the relational engine. The relational engine combines the data from the storage engine rowsets into the final resultset transmitted back to the user.

Not all communication between the relational engine and the storage engine uses OLE DB. Some commands cannot be expressed in terms of OLE DB rowsets. The most obvious and common example is when the relational engine processes data definition language (DDL) requests to create a table or other SQL Server object.

A session opens a table, requests and evaluates a range of rows against the conditions in the **WHERE** clause, and then closes the table. A session descriptor data structure (SDES) keeps track of the current row and the search conditions for the object being operated on (which is identified by the object descriptor data structure, or DES).

The Row Operations Manager And The Index Manager

The row operations manager and the index manager can be considered components of the access methods manager, because they carry out the actual method of access. Each is responsible for manipulating and maintaining its respective on-disk data structures, namely rows of data or B-tree indexes. They understand and manipulate information on data and index pages.

The Row Operations Manager

The row operations manager retrieves, modifies, and performs operations on individual rows. It performs an operation within a row, such as "retrieve column 2" or "write this value to column 3." As a result of the work performed by the access methods manager, lock manager, and transaction manager, the row will have been found and will be appropriately locked and part of a transaction. After formatting or modifying a row in memory, the row operations manager inserts or deletes a row.

The row operations manager also handles updates. SQL Server 7 offers three methods for handling updates. All three are direct, which means that there is no need for two passes through the transaction log, as was the case with deferred updates in earlier versions of SQL Server. SQL Server 7 has no concept of a deferred data modification operation.

The three update modes in SQL Server 7 are:

♦ *In-place mode*—This mode is used to update a heap or clustered index when none of the clustering keys change. The update can be done in place, and the new data is written to the same slot on the data page.

♦ *Split mode*—This mode is used to update nonunique indexes when the index keys change. The update is split into two operations—a delete followed by an insert—and these operations are performed independently of each other.

♦ *Split with collapse mode*—This mode is used to update a unique index when the index keys change. After the update is rewritten into delete and insert operations, if the same index key is both deleted and then reinserted with a new value, it is "collapsed" into a single update operation.

If you want to reorganize a table—for example, to reestablish a **FILLFACTOR** value or to make data more contiguous after a lot of data modification has occurred—you can use a *clustered index*, which makes the reorganization easy. You simply rebuild the clustered index, which rebuilds the entire table. In the case of a delete, if the row deleted is the last row on a data page, that page is deallocated. (The only exception occurs if that page is the only one remaining in the table. A table always contains at least one page, even if it is empty.)

The Index Manager

The index manager maintains and supports searches on B-trees, which are used for SQL Server indexes. An index is structured as a tree, with a root page and intermediate- and lower-level pages (or branches). A B-tree groups records that have similar index keys, thereby allowing fast access to data by searching on a key value. The B-tree's core feature is its ability to balance the index tree. (*B* stands for *balanced.*) Branches of the index tree are spliced together or split apart as necessary so that the search for any given record always traverses the same number of levels and thus requires the same number of page accesses.

The traverse begins at the root page, progresses to intermediate index levels, and finally moves to bottom-level pages called *leaf pages.* The index is used to find the correct leaf page. On a qualified retrieval or delete, the correct leaf page is the lowest page of the tree at which one or more rows with the specified key or keys reside. SQL Server supports both clustered and nonclustered indexes. In a nonclustered index, shown in Figure 7.3, the leaf level of the tree (the leaf page of the index) contains every key value in the index, along with a row locator for each key value. The row locator is also called a *bookmark* and indicates where to find the referenced data. A row locator can have one of two forms. If the base table has no clustered index, the table is referred to as a *heap.* The row locators in nonclustered index leaf pages for a heap are pointers to the actual rows in which the data can be found, and these pointers consist of a Row ID (RID), which is a file number, a page number, and a row number on the page. If the base table has a clustered index, the row locators in any nonclustered index leaf pages contain the clustered index key value for the row.

After reaching the leaf level in a nonclustered index, you can find the exact location of the data, although the page on which that data resides must still be separately retrieved. Because you can access the data directly, you don't need to scan all the data pages for a qualifying row. Better yet, in a clustered index, shown in Figure 7.4, the leaf level actually contains the data row, not simply the index key. A clustered index keeps the data in a table physically ordered around the key of the clustered index, and the leaf page of a clustered index is in fact the data page itself.

Because data can be physically ordered in only one way, only one clustered index can exist per table. This makes the selection of the appropriate key value on which to cluster data an important performance consideration.

You can also use indexes to ensure the uniqueness of a particular key value. In fact, the **PRIMARY KEY** and **UNIQUE** constraints on a column work by creating a unique index on the column's values. The optimizer can use the knowledge that an index is unique in formulating an effective query plan.

Internally, SQL Server always ensures that clustered indexes are unique by adding a 4-byte "uniqueifier" to clustered index key values that occur more than once. This uniqueifier becomes part of the key and is used in all levels of the clustered index and in references to the clustered index key through all nonclustered indexes.

Because SQL Server maintains ordering in index leaf levels, you do not need to unload and reload data to maintain clustering properties as data is added and moved. SQL Server will always insert rows into the correct page in clustered sequence. For a clustered index, the correct leaf page is the data page in which a row will be inserted. For a nonclustered index,

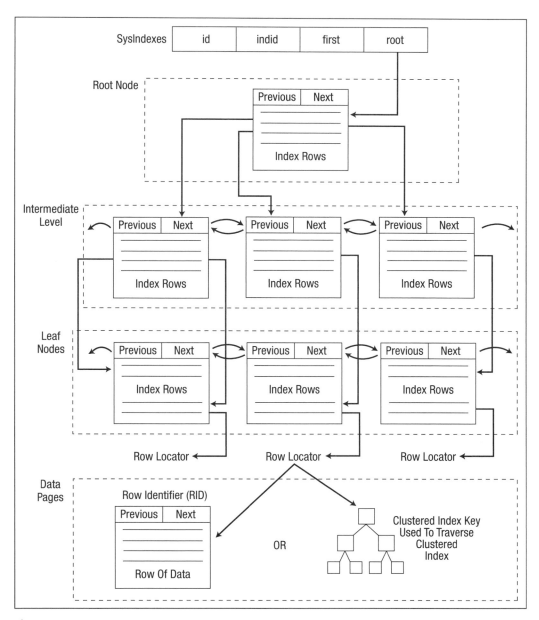

Figure 7.3
A simple diagram of a nonclustered index.

the correct leaf page is the one into which SQL Server inserts a row containing the key value (and data row locator) for the newly inserted row. If data is updated and the key values of an index change, or if the row is moved to a different page, SQL Server's transaction control ensures that all affected indexes are modified to reflect these changes. Under

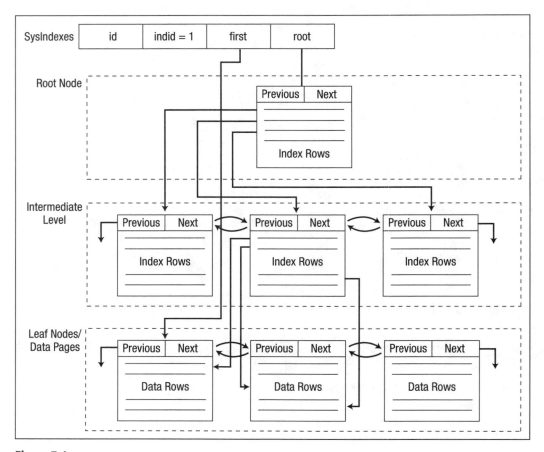

Figure 7.4
A simple diagram of a clustered index.

transaction control, index operations are performed as atomic operations. The operations are logged and fully recovered in the event of a system failure.

Locking And Index Pages

As we'll see in the section on the lock manager, pages of an index use a slightly different locking mechanism than regular data pages. A lightweight lock called a *latch* is used to lock upper levels of indexes. Latches are not involved in deadlock detection, because SQL Server 7 uses "deadlock-proof" algorithms for index maintenance.

You can customize the locking strategy for indexes on a table basis or index basis. The system stored procedure **sp_indexoption** lets you enable or disable page or row locks with any particular index or, by specifying a table name, for every index on that table. The settable options are **AllowPageLocks** and **AllowRowLocks**. If both of these options are set to false for a particular index, only table level locks are applied.

The Page Manager And The Text Manager

The page manager and the text manager cooperate to manage a collection of pages as named databases. Each database is a collection of 8K disk pages, which are spread across one or more physical files.

SQL Server uses six types of disk pages: data pages, text/image pages, index pages, Page Free Space (PFS) pages, Global Allocation Map (GAM and SGAM) pages, and Index Allocation Map (IAM) pages. All user data, except for the **text** and **image** data types, are stored on data pages. The **text** and **image** data types, which are used for storing large objects (up to 2GB each of text or binary data), use a separate collection of pages, so the data is not stored on regular data pages with the rest of the rows. A pointer on the regular data page identifies the starting page and offset of the text/image data. Index pages store the B-trees that allow fast access to data. PFS pages keep track of which pages in a database are available to hold new data. Allocation pages (GAMs, SGAMs, and IAMs) keep track of the other pages. They contain no database rows and are used only internally.

The page manager allocates and deallocates all types of disk pages, organizing extents of eight pages each. An extent can be either a uniform extent, for which all eight pages are allocated to the same object (table or index), or a mixed extent, which can contain pages from multiple objects. If an object uses less than eight pages, the page manager allocates new pages for that object from mixed extents. When the size of the object exceeds eight pages, the page manager allocates new space for that object in units of entire uniform extents. This optimization prevents the overhead of allocation from being incurred every time a new page is required for a large table; it is incurred only every eighth time. Perhaps most important, this optimization forces data of the same table to be contiguous for the most part. At the same time, the ability to use mixed extents keeps SQL Server from wasting too much space if a database contains many small tables.

To determine how contiguous a table's data is, you use the **DBCC SHOWCONTIG** command. A table with a lot of allocation and deallocation can get fairly fragmented, and rebuilding the clustered index (which also rebuilds the table) can improve performance, especially when a table is accessed frequently using table scans.

The Transaction Manager

A core feature of SQL Server is its ability to ensure that transactions follow the ACID properties rule (see the following section). Transactions must be *atomic*—that is, all or nothing. If a transaction has been committed, it must be recoverable by SQL Server no matter what—even if a total system failure occurs one millisecond after the commit was acknowledged. In SQL Server, if work was in progress and a system failure occurred before the transaction was committed, all the work is rolled back to the state that existed before the transaction began. Write-ahead logging makes it possible to always roll back work in progress or roll forward committed work that has not yet been applied to the data pages. Write-ahead logging assures that a transaction's changes—the "before and after" images of data—are captured on disk in the transaction log before a transaction is acknowledged as committed. Writes to the transaction log are always synchronous—that is, SQL Server must wait for them to complete. Writes to the data pages can be asynchronous, because all the effects can be reconstructed from the log if necessary. The transaction manager coordinates logging, recovery, and buffer management. These topics are discussed later in this chapter; at this point, we'll just look at transactions themselves.

Understanding The ACID Test

The ACID test for transaction processing is that the system be Atomic, Consistent, Isolated, and Durable. Atomic means indivisible—that is, an effect is atomic if it cannot be partially implemented. The system must either complete the transaction or return to a state that is indistinguishable from the state it was in before the transaction began. Of course, a transaction takes system resources even if it aborts. It clearly has an effect on the database, if only on its performance. When we say it has no effect on the database, we mean that none of the tables in the database are changed, none of the IDs are used or retired, and so on. It is as if you went to sleep for a few milliseconds and nothing happened—the transaction had no permanent effects on the system (usually meaning the database). Other transactions might have been processed during the same time, and these might have affected the database, but the point is that the effects that these other transactions have on the database are the same as if the aborted transaction had never existed.

Atomic transactions are designed to leave the database in a consistent state—the information in each of the tables is consistent with the information in all of the other tables. Transaction-based systems become complicated in multitasking environments, so the developer must take steps to protect the integrity or consistency of the database tables.

It is assumed that a database is initially *consistent* and that all transactions leave it consistent. This assumption is realized in the database world through the use of integrity constraints. In the object world, we assume that the objects represented in the database satisfy all of the constraints that are defined in the static object model for the database.

In general, I speak about transactions as if they were processed one at a time. No system processing transactions could afford to do this: It would make the cost-per-transaction of the software and hardware an order of magnitude higher. Instead, transactions are interleaved like any other activity in a modern multiuser multitasking computer system. That said, the effects of a transaction must be the same whether it is run alone or at the same time as other transactions. A set of transactions that *could* run one after the other, that is in series, is said to be *serializable*. A system is *isolated* if each transaction is serializable; that is, to the system, it appears as if this transaction occurred in isolation of all the other transactions. Nothing in this transaction requires any activity in another transaction. If no other transaction occurred, this transaction would remain consistent and valid.

Finally, once a transaction commits, the effect it has on the database is permanent—it does not matter if the hardware or software fails. This can be accomplished through redundancy, backups, and so forth. No failure of memory, disk storage or system software should be able to undo the effects of a transaction. The transaction is *durable*.

It is possible to create this durability by ensuring that the transaction can be replicated. That is, if you know the starting state before corruption and you know the details of the transaction, you may be able to restore the transaction by re-enacting it. In any case, when restoration is complete, the transaction's effects have been sustained.

The transaction manager delineates the boundaries of statements that must be grouped together to form an operation. It handles transactions that cross databases within the same SQL Server, and it allows nested transaction sequences. (However, nested transactions simply execute in the context of the first-level transaction; no special action occurs when they are committed. And a rollback specified in a lower level of a nested transaction undoes the entire transaction.) For a distributed transaction to another SQL Server (or to any other resource manager), the transaction manager coordinates with the Microsoft Distributed Transaction Coordinator (MS DTC) service using operating system remote procedure calls. The transaction manager marks *savepoints*, which let you designate points within a transaction at which work can be partially rolled back or undone.

The transaction manager also coordinates with the lock manager regarding when locks can be released, based on the isolation level in effect. The isolation level in which your transaction runs determines how sensitive your application is to changes made by others and consequently how long your transaction must hold locks to protect against changes made by others. Four isolation-level semantics are available in SQL Server 7: Uncommitted Read (also called "dirty read"), Committed Read, Repeatable Read, and Serializable.

Your transactions' behavior depends on the isolation level. We'll look at these levels now, but a complete understanding of isolation levels also requires an understanding of locking because the topics are so closely related. The next section provides an overview of locking.

Uncommitted Read

Uncommitted Read, or "dirty read," lets your transaction read any data that is currently on a data page, whether or not that data has been committed. For example, another user might have a transaction in progress that has updated data, and even though it is holding exclusive locks on the data, your transaction can read it anyway. The other user might then decide to roll back his or her transaction, so logically those changes were never made. If the system is a single-user system and everyone is queued up to access it, the changes would never have been visible to other users. In a multiuser system, however, you read the changes and possibly took action on them. Although this scenario isn't desirable, with Uncommitted Read you won't get stuck waiting for a lock, nor will *your* reads issue share locks (described in the section entitled "The Lock Manager") that might affect others.

When using Uncommitted Read, you give up assurances of having strongly consistent data so that you can have the benefit of high concurrency in the system without users locking each other out. So when should you choose Uncommitted Read? Clearly, you don't want to choose it for financial transactions in which every number must balance. But it might be fine for certain decision-support analyses—for example, when you look at sales trends— for which complete precision is not necessary and the tradeoff in higher concurrency makes it worthwhile.

Committed Read

Committed Read is SQL Server's default isolation level. It ensures that an operation will never read data that another application has changed but not yet committed. (That is, it will never read data that logically never existed.) With Committed Read, if a transaction is updating data and consequently has exclusive locks on data rows, your transaction must wait for those locks to be released before you can use that data (whether you are reading or modifying). Also, your transaction must put share locks (at a minimum) on the data that will be visited, which means that data is potentially unavailable to others to use. A share lock doesn't prevent others from reading the data, but it makes them wait to update the data. Share locks can be released after the data has been sent to the calling client—they do not have to be held for the duration of the transaction.

Warning
Although you can never read uncommitted data, if a transaction running with Committed Read isolation subsequently revisits the same data, that data might have changed or new rows might suddenly appear that meet the criteria of the original query. Rows that appear in this way are called phantoms.

Repeatable Read

The Repeatable Read isolation level adds to the properties of Committed Read by ensuring that if a transaction revisits data or if a query is reissued, the data will not have changed. In other words, issuing the same query twice within a transaction will not pick up any changes to data values made by another user's transaction.

Preventing nonrepeatable reads from appearing is a desirable safeguard—but there's no free lunch. The cost of this extra safeguard is that all the shared locks in a transaction must be held until the completion (**COMMIT** or **ROLLBACK**) of the transaction. (Exclusive locks must always be held until the end of a transaction, no matter what the isolation level, so that a transaction can be rolled back if necessary. If the locks were released sooner, it might be impossible to undo the work.) No other user can modify the data visited by your transaction as long as your transaction is outstanding. Obviously, this can seriously reduce concurrency and degrade performance. If transactions are not kept short or if applications are not written to be aware of such potential lock contention issues, SQL Server can appear to "hang" when it is simply waiting for locks to be released.

Tip
*You can control how long SQL Server waits for a lock to be released by using the session option **LOCK_TIMEOUT**.*

Serializable

The Serializable isolation level adds to the properties of Repeatable Read by ensuring that if a query is reissued, rows will not have been added in the interim. In other words, phantoms will not appear if the same query is issued twice within a transaction. More precisely, Repeatable Read and Serializable affect sensitivity to another connection's changes, whether or not the user ID of the other connection is the same. Every connection within SQL Server has its own transaction and lock space. In this context, I use the term *user* loosely so as not to obscure the central concept.

Preventing phantoms from appearing is another desirable safeguard. But once again, there's no free lunch. The cost of this extra safeguard is similar to that of Repeatable Read—all the shared locks in a transaction must be held until completion of the transaction. In addition, enforcing the Serializable isolation level requires that you not only lock data that has been read, but also lock data that *does not exist*! For example, suppose that within a transaction we issue a **SELECT** statement to read all the customers whose ZIP code is between 98000 and 98100, and on first execution, no rows satisfy that condition. To enforce the Serializable isolation level, we must lock that "range" of *potential* rows with ZIP codes between 98000 and 98100 so that if the same query is reissued, there will still be no rows that satisfy the condition. SQL Server handles this by using a special kind of lock called a *range lock*.

The Serializable level gets its name from the fact that running multiple serializable transactions at the same time is the equivalent of running them one at a time—that is, serially—without regard to sequence. For example, transactions A, B, and C are serializable only if the result obtained by running all three simultaneously is the same as if they were run one at a time, in any order. Serializable does not imply a known order in which the transactions are to be run. The order is considered a chance event. Even on a single-user system, the order of transactions hitting the queue would be essentially random. If the batch order is important to your application, you should implement it as a pure batch system.

The tough part of transaction management, of course, is dealing with roll-back/roll-forward and recovery operations. We'll return to the topic of transaction management and recovery a bit later. But first let's further discuss locking and logging.

The Lock Manager

Locking is a crucial function of a multiuser database system such as SQL Server. Recall that SQL Server lets you manage multiple users simultaneously and ensures that the transactions observe the properties of the chosen isolation level. At the highest level, Serializable, SQL Server must make the multiuser system perform like a single-user system—as though every user is queued up to use the system alone with no other user activity. Locking guards data and the internal resources that make this possible, and it allows many users to simultaneously access the database and not be severely affected by others' use.

The lock manager acquires and releases various types of locks, such as shared read locks, exclusive locks for writing, intent locks to signal a potential "plan" to perform some operation, extent locks for space allocation, and so on. It manages compatibility between the lock types, resolves deadlocks, and escalates locks if needed. The lock manager controls table, page, and row locks as well as system data locks. (System data, such as page headers and indexes, is private to the database system.)

The lock manager provides two separate locking systems. The first enables row locks, page locks, and table locks for all fully shared data tables, data pages and rows, text pages, and leaf-level index pages and index rows. The second locking system is used internally only for restricted system data; it protects root and intermediate index pages while indexes are being traversed. This internal mechanism uses *latches*, a lightweight, short-term variation of a lock for protecting data that does not need to be locked for the duration of a transaction. Full-blown locks would slow the system down. In addition to protecting upper levels of indexes, latches protect rows while they are being transferred from the storage engine to the relational engine. If you examine locks by using the **sp_lock** stored procedure or a similar mechanism that gets its information from the **syslockinfo** table, you won't see or be aware of latches; you'll see only the locks for fully shared data. However, some counters are available in Performance Monitor to monitor latch requests, acquisitions, and releases. Locking is an important feature of SQL Server, primarily for the many developers who are keenly interested in locking because of its potential effect on application performance.

Other Managers In SQL Server

Also included in the storage engine are managers for controlling utilities such as bulk load, DBCC commands, backup and restore operations, and the Virtual Device Interface (VDI). VDI allows developers to write their own backup and restore utilities and to access the SQL Server data structures directly, without going through the relational engine. There is also a manager to control sorting operations and one to physically manage the files and backup devices on disk.

Managing Memory

One of the major goals of SQL Server 7 was to scale easily from a laptop installation on Windows 95 or Windows 98 to an SMP server running on Windows NT Enterprise Edition. This requires a very robust policy for managing memory. By default, SQL Server 7 adjusts its use of system memory to balance the needs of other applications running on the machine and the needs of its own internal components. SQL Server can also be configured to use a fixed amount of memory. Whether memory allocation is fixed or dynamically adjusted, the total memory space is considered one unified cache and is managed as a collection of various pools with their own policies and purposes. Memory can be requested by and granted to any of several internal components.

The Buffer Manager And Memory Pools

The buffer pool is a memory pool that's the main memory component in the server; all memory not used by another memory component remains in the buffer pool. The buffer manager manages disk I/O functions for bringing data and index pages into memory so that data can be shared among users. When other components require memory, they can request a buffer from the buffer pool.

Another memory pool is the operating system itself. Occasionally, SQL Server must request contiguous memory in larger blocks than the 8K pages that the buffer pool can provide. Typically, use of large memory blocks is kept to a minimum, so direct calls to the operating system account for a very small fraction of SQL Server's memory usage.

The procedure cache can be considered another memory pool, in which query trees and plans from stored procedures, triggers, or ad hoc queries can be stored. Other pools are used by memory-intensive queries that use sorting or hashing, and by special memory objects that need less than one 8K page.

Access To In-Memory Pages

Access to pages in the buffer pool must be fast. Even with real memory, it would be ridiculously inefficient to have to scan the whole cache for a page when you're talking about hundreds of megabytes, or even gigabytes, of data. To avoid this inefficiency, pages in the buffer pool are hashed for fast access. *Hashing* is a technique that uniformly maps a key (in this case, a **dbid-fileno-pageno** identifier) via a hash function across a set of hash buckets. A *hash bucket* is a page in memory that contains an array of pointers (implemented as a linked list) to the buffer pages. If all the pointers to buffer pages do not fit on a single hash page, a *linked list* chains to additional hash pages.

Given a **dbid-fileno-pageno** value, the hash function converts that key to the hash bucket that should be checked; in essence, the hash bucket serves as an index to the specific page needed. By using hashing, even when large amounts of memory are present, you can find a specific data page in cache with only a few memory reads (typically one or two).

Tip

Finding a data page might require that multiple hash buckets be accessed via the chain (linked list). The hash function attempts to uniformly distribute the ***dbid-fileno-pageno*** *values throughout the available hash buckets. The number of hash buckets is set internally by SQL Server and depends on the total size of the buffer pool.*

Understanding The Lazywriter

A data page or an index page can be used only if it exists in memory. Therefore, a buffer in the buffer pool must be available for the page to be read into. Keeping a supply of buffers available for immediate use is an important performance optimization. If a buffer isn't readily available, many memory pages might have to be searched simply to locate a buffer to use as a workspace.

The buffer pool is managed by a process called the *lazywriter* that uses a clock algorithm to sweep through the buffer pool. Basically, the lazywriter thread maintains a pointer into the buffer pool that "sweeps" sequentially through it (like the hand on a clock). As it visits each buffer, it determines whether that buffer has been referenced since the last sweep by examining a reference count value in the buffer header. If the reference count is not 0, the buffer stays in the pool and its reference count is adjusted in preparation for the next sweep; otherwise, the buffer is made available for reuse: It is written to disk if dirty, removed from the hash lists, and put on a special list of buffers called the *free list*.

Tip

The set of buffers that the lazywriter sweeps through is sometimes called the LRU (for least recently used list). However, it does not function as a traditional LRU, because the buffers do not move within the list according to their use or lack of use; the lazywriter clock hand does all the moving. Also note that the set of buffers that the lazywriter inspects actually includes more than pages in the buffer pool. The buffers also include pages from compiled plans for procedures, triggers, or ad hoc queries.

The reference count of a buffer is incremented each time the buffer's contents are accessed by any process. For data or index pages, this is a simple increment by one. But objects that are expensive to create, such as stored procedure plans, get a higher reference count that reflects their "replacement cost." When the lazywriter clock hand sweeps through and checks which pages have been referenced, it does not use a simple decrement. It divides the reference count by 4. This means that frequently referenced pages (those with a high reference count) and those with a high replacement cost are "favored" and their count will not reach 0 any time soon, keeping them in the pool for further use.

The lazywriter hand sweeps through the buffer pool when the number of pages on the free list falls below its minimum size. The minimum size is computed as a percentage of the overall buffer pool size but is always between 128K and 4MB. Currently, the percentage is set at 3 percent, but that could change in future releases.

User threads also perform the same function of searching for pages for the free list. This happens when a user process needs to read a page from disk into a buffer. Once the read has been initiated, the user thread checks to see if the free list is too small. (Note that this process consumes one page of the list for its own read.) If so, the user thread performs the same function as the lazywriter: It advances the clock hand and searches for buffers to free. Currently, it advances the clock hand through 16 buffers, regardless of how many it actually finds to free in that group of 16. The reason for having user threads share in the work of the lazywriter is so that the cost can be distributed across all of the CPUs in an SMP environment.

Keeping Pages In The Cache Permanently

Tables can be specially marked so that their pages are never put on the free list and are therefore kept in memory indefinitely. This process is called *pinning* a table. Any page (data, index, or text) belonging to a pinned table is never marked as free and reused unless it is unpinned. Pinning and unpinning is accomplished using the **pintable** option of the **sp_tableoption** stored procedure. Setting this option to true for a table doesn't cause the table to be brought into cache, nor does it mark pages of the table as "favored" in any way; instead, it avoids the unnecessary overhead and simply doesn't allow any pages belonging to a pinned table to be put on the free list for possible replacement.

Because mechanisms such as write-ahead logging and checkpointing are completely unaffected, such an operation in no way impairs recovery. Still, pinning too many tables can result in few or even no pages being available when a new buffer is needed. In general, you should pin tables only if you have carefully tuned your system, plenty of memory is available, and you have a good feel for which tables constitute hot spots.

Pages that are "very hot" (accessed repeatedly) are never placed on the free list. A page in the buffer pool that has a nonzero use count, such as one that is newly read or newly created, is not added to the free list until its use count falls to 0. Prior to that point, the page is clearly hot and isn't a good candidate for reuse. Very hot pages might never get on the free list, even without their objects being pinned—which is as it should be.

Protection against media failure is achieved using whatever level of RAID (redundant array of independent disks) technology you choose. Write-ahead logging in conjunction with RAID protection ensures that you never lose a transaction. (However, a good backup strategy is still essential in case of certain situations, such as when an administrator accidentally clobbers a table.) SQL Server always opens its files by instructing the operating system to write through any other caching that the operating system might be doing. Hence, SQL Server ensures that transactions are atomic—even a sudden interruption of power results in no partial transactions existing in the database, and all completed transactions are guaranteed to be reflected. (It is crucial, however, that a hardware disk-caching controller not "lie" and claim that a write has been completed unless it really has or will be.)

Checkpoints

Checkpoint operations minimize the amount of work that SQL Server must do when databases are recovered during system startup. Checkpoints are run on a database-by-database basis. They flush dirty pages from the current database out to disk so that those changes will not have to be redone during database recovery. (A *dirty page* is one that has been modified since it was brought from disk into the buffer pool.) When a checkpoint occurs, SQL Server writes a checkpoint record to the transaction log, which lists all the transactions that are active. This allows the recovery process to build a table containing a list of all the potentially dirty pages.

Checkpoints are triggered when any of the following occurs:

♦ A database owner explicitly issues a checkpoint command to perform a checkpoint in that database.

◆ The log is getting full (more than 70 percent of capacity) and the database option **trunc. log on chkpt.** is set. A checkpoint is triggered to truncate the transaction log and free up space.

◆ A long recovery time is estimated. When recovery time is predicted to be longer than the *recovery interval* configuration option, a checkpoint is triggered. SQL Server 7 uses a simple metric to predict recovery time, because it can recover, or redo, in less time than it took the original operations to run. Thus, if checkpoints are taken at least as often as the recovery interval frequency, recovery will complete within the interval. A recovery interval setting of 1 means checkpoints occur every minute. A minimum amount of work must be done for the automatic checkpoint to fire; this is currently 10MB of log per minute. In this way, SQL Server doesn't waste time taking checkpoints on idle databases. A default recovery interval of 0 means that SQL Server will choose an appropriate value automatically; for the current version, this is one minute.

Checkpoints And Performance Issues

A checkpoint is issued as part of an orderly shutdown, so a typical recovery upon restart takes only seconds. (An orderly shutdown occurs when you explicitly shut down SQL Server, unless you do so via the **SHUTDOWN WITH NOWAIT** command. An orderly shutdown also occurs when the SQL Server service is stopped through the Windows NT Service Control Manager or the **net stop** command from an operating system prompt.) Although a checkpoint speeds up recovery, it does slightly degrade runtime performance.

Unless your system is being pushed with high transactional activity, the runtime impact of a checkpoint probably won't be noticeable. It is minimized via the *fuzzy checkpoint* technique, which reflects the changes to the data pages incrementally. You can also use the recovery interval option of **sp_configure** to influence checkpointing frequency, balancing the time to recover versus any impact on runtime performance. If you are interested in tracing how often checkpoints actually occur, you can start your SQL Server with trace flag 3502, which writes information to SQL Server's error log every time a checkpoint occurs.

Accessing Pages Via The Buffer Manager

The buffer manager handles the in-memory version of each physical disk page and provides all other modules access to it (with appropriate safety measures). The memory image in the buffer pool, if one exists, takes precedence over the disk image. That is, the copy of the data page in memory might include updates that have not yet been written to disk. (It might be dirty.) When a page is needed for a process, it must exist in memory (in the buffer pool). If the page is not there, a physical I/O is performed to get it. Obviously, because physical I/Os are expensive, the fewer the better. The more memory there is (the bigger the buffer pool), the more pages can reside there and the more likely a page can be found there.

A database appears as a simple sequence of numbered pages. The database ID (**dbid**), file number (**fileno**), and page number (**pageno**) uniquely specify a page for the entire SQL

Server environment. When another module (such as the access methods manager, row manager, index manager, or text manager) needs to access a page, it requests access from the buffer manager by specifying the **dbid**, **fileno**, and **pageno**.

The buffer manager responds to the calling module with a pointer to the memory buffer holding that page. The response might be immediate if the page is already in the cache, or it might take an instant for a disk I/O to complete and bring the page into memory. Typically, the calling module also requests that the lock manager perform the appropriate level of locking on the page. The calling module notifies the buffer manager if and when it is finished dirtying, or making updates to, the page. The buffer manager is responsible for writing these updates to disk in a way that coordinates with logging and transaction management.

Large Memory Issues

Systems with hundreds of megabytes of RAM are not uncommon. In fact, for benchmark activities, Microsoft runs with a memory configuration of as much as 2GB of physical RAM. Using SQL Server on a DEC Alpha processor, or using the Enterprise Edition of SQL Server, allows even more memory to be used. In the future, Windows NT will support a 64-bit address space and memory prices probably will continue to decline, so huge data caches of many gigabytes will not be so unusual. The reason to run with more memory is, of course, to reduce the need for physical I/O by increasing your cache-hit ratio.

Read Ahead

SQL Server supports a mechanism called *read ahead*, whereby the need for data and index pages can be anticipated and pages can be brought into the buffer pool before they are actually read. This performance optimization allows large amounts of data to be processed effectively. Unlike in previous versions of SQL Server, read ahead is managed completely internally, and no configuration adjustments are necessary. In addition, read ahead does not use separate Windows NT threads. This ensures that read ahead stays far enough—but not too far—ahead of the scan of the actual data.

There are two kinds of read ahead: one for table scans and one for index ranges. For table scans, the table's allocation structures are consulted to read the table in disk order. Up to 32 extents (32×8 pages/extent $\times 8,192$ bytes/page = 2MB) of read ahead can be outstanding at a time. The extents are read with a single 64K scatter read. If the table is spread across multiple files in a file group, SQL Server attempts to keep at least eight of the files busy with read ahead instead of sequentially processing the files.

Tip

*Scatter-gather I/O was introduced in Windows NT 4, Service Pack 2, with the Win32 functions **ReadFileScatter** and **WriteFileScatter**. These functions allow SQL Server to issue a single read or write to transfer up to eight pages of data directly to or from SQL Server's buffer pool.*

For index ranges, the scan uses level one of the index structure, which is the level immediately above the leaf, to determine which pages to read ahead. It tries to stay a certain number of pages ahead of the scan; that number is currently about 40 plus the configuration value for *max async I/O*. When the index scan starts, read ahead is invoked on the initial descent of the index to minimize the number of reads performed. For instance, for a scan of **WHERE state = 'NV'**, read ahead searches the index for **key = 'NV'**, and it can tell from the level one nodes how many pages have to be examined to satisfy the scan. If the anticipated number of pages is small, all the pages are requested by the initial read ahead; if the pages are contiguous, they are fetched in scatter reads. If the range contains a large number of pages, the initial read ahead is performed and thereafter every time another 16 pages are consumed by the scan, the index is consulted to read in another 16 pages. This has several interesting effects:

♦ Small ranges can be processed in a single read at the data page level whenever the index is contiguous.

♦ The scan range (for example, **state = 'NV'**) can be used to prevent reading ahead of pages that will not be used because this information is available in the index.

♦ Read ahead is not slowed by having to follow page linkages at the data page level. (Read ahead can be done on both clustered indexes and nonclustered indexes.)

> **Tip**
>
> *Scatter-gather I/O and asynchronous I/O are available only to SQL Server running on Windows NT. This includes the desktop edition of SQL Server if it has been installed on Windows NT Workstation.*

The Log Manager

All changes are "written ahead" by the buffer manager to the transaction log. Write-ahead logging ensures that all databases can be recovered to a consistent state even in the event of a complete server failure, as long as the physical medium (hard disk) survives. A process is never given acknowledgment that a transaction has been committed unless it is on disk in the transaction log. For this reason, all writes to the transaction log are synchronous—SQL Server must wait for acknowledgment of completion. Writes to data pages can be made asynchronously, without waiting for acknowledgment, because if a failure occurs, the transactions can be undone or redone from the information in the transaction log.

The log manager formats transaction log records in memory before writing them to disk. To format these log records, the log manager maintains regions of contiguous memory called *log caches*. Unlike in previous versions, in SQL Server 7 log records do not share the buffer pool with data and index pages. Log records are maintained only in the log caches.

To achieve maximum throughput, the log manager maintains two or more log caches. One is the current log cache, in which new log records are added. The log manager also has two queues of log caches: a *flushQueue*, which contains log caches waiting to be flushed, and a *freeQueue*, which contains log caches that have no data and can be reused.

When a user process requires that a particular log cache be flushed (for example, when a transaction commits), the log cache is placed into the flushQueue (if it isn't already there). Then the thread (or fiber) is put into the list of connections waiting for the log cache to be flushed. The connection does not do further work until its log records have been flushed.

The *log writer* is a dedicated thread that goes through the flushQueue in order and flushes the log caches out to disk. The log caches are written one at a time. The log writer first checks to see if the log cache is the current log cache. If it is, the log writer pads the log cache to sector alignment and updates some header information. It then issues an I/O event for that log cache. When the flush for a particular log cache is completed, any processes waiting on that log cache are woken up and can resume work.

The SQL Server Kernel And Its Interaction With The Operating System

The SQL Server *kernel* is responsible for interacting with the operating system. It's a bit of a simplification to suggest that SQL Server has one module for all operating system calls, but for ease of understanding, you can think of it this way. All requests to operating system services are made via the Win32 API and C runtime libraries. When SQL Server runs under Windows NT, it runs entirely in the Win32 protected subsystem. Absolutely no calls are made in Windows NT Privileged Mode; they are made in User Mode. This means that SQL Server cannot crash the entire system, it cannot crash another process running in User Mode, and other such processes cannot crash SQL Server. SQL Server has no device-driver–level calls, nor does it use any undocumented calls to Windows NT. If the entire system crashes (giving you the so-called "Blue Screen of Death") and SQL Server happens to have been running there, one thing is certain: SQL Server did not crash the system. Such a crash must be the result of faulty or incompatible hardware, a buggy device driver operating in Privileged Mode, or a critical bug in the Windows NT operating system code (which is doubtful).

Tip

The Blue Screen of Death—a blue "bug check" screen with some diagnostic information—appears if a crash of Windows NT occurs. It looks similar to the screen that appears when Windows NT initially boots up.

A key design goal of both SQL Server and Windows NT is scalability. The same binary executable files that run on notebook computer systems run on symmetric multiprocessor super servers with loads of processors. SQL Server includes versions for Intel and RISC hardware architectures on the same CD. Windows NT is an ideal platform for a database server because it provides a fully protected, secure 32-bit environment. The foundations of a great database server platform are preemptive scheduling, virtual paged memory management, symmetric multiprocessing, and asynchronous I/O. Windows NT provides these, and SQL Server uses them fully. The SQL Server engine runs as a single process on Windows NT. Within that process are multiple threads of execution. Windows NT schedules each thread to the next processor available to run one.

Threading And Symmetric Multiprocessing

SQL Server approaches multiprocessor scalability differently than most other symmetric multiprocessing (SMP) database systems. Two characteristics separate this approach from other implementations:

◆ *Single-process architecture*—SQL Server maintains a single-process, multithreaded architecture that reduces system overhead and memory use. This is called the Symmetric Server Architecture.

◆ *Native thread-level multiprocessing*—SQL Server supports multiprocessing at the thread level rather than at the process level, which allows for preemptive operation and dynamic load balancing across multiple CPUs. Using multiple threads is significantly more efficient than using multiple processes.

To understand how SQL Server works, it is useful to compare its strategies to strategies generally used by other products. On a nonthreaded operating system, such as some Unix variants, a typical SMP database server has multiple DBMS processes, each bound to a specific CPU. Some implementations even have one process per user, which results in a high memory cost. These processes communicate using shared memory, which maintains the cache, locks, task queues, and user context information. The DBMS must include complex logic that takes on the role of an operating system: It schedules user tasks, simulates threads, coordinates multiple processes, and so on. Because processes are bound to specific CPUs, dynamic load balancing can be difficult or impossible. For the sake of portability, products often take this approach even when they run on an operating system that offers native threading services, such as Windows NT. SQL Server, on the other hand, uses a clean design of a single process and multiple operating system threads. The threads are scheduled onto a CPU by a User Mode Scheduler.

SQL Server always uses multiple threads, even on a single-processor system. Threads are created and destroyed depending on system activity, so thread count is not constant. Typically, the number of active threads in SQL Server ranges from 16 to 100, depending on system activity and configuration. A pool of threads handles each of the networks that SQL Server simultaneously supports, another thread handles database checkpoints, another handles the lazywriter process, and another handles the log writer. A separate thread is also available for general database cleanup tasks, such as periodically shrinking a database that is in autoshrink mode. Finally, a pool of threads handles all user commands.

The Worker Thread Pool

Although SQL Server might seem to offer each user a separate operating system thread, the system is actually a bit more sophisticated than that. Because it is inefficient to use hundreds of separate operating system threads to support hundreds of users, SQL Server establishes a pool of worker threads.

When a client issues a command, the SQL Server network handler places the command in a queue and the next available thread from the worker thread pool takes the request. Technically, this queue is a Windows NT facility called an *IOCompletion port*. The SQL Server worker thread waits in the completion queue for incoming network requests to be posted to the IOCompletion port. If no idle worker thread is available to wait for the next incoming request, SQL Server dynamically creates a new thread until the maximum configured worker thread limit has been reached. The client's command must wait for a worker thread to be freed.

Even in a system with thousands of connected users, most are typically idle at any given time. As the workload decreases, SQL Server gradually eliminates idle threads to improve resource and memory use.

The worker thread pool design is efficient for handling thousands of active connections without the need for a transaction monitor. Most competing products, including those on the largest mainframe systems, need to use a transaction monitor to achieve the level of active users that SQL Server can handle without such an extra component. If you support a large number of connections, this is an important capability.

Tip

In many cases, you should allow users to stay connected—even if they will be idle for periods of, say, an hour—rather than have them continually connect and disconnect. Repeatedly incurring the overhead of the logon process is more expensive than simply allowing the connection to remain live but idle.

Active Vs. Idle

In the previous context, a user is considered idle from the database perspective. The human end user might be quite active, filling in the data entry screen, getting information from customers, and so forth. But those activities don't require any server interaction until a command is actually sent. So from the SQL Server engine perspective, the connection is idle.

When you think of an active user versus an idle user, be sure to consider the user in the context of the back-end database server. In practically all types of applications that have many end users, at any given time the number of users who have an active request with the database is relatively small. A system with 1,000 active connections might reasonably be configured with 150 or so worker threads. But this doesn't mean that all 150 worker threads are created at the start—they're created only as needed, and 150 is only a high-water mark.

In fact, fewer than 100 worker threads might be active at a time, even if end users all think they are actively using the system all the time.

A thread from the worker thread pool services each command to allow multiple processors to be fully utilized as long as multiple user commands are outstanding. In addition, with SQL Server 7, a single user command with no other activity on the system can benefit from multiple processors if the query is complex. SQL Server can break complex queries into component parts that can be executed in parallel on multiple CPUs. Note that this intraquery parallelism occurs only if there are processors to spare—that is, if the number of processors is greater than the number of connections. In addition, intraquery parallelism is not considered if the query is not expensive to run, and the threshold for what constitutes "expensive" can be controlled with a configuration option called *cost threshold for parallelism*.

Under the normal pooling scheme, a worker thread runs each user request to completion. Because each thread has its own stack, stack switching is unnecessary. If a given thread performs an operation that causes a page fault, only that thread, and hence only that one client, is blocked. (A page fault occurs if the thread makes a request for memory and the virtual memory manager of the operating system must swap that page in from disk because it had been paged out. Such a request for memory must wait a long time relative to the normal memory access time, because a physical I/O is thousands of times more expensive than reading real memory.)

Now consider something more serious than a page fault. Suppose that while a user request is being carried out, a bug is exposed in SQL Server that results in an illegal operation that causes an access violation (for example, the thread tries to read some memory outside the SQL Server address space). Windows NT immediately terminates the offending thread—an important feature of a truly protected operating system. Because SQL Server makes use of structured exception handling in Windows NT, only the specific SQL Server user who made the request is affected. All other users of SQL Server or other applications on the system are unaffected and the system at large will not crash. Of course, such a bug should never occur and in reality is indeed rare. But this is software, and software is never perfect. Having this important reliability feature is like having an air bag in your car—you hope you never need it, but you're glad it's there in case of a crash.

Tip

Because Windows 95 and Windows 98 do not support SMP systems or thread pooling, the previous discussion is relevant only to SQL Server running on Windows NT. The following discussion of disk I/O is also relevant only to SQL Server on Windows NT.

Disk I/O On Windows NT

SQL Server 7 uses two Windows NT features to improve its disk I/O performance: scatter-gather I/O and asynchronous I/O. The following list briefly explains these two techniques:

♦ *Scatter-gather I/O*—As just mentioned, scatter-gather I/O was introduced in Windows NT 4, Service Pack 2. Previously, all the data for a disk read or write on Windows NT had to be in a contiguous area of memory. If a read transferred in 64K of data, the read request had to specify the address of a contiguous area of 64K of memory. Scatter-gather I/O allows a read or write to transfer data into or out of discontiguous areas of memory. If SQL Server 7 reads in a 64K extent, it does not have to allocate a single 64K area and then copy the individual pages to buffer cache pages. It can locate eight buffer pages and then do a single scatter-gather I/O that specifies the address of the eight buffer pages. Windows NT places the eight pages directly into the buffer pages, eliminating the need for SQL Server to do a separate memory copy.

♦ *Asynchronous I/O*—In an asynchronous I/O, after an application requests a read or write operation, Windows NT immediately returns control to the application. The application can then perform additional work, and it can later test to see if the read or write has completed. By contrast, in a synchronous I/O, the operating system does not return control to the application until the read or write completes. SQL Server supports multiple concurrent asynchronous I/O operations against each file in a database. The maximum number of I/O operations for any file is controlled by the *max async io* configuration option. If max async io is left at its default of 32, a maximum of 32 asynchronous I/O operations can be outstanding for each file at any time.

Types Of Databases

Each SQL Server has two types of databases: system databases and user databases. Structurally, there is no difference between system and user databases—both store data. However, SQL Server recognizes and requires system databases for its own use. System databases store information about SQL Server as a whole. SQL Server uses these databases to operate and manage the system. User databases are databases that users create. One copy of SQL Server can manage one or more user databases. When SQL Server is installed, SQL Server Setup creates four system databases and two sample user databases. Table 7.1 describes the system databases.

Table 7.1 SQL Server's system databases.

Database	Description
master	Controls the user databases and operation of SQL Server as a whole by keeping track of information such as login accounts, configurable environment variables, database locations, and system error messages.
model	Provides a template, or prototype, for new user databases.
tempdb	Provides a storage area for temporary tables and other temporary working storage needs.
msdb	Supports SQL Server Agent and provides a storage area for scheduling information and job history.
distribution	Stores history and transaction data used in replication. The distribution database is installed only when you configure SQL Server for replication activities (not at initial setup and installation).

It is possible to modify and delete data in the system databases, but this is not recommended. You should create all user objects in user databases and use system stored procedures only to read and modify data in the system databases.

There is one case in which you can modify a system database directly. If you want certain objects that you create (such as stored procedures, data types, defaults, and rules) to be added to every new user database, you can add these objects to the model database. The contents of the model database are copied into every new database.

User Databases

The pubs and Northwind sample databases are installed when you install SQL Server. These provide useful examples for you to use when learning how to work with SQL Server. They are not required for SQL Server to operate correctly.

Database Objects

A database is a collection of data stored in tables, along with objects that support the storage, retrieval, security, and integrity of this data. Table 7.2 summarizes the SQL Server database objects.

Tip

In Enterprise Manager, system databases and system objects are hidden by default. You can change the default by editing the server registration information and checking the Show System Databases And System Objects option.

Table 7.2   The different types of database objects supported by SQL Server 7.

Database Object	Description
Constraint	Used to define integrity rules for a column or set of columns in a table; the standard mechanism for enforcing data integrity.
Data type	Defines the type of data values allowed for a column or variable. SQL Server provides system-supplied data types. Users can create user-defined data types.
Default	Defines a value that is stored in a column if no other value is supplied.
Index	A storage structure that provides ordering and fast access for data retrieval and that can enforce data uniqueness.
Rule	Defines an expression that is used to check the validity of values that are stored in a column or data type.
Stored procedure	A named collection of Transact-SQL statements or batches that execute together.
Table	Stores data as a collection of rows and columns.
Trigger	A special form of a stored procedure that is executed automatically when a user modifies data in a table.
View	Provides a way to look at data from one or more tables or other views in a database.

Referring To SQL Server Objects

You can refer to SQL Server objects in several ways. You can specify the full name of the object (its fully qualified name), or you can specify only part of the object's name and have SQL Server determine the rest of the name from the context in which you are working.

Fully Qualified Names

The complete name of a SQL Server object includes four identifiers: the server name, the database name, the owner name, and the object name, in the following format:

```
server.database.owner.object
```

Any name that specifies all four parts is known as a *fully qualified name*. Each object created in SQL Server must have a unique, fully qualified name. For example, there can be two tables named **Orders** in the same database only as long as they belong to different owners. In addition, column names must be unique within a table or view.

Partially Specified Names

When referencing an object, you do not always have to specify the server, database, and owner. Leading identifiers can be omitted. Intermediate identifiers can also be omitted as long as their position is indicated by periods. The valid formats of object names are as follows:

```
server.database.owner.object
server.database..object
server..owner.object
server...object
database.owner.object
database..object
owner.object
object
```

When you create an object, SQL Server uses the following defaults if different parts of the name are not specified:

♦ The server defaults to the local server.

♦ The database defaults to the current database.

♦ The owner defaults to the username in the specified database associated with the login ID of the current connection. (Usernames are mapped to login IDs when they are created.)

A user who is a member of a role can explicitly specify the role as the object owner. A user who is a member of the **db_owner** or **db_ddladmin** role in the Northwind database, for example, can specify the **dbo** user account as the owner of an object. This practice is strongly recommended—both by developers and by Microsoft, primarily to assist in avoiding the issue of *broken ownership chains*, discussed in Chapter 10.

The following example creates an **order_history** table in the Northwind database:

```
CREATE TABLE northwind.dbo.order_history
(
  OrderID int,
  ProductID int,
  UnitPrice money,
  Quantity int,
  Discount decimal
)
```

Most object references use three-part names and default to the local server. Four-part names are generally used for distributed queries or remote stored procedure calls. Needless to say, this syntax for table creation looks very similar to the syntax that you are accustomed to using with Access—the primary difference coming in the support for some different data types that are not supported in Access.

System Tables

System tables store information, called *metadata*, about the system and objects in databases. Metadata is information about data.

Each database (including the master database) contains a collection of system tables that store metadata about that specific database. This collection of system tables is called the *database catalog*.

The *system catalog*, found only in the **master** database, is a collection of system tables that stores metadata about the entire system and all other databases. System tables all begin with the **sys** prefix. Table 7.3 identifies some frequently used system tables.

Table 7.3 Frequently used system tables in the SQL Server environment.

System Table	Database	Function
sysxlogins	master	Contains one row for each login account that can connect to SQL Server. If you need to access information in **sysxlogins**, you should do so through the **syslogins** view.
sysmessages	master	Contains one row for each system error or warning that SQL Server can return.
sysdatabases	master	Contains one row for each database on a SQL Server.
sysusers	All	Contains one row for each Windows NT user, Windows NT group, SQL Server user, or SQL Server role in a database.
sysobjects	All	Contains one row for each object in a database.

Metadata Retrieval

You can query a system table as you would any other table to retrieve information about the system. However, you should not write scripts that directly query the system tables, because if the system tables are changed in future product versions, your scripts may fail or may not provide accurate information.

Warning

Writing scripts that directly modify the system tables is generally not a good idea. Changing a system table may make it impossible for SQL Server to operate normally—in some extreme cases, it may even make it impossible for SQL Server to boot.

When you write applications that retrieve metadata from system tables, you should use system stored procedures, system functions, or system-supplied information schema views. Each of these is described in the sections that follow.

System Stored Procedures

To make it easier for you to gather information about the state of the server and database objects, SQL Server provides a collection of prewritten queries called *system stored procedures*. The names of most system stored procedures begin with the **sp_** prefix. Table 7.4 describes three commonly used system stored procedures.

Many other stored procedures are used to create or modify system information or database objects by modifying the system tables. For example, the system stored procedure **sp_addlogin** creates a new login account in the **master..sysxlogins** system table. As you have seen, some system stored procedures modify and query the system tables for you so you don't have to do so directly.

Information Schema Views

Information schema views provide an internal, system-table–independent view of the SQL Server metadata. These views conform to the ANSI SQL standard definition for information schema. Information schema views allow applications to work properly even if future product versions change the system tables significantly.

Table 7.4   Three of the stored procedures most frequently used by new and experienced developers.

System Stored Procedure	Description
sp_help [*object_name*]	Provides information on the specified database object.
sp_helpdb [*database_name*]	Provides information on the specified database.
sp_helpindex [*table_name*]	Provides information on the index for the specified table.

In SQL Server, all information schema views are owned by a predefined **information_schema** user. Each information schema view contains metadata for the data objects stored in a particular database. Three information schema views are the most commonly used:

♦ **information_schema.tables**—List of tables in the database

♦ **information_schema.columns**—Information on columns defined in the database

♦ **information_schema.tables_privileges**—Security information for tables in the database

Where To Go From Here

In this chapter, we've looked at the general workings of the SQL Server engine, including the key modules and functional areas that make up the engine. We've also covered issues dealing with integration with Windows NT. By necessity, we've made some simplifications throughout the chapter, but the information should provide some insight into the roles and responsibilities of the major subsystems in SQL Server, the general flow of the system, and the interrelationships among subsystems.

The retrieval of metadata—information about objects and their configuration—has been made much easier in SQL Server 7. Information schema views, new to this version, allow you to retrieve valuable information from system tables without having to write a query against these tables yourself. SQL Server continues to support the use of system stored procedures, which can be recognized by their **sp_** prefix, to gather valuable information for database objects.

In Chapter 8, I will continue the preliminary examination of server-side database products with the consideration of Oracle, and its uses with Access 2000 as a front end. In Chapter 9, we will return to working with SQL Server, attacking development through the use of the new Access Data Project (ADP) file type.

Chapter 8
Using Oracle And Access For Client/Server

In Chapter 7, you learned more about using Access to build front ends for the SQL Server client/server architecture. In that chapter, we focused specifically on implementing Access with SQL Server back ends. However, Oracle is another very common back-end architecture. In this chapter, you'll learn more about using Access for client/server, specifically in the context of the Oracle architecture. We'll begin by examining Oracle, with an eye toward some of the differences between Oracle and Access, as well as differences between Oracle and SQL Server. Next, we'll address some of the issues surrounding conversion of existing Access databases to Oracle databases. Finally, we'll look at using open database connectivity (ODBC) and ActiveX Data Objects (ADO) to attach to Oracle database back ends, and we'll consider some issues to keep in mind when working with Oracle back ends.

Tip

The work in this chapter requires that you have Oracle8 installed on a Windows NT or Unix server on your network. If you don't use Oracle within your environment, you may want to skip this chapter entirely. Many of the techniques for client/server presented here are similar to those you saw in Chapter 7 when working with SQL Server databases.

Before considering Access-specific issues, we'll take some time to describe most of the components of the Oracle database software present (in one form or another) on all machines on which the Oracle database can run. Although we'll only briefly touch on some of the various components (such as memory, process, hardware, and network components) and discuss the interaction between them, we'll spend more time discussing some of the internal objects (such as rollback segments) of Oracle databases.

Global View Of The Oracle Architecture

The Oracle architecture described in this section is the generic architecture that applies to all platforms on which Oracle runs. There might be differences in the architecture between various platforms, but the fundamentals are the same.

Understanding Oracle Databases

As you've learned in previous chapters, a *database* is a collection of related data that's used and retrieved together for one or more application systems. The physical location and implementation of the database is transparent to the application programs, and in fact, you could move and restructure the physical database without affecting the programs.

Physically, in its simplest form, an Oracle database is nothing more than a set of files somewhere on disk. The physical location of these files is irrelevant to the function (although important for the performance) of the database. The files are binary files that you can access only by using the Oracle kernel software. Querying data in the database files is typically done with one of the Oracle tools (such as SQL*Plus) using structured query language (SQL). The first major difference between Oracle databases and Access 2000 databases occurs here at the physical layer.

The Access database, together with all the information associated with it (with the notable exception of the entries within the system.mdw file) is stored within a single file. The Oracle database, on the other hand, stores each table within its own physical file—a structure more in line with what you learned about other server-based database products in Chapter 7.

Logically, the database is divided into a set of Oracle user accounts (schemas), each of which is identified by a username and password unique to that database. Tables and other objects are owned by one of these Oracle users, and access to the data is available only by logging in to the database using an Oracle username and password. Without a valid username and password for the database, you're denied access to anything on the database.

It's important to note that the Oracle username and password are different from the operating system username and password. For example, a database residing on a Windows NT server requires that the user log in to the system with his or her system-defined login. If the user then wants to connect to the Oracle database, he or she has to log in to Oracle as well, using another ID and password set. This process of logging in, or connecting to, the database is required whether you're using an Oracle or non-Oracle tool to access the database.

The differences between the Oracle construction and the Access construction are obvious at the logical layer. In general, you can visualize the difference between the two by recognizing that Oracle's construction is designed to manage a much larger number of users than the Access construction, and also to be more secure from unauthorized access to the data.

The same table name can coexist in two separate Oracle user accounts. Even though the tables might have the same name, they're different tables. Sometimes, the same database (same set of physical database files) is used for holding different versions of tables (in separate Oracle accounts) for the developers, system testing, or user testing. Alternately, different applications systems may use the same table name for different purposes within a single database.

Often, people refer to an Oracle user account as a database, but this isn't strictly correct. You could use two Oracle user accounts to hold data for two entirely different application systems. In such a construction, you would have two logical databases implemented in the same physical database using two Oracle user accounts.

In addition to physical files, Oracle processes and memory structures must also be present before you can use the database. Figure 8.1 shows the basic Oracle architecture that you'll review throughout this chapter.

Whereas the architecture consists of many components, the Oracle database files are the root of what comprises a database. The next section discusses the files that make up a database in Oracle.

Understanding The Oracle Files That Comprise A Database

As you've learned, Oracle implements databases in a manner significantly different from what you're used to with Access. Each database consists of a series of files, each of which corresponds loosely to one or more database objects. Three major sets of files comprise a database:

♦ Database files

♦ Control files

♦ Redo logs

The most important of these files are the database files, because they contain the actual data itself, whereas the control files and the redo logs support the functioning of the architecture. In the event of an operating system failure or other problem, the control files and the redo files can be mostly reconstructed.

However, all three sets of files must be present, open, and available to Oracle for any data on the database to be useable. Without these files, you can't access the database, and the database administrator (DBA) might have to recover some or all of the database using a

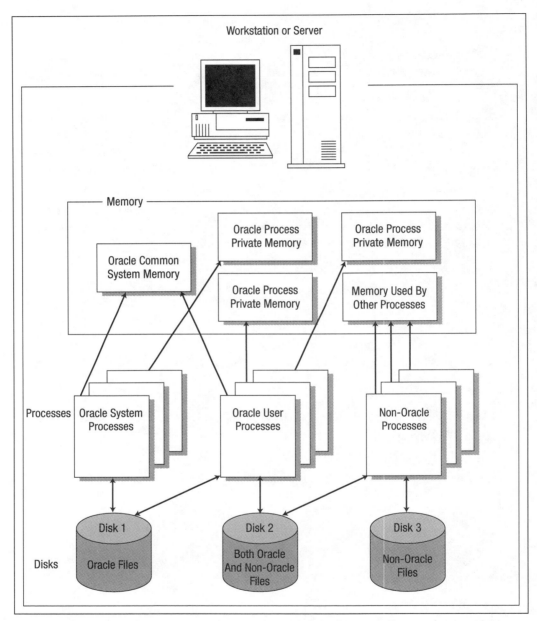

Figure 8.1
The basic Oracle architecture.

backup. All the files are binary—meaning that users can't, for all intents and purposes, access the information that the files contain without going through the Oracle kernel to do so.

System And User Processes

For database files to be useable, you must have the Oracle system processes and one or more user processes running on the machine. The Oracle system processes, also known as Oracle background processes, provide functions for the user processes—functions that would otherwise be executed by the user processes themselves. You can initiate many background processes, but as a minimum, only the PMON, SMON, DBWR, and LGWR processes (all described later in the chapter) must be up and running for the database to be useable. Other background processes support optional additions to the way the database runs.

In addition to the Oracle background processes, there is one user process per connection to the database in its simplest setup. The user must make a connection to the database before he can access any of the objects. If one user logs into Oracle using SQL*Plus, another user chooses Oracle Designer/2000, and yet another user employs an Access front end that gets its data from Oracle, then you have three user processes against the database—one for each connection. Like other operating system processes, Oracle runs within the computer's memory. Oracle divides the memory that it uses into two general categories:

♦ *Oracle system memory*—Oracle database-wide system memory is known as the *system global area* or *shared global area (SGA)*. The data and control structures in the SGA are shareable, and all the Oracle background and user processes can use them.

Tip

The combination of the SGA and the Oracle background processes is known as an Oracle instance, a term that you'll encounter often with Oracle. Although there's typically one instance for each database, it's common to find many instances (running on different processors or even on different machines) all running against the same set of database files.

♦ *User process memory*—For each connection to the database, Oracle allocates a *process global area* or *program global area (PGA)* in the machine's memory. Oracle also allocates a PGA for the background processes. This memory area contains data and control information for one process and isn't shareable between processes.

As you saw earlier in this chapter, the Oracle architecture in and of itself does not include network support. In fact, you must use the SQL*Net process and stubs that talk to network protocols to support network connections to your Oracle database. The next section discusses network considerations in more detail.

Network Software And SQL*Net

A simple configuration for an Oracle database has the database files, memory structures, and Oracle background and user processes all running on the same machine, without any networking involved. However, a much more common configuration is one that implements the database on a server machine, and the Oracle tools or a database front end on a different machine (such as a PC with Microsoft Windows). For this type of client/server configuration, the machines are connected with some non-Oracle networking software that enables the two machines to communicate. Also, you might want two databases running on different machines to talk to each other—perhaps you're accessing tables from both databases in the same transaction or even in the same SQL statements. Again, the two machines need some non-Oracle networking software to communicate.

Warning

Oracle can support many different types of networks and protocols. However, if you require communication between machines running Oracle software, you must install the Oracle SQL*Net software on all machines that need network access.

Whatever type of networking software and protocols you use to connect the machines (such as Transmission Control Protocol/Internet Protocol [TCP/IP]) for either the client/server or server/server setup mentioned previously, you must have the Oracle SQL*Net product to enable Oracle to interface with the networking protocol. SQL*Net supports most of the major networking protocols for both PC LANs (such as Internetwork Packet Exchange/Sequenced Packet Exchange [IPX/SPX]) and the largest mainframes (such as Systems Network Architecture [SNA]). Essentially, SQL*Net provides the software layer between Oracle and the networking software, providing seamless communication between an Oracle client machine (running SQL*Plus) and the database server, or between one database server and another.

You must install the SQL*Net software on both machines on top of the underlying networking software for both sides to talk to each other. SQL*Net software options enable a client machine supporting one networking protocol to communicate with another supporting a different protocol.

You don't need to change the application system software itself if the networking protocols or underlying networking software changes. You can make the changes transparently with the DBA, installing a different version of SQL*Net for the new network protocol.

Figure 8.2 shows the role of SQL*Net in a client/server environment with two server database machines.

Now that you have learned about the generalities of the Oracle architecture, let's take a moment to consider the specifics of the different types of files that Oracle uses to perform its processing. The following section discusses Oracle file types.

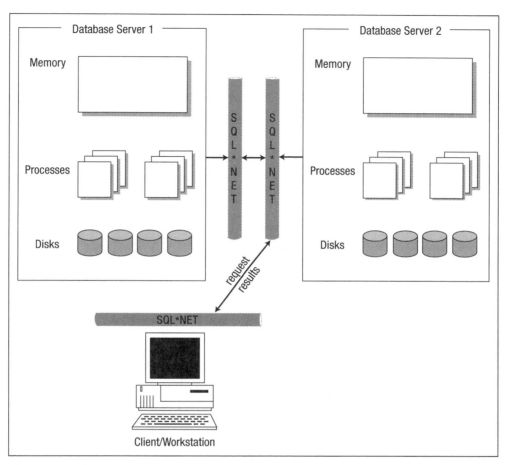

Figure 8.2
SQL*Net diagram in a client/server environment.

Considering Oracle's File Types

As you saw earlier in this chapter, Oracle uses three general types of files to construct and administer the database. The following sections discuss each of the different file types in greater detail.

Database Files

Database files hold the actual data and are typically the largest in size (from a few megabytes to many gigabytes). The other files (control files and redo logs) support the rest of the architecture. Depending on their sizes, the tables (and other objects) for all the user accounts can obviously go in one database file. However, such a construction isn't ideal, because it doesn't make the database structure very flexible. Issues such as controlling access to storage for different Oracle users, putting the database on different disk drives, or backing up and restoring just part of the database become significantly more complex when all the information resides within a single database file.

You must have at least one database file (adequate for a small or testing database), but usually, you'll have many more than one. In terms of accessing and using the data in the tables and other objects, the number (or location) of the files is immaterial. The database files are fixed in size and never grow bigger than the size at which they were created. As with a SQL Server, this is an important issue, because you must make sure that initially you create the files big enough to handle whatever you fill the files with.

Control Files

Any Oracle database must have at least one control file, although you typically have more than one to guard against loss. The control file records the name of the database, the date and time it was created, the location of the database and redo logs, and the synchronization information for the database. Oracle uses the synchronization information to ensure that all three sets of files are always in step. Every time you add a new database file or redo log file to the database, the information is recorded in the control files.

Redo Logs

Any database must have at least two redo logs. These are the journals for the database, recording all changes to the user objects or system objects. If any type of failure occurs, such as loss of one or more database files, you can use the changes recorded in the redo logs to bring the database to a consistent state without losing any committed transactions. Were a machine to crash or fail without losing data, Oracle could then apply the information in the redo logs automatically without intervention from the DBA. The SMON background process automatically reapplies the committed changes in the redo logs to the database files. Like the other files used by Oracle, the redo log files are fixed in size and never grow dynamically from the size at which they were created.

Online Redo Logs

The online redo logs are the two or more redo log files always in use while the Oracle instance is up and running. Changes you make are recorded to each of the redo logs in turn. When one is full, the other is written to. When the second one becomes full, the first is overwritten, and the cycle continues.

Offline/Archived Redo Logs

The offline or archived redo logs are exact copies of the online redo logs that have been filled. It's optional to ask Oracle to create these. Oracle creates them only when the database is running in **ARCHIVELOG** mode. If the database is running in **ARCHIVELOG** mode, the ARCH background process wakes up and copies the online redo log to the offline destination (typically another disk drive) once it becomes full. While this copying is in progress, Oracle uses the other online redo log. If you have a complete set of offline redo logs since the database was last backed up, you have a complete record of changes that have been made. You could then use this record to reapply the changes to the backup copy of the database files if one or more online database files are lost.

In general, particularly for critical business processes, it's a good idea to use Oracle's archiving features. If you use them together with Oracle's built-in backup support, the system will automatically retain what actions occurred before and after the backup, which can radically speed restorations in the event of a failure.

Other Supporting Files

When you start an Oracle instance (in other words, when the Oracle background processes are initiated and the memory structures allocated), the instance parameter file determines the sizes and modes of the database. This parameter file is known as the INIT.ORA file (the actual name of the file has the Oracle instance identifier appended to the file name). This is an ordinary text file containing parameters for which you can override the default settings. The DBA is responsible for creating and modifying the contents of this parameter file. On some Oracle platforms, a SGAPAD file is also created, which contains the starting memory address of the Oracle SGA.

No matter what platform you use, or how many of these files are present on the platform, all these files are important for the long-term usability of the Oracle database—deleting or otherwise corrupting one of these files may make the Oracle database unreadable, unupdateable, or both. However, the actual processing occurs within the Oracle system and user processes, which the following sections discuss in detail.

A sample INIT.ORA file can be found on the companion CD-ROM.

System And User Processes

The following sections discuss some of the Oracle system processes that must be running for the database to be useable, including the optional processes and the processes created for users connecting to the Oracle database. These sections are not, by any means, a definitive treatment of all the system processes in Oracle; rather, they explain the most important processes that *must* run for Oracle to work correctly.

Mandatory System Processes

The four Oracle system processes that must always be up and running for the database to be useable include database writer (DBWR), log writer (LGWR), system monitor (SMON), and process monitor (PMON).

The Database Writer (DBWR)

The database writer background process writes modified database blocks in the SGA to the database files. It reads only the blocks that have changed (for example, if the block contains a new record, a deleted record, or a changed record). These blocks are also called *dirty* blocks. The database writer writes out the least recently used blocks first. These blocks aren't necessarily written to the database when the transaction commits; the only thing that always happens on a commit is that the changes are recorded and written to the online redo log files. The database blocks will be written out later when there aren't enough buffers free in the SGA to read in a new block—that is, when the SGA's buffers fill, the Oracle processes will write out blocks to create space for the new, incoming blocks.

The Log Writer (LGWR)

The log writer process writes the entries in the SGA's redo buffer for one or more transactions to the online redo log files. For example, when a transaction commits, the log writer must write out the entries in the redo log buffer to the redo log files on disk before the process receives a message indicating that the commit was successful. Once committed, the changes are safe on disk even though the modified database blocks are still in the SGA's database buffer area waiting to be written out by DBWR. The SMON can always reapply the changes from the redo logs if the memory's most up-to-date copy of the database blocks is lost.

The System Monitor (SMON)

The system monitor process looks after the instance. If two transactions are both waiting for each other to release locks and neither of them can continue (known as a *deadlock* or *deadly embrace*), SMON detects the situation and sends one of the processes an error message indicating that a deadlock has occurred. SMON also releases temporary segments no longer in use by the user processes that caused them to be created.

During idle periods, SMON compacts the free-space fragments in the database files, making it easier and simpler for Oracle to allocate storage for new database objects or for existing database objects to grow.

In addition, SMON automatically performs recovery when the Oracle instance is first started up (if none of the files have been lost). You won't see a message indicating that instance recovery is occurring, but the instance might take longer to come up.

The Process Monitor (PMON)

The process monitor monitors the user processes. If any failure occurs with the user processes (for example, if the process is killed in the middle of a transaction), PMON automatically rolls back the work of the user process since the transaction started (anything since the last **COMMIT** or **ROLLBACK**). It releases any locks taken out and other system resources taken up by the failed process. PMON also monitors the dispatcher and shared server processes, which are part of the multithreaded server setup, and restarts them if they have died.

Optional System Processes

Besides the four mandatory system processes, you can initiate a number of optional system processes. The following sections describe the most common of these.

The Archiver Process (ARCH)

When the database is running in **ARCHIVELOG** mode and you've started the Archiver background process, it makes a copy of one of the online redo log files to the archive destination (the exact location is specified in an INIT.ORA parameter). In this way, you can have a complete history of changes made to the database files recorded in the offline and online redo logs. Just remember, there's no point in keeping the Archiver background process running if the database isn't running in **ARCHIVELOG** mode.

The Checkpoint Process (CKPT)

A checkpoint occurs when one of the online redo log files fills. Oracle will overwrite the checkpoint when one of the other online redo logs fills. If the redo log file is overwritten, the changes recorded in that file aren't available for reapplying in case of system failure. At a checkpoint, the modified database buffer blocks are written down to the relative safety of the database files on disk by the database writer background process. In effect, this means that you won't need the record of changes in the event of system failure with lost memory areas. After a checkpoint occurs, the redo log can be reused.

At a checkpoint, all the database file headers and redo log file headers are updated to record the fact that a checkpoint has occurred. The LGWR background process performs the actual updating task, which could be significant if a large number of database and redo log files exist. The entire database might have to wait for the checkpoint to complete before the redo logs can record further database changes. To reduce the time it takes for LGWR to update the database and redo log file headers, you can initiate the checkpoint process.

A checkpoint can occur at other times, such as when the entries in the redo log files reach a limit defined by the DBA. Such a construction is generally sensible in environments where most processing occurs during a specified block of time, and the database has time for other tasks at other times. In other words, the administrator might want to initiate a checkpoint at night or during the early morning hours, rather than letting the database reach a natural checkpoint during the day, when most database access is occurring.

Tip

Whether or not the CKPT background process is initiated, checkpointing still occurs when one of the redo log files fills.

The Recoverer Process (RECO)

You use the Recoverer background process when a failure in a distributed transaction has occurred (a transaction where two or more databases are updated) and one or more of the databases involved needs to either commit or roll back their changes. If initiated, the

Recoverer attempts to automatically commit or roll back the transaction on the local database at timed intervals in synchronization with the Recoverer processes on the other Oracle databases. And as a reminder, there's no point in keeping the Recoverer background process running if you're not using distributed transactions on the database.

The Lock Process (LCK)

Use the Lock background process in the parallel server setup of Oracle in which more than one instance is running against the same set of database files. The LCK processes running on all instances will synchronize locking between the instances. If a user connects to one instance and locks a row, the row remains locked for a user attempting to make a change on another instance. Other users can always query the rows regardless of how the rows are locked by other users.

You can initiate up to 10 LCK background processes to reduce the bottleneck of synchronizing locking, but one is usually more than enough. However, you shouldn't initiate the LCK background processes unless you're implementing a parallel server (multi-instance) setup of Oracle.

SQL*Net Listener

The SQL*Net listener is a process running on the machine that routes requests coming in from client machines through to the correct Oracle instance. It communicates with the underlying networking software to route requests to and from the database server and the client machine (whether that client machine is a machine running an Oracle tool or even another database server).

For example, the communications between a client machine running an Access 2000 front end on a PC with Windows 98 and a database server on a Unix machine with TCP/IP as the networking protocol would involve the following major steps:

1. The client machine sends the SQL statement execution request to the Unix database server machine.
2. The non-Oracle TCP/IP listener process picks up the request and recognizes it as a request for Oracle.
3. The request is sent to the Oracle SQL*Net listener, which routes the request to the correct Oracle instance on the machine. (The machine might be running many instances for many different databases.)
4. A process on the instance executes the statement.
5. The results are then sent back up the communications link to the client machine, using a similar process.

The SQL*Net listener isn't related to the Oracle instance itself, but rather is related systemwide and will process requests for all instances running on the machine. You can initiate more than one SQL*Net listener, but this is uncommon.

Considering User Processes

User processes logically consist of two halves: the Oracle server code, which translates and executes SQL statements and reads the database files and memory areas, and the tool-specific code, which is the executable code for the tool that's used. The server code is the same regardless of the tool that's executing the SQL statement—that is, the same steps are involved. The server code is sometimes known as the Oracle *kernel code*.

You can configure the user processes in Oracle three different ways, all of which could coexist for the same instance. These three configurations are single-task, dedicated server, or multithreaded server.

Single-Task Configuration

In the single-task configuration, the tool-specific code and database server code are both configured into one process running on the machine. Each connection to the database has one user process running on the machine. This is common on the virtual address extension (VAX) Virtual Memory System (VMS) platforms without a client/server environment. It isn't a typical configuration that you'll encounter when writing Access front ends for Oracle back ends, because the tool-specific code will run in its own process (the Access process) on the client machine.

Dedicated Server Processes

In the dedicated server configuration (also known as *two-task* or *running with shadow processes*), the two parts of a user process are implemented as two separate processes running on the machine. They communicate with each other using the machine's interprocess communication mechanisms. Each connection to the database has two processes running on the machine. The Oracle kernel software in one process is sometimes called the *shadow process*.

This configuration is common for Unix platforms, because the operating system can't (in some implementations of Unix) protect the Oracle code and memory areas from the application code. It's also common for client/server configurations in which the server code resides on the server machine and the tool-specific code runs on the client machine, with communication over a network. This, of course, is the way that the vast majority of your Windows applications will interact with the Oracle database. The way the two component parts of one logical process communicate is fundamentally the same as if one process were implemented on the same machine. However, the two halves of the logical process happen to reside on two different machines and communicate over the network using SQL*Net rather than the interprocess communication mechanisms of the operating system.

The dedicated server configuration can be wasteful, because memory is allocated to the shadow process and the number of processes that must be serviced on the machine increases, even when the user isn't making any database requests. The dedicated server (shadow process) will process requests only from one associated client process.

Multithreaded Server Configuration

The multithreaded server configuration enables one Oracle server process to perform work for many user processes. This overcomes the drawbacks of the dedicated server configuration. It reduces the number of processes running and the amount of memory used on the machine and can improve system performance. The multithreaded server introduces two new types of system processes that support this part of the architecture.

Using one of the shared server processes that comes as part of the multithreaded server configuration isn't appropriate when a user process is making many database requests (such as an export backup of the database); for that process, you could use a dedicated server. A mixture of both configurations can coexist.

Dispatchers

One or more dispatcher processes retrieves requests for the client processes from the SQL*Net listener and routes the request to one of the shared server processes. The SQL*Net listener is required for the multithreaded server configuration even if no networking is involved.

You must configure at least one dispatcher for each network protocol that's used to route requests to the instance. The number of dispatchers configured doesn't increase if the system load increases, because the dispatchers are only providing the routing. The actual work is done by the shared servers.

Tip

*The multithreaded server requires SQL*Net 2 or newer even if both the dispatcher and the user process are running on the same machine.*

Shared Servers

The shared servers provide the same functionality as the dedicated server processes and contain the Oracle server code that performs the work for the client. They can service requests from many different user processes. The actual shared server used might differ from one call to another, so no user process can monopolize any one particular shared server process. Oracle uses an area in the SGA for messaging between the different processes involved.

The number of shared server processes is automatically increased (or decreased to an initial number defined by the DBA) according to the system activity. Note, however, that although the number of shared servers is increased or decreased automatically, the number of dispatchers isn't.

Just as Oracle performs certain actions while managing server processes, it also manages memory in specific fashions. The following sections discuss how Oracle uses memory in detail.

Understanding How Oracle Uses Memory

In this section, you'll learn a little about how Oracle uses the computer's memory. Generally, the more real memory is available to Oracle, the quicker the system runs. Although these issues are significant for Oracle development, we'll really only touch on them here, with the presumption that you have other Oracle knowledge with which to flesh out these broad strokes. If you're using Oracle for your back end, it's likely that your company has an Oracle DBA whose job it is to manage the Oracle server process—if you run into trouble, you may wish to consult that person for assistance in connecting. However, understanding the memory usage of Oracle is important whether you are the front-end developer, the back-end DBA, or both. The most important area of memory for Oracle is the system global area (SGA), discussed in the next section.

System Global Area (SGA)

The system global area, sometimes known as the shared global area, is for data and control structures in memory that can be shared by all the Oracle background and user processes running on that instance. Each Oracle instance has its own SGA. In fact, the SGA and affiliated background processes are what define an instance. The SGA memory area is allocated when the instance is started, and Oracle flushes and deallocates the memory when it shuts the instance down.

The contents of the SGA are divided into three main areas: the database buffer cache, the shared pool area, and the redo cache. The size of each is controlled by parameters in the INIT.ORA file. The bigger you can make the SGA and the more of it that can fit into the machine's real memory (as opposed to virtual memory), the quicker your instance will run. Figure 8.3 shows the Oracle SGA in memory.

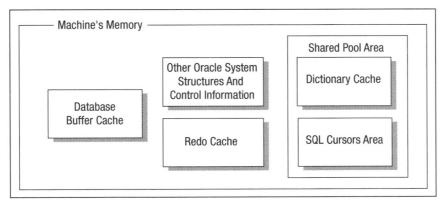

Figure 8.3
The Oracle SGA in the computer's memory.

Database Buffer Cache

The SGA's database buffer cache holds Oracle blocks that have been read in from the database files. When one process reads the blocks for a table into memory, all the processes for that instance can access these blocks.

If a process needs to access some data, Oracle checks to see if the block is already in this cache (thereby avoiding a disk read). If the Oracle block isn't in the buffer, it must be read from the database files into the buffer cache. The buffer cache must have a free block available before the data block can be read from the database files.

The Oracle blocks in the database buffer cache in memory are arranged with the most recently used at one end and the least recently used at the other. This list is constantly changing as the database is used. If data must be read into memory from the database files, the blocks at the least recently used end are written back to the database files first (if they've been modified). The DBWR process is the only process that writes the blocks from the database buffer cache to the database files.

As you might expect, the more database blocks your instance can hold in real memory, the quicker it will run.

Redo Cache

The online redo log files record all the changes made to user objects and system objects. Before the changes are written to the redo logs, Oracle stores them in the redo cache memory area. The entries in the redo log cache are written to the online redo logs when, for example, the cache becomes full or a transaction issues a commit.

The entries for more than one transaction can be included together in the same data writing to the disk as the redo log files. The LGWR background process is the only process that writes out entries from this redo cache to the online redo log files.

Shared Pool Area

The shared pool area of the SGA has two main components: the SQL area and the dictionary cache. You can alter the size of these two components only by changing the size of the entire shared pool area.

A SQL statement sent for execution to the database server must be parsed before it can execute. The SQL area of the SGA contains the binding information, runtime buffers, parse tree, and execution plan for all the SQL statements sent to the database server. Because the shared pool area is a fixed size, you might not see the entire set of statements that have been executed since the instance first came up; Oracle might have flushed out some statements to make room for others.

If a user executes a SQL statement, that statement takes up memory in the SQL area. If another user executes exactly the same statement on the same objects, Oracle doesn't need to reparse the second statement, because the parse tree and execution plan are already in the SQL area. This part of the architecture saves on reparsing overhead. The SQL area is also used to hold the parsed, compiled form of programming language/structured query language (PL/SQL) blocks, which can also be shared between user processes on the same instance.

Tip

Write all your SQL statements exactly the same way in application code (using procedures) to avoid reparsing overhead.

The dictionary cache in the shared pool area holds entries retrieved from the Oracle system tables, otherwise known as the Oracle data dictionary. The data dictionary is a set of tables located in the database files; because Oracle accesses these files often, it sets aside a separate area of memory to avoid disk input/output (I/O).

The cache itself holds a subset of the data from the data dictionary. It's loaded with an initial set of entries when the instance is first started, then populated from the database data dictionary as further information is required. The cache holds information about all the users, tables, and other objects, structure, security, storage, and so on. The data dictionary cache grows to occupy a larger proportion of memory within the shared pool area as needed, but the size of the shared pool area remains fixed.

In addition to the system global area, Oracle manages separate areas of memory for each user or server process. These areas, called process global areas, are discussed in the following section.

Process Global Area (PGA)

The process global area, sometimes called the *program global area* or PGA, contains data and control structures for one user or server process. One PGA is allocated for each user process (connection) to the database.

The actual contents of the PGA depend on whether the multithreaded server configuration is implemented, but it typically contains memory to hold the session's variables, arrays, some row results, and other information. If you're using the multithreaded server, some of the information that's usually held in the PGA is instead held in the common SGA.

The size of the PGA depends on the operating system used to run the Oracle instance, and once allocated, it remains the same. Memory used in the PGA doesn't increase according to the amount of processing performed in the user process. The DBA can control the size of the PGA by modifying some of the parameters in the instance parameter file INIT.ORA. For example, one of the parameters that DBAs most often change is the **SORT_AREA_SIZE** parameter.

The Oracle Programs

The Oracle server code mentioned previously is code that performs the same function regardless of which tool the front-end programs are using (such as SQL*Plus, Oracle Designer/2000,

Reports, Excel, and so on). On some platforms, the server code is loaded only once into the machine's memory, and all the processes using the instance can share it—even across instances (as long as you are running the same version of Oracle for both instances). This kernel code, also known as *reentrant code*, saves memory because it requires that only one copy of the code be loaded into memory.

Understanding Oracle Data Storage

You've already learned that database files are binary, fixed-size files on disk. However, it's worthwhile, if you're going to be working closely with Oracle databases, to understand a little more detail about the construction of the binary files themselves. In the following sections, you'll learn more about these constructions.

Understanding The Relationship Between Tablespaces And Database Files

For management, security, and performance reasons, the database is logically divided into one or more tablespaces that each contain one or more database files. A *tablespace* is a logical division of a database that contains one or more physical database files. A database file is always associated with only one tablespace.

Every Oracle database has a tablespace named **SYSTEM** to which Oracle allocates the very first file of the database. The **SYSTEM** tablespace is the default location of all objects when a database is first created. The simplest database setup is one database file in the **SYSTEM** tablespace (simple, but not recommended).

Typically, you create many tablespaces to partition the different parts of the database. For example, you might have one tablespace for tables, another to hold indexes, and so on, and each of these tablespaces would have one or more database files associated with them.

When you create objects that use storage in the database (such as tables), you should specify the tablespace location of the object as part of the **CREATE** statement for the object. Only system tables should occupy storage in the **SYSTEM** tablespace. The system tables are tables such as **tab$**, **col$**, **ind$**, **fet$**, and other internal tables. Objects, such as synonyms and views, don't take up storage within the database other than the storage in the data dictionary table for their definitions, along with the definitions for all other types of objects.

Tablespaces can be added, dropped, taken offline and online, and associated with additional database files. By adding another file to a tablespace, you increase the size of the tablespace and, therefore, the database itself. However, you can't drop the **SYSTEM** tablespace; doing so would destroy the database because it contains the system tables. You also can't take the **SYSTEM** tablespace offline.

Tablespaces, along with other storage objects, are all placed within *segments*. The following section explains segments.

Understanding Segments

A *segment* is a generic name given to any object that occupies storage in the database files. Some examples of segments are table segments (data segments), index segments, rollback segments, temporary segments, and the cache (bootstrap) segment. A segment uses a number of Oracle blocks in the same tablespace (although the blocks themselves can be in different files that make up the tablespace).

Extents And Their Composition

The storage for any object on the database is allocated in a number of blocks that must be contiguous in the database files. These contiguous blocks are known as *extents*. For example, when a table is first created using default settings, five Oracle blocks are allocated to the table for the very first extent (otherwise known as the initial extent). As rows are inserted and updated into the table, the five blocks fill with data. When the last block has filled and new rows are inserted, the database automatically allocates another set of five blocks for the table, and the new rows are inserted into the new set of blocks. This allocating of additional storage (additional extents) continues until no more free space is available in the tablespace. The table starts with the one initial extent and is then allocated other secondary (or next) extents. The blocks for an extent must be contiguous within the database files.

Once an extent is allocated to a segment (table), these blocks can't be used by any other database object, even if all the rows in the table are deleted. The table must be dropped or truncated to release the storage allocated to the table. The exception to this is *rollback segments*, which can dynamically release storage that was allocated to them.

The Lowest Level Of Construction: Oracle Blocks

Oracle "formats" the database files into a number of Oracle blocks when they're first created—making it easier for the relational database management system (RDBMS) software to manage the files and easier to read data into the memory areas. These blocks are usually 1K (the default for Windows NT systems), 2K (the default for most Unix machines and VAX VMS), 4K (the default for IBM mainframes), or larger. For a 50MB database file, there would be 25,600 Oracle blocks, assuming a block size of 2K (50MB/2K). The block size should be a multiple of the operating system block size (a figure that represents how the operating system stores data onto disk media). Regardless of the block size, not all of the block is available for holding data, because Oracle takes up some space to manage the contents of the block. This block header has a minimum size, but it can grow.

These Oracle blocks are the smallest unit of storage in the Oracle environment. Increasing the Oracle block size can improve performance, but you should do this only when the database is first created, because changing block size later can corrupt or even destroy the database. In fact, some installations of Oracle don't even provide you with the opportunity to increase block size after the database is created.

When you first create a database, it uses some of the blocks within the first file, and the rest of the blocks are free. In the data dictionary, Oracle maintains a list of the free blocks for each data file in each tablespace.

Each Oracle block is numbered sequentially for each database file, starting at 1. Two blocks can have the same block address if they're in different database files.

Warning
Again, as just noted, it's a very bad idea to modify the Oracle block size once you've created the database. Doing so can corrupt or destroy the data within your database.

Understanding ROWIDs

The **ROWID** is a unique database-wide physical address for every row on every table. Once assigned (when the row is first inserted into the database), it never changes until the row is deleted or the table is dropped.

The **ROWID** consists of the following three components, the combination of which uniquely identifies the physical storage location of the row:

♦ Oracle database file number, which contains the block with the row

♦ Oracle block address, which contains the row

♦ The row within the block (because each block can hold many rows)

The **ROWID** is used internally in indexes as a quick means of retrieving rows with a particular key value. Application developers also use it in SQL statements as a quick way to access a row once they know the **ROWID**.

Free Space And Automatic Compaction

When a database file is first created or added to a tablespace, all the blocks within that file are empty blocks that have never been used. As time goes by, the blocks within a database file are used by a segment (table), or they remain free blocks. Oracle tracks the file's free blocks in a list in the data dictionary. As you create and drop tables, the free space becomes fragmented, with free space in different parts of the database file. When the free blocks are scattered in this way, Oracle has no way to automatically bring the free storage together.

When two fragments of free space are physically next to each other in the database file, the two smaller fragments can be compacted together into one larger fragment, which is recorded in the free space list. This compacting reduces the overhead when Oracle actually needs the free space (when a table wants to allocate another extent of a certain size, for example). The SMON background process performs this automatic compaction.

Understanding Some Of The System Database Objects

Now that you've learned how Oracle constructs the database and its components, it's worthwhile to learn more about some of the system objects that Oracle uses to implement the construction. The following sections discuss some of the system objects that support the workings of the architecture and, in turn, provide the user or administrator with information about the structure of the database.

The Data Dictionary

The first tables created on any database are the system tables, also known as the Oracle data dictionary. These tables are owned by the first Oracle user account that's created automatically—that is, by the user SYS. The system tables record information about the structure of the database and the objects within it, and Oracle accesses them when it needs information about the database or every time it executes a data definition language (DDL) or data manipulation language (DML) statement. It's important to note that these tables are never directly updated. However, updates to them occur in the background whenever a DDL statement is executed.

The core data dictionary tables hold normalized information that's cryptic to understand, so Oracle provides a set of views to make the information in the core system tables more meaningful. You can use the following command to access the names of more than 170 of the views in the data dictionary:

```
SELECT * FROM DICT
```

Oracle requires the information in the data dictionary tables to parse any SQL statement. The information is cached in the data dictionary area of the shared pool in the SGA. Because the very first tablespace created is the **SYSTEM** tablespace, the data dictionary tables use storage in the database files associated with the **SYSTEM** tablespaces.

Rollback Segments

Whenever you change data in Oracle, the change must be either committed or reversed. If a change is reversed, or *rolled back*, the contents of the data block are restored back to the original state before the change. Rollback segments are system-type objects that support this reversing process. Whenever you make any kind of change to either application tables or system tables, a rollback segment automatically holds the previous version of the data that's being modified, so the old version of the data is available if a rollback is required.

If other users want to see the data while the change is pending, they always have access to the previous version from the rollback segment. They're provided with a *read-consistent* version of the data. Once the change is committed, the modified version of the data is available. Keep a few important things in mind when considering rollback segments:

♦ Rollback segments are always owned by the user SYS, and no Oracle user can access them for viewing.

♦ Rollback segments use storage in the same way as other segments in terms of extents. With a rollback segment, however, you must initially allocate a minimum of two extents instead of only one.

♦ The first rollback segment is created automatically when the database is first created and has a name of **SYSTEM**; it uses storage in the first tablespace, which also has a name of **SYSTEM**.

Warning
*The fact that Oracle uses the same name for three different types of objects can get confusing; the first tablespace is called **SYSTEM**, the first rollback segment is called **SYSTEM**, and one of the first Oracle accounts created also is called **SYSTEM**. They're different types of objects, so don't confuse them.*

Temporary Segments

Temporary segments use storage in the database files to provide a temporary work area for intermediate stages of SQL processing and for large sort operations. Oracle creates temporary segments on the fly, and they are automatically deleted when the SMON background process no longer needs them. If only a small working area is required, Oracle doesn't create a temporary segment, but instead uses a part of the PGA memory as a temporary work area.

The following operations might cause Oracle to create a temporary segment:

♦ Creating an index

♦ Using the **ORDER BY, DISTINCT**, or **GROUP BY** clause in a **SELECT** statement

♦ Using the set operator **UNION, INTERSECT**, or **MINUS**

♦ Creating joins between tables

♦ Using some subqueries

The DBA can control which tablespaces contain the temporary segments on a user-by-user basis. However, Oracle automatically allocates and manages certain types of segments on its own. One of these segments is the bootstrap segment, discussed in the following section.

Bootstrap/Cache Segment

A bootstrap or cache segment is a special type of object on the database that's used to perform an initial load of the data dictionary cache in the shared pool area of the SGA. Oracle uses the cache segment only when the instance first starts and doesn't use it again until the instance restarts. Once the segment is used to perform the initial load of the data dictionary cache, the remainder of the cache in memory is steadily populated as statements are executed against the database.

Now that you have learned some of the fundamentals of Oracle databases, and some of the issues you must consider when creating those databases, its time to move on to working with the actual data within the database. The following sections discuss some of the specific issues that you must keep in mind when working with Oracle back ends from your Access front end.

Oracle Data Management Considerations

Although you've spent quite a bit of time in recent chapters learning how to manage data in your Access databases, and even learned a little bit about how to manage data in SQL Server databases in the preceding chapter, some differences occur when dealing with Oracle. The following sections discuss some of these considerations in the Oracle environment to help you better manage your development.

Transactions And Using The Commit And Rollback Actions

Database changes aren't saved until the user explicitly decides that the **INSERT**, **UPDATE**, and **DELETE** statements should be made permanent. Up until that point, the changes are in a pending status, and any failures, such as a machine crash, will reverse the changes.

A *transaction* is an atomic unit of work comprising one or more SQL statements; it begins when the user first connects to the database and ends when a **COMMIT** or **ROLLBACK** statement is issued. Upon a **COMMIT** or **ROLLBACK**, the next transaction automatically begins. All the statements within a transaction are either all saved (committed) or all reversed (rolled back).

Committing a transaction makes changes in the entire transaction to the database permanent; once committed, the changes can't be reversed. Rolling back reverses all the inserts, updates, deletes in the transaction; again, once rolled back, these changes can't then be committed. Internally, the process of committing means writing out the changes recorded in the SGA's redo log buffer cache to the online redo log files on disk. If this disk I/O succeeds, the application receives a message indicating a successful commit. (The text of the message changes from one tool to another.) The DBWR background process can write out the actual Oracle data blocks in the SGA's database buffer cache at a later time. If the system should crash, Oracle can automatically reapply the changes from the redo logs files even if the Oracle data blocks weren't written back to the database files before the failure.

Tip

*DDL statements such as **CREATE TABLE** will automatically issue a **COMMIT**, even if the DDL statement itself fails.*

Oracle also implements statement-level rollback. If a single statement fails during a transaction, the entire statement will fail. In other words, an **INSERT** statement for 1,000 rows will insert either all 1,000 rows or none at all. If a statement does fail within a transaction, the rest of the statements in the transaction are still in a pending state and must be committed or rolled back.

If a user process terminates abnormally (the process is killed, for example), the PMON background process automatically rolls back changes. Any changes that the process had committed up to the point of failure remain committed, and only the changes for the current transaction are rolled back.

All locks held by the transaction are automatically released when the transaction commits or rolls back or when the PMON background process rolls back the transaction. In addition, other system resources (such as rollback segments) are released for other transactions to use.

Savepoints enable you to set up markers within a transaction so that you have the option of rolling back just part of the work performed in the transaction. You can use savepoints in long and complex transactions to provide the reversing option for certain statements. However, this causes extra overhead on the system to perform the work for a statement and then reverse the changes; usually, changes in the logic can produce a more optimal solution. When Oracle performs a rollback to a savepoint, the rest of the statements in the transaction remain in a pending state and must be committed or rolled back. Oracle releases the locks taken by these statements that were rolled back.

Data Integrity

As you've learned, data integrity is about enforcing data validation rules—such as checking that a percentage amount is between 0 and 100—to ensure that invalid data doesn't get into your tables. Historically, these rules were enforced by the application programs themselves (and the same rules were checked repeatedly in different programs). In many cases, this will still be the most efficient way to enforce rules—it makes no sense, for example, to generate network traffic if the application itself can determine the invalidity of the data.

However, Oracle enables you to define and store data validation rules against the database objects to which they relate. The major benefit of such a construction is that you need to code them only once—which ensures that they're enforced whenever any kind of change is made to the table, regardless of which tool issues the **INSERT**, **UPDATE**, or **DELETE** statement. This checking takes the form of *integrity constraints* and *database triggers*.

Understanding Integrity Constraints

Integrity constraints enforce business rules at the database level by defining a set of checks for the tables in your system. These checks are automatically enforced whenever you issue an **INSERT**, **UPDATE**, or **DELETE** statement against the table. If any of the constraints are violated, the **INSERT**, **UPDATE**, or **DELETE** statement is rolled back. The other statements within the transaction remain in a pending state and can be committed or rolled back according to application logic.

Because integrity constraints are checked at the database level, they're performed regardless of where the **INSERT, UPDATE,** or **DELETE** statement originated—whether it was an Oracle or a non-Oracle tool. Defining checks using these constraints is also quicker than performing the same checks using SQL. In addition, the information provided by declaring constraints is used by the Oracle optimizer to make better decisions about how to run a statement against the table. The Oracle Designer/2000 product can also use constraints to automatically generate code in the front-end programs to provide an early warning to the user of any errors.

The types of integrity constraints that you can set up on a table are **NOT NULL, PRIMARY KEY, UNIQUE, FOREIGN KEY, CHECK,** and indexes. Most of these are consistent with their similar definitions in the Access 2000 product. In general, constraints over Oracle are completely consistent with constraints over SQL Server 7, because both are fully ANSI SQL-92 compliant. Because we discussed constraints in Chapter 7, and I will revisit them at length in several later chapters, I will not discuss them again here.

Database Triggers

A database trigger is a PL/SQL block that you can define to automatically execute for **INSERT, UPDATE,** and **DELETE** statements against a table. You can define the trigger to execute once for the entire statement or once for every row that's inserted, updated, or deleted. For any one table, you can define database triggers for up to 12 events. However, each event can have many different database triggers.

A database trigger also can call database procedures that are written in PL/SQL. Unlike database triggers, procedures on the database are stored in a compiled form. For this reason, you should put the longer code segments into a procedure, then call the procedure from the database trigger.

In addition to implementing complex business rules, checking, and defaulting, you can use database triggers to insert, update, and delete other tables. An example of this use is providing an auditing facility where an audit trail is automatically created in an audit table whenever a row is changed on a table. Without database triggers, this function would be implemented in the front-end programs that make the change to the database; however, someone bypassing the code in the front-end programs (using SQL*Plus, for example) wouldn't go through the checks and processing defined.

Database triggers differ from constraints in that they enable you to embed SQL statements within them, whereas constraints don't. Whenever possible, use constraints for checking; they're quicker than using database triggers.

System-Level Privileges

Each Oracle user defined on the database can have one or more of over 80 system-level privileges. These privileges control on a very fine level the right to execute SQL commands. The DBA assigns system privileges either directly to Oracle user accounts or to roles. The roles are then assigned to the Oracle user accounts.

For example, before you can create a trigger on a table (even if you own the table as an Oracle user), you must have the system privilege called **CREATE TRIGGER** either assigned to your Oracle user account or assigned to a role given to the user account.

The **CREATE SESSION** privilege is another frequently used system-level privilege. To make a connection to the database, an Oracle account must have the **CREATE SESSION** system-level privilege assigned to it. This gives the account the privilege to make connections to the database.

Object-Level Privileges

Object-level privileges provide the capability to perform a particular type of action (select, insert, update, delete, and so on) on a specific object. The owner of the object has full control over the object and can perform any action on it; he or she doesn't need to have object-level privileges assigned. In fact, the owner of the object is the Oracle user who grants object-level privileges to others.

For example, if the user who owns a table wants another user to be able to select and insert rows from his or her table (but not update or delete), the owner grants the **SELECT** and **INSERT** object-level privileges on that table to the other user. You can assign object-level privileges either directly to users or to roles that are then assigned to one or more Oracle user accounts.

However, in general you should administer privileges through a level of indirection. Rather than assigning them directly to users, you should use *roles* to specify privileges. Roles are conceptually similar to Access *groups*. The following section discusses roles in detail.

Users And Roles

A *role* is a type of object that you can use to simplify the administration of system- and object-level privileges. Instead of assigning privileges directly to user accounts, you can assign the privileges to roles that are then assigned to users. (The metaphor of roles and users is similar to Windows NT Groups and Users.)

Roles are essentially groupings of system and object-level privileges. They make the administration of privileges much easier, because you can configure the privileges for a particular type of user once and assign these privileges to a role. When a user needs that set of privileges, you can use a single role assignment command to set that user up. Without the use of roles, you'd need to issue many commands for each of the different privileges required.

In addition, you can set up different roles with the correct privileges even though you don't yet have Oracle user accounts that require these assignments. You can assign a role to another role, building hierarchies of roles. Also, you can protect a role with a password that the user must supply when he or she wants to enable the role.

As already discussed, a physical database could contain many Oracle user accounts that are protected by passwords. You must supply the username and password regardless of which tool you use to gain access to the database. Roles aren't the same as Oracle users; you can't connect to the database by supplying a role name and password.

Auditing

Oracle's auditing mechanism provides three types of audit trails. One audit trail (the *system audit trail*) tracks which system privileges are used. *Statement auditing* keeps track of which SQL statements are used without regard to specific objects. *Object-level auditing* audits access to specific objects. You can initiate these audit trails to track when statements succeed, when they fail, or both, so all accesses are audited. You can use auditing to keep track of anyone attempting to break into the system.

In addition, you can set up how all the different types of auditing record the entries. The audit trail can record one entry per operation regardless of how many attempts are made on the operation during the connection session. Alternatively, request one entry in the audit trail for every attempt (successful or not) on the operation during the session.

If it's set up and enabled, the audit trail keeps the audit information in a data dictionary table owned by the user SYS. This table indicates the operation being audited, the user performing the operation, and the date and time of the operation. Oracle provides a set of data dictionary views to make the information in the dictionary audit table more meaningful. Although the audit trail is implemented in a data dictionary table, it keeps the insertion of rows in the audit trail even if the user rolls back his transaction. The DBA can clear out or archive the audit trail periodically.

One of the most important tasks in data management is protecting not only the integrity, but also the existence of the data within your systems. Many enterprises find that they need to split their databases up into multiple physical components—for security, for protection from failure, or for enterprise-specific concerns. Oracle supports *distributed databases* to help address this issue. The following section addresses distributed databases in detail.

Distributed Databases

A distributed database is one logical database that's implemented as two or more physical databases on either the same machine or separate machines. In some cases, the separate machines could be right next to each other—in other cases, they could be thousands of miles away. The system's designers decide where the tables should physically reside.

Each physical database has its own instance and sets of files, and the machines on which the databases reside are connected over a network. The location of tables can be made transparent to the application by using database links and synonyms.

Oracle enables a transaction and even a single statement to access tables on two or more distributed databases. This doesn't necessitate any more coding by the application developers.

A *distributed transaction* modifies tables on more than one database, then expects all the changes to be committed. With any kind of failure, all the changes on all the databases are rolled back. A distributed transaction can involve many Oracle databases and only one non-Oracle database. The Oracle two-phase commit mechanism controls the synchronization of commits across all databases and can automatically roll back changes on all the databases if any kind of failure occurred. The RECO background process synchronizes this operation.

In addition to this functionality, Oracle also provides the capability to replicate tables from one database to others. This is called *creating a snapshot* of the table.

You create a snapshot with the **CREATE SNAPSHOT** command on the database where you want to have the copy of the data. The Oracle RDBMS software automatically sends down any changes made to the master copy of the table to each of the snapshot copies at user-defined intervals without any manual intervention. The snapshot mechanism enables you to make updates to the snapshot copy of the table, in which case the changes are sent from the copy table back to the master table.

Needless to say, the Oracle architecture is significantly more complex than the Access architecture—as you would expect it to be to support the number and volume of transactions it is intended for. Understanding the steps a SQL statement proceeds through in this more complex environment is therefore useful. The following section describes those steps in detail.

Following A SQL Statement Through The Architecture

Before we move on to a consideration of the Access connection to the Oracle back end, it's worthwhile to consider the steps a typical SQL statement might go through to be executed on the Oracle machine. The discussion uses a simple scenario with both the client and the Oracle database server machine on Windows NT Server, without any networking involved. Using a single-task configuration makes tracking the steps a little simpler. However, the knowledge that you've put together in previous chapters should help you recognize some of the places where network communications would be appropriate.

The following process shows some of the steps involved in executing SQL statements:

1. The user executes the client and enters the Oracle username and password.
2. Oracle validates the username and password against the data dictionary and sends a response to the user process to indicate connection.
3. The user enters a **SELECT** statement.

4. Oracle must translate the **SELECT** statement before it executes it, so the Oracle parser and optimizer are called. If any user has issued *exactly* the same statement before, the parsed version might be in the shared pool area in memory. In such a case, Oracle uses the parsed version, so no extra parsing is done for this statement.

5. To translate the **SELECT** statement, Oracle must obtain the names of the objects, privileges, and other information from the data dictionary. The data dictionary cache area in the shared pool in the SGA doesn't have the information on the tables, so parsing of the **SELECT** statement is suspended while the information is read in.

6. Oracle runs a recursive SQL statement (a system-generated statement) to load information about the objects from the data dictionary tables in the database files into the data dictionary cache in memory.

7. Parsing of the original user **SELECT** statement resumes, and Oracle constructs an optimization plan to control the way the statement runs.

8. The statement accesses a table. If you assume the Oracle blocks for the table aren't in the database buffer cache in the SGA, the required Oracle blocks are then read in from the database files and held in the cache area of the SGA. (If they're already in the cache, Oracle simply moves on to Step 9.)

9. Oracle runs the statement and returns the results to the user.

Now let's consider what happens when the user then issues an **UPDATE** statement to modify some of the fields on the rows he or she has just selected. Oracle will, in such a case, perform the following steps:

1. Because the data dictionary cache already has the information about the table in memory, no more recursive SQL is generated (assuming that the information hasn't been flushed out by another process requiring space in the cache area). Also, the Oracle blocks for the table are in the database buffer cache, so you won't do another disk I/O to read these blocks in.

2. Oracle locks the rows to be updated.

3. Before Oracle makes the **UPDATE**, information about the old state of the blocks is recorded in a rollback segment, and the original version of the values is also recorded in the redo buffers cache.

4. Oracle updates the rows and records the new version of the values in the redo buffer cache in the SGA.

5. The user issues the **COMMIT** command to make the change permanent to the database.

6. Oracle records an entry indicating a commit in the redo buffer cache, and the old, new, and commit entry are all flushed down to the online redo log (whichever one is the current one in use).

7. The rollback segment is released (but not overwritten) for other processes to use.

8. Oracle releases the locks on the table.

9. The user receives a commit successful message (the exact wording of this message varies from tool to tool).

10. If the user issues a **ROLLBACK** instead of a **COMMIT**, the old versions of the changed values are restored back to the Oracle data blocks from the rollback segment. Oracle also writes an entry to the redo buffer cache indicating that a rollback was performed.

Creating A Data Source Name (DSN)

As you know, the first step before you can connect to any data source that isn't an Access data source is to locate it and make sure drivers for connection are present on the client machine. Although Active Data Objects (ADOs) let you connect to a data source without defining a DSN (as you saw in previous chapters), it's still worthwhile to create the data source in the ODBC administrator.

As you saw in Chapter 7, ODBC data sources are set up in the ODBC administrator. Depending on your installation, the ODBC administrator could be a standalone application, or it could appear as a Control Panel icon. It enables you to create, modify, and delete data sources and to obtain information about existing drivers. Remember that a data source is simply a user-definable name that stores settings that can be used to access a back end located on a particular server using a specified driver. Figure 8.4 shows the Drivers tab within the ODBC administrator. Note the existence of two Microsoft-designed Oracle drivers in the figure. Your installation may differ.

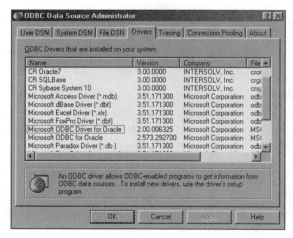

Figure 8.4
The Drivers tab within the ODBC administrator showing the Oracle drivers.

To define a new data source, change back to the User DSN tab and click on the Add button in the ODBC Administrator dialog box. The Create New Data Source dialog box, where you must select the name of the driver that the data source will use, will appear. In this case, we're opting to use the Oracle8 drivers provided by Oracle, as shown in Figure 8.5.

After you select a data source and click on Finish, you're shown another dialog, which varies depending on which driver you've selected. It enables you to define specific information about the data source that you're creating. An example is the Oracle8 ODBC Driver Setup dialog box shown in Figure 8.6.

As you can see, the Oracle8 ODBC Driver Setup dialog box enables you to specify information, such as the data source name, a description of the data source, and the network name of the Oracle database to connect to.

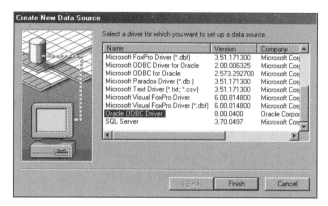

Figure 8.5
The Create New Data Source dialog box after the selection of the Oracle drivers.

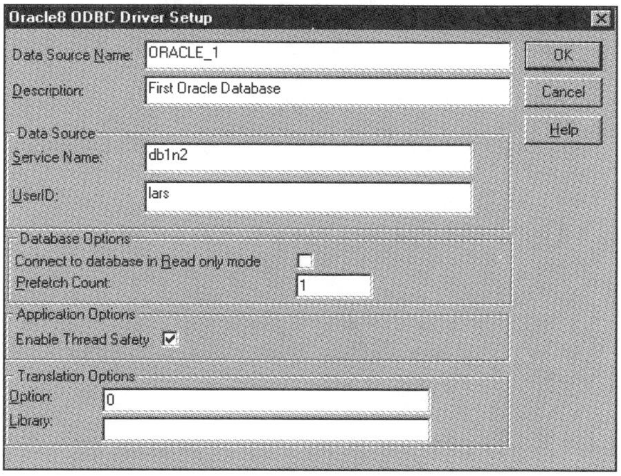

Figure 8.6
The Oracle8 ODBC Driver Setup dialog box.

Connecting To The Database

No additional configuration is required to connect to an ODBC data source from Visual Basic for Applications (VBA) (except through the ODBC administrator). Any drivers and data sources installed and configured using the ODBC administration program are accessible. If you're using DAO, the **Database** object is used to establish connections through its **OpenDatabase** method. As you've learned, the **OpenDatabase** method takes four arguments, three of which apply only to local desktop databases:

♦ *Database name parameter*—An empty string for ODBC data sources.

♦ *Open exclusive Boolean parameter*—Always set to false for ODBC data sources.

♦ *Read-only Boolean parameter*—Always set to false for ODBC data sources.

♦ *Connect string parameter*—Contains the ODBC connect string. The string includes the word "ODBC;", the data source name, user ID, password, and any additional database-specific parameters.

To connect to Oracle, the connect string requires no special parameters. The code fragment shown here uses values from a generic ODBC login form to build a connect string:

```
Private Sub ConnectWithDAO()
  Dim dbOracle As Database
  Dim szConnect As String

  szConnect = "ODBC;DSN=" & lstDSNs.Text & ";" & "UID=" & _
    txtID.Text & ";" & "PWD=" & txtPassword.Text & ";"
  Set dbOracle = OpenDatabase("", False, False, szConnect)
  ' Do work here
End Sub
```

The connect string from this example might look something like the following:

```
"ODBC;DSN=ORACLE_1;UID=lars;PWD=kimba;"
```

This code looks pretty similar when you use it with ADO, as shown in the following code:

```
Sub cmdOpenRecordset_Click()
  Dim cnOracle As Connection
  Dim rsOracle As Recordset

  Set cnOracle = New Connection
  With cnOracle
    .Provider = "MSORAOLE"
    .ConnectionString = "ODBC;DSN=" & lstDSNs.Text & ";" & "UID=" & _
      txtID.Text & ";" & "PWD=" & txtPassword.Text & ";"
    .Open
```

```
    End With
    Set rsOracle = New Recordset
    rsOracle.Open "SELECT StudentID FROM Students", cnOracle, _
        adOpenKeyset, adLockPessimistic
End Sub
```

Using Create Snapshot With Oracle

The primary means of retrieving results from an ODBC data source is the Snapshot-type **Recordset** object. This **Recordset** object is created using the **OpenRecordset** method of the **Database** object. As you've learned previously, the **OpenRecordset** method takes a series of arguments, one of which lets you specify the **Recordset** type—in this case, **dbOpenSnapshot** is the constant to pass. Additionally, you can pass a SQL **SELECT** statement or other query definition, and a numeric constant used to control processing of the SQL. Unless the application needs to be portable to different RDBMSs, this numeric constant should be set to **dbSQLPassThrough**, which sends the statement directly to the server for processing. This mode allows the developer to use the native syntax of the RDBMS, and it prevents the local Microsoft Access engine from attempting to parse and process the SQL. (As you've seen in previous chapters, this is known as the ODBC Direct model.) The following code in the **OpenOracleODBCDirect** procedure provides a simple example of the use of the **OpenRecordset** method to create a snapshot against an Oracle database (note that **dbOracle** must be defined before this routine is called):

```
Private Sub OpenOracleODBCDirect()
    '  Other code to open the workspace and connect to
    '  the database must come first

    Dim dsContacts As Recordset
    Dim rsString as String

    rsString = "SELECT a.last_name, a.first_name, b.phone_nbr " & _
        "FROM individual a, phone b " & _
        "WHERE a.ID = b.IndividualID(+) " & _
        "ORDER BY 1, 2"
    Set dsContacts = dbOracle.OpenRecordset(rsString, dbOpenSnapshot, _
        dbSQLPassThrough)
End Sub
```

The example assumes that the **Database** object has already connected to the data source. Note that if **dbSQLPassThrough** isn't specified, a syntax error results, because the local Access engine attempts to parse the SQL and doesn't recognize the Oracle-specific outer join syntax.

After applying the SQL and creating the resultset, numerous methods can be applied to position the record pointer in the cursor. The **MoveFirst**, **MoveLast**, **MoveNext**, and **MovePrevious** methods are the most commonly used—you've learned about them in previous chapters.

Using The ODBC Application Programming Interface (API) From VBA With Oracle

When working with Oracle data sources, it's possible that you may want to use the ODBC API directly (although you're generally better served using ADO). Doing so opens numerous possibilities, including the creation of a truly portable client application.

A small subset of the ODBC API can be used to provide transaction control in Access applications accessing ODBC data sources. The ODBC API functions shown in Table 8.1 provide access to all functions needed to connect, apply transactions through embedded SQL, and roll back or commit them, as needed.

Table 8.1   ODBC API declarations for Visual Basic.

Function	Description
SQLAllocConnect	Allocates memory for a connection handle within the environment returned from **SQLAllocEnv**.
SQLAllocEnv	Allocates memory for an environment handle and initializes the ODBC call-level interface for use by an application. An application must call **SQLAllocEnv** before calling any other ODBC function.
SQLAllocStmt	Allocates memory for a statement handle and associates the statement handle with the connection returned from **SQLAllocConnect**. An application must call **SQLAllocStmt** before submitting SQL statements.
SQLDisconnect	Closes the connection associated with a specific connection handle.
SQLDriverConnect	An alternative to the **SQLConnect** function. **SQLDriverConnect** supports data sources that require more connection information than the three arguments in **SQLConnect** dialog boxes to prompt the user for all connection information and data sources that aren't defined in the ODBC.INI file or Registry.
SQLExecDirect	Executes a preparable statement using the current values of the parameter marker variables if any parameters exist in the statement. **SQLExecDirect** is the fastest way to submit a SQL statement for one-time execution.
SQLFreeConnect	Releases a connection handle and frees all memory associated with that handle.
SQLFreeEnv	Releases an environment handle and frees all memory associated with that handle.

(continued)

Table 8.1   ODBC API declarations for Visual Basic *(continued)*.

Function	Description
SQLFreeStmt	Releases a statement handle and frees all memory associated with that handle.
SQLSetConnectOption	Sets options that govern aspects of connections. For example, the **SQLAutocommit** option can be set with this function.
SQLTransact	Requests a **COMMIT** or **ROLLBACK** operation for all active operations on all statements associated with a connection. **SQLTransact** can also request that a **COMMIT** or **ROLLBACK** operation be performed for all connections associated with an environment.

The companion CD-ROM contains the odbc_api.bas module, which includes the definitions for these functions and the constants they use for execution.

Using The ODBC API Calls

Assume for the moment that you wanted to disable the SQL **AUTOCOMMIT** function. After establishing a connection for retrieving results with the **OpenDatabase** method, the application should establish a second connection to the database using the API functions— for applying transactions. After establishing this connection, **SQLSetConnectOption** should be used to disable **AUTOCOMMIT**. The following listing shows how all this might be accomplished:

```
Private Sub OpenOracleWithSQLAPI()
  Dim hEnv As Long
  Dim hDBc As Long
  Dim szConnectString As String
  Dim iError As Integer
  Dim hWnd As Integer
  Dim iLenCSOut As Integer
  Dim szCSOut As String * 254

  szConnectString = "ODBC;DSN=ORACLE_1;UID=lars;PWD=kimba;"
  hWnd = frmMDIChild.hWnd
  iError = SQLAllocEnv(hEnv)              ' Allocate environment
  iError = SQLAllocConnect(hEnv, hDBc)   ' Allocate connection

  ' Load driver & connect to ODBC data source
  iError = SQLDriverConnect(hDBc, hWnd, szConnectString, SQL_NTS, _
      szCSOut, 254, iLenCSOut, SQL_DRIVER_NOPROMPT)

  ' Disable autocommit
  iError = SQLSetConnectOption(hDBc, SQL_AUTOCOMMIT, 0)
  ' Invoke SQL statements now...
End Sub
```

In practice, the connect string wouldn't be hard-coded and the return value of each function should be checked.

Applying A Transaction Using Embedded SQL

Once a connection has been established, the application can apply transactions using **SQLExecDirect** after allocating a statement handle with **SQLAllocStmt**. **SQLTransact** can then be used to commit or roll back a transaction based on the return value of **SQLExecDirect**. After applying the transaction, the application should call **SQLFreeStmt** to free the resources allocated to the statement handle. The following code shows an example of the calls to these functions:

```
Public Sub InvokeSQLAgainstOracle()
  Dim hStmt As Long

  iError = SQLAllocStmt(hDBc, hStmt)            ' Allocate a statement handle
  For i = 0 To iStmts
    iError = SQLExecDirect(hStmt, szSQL(i), SQL_NTS)      ' Apply SQL
    If iError Then                              ' Rollback transaction
      iNextErr = SQLTransact(hEnv, hDBc, SQL_ROLLBACK)
      Exit For
    End If
  Next i
  If (iError = 0) Then                          ' Commit transaction
    iError = SQLTransact(hEnv, hDBc, SQL_COMMIT)
  End If
  iError = SQLFreeStmt(hStmt, SQL_DROP)
End Sub
```

The sample code assumes that the environment and connection handles, **hEnv** and **hDBc**, are valid and connected to the data source, and that **szSQL** is an array of **iStmts** SQL statements. If any statement in the transaction fails, a rollback is issued and processing of the transaction is discontinued. If all statements are processed without errors, the entire transaction is committed. Regardless of whether the transaction is committed or rolled back, the application frees the statement handle.

When the application exits, it needs to disconnect from the data source and free all resources allocated to the environment and connection handles. This can be accomplished with three functions calls, as illustrated in the following lines:

```
Public Sub ApplicationCleanUp()
  iError = SQLDisconnect(hDBc)
  iError = SQLFreeConnect(hDBc)
  iError = SQLFreeEnv(hEnv)
End Sub
```

The full capabilities of ODBC are far beyond the scope of this discussion, but many additional capabilities can be provided, and an application can be constructed in a manner that's completely database-independent using embedded SQL. However, if an application doesn't need to be portable to other database platforms, it may be easier to use stored procedures or a third-party product to apply transactions from Visual Basic.

Using ADO Objects With Oracle

Not surprisingly, the way that you manipulate Oracle databases with ADO is almost identical to the way you manipulate SQL Server databases with ADO—that, of course, is ADO's intention. For example, the following code connects to an Oracle database and iterates through every record that meets certain criteria, adjusting these record values accordingly. By making a change to the connection string, the code could just as easily connect to a SQL Server database.

Because most databases don't support the Jet engine **Find** methods, when working with ADO objects, you must create the recordset to update with a SQL **SELECT** statement, then move through the records in order, as shown here:

```
Sub IncreaseBaseCharges()
  Dim cnnLocal As ADODB.Connection
  Dim cmdLocal As ADODB.Command
  Dim rstLocal As ADODB.Recordset
  Dim intUpdated As Integer

  ' Create Connection object and open it on the Oracle database
  Set cnnLocal = New ADODB.Connection

  cnnLocal.ConnectionString = "dsn=ORACLE_1;UID=lars;PWD=kimba;"
  cnnLocal.Open

  Set cmdLocal = New ADODB.Command
  Set cmdLocal.ActiveConnection = cnnLocal
  cmdLocal.CommandText = "SELECT * FROM tblCustomerQuotations " _
      & "WHERE BaseEstimate < 10000"
  rstLocal.CursorType = adOpenForwardOnly
  Set rstLocal = cmdLocal.Execute()

  intUpdated = 0
  Do While Not rstLocal.EOF
    intUpdated = intUpdated + 1
    rstLocal.Fields("BaseEstimate") = 10000
    rstLocal.Update
    rstLocal.MoveNext
  Loop
```

```
    Debug.Print intUpdated & " Records Updated"
    rstLocal.Close
End Sub
```

Of course, in the case of this particular example, you would probably be just as well served to simply run an **UPDATE** query against the Oracle table. However, the example's intention is simply to show how to use ADO with Oracle tables.

Tip

*Changing the line **cnnLocal.ConnectionString** to point to a SQL Server database definition is the only change that you would have to make to use the code against a different data source (assuming, or course, that the SQL Server contains the same tables and field definitions).*

Where To Go From Here

After our all-to-brief discussion of Oracle in this chapter, we will return to a consideration of SQL Server in Chapter 9, using the new Access 2000 Access Data Projects (ADPs). Throughout the rest of the book, our focus will remain on SQL Server, primarily because of the close integration of the Access 2000 product. We will discuss the use of Access 2000 with Jet-based databases and with SQL Server databases, but not with Oracle, simply because it is a relatively nonstandard configuration. However, much of the Web-based and ADO-based programming that we will discuss throughout the rest of this book can be easily applied to the Oracle back-end product, with only changes to the drivers, and sometimes a slight tweaking of the program code itself.

Part III

Access Data Project
As Front End

Chapter 9

Introduction To Access Data Projects

In previous chapters, we discussed some of the common issues that you may encounter when using Access in either of the classic manners to connect with SQL Server or Oracle databases—the classic manners, of course, being linking through the Interactive Development Environment (IDE) and connecting via code.

However, Access 2000 provides you with a third means of connecting to SQL Server databases—the Access Data Project (ADP). This tool is part of Microsoft's future strategy of moving Access off of the Jet engine and entirely onto a SQL Server architecture. However, we will focus on it as a tool for client/server design—a tool that lets us create and define databases in their entirety on the remote server using the Access IDE. For those of you who are relatively new to Access, this may not seem like a particularly big deal. However, what you must understand is that the project is essentially a very thin client against the back-end database.

Considering ADPs And SQL Server Objects

The support within Access for ADPs makes designing effective client/server applications easier than ever before. The Access Database window even supports new objects to help you work with SQL Server databases when you create an ADP, as shown in Figure 9.1.

As you can see, when you are working with an ADP, the Database window adds support for views, database diagrams, and stored

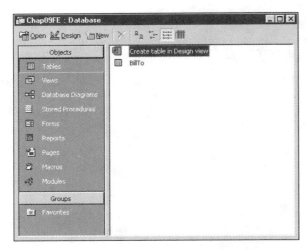

Figure 9.1
Working with an ADP within the Database window.

procedures, and removes queries from the accessible objects. The following sections discuss these new objects, and we'll also look briefly at database diagrams.

Views allow you to specify exactly how a user will see data. They can be thought of as stored queries—they are, functionally, equivalent to Jet **QueryDef** objects created in Access. *Stored procedures* are precompiled SQL statements. Because stored procedures are precompiled, they run much more quickly than straight SQL queries do. *Triggers* are a special kind of stored procedure that can be very complex, and they have several rules about how and when they should be created. Triggers allow you to apply complex data integrity, domain integrity, and referential integrity rules within your database.

Creating And Manipulating Views

Views allow you to horizontally and vertically partition information from one or more tables in the database. In other words, with a view, you can allow the user to see only selected fields and rows. Views can also be created to show derived information. In addition, views have the following advantages:

♦ You have more control over what the user can see. This is useful for both security and ease of use. Users don't have to look at "extra" information that they don't require.

♦ You can simplify the user interface by creating views of often-used queries. This will allow a user to run a view with a simple statement rather than supplying parameters every time the query is run.

♦ You can heighten security. Users can affect only what you let them see. This may be a subset of rows or columns, statistical information, or a subset of information from another view.

♦ You can use the Bulk Copy Program (BCP) utility to export data from a view.

You should be aware of the following rules and restrictions when creating views:

♦ When you are creating a view, any database objects that are referenced by the view are verified.

♦ When you are running a view, you must have SQL Server's **SELECT** permission on the objects referenced in the view definition. This means that you could potentially create a view that you can't run. Permissions on views are checked each time that view is run, not when it is created.

♦ If you drop objects referenced within a view, the view still remains. You will receive an error message the next time you attempt to run that view.

♦ Temporary tables can't be referenced in a view. This also means that you cannot use a **SELECT INTO** clause in a view.

♦ If you create a child view based on a parent view, you should be aware of what the parent view is doing. You could run into problems if the parent view is large and complex.

♦ Data in a view is not stored separately. This means that if you modify data in a view, you are modifying the data in the base tables.

♦ Triggers and indexes can't be created on a SQL Server view.

You will learn more about views in Chapter 10.

Stored Procedures

Stored procedures are precompiled SQL statements that are stored at the SQL Server (on the server machine). Because stored procedures are precompiled, they provide the best performance of any type of query. There are many system-stored procedures defined with an **sp_** prefix that gather information from system tables and are especially useful for administration. You can create your own user-defined stored procedures as well.

When you run a stored procedure for the first time, it runs in the following manner:

1. The procedure is parsed into its component pieces.

2. The components that reference other objects in the database (tables, views, and so on) check for the existence of these objects. This is also known as *resolving*.

3. Once resolving is complete, the name of the procedure will be stored in the **sysobjects** table and the code to create the stored procedure will be saved in **syscomments**.

4. Compilation continues and, during compilation, a blueprint that defines how to run the query is created. This blueprint is often called a *normalized plan*, a *query tree*, or a *query plan*. The query plan is saved in the **sysprocedures** table.

5. When the stored procedure is first executed, the query plan is read, fully compiled into a procedure plan, and then run. This saves you the time of reparsing, resolving, and compiling a query tree every time you run the stored procedure.

Another added benefit of using a stored procedure is that, once the stored procedure is executed, the procedure plan will be stored in the procedure cache. This means that the next time you use that stored procedure, it will be read directly from the cache and run. This gives you a huge performance boost over running a standard SQL query again and again.

You can use stored procedures to encapsulate business rules. Once encapsulated, these rules can be used by multiple applications, thus giving you a consistent data interface. This is also advantageous in that, if functionality needs to change, you only need to change it in one place rather than once for each application. All in all, stored procedures offer the following benefits:

♦ Performance is boosted for all stored procedures, but even more so for stored procedures that are run more than once because the query plan is saved in the procedure cache.

♦ With stored procedures, you can pass in arguments and return data, too.

♦ Stored procedures can be designed to run automatically when SQL Server starts up.

♦ Stored procedures can be used to extract data or modify data (not at the same time).

♦ Stored procedures are explicitly invoked. Unlike triggers, stored procedures must be called by your application, script, batch, or task.

Working With Triggers

In this section, you'll learn about a special type of stored procedure called a *trigger*. Triggers are automatically invoked when you try to modify data that a trigger is designed to protect. Triggers help secure the integrity of your data by preventing unauthorized or inconsistent changes from being made. For example, suppose you have a **customers** table and an **orders** table. You can create a trigger that will ensure that when you create a new order, it will have a valid customer ID to which it can attach. Likewise, you could create the trigger so that if you tried to delete a customer from the **customers** table, the trigger would check to see if there were any orders still attached to that customer and, if so, halt the delete process.

Triggers don't have parameters and can't be explicitly invoked. This means that you must attempt a data modification to fire off a trigger. Triggers can also be nested up to 16 levels. Nested triggers work like this: A trigger on your **orders** table might add an entry to your **accounts receivable** table that would, in turn, fire a trigger that checks to see if the customer has any overdue accounts receivable and notifies you if he or she does.

Performance-wise, triggers have a relatively low amount of overhead. Most of the time involved in running a trigger is spent referencing other tables. The referencing can be fast if the other tables are in memory or a bit slower if they need to be read from disk.

Triggers are always considered a part of the transaction. If the trigger or any other part of the transaction fails, it is rolled back.

In the past (before SQL Server 6.5), triggers were the only means of enforcing referential integrity. However, you now have the ability to use Declarative Referential Integrity (DRI), which makes most triggers unnecessary. You can create triggers directly from the Access IDE without using any of the SQL Server management tools.

Essentially, you'll use triggers (rather than the Relationships window that you use with Access-created databases) to enforce complex referential integrity, while a different SQL Server object, known as a constraint, will enforce simple referential integrity.

Using Database Diagrams To Create Databases

You can use database diagrams to create, edit, or delete database objects for SQL Server or Microsoft Database Engine (MSDE) databases while you're directly connected to the database in which those objects are stored. Database diagrams graphically represent tables, the columns they contain, and the relationships between them. You can use database diagrams to:

◆ View the tables in your database and their relationships

◆ Perform complex operations to alter the physical structure of your database

When you modify a database object through a database diagram, the modifications you make are not saved in the database until you save the table or the database diagram. Thus, you can experiment with "what if" scenarios on a database's design without permanently affecting its existing design or data.

In any event, when you finish working with a database diagram, you can then:

◆ Discard your changes.

◆ Save the changes to selected tables in the diagram or the entire database diagram and have the changes modify the server database.

◆ Save the Transact-SQL code that your changes to the diagram would invoke against the database in a change script. If you save a change script instead of saving your changes to the database, you then have more options as to its application. You can either apply the change script to the database at another time using a tool such as Microsoft SQL Server's osql command-line utility, or further edit the change script in a text editor and then apply the modified script to the database from osql or Query Analyzer.

You control the timing, type, and extent of the changes to your database by choosing how changes to the database diagram affect the server database.

Creating And Modifying Database Objects

As noted previously, you can use a database diagram to create and modify database objects, including the following objects:

◆ Tables

◆ Table columns and their properties

◆ Indexes

◆ Constraints

◆ Table relationships

You can modify tables and their columns directly in a database diagram. You modify indexes, constraints, and relationships through the Properties window for a table in your diagram.

Creating And Managing Database Diagrams

Needless to say, database diagrams duplicate functionality available to you elsewhere from the Access Database window. However, database diagrams simplify your interaction with SQL Server by letting you view both abstract and detailed information simultaneously in a somewhat more intuitive interface. In general, you can use database diagrams to:

♦ Manipulate database objects without having to write Transact-SQL code

♦ Visualize the structure of your database tables and their relationships

♦ Provide different views of complex databases

♦ Experiment with database changes without modifying the underlying database

♦ Create new objects and relationships

♦ Alter the structure of your database

Using Database Diagrams To Perform Database Operations

You can create database diagrams of varying complexity, from diagrams that contain just one table to diagrams that contain hundreds of tables. When you first create a diagram, you are presented with a blank diagram surface to which you can add tables. In the diagram, you can:

♦ Add tables by dragging them from the Show Table window, other open diagrams, or the view designer

♦ Create new tables that have not yet been defined in the database

♦ Edit the tables you have added to or created within the diagram and their properties

♦ Edit the database objects, such as constraints and indexes, that are attached to the tables in the diagram

♦ Create relationships between tables

♦ Delete tables or relationships from the diagram

♦ As mentioned previously, save a SQL change script, which places the Transact-SQL code for your changes in a file so that you can later apply them to the database or perform further editing upon them

♦ Save your diagram and update the database with your changes

It is important to note that changes that you make outside of the database diagram will pass through to the diagram. For example, if you add a table to the diagram, then proceed to add additional fields (columns) to the table from the table designer, when you return to the diagram, that table will indicate your new fields (columns) within the designer.

Using Database Diagrams To Graphically Lay Out Your Tables

You can perform a variety of diagramming operations in a database diagram without affecting the object definitions in your database. You can customize the appearance of your diagram to meet your development needs in the following ways:

♦ Use the keyboard or mouse to move around in a diagram

♦ Select and move tables and relationship lines

♦ Change the size and shape of tables

♦ Remove tables from the diagram without deleting them from the database

♦ Change the magnification of a diagram

♦ Open the Properties window to view properties for the objects in your diagram

These operations affect the appearance of your diagram, but they do not affect the structure of your database. We will further explore database diagrams, as well as other advanced features of working with SQL Server and the MSDE, in Chapter 12.

Working With Basic ADPs

You now know the basics of what an ADP is, and you've read about—albeit briefly—the SQL Server database objects that you will manipulate from the ADP. In the next several sections, we will look at some of the most important issues that you should be comfortable with when working with ADPs. We will begin, in the next section, by considering the MSDE, a local version of SQL Server designed for standalone machines.

Installing The MSDE

If your network already uses SQL Server 7, you can create ADPs directly against the SQL Server across the network. Alternatively, you can use the MSDE, installed locally, to create the connections and the SQL Server database. For simplicity's sake, in this chapter we'll create a database with the MSDE.

You must first install the MSDE onto your local development machine (Access will not do it automatically). To install the engine, insert the Office 2000 CD-ROM 1 into the CD-ROM drive. Using Windows Explorer, navigate to the \SQL\X86\Setup directory, and then double-click on the file named SetupSQL.exe. Windows will start to run the MSDE installation program.

Warning

If you have installed one of the SQL Server 7 Betas onto your development machine, and the build is earlier than Build 516, the MSDE will not install. In some cases, removing the SQL Server Beta from the machine may not be enough; you may actually need to install either a later Beta of SQL Server or the release version so that the MSDE will recognize the program code and helper DLLs that it needs.

After executing the file, follow the prompts to install MSDE onto your computer. When you finish the installation, the installer will prompt you to reboot your machine. You must do so before you can use the MSDE for project design.

Warning

If you have already installed the desktop version of SQL Server 7, the MSDE installation will fail because it would write over the existing install. However, you can nevertheless perform all the actions detailed herein regarding the MSDE—just use the MS SQL Server 7 icon set to perform the required activities.

Starting The SQL Server Service

After you install the MSDE and reboot the system, your computer will come back up with the SQL Server service icon in the system tray. However, you will notice that the icon has a red circle over it, which indicates that the service is not currently running. To start the service (a necessary step to use the MSDE), double-click on the SQL Server service icon in the system tray. Windows will display the SQL Server Service Manager.

The Server combo box should contain the name of the computer on which the service is running, and the dialog box should indicate that the service is stopped. Click on the Start/Continue button to start the service. Additionally, if you plan to use the MSDE regularly during development, you may want to instruct the service to start automatically when the operating system boots. If so, click on the checkbox to instruct the Service Manager. When you finish, the dialog box should look similar to the one in Figure 9.2. In addition, the icon in the system tray should change to a green arrow pointing right. You can either close the Service Manager dialog box entirely or minimize it, depending on whether you plan to use the Service Manager regularly.

Upsizing An Existing Database To SQL Server

One of the new features of Access 2000 is its provision for easily upsizing your databases to SQL Server 7. The easiest way to perform an upgrade of this type from within the Access

Figure 9.2
The SQL Server Service Manager after you start the service.

IDE is through the Database Upsizing Wizard. To use the Upsizing Wizard on the Chap09Upsize.mdb database (contained on the companion CD-ROM), perform the following steps:

1. Choose File | Open and open the Chap09Upsize.mdb database.

2. Choose Tools | Database Utilities Upsizing Wizard. Access will display the dialog box shown in Figure 9.3.

3. For this exercise, use the Create New Database option (although you can upsize into an existing database if you so choose). Click on Next to move to the next dialog box.

4. You will be prompted to select a SQL Server to use for the database, as well as a login ID and password for a user who has create rights on the database. Finally, it prompts you to name the new SQL Server database. After you perform these actions, click on Next to move to the next dialog box.

5. You will be prompted to select which tables to export to the SQL Server. Click on the >> button to export all the tables. Click on Next to move to the next dialog box.

6. The next dialog box lets you export table attributes in addition to data (see Figure 9.4). Accept the defaults and click on Next to move to the next dialog box.

7. In the next dialog box, you can opt to keep your existing application as is, change the application to support links to the SQL Server tables, or create an ADP to connect to the table. Select the Create A New Access Client/Server Application option and accept the default name. Click on Next to move to the next dialog box.

8. After you click on Finish in the last dialog box (you can, of course, click on the Back button if you want to re-think any of your choices), the Upsizing Wizard will use the information that you have entered to create the new SQL Server database and the ADP to access the database.

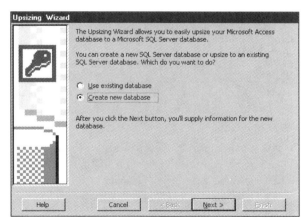

Figure 9.3
The opening dialog box of the Upsizing Wizard.

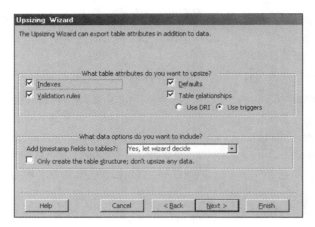

Figure 9.4
The data export selection options in the Upsizing Wizard dialog box.

The new ADP will maintain all of your current forms and reports, but it will not maintain any data locally—instead, all data will be maintained in the new SQL Server.

Warning
Before you upsize a database to SQL Server, make sure all of the table names correspond to SQL Server naming rules. Specifically, in the Chap09Upsize.mdb database, you will note that there are no spaces in any of the table names. Because of new features in Access 2000, you can rename the tables without having to rebuild all the queries and other objects in the database.

Working With The Access Data Project

As with standard Access databases, you must first create the data project before you can begin to work with it. To create an ADP, perform the following steps:

1. Choose File | New. Access will display the New dialog box.

2. Within the General tab of the dialog box, double-click on the Project (New Database) icon. If you are designing a project to work with an existing SQL Server 7 back end, you can choose the Project (Existing Database) icon. We'll be creating a new database as we create the project.

3. After you double-click on the Project (New Database) icon, Access will display the File New Database dialog box. Click on Create to save the new project as Chap09FE.adp. Access will display the Microsoft SQL Server Database Wizard.

4. Within the first combo box, enter the name of the server for the SQL Server database (which you can obtain from the SQL Server Service Manager or from your network administrator).

5. Enter the login ID and password of an account with Create Database privileges on the server. Finally, enter "Chap09BESQL" as the name of the new database. Click on Next to move to the last dialog box in the wizard.

6. Click on Finish. The MSDE will create the SQL Server database and return you to the Database window.

As you saw earlier in this chapter, the Database window has some additional objects that a normal MDB window doesn't have—views, database diagrams, and stored procedures. You saw these objects earlier in this chapter—and you'll learn more detail about many of these objects in later chapters.

Creating The Tables

As you saw earlier, the first step to creating the database is to create the tables that will reside in the database. When you do this through an ADP, the tables are automatically created on the SQL Server, and the links to the server data are automatically created in the project. We'll use a database example similar to others that you have seen—a simple order entry database. The following sections detail how to create the tables in the database.

Creating The BillTo Table

The first table to create is the **BillTo** table. This table will maintain address information about the customer, which the program will (ultimately) use to maintain billing information for each customer. The design of the table is pretty straightforward—as will be the design of the most of the tables. To design the table, perform the following steps:

1. Double-click on the Create Table In Design View option within the Database window. When you do so, Access may display the prompt shown in Figure 9.5. If it does, go ahead and install the Client Server Visual Design Tools. You will need to insert the Office 2000 CD-ROM 1 into the drive to do so.

2. After installing the Design Tools, Access will display the Table 1:Table Design view window. It will also prompt you to enter a name for the table. Enter the name as "BillTo" and click on OK.

3. As you can see, the Design window is somewhat different than the Access table Design window. However, most of what you know will translate. Within the window, specify the fields in the table as shown in Table 9.1.

4. Scroll to the right and click in the Allow Nulls checkbox for the **CustomerNum** field. The designer will remove the checkmark in the box.

5. Click in the Identity checkbox for the **CustomerNum** field. The designer will add a checkmark to the box and place a default value of 1 in the **Identity Seed** and **Identity Increment** fields.

Figure 9.5
The Client Server Visual Design Tools installation prompt.

Table 9.1   The fields in the BillTo table.

Field Name	Data Type	Length
CustomerNum	int	4
CustomerFirst	char	25
CustomerLast	char	25
Address1	char	25
Address2	char	25
City	char	25
State	char	2
Zip	char	10
Phone	char	14
Fax	char	14

6. Click on the gray selector box to the left of the **CustomerNum** field. Access will high-light the entire field.

7. Click on the primary key button on the toolbar. Access will display a primary key symbol in the selector. When you finish the steps, the designer will look similar to Figure 9.6.

8. Click on the Close button in the window to close the designer. Access will prompt you to save the design changes.

Creating The ShipTo Table

The second table to create is the **ShipTo** table. This table will maintain shipping address information about the customer, which the program will (ultimately) use to keep records about where orders were shipped. As with the **BillTo** table, the design of the table is pretty straightforward. To design the table, perform the following steps:

1. Double-click on the Create Table In Design View option within the Database window. Access will display the Table 1:Table Design view window. It will also prompt you to enter a name for the table. Enter the name as "ShipTo" and click on OK.

2. Within the window, specify the fields within the table as shown in Table 9.2.

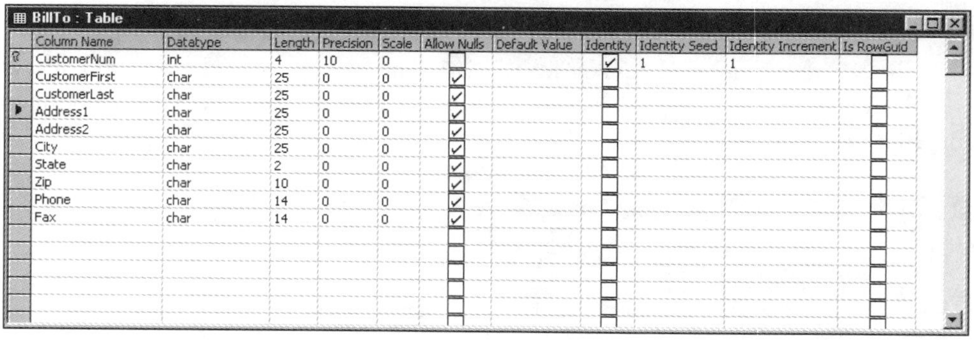

Figure 9.6
The designer after you create the **BillTo** table.

Table 9.2   The fields in the ShipTo table.

Field Name	Data Type	Length
ShipToNum	int	4
CustomerNum	int	4
CustomerFirst	char	25
CustomerLast	char	25
Address1	char	25
Address2	char	25
City	char	25
State	char	2
Zip	char	10
Phone	char	14
Fax	char	14

3. Click in the Allow Nulls checkbox for the **ShipToNum** field. The designer will remove the checkmark from the box.

4. Scroll to the right and click in the Identity checkbox for the **ShipToNum** field. The designer will place a checkmark in the box and place a default value of 1 in the **Identity Seed** and **Identity Increment** fields.

5. Click on the gray selector box to the left of the **ShipToNum** field. Access will highlight the entire field.

6. Click on the primary key button on the toolbar. Access will display a primary key symbol in the selector.

7. Click on the Close button on the window to close the designer. Access will prompt you to save the design changes.

Creating The OrderLookup Table

The next table to create is the **OrderLookup** table. This table will maintain shipping address information about the customer, which the program will use to link the customer information to the order information. To design the table, perform the following steps:

1. Double-click on the Create Table In Design View option within the Database window. Access will display the Table 1:Table Design view window. It will also prompt you to enter a name for the table. Enter the name as "OrderLookup" and click on OK.

2. Within the window, specify the fields within the table as shown in Table 9.3.

Table 9.3   The fields in the OrderLookup table.

Field Name	Data Type	Length	Allow Nulls
CustomerNum	int	4	False (unchecked)
ShipToNum	int	4	False (unchecked)
OrderNum	int	4	False (unchecked)

3. Click on the gray selector box to the left of the **CustomerNum** field. Hold the Shift key down and click on the gray selector box to the left of the **OrderNum** field. The designer will highlight all three fields.

4. Click on the primary key button on the toolbar. Access will display a primary key symbol in the selector next to the three fields, indicating that the primary key will be derived from their combined values.

5. Click on the Close button on the window to close the designer. Access will prompt you to save the design changes.

Creating The Orders Table

Next, we'll create the **Orders** table. This table will maintain order information and combine the line items from the **OrderDetail** table with the date and total information it contains when it displays the invoice. To design the table, perform the following steps:

1. Double-click on the Create Table In Design View option within the Database window. Access will display the Table 1:Table Design view window. It will also prompt you to enter a name for the table. Enter the name as "Orders" and click on OK.

2. Within the window, specify the fields within the table as shown in Table 9.4.

3. Click in the Allow Nulls checkbox for the **OrderNum** field. The designer will remove the checkmark from the box.

4. Scroll to the right and click in the Identity checkbox for the **OrderNum** field. The designer will place a checkmark in the box and place a default value of 1 in the **Identity Seed** and **Identity Increment** fields.

5. Click on the gray selector box to the left of the **OrderNum** field. Access will highlight the entire field.

6. Click on the primary key button on the toolbar. Access will display a primary key symbol in the selector.

7. Click on the Close button on the window to close the designer. Access will prompt you to save the design changes.

Creating The ItemInformation Table

The next table to create is the **ItemInformation** table. This table will maintain specific information about items. You should create this table before creating the **OrderDetail** table

Table 9.4 The fields in the Orders table.

Field Name	Data Type	Length
OrderNum	int	4
OrderDate	datetime	8
DeliveryDate	datetime	8
Total	money	8

so that you can simply use a lookup between the tables to fill in the **ItemNumber** field in the **OrderDetail** table. To design the **ItemInformation** table, perform the following steps:

1. Double-click on the Create Table In Design View option within the Database window. Access will display the Table 1:Table Design view window. It will also prompt you to enter a name for the table. Enter the name as "ItemInformation" and click on OK.

2. Within the window, specify the fields within the table as shown in Table 9.5.

3. Click in the Allow Nulls checkbox for the **ItemNum** field. The designer will remove the checkmark from the box.

4. Scroll to the right and click in the Identity checkbox for the **ItemNum** field. The designer will place a checkmark in the box and place a default value of 1 in the **Identity Seed** and **Identity Increment** fields.

5. Click on the gray selector box to the left of the **ItemNum** field. Access will highlight the entire field.

6. Click on the primary key button on the toolbar. Access will display a primary key symbol in the selector.

7. Click on the Close button on the window to close the designer. Access will prompt you to save the design changes.

Creating The Discount Table

Next, we'll create the **Discount** table (which is the next-to-last table in the database). This table will maintain specific information about discounts. You should create this table before the **OrderDetail** table so you can simply use a lookup between the tables to fill in the **DiscountNum** field in the **OrderDetail** table. To design the **Discount** table, perform the following steps:

1. Double-click on the Create Table In Design View option within the Database window. Access will display the Table 1:Table Design view window. It will also prompt you to enter a name for the table. Enter the table's name as "Discount" and click on OK.

2. Within the window, specify the fields within the table as shown in Table 9.6.

Table 9.5   The fields in the ItemInformation table.

Field Name	Data Type	Length
ItemNum	int	4
Description	varchar	50
Price	money	8

Table 9.6   The fields in the Discount table.

Field Name	Data Type	Length
DiscountNum	int	4
DiscountValue	decimal	9
DiscountDescription	varchar	50

3. Click in the Allow Nulls checkbox for the **DiscountNum** field. The designer will remove the checkmark from the box.

4. Scroll to the right and click in the Identity checkbox for the **DiscountNum** field. The designer will place a checkmark in the box and place a default value of 1 in the **Identity Seed** and **Identity Increment** fields.

5. Click on the gray selector box to the left of the **DiscountNum** field. Access will highlight the entire field.

6. Click on the primary key button on the toolbar. Access will display a primary key symbol in the selector.

7. Click on the Close button on the window to close the designer. Access will prompt you to save the design changes.

Creating The OrderDetail Table

The last table to create is the **OrderDetail** table. This table will maintain specific line information about orders. To design the **OrderDetail** table, perform the following steps:

1. Double-click on the Create Table In Design View option within the Database window. Access will display the Table 1:Table Design view window. It will also prompt you to enter a name for the table. Enter the table's name as "OrderDetail" and click on OK.

2. Within the window, specify the fields within the table as shown in Table 9.7.

3. Click in the Allow Nulls checkbox for the **OrderItemID** field. The designer will remove the checkmark from the box.

4. Scroll to the right and click in the Identity checkbox for the **OrderItemID** field. The designer will place a checkmark in the box and place a default value of 1 in the **Identity Seed** and **Identity Increment** fields.

5. Click on the gray selector box to the left of the **OrderItemID** field. Access will highlight the entire field.

6. Click on the primary key button on the toolbar. Access will display a primary key symbol in the selector.

7. Click on the Close button on the window to close the designer. Access will prompt you to save the design changes.

Table 9.7 The fields in the OrderDetail table.

Field Name	Data Type	Length
OrderItemID	int	4
OrderNum	int	4
ItemNum	int	4
DiscountNum	int	4

Creating Data Types

Before you can create a table, you must define the data types for the table. Data types specify the type of information (characters, numbers, or dates) that a column can hold, as well as how the data is stored. Microsoft SQL Server supplies various system data types. SQL Server also allows user-defined data types that are based on system data types.

System-Supplied Data Types

As you saw in the previous section, SQL Server provides several different data types. Certain types of data have several associated SQL Server system-supplied data types. For example, you could use the **int**, **decimal**, or **float** data type to store numeric data. However, you should choose appropriate data types to optimize performance and conserve disk space—if a number will always contain a whole value, for example, there is no reason to use a **float**, and doing so can actually impede performance.

Table 9.8 maps common types of data to SQL Server system-supplied data types. The table includes data type synonyms for ANSI compatibility.

> **Note**
>
> *SQL Server supports multiple languages with the **nchar**, **nvarchar**, and **ntext** Unicode string data types. Unicode strings use two bytes per character.*

Table 9.8   The common types of data and their SQL Server and ANSI counterparts.

Type Of Data	System-Supplied Data Types	ANSI Synonym	Number Of Bytes
Binary	**binary[(n)]**, **varbinary[(n)]**	--, **binary varying[(n)]**	1–8,000
Character	**char[(n)]**, **varchar[(n)]**	**character[(n)]**, **char[acter] varying[(n)]**	1–8,000 (8,000 characters)
Unicode character	**nchar[(n)]**, **nvarchar[(n)]**	**national char[acter][(n)]**, **national char[acter] varying[(n)]**	2–8,000 (1 –4,000 characters)
Date and time integers),	**Datetime**,	--, --	8 (two 4-byte
	smalldatetime		4 (two 2-byte
integers)			
Exact numeric	**decimal[(p[, s])]** , **numeric[(p[, s])]**	**dec**	5–17
Approximate numeric	**float[(n)]**, **real**	**Double precision or float[(n)]**, **float[(n)]**	4–8, 4
Global identifier	**uniqueidentifier**	---	16
Integer	**int, smallint, tinyint**	**integer**, ---	4, 2, 1
Monetary	**money, smallmoney**	---, ---	8, 4
Special	**bit, cursor, sysname, timestamp**	---, ---, ---, ---	1, 1, 0–8, 0–8
Text and image	**text**, **image**	---, ---	0–2GB
Unicode text	**ntext**	**national text**	0–2GB

Exact And Approximate Numeric Data

The terms *exact numeric data* and *approximate numeric data* can be confusing because, in practice, they are often used differently than their names imply.

Exact Numeric Data Types

Exact numeric data types let you specify *exactly* the scale and precision to use. For example, you can specify three digits to the right of the decimal and four to the left. A query always returns exactly what you entered. SQL Server supports exact numeric data with two synonymous data types, **decimal** and **numeric**, for ANSI compatibility.

Most of the time, you would use exact numeric data types for financial applications in which you want to portray the data consistently (always two decimal places) and to query on that column (for example, to find all loans with an interest rate of 8.75 percent).

Approximate Numeric Data Types

Approximate numeric data types store data as accurately as is possible using binary numbers. For example, the fraction 1/3 is represented in a decimal system as .33333 (repeating). The number cannot be stored accurately, so an approximation is stored.

The approximate numeric data types, **real** and **float**, are unable to store all decimal numbers with complete accuracy. Therefore, it is necessary to store an approximation of the decimal number. Most of the time, you would use approximate numeric data types for scientific or engineering applications.

Tip

*Avoid referencing columns with the **float** or **real** data types in **WHERE** clauses. Calculations performed on **float** and **real** decimal values are likely to have small rounding errors due to the approximate representation of decimal numbers.*

Creating And Dropping User-Defined Data Types

User-defined data types are based on system-supplied data types. They allow you to refine data types further to ensure consistency when you're working with common data elements in different tables or databases. User-defined data types do not allow you to define structures or complex data types. A user-defined data type is defined for a specific database.

Note

*User-defined data types that you create in the model database are automatically included in all databases that are subsequently created. Each user-defined data type is added as a row in the **systypes** table.*

You can create and drop user-defined data types with system stored procedures. Data type names must follow the rules for identifier names and must be unique to each database.

Define each user-defined data type in terms of a system-supplied data type. Specify a default null type of **NULL** or **NOT NULL**, which indicates whether the user-defined data type may or may not store nulls. The default null type can be overridden when the user-defined data type is used in a column definition.

Creating A User-Defined Data Type

The **sp_addtype** system stored procedure creates user-defined data types. You can access the **sp_addtype** stored procedure either by calling it down an ADO connection, or, more commonly, during the design phase of database creation by invoking the stored procedure from within the SQL Server Query Analyzer. The prototype for the stored procedure is as follows:

```
sp_addtype type, system_data_type [,'NULL' | 'NOT NULL']
```

The following example code, then, creates three user-defined data types:

```
EXEC sp_addtype isbn, 'smallint', 'NOT NULL'
EXEC sp_addtype zipcode, 'char(10)', 'NULL'
EXEC sp_addtype longstring, 'varchar(63)', 'NULL'
```

Note

*The types defined in these three lines are used throughout the **library** database discussed in the next several chapters. If you have not defined these types, you will receive error messages when trying to create tables and views in later chapters.*

Dropping A User-Defined Data Type

The **sp_droptype** system stored procedure deletes user-defined data types from the **systypes** system table. A user-defined data type cannot be dropped if it is referenced by tables or other database objects. The prototype for the stored procedure is as follows:

```
sp_droptype type
```

The following example code, then, drops the **isbn** user-defined data type created previously:

```
EXEC sp_droptype isbn
```

To better understand how this whole process works, it is a valuable exercise for you to write and execute statements that create user-defined data types in the **library** database that you will be using in later chapters.

Obtaining Information About Data Types

Execute the **sp_help** system stored procedure or query the **information_schema.domains** view to retrieve a list of user-defined data types for the current database. As any good book about SQL Server will teach you, the information schema views that SQL Server defines are excellent sources of information in your management of databases. There are several of these views; for more information, check the SQL Server Books Online under "Information Schemas."

Try the following exercise:

1. Log on to your computer as Administrator or another account that is a member of the Administrators group (alternately, log on to your computer as whoever you are, and then connect to the SQL Server using standard authentication).

2. Open SQL Server Query Analyzer and log on to either the local server or whatever server hosts the **library** database with Microsoft Windows NT authentication (or standard authentication, if you have chosen to use that). If you use Windows NT authentication, your account must be a member of the Windows NT Administrators group, which is automatically mapped to the SQL Server **sysadmin** role. Otherwise, make sure you log on with a system administrator-level role to the database.

3. From the DB list box, click on library.

4. Write and execute statements to create the user-defined data types described in Table 9.9.

5. The following statements are used to create these user-defined data types:

```
EXEC sp_addtype zipcode, 'char(10)'
EXEC sp_addtype member_no, 'smallint'
EXEC sp_addtype phonenumber, 'char(13)', NULL
EXEC sp_addtype shortstring, 'varchar(15)'
```

6. Type and execute the following statement to verify that the data type was created:

```
SELECT domain_name, data_type, character_maximum_length
   FROM information_schema.domains
   ORDER BY domain_name
```

Table 9.9   User-defined data types and their descriptions.

Data Type	Description Of Data
Zipcode	Character data of 10 characters
Member_no	A whole number that will not exceed 30,000
Phonenumber	Character data of 13 characters that allows **NULL**
Shortstring	Variable character of up to 15 characters

Guidelines For Creating User-Defined Data Types

Consider the following guidelines for creating user-defined data types and balancing storage size with requirements:

♦ If column length varies, use one of the variable data types. For example, if you have a list of names, you can set it to **varchar** instead of **char (fixed)**. Using a variable data type will limit space usage.

♦ Integer, date and time, and monetary data all support different ranges based on storage size. For example, if you use the **tinyint** data type for a **store** identifier in a database, you will have problems when you decide to open **store** number 256.

♦ For numeric data types, the size and required level of precision helps to determine your choice. In general, use **decimal**.

♦ If the storage is greater than 8,000 bytes, use the **text** or **image** data type. If it is less than 8,000, use **binary**, **char**, or **varchar**. When possible, it is best to use **char** or **varchar** because they have more functionality than **text** and **image**.

Where To Go From Here

Clearly, the new Access Data Project (ADP) file format opens a whole new world of possibility for Access client/server development. The ability to create database objects directly against a SQL Server from your Access 2000 front end is a benefit substantial enough that you may not even realize the extent to which it changes the way you work until long after you have gotten comfortable with it.

User-defined data types are useful when a number of tables in a database will use a field with the same data type, size, and possibly the same validity restrictions or defaults. User-defined data types are mapped to system data types. These data types can have rules and defaults bound to them.

In the next several chapters that comprise this section, you will work with ADPs in more depth, as well as with all of the different SQL Server database objects. In Chapter 10, you will learn about table construction, constraints, and views, and the creation, modification, and management of each.

Creating Databases, Tables, And Views With SQL Server

Clearly, as you saw in Chapter 9—and as you likely knew already—SQL Server is a product and a programming platform entirely unto itself. This book is really about Access client/server, so we won't spend an extensive amount of time discussing the issues surrounding SQL Server programming. The fact that Microsoft is really transitioning the Access product to run on the local version of SQL Server (the Microsoft Data Engine, or MSDE, that you learned about in Chapter 9), and the fact that Access Data Projects (ADPs) have been added to Access to allow for the direct management of database design against the SQL Server, demands that you understand some of the different objects and techniques that SQL Server supports. In this chapter, we will begin that exploration with a discussion of databases, tables, and views—the basic objects that make up the SQL Server installation. Along the way, the text will introduce such issues as constraints, security actions with views, and more. In Chapter 11, we will move on to a consideration of stored procedures and triggers.

Creating And Dropping Databases

The **CREATE DATABASE** and **DROP DATABASE** statements allow you to create and remove databases. In the following sections, you will learn how to use these statements. Databases are, of course, the root means of storage for all data on a SQL Server—just as they are in Access. However, databases are constructed a little differently in SQL Server, both physically and conceptually. Let's take a look at creating and manipulating some databases to better understand these issues.

Creating Databases

You can create a database using the Database Creation wizard, SQL Server Enterprise Manager, or the **CREATE DATABASE** statement. The process of creating a database also creates a transaction log for that database.

Creating a database is a process of specifying the name of the database and designating the size and location of the database files. When the new database is created, it is a duplicate of the model database. Any options or settings in the model database are copied into the new database. New databases can be created by default by members of the **sysadmin** and **dbcreator** fixed server roles; however, permissions to create databases can be given to other users.

Tip

*Information about each database in SQL Server is stored in the **sysdatabases** system table in the master database. Therefore, you should back up the master database each time you create, modify, or drop a database.*

To create databases, you can use the **CREATE DATABASE** Transact-SQL statement. The prototype looks like the following (as always, items in brackets are optional):

```
CREATE DATABASE database_name
[ON
    {[PRIMARY] (NAME = logical_file_name,
        FILENAME = ' os_file_name'
        [, SIZE = size]
        [, MAXSIZE = max_size]
        [, FILEGROWTH = growth_increment] )
    } [, ...n]
]
[LOG ON
    { ( NAME = logical_file_name,          FILENAME = ' os_file_name'
        [, SIZE = size] )
    } [, ...n]
]
[FOR RESTORE]
```

Tip

*The **CREATE DATABASE** syntax has changed significantly from SQL Server version 6.5. SQL Server version 7 does not use devices, so it is no longer necessary to create a device using the **DISK INIT** statement before creating a database. You now specify file information as part of the **CREATE DATABASE** statement.*

When you create a database, you can set the following options:

♦ **PRIMARY**—This option specifies the files in the primary filegroup. The primary filegroup contains all the database system tables. It also contains all objects not assigned to user filegroups (covered later in this chapter). A database can have only one primary data file. The primary data file is the starting point of the database and points to the rest of the files in the database. Every database has one primary data file. The recommended file extension for a primary data file is .mdf. If the **PRIMARY** keyword is not specified, the first file listed in the statement becomes the primary data file. Note this first difference from an Access database: The SQL Server database can be spread across multiple component files, allowing you to even go so far as to distribute the database across multiple physical hard drives. This construction means that your databases can grow substantially, and that they are much more robust than an Access database.

♦ **FILENAME**—This option specifies the operating system file name and path for the file. The path specified in the place of the *os_file_name* placeholder must specify a folder on a local hard drive of the server on which SQL Server is installed.

Tip

If your computer has more than one disk and you are not using RAID (Redundant Array of Inexpensive Disks), place the data file and transaction log file on separate physical disks. This separation increases performance and can be used, in conjunction with disk mirroring, to decrease the likelihood of data loss in case of media failure.

♦ **SIZE**—This option specifies the size of the file. You can specify sizes in megabytes using the MB suffix (the default), or kilobytes using the KB suffix. The minimum value is 512KB. If size is not specified for the primary data file, it defaults to the size of the model database primary data file. If no log file is specified, a default log file that is 25 percent of the total size of the data files is created. If size is not specified for secondary data files or log files, it defaults to a size of 1MB.

The **SIZE** option sets the minimum size of the file. The file can grow larger, but cannot shrink smaller than this size. To reduce the minimum size of a file, use the **DBCC SHRINKFILE** statement.

Tip

SQL Server 7 has a maintenance wizard that can be set to control the size of databases.

♦ **MAXSIZE**—This option specifies the maximum size to which the file can grow. You can specify sizes using the MB suffix (the default), or the KB suffix. If no size is specified, the file grows until the disk is full.

♦ **FILEGROWTH**—This option specifies the growth increment of the file. When SQL Server needs to increase the size of a file, it will increase the file by the amount specified by the **FILEGROWTH** option. A value of 0 indicates no growth. The value can be specified in megabytes (the default), in kilobytes, or as a percentage (%). The default value, if **FILEGROWTH** is not specified, is 10 percent, and the minimum value is 64KB. The specified size is rounded to the nearest 64KB.

To see how all this works, consider the following Transact-SQL statement, which creates a database called **sample**. The database contains a 10MB primary data file and a 3MB log file. The primary data file can grow to a maximum of 15MB and it will grow in 20 percent increments; for example, it would grow by 2MB the first time that it needed to grow. The log file can grow to a maximum of 5MB and it will grow in 1MB increments.

```
CREATE DATABASE sample
ON
  PRIMARY (NAME=sample_data,
  FILENAME='c:\mssql7\data\sample.mdf',
  SIZE=10MB,
  MAXSIZE=15MB,
  FILEGROWTH=20%)
LOG ON
  (NAME=sample_log,
  FILENAME='c:\mssql7\data\sample.ldf',
  SIZE=3MB,
  MAXSIZE=5MB,
  FILEGROWTH=1MB)
```

Dropping A Database

You can drop a database when you no longer need it. When you drop a database, you permanently delete the database and the disk files used by the database. Permission to drop a database defaults to the database owner and members of the **sysadmin** fixed server role. Permission to drop a database cannot be transferred.

You can drop databases using SQL Server Enterprise Manager or by executing the **DROP DATABASE** statement, which is constructed as shown in the following prototype:

```
DROP DATABASE database_name [,...n]
```

For example, the following code drops multiple databases by using one statement:

```
DROP DATABASE mydb1, mydb2
```

When you drop a database, consider the following facts and guidelines:

♦ With SQL Server Enterprise Manager, you can drop only one database at a time.

♦ With Transact-SQL, you can drop several databases at one time.

♦ After you drop a database, login IDs for which that particular database was the default database will not have a default database.

♦ Back up the master database after you drop a database.

◆ SQL Server does not let you drop the master, model, and tempdb databases, but does allow you to drop the msdb system database.

◆ You cannot drop a database from within the ADP design environment.

In addition to these guidelines, there are some limitations on when you can drop a database. You cannot drop a database that is:

◆ In the process of being restored

◆ Open for reading or writing by any user

◆ Publishing any of its tables as part of SQL Server replication

Although SQL Server allows you to drop the msdb system database, you should not drop it if you use or intend to use any of the following:

◆ SQL Server Agent

◆ Replication

◆ SQL Server Web wizard

◆ Data Transformation Services (DTS)

Tip

After deleting a database in SQL Server Query Analyzer, it may still show in SQL Server Enterprise Manager. This is because Enterprise Manager does not automatically refresh information that has been changed by other connections. You will need to use the Refresh option, which is available from the right-click shortcut menu on the various folders, to see updated information.

Creating Tables

SQL Server uses the ANSI SQL standard **CREATE TABLE** syntax. SQL Server Enterprise Manager provides a front-end, fill-in-the-blanks table designer (with ADPs, you can use the Project—New Database option from the Access New dialog box), which might make your job easier. Ultimately, the SQL syntax is always sent to SQL Server to create a table. You can create a table directly using a tool such as osql, ISQL, or the Query Analyzer; from SQL Server Enterprise Manager; from the Access Project window; or using a third-party data modeling tool (such as Visual InterDev or Visual Basic) that transmits the SQL syntax under the cover of a friendly interface.

In this chapter, I emphasize direct use of the data definition language (DDL) rather than discuss the interface tools. This is, in part, because I discussed the ADP interface from a basic perspective in Chapter 9, in part because I will get into more depth in Chapter 13, and in part because I will talk about using some other tools—most notably, Visual Basic—to create databases in SQL Server later in this chapter. You should keep all DDL commands that you embed in a script so that you can run them easily at a later time to re-create the table.

Warning

Even if you use one of the friendly front-end tools to create the tables initially, it's critical that you understand and have access to the script involved so that you can later re-create the table. Re-creating tables is an important issue that comes up from time to time in SQL Server as the result of data or table corruption, server corruption, or other similar issues.

SQL Server Enterprise Manager and other front-end tools can create and save operating system files with the SQL DDL commands necessary to create the object. This DDL is essentially source code, and you should treat it as such. Keep a backup copy. You should also consider keeping these files under version control using a source control product such as Visual SourceSafe.

At the basic level, creating a table requires little more than knowing what you want to name it, what columns it will contain, and what range of values (domain) each column will be able to store. Here's the basic syntax for creating the **customer** table, with three fixed-length character (**char**) columns. (Note that this table definition isn't necessarily the most efficient way to store data, because it always requires 46 bytes per entry plus a few bytes of overhead regardless of the actual length of the data.)

```
CREATE TABLE customer (
   name    char(30),
   phone   char(12),
   emp_id char(4)
   )
```

This example shows each column on a separate line for readability. As far as the SQL Server parser is concerned, whitespaces created by tabs, carriage returns, and the spacebar are identical. From the system's standpoint, the following **CREATE TABLE** example is identical to the previous one, but it's harder to read from a user's standpoint:

```
CREATE TABLE customer (name char(30), phone char(12), emp_id char(4))
```

This simple example shows just the basics of creating a table. We'll see many more detailed examples later in this chapter.

Naming Tables And Columns

A table is always created within a database and is owned by one particular user. Normally, the owner is the user who created the table, but anyone with the **sysadmin** or **db_owner** role can create a table owned by another user. A database can contain multiple tables with the same name, as long as the tables have different owners. The full name of a table has three parts, in this form:

```
database.owner.tablename
```

For example, say that a user (with the username LKlander) created a sample **customer** table in the **pubs** sample database. This user's table would have the **pubs.LKlander.customer** three-part name. (If this user is also the database owner, **pubs.dbo.customer** would be his table's name, because **dbo** is the special username for the database owner in every database.)

The first two parts of the three-part name specification have default values. The default for the name of the database is whatever database context you're currently working in. The table owner actually has two possible defaults. If no table owner name is specified when referencing a table, SQL Server will assume that either you or the owner of the database owns the table. For example, if our hypothetical user owns the **customer** table and her database context is the **pubs**, she can refer to the table simply as **customer**.

Tip

To access a table owned by anyone other than yourself or the database owner, you must include the owner name along with the table name.

Column names should be descriptive, and because you'll use them repeatedly, you should avoid wordiness. The name of the column (or any object in SQL Server, such as a table or a view) can be whatever you choose, as long as the name conforms to the SQL Server rules for identifiers: It must consist of a combination of 1 through 128 letters, digits, or the symbols #, $, @, or _. (For more specific identifier rules, see "Using Identifiers" in SQL Server Books Online—accessible from the Start menu Microsoft SQL Server 7.0 program group. The discussions contained therein are true for all SQL Server object names, not just for column names.)

Reserved Keywords

Certain reserved keywords, such as **table**, **create**, **select**, and **update**, have special meaning to the SQL Server parser, and collectively they make up the SQL language implementation. If at all possible, you shouldn't use reserved keywords for your object names—in fact, you shouldn't even use them *within* your object names. In addition to the SQL Server reserved keywords, the SQL-92 standard has its own list of reserved keywords. In some cases, this list is more restrictive than SQL Server's list; in other cases, it's less restrictive. SQL Server Books Online has a complete list of both SQL Server's reserved keywords and the SQL-92 standard's list.

Watch out for SQL-92's reserved keywords. They aren't reserved keywords in SQL Server yet, but they could become reserved keywords in a future SQL Server version. Using a SQL-92 reserved keyword might require that you alter your application before upgrading it if the word has become a SQL Server reserved keyword.

Delimited Identifiers

You can't use keywords in your object names unless you use a delimited identifier. In fact, if you use a delimited identifier, not only can you use keywords as identifiers, but you can also use any other string—whether it follows the rules for identifiers or not—as an object name. This includes spaces and other nonalphanumeric characters normally not allowed. Two types of delimited identifiers exist:

♦ Bracketed identifiers are delimited by square brackets ([*object name*]).

♦ Quoted identifiers are delimited by double quotation marks ("*object name*").

You can use bracketed identifiers in any environment, but to use quoted identifiers, you must enable a special option using **SET QUOTED_IDENTIFIER ON**. Once you have turned on **QUOTED_IDENTIFIER**, double quotes will always be interpreted as referencing an object. To delimit string or date constants, you have to use single quotes. Let's look at some examples. Because **column** is a reserved keyword, the first statement that follows would be illegal in all circumstances, and the second one would be illegal unless **QUOTED_IDENTIFIER** was on. The third statement would be legal in any circumstances.

```
CREATE TABLE customer (name char(30), column char(12), emp_id char(4))
CREATE TABLE customer (name char(30), "column" char(12), emp_id char(4))
CREATE TABLE customer (name char(30), [column] char(12), emp_id char(4))
```

The ODBC driver that comes with SQL Server sets the option **QUOTED_IDENTIFIER** to **ON** by default, but some of the SQL Server-specific tools will set it to **OFF**. You can determine whether to set this option on or off for your session by executing the following command:

```
DBCC useroptions
```

Data Types

SQL Server provides many data types. A discussion about the data types was provided (briefly) in Chapter 9, but for more in-depth information, refer to Books Online. Choosing the appropriate data type is simply a matter of mapping the domain of values you need to store to the corresponding data type. In choosing data types, you want to avoid wasting storage space while allowing enough space for a sufficient range of possible values over the life of your application.

Data Type Synonyms

SQL Server syntactically accepts as data types both synonym data type names and base data type names when creating or altering a table, but it uses only the type listed as the data type within the actual definition. For example, you can define a column as **character(1)**, **character**, or **char(1)**, and SQL Server will accept them all as valid syntax. Internally, however, the expression is considered **char(1)**, and subsequent querying of the SQL Server system catalogs for the data type will show it as **char(1)**, regardless of the syntax that you used when you created it.

Naming Conventions

Many organizations and multiuser development projects adopt standard naming conventions, which is generally good practice. For example, assigning a standard moniker of **cust_id** to represent a customer number in every table clearly shows that all the tables share common data. On the other hand, if an organization used several monikers in the tables to represent a customer number, such as **cust_id**, **cust_num**, **customer_number**, and **customer_#**, it wouldn't be as obvious that these monikers represented common data.

One naming convention is the Hungarian-style notation for column names. Hungarian-style notation is a widely used practice in C programming, whereby variable names include information about their data types. Hungarian-style notation uses names such as **sint_nn_custnum** to indicate that the **custnum** column is a small integer (**smallint** of 2 bytes) and is **NOT NULL** (doesn't allow nulls). Although this practice makes good sense in C programming, it defeats the data type independence that SQL Server provides; therefore, I recommend *against* using it.

Suppose, for example, that after the table is built and applications have been written, you discover that the **custnum** column requires a 4-byte integer (**int**) instead of a 2-byte small integer. You can re-create the table relatively easily and define the column as an **int** instead of a **smallint**. (Alternatively, you can use the **ALTER TABLE** command to modify the data type of the existing table.) SQL Server stored procedures will handle the different data type automatically. Applications using ODBC, OLE DB, or DB-Library that bind the retrieved column to a character or integer data type will be unaffected. The applications would need to change if they bound the column to a small integer variable because the variable's type would need to be larger. Therefore, you should try not to be overly conservative with variable data types, especially in your client applications. You should be most concerned with the type on the server side; the type in the application can be larger and will automatically accommodate smaller values. By overloading the column name with data type information, which is readily available from the system catalogs, the insulation from the underlying data type is compromised. (You could, of course, change the data type from a **smallint** to an **int**, without changing the column name, but then the Hungarian-style name would no longer accurately reflect the column definition. Changing the column name would then result in the need to change application code, stored procedures, or both.)

Globally Unique Identifiers

Most available data types in SQL Server are well documented, so we'll leave it up to you to find additional details in the product documentation. However, one special data type merits a bit more discussion.

Using a globally unique identifier (GUID)—also called a universal unique identifier (UUID)—is becoming an important way to identify data, objects, software applications, and applets in distributed systems. A GUID is a 128-bit (16-byte) value generated in a way that, for all practical purposes, guarantees uniqueness worldwide, even among disconnected computers. SQL Server 7 supports a data type called **uniqueidentifier** for storing a globally unique identifier. The Transact-SQL language supports the system function **NEWID**, which can be used to generate a **uniqueidentifier** value. A column or variable of data type **uniqueidentifier** can be initialized to a value in one of the following two ways:

- Using the system-supplied function **NEWID**.
- Using a string constant in the following form (32 hexadecimal digits separated by hyphens): xxxxxxxx-xxxx-xxxx-xxxx-xxxxxxxxxxxx. (Each x is a hexadecimal digit in the range 0 through 9 or a through f.)

This data type can be quite cumbersome to work with, and the only operations that are allowed against a **uniqueidentifier** value are comparisons (=, <>, <, >, <=, >=) and checking for **NULL**. (The online product documentation states that only the equality and inequality operators, = and <>, are allowed for **uniqueidentifier** columns, but this is incorrect. In fact, you can even sort by a **uniqueidentifier** column.) However, using this data type internally can have several advantages.

One advantage is that the values are guaranteed to be globally unique for any machine on a network, because the last six bits of a **uniqueidentifier** value make up the node number for the machine. On a machine with a network interface card (NIC), the node is the unique IEEE 802 identifier of that card. On a machine without a NIC (for example, a home computer that connects to the Internet via modem), the node is a pseudo-random, 48-bit value that isn't guaranteed to be unique, but is highly likely to be unique for the near future.

Another advantage is that the list of **uniqueidentifier** values can't be exhausted. This is not the case with other data types frequently used as unique identifiers. In fact, this data type is used internally by SQL Server for row-level merge replication. A **uniqueidentifier** column can have a special property called the **ROWGUIDCOL** property; at most, one **uniqueidentifier** column can have this property per table. The **ROWGUIDCOL** property can be specified as part of the column definition in **CREATE TABLE** and **ALTER TABLE ADD COLUMN** or added or dropped for an existing column through **ALTER TABLE ALTER COLUMN**.

A **uniqueidentifier** column with the **ROWGUIDCOL** property can be referenced using the keyword **ROWGUIDCOL** in a query. This is similar to referencing an identity column through the **IDENTITYCOL** keyword. The **ROWGUIDCOL** property does not imply any automatic value generation, and if automatic value generation is needed, the **NEWID** function should be defined as the default value of the column. You can have multiple **uniqueidentifier** columns per table, but only one of them can have the **ROWGUIDCOL** property. You can use the **uniqueidentifier** data type for whatever reason you come up with, but if you're using one to identify the current row, an application must have a generic way to ask for it without needing to know the column name. That's what the **ROWGUIDCOL** property does.

Note
*The **uniqueidentifier** column is also commonly used with merge replication when you are merging rows from several different publishers into a single or multiple subscriber(s).*

Variable-Length Vs. Fixed-Length Data Types

Deciding to use a variable-length or a fixed-length data type isn't always straightforward or obvious. As a general rule, variable-length data types are most appropriate when you expect significant variance in the size of the data for a column and when the data in the column won't be frequently changed.

Using variable-length data types can yield important storage savings. Choosing them can sometimes result in a minor performance loss and at other times can result in improved performance. A row with variable-length columns requires special offset entries to be internally maintained. These entries keep track of the actual length of the column. Calculating and maintaining the offsets requires slightly more overhead than a pure fixed-length row, which needs no such offsets at all. This task requires a few addition and subtraction operations to maintain the offset value. However, the extra overhead of maintaining these offsets is generally inconsequential, and this alone would not make a significant difference on most, if not all, systems.

On the other hand, using variable-length columns can sometimes improve performance because they can allow more rows to fit on a page. But the efficiency results from more than simply requiring less disk space. A data page for SQL Server is 8K (8,192 bytes), of which 8,096 bytes are available to store data. (The rest is for internal use to keep track of structural information about the page and the object to which it belongs.) One I/O operation brings back the entire page. If you can fit 80 rows on a page, a single I/O operation brings back 80 rows. But if you can fit 160 rows on a page, one I/O operation is essentially twice as efficient. In operations that scan for data and return lots of adjacent rows, this can amount to a significant performance improvement. The more rows you can fit per page, the better your I/O and cache-hit efficiency will be.

For example, consider a simple customer table. Suppose you could define it in two ways, fixed-length and variable-length, as shown in Figures 10.1 and 10.2.

Columns that contain addresses, names, or URLs all have data that varies significantly in length. Let's look at the differences between choosing fixed-length columns versus choosing variable-length columns. In Figure 10.1, using all fixed-length columns, every row uses 304 bytes for data, regardless of the number of characters actually inserted into the row. Furthermore, SQL Server needs an additional 10 bytes of overhead for every row in this table, so the rows will need a total of 314 bytes for storage. But assume that even though the table must accommodate addresses and names up to the specified size, on average, the actual entries are only half the maximum size.

In Figure 10.2, assume that for all the variable-length (**varchar**) columns, the average entry is actually only about half the maximum. Instead of a row length of 304 bytes, the average length is 184 bytes. This length is computed as follows: the **smallint** and **char(2)** columns total 4 bytes. The **varchar** columns' maximum total length is 300, half of which is 150 bytes. And a 2-byte overhead exists for each of 9 **varchar** columns, for 18 bytes. Add 2 more bytes for any row that has one or more variable-length columns. In addition, this row

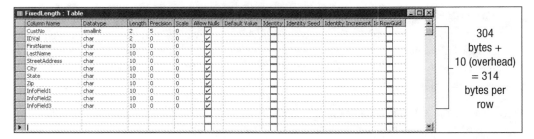

Figure 10.1
A customer table with fixed-length columns.

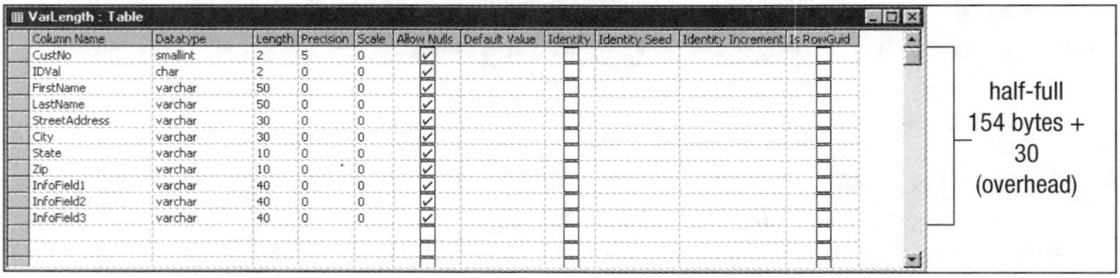

Figure 10.2
A customer table with variable-length columns.

requires another 10 bytes of overhead, regardless of the presence of variable-length fields. (This is the same 10 bytes of overhead needed in the case of all fixed-length columns; in other words, all rows have these same 10 bytes of constant overhead.) So the total is 4 + 150 + 18 + 2 + 10, or 184. (The actual meaning of each of these bytes of overhead will be discussed later in this chapter.)

In the fixed-length example in Figure 10.1, you always fit 25 rows on a data page (8,096 divided by 314, discarding the remainder). In the variable-length example in Figure 10.2, you can fit an average of 44 rows per page (8,096 divided by 184). The table using variable-length columns will consume about half as many pages in storage, a single I/O operation will retrieve almost twice as many rows, and a page cached in memory is twice as likely to contain the row you're looking for.

When choosing lengths for columns, don't be wasteful—but don't be cheap, either. Allow for future needs, and realize that if the additional length doesn't change how many rows will fit on a page, the additional size is free anyway. Consider again the examples in Figures 10.1 and 10.2. The **CustNo** was declared as a **smallint**, meaning that its maximum positive value is 32,767 (unfortunately, SQL Server doesn't provide any unsigned **int** or unsigned **smallint** data types), and it consumes 2 bytes of storage. Although 32,767 customers might seem like a lot to a new company, the company might be surprised by its own success and, in a couple of years, find out that 32,767 is too limited.

The database designers might regret that they tried to save 2 bytes and didn't simply make the data type an **int**, using 4 bytes but with a maximum positive value of 2,147,483,647. They'll be especially disappointed if they realize they didn't really save any space. If you compute the rows-per-page calculations just discussed, increasing the row size by 2 bytes, you'll see that the same number of rows still fit on a page. The additional 2 bytes are free—they were simply wasted space before. They never cause fewer rows per page in the fixed-length example, and they'll rarely cause fewer rows per page even in the variable-length case.

So which strategy wins? Potentially better update performance, or more rows per page? Like most questions of this nature, no single answer is right. It depends on your application. If you understand the tradeoffs, you'll be able to make the best choice. Now that you know the issues, this general rule merits repeating: Variable-length data types are most appropriate when you expect significant variance in the size of the data for that column and when the column won't be updated frequently.

Much Ado About NULL

The issue of whether to allow **NULL** has become an almost religious one for many in the industry, and no doubt any discussion about **NULL** will outrage a few people, no matter which side of the issue you take. Pragmatically, dealing with **NULL** brings added complexity to the storage engine, because SQL Server keeps a special bitmap in every row to indicate which nullable columns actually *are* **NULL**. If **NULL**s are allowed, SQL Server must decode this bitmap for every row accessed. Allowing **NULL** also adds complexity in application code, which can often lead to bugs. You must always add special logic to account for the case of **NULL**.

You, as the database designer, might understand the nuances of **NULL** and three-valued logic when used in aggregate functions, when doing joins, and when searching by values. However, you need to consider whether your development staff understands as well. If possible, it is recommended that you use all **NOT NULL** columns and define default values (discussed later in this chapter) for missing or unknown entries (and possibly make such character columns **varchar** if the default value is significantly different in size from the typical entered value).

In any case, it's good practice to explicitly declare **NOT NULL** or **NULL** when creating a table. If no such declaration exists, SQL Server assumes **NOT NULL**. (In other words, no **NULL**s will be allowed.) However, you can set the default to allow **NULL**s by using a session setting or a database option. The ANSI SQL standard says that if neither is specified, **NULL** should be assumed, but as mentioned, this isn't SQL Server's default. If you script your DDL and then run it against another server that has a different default setting, you'll get different results if you don't explicitly declare **NULL** or **NOT NULL** in the column definition.

Several database options and session settings can control SQL Server's behavior regarding **NULL** values. You set database options using the system procedure **sp_dboption**. And you enable session settings for one connection at a time using the **SET** command.

The database option *ANSI null default* corresponds to the two session settings **ANSI_NULL_DFLT_ON** or **ANSI_NULL_DFLT_OFF**. When the ANSI null default database option is false (the default setting for SQL Server), new columns created with the **ALTER TABLE** and **CREATE TABLE** statements are, by default, **NOT NULL** if the nullability status of the column isn't explicitly specified. **SET ANSI_NULL_DFLT_OFF** and **SET ANSI_NULL_DFLT_ON** are mutually exclusive options, yet both options exist to determine whether the database option should be overridden. When on, each option forces the opposite option off. Neither option, when set off, turns the opposite option on.

Use the function **GETANSINULL** to determine the default nullability for your current session. This function returns 1 when new columns will allow null values and the column or data type nullability isn't explicitly defined when the table is created or altered. We strongly recommend declaring **NULL** or **NOT NULL** explicitly when you create a column. This removes all ambiguity and ensures that you're in control of how the table will be built regardless of the default nullability setting.

The database option **CONCAT NULL** corresponds to the session setting **SET CONCAT_NULL_YIELDS_NULL**. When **CONCAT_NULL_YIELDS_NULL** is on, concatenating a **NULL** value with a string yields a **NULL** result. For example, **SELECT 'abc' + NULL** yields **NULL**. When **SET CONCAT_NULL_YIELDS_NULL** is off, concatenating a **NULL** value with a string yields the string itself. (The **NULL** value is treated as an empty string.) For example, **SELECT 'abc' + NULL** yields **abc**. If the session level setting isn't specified, the value of the database option *concat null yields null* applies. Also, if **SET CONCAT_NULL_YIELDS_NULL** is off, SQL Server uses the *concat null yields null* setting of **sp_dboption**.

> **Note**
>
> *The reason why some of these options are represented in bold and others in italics is because of the different names for the options in the different interfaces to SQL Server. Setting an option from the Query Analyzer—or any front end that uses Transact-SQL—requires the specification of one option. On the other hand, setting that option from Enterprise Manager, or through any application that uses SQL Distributed Management Objects (SQL-DMO) requires the use of the italicized option name.*

The database option *ANSI nulls* corresponds to the session setting **SET ANSI_NULLS**. When true, all comparisons to a null value evaluate to **NULL** (unknown). When false, comparisons of non-Unicode values to a **NULL** value evaluate to **TRUE** if both values are **NULL**. In addition, when this value is **TRUE**, your code must use the condition **IS NULL** to determine whether a column has a **NULL** value. When this value is **FALSE**, SQL Server allows = **NULL** as a synonym for **IS NULL** and <> **NULL** as a synonym for **IS NOT NULL**. You can see this behavior yourself by looking at the **titles** table in the **pubs** database. The **titles** table has two rows with a **NULL** price. The first batch of statements that follows, when executed from the Query Analyzer, should return two rows, and the second batch should return no rows:

```
-- First batch will return 2 rows
use pubs
set ansi_nulls off
go
select * from titles where price = null
go

--Second batch will return no rows
use pubs
set ansi_nulls on
go
select * from titles where price = null
go
```

A fourth session setting is **ANSI_DEFAULTS**. Setting this to **ON** is a shortcut for enabling both **ANSI_NULLS** and **ANSI_NULL_DEFAULT_ON**, as well as other session settings not related to **NULL** handling. SQL Server's ODBC driver and the SQL Server OLE DB provider automatically set **ANSI_DEFAULTS** to **ON**. You can change the **ANSI_NULLS** setting when defining your DSN. Two of the client tools supplied with SQL Server (Query Analyzer and the text-based osql) use the SQL Server ODBC driver but then internally turn off some of these options. To see which options are enabled for the tool you're using, run the following command:

```
DBCC USEROPTIONS
```

Warning

*Although internally SQL Server's default behavior is to not allow **NULLs** unless specifically declared in the **CREATE TABLE** statement, you might never see this behavior in action. Because SQL Server Query Analyzer, the basic tool for submitting SQL code to SQL Server, is ODBC-based, it automatically turns on the **ANSI_NULL_ DEFAULT_ON** option. This setting means that all your new columns will allow **NULLs** by default. It cannot be overemphasized that your best bet for avoiding confusion is to always state explicitly in your table definition whether **NULLs** should be allowed.*

The database compatibility level controls two additional aspects of how SQL Server handles **NULL** values, as determined by the system procedure **sp_dbcmptlevel**. If the compatibility level is set to 70, the nullability of bit columns without explicit nullability is determined by either the session setting of **SET ANSI_NULL_DFLT_ON** or **SET ANSI_NULL_ DFLT_OFF** or the database setting of *ANSI null default*. In 60 or 65 compatibility mode, bit columns created without an explicit **NULL** or **NOT NULL** option in **CREATE TABLE** or **ALTER TABLE** are created as **NOT NULL**.

The database compatibility level also controls whether SQL Server interprets an empty string (two single quotes with nothing between them) as a single space or a true empty string. In compatibility level 60 or 65, SQL Server interprets empty strings as single spaces. If the compatibility level is 70, SQL Server interprets empty strings as truly empty—that is, a character string with no characters in it. Sometimes this empty space is referred to as a **NULL**, but SQL Server doesn't treat it like a **NULL**. SQL Server marks **NULL**s internally as **NULL**s, but an empty string is actually stored as a variable-length character field of 0 length.

In 60 or 65 compatibility mode, the empty string ('') is interpreted as a single space in **INSERT** or assignment statements on **varchar** data. In concatenating **varchar**, **char**, or **text** data, the empty string is interpreted as a single space. This means that you can never have a truly empty string. The only alternative in 60 or 65 compatibility mode would be to define the field as allowing **NULL**s, and use a **NULL** in place of an empty string.

As you can see, you can configure and control the treatment and behavior of **NULL** values several ways, and you might think it would be impossible to keep track of all the variations. If you try to control every aspect of **NULL** handling separately within each individual session, you can cause immeasurable confusion and even grief. However, you'll notice that most of the issues become moot if you follow a few basic recommendations:

♦ Never allow **NULL** values inside your tables.

♦ Include a specific **NOT NULL** qualification in your table definitions.

♦ Make sure all your databases are running in 70 compatibility mode.

If you must use **NULL**s in some cases, you can minimize problems by always following the same rules, and the easiest rules to follow are the ones that ANSI already specifies.

Types Of Data Integrity

An important step in database planning is deciding the best way to enforce the integrity of the data. Data integrity refers to the consistency and accuracy of data that is stored in a database. There are four types of data integrity: domain integrity, entity integrity, referential integrity, and user-defined integrity. Figure 10.3 illustrates how domain integrity, entity integrity, and referential integrity relate to each other.

♦ *Domain integrity*—Domain (or *column*) integrity specifies the set of data values that are valid for a column and determines whether **NULL** values are allowed. Domain integrity is enforced by validity checking and by restricting the data type, format, or range of possible values allowed in a column.

♦ *Entity integrity*—Entity (or *table*) integrity requires that all rows in a table have a unique identifier, known as the *primary key value*. Whether the primary key value can be changed, or whether the whole row can be deleted, depends on the level of integrity required between the primary key and any other tables.

♦ *Referential integrity*—Referential integrity ensures that the relationship between the primary key (in a referenced table) and the foreign key (in each of the referencing tables) is always maintained. The maintenance of this relationship means that the following conditions must be met:

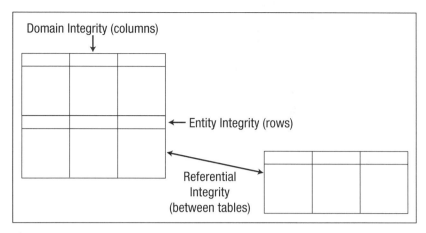

Figure 10.3
Types of data integrity.

- ◆ A row in a referenced table cannot be deleted, nor can the primary key be changed, if a foreign key refers to the row. For example, you cannot delete a customer that has placed one or more orders.

- ◆ A row cannot be added to a referencing table if the foreign key does not match the primary key of an existing row in the referenced table. For example, you cannot create an order for a customer that does not exist.

- ◆ *User-defined integrity*—User-defined integrity allows you to define specific business rules that do not fall into one of the other integrity categories. All the integrity categories support user-defined integrity. Constraints, stored procedures, and triggers are available for enforcing user-defined integrity. We will discuss these in depth later in this chapter and in Chapter 11.

Enforcing Data Integrity

You can enforce data integrity through two methods: declarative data integrity and procedural data integrity.

Declarative Data Integrity

With *declarative integrity*, you define the criteria that the data must meet as part of an object definition, and then SQL Server 7 automatically ensures that the data conforms to the criteria. The preferred method of implementing basic data integrity is to use declarative integrity. Consider the following facts about the declarative method:

- ◆ Declarative integrity is part of the database definition created by using declared constraints that are defined directly on tables and columns.

- ◆ You can implement declarative integrity by using constraints.

- ◆ SQL Server 7 constraints are fully ANSI SQL-92 compliant.

Procedural Data Integrity

With *procedural integrity*, you write scripts that both define and enforce the criteria that data must meet. You should limit your use of procedural integrity to more complicated business logic and exceptions. For example, use procedural integrity when you want to have a cascading delete. The following facts apply to procedural integrity:

♦ You can implement procedural integrity on the client or the server by using other programming languages and tools.

♦ You can implement procedural integrity on SQL Server with defaults, rules, triggers, and stored procedures.

Using Constraints

Constraints are the preferred method of enforcing data integrity. This section discusses how to determine the type of constraint to use, what type of data integrity each type of constraint enforces, how to define constraints, and how to disable constraint checking.

Determining Which Type Of Constraint To Use

Constraints are an ANSI-standard method of enforcing data integrity. Each type of data integrity—domain, entity, referential, and user defined—is enforced with separate types of constraints. Constraints ensure that valid data values are entered in columns and that relationships are maintained between tables.

Table 10.1 describes the different types of constraints.

Table 10.1   The different types of SQL Server constraints.

Type Of Integrity	Constraint Type	Description
Domain	DEFAULT	Specifies the value that will be provided for the column when a value has not been supplied explicitly in an **INSERT** statement.
	CHECK	Specifies a validity rule for the data values in a column.
	FOREIGN KEY	Values in the foreign key column(s) must match values in the primary key column(s) of the referenced table.
Entity	PRIMARY KEY	Uniquely identifies each row—ensures that users do not enter duplicate values and that an index is created to enhance performance. **NULL** values are not allowed.
	UNIQUE	Prevents duplicates in nonprimary keys and ensures that an index is created to enhance performance. **NULL** values are allowed.
Referential	FOREIGN KEY	Defines a column or combination of columns whose values match the primary key of either the same or another table.
User-defined	CHECK	Specifies a validity rule for the data values in a column.

Defining Constraints

You define constraints by using the **CREATE TABLE** or **ALTER TABLE** statement. You can add constraints to a table that has existing data, and you can place constraints on single or multiple columns. When you're adding single or multiple column constraints, use the following criteria:

♦ If the constraint is defined on a single column, it can reference only that column and is called a *column-level constraint*.

♦ If a constraint is not defined on a single column, it can reference multiple columns and is called a *table-level constraint*.

♦ **DEFAULT** constraints must be column-level.

♦ Column-level **CHECK** constraints can reference only a single column.

♦ Table-level **CHECK** constraints can reference all columns in the table.

♦ Constraints cannot reference columns in other tables.

You can find the syntax for creation of constraints in the Books Online help file; however, it is rather confusing if you look at the prototype. Instead, let's consider some statements that create constraints on tables. For example, the following code creates an **authors** table and defines column-level **PRIMARY KEY** and **CHECK** constraints on two of the columns in the table. The **CHECK** constraint ensures that the status for an author can only be **'CONTRACT'** or **'EMPLOYEE'**:

```
CREATE TABLE authors
   (au_id      int      NOT NULL CONSTRAINT au_PK PRIMARY KEY,
    firstname  char(30) NOT NULL,
    lastname   char(30) NOT NULL,
    status     char(10) NOT NULL
    CONSTRAINT cat_CHK CHECK (status IN ('CONTRACT', 'EMPLOYEE'))
   )
```

As you can see, the last statement in the table's definition—which is actually part of the column definition for **status** (a fact that you can easily discern because the constraint falls within the column-definition parentheses for the **CREATE TABLE** statement and there is no comma after the **status** column's definition)—includes the **CONSTRAINT** keyword, the name of the constraint, and the type of constraint (in this case, **CHECK**). The information within the parentheses specifies the possible incoming values for new rows in the table, indicating that only **CONTRACT** or **EMPLOYEE** status will be accepted, and if the user tries to input a different value, the database will generate and return an error to the user.

Let's take a look at another brief example; this one creates an **employee** table and defines table-level **PRIMARY KEY** and **CHECK** constraints on the table. The **CHECK** constraint ensures that the date the employee was employed is earlier than the date the employee was terminated:

```
CREATE TABLE employee
    (emp_num     int     NOT NULL,
     lastname    char(30) NOT NULL,
     firstname   char(30) NOT NULL,
     employed    datetime NOT NULL,
     terminated  datetime NULL,
     CONSTRAINT emp_PK PRIMARY KEY (emp_num),
     CONSTRAINT date_CHK CHECK (employed < terminated))
```

Considerations For Using Constraints

Consider the following facts when you implement or modify constraints:

♦ You can create, change, and drop constraints without having to drop and re-create a table.

♦ You must build error-handling logic into your client applications to test whether a constraint has been violated whenever data is modified on the server.

♦ By default, SQL Server verifies existing data when you add a constraint to a table.

♦ You should specify names for constraints when you create them, because SQL Server provides complicated, system-generated names. Names must be unique to the database object owner and follow the rules for SQL Server identifiers.

♦ To obtain information about constraints, execute the **sp_helpconstraint** or **sp_help** system stored procedures or query information schema views, such as **check_constraints**, **referential_constraints**, **table_constraints**, **constraint_column_usage**, and **constraint_table_usage**.

♦ The following system tables store constraint definitions: **syscomments**, **sysreferences**, and **sysconstraints**.

DEFAULT Constraints

A **DEFAULT** constraint enters a value in a column when one is not specified in an **INSERT** statement. **DEFAULT** constraints enforce domain integrity. For example, the following code adds a **DEFAULT** constraint that inserts the value **'Unknown'** into the **firstname** column if a value is not provided when a row is inserted into the **member** table:

```
USE library
ALTER TABLE member
ADD
CONSTRAINT firstname DEFAULT 'Unknown' FOR firstname
```

Consider the following facts when you apply a **DEFAULT** constraint:

♦ It only applies to **INSERT** statements.

♦ Only one **DEFAULT** constraint can be defined per column.

♦ It cannot be placed on columns with the **IDENTITY** property or on columns with the **timestamp** data type.

♦ You can use functions to supply default values. For example, you can use the **SUSER_SNAME** function to record which users insert data or the **GETDATE** function to record the date and time that data was inserted.

CHECK Constraints

A **CHECK** constraint restricts the data values that can be stored in one or more columns. A **CHECK** constraint specifies a logical expression that must be true for data to be accepted. For example, the following code adds a **CHECK** constraint to ensure that a phone number is in the Las Vegas area code and conforms to accepted phone number formatting:

```
USE library
ALTER TABLE adult
ADD CONSTRAINT phone_no
CHECK (phone_no LIKE '(702)[0-9][0-9][0-9]-[0-9][0-9][0-9][0-9]')
```

Consider the following facts when you apply a **CHECK** constraint:

♦ It verifies data every time you execute an **INSERT** or **UPDATE** statement.

♦ It can reference other columns in the same table. For example, a **salary** column could reference a value in a **job_grade** column.

♦ It cannot be placed on columns with the **IDENTITY** property or columns with the **timestamp** or **uniqueidentifier** data type.

♦ It cannot contain **subqueries**.

The following statement adds a table-level **CHECK** constraint to the loan table called **loan_date_check**. The constraint validates that the value in the **due_date** column is greater than or equal to the value in the **out_date** column:

```
USE library
ALTER TABLE loan
  ADD CONSTRAINT loan_date_check
  CHECK (due_date >= out_date)
GO
```

PRIMARY KEY Constraints

A **PRIMARY KEY** constraint defines a primary key on a table. The value in the primary key uniquely identifies each row in the table. This constraint enforces entity integrity.

Tip

*A unique index is automatically created to support primary key and unique key constraints. The syntax for **PRIMARY KEY** and **UNIQUE** constraints allows you to specify characteristics for this index.*

For example, the following statement adds a constraint that specifies that the primary key value of the **member** table is the member number and indicates that a clustered index will be created to enforce the constraint:

```
USE library
ALTER TABLE member
  ADD CONSTRAINT PK_member_member_no
  PRIMARY KEY CLUSTERED (member_no)
```

Consider the following facts when you apply a **PRIMARY KEY** constraint:

◆ Only one **PRIMARY KEY** constraint can be defined per table.

◆ The primary key values must be unique.

◆ **NULL** values are not allowed.

◆ You can specify whether a *clustered* or *nonclustered index* is created (clustered is the default if it does not already exist). If a clustered index does exist, you must drop it first or specify that a nonclustered index be created.

UNIQUE Constraints

A **UNIQUE** constraint specifies that two rows in a column cannot have the same value. This constraint enforces entity integrity. A unique index is created automatically to support the constraint.

A **UNIQUE** constraint is helpful when you already have a primary key (such as an employee number) but you want to guarantee that other columns (such as an employee's driver's license number) are also unique.

For example, in an **employee** database, the following statement creates a **UNIQUE**, nonclustered constraint on the driver's license column in the **employee** table:

```
ALTER TABLE employee
  ADD CONSTRAINT u_driver_lic_no
  UNIQUE NONCLUSTERED (driver_lic_no)
```

Consider the following facts when you apply a **UNIQUE** constraint:

◆ It can allow **NULL** values.

◆ You can place multiple **UNIQUE** constraints on a table.

◆ You can apply the **UNIQUE** constraint to one or more columns that must have unique values but are not the primary key of a table.

♦ The **UNIQUE** constraint is enforced through the creation of a unique index on the specified column or columns.

♦ The **UNIQUE** constraint defaults to using a unique nonclustered index unless a clustered index is specified.

FOREIGN KEY Constraints

A **FOREIGN KEY** constraint enforces referential integrity. The **FOREIGN KEY** constraint defines a reference to the column(s) of a **PRIMARY KEY** constraint or a **UNIQUE** constraint of either the same or another table.

The following T-SQL statement uses a **FOREIGN KEY** constraint to ensure that any juvenile member is associated with a valid adult member:

```
USE library
ALTER TABLE juvenile
  ADD CONSTRAINT FK_adult_memberno
  FOREIGN KEY (adult_member_no)
  REFERENCES adult(member_no)
```

Consider the following facts and guidelines when you apply a **FOREIGN KEY** constraint:

♦ It provides single or multicolumn referential integrity. The number of columns and data types that are specified in the **FOREIGN KEY** statement must match the number of columns and data types in the **REFERENCES** clause. Column names do not need to match.

♦ Unlike **PRIMARY KEY** or **UNIQUE** constraints, **FOREIGN KEY** constraints do not create indexes automatically. Nevertheless, a **FOREIGN KEY** is a good candidate for indexing and you should consider adding an index on the **FOREIGN KEY** column(s) to improve join performance.

♦ To modify data in a table that has a **FOREIGN KEY** constraint defined on it, users must have **SELECT** or **REFERENCES** permissions on the tables that are referenced by the **FOREIGN KEY** constraint.

♦ You must use only the **REFERENCES** clause without the **FOREIGN KEY** clause when you reference a column in the same table.

Disabling Data Checking When Adding Constraints

When you define a constraint on a table that already contains data, SQL Server checks the data automatically to verify that it meets the constraint requirements. However, you can disable constraint checking of existing data, if you do so at the time that the constraint is added to the table. Consider the following guidelines for disabling constraint checking on existing data:

♦ You can disable checking only when adding **CHECK** and **FOREIGN KEY** constraints. Data is always checked when **PRIMARY KEY** and **UNIQUE** constraints are added.

♦ To disable constraint checking when you add a **CHECK** or **FOREIGN KEY** constraint to a table with existing data, include the **WITH NOCHECK** option in the **ALTER TABLE** statement.

♦ Use the **WITH NOCHECK** option only if existing data is known to conform to the new constraint or if existing data will never be updated.

Tip

*Data modifications that are made after you add the constraint must satisfy the constraint even if the columns used in the constraint are not modified. For example, if you add a **CHECK** constraint to **ColumnA** and specify the **WITH NOCHECK** option, the existing values in **ColumnA** are not checked. If you later update the value of **ColumnB**, and the existing value of **ColumnA** for the row being updated does not meet the **CHECK** constraint requirements, the update fails.*

Disabling Constraint Checking

Constraint checking can be disabled for existing **CHECK** and **FOREIGN KEY** constraints so that any data that you modify or add to the table is not checked against the constraint. To avoid the overhead of constraint checking, you might want to disable constraints when either of the following considerations is true:

♦ You are loading a large amount of data that is known to conform to the constraints.

♦ You want to load a large amount of data that does not conform to the constraints. Later, you can execute queries to change the data and then re-enable the constraints.

To disable a constraint, use the **ALTER TABLE** statement and the **NOCHECK CON-STRAINT** clause. To enable a disabled constraint, use the **ALTER TABLE** statement and the **CHECK CONSTRAINT** clause. You can disable or enable all the constraints on a table with the **ALTER TABLE** statement and either the **NOCHECK CONSTRAINT ALL** or the **CHECK CONSTRAINT ALL** clause.

The following statement disables the **correct_amount** constraint on the **sales** table in the **pubs** database.

```
USE pubs
  ALTER TABLE sales
  NOCHECK CONSTRAINT correct_amount
```

You can re-enable the constraint by executing another **ALTER TABLE** statement with the **CHECK CONSTRAINT** clause.

```
USE pubs
  ALTER TABLE sales
  CHECK CONSTRAINT correct_amount
```

To determine whether a constraint is enabled or disabled on a table, execute the **sp_help** *table_name* or the **sp_helpconstraint** *table_name* system stored procedure.

Introduction To Views

When you use a *view*, you can store a predefined query as an object in the database for later use, as shown in Figure 10.4. The tables queried in a view are called *base tables*. With a few exceptions, any **SELECT** statement can be named and stored as a view.

Common examples of views include the following:

♦ A subset of rows or columns of a base table

♦ A union of two or more base tables

♦ A join of two or more base tables

♦ A statistical summary of a base table

♦ A subset of another view, or some combination of views and base tables

The following statement creates the **TitleView** view in the library database. The view displays two columns in the **title** table:

```
USE library
GO

CREATE VIEW dbo.TitleView AS
  SELECT title, author
  FROM title
```

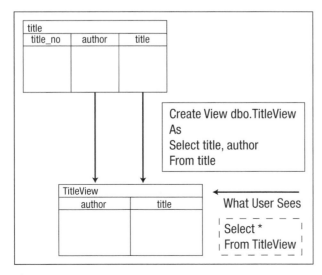

Figure 10.4
How a view works.

Then, if you execute a **SELECT** statement against the view, as shown in the following statement, the returned information will show only the **title** and **author** columns:

```
SELECT * FROM TitleView
```

Advantages Of Views

Views offer several advantages, including focusing data for users, masking data complexity, simplifying permission management, and organizing data for export to other applications.

Focus The Data For Users

Views create a controlled environment that allows access to specific data and conceals other data. Data that is unnecessary, sensitive, or inappropriate can be left out of a view. Users can manipulate the display of data in a view, similarly to a table. In addition, with the proper permissions and a few restrictions, users can modify the data that a view produces.

Mask Database Complexity

Views shield the complexity of the database design from the user. This means that developers can change the design without affecting user interaction with the database. In addition, users can see a friendlier version of the data by using names that are easier to understand than the cryptic names that are often used in databases.

Complex queries, including distributed queries to heterogeneous data, can also be masked through views. The user queries the view instead of writing the query or executing a script.

Simplify Management Of User Permissions

Instead of granting permission for users to query specific columns in base tables, database owners can grant permission for users to query data through views only. This type of querying also protects changes in the design of the underlying base tables. Users can continue to query the view without interruption.

Organize Data For Export To Other Applications

You can create a view based on a complex query that joins two or more tables and then export the data to another application for further analysis.

Information Schema Views

Information schema views are a good example of the benefits of using views instead of querying base tables directly. With information schema views, SQL Server can present system data in a consistent manner, even when significant changes have been made to the system tables. This ability allows applications that retrieve system information from information schema views to work properly.

For example, to retrieve information about the tables in the current database, query the **information_schema.tables** information schema view rather than the **sysobjects** system table.

Creating, Altering, And Dropping Views

Before users can use views, the views must be created in the database. The following sections discuss how you can create, alter, and drop views.

Creating Views

You can create views with the Create View wizard, Microsoft SQL Server Enterprise Manager, Transact-SQL, or from within the database manager in the ADP window. Views can be created in the current database only.

Creating A View

When you create a view, SQL Server verifies the existence of objects that are referenced in the view definition. Your view name must follow the rules for identifiers. Specifying a view owner name is optional. You should develop a consistent naming convention to distinguish views from tables. For example, you might add the word **View** as a suffix to each view object that you create. This naming convention allows similar objects (tables and views) to be easily distinguished. Let's consider briefly, then, the prototype for the **CREATE VIEW** statement:

```
CREATE VIEW [view_owner.]view_name
  [(column[, ...n])]
  [WITH ENCRYPTION]
AS
  select_statement
 [WITH CHECK OPTION]
```

To execute the **CREATE VIEW** statement, you must be a member of the **sysadmin**, **db_owner**, or **db_ddladmin** role, or you must have been granted the **CREATE VIEW** permission by a member of the **sysadmin** or **db_owner** role. You must also have the **SELECT** permission on all tables or views that are referenced within the view; otherwise, the view will return an empty resultset when queried.

To avoid situations in which the owner of a view and the owner of the underlying tables differ, it is recommended that the **dbo** user own all objects in a database. Always specify the **dbo** user as the owner name when you create the object; otherwise, the object will be created with your username as the object owner.

The contents of a view are specified with a **SELECT** statement. With a few limitations, views can be as complex as you like. Column names for the columns in the view can be specified in one of two ways: in the **SELECT** statement, by using column aliasing, or in the **CREATE VIEW** statement. You must specify column names if any of the following conditions are true:

♦ Any of the columns of the view are derived from an arithmetic expression, built-in function, or constant.

♦ Any columns in the base tables share the same name.

♦ You want to use a name for a column that is different than the column's name in the base table.

When you create views, it is important to test the **SELECT** statement that defines the view to ensure that SQL Server returns the expected resultset. Create the view after you have written and tested the **SELECT** statement and verified the results.

You can use the Create View Wizard within the SQL Server Enterprise Manager to create a view quickly. To do so, perform the following steps:

1. Open SQL Server Enterprise Manager.

2. In the console tree, click on your server.

3. On the SQL Server Enterprise Manager Tools menu, click on Wizards.

4. Expand Database, click on Create View Wizard, and then click on OK.

5. Use the information in Table 10.2 to create a view that lists books written by Jane Austen.

Warning

*Due to an error in the Create View Wizard, you cannot specify the owner when you specify the view name in the Create View Wizard. Do not try to specify an owner name when you name the view in the Create View Wizard; instead of the owner being set, the view name will include the owner name. You can specify the owner name by editing the **CREATE VIEW** statement manually in the last step of the wizard.*

6. Query the view to ensure that you received the expected resultset.

Note

Clearly, we will generally want to create and manage views using the Da Vinci tools that come with Access 2000. Although understanding how to create views from the Enterprise Manager is useful and important, you will see in Chapter 11 exactly how to go about creating a view from the Access 2000 IDE.

Table 10.2   Creating a view that lists books written by Jane Austen.

Option	Value
Select Database	library
Select Tables	title
Select Columns	title.title, title.author
Define Restriction	WHERE author = 'Jane Austen'
Name The View	AustenBooksView

Restrictions On Defining Views

When you create views, consider the following restrictions:

♦ The **CREATE VIEW** statement cannot include the **ORDER BY**, **COMPUTE**, or **COMPUTE BY** clause or the **INTO** keyword.

♦ Views cannot reference temporary tables.

♦ Views cannot reference more than 1,024 columns.

♦ The **CREATE VIEW** statement cannot be combined with other Transact-SQL statements in a single batch.

Views Of Joined Tables

Views are often created to provide a convenient way of looking at information from two or more joined tables in one central location, as shown in Figure 10.5.

In the following example code, we create the **BirthdayView** view, whose purpose is to join the member and juvenile tables and control the fields that are displayed:

```
USE library
GO

 CREATE VIEW dbo.BirthdayView
  (Lastname, Firstname, BirthDate)
AS
  SELECT lastname, firstname,
      CONVERT(char(8), birth_date, 2)
  FROM member JOIN juvenile
  ON member.member_no = juvenile.member_no
```

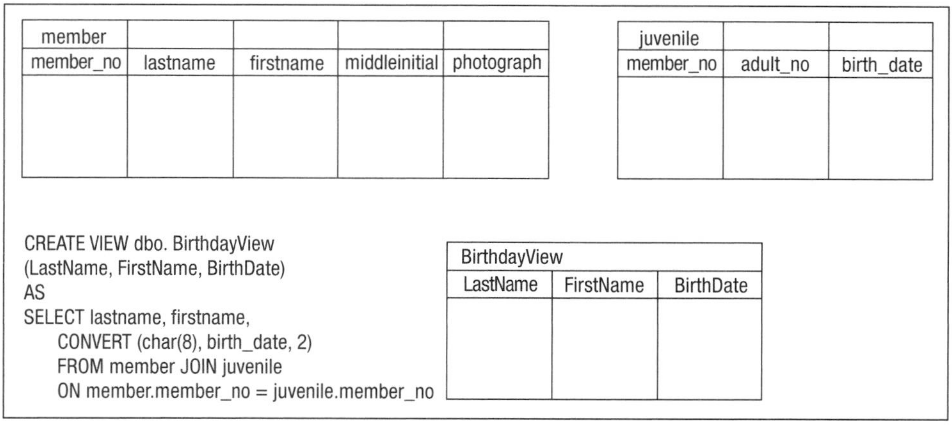

Figure 10.5
View of joined tables.

After the view is created, you can then query the view to see the contents:

```
SELECT * FROM BirthdayView
```

Avoiding Outer Joins In Views

You should create views only on tables that have been joined with an inner join. SQL Server allows you to include an outer join in a view definition, but an outer join is not a relational command and thus may produce unexpected results when users query the view. As you know, outer joins return **NULL** values in columns from the outer table and users will typically not know what these nulls represent.

Altering And Dropping Views

Views are often altered in response to requests from users for additional information or to changes in the underlying table definition. You can alter a view by dropping and re-creating it or by executing the **ALTER VIEW** statement.

Warning
The **ALTER VIEW** statement is not included in the ANSI SQL-92 standard.

Altering Views

The **ALTER VIEW** statement changes the definition of a view while allowing you to retain permissions for the view. This statement is subject to the same restrictions as the **CREATE VIEW** statement. If you drop a view and then re-create it, you must reassign permissions to it. The following prototype shows how you will issue the **ALTER VIEW** statement:

```
ALTER VIEW view_name [(column
  [, ...n])]
  [WITH ENCRYPTION]
AS
  select_statement
  [WITH CHECK OPTION]
```

If you use the **WITH ENCRYPTION** or **WITH CHECK OPTION** clause when you create the view, you must include it in the **ALTER VIEW** statement if you want to retain the functionality that the option provides.

When the view is created, the column list that the view will return is stored in the **syscolumns** system table. If you define a view with a **SELECT *** statement and then alter the structure of the underlying tables by adding columns, the new columns do not appear in the view. When all columns are selected in a **CREATE VIEW** statement, the list of all columns is interpreted only when you first create the view. To see the new columns in the view, you must alter the view. For example, the following program code alters the **TitleView** view to add the **synopsis** column:

```
USE library
GO

ALTER VIEW dbo.TitleView
AS
  SELECT title, author, synopsis
  FROM title
```

Dropping Views

If you no longer need a view, you can remove its definition from the database by executing the **DROP VIEW** statement. Dropping a view removes its definition and all permissions assigned to it. Furthermore, if users query any secondary views that reference the dropped view, they receive an error message. Dropping a table that is referenced by a view does not drop the view automatically; you must drop the view explicitly.

The permission to drop a view defaults to the view owner and is nontransferable. However, members of the **sysadmin** or **db_owner** role can drop any object by specifying the owner name in the **DROP VIEW** statement.

Nested Views

When views that join several tables and evaluate complex expressions are nested within another view, as shown in Figure 10.6, the immediate source of any performance problems may be difficult to determine. Therefore, you should consider creating separate view definitions rather than nesting views.

You can nest views up to 32 levels deep. However, if you do decide to nest views, you should not nest more than three levels in order to minimize the effect of hiding performance problems. To understand how nested views work, consider the following example, in which the **LoanableView** view queries a subset of rows from the **CopywideView** view.

```
USE library
GO
CREATE VIEW dbo.LoanableView
AS
  SELECT *
  FROM CopywideView
  WHERE loanable = 'y'
```

The view definition of **LoanableView** hides the complexity of the underlying query that is used to create **CopywideView**, which joins three underlying tables, and is constructed as shown here:

```
USE library
GO
```

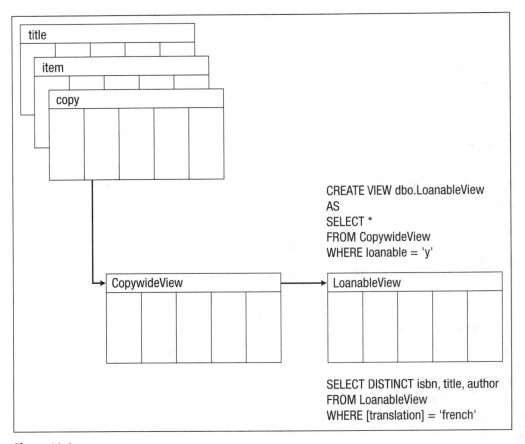

Figure 10.6
Nested views.

```
CREATE VIEW dbo.CopywideView
AS
  SELECT copy.isbn, copy.copy_no,
      title.title, title.author,
      item.[translation], item.loanable, copy.on_loan
  FROM copy JOIN item
      ON item.isbn = copy.isbn
      JOIN title
      ON title.title_no = copy.title_no
```

Because of the level of indirection provided by having the intermediate table, if users experience any performance problems when they execute the following query to list the available French books, the source of the problem will not be readily apparent:

```
SELECT DISTINCT isbn, title, author
  FROM LoanableView
```

```
WHERE [translation] = 'french'
ORDER BY title
```

Avoiding Broken Ownership Chains

SQL Server allows the owner of an object to retain control over the users who are authorized to access the object. In the following sections, we will consider some of the ways this issue has importance in a SQL Server installation.

Dependent Objects With Different Owners

View definitions depend on underlying objects (views or tables). These dependencies can be thought of as the ownership chain. If the owner of a view also owns the underlying objects, the owner only has to grant permission on the view. When the object is used, permissions are checked only on the view.

If the same user does not own all objects in the chain, the ownership chain is broken. When the object is used, permissions are checked on each dependent object with a different owner.

For example, consider Figure 10.7. As the figure indicates, Brett creates **view2**. With the following statement, she grants permission to George to query **view2**.

```
GRANT select ON view2 TO George
```

However, **brett.view2** depends on an object (**view1**) owned by another user (Sue). Permissions will be checked on each dependent object with a different owner when **view2** is queried. Therefore, when George queries **brett.view2** using the following statement, one of several things is going to happen:

```
SELECT * FROM brett.view2
```

Because **brett.view2** depends on **sue.view1**, SQL Server checks George's permissions on **brett.view2** and **sue.view1**. If Sue has previously granted permission to George on **view1**,

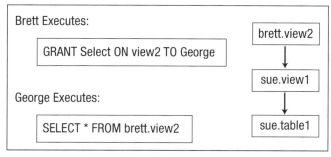

Figure 10.7
Broken ownership chain example.

George is allowed access. If Sue has not previously granted permission to George, access is denied, allowing Sue to retain control over the users who are authorized to access the objects that she creates.

To prevent broken ownership chains and simplify permissions management, you should always create objects with the same owner by specifying the object owner when you create new objects, such as views. The default object owner in SQL Server is **dbo**. It is a good idea to specify **dbo** as the owner of objects that you create.

Locating View Definition Information

You may want to see the definition of a view to alter the view definition or to understand how its data is derived from the base tables. Both the Enterprise Manager and Transact-SQL provide you with the means to gather or alter view information. In the next sections, we will look at accessing different types of view information.

Locating View Definitions

You can locate view definition information with SQL Server Enterprise Manager or by querying the information schema views, system stored procedures, and system tables detailed in Table 10.3. Querying system tables is not recommended because the structure of system tables could change in future versions of SQL Server, and the system tables are intended for internal use by SQL Server only.

To display the text that is used to create a view, use SQL Server Enterprise Manager, query the **information_schema.views** view, or execute the **sp_helptext** system stored procedure with the view name as the parameter. For example, you might issue the following command from the Query Analyzer:

```
EXEC sp_helptext BirthdayView
```

Table 10.3   Tools SQL Server provides to help you obtain system information.

Information Schema View Or System Table	Displays Information On
information_schema.tables or **sysobjects**	View names
information_schema.view_table_usage	Underlying table names
information_schema.views, **sp_helptext**, or **syscomments**	View definition
information_schema.view_column_usage or **syscolumns**	Columns that are defined in a view
sp_depends or **sysdepends**	View dependencies
information_schema.table_privileges or **sysprotects**	Permissions

Doing so will result in output similar to the following:

```
Text
- - - - - - - - - - - - - - - - - - - - - - - - - - - - - - - - - - - - - - - - -
CREATE VIEW dbo.BirthdayView
    (Lastname, Firstname, [Birth Date])
AS
SELECT lastname, firstname,
    CONVERT(char(8), birth_date, 2)
FROM member INNER JOIN juvenile
    ON member.member_no = juvenile.member_no
```

Locating View Dependencies

To retrieve a report of the tables or views on which a view depends and of objects that depend on a particular view, use SQL Server Enterprise Manager or execute the **sp_depends** system stored procedure. Before you alter or drop a table, use **sp_depends** to determine whether any objects reference the table. For example, let's see what type of resultset might be returned when we look at the dependencies for the **BirthdayView** view:

```
In the current database, the specified object references the following:
name                    type                updated selected column
- - - - - - - - - - -   - - - - - - - - -   - - - - - - - - - - -  - - - - - - - -
dbo.member              user table          no      no       member_no
dbo.member              user table          no      no       lastname
dbo.member              user table          no      no       firstname
dbo.juvenile            user table          no      no       member_no
dbo.juvenile            user table          no      no       birth_date
```

Additionally, you can use it the other way—passing in a lower-level object, like the **member** table—and seeing what views are defined that use that object. This might return a resultset similar to the following:

```
In the current database, the specified object is referenced by the following:
name                                        type
- - - - - - - - - - - - - - - - - - - - -   - - - - - - - - - - -
dbo.BirthdayView                            view
dbo.ChildwideView                           view
dbo.AdultwideView                           view
dbo.OnLoanView                              view
```

Hiding View Definitions

Users can see the definition of a view by using SQL Server Enterprise Manager or by querying the **information_schema.views** view or the **syscomments** system table. If you prefer that users not be able to do this, use the **WITH ENCRYPTION** option with the **CREATE VIEW** statement.

Before you encrypt a view, ensure that the view definition (script) is saved to a file. To unencrypt the text of a view, you must drop the view and re-create it or alter the view and use the original syntax. You cannot retrieve the unencrypted version of the text after using the **WITH ENCRYPTION** option.

For example, let's create the **dbo.UnpaidFinesView** view using the **WITH ENCRYPTION** option so that the view definition is hidden from prying eyes:

```
USE library
GO

CREATE VIEW dbo.UnpaidFinesView (Member, TotalUnpaidFines)
  WITH ENCRYPTION
AS
  SELECT member_no, (SUM(fine_assessed-fine_paid))
  FROM loanhist
  GROUP BY member_no
  HAVING SUM(fine_assessed-fine_paid) > 0
```

If you then execute the **sp_helptext** system stored procedure on the **UnpaidFinesView**, SQL Server will produce the following result:

```
The object comments have been encrypted.
Do Not Delete Entries in the syscomments Table
```

When security considerations require that the view definition is unavailable to users, use encryption. Never delete entries from the **syscomments** table. You will not be able to use your view, and it can prevent SQL Server from re-creating the view when you upgrade a database to a newer version of SQL Server.

Modifying Data Through Views

Views do not maintain a separate copy of data. Instead, they show the resultset of a query on one or more base tables. Therefore, whenever you modify data in a view, you actually are modifying the base table.

With some restrictions, you can insert, update, or delete table data freely through a view. In general, the view must be defined on a single table and must not include aggregate functions or **GROUP BY** clauses in the **SELECT** statement. Specifically, modifications that are made by using views will have the following limitations:

♦ *They cannot affect more than one underlying table.* You can modify views that are derived from two or more tables, but each update or modification can affect only one table.

♦ *They cannot be made to certain columns.* SQL Server does not allow you to change a column that is the result of a calculation, such as columns that contain computed values, built-in functions, or row aggregate functions.

♦ *They can cause errors if they affect tables with columns that do not have default values or accept* **NULL** *values.* For example, you will receive an error message if you insert a row into a view where the underlying table has a column that is not included in the view and does not allow **NULL**s or have a default value.

♦ *They are verified if the* **WITH CHECK OPTION** *setting has been specified in the view definition.* The **WITH CHECK OPTION** setting forces all data modification statements that are executed against the view to adhere to the criteria set within the **SELECT** statement that defines the view. If the changed values are out of the range of the view definition, SQL Server rejects the modifications. In other words, if you try to add a row that contains valid data but will not be visible through the view, the update fails.

Where To Go From Here

The knowledge of good SQL Server database design is not necessarily a turning point throughout this book; however, later chapters that use SQL Server as the back end for whatever technology we are discussing as the front end will assume that you have carefully examined and learned the information that is presented within this chapter.

In Chapter 11, we will look at how you can use stored procedures, and a special kind of stored procedure known as a trigger, to better administer your SQL Server databases and to simplify complex programming tasks and issues. As you will learn in later chapters, stored procedures are especially critical when you're designing complex, distributed systems that use the Microsoft Transaction Server (MTS)-based programming model. For now, in Chapter 11, we will focus on how to create, modify, and remove stored procedures and triggers, and why you should use them with your SQL Server back end.

Understanding, Managing, And Working With Stored Procedures And Triggers

In Chapter 10, we discussed some of the objects that are common to SQL Server databases and their effective design and management. In this chapter, we continue that theme with a close evaluation of stored procedures and triggers, two of the most powerful weapons in your toolkit for effective database design. This chapter considers stored procedures and triggers together for one simple reason: A trigger is a special kind of stored procedure that executes automatically when a certain condition is met. Because they are both written almost entirely in Transact-SQL, and because the processing performed by both is similar, they are good candidates for discussion together. We will start the discussion with stored procedures, because understanding them will greatly simplify your work with triggers.

Introduction To Stored Procedures

A *stored procedure* is a named collection of SQL statements that is stored on the server. Stored procedures are an efficient method of encapsulating statements for repeated execution. Stored procedures support user-declared variables, conditional execution, and other powerful programming features.

Stored procedures in SQL Server are similar to procedures in other programming languages because they can:

♦ Contain groups of statements and call other stored procedures

♦ Accept input parameters

♦ Return a status value to a calling stored procedure or batch to indicate success or failure (and the reason for failure)

◆ Return multiple values to the calling stored procedure or batch in the form of output parameters

SQL Server supports five types of stored procedures: system, user-defined, temporary, remote, and extended:

◆ *System stored procedures*—These are stored in the master database and are identified by the **sp_** prefix. System stored procedures are used for activities such as general maintenance, replication administration, security administration, and other more specialized tasks.

◆ *User-defined stored procedures*—These are created in individual user databases. They are used for all types of activities, any of which would benefit from the use of a compiled T-SQL statement rather than a passed-in SQL statement or script. User-defined stored procedures are typically prefaced with a **usp_** prefix.

◆ *Temporary stored procedures*—These are stored in the tempdb database and are automatically removed when their execution completes. Local temporary stored procedures have names that start with a single pound symbol (**#**) and are available to the session that creates the local temporary stored procedure until the session is closed.

◆ *Global temporary stored procedures*—These have names that start with a double pound symbol (**##**) and are available to all user sessions until the session that created the global temporary stored procedure is closed.

◆ *Remote stored procedures*—These are stored procedures that are called from a remote server or from a client that is connected to a remote server. By nature, most remote stored procedures are also user-defined stored procedures. Most developers prefix remote stored procedures with **rsp_**.

◆ *Extended stored procedures*—These are DLLs executed outside the SQL Server environment. However, they can be loaded and executed in a manner similar to that of stored procedures. Extended stored procedures usually have an **xp_** prefix. Some system stored procedures call extended stored procedures.

Initial Processing Of Stored Procedures

Processing a stored procedure includes creating it and then executing it the first time, which places its query plan in the procedure cache, as shown in Figure 11.1. The procedure cache is the area of memory that SQL Server uses to store compiled query plans for the execution of a stored procedure. The size of the procedure cache fluctuates according to activity levels. When the procedure cache becomes full, the least recently used plans are removed to make space for new plans.

Creation Of Stored Procedures

When you create a stored procedure, the statements in it are parsed for syntactical accuracy. SQL Server then stores the name of the stored procedure in the **sysobjects** system table and

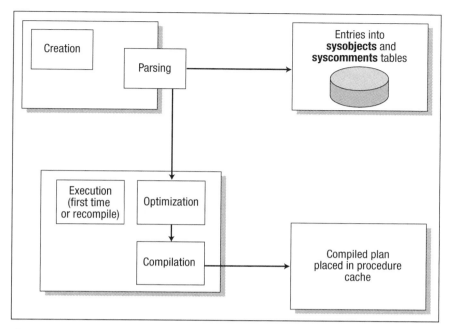

Figure 11.1
Initial processing of stored procedures.

the text of the stored procedure in the **syscomments** system table in the current database. An error is returned if a syntax error is encountered, and the stored procedure is not created.

A process called *deferred name resolution* allows stored procedures to refer to objects that do not exist when the stored procedure is created. This process permits flexibility, because stored procedures and the objects that they reference do not have to be created in a particular order. The objects must exist by the time the stored procedure is executed.

Execution (First Time Or Recompile) Of Stored Procedures

The first time that a stored procedure is executed, or if the stored procedure must be recompiled, the query processor reads the stored procedure from the **syscomments** system table and then performs the name resolution process.

Stored procedures are recompiled automatically in the following circumstances:

♦ Whenever the schema versions change—for example, any time that a table or index is modified

♦ When the environment in which the stored procedure was compiled is different than the one in which it is executing

♦ When the statistics have changed for an index or a table that the stored procedure is referencing

Optimization Of Stored Procedures

When a stored procedure successfully passes the name resolution stage, the SQL Server *query optimizer* analyzes the Transact-SQL statements in the stored procedure and creates a plan that contains the fastest method to access the data. To do so, the query optimizer considers the following:

♦ The amount of data in the tables

♦ The presence and nature of table indexes and the distribution of data in the indexed columns

♦ The comparison operators and comparison values that are used in **WHERE** clause conditions

♦ The presence of joins and the **UNION**, **GROUP BY**, or **ORDER BY** clauses

Compilation Of Stored Procedures

Compilation refers to the process of analyzing the stored procedure and creating a query plan. After the query optimizer places the compiled plan in the procedure cache, the stored procedure is executed.

Subsequent Processing Of Stored Procedures

Subsequent processing of stored procedures is faster than initial processing, because SQL Server uses the optimized query plan in the procedure cache, as shown in Figure 11.2.

SQL Server uses the in-memory plan for subsequent executions of the query if the following conditions apply:

♦ The current environment is the same as the environment in which the plan was compiled. Server, database, and connection settings determine the environment.

♦ Objects to which the stored procedure refers do not require name resolution. Objects require name resolution when objects that are owned by different users have the same names. For example, if the sales role owns a product table and the development role owns a product table, SQL Server must determine which table to operate on each time a product table is referenced.

Advantages Of Stored Procedures

Stored procedures offer numerous advantages. For example, they can share application logic with other applications, thereby ensuring consistent data access and manipulation. Additionally, stored procedures can encapsulate business functionality. Business rules or policies encapsulated in stored procedures can be changed in a single location. All clients can use the same stored procedures to ensure consistent data modification.

Stored procedures offer an excellent way to provide security mechanisms. Users can be granted permission to execute a stored procedure even if they do not have permission to access the tables or views that are referred to in the stored procedure.

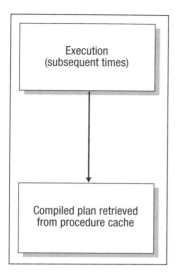

Figure 11.2
Subsequent processing of stored procedures.

Stored procedures can automatically execute at startup if the startup option for the stored procedure is set to **TRUE** using the **sp_procoption** system stored procedure. Stored procedures that have their startup option set to **TRUE** are executed when the last database has been recovered at startup. Each automatically executed stored procedure uses a single thread. It is a good idea to have only one stored procedure identified at startup for automatic execution. This stored procedure can call additional stored procedures so that you do not use unnecessary threads.

Stored procedures often increase performance because execution plans reside in the cache after they are executed the first time. For similar reasons, stored procedures also substantially reduce network traffic. Rather than send hundreds of Transact-SQL statements over the network, users can perform a complex operation by executing a single stored procedure, which reduces the number of requests that pass between the client and server.

Creating, Executing, And Modifying Stored Procedures

Now that we have considered some of the basics about stored procedures and the reasons *why* you should use them, let's talk about *how* you create and manage them. Stored procedures are easy to develop—but like many other programming techniques, true mastery takes time. Recognize going in that most of the examples in this chapter are very simple stored procedures—I have, in the field, created stored procedures and nested stored procedures that perform thousands of lines of execution before they finish.

Creating Stored Procedures

You create stored procedures in the current database. Creating a stored procedure is similar to creating a view. First, you write and test the Transact-SQL statements that you want to include in the stored procedure. Then, if you receive the results that you expect, create the stored procedure.

You create stored procedures with the **CREATE PROCEDURE** statement (which you can abbreviate within your code as **CREATE PROC**). Consider the following facts when you create stored procedures:

◆ Stored procedures can reference tables, views, stored procedures, and temporary tables.

◆ If a stored procedure creates a local temporary table, the temporary table only exists for the purpose of the stored procedure. The table is removed when the stored procedure execution completes.

◆ A **CREATE PROCEDURE** statement cannot be combined with other SQL statements in a single batch.

◆ The **CREATE PROCEDURE** definition can include any number and type of Transact-SQL statements, with the exception of the following object creation statements: **CREATE DEFAULT, CREATE PROCEDURE, CREATE RULE, CREATE TRIGGER**, and **CREATE VIEW**. Other database objects can be created within a stored procedure.

◆ To execute the **CREATE PROCEDURE** statement, you must be a member of the **sysadmin** role, **db_owner** role, or **db_ddladmin** role, or you must have been granted **CREATE PROCEDURE** permission on the database to which the procedure will apply by a member of the **sysadmin** or **db_owner** roles.

◆ The maximum size of a stored procedure is 128MB.

The partial syntax of the **CREATE PROCEDURE** statement is as follows:

```
CREATE PROC[EDURE] procedure_name
[;number]
    [
        {@parameter data_type} [= default] [OUTPUT]
    ]
    [,...n]
    [WITH {RECOMPILE | ENCRYPTION | RECOMPILE,ENCRYPTION}]
AS
    sql_statement [...n]
```

Looks pretty complex—especially when you realize that the text after the **AS** clause can be as long as you need it to be. The best way to get a handle on the use of stored procedures is to look at one. The following statements, for example, create a stored procedure in the **library** database called **overdue_books** that lists all overdue books.

*You restored the **library** database from the CD-ROM that accompanies this book in Chapter 10.*

```
USE library
GO
CREATE PROC dbo.overdue_books
  AS
    SELECT * FROM loan
    WHERE due_date < GETDATE()
GO
```

After you execute the previous example, you can call the following statement to execute the **overdue_books** stored procedure:

```
EXEC overdue_books
```

Guidelines For Creating Stored Procedures

Consider the following facts and guidelines when you create stored procedures:

♦ To avoid situations in which the owner of a stored procedure and the owner of the underlying tables differ, the dbo user should own all objects in a database. Because a user can be a member of multiple roles, always specify the dbo user as the owner name when you create the object. Otherwise, the object will be created with your user name as the owner.

♦ Design each stored procedure to accomplish a single task.

♦ Create, test, and debug your stored procedure on the server; then test it from the client.

♦ To distinguish system stored procedures easily, avoid using the **sp_** prefix when you name user-defined stored procedures.

♦ If you do not want users to be able to view the text of your stored procedures, you must create them using the **WITH ENCRYPTION** option. Do not delete entries from the **syscomments** system table. If you do not use **WITH ENCRYPTION**, users can use SQL Server Enterprise Manager or execute the **sp_helptext** system stored procedure to view the text of stored procedures in the **syscomments** system table.

♦ Stored procedures that require a particular option setting should issue a **SET** statement at the start of the stored procedure. For example, when an Open Database Connectivity (ODBC) application connects to SQL Server, ODBC automatically sets the following options for the session:

```
SET QUOTED_IDENTIFIER ON
SET TEXTSIZE 2147483647
SET ANSI_DEFAULTS ON
```

```
SET CURSOR_CLOSE_ON_COMMIT OFF
SET IMPLICIT_TRANSACTIONS OFF
```

These options are set to increase the portability of ODBC applications. Because DB-Library-based applications generally do not set these options, stored procedures should be tested with the **SET** options turned both on and off. This ensures that the stored procedures work correctly when they are invoked, regardless of the options that a particular connection may have set.

Nesting Stored Procedures

Stored procedures can be *nested*, a process in which one stored procedure calls another. As you will learn later in this chapter, triggers can also be nested. Characteristics of nesting include the following:

♦ Stored procedures can be nested to 32 levels. Attempting to exceed 32 levels of nesting causes the entire calling stored procedure chain to fail.

♦ The current nesting level is returned by the ****NESTLEVEL** function.

♦ If one stored procedure calls a second stored procedure, the second stored procedure can access all the objects that are created by the first stored procedure, including temporary tables.

♦ If a stored procedure starts a transaction and later calls a second stored procedure that issues a **ROLLBACK TRAN** statement, the transaction and all modifications made in both stored procedures are rolled back.

Viewing Information About Stored Procedures

You can use the system stored procedures in Table 11.1 to find additional information about all types of stored procedures. You can also use SQL Server Enterprise Manager.

Executing Stored Procedures

You can execute a stored procedure by itself or as part of an **INSERT** statement. Before you execute the procedure, however, you must first have been granted **EXECUTE** permission on the stored procedure.

Table 11.1   System stored procedures that you can use to find out more information.

Stored Procedure	Information
sp_help *procedure_name*	Displays a list of parameters and their data types for the specified stored procedure.
sp_helptext *procedure_name*	Displays the text of the specified stored procedure if it is not encrypted.
sp_depends *procedure_name*	Lists objects that are dependent upon the specified stored procedure and objects upon which the specified stored procedure is dependent.
sp_stored_procedures	Returns a list of stored procedures in the current database.

You can execute system stored procedures from any database, because SQL Server always searches the master database when a stored procedure with the **sp_** prefix is executed. Before executing other stored procedures, you must make the database in which the stored procedure was created current. Otherwise, you can execute a stored procedure by specifying a full three-part name for the stored procedure.

Executing A Stored Procedure By Itself

You can execute a stored procedure by issuing the **EXECUTE** statement along with the name of the stored procedure and any parameters. The following prototype shows how to do this:

```
[EXEC[UTE]]
    {
        [@return_status =] {procedure_name [;number] @procedure_name_var}
    }
    [[@parameter =] {value | @variable [OUTPUT] | [DEFAULT]] [, ...n]}
    [WITH RECOMPILE]
```

For example, consider the following statement, which executes the **overdue_books** stored procedure that we created earlier in this chapter. If you recall, the stored procedure lists all overdue books in the **library** database after making the **library** database the currently selected database.

```
USE library
EXEC overdue_books
```

The following statement uses a three-part name to execute the **overdue_books** stored procedure that lists all overdue books in the **library** database, without making the **library** database the currently selected database.

```
EXEC library.dbo.overdue_books
```

Tip

*You can execute a stored procedure by specifying its name without the **EXEC[UTE]** statement if it is the first line of a batch. However, you should always use the **EXEC[UTE]** statement to prevent errors from occurring if you insert another line at the beginning of the batch. If you try to execute a stored procedure on any line other than the first line in a batch and you do not specify the **EXEC[UTE]** statement, an "Incorrect syntax" error is returned.*

Executing A Stored Procedure Within An INSERT Statement

The **INSERT** statement can use a resultset that is returned from a local or remote stored procedure. The **INSERT** statement loads a table with data that is returned from **SELECT** statements in the stored procedure. The data types returned by the stored procedure must match those of the table referenced in the **INSERT** statement.

Stored procedures that are executed within an **INSERT** statement must return a relational resultset. For example, you could not use a **COMPUTE BY** clause in a **SELECT** statement in a stored procedure that will be called from an **INSERT** statement.

To better understand how this works, consider the following statements, which create the **Employee_Customer** stored procedure. The stored procedure, as we will see in a moment, is then called from an **INSERT** statement to insert employees into the **Customers** table of the **Northwind** database:

```
USE Northwind
GO
CREATE PROC dbo.Employee_Customer
  AS
    SELECT
        UPPER(SUBSTRING(LastName, 1, 4) + SUBSTRING(FirstName, 1, 1)),
        'Northwind Traders', RTRIM(FirstName) + ' ' + LastName,
        'Employee', Address, City, Region, PostalCode, Country,
        ('(206) 555-1234' + ' x' + Extension), NULL
    FROM Employees
    WHERE CONVERT(varchar(10), HireDate, 101) =
        CONVERT(varchar(10), GETDATE(), 101)
GO
```

The following statements execute the stored procedure:

```
INSERT Customers
EXEC Employee_Customer
```

The number of employees hired on today's date is added to the **Customers** table after the execution completes.

Explicitly Recompiling Stored Procedures

As you have learned, stored procedures will generally not need to be recompiled once you create them. However, in certain situations you will need to recompile stored procedures to help ensure that you achieve the best possible performance. You may need to recompile a stored procedure explicitly when:

♦ The stored procedure executes infrequently.

♦ You want to execute the stored procedure with very different parameter values. When you pass values that cause the return of substantially varying resultsets to the stored procedure from the underlying database or to the caller of the stored procedure, it is not always optimal to execute the cached execution plan.

SQL Server provides three methods for recompiling a stored procedure explicitly: the **CRE-ATE PROCEDURE...WITH RECOMPILE** statement, the **EXECUTE...WITH RECOMPILE** statement, and the **sp_recompile** system stored procedure. We will consider the use of each of these three methods in the following sections.

Creating Stored Procedures That Automatically Recompile

The **CREATE PROCEDURE...WITH RECOMPILE** statement creates a stored procedure for which the query plan is not cached when the stored procedure is executed. Instead, the stored procedure is recompiled and optimized, and a new query plan is created each time the stored procedure is executed.

Use this method if the stored procedure that you are creating is executed only periodically, such as monthly or quarterly. For example, the following statement creates a stored procedure called **usp_titlecount** that is recompiled each time it is executed:

```
USE library
GO
CREATE PROC usp_titlecount @title_no title_no WITH RECOMPILE
  AS
    SELECT COUNT(*) FROM loanhist
    WHERE title_no = @title_no
GO
```

Forcing Stored Procedures To Recompile At Execution

The **EXECUTE...WITH RECOMPILE** statement creates a new query plan during execution of the stored procedure. The new execution plan is placed in the cache.

Use this method if the parameter that you are passing varies greatly from those that are usually passed to the stored procedure. Because this optimized plan is the exception rather than the rule, the first time you execute the stored procedure with a typical parameter, you should specify the **WITH RECOMPILE** option with the **EXECUTE** statement again. For example, the following statement recompiles the **sp_help** system stored procedure at the time it is executed.

```
EXEC sp_help WITH RECOMPILE
```

Executing The sp_recompile System Stored Procedure

Finally, you can execute the **sp_recompile** system stored procedure to force a recompile of a specific stored procedure or of all stored procedures or triggers that reference a specified object in the current database. The stored procedures are recompiled the next time they are executed.

For example, if you have added a new index to a table that is referenced by a stored procedure and you believe that the performance of the stored procedure will benefit from the new index, execute the **sp_recompile** system stored procedure and specify the name of the table. The following statement forces a recompile of stored procedures that reference the **title** table in the **library** database:

```
EXEC sp_recompile title
```

Executing Extended Stored Procedures

Extended stored procedures are DLLs that increase SQL Server functionality. They are executed the same way as stored procedures, and they support return status codes and output parameters. Note that extended stored procedures have the following characteristics:

- They communicate with SQL Server by using the Open Data Services application programming interface (ODS API), not ODBC or OLE DB.

- They can include C and C++ features that are not available in Transact-SQL.

- They can contain multiple functions.

- They can be called from a client or SQL Server.

- They must be executed from the master database or by explicitly specifying *master* as part of the extended stored procedure name. You can call extended stored procedures from user-defined system stored procedures that you create.

The following example statement executes the **xp_cmdshell** extended stored procedure, which makes it possible to execute operating system commands from within SQL Server. The command returns a list of files and subdirectories:

```
EXEC master..xp_cmdshell 'dir c:\mssql7'
```

Table 11.2 lists some commonly used extended stored procedures. You can also create your own extended stored procedures. Generally, you call extended stored procedures to communicate with other applications or the operating system. For example, extended stored procedures in Sqlmap70.dll, such as **xp_sendmail** and **xp_readmail**, allow you to work with email messages from within SQL Server.

Altering And Dropping Stored Procedures

Stored procedures are often modified in response to requests from users or changes in the underlying table definitions. You will use the **ALTER PROCEDURE** and **DROP**

Table 11.2   Some commonly used extended stored procedures.

Extended Stored Procedure	Description
xp_cmdshell	Executes a given command string as an operating system command shell and returns output as rows of text.
xp_logevent	Logs a user-defined message in the SQL Server error log and in the Microsoft Windows NT application log.

PROCEDURE statements to alter and drop stored procedures, as discussed in the following sections.

Altering Stored Procedures

To modify an existing stored procedure and retain permission assignments, use the **ALTER PROCEDURE** statement. SQL Server replaces the previous definition of the stored procedure when it is altered with **ALTER PROCEDURE**.

Warning

You should not modify system stored procedures. If you want to change the functionality of a system stored procedure, create a new user-defined stored procedure by copying the statements from an existing system stored procedure, and then modifying it to meet your needs.

Consider the following facts when you use the **ALTER PROCEDURE** statement:

♦ If you want to modify a stored procedure that was created with any options, such as the **WITH ENCRYPTION** option, you must include the option in the **ALTER PROCEDURE** statement to retain the functionality that the option provides.

♦ **ALTER PROCEDURE** alters only a single procedure. If your procedure calls other stored procedures, the nested stored procedures are not affected.

♦ Permission to execute this statement defaults to the creators of the initial stored procedure and members of the **sysadmin**, **db_owner**, and **db_ddladmin** roles. You cannot grant permission to execute **ALTER PROCEDURE**.

Implement the **ALTER PROCEDURE** statement as shown in the following prototype:

```
ALTER PROC[EDURE] procedure_name [;number]
    [{@parameter data_type }[VARYING][ = default] [OUTPUT]]
        [,...n]
 [WITH {RECOMPILE | ENCRYPTION | RECOMPILE,ENCRYPTION}]

[FOR REPLICATION]
 AS
    sql_statement [...n]
```

To understand this better, let's consider a statement that modifies the **usp_overdue_books** stored procedure to select specific columns from the **OverdueView** view rather than all columns from the **loan** table, as shown here:

```
USE library
GO
ALTER PROC usp_overdue_books
  AS
    SELECT CONVERT(char(8), due_date, 1) date_due,
        isbn, copy_no,
```

```
        SUBSTRING(title, 1, 30) title, member_no, lastname
    FROM OverdueView
    ORDER BY due_date
GO
```

Dropping Stored Procedures

Once you create a stored procedure, you can later use the **DROP PROCEDURE** statement to remove user-defined stored procedures from the current database. Before you drop a stored procedure, execute the **sp_depends** stored procedure to determine whether objects depend on the stored procedure you want to drop. Use the **DROP PROCEDURE** statement as shown in the following prototype:

```
DROP PROC[EDURE]  procedure [, ...n]
```

The following statement drops the **usp_overdue_books** stored procedure:

```
USE library
GO
DROP PROC usp_overdue_books
```

Using Parameters And Error Messages With Stored Procedures

Parameters extend the functionality of stored procedures. You can pass information into and out of stored procedures with parameters. You can use the same stored procedure many times with different parameter values, thereby avoiding the necessity to create a separate stored procedure for each value.

When an error or an illegal condition occurs in a stored procedure, the stored procedure should generate an *error message* indicating the nature of the problem.

Using Input Parameters

Input parameters allow information to be passed into a stored procedure. To define a stored procedure that accepts input parameters, declare one or more variables as parameters in the **CREATE PROCEDURE** statement, as shown in the prototype for the statement detailed earlier in this chapter.

Consider the following facts and guidelines when you specify parameters:

♦ You should provide an appropriate default value for a parameter. If a default value is defined, a user can execute the stored procedure without specifying a value for that parameter. Parameter default values must be constants or **NULL**.

♦ All incoming parameter values should be checked at the beginning of the stored procedure to trap missing and invalid values early.

♦ The maximum number of parameters to a stored procedure is 1,024.

♦ The maximum number of local variables that may be declared within a stored procedure is limited by the available memory on the server.

♦ Parameters are local to a stored procedure. The same parameter names can be used in other stored procedures.

♦ Parameter information is stored in the **syscolumns** system table.

The following statement finds the ISBN number for a title that is written in a specific language. The title is passed to the **@title** input parameter and the language is passed to the **@translation** input parameter. The language information is stored in the **translation** column. The stored procedure checks the input parameter value to ensure that a title has been supplied. If a specific language is not provided, the default language for the title is English:

```
USE library
GO
CREATE PROC dbo.find_isbn
    @title longstring = NULL,
    @translation char(8) = 'English'
AS
  IF @title IS NULL
    BEGIN
      PRINT 'Please provide a title (or partial title) and the language'
      PRINT 'For example: EXEC find_isbn ''Oliver'', ''Japanese'''
      PRINT 'If you''re looking for a book in English, ' +
            'you do not have to specify the language.'
      RETURN --Breaks out of stored procedure unconditionally.
    END
  SET *title = '%' + *title + '%'
  SELECT isbn, title, [translation], cover
  FROM item i JOIN title t
  ON t.title_no = i.title_no
  WHERE t.title LIKE *title
  AND i.[translation] LIKE *translation
```

Note

*If you try to run this code, or any code described within this chapter, without first creating the **library** database as discussed in Chapter 9, you will receive type definition errors, because the **library** database uses a series of user-defined data types to describe strings within the database. We discussed user-defined data types, and how to implement them, in-depth in Chapter 9.*

Executing Stored Procedures With Input Parameters

You can set the value of a parameter by passing the value to the stored procedure by reference or by position. You should not mix the different formats when you supply values.

Passing Values By Reference

Specifying a parameter in an **EXECUTE** statement in the format *@parameter = value* is referred to as *passing by reference*. When you pass values by reference, the parameter values can be specified in any order, and you can omit parameters that have a default value.

The **usp_addadult** stored procedure adds a new adult member to the **library** database. The parameter declaration portion of the **CREATE PROC** statement for the stored procedure is shown here:

```
USE library
GO
CREATE PROC dbo.addadult
    @lastname       shortstring,
    @firstname      shortstring,
    @middleinitial  letter = NULL,
    @street         shortstring = NULL,
    @city           shortstring = NULL,
    @state          statecode = NULL,
    @zip            zipcode = NULL,
    @phone_no       phonenumber = NULL
  AS
    ...
```

The following script passes values by reference to the **usp_addadult** stored procedure. Notice that the order is different from the **CREATE PROC** statement and that two of the parameters, **@middleinitial** and **@phone_no**, are not specified.

```
EXEC addadult @firstname = 'George', @lastname = 'Klander',
    @street = 'Old and Grey Lane', @city = 'HomeTown',
    @state = 'NV', @zip = '89999'
```

Tip

Most programming languages—including VBA—use the term pass by reference differently than SQL Server. The usual meaning of the term is to pass a reference or pointer to a parameter. Passing parameters by reference in SQL Server is akin to passing named parameters in VBA.

Passing Values By Position

Passing values without a reference to the parameter names is referred to as *passing values by position*. When you specify only values, they must be listed in the order in which they are defined in the **CREATE PROC** statement.

When you pass values by position, you can omit parameters where default values exist, but you cannot interrupt the sequence. For example, if a stored procedure has five parameters, you can omit both the fourth and fifth parameters, but you cannot omit the fourth parameter and specify the fifth.

The following script passes values by position to the **usp_addadult** stored procedure:

```
EXEC addadult 'Klander', 'George', NULL, 'Old And Grey Lane',
    'HomeTown', 'NV', '89999', NULL
```

Returning Values With Output Parameters

Stored procedures can return information to the calling stored procedure or client with output parameters (parameters designated with the **OUTPUT** keyword). Any changes to the parameter that occur during the execution of the stored procedure are retained, even after the stored procedure completes execution.

To use an output parameter, the **OUTPUT** keyword must be specified in both the **CREATE PROC** and **EXECUTE** statements. If **OUTPUT** is omitted when the stored procedure is executed, the stored procedure still executes, but it produces an error condition. Output parameters have the following characteristics:

♦ The calling statement must specify a variable name for the output parameter. The variable will hold the output value after the stored procedure executes. You may not specify a constant for an output parameter in the calling statement.

♦ You can use the variable subsequently in additional SQL statements in the calling batch or the calling stored procedure.

♦ The parameter can be of any data type except **text** or **image**.

♦ A stored procedure can have any number of output parameters (as long as the total number of parameters does not exceed 1,024).

The following T-SQL code creates the **usp_mathtutor** stored procedure that calculates the product of two numbers:

```
USE library
GO
CREATE PROCEDURE dbo.usp_mathtutor
    @m1 smallint,
    @m2 smallint,
    @result smallint OUTPUT
AS
    SET @result = @m1 * @m2
```

The **CREATE PROCEDURE** statement declares three parameters. The first two parameters, **@m1** and **@m2**, are used to pass two values into the stored procedure. The third parameter, **@result**, is designated as an output parameter with the **OUTPUT** keyword. In the body of the stored procedure, the value of **@result** is set equal to the product of **@m1** and **@m2**. To execute the stored procedure after its creation, you would execute a statement sequence similar to the following:

```
DECLARE @answer smallint
EXECUTE usp_mathtutor 5, 6, @answer OUTPUT
SELECT 'The result of the execution is: ', @answer
```

A variable called **@answer** is declared for the output parameter. In the **EXECUTE** statement, constants are specified for the first two parameters, and the **@answer** variable and **OUTPUT** keyword are specified for the output parameter. After this statement is executed, **@answer** holds the value from the output parameter. The batch then uses the **SELECT** statement to display the value of **@answer**—in this case, 30.

The result displayed by the **SELECT** statement shows that the **@answer** variable holds the value passed from the stored procedure through the output parameter.

Handling Error Messages

To enhance the effectiveness of stored procedures, you should include return codes, error messages, or a combination of both to communicate status (success or failure) to the user. Perform tasks, business logic, and error checking *before* you begin transactions; this helps to keep your transactions short and exit the stored procedure, if necessary, before incurring the overhead of a transaction.

You can use coding strategies, such as existence checks, to recognize errors. When an error occurs, provide as much information as possible to the client. You should include provisions for the following in your error-handling logic: return codes, SQL Server errors, and error messages returned by user-defined stored procedures.

Using Return Codes

The **RETURN** statement exits unconditionally from a query or stored procedure. It can return an integer status value (return code). A return value of 0 indicates success; values –1 through –14 are currently used to indicate different reasons for failure, and values from –15 through –99 are reserved for future use. If a user-defined return value is not provided, 0 is returned.

To help you understand this better, the following example code creates a stored procedure called **usp_MemberType** that takes a single number as a parameter. It checks to see if the number is that of an adult or juvenile member. If the number is not the number of a member, the stored procedure returns a value of –100. If the number is the member number of an adult, a value of 1 is returned; if the number is the member number of a juvenile, a value of 2 is returned.

```
USE library
GO
CREATE PROC dbo.usp_MemberType
    @memberno int
AS
    IF NOT EXISTS(SELECT member_no FROM member WHERE member_no = @memberno)
        RETURN -100 --Member does not exist
    IF EXISTS(SELECT member_no FROM adult WHERE member_no = @memberno)
        RETURN 1    --Member is an adult
    IF EXISTS(SELECT member_no FROM juvenile WHERE member_no = @memberno)
        RETURN 2    --Member is a juvenile
```

The following code shows how to call the **usp_MemberType** stored procedure. After executing this code, the **@returnvalue** variable will hold a value of –100, 1, or 2, depending on whether a member with the number 4315 exists and is an adult or a juvenile.

```
DECLARE @returnvalue int
EXEC @returnvalue = usp_MemberType 4315
```

The @@ERROR Function

The **@@ERROR** function contains the error number for the most recently executed Transact-SQL statement. It is cleared and reset with each statement that is executed. A value of 0 is returned if the statement executes successfully. You can use the **@@ERROR** function to detect a specific error number or to exit a stored procedure conditionally.

The following code creates the **usp_addadult** stored procedure that uses the **@@ERROR** function to determine whether an error occurs when each **INSERT** statement is executed. If an error does occur, the transaction is rolled back:

```
CREATE PROCEDURE dbo.usp_addadult
    @lastname shortstring, @firstname shortstring,
    @middleinitial letter = NULL, @street shortstring,
    @city shortstring, @state statecode, @zip zipcode,
    @phone_no phonenumber = NULL
AS
  BEGIN TRANSACTION
    INSERT member (lastname,  firstname,  middleinitial)
        VALUES (@lastname, @firstname, @middleinitial)
    IF @@ERROR <> 0
      BEGIN
        ROLLBACK TRAN
        RETURN
      END
    DECLARE @insertmem_no member_no
    SET @insertmem_no = @@identity
```

```
      INSERT adult (member_no, street, city, state, zip,
          phone_no, expr_date)
      VALUES (@insertmem_no, @street, @city, @state, @zip,
          @phone_no, dateadd(year, 1, GETDATE()) )
    IF @@ERROR <> 0
      BEGIN
        ROLLBACK TRAN
        RETURN
      END
  COMMIT TRANSACTION
```

RAISERROR Statement

The **RAISERROR** statement returns a user-defined error message and sets a system flag to record that an error has occurred. **RAISERROR** allows the application to retrieve an entry from the **sysmessages** system table or build a message dynamically with user-specified severity and state information. **RAISERROR** can write error messages to the SQL Server error log and to the Windows NT application log.

The following statement raises a user-defined error message and writes the message to the Windows NT application log as well as the SQL Server error log:

```
RAISERROR('Invalid member number', 10, 1) WITH LOG
```

Creating Custom Error Messages

The **sp_addmessage** system stored procedure allows developers to create custom error messages. SQL Server treats both system and custom error messages the same way. All messages are stored in the **sysmessages** table. These error messages can be written automatically to the Windows NT application log and the SQL Server error log.

The following code creates a custom error message that requires the message to be written to the Windows NT application log and the SQL Server error log when it occurs:

```
EXEC sp_addmessage @msgnum = 50011, @severity = 10,
    @msgtext = 'Member cannot be deleted.', @with_log = 'true'
```

To use this error message, execute the **RAISERROR** statement and specify the error number instead of a message, as follows:

```
RAISERROR(50011, 10, 1)
```

Introducing Triggers

Now we'll consider triggers, describe the circumstances in which you may want to use triggers, discuss various issues to consider when you use triggers, and show you how to create, alter, and drop triggers.

A *trigger* is a special kind of stored procedure that executes automatically whenever an attempt is made to modify data in a table that the trigger protects. Triggers can include most Transact-SQL statements. The query plan for a trigger is stored in the procedure cache. Triggers have some important uniform characteristics, as discussed in the following list:

♦ Triggers are defined on a specific table, which is referred to as the *trigger table*. In other words, you can create a trigger **Trigger1** on the **Autos** table and then create another trigger **Trigger1** on the **Trucks** table, and SQL Server won't mind a bit.

♦ When an attempt is made to insert, update, or delete data in a table and a trigger for that particular action has been defined on the table, the trigger executes automatically. A trigger cannot be circumvented. Moreover, unlike standard stored procedures, triggers cannot be called directly and do not pass or accept parameters.

♦ The trigger and the statement that causes it to fire are treated as a single transaction that can be rolled back from anywhere within the trigger. Trigger definitions can include a **ROLLBACK TRANSACTION** statement even if an explicit **BEGIN TRANSACTION** statement does not exist. The statement that causes the trigger to fire begins an implicit transaction if an explicit **BEGIN TRANSACTION** statement has not been executed.

♦ If a trigger that includes a **ROLLBACK TRANSACTION** statement is fired from within a user-defined transaction, the **ROLLBACK TRANSACTION** rolls back the entire transaction. If a trigger that includes a **ROLLBACK TRANSACTION** statement is fired from within a batch, the **ROLLBACK TRANSACTION** statement cancels the entire batch; subsequent statements in the batch are not executed.

♦ You should minimize or avoid the use of **ROLLBACK TRANSACTION** in your trigger code. Rolling back a transaction creates additional work because all the work that is completed up to that point in the transaction has to be undone. This will have a negative impact on performance. If possible, check and validate information before starting the transaction. For example, attempting to delete a customer that has outstanding orders may be prevented by a trigger that issues a **ROLLBACK TRANSACTION** statement. In a transaction that deletes a customer, you might check to see that the customer has no outstanding orders before issuing the **DELETE** statement. This step will prevent the **DELETE** statement from failing and causing the rollback of the transaction.

Uses Of Triggers

Triggers are used to maintain low-level data integrity, not to return query results. The primary benefit of triggers is that they can contain complex processing logic. You should use triggers only when constraints do not provide the functionality you require. For more information about choosing between constraints and triggers, refer to the discussion on constraints and their benefits over triggers in Chapter 10. The following sections detail some of the most common reasons to use triggers.

Cascade Modifications Through Related Tables In A Database

Cascading modifications with a trigger reduces the amount of code that needs to be executed to perform updates to related tables and ensures that changes to related tables always occur together. For example, a delete trigger on the **title** table in the **library** database can delete rows in other tables that correspond to the deleted title. The trigger does this by using the **title_no** foreign key column to locate rows in the **loan**, **item**, and **copy** tables. The trigger ensures that no rows exist anywhere for a title that has been deleted.

> **Note**
> *You can find the SQL script that creates this trigger in the title_delete_trig.sql file on the companion CD-ROM.*

Enforce More Complex Data Integrity Than A CHECK Constraint

Unlike **CHECK** constraints, triggers can reference columns in other tables. For example, when a member checks out a book, a row is inserted into the **loan** table. An **INSERT** trigger on that table determines whether the book is loanable. It does this by checking the value of the **loanable** column in the item table. If the value is **'N'** (no), the trigger will roll back the book checkout and notify the librarian.

> **Note**
> *You can find the SQL script that creates this trigger in the loan_title_loanable.sql file on the companion CD-ROM.*

You can also use triggers to enforce complex referential integrity. Referential integrity is generally enforced using **FOREIGN KEY** constraints, but constraints do not perform an action; they prevent a data modification that will compromise referential integrity. Use triggers to perform cascading deletions or updates in related tables. If constraints exist on the trigger table, they are checked prior to the trigger execution. If constraints are violated, the trigger is not executed.

Raise Custom Error Messages

Occasionally, your implementation may benefit from custom error messages that indicate the status of an action. Use triggers to raise predefined or dynamic custom error messages when certain conditions occur as a trigger executes.

Constraints, rules, and defaults can communicate errors through standardized system error messages only. If your application requires (or can benefit from) customized messages and more complex error handling, you must use a trigger.

Maintain Denormalized Data

Triggers can be used to maintain low-level data integrity in denormalized database environments. Maintaining denormalized data is different from cascading, because cascading typically refers to maintaining relationships between primary and foreign key values. Denormalized data typically contains contrived or derived values. For example, use a trigger if:

♦ A deletion from one table requires a deletion from another table, without a direct relation between the two.

♦ Referential integrity is based on something other than an exact match, such as maintaining derived data (such as year-to-date sales) or flagging columns (such as Y or N to indicate whether a book is on loan).

♦ You require customized messages and complex error messaging.

Compare Or Record Before And After States Of Data

Triggers provide the ability to reference the changes that are made to the data by the **INSERT**, **UPDATE**, and **DELETE** statements. This ability allows you to reference the rows that are being affected by the modification statements inside the trigger. You can use a trigger to compare the current values in the row that is being modified to the values that will be in the row if the modification occurs. If the comparison is invalid, the trigger can roll back the changes. You can also use the before and after values to record changes to an audit trail or log.

Considerations For Using Triggers

Consider the following facts and guidelines when you work with triggers:

♦ Triggers are reactive, whereas constraints are proactive.

♦ Triggers are executed in response to an **INSERT**, **UPDATE**, or **DELETE** statement being executed on the table in which the trigger is defined.

♦ Constraints are checked first.

♦ If constraints exist on the trigger table, they are checked prior to the trigger execution. If constraints are violated, the trigger does not execute because the **INSERT**, **UPDATE**, or **DELETE** statement is cancelled.

♦ Tables can have multiple triggers for any action.

♦ With SQL Server 7, you can create several triggers on a single table for the same action. For example, a table can have multiple **INSERT** triggers defined for it. Because the triggers are not fired in any particular order, they must be independent of each other.

♦ Permissions are necessary to perform all trigger-defined statements. The table owner and members of the **db_owner**, **db_ddladmin**, and **sysadmin** roles can create and drop triggers for a table. These permissions cannot be transferred. In addition, the creator of the trigger must have permission to perform all the statements on all the affected tables. If permissions are denied to any portion of the Transact-SQL statements inside the trigger, the entire transaction is rolled back.

- Triggers cannot be created on views or temporary tables, but they can reference views and temporary tables.

- Triggers should not return resultsets. Triggers contain Transact-SQL statements in the same way that stored procedures do. Like stored procedures, triggers can contain statements that return a resultset. However, including statements that return values in triggers is not recommended, because the **UPDATE**, **INSERT**, and **DELETE** statements are not expected to return resultsets.

- Triggers can handle multirow actions.

- An **INSERT**, **UPDATE**, or **DELETE** action that invokes a trigger can affect multiple rows. To determine whether multiple rows are affected, use the **@@ROWCOUNT** function.

Tip

Although you can create multiple triggers for the same action, most of the time you should create only one trigger for an action. The benefit of having multiple triggers for the same action is that other triggers can be automatically generated without affecting your trigger. For example, suppose you have a table on which you have created a trigger and you then use the Web Assistant Wizard to publish data from the table to a Web page whenever data in the table changes. The Web Assistant Wizard needs to add triggers to the table to achieve the automatic Web page updates. If multiple triggers were not allowed for an action, the Web Assistant Wizard would have to add code to your trigger, or delete it.

The Inserted And Deleted Tables

Two special tables are available within triggers: the *deleted table* and the *inserted table*. You use the names **deleted** and **inserted** (or aliases, such as **d** and **i**, which are much more common) to refer to these tables in a trigger.

The deleted table stores copies of the rows affected by **DELETE** and **UPDATE** statements. When a **DELETE** or an **UPDATE** statement is executed, rows are deleted from the trigger table and transferred to the deleted table. The deleted table and the trigger table ordinarily have no rows in common.

The inserted table stores copies of the rows affected by **INSERT** and **UPDATE** statements. When an **INSERT** or **UPDATE** statement is executed, new rows are added simultaneously to both the inserted table and the trigger table. The rows in the inserted table are copies of the new rows in the trigger table.

Note

*As you can see from the preceding text, when you perform an **UPDATE**, you actually end up with deleted row(s) and inserted row(s); this is because SQL Server actually*

*places the un-updated row into the **deleted** table, and the updated row into the*
***inserted** table. This is necessary so that you can roll back to the state prior to the*
change, if necessary.

You can use the rows from the deleted and inserted tables to reference rows in related tables
or to test values in the rows that are being deleted or inserted. You cannot alter the data in
the deleted or inserted tables directly, but you can use the tables in **SELECT** statements.

Creating Triggers

Triggers are created with the **CREATE TRIGGER** statement. The statement specifies the
table on which a trigger is defined, the event for which the trigger executes, and the statements for the trigger. The following prototype shows how to implement the **CREATE
TRIGGER** statement:

```
CREATE TRIGGER trigger_name
  ON table [WITH ENCRYPTION]
  {FOR {[INSERT][,][UPDATE][,][DELETE]}
    [WITH APPEND]
    [NOT FOR REPLICATION]
AS
    sql_statement [,...n]}
```

When you create a trigger, information about the trigger is inserted into the **sysobjects** and
syscomments system tables. With deferred name resolution, you can reference tables and
views in a trigger that does not yet exist.

Triggers Cannot Contain Certain Statements

SQL Server does not allow the following statements to be used in a trigger:

♦ All **CREATE**, **ALTER**, and **DROP** statements

♦ **GRANT**, **REVOKE**, and **DENY**

♦ **LOAD** and **RESTORE**

♦ **RECONFIGURE**

♦ **TRUNCATE TABLE**

♦ **UPDATE STATISTICS**

♦ **SELECT INTO** (because it creates a table)

The following code fragment creates a trigger that generates a contrived customer ID for
every row that is inserted into a customer table. The contrived customer ID consists of the
identity value from the ID column concatenated with the first three letters of the customer's
last name and the first letter of the customer's first name. Notice that the identity value is

padded with leading zeros to provide a 10-character, fixed-length, contrived customer ID. The value of the new ID that is being inserted is obtained from the special inserted table that is available in an **INSERT** trigger:

```
CREATE TRIGGER gen_cust_id ON customer FOR INSERT
AS
    UPDATE c SET cust_id = (SELECT
        UPPER(SUBSTRING(i.lastname, 1, 3) + SUBSTRING(i.firstname, 1, 1)) +
        REPLICATE('0', 6 - (DATALENGTH(CAST(i.id AS varchar(6))))) +
        CAST(i.id AS varchar(6))
        FROM customer c INNER JOIN inserted i ON i.id = c.id)
        FROM customer c INNER JOIN inserted i ON i.id = c.id
```

The following **INSERT** statement fires the trigger:

```
INSERT customer (lastname, firstname)
VALUES ('Axelrod', 'Brett')
```

The following **SELECT** statement and resultset verifies that the trigger fired:

```
SELECT * FROM customer

cust_id     id          lastname             firstname
----------  ----------  -------------------  --------------------
AXEL000001  1           Axelrod              Brett

(1 row(s) affected)
```

Viewing Information About Triggers

You can use the system stored procedures in Table 11.3 to find additional information about triggers. You can also use SQL Server Enterprise Manager.

Altering And Dropping Triggers

You can alter or drop an existing trigger. You can also temporarily disable a trigger and then enable it again later. Use the **ALTER TRIGGER** and **DROP TRIGGER** statements to perform these actions, as discussed in the following sections.

Table 11.3   Stored procedures that provide additional information about triggers.

Stored Procedure	Information
sp_helptext *trigger_name*	Displays the text of the specified trigger if it is not encrypted.
sp_depends *trigger_name*	Lists objects that are referenced by the trigger.
sp_helptrigger *table_name*	Returns a list of triggers defined on the specified table.

Altering A Trigger

If you must change the definition of an existing trigger, you can alter it without having to drop it. The altered definition replaces the definition of the existing trigger with the new definition. Trigger action also can be altered. For example, if you create a trigger for **IN-SERT** and then alter the trigger for **UPDATE**, the trigger no longer fires when rows are inserted into the table, but it fires when rows in the table are updated. The following prototype shows how to implement the **ALTER TRIGGER** statement:

```
ALTER TRIGGER trigger_name
  ON table [WITH ENCRYPTION]
    {FOR {[INSERT][,][UPDATE][,][DELETE]}
    [NOT FOR REPLICATION]
  AS
    sql_statement [,...n]}
```

The following code examples first create the **loan_insert** trigger for the **INSERT** action on the **loan** table. When a row is inserted into the **loan** table, the trigger updates the **on_loan** column of the **copy** table with **'Y'** (yes). The second code sample alters the trigger to include checking for the **DELETE** action and includes the Transact-SQL statements that are required to update the **on_loan** column in the **copy** table when the book is returned. This code initially creates the trigger:

```
USE library
GO
CREATE TRIGGER loan_insert
  ON loan
  FOR INSERT
AS
  UPDATE c SET on_loan = 'Y'
    FROM copy c INNER JOIN inserted i
    ON c.isbn = i.isbn AND c.copy_no = i.copy_no
```

Now that the trigger is created, the following code then alters the trigger:

```
USE library
GO
ALTER TRIGGER loan_insert
  ON loan FOR INSERT, DELETE
AS
  IF EXISTS (SELECT * FROM inserted)
    BEGIN
      UPDATE c SET on_loan = 'Y'
          FROM copy c INNER JOIN inserted i
          ON c.isbn = i.isbn AND c.copy_no = i.copy_no
```

```
    END
  ELSE
    BEGIN
      UPDATE c SET on_loan = 'N'
          FROM copy c INNER JOIN deleted d
          ON c.isbn = d.isbn AND c.copy_no = d.copy_no
    END
```

Disabling Or Enabling A Trigger

You can disable or enable a specific trigger or all triggers on a table. When a trigger is disabled, it is still defined for the table; however, when an **INSERT**, **UPDATE**, or **DELETE** statement is executed against the table, the trigger is not fired. You will use the **ALTER TABLE** statement to enable or disable specific triggers or all triggers on a table, as shown in the following prototype:

```
ALTER TABLE table
{ENABLE | DISABLE} TRIGGER
{ALL | trigger_name[,...n]}
```

Dropping A Trigger

You can remove a trigger by dropping it. Triggers are dropped automatically if their associated table is dropped. Permission to drop a trigger defaults to the table owner and is nontransferable. Members of the **sysadmin**, **db_owner**, and **db_ddladmin** roles can drop any object by specifying the owner in the **DROP TRIGGER** statement. Implement the **DROP TRIGGER** statement as shown in the following prototype:

```
DROP TRIGGER {trigger} [,...n]
```

How Triggers Work

When you design triggers, it is important to understand how they work—not just what they do, but the exact means and method that they use to do it. This section discusses how triggers work when they are defined on **INSERT**, **DELETE**, and **UPDATE** statements, the inserted and deleted tables, and nested and recursive triggers.

How An INSERT Trigger Works

The following steps describe how an **INSERT** trigger is fired when an **INSERT** statement is executed:

1. An **INSERT** statement is executed on a table with an **INSERT** trigger defined.
2. The **INSERT** statement is logged.
3. The trigger is fired and the trigger statements are executed.

When an **INSERT** trigger is fired, new rows are added to both the trigger table and the inserted table. The inserted table is a logical in-memory table that holds a copy of the rows that have been inserted. The inserted table contains the logged insert activity from the **INSERT** statement. The inserted table allows you to reference logged data from the initiating **INSERT** statement. The trigger can examine the inserted table to determine whether or how the trigger actions should be carried out. The rows in the inserted table are always duplicates of one or more rows in the trigger table.

All data modification activity (**INSERT**, **UPDATE**, and **DELETE** statements) is logged by SQL Server, but the information in the transaction log is unreadable. However, the inserted table allows you to reference the logged changes that the **INSERT** statement caused. You can validate the inserted data or use the inserted data values to take further action. You also can reference inserted data without having to store the information in variables.

To understand these principles better, let's consider the **loan_insert** trigger on the **loan** table. The **loan_insert** trigger updates a derived column (**on_loan**) in the **copy** table whenever a book is checked out (whenever a record is inserted into the **loan** table). Users can quickly search the **copy** table to determine whether a particular book is available or is already on loan without having to join the **copy** and **loan** tables. This is an example of using a trigger to support denormalization, because the **on_loan** column in the **copy** table is denormalized data. The following code shows the implementation of the **loan_insert** trigger:

```
USE library
GO
CREATE TRIGGER loan_insert
  ON loan
  FOR INSERT
AS
  UPDATE c SET on_loan = 'Y'
    FROM copy c INNER JOIN inserted i
    ON c.isbn = i.isbn AND c.copy_no = i.copy_no
```

Now that you have seen how to use an **UPDATE** statement in conjunction with an **INSERT** trigger, let's take a look at another **INSERT** trigger, this time one that generates output. The following code creates an **INSERT** trigger named **adult_insert**:

```
USE library
GO
CREATE TRIGGER adult_insert
  ON adult
  FOR INSERT
AS
  DECLARE @rcnt int
  SELECT @rcnt = @@ROWCOUNT
```

```
IF (SELECT COUNT(i.member_no)
    FROM member m INNER JOIN inserted I
    ON m.member_no = i.member_no) = 0
  BEGIN
    PRINT 'Transaction cannot be processed.'
    PRINT 'No entry in Member for this adult.'
    ROLLBACK TRANSACTION
  END
IF (SELECT COUNT(*)
    FROM member m INNER JOIN inserted I
    ON m.member_no = i.member_no) <> @rcnt
  BEGIN
    PRINT 'Not all adults have an entry in the Member table'
    PRINT 'The multi row Adult insert has been rolled back.'
    ROLLBACK TRANSACTION
  END
```

This trigger determines whether a matching row in the **member** table exists for an adult before the row is inserted into the **adult** table. It also checks whether multiple adults are inserted. For example, if three adults are inserted into the **adult** table, the trigger determines whether all three adults exist in the **member** table. If one or more of the adults does not have a match in the **member** table, the transaction is rolled back and no adults are added to the **adult** table.

How A DELETE Trigger Works

The following steps describe how a **DELETE** trigger is fired when a **DELETE** statement is executed:

1. A **DELETE** statement is executed on a table with a **DELETE** trigger defined.

2. The **DELETE** statement is logged.

3. The trigger is fired and the trigger statements are executed.

When a **DELETE** trigger is fired, deleted rows from the affected table are placed in a special deleted table. The deleted table is a logical in-memory table that holds a copy of the rows that have been deleted. The deleted table allows you to reference logged data from the initiating **DELETE** statement.

Consider the following facts when you use the **DELETE** trigger:

◆ Rows in the deleted table no longer exist in the database table; therefore, the deleted table and the database table have no rows in common.

◆ A trigger that is defined for a **DELETE** action does not execute for the **TRUNCATE TABLE** statement, because **TRUNCATE TABLE** is not logged.

Let's consider another trigger on the **loan** table in the **library** database. This trigger updates a derived column (**on_loan**) in the **copy** table whenever a book is returned (whenever a record is deleted from the **loan** table). In other words, this trigger lets us directly support denormalization from within the database, without user interaction; an important process, because it lets users quickly search the **copy** table to determine whether a particular book is available or is already on loan. Most notably, it lets the users search the **copy** table without having to join the **copy** and **loan** tables:

```
USE library
GO
CREATE TRIGGER loan_delete
  ON loan
  FOR DELETE
AS
  UPDATE c SET on_loan = 'N'
      FROM copy c INNER JOIN deleted d
      ON c.isbn = d.isbn AND c.copy_no = d.copy_no
```

How An UPDATE Trigger Works

The following steps describe how an **UPDATE** trigger is fired when an **UPDATE** statement is executed:

1. An **UPDATE** statement is executed on a table with an **UPDATE** trigger defined.
2. The **UPDATE** statement is logged as **INSERT** and **DELETE** statements.
3. The trigger is fired and the trigger statements are executed.

You can think of an **UPDATE** statement as two steps: the **DELETE** step that captures the before image of the data and the **INSERT** step that captures the after image of the data. When an **UPDATE** statement is executed on a table that has a trigger defined on it, the original rows (before image) are moved into the deleted table and the updated rows (after image) are inserted into the inserted table.

The trigger can examine the deleted and inserted tables, as well as the trigger table, to determine whether multiple rows have been updated and how the trigger actions should be carried out.

Using IF UPDATE On A Column

You can define a trigger to monitor data updates on a specific column by using the **IF UPDATE** statement in the trigger. Using the **IF UPDATE** statement allows the trigger to selectively execute statements only when values in a specific column or columns are modified. If a specific column has been updated, the trigger can take proper action, such as raising an error message that says that the column cannot be updated or processing a series of statements based on the newly updated column value. You can use the **IF UPDATE** statement as shown in the following prototype:

```
IF UPDATE (column) [{AND | OR} UPDATE (column)] [...n]
```

The following code fragment uses the **IF UPDATE** statement to prevent a user from modifying the member number of a row in the **loanhist** table:

```
USE library
GO
CREATE TRIGGER loanhist_member_update
    ON loanhist
    FOR UPDATE
AS
    IF UPDATE (member_no)
      BEGIN
        RAISERROR ('Member number cannot be modified.', 10, 1)
        ROLLBACK TRANSACTION
      END
```

Nested Triggers

Any trigger can contain an **UPDATE, INSERT,** or **DELETE** statement that affects another table. With nesting enabled, a trigger that changes a table can activate a second trigger, which in turn can activate a third trigger, and so on. Figure 11.3 illustrates nested triggers in the **library** database.

Triggers can be nested up to 32 levels deep (just like stored procedures). If any trigger in a nested chain sets off an infinite loop, the nesting level is exceeded and the trigger terminates and rolls back the transaction. Consider the following facts when you use nested triggers:

♦ By default, the nested triggers configuration option is set to **ON**.

♦ A nested trigger will not fire twice in the same transaction. In other words, a trigger does not cause itself to fire in response to a modification to the trigger table within the trigger.

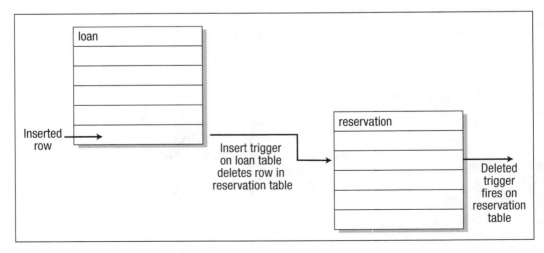

Figure 11.3
Nested triggers in the **library** database.

For example, if a trigger modifies a table that, in turn, modifies the original trigger table, the trigger does not fire again. It is possible to have triggers fire again in the same transaction; this is called a *recursive trigger*. Recursive triggers are discussed later in this chapter.

♦ Because a trigger is a transaction, a failure at any level of a set of nested triggers cancels the entire transaction and all data modifications are rolled back. You can include **PRINT** statements when you test your triggers so that you can determine where the failure occurred.

Checking The Nesting Level

Each time a nested trigger fires, the nesting level increments. SQL Server supports up to 32 levels of nesting, but you may want to limit the levels of nesting to avoid exceeding the maximum nesting level. You can use the **@@NESTLEVEL** function to see the current levels of nesting. Although the **@@NESTLEVEL** function is useful when testing and debugging triggers, it is not typically used in a production environment.

Determining Whether To Use Nesting

Nesting is a powerful feature that you can use to maintain data integrity throughout a database. Nesting is enabled when SQL Server is installed. Occasionally, however, you may want to disable nesting. If nesting is disabled, a trigger that modifies another table does not invoke any of the triggers on the second table. Nesting can be enabled/disabled using the **sp_configure** system stored procedure or using the Server Settings tab of the SQL Server Properties dialog box in SQL Server Enterprise Manager.

Use the following statement to disable nesting:

```
sp_configure 'nested triggers', 0
```

Use the following statement to enable nesting if you have previously disabled nesting:

```
sp_configure 'nested triggers', 1
```

You may decide to disable nesting because of any number of reasons; however, most commonly you will disable nesting because nested triggers require a complex and well-planned design. Cascading modifications can modify data that you did not intend to affect. Moreover, the other thing to watch out for with nested triggers is that data modification at any point in a series of nested triggers sets off the trigger series. Although this offers powerful protection for your data, it can be a problem if your tables must be updated in a specific order.

You can create the same functionality with or without the nesting feature; however, your trigger design will differ substantially. In designing nested triggers, each trigger should initiate the next data modification only—the design should be modular. In designing non-nested triggers, each trigger should initiate all data modifications that you want it to make. Another alternative to using nested triggers is to create a stored procedure that modifies all the tables, and then allow changes to the tables using the stored procedure only.

Recursive Triggers

Any trigger can contain an **UPDATE, INSERT,** or **DELETE** statement that affects the same table or another table. With the *recursive trigger* database option enabled, a trigger that changes data in a table causes itself to fire again, in a recursive execution. No fixed order exists in which multiple triggers that are defined for a given event are executed. Each trigger should be self-contained.

The recursive trigger database option is disabled by default when a database is created, but you can enable it by using the **sp_dboption** system stored procedure or by using the Options tab of the database Properties dialog box in SQL Server Enterprise Manager.

Enabling Recursive Triggers

Use the following statement to enable or disable recursive triggers:

```
sp_dboption database, 'recursive triggers', TRUE | FALSE
```

If the nested trigger configuration option is off, the recursive trigger database option is also disabled, regardless of the setting of the recursive trigger database option. The inserted and deleted tables for a given trigger contain rows that correspond only to the **UPDATE, IN-SERT,** or **DELETE** statement that last invoked the trigger.

As mentioned previously, trigger recursion can occur up to 32 levels deep. If any trigger in a recursive loop sets off an infinite loop, the nesting level is exceeded, and the trigger terminates and rolls back the transaction.

Types Of Recursion

There are two different types of recursion:

♦ Direct recursion, which occurs when a trigger fires and performs an action that causes the same trigger to fire again. For example, an application updates table **T1**, which causes trigger **Trig1** to fire. **Trig1** updates table **T1** again, which causes trigger **Trig1** to fire again.

♦ Indirect recursion, which occurs when a trigger fires and performs an action that causes a trigger on another table to fire, subsequently causing a modification to occur in the original table. This modification then causes the original trigger to fire again. For example, an application updates table **T2**, which causes trigger **Trig2** to fire. **Trig2** updates table **T3**, which causes trigger **Trig3** to fire. **Trig3** in turn updates table **T2**, which causes **Trig2** to fire again.

Determining Whether To Use Recursive Triggers

Recursive triggers are a complex feature that you can use to solve complex relationships, such as self-referencing relationships (also known as *transitive closures*). In these special situations, you may want to enable recursive triggers. Some examples of when recursive triggers might be useful would include the following:

♦ Maintaining the number of reports columns in an employee table where the table contains an employee ID column and a manager ID column. For example, assume that two update triggers, **tr_update_employee** and **tr_update_manager**, are defined on the **employee** table. The **tr_update_employee** trigger updates the **employee** table. An **UPDATE** statement causes both the **tr_update_employee** and the **tr_update_manager** triggers to fire. Because the **tr_update_employee** trigger updates the employee table, it causes the **tr_update_employee** and the **tr_update_manager** triggers to fire again (recursively).

♦ Maintaining a Gantt chart for production scheduling data in which an implied scheduling hierarchy exists.

♦ Maintaining a parts explosion tree in which subparts are tracked to parent parts.

Consider the following very important guidelines before you use recursive triggers:

♦ Recursive triggers are complex and need to be designed well and thoroughly tested. Recursive triggers require controlled looping logic code (that is, an effective termination check). Otherwise, you will exceed the 32-level nesting limit.

♦ A data modification at any point can set off the trigger series. Although this provides the ability for processing complex relationships, it can be a problem if your tables must be updated in a specific order.

You can create similar functionality without the recursive trigger feature; however, your trigger design will differ substantially. In designing recursive triggers, each trigger must contain a conditional check to stop recursive processing when the condition becomes false. In designing nonrecursive triggers, each trigger must contain the full programming looping structures and checks.

Examples Of Triggers

Some of the actions that triggers perform can be accomplished using constraints, and you should always consider constraints first. However, triggers are necessary to enforce various degrees of denormalization, to cascade updates and deletes to maintain referential integrity, and to enforce complex business rules.

Enforcing Data Integrity

Figure 11.4 shows the **reservation_delete** trigger that maintains the members in the **members** table.

This example shows how a trigger can maintain data integrity on the **reservation** table by deleting a reservation entry when the member who holds the reservation checks out the book that was on reserve. This trigger enforces data integrity by deleting the reservation

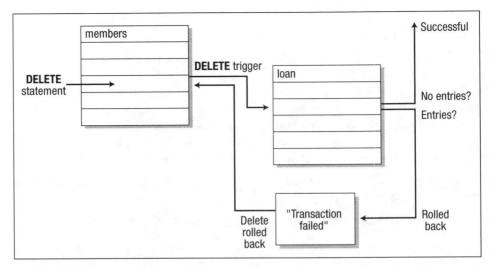

Figure 11.4
Enforcing data integrity.

row entry (if one exists) in the **reservation** table when a row is inserted into the **loan** table (when the book is checked out):

```
USE library
GO
CREATE TRIGGER reservation_delete
  ON loan
  FOR INSERT
AS
  IF (SELECT r.member_no FROM reservation r JOIN inserted i
      ON r.member_no = i.member_no
      AND r.isbn = i.isbn ) > 0
    BEGIN
      DELETE r FROM reservation r INNER JOIN inserted i
          ON r.member_no = i.member_no
          AND r.isbn = i.isbn
    END
```

Enforcing Business Rules

You can use triggers to enforce particular business rules that require more complexity than a **CHECK** constraint can define. Figure 11.5 shows how you can ensure that members' outstanding fines are paid before they are allowed to discontinue membership.

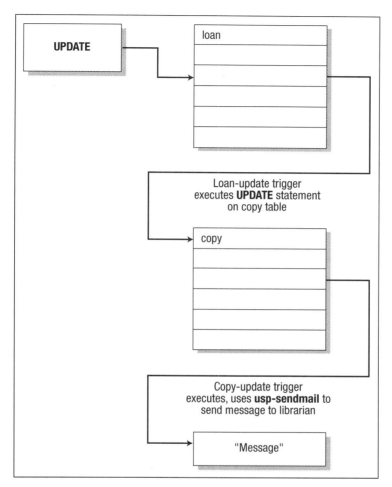

Figure 11.5
Enforcing business rules.

The following code fragment creates a trigger that determines whether a member who is discontinuing membership has any outstanding loans. If no outstanding loans exist, the member can be deleted from the database, along with any book reservations that the member might have. If the member has books checked out, the trigger returns a custom error message:

```
USE library
GO
CREATE TRIGGER member_delete
    ON member FOR DELETE
```

```
AS
  IF (SELECT COUNT (*) FROM loan INNER JOIN deleted
      ON loan.member_no = deleted.member_no) > 0
    BEGIN
      PRINT 'Transaction cannot be processed.'
      PRINT 'This member still has books on loan.'
      ROLLBACK TRANSACTION
    END
  ELSE
    DELETE reservation FROM reservation INNER JOIN deleted
        ON reservation.member_no = deleted.member_no
```

Performance Considerations

You should consider the following performance issues when you use triggers:

◆ Triggers work quickly because the inserted and deleted tables are in the SQL Server cache.

◆ The **inserted** and **deleted** tables are always in memory rather than on disk. It is possible to store these tables in memory because they are logical tables, are usually small, and only exist for a short time.

◆ Execution time of a trigger or nested trigger series is determined by the number of tables referenced and the number of rows affected.

◆ Time that is spent invoking a trigger is minimal. The largest portion of execution time occurs as a result of referencing other tables (which may be either in memory or on disk) and modifying data, if the trigger statements perform data modifications.

◆ Actions contained in triggers are implicitly part of a transaction.

◆ After a trigger is defined, the user action (**INSERT**, **UPDATE**, or **DELETE** statement) on the table that causes the trigger to fire is always implicitly part of a transaction, along with the trigger itself. If a **ROLLBACK TRANSACTION** statement is encountered, the whole transaction rolls back. If any statements exist in the trigger script after the **ROLLBACK TRANSACTION** statement, those statements are executed. Therefore it may be necessary to use a **RETURN** clause in an **IF** statement to prevent the processing of other statements.

Where To Go From Here

Stored procedures provide full programmability to SQL Server. Many system tasks are performed using system stored procedures that are installed with SQL Server. Stored procedures, which you can create, are stored in databases and loaded into the procedure cache the first time they are executed. Subsequent executions use the copy of the stored procedure already loaded in the procedure cache.

A special kind of stored procedure—triggers—make it possible to enforce complex business logic and data integrity that constraints cannot. Use triggers when you can't achieve the desired functionality using constraints. Although you can use most Transact-SQL statements in triggers, certain statements are not allowed. Triggers are always part of a transaction and can roll back the transaction to prevent data modification.

Special tables called **inserted** and **deleted** are available inside a trigger. These tables contain the rows affected by the statement that caused the trigger to fire. An **UPDATE** statement on a table with an **UPDATE** trigger works by deleting the rows from the table and inserting changed rows back into the table; for this reason, an **UPDATE** trigger also uses the **inserted** and **deleted** tables.

The topics discussed in this chapter are closely supplemented by topics discussed in Chapters 7, 9, and 10, as well as supporting information on common uses for stored procedures in other chapters within this book where we use them.

Now that we have reviewed most of the important components in SQL Server database design and management—even though we have barely scratched the surface—it's time to move on to a more complete discussion of using Access 2000 with SQL Server. In Chapter 13, we will discuss the use of Access Data Projects (ADPs), a new project type in Access 2000, for the design of front-ends to SQL Server databases.

Chapter 12

Additional Programming And ADP Issues With Client/Server Development

Throughout the previous chapters, you've been exposed to a brief overview of the techniques that you can use with Access to connect to a server-side database. You've explored the basics of how to work with both SQL Server and Oracle (the two most commonly used server-side databases for the Windows environment). You've also looked at the majority of the SQL Server objects, and how their use affects your client/server design with Access 2000 as the front end. We're going to consider these concepts more in just a little bit—that is, how to work with the SQL Server back end—but first, it is worth taking a few pages to discuss one of the most important concepts in client/server design, the transaction.

A *transaction* is an atomic group of actions against a database that either all succeed or all fail. In the following sections, we'll begin our exploration of some of the other client/server processing issues with a discussion of transaction processing.

Understanding Transaction Processing

Transaction processing refers to the grouping of a series of changes into a single batch. The entire batch of changes is either accepted or rejected as a group. One of the most common explanations used for transaction processing is a bank automated teller machine (ATM) transaction. Imagine that you go to the ATM machine to deposit your paycheck. In the middle of processing, a power outage occurs. Unfortunately, the bank recorded the incoming funds before the outage, but the funds hadn't yet been credited to *your* account when the power outage occurred. In other words, the bank had your money, so you couldn't redeposit the check, but they didn't credit the money to your account, so you couldn't access the money either.

Needless to say, you'd likely be pretty unhappy with this particular outcome. Transaction processing would prevent this scenario from occurring. With transaction processing, the whole process either succeeds or fails as a unit. If a group of operations is considered a transaction, then it must meet the following criteria (the so-called ACID test):

♦ *It's Atomic*—The group of operations should complete as a unit or not at all.

♦ *It's Consistent*—The group of operations, when completed as a unit, retains the consistency of the application.

♦ *It's Isolated*—The group of operations is independent of anything else going on in the system.

♦ *It's Durable*—After the group of operations is committed, the changes persist, even if the system crashes.

If your application contains a group of operations that are atomic and isolated, and if to maintain the consistency of your application all changes must persist even if the system crashes, then you should place the group of operations in a transaction loop.

With Access 2000, the primary benefit of transaction processing is data integrity. As you'll see in the following section, with prior versions of Access, transaction processing also provided significant performance benefits. Transaction processing still provides performance benefits in Access 2000, but they're minor and generally aren't the primary reason why you'll use transaction processing in your development.

Understanding The Benefits Of Transaction Processing

In Access 2, the benefits of transaction processing were many, above and beyond simple integrity issues. In general, these benefits were so much more significant because Access 2 did no implicit transaction processing. If you were to run the following code in Access 2, for example, each time the **Update** method occurs within the loop, the data would be written to disk. These disk writes are costly in terms of performance, especially if the tables aren't located on a local machine:

```
Sub IncreaseQuantity()
  On Error GoTo IncreaseQuantity_Err
  Dim db As Database
  Dim rst As Recordset

  Set db = CurrentDb
  Set rst = db.OpenRecordset("Select OrderId, Quantity From tblOrderDetails", _
    dbOpenDynaset)
```

```
  'Loop through recordset increasing Quantity field by 1
  Do Until rst.EOF
    rst.Edit
      rst!Quantity = rst!Quantity + 1
    rst.Update
    rst.MoveNext
  Loop

IncreaseQuantity_Exit:
  Set db = Nothing
  Set rst = Nothing
  Exit Sub

IncreaseQuantity_Err:
  MsgBox "Error # " & Err.Number & ": " & Error.Description
  Resume IncreaseQuantity_Exit
End Sub
```

You can find this code in the Chap12trans.mdb database on the companion CD-ROM. This particular code fragment can be found in the module called **basTransactionRoutines**.

This same code, when run in Access 2000, performs much differently. In addition to any *explicit* transaction processing you might implement for data-integrity reasons, Access 2000 does its own behind-the-scenes transaction processing. This *implicit transaction processing* is done solely to improve the performance of your application. As the processing loop in the **IncreaseQuantity** routine executes, Access buffers periodically write the data to disk. In a multiuser environment, by default, Jet automatically (implicitly) commits transactions every 50 milliseconds. This period of time is optimized for concurrency rather than performance. If you think it's necessary to sacrifice concurrency for performance, you can modify a few Windows Registry settings to achieve the specific outcome you want. These settings are covered in the next section, "Modifying The Default Behavior Of Transaction Processing."

In general, implicit transaction processing, along with the modifiable Windows Registry settings, afford you better performance than explicit transaction processing; however, it's not a cut-and-dried situation. Many factors, including those in the following list, affect the performance benefits gained by *both* implicit and explicit transaction processing:

♦ The amount of free memory

♦ The number of columns and rows being updated

♦ The size of the rows being updated

♦ Network traffic

If you plan to implement explicit transaction processing solely for the purpose of improving performance, you should make sure you benchmark your application's performance using both implicit and explicit transactions. It's critical that your application-testing environment be as similar as possible to the production environment within which the application will run—otherwise, your benchmarking is relatively useless.

However, the likelihood is that you will implement explicit transaction processing for reasons pertaining to the way you manage the data. In such cases, you will have several different options for how to implement the transaction processing. The following section discusses how to modify the default behaviors of transaction processing in Access.

Modifying The Default Behavior Of Transaction Processing

Before you learn how to implement transaction processing, let's see what you can do to modify the default behavior of the transaction processing built into Access 2000. Three Registry settings affect *implicit* transactions within Access 2000: ImplicitCommitSync, ExclusiveAsyncDelay, and SharedAsyncDelay. These keys aren't automatically found in the System Registry. Instead, you must add them to the Registry using the Registry Editor if you determine that you want to control the implicit settings.

The ImplicitCommitSync setting determines whether implicit transactions are used. The default is No, which might seem to imply that no implicit transactions occur. Actually, because of a documented Jet 3.x bug, which seems to have carried over to Jet 4, the value of No means that implicit transactions *are* used. You generally won't want to change this setting, because implicit transactions are typically very beneficial to application performance. Furthermore, by placing a series of commands within an *explicit* transaction loop, any *implicit* transaction processing is disabled for that loop.

The ExclusiveAsyncDelay setting specifies the maximum number of milliseconds that elapse before Jet commits an implicit transaction when a database is opened for exclusive use. The default value for this setting is 2,000 milliseconds. This setting doesn't in any way affect databases that are open for shared use.

The SharedAsyncDelay setting is similar to ExclusiveAsyncDelay. It determines the maximum number of milliseconds that elapse before Jet commits an implicit transaction when a database is opened for shared use. The default value for this setting is 50 milliseconds. The higher this value, the greater the performance benefits reaped from implicit transactions, but the higher the chances that concurrency problems will result. These concurrency issues are discussed in detail in the section entitled "Transaction Processing In A Multiuser Environment."

Besides the settings that affect implicit transaction processing in Access 2000, an additional Registry setting affects explicit transaction processing. The UserCommitSync setting controls whether explicit transactions are completed synchronously or asynchronously. With the default setting of Yes, control doesn't return from a **CommitTrans** statement until the transactions are actually written to disk. When this value is changed to No, a series of changes are queued, and control returns before the changes are complete.

However, despite the simple model of transaction processing, when you use explicit processing you need to consider certain issues to ensure that the processing occurs correctly. Issues such as record locks, field locks, and more all carry over with special significance during transaction processing. The next section begins the discussion of how to properly implement transaction processing.

Properly Implementing Explicit Transaction Processing

Now that you're aware of the settings that affect transaction processing, you're ready to see how transaction processing is implemented. From DAO, three methods of the **Workspace** object control transaction processing:

♦ **BeginTrans**

♦ **CommitTrans**

♦ **Rollback**

The **BeginTrans** method of the **Workspace** object begins the transaction loop. The moment Access encounters **BeginTrans**, the program begins writing all changes to a log file in memory. Unless the **CommitTrans** method is issued on the **Workspace** object, the changes are never actually written to the database file. After the **CommitTrans** method is issued, the updates are permanently written to the database object. If a **Rollback** method of the **Workspace** object is encountered, the log in memory is released. Here's an example of simple transaction processing using our old friends, the DAO objects:

```
Sub IncreaseQuantityTrans()
  On Error GoTo IncreaseQuantityTrans_Err
  Dim wrk As Workspace
  Dim db As Database
  Dim rst As Recordset

  Set wrk = DBEngine(0)
  Set db = CurrentDb
  Set rst = db.OpenRecordset("Select OrderId, Quantity From tblOrderDetails", _
    dbOpenDynaset)
  'Begin the transaction loop
  wrk.BeginTrans
    'Loop through recordset increasing Quantity field by 1
    Do Until rst.EOF
      rst.Edit
        rst!Quantity = rst!Quantity + 1
      rst.Update
      rst.MoveNext
    Loop
  'Commit the transaction; everything went as planned
  wrk.CommitTrans
```

```
IncreaseQuantityTrans_Exit:
  Set wrk = Nothing
  Set db = Nothing
  Set rst = Nothing
  Exit Sub

IncreaseQuantityTrans_Err:
  MsgBox "Error # " & Err.Number & ": " & Error.Description
  'Rollback the transaction; an error occurred
  wrk.Rollback
  Resume IncreaseQuantityTrans_Exit
End Sub
```

This code uses a transaction loop to ensure that everything completes as planned or not at all. Notice that the loop that moves through the recordset, increasing the quantity field within each record by one, is placed within a transaction loop. If all processing within the loop completes successfully, the **CommitTrans** method is executed. If the routine invokes the error-handling code for any reason, the error handler issues the **Rollback** method, ensuring that none of the changes are written to disk.

When working with ActiveX Data Objects (ADO), you'll generally use the **BeginTrans**, **CommitTrans**, and **RollbackTrans** methods of the **Connection** object to perform your transaction processing. The following program code demonstrates, briefly, how you can use ADO objects to perform the same processing shown previously using DAO (note that you must create a ODBC Data Source Name [DSN] called "Chap12" that connects to the Northwind database on your SQL Server):

```
Sub ADOIncreaseQuantityTrans()
  On Error GoTo ADOIncreaseQuantityTrans_Err
  Dim cnnLocal As ADODB.Connection
  Dim cmdLocal As ADODB.Command
  Dim rstLocal As ADODB.Recordset

  ' Create Connection Object and open it on CHAP12 catalog
  Set cnnLocal = New ADODB.Connection
  cnnLocal.ConnectionString = "dsn=Chap12;User ID=sa;Password=;"
  cnnLocal.Open

  Set cmdLocal = New ADODB.Command
  Set cmdLocal.ActiveConnection = cnnLocal

  cmdLocal.CommandText = "Select OrderId, Quantity From tblOrderDetails"
  rstLocal.CursorType = adOpenForwardOnly
  Set rstLocal = cmdLocal.Execute()
```

```
'Begin the transaction loop
cnnLocal.BeginTrans
  'Loop through recordset increasing Quantity field by 1
    Do Until rstLocal.EOF
      rstLocal.Fields("Quantity") = rstLocal.Fields("Quantity") + 1
      rstLocal.MoveNext
    Loop
  'Commit the transaction; everything went as planned
  cnnLocal.CommitTrans

ADOIncreaseQuantityTrans_Exit:
  Set cnnLocal = Nothing
  Set cmdLocal = Nothing
  Set rstLocal = Nothing
  Exit Sub

ADOIncreaseQuantityTrans_Err:
  MsgBox "Error # " & Err.Number & ": " & Error.Description
  'Rollback the transaction; an error occurred
  cnnLocal.RollbackTrans
  Resume ADOIncreaseQuantityTrans_Exit
End Sub
```

Needless to say, although transaction processing is still a relatively straightforward activity (as are most things from within VBA), its basic nature nevertheless introduces certain issues. The following sections discuss some of the issues that you might encounter when performing transaction processing.

Potential Issues With Transaction Processing

Before you decide that transaction processing is the greatest thing in the history of database design, you should keep several issues in mind. These issues are outlined within this section.

Making Sure The Data Source Supports Transactions

Not all recordsets (such as older FoxPro and dBASE files) support transaction processing. Neither do certain back-end, open database connectivity (ODBC) database servers. To make matters worse, you won't encounter any errors when using the transaction processing methods on FoxPro or dBASE tables. It'll appear as if everything processed as planned, but actually, all references to transactions are ignored. When in doubt, you can use the **Transactions** property of the DAO **Database** or **Recordset** object to determine whether the data source supports transaction processing. The **Transactions** property is equal to **True** if the data source supports transaction processing and **False** if the data source doesn't support transaction processing.

Checking A Database Object For Transaction Support

As you've learned, some databases won't support transactions. Ensuring that a database does before your code tries to send transaction-processing code to the object is an important task. You can check these capabilities from both DAO and ADO. To do so from DAO, you'll use code similar to the following:

```
Sub SupportsTrans(strTableName)
  On Error GoTo SupportsTrans_Err
  Dim wrk As Workspace
  Dim db As Database
  Dim rst As Recordset
  Dim fSupportsTrans As Boolean

  fSupportsTrans = False
  Set wrk = DBEngine(0)
  Set db = CurrentDb
  Set rst = db.OpenRecordset(strTableName, _
      dbOpenDynaset)
  'Begin the transaction loop only if recordset supports transaction
  If rst.Transactions Then
    fSupportsTrans = True
    wrk.BeginTrans
  End If
  'Loop through recordset decreasing Quantity field by 1
  Do Until rst.EOF
    rst.Edit
      rst!Quantity = rst!Quantity - 1
    rst.Update
    rst.MoveNext
  Loop
  'Issue the CommitTrans if everything went as planned
  'and Recordset Supports Transactions
  If fSupportsTrans Then
    wrk.CommitTrans
  End If

SupportsTrans_Exit:
  Set wrk = Nothing
  Set db = Nothing
  Set rst = Nothing
  Exit Sub

SupportsTrans_Err:
  MsgBox "Error # " & Err.Number & ": " & Error.Description
  'Rollback the transaction if an error occurred
```

```
'and recordset supports transactions
If fSupportsTrans Then
  wrk.Rollback
End If
Resume SupportsTrans_Exit
End Sub
```

Notice that this code uses a Boolean variable called **fSupportsTrans** to track whether the recordset supports transactions. The code tests the recordset to see whether the **SupportsTrans** property evaluates to **True**. If so, the **BeginTrans** is issued and the **fSupportsTrans** variable is set equal to **True**. The **fSupportsTrans** variable is evaluated two different times in the remainder of the routine. The **CommitTrans** method is issued only if **fSupportsTrans** evaluates to **True**. Within the error-handling routine, the **Rollback** method is issued only if the **fSupportTrans** variable is equal to **True**.

> **Note**
>
> *Implementing these techniques using ADO is left as an exercise for you—though it is important to emphasize, once again, that transactions are implemented in ADO through the use of the **BeginTrans** and related methods of the **Connection** object.*

Nesting Transactions

Another issue to be aware of with transactions is that you can nest transactions up to five levels deep. The inner transactions must always be committed or rolled back before the outer transactions. Furthermore, nested transactions aren't supported at all for ODBC data sources. This is covered in the section of this chapter entitled "Transaction Processing In A Client/Server Environment." Note as well that nested transactions are somewhat nonsensical in most contexts.

Neglecting To Explicitly Commit Transactions

When a transaction loop is executing, all updates are written to a log file in memory. If a **CommitTrans** is never executed, the changes are, in effect, rolled back. In other words, a **Rollback** is the default behavior if the changes are never explicitly written to disk with the **CommitTrans** method. This generally works to your advantage. If the power is interrupted or the machine "hangs" before the **CommitTrans** is executed, all changes are, in effect, rolled back. But this behavior can get you into trouble if you forget the **CommitTrans** method. If the workspace is closed without the **CommitTrans** method being executed, the memory log is flushed and the transaction is implicitly rolled back.

Available Memory And Transactions

Another problem to watch out for with transactions occurs when the computer's physical memory is exhausted (or filled) by the transaction log. In such a situation, Access first attempts to use virtual memory. The transaction log is written to the temporary directory specified by the **TEMP** environment variable of the user's machine. This has the effect of dramatically slowing down the transaction process. However, if the transaction process exhausts both physical and virtual memory, an error 2004 results from DAO processing. The error number returned from ADO may vary. You must issue a **Rollback** at this point; otherwise, you're in danger of violating the consistency of the database.

Warning
If your DAO code attempts to commit the transaction after a 2004 error has occurred, the Jet engine commits as many changes as possible, leaving the database in an inconsistent state. In general, ADO won't let you commit transactions after this type of error occurs.

Transactions And Forms

Access handles its own transaction processing on bound forms—unless you have used the new support within Access for thin-form binding to SQL Server databases. In such cases, you'll have some control of the transaction processing Access performs.

Except as noted, you can't control the transaction processing Access performs on bound forms in any way. If you want to utilize transaction processing with forms, you must create unbound forms.

Transaction Processing In A Multiuser Environment

In a multiuser environment, transaction processing has implications beyond the protection of data. By wrapping a process in a transaction loop, you ensure that you're in control of all records involved in the process. The cost of this additional control is reduced concurrency for the rest of the users of the application. The following code illustrates this scenario:

```
Sub MultiPessimistic()
  On Error GoTo MultiPessimistic_Err
  Dim wrk As Workspace
  Dim db As Database
  Dim rst As Recordset
  Dim intCounter As Integer, intChoice As Integer
  Dim intTry As Integer

  Set wrk = DBEngine(0)
  Set db = CurrentDb
  Set rst = db.OpenRecordset("Select OrderId, ProductID, UnitPrice " & _
      "From tblOrderDetails Where ProductID > 50", dbOpenDynaset)
  rst.LockEdits = True
  'Begin the transaction loop
  wrk.BeginTrans
    'Loop through recordset increasing UnitPrice
    Do Until rst.EOF
```

```
      'Lock occurs here for each record in the loop
      rst.Edit
        rst!UnitPrice = rst!UnitPrice * 1.1
      rst.Update
      rst.MoveNext
    Loop
  'Commit the transaction; everything went as planned
  'All locks released for ALL records involved in the process
  wrk.CommitTrans
  Set wrk = Nothing
  Set db = Nothing
  Set rst = Nothing
  Exit Sub

MultiPessimistic_Err:
  Select Case Err.Number
    Case 3260
      intCounter = intCounter + 1
      If intCounter > 2 Then
        intChoice = MsgBox(Err.Description, vbRetryCancel + vbCritical)
        Select Case intChoice
          Case vbRetry
            intCounter = 1
          Case vbCancel
            'User selected cancel, roll back
            Resume TransUnsuccessful
        End Select
      End If
      DoEvents
      For intTry = 1 To 100
      Next intTry
      Resume
    Case Else
      MsgBox "Error # " & Err.Number & ": " & Err.Description
  End Select

TransUnsuccessful:
  wrk.Rollback
  MsgBox "Warning: Entire Process Rolled Back"
  Set wrk = Nothing
  Set db = Nothing
  Set rst = Nothing
  Exit Sub
End Sub
```

The **MultiPessimistic** routine employs Pessimistic locking. This means that each time the **Edit** method is issued, the record on which the edit is issued is locked. If all goes well and no error occurs, the lock is released when the **CommitTrans** is reached. The error-handling code traps for a 3260 error (you should, of course, trap for all possible errors in your code). This error means that the record is locked by another user. The user running the transaction processing is given the opportunity to retry or cancel. If the user selects retry, the code once again tries to issue the **Edit** method on the record. If the user selects cancel, a **Rollback** occurs. This causes the changes made to any of the records involved in the process to be canceled.

You should recognize and understand two key points about the **MultiPessimistic** routine. The first point is that as this routine executes, each record involved in the process is locked. This potentially means that all other users will be unable to edit a large percentage, or even any, of the records until the transaction process is complete. This is wonderful from a data-integrity standpoint, but it might not be practical within an environment in which users must update data on a frequent basis. For this reason, it's a good idea to keep transaction loops as short in duration as possible. The second point is that if any of the lock attempts are unsuccessful, the entire transaction must be canceled. Once again, this might be what you want or need from a data-integrity standpoint, but it might require that all users refrain from editing data while an important process completes.

With Optimistic locking, the lock attempt occurs when the **Update** method is issued rather than when the **Edit** method is issued. In general, this doesn't make too much of a difference—all of the records involved in the transaction remain locked until the **CommitTrans** or **Rollback** occurs. An additional difference is in the errors that you must trap for. The DAO code looks like this:

```
Sub MultiOptimistic()
  On Error GoTo MultiOptimistic_Err
  Dim wrk As Workspace
  Dim db As Database
  Dim rst As Recordset
  Dim intCounter As Integer, intChoice As Integer
  Dim intTry As Integer

  Set wrk = DBEngine(0)
  Set db = CurrentDb
  Set rst = db.OpenRecordset("Select OrderId, ProductID, UnitPrice " & _
      "From tblOrderDetails Where ProductID > 50", dbOpenDynaset)
  rst.LockEdits = False
  'Begin the Transaction Loop
  wrk.BeginTrans
    'Loop through recordset increasing UnitPrice
    Do Until rst.EOF
```

```
          rst.Edit
            rst!UnitPrice = rst!UnitPrice * 1.1
            'Lock occurs here for each record in the loop
          rst.Update
          rst.MoveNext
        Loop
      'Commit the transaction; everything went as planned
      'All locks released for ALL records involved in the process
      wrk.CommitTrans
      Set wrk = Nothing
      Set db = Nothing
      Set rst = Nothing
      Exit Sub

  MultiOptimistic_Err:
      Select Case Err.Number
        Case 3197  'Data Has Changed Error
          If rst.EditMode = dbEditInProgress Then
            intChoice = MsgBox("Overwrite Other User's Changes?", _
                vbYesNoCancel + vbQuestion)
            Select Case intChoice
              Case vbCancel, vbNo
                MsgBox "Update Canceled"
                Resume TransNotSuccessful
              Case vbYes
                rst.Update
                Resume
            End Select
          End If
        Case 3186, 3260   'Locked or can't be saved
          intCounter = intCounter + 1
          If intCounter > 2 Then
            intChoice = MsgBox(Err.Description, vbRetryCancel + vbCritical)
            Select Case intChoice
              Case vbRetry
                intCounter = 1
              Case vbCancel
                'User selected cancel, roll back
                Resume TransNotSuccessful
            End Select
          End If
          DoEvents
          For intTry = 1 To 100
          Next intTry
          Resume
        Case Else
```

```
      MsgBox "Error # " & Err.Number & ": " & Err.Description
   End Select

TransNotSuccessful:
  wrk.Rollback
  MsgBox "Warning: Entire process rolled back"
  Set wrk = Nothing
  Set db = Nothing
  Set rst = Nothing
  Exit Sub
End Sub
```

Notice that in the **MultiOptimistic** routine, the lock occurs each time the **Update** method is issued. All of the locks are released when the **CommitTrans** is executed. Furthermore, the error handling checks for a 3197 (data has changed) error. The 3197 occurs when the data is changed by another user after the **Edit** method is issued and just before the **Update** method is issued.

Tip

*The Chap12trans.mdb file on the companion CD-ROM contains example code (in the routines **ADOMultiPessimistic** and **ADOMultiOptimistic**) that shows how to perform this type of processing and locking with ADO objects rather than with DAO objects.*

Transaction processing, then, clearly has its own set of issues in any environment. However, in a client/server environment, some issues are different, some are more serious, and some are less serious. The following sections discuss some of the issues surrounding transaction processing in a client/server environment.

Transaction Processing In A Client/Server Environment

When you're utilizing transactions in a client/server environment, you must consider several additional issues. These issues concern when and how transactions occur, what types of transactions are supported, and what potential problems can occur.

Implicit Transactions And The Client/Server Environment

When explicit transactions aren't used, the way that transactions are committed on the database server depends upon what types of commands are being executed. In general, each and every line of code has an implicit transaction around it. This means that there isn't a way to roll back an action, because it's immediately committed on the database server. The exceptions to this rule are any issued SQL statements that modify data. These SQL statements (**UPDATE, INSERT**, and **APPEND**) are executed in batches. This means a transaction loop is implicitly placed around the entire statement. If any records involved in the SQL statement can't be updated successfully, the entire **UPDATE, INSERT**, or **APPEND** is rolled back.

Explicit Transactions And The Client/Server Environment

When explicit transactions are used, ODBC or OLE DB (depending on which object set you're using) translates the **BeginTrans**, **CommitTrans**, and **Rollback** methods to the appropriate syntax of the back-end server and the transaction processes as expected. The main exception to this rule is when transactions aren't supported by the specific back end that you're using. An example of transaction processing with a SQL Server back end is shown in the following code:

```
Sub TransSQLServer()
  Dim cnnBack As Connection
  Dim cmdBack As Command

'Open connection to Pubs database
'on SQLSERVER server.
    Set cnnBack = New ADODB.Connection
    strCnn = "Provider=sqloledb;" & _
        "Data Source=SQLSERVER;" & _
        "Initial Catalog=Pubs;" & _
        "User Id=sa;Password=;"
    cnnBack.Open strCnn

  cnnBack.BeginTrans

    Set cmdBack = new ADODB.Command
    set cmdBack.ActiveConnection = cnnBack
    cmdBack.CommandText = "UPDATE sales Set qty = qty + 1 " & _
        "Where Stor_ID = '7067';"
    cmdBack.Execute
    cmdBack.CommandText = "Update titles Set price = price + 1 " & _
        "Where Type = 'Business'"
    cmdBack.Execute
  cnnBack.CommitTrans

TransSQLServer_Exit:
  Set cnnBack = Nothing
  Set cmdBack = Nothing
  Exit Sub

TransSQLServer_Err:
  ' Note that, in most cases, you would probably use the ADO
  ' Errors collection, and not the VB error object—I have just
  ' tried to keep it simple.

  MsgBox "Error # " & Err.Number & ": " & Err.Description
  cnnBack.Rollback
```

```
    Resume TransSQLServer_Exit
End Sub
```

The **TransSQLServer** routine begins by creating both **Connection** and **Command** object variables. Next, it executes the **BeginTrans** method on the connection. It then uses the **CommandText** property of the **Command** object to execute a temporary query on the SQL Server. The **CommandText** property of the **Command** object is modified and the query is executed again. If both **Execute** methods complete successfully, the **CommitTrans** method is issued on the **Connection** object. If any error occurs during processing, the **Rollback** method is issued.

Nested Transactions In A Client/Server Environment

One occasion in which transactions might not perform as expected is when your code employs nested transactions. ODBC doesn't support them. If your code includes nested transactions, all but the outermost transaction loop will be ignored.

Lock Limits In A Client/Server Environment

A potential pitfall when dealing with client/server databases involves lock limits. Many database servers impose strict limits upon how many records can be concurrently locked. As you saw in the code examples within the "Properly Implementing Explicit Transaction Processing" section earlier in this chapter, a transaction loop can potentially lock a significant number of records. It's important to consider the maximum number of locks supported by your back end when employing transaction loops in your Visual Basic for Applications (VBA) code.

Negative Interactions With Server-Specific Transaction Commands

You should never utilize server-specific transaction commands when building pass-through queries. These server-specific commands can conflict with the **BeginTrans**, **CommitTrans**, and **Rollback** methods, causing confusion and potential data corruption.

All the discussions that we've had so far about what to do to improve your application's client/server processing have focused, for the most part, on what to do from the client side of the communication. However, you can use some important techniques at the server, as well, to improve processing. The following sections discuss some of these techniques, with a specific eye toward SQL Server because of Access 2000's close integration with SQL Server 7. Although the techniques discussed in the remainder of this chapter may have different names or specific implementations within other database server products, the logic is the same. Check your server product for specifics.

Now that we have briefly considered some of the issues surrounding transaction processing, both at the local level and in the client/server environment, let's move on to more specific considerations of some of the issues surrounding the use of client/server database products. One of the biggest differences between programming for Access and programming for client/server is the use of stored procedures and extended SQL code in the client/server environment. The following sections continue our discussion of client/server issues with stored procedures.

Managing Stored Procedures And Using Flow-Control Statements

As your systems become more complex, you'll need to spend more time carefully integrating SQL code with your host application code. In the following sections, you'll review some of the logic and flow-control statements that you have available to you in your SQL code.

At a high level, stored procedures are a way you can create routines and procedures that are run on the server, by server processes. These routines can be started when an application calls them or when they're called by data integrity rules or triggers (triggers are explained in detail later in this chapter).

The benefit of stored procedures comes from the fact that they run within the server environment on the server. Although this might not seem to be an obvious advantage at first, it goes to the heart of the client/server model. Because the server environment is the manager of any databases in your system once you fully transition to the client/server model, it makes sense that it would be the best place to run the stored procedures against that data. Stored procedures can return values, modify values, and can be used to compare a user-supplied value against the prerequisites for information in the system. They run quickly, with the added horsepower of the average server hardware, and they're database-aware and able to take advantage of most servers' optimizers for best performance at runtime. In general, you can think of a stored procedure as being similar to a query definition in Access 2000.

You can also pass values to a stored procedure, and it can return values that aren't necessarily part of an underlying table but are, instead, calculated during the running of the stored procedure. The benefits of stored procedures in a client/server implementation, from a high-level perspective, include the following:

- *Performance*—Because stored procedures run on the server, typically a more powerful machine, the execution time is generally much less than at the workstation. In addition, because the database information is readily at hand and on the same system physically, there's no wait for records to pass over the network for processing. Instead, the stored procedure has immediate, ready access to the database, which makes working with the information extremely fast.

- *Client/server development benefits*—By breaking apart the client and server development tasks, you can sometimes help to decrease the time needed to bring your projects to completion. You can develop the server-side pieces separately from the client-side, and you can reuse the server-side components between client-side applications.

♦ *Security*—You can use stored procedures as a tool to apply some serious security to your server-side databases. You can create stored procedures for all add, change, delete, and list operations and make it so you can programmatically control each of these aspects of information access.

♦ *Server-side enforcement of data-oriented rules*—This is ultimately one of the most important reasons for using an intelligent database engine. The stored procedures let you put into place the rules and other logic that help control the information that goes into your system.

Warning

When you design for the client/server model, it's critical that you keep the model in mind when you're building your systems. Remember, data management belongs on the server, and data presentation and display manipulation for reports and inquiries should reside on the client in the ideal model. As you build systems, be on the lookout for those items that can be moved to the different ends of the model to optimize the user's experience with your application.

Although SQL is defined as a nonprocedural language, SQL Server permits the use of flow-control keywords. You use flow-control keywords to create a procedure you can store for subsequent execution. You can use these stored procedures to perform operations with a SQL Server database and its tables instead of writing programs using VBA to perform these operations.

Stored procedures are compiled the first time that they're run and are stored in a system table of the current database. When they're compiled, they're optimized to select the best path to access information in the tables. This optimization takes into account the actual data patterns in the table, indexes that are available, table loading, and more. These compiled stored procedures can greatly enhance the performance of your system.

Another benefit of stored procedures is that you can execute a stored procedure on either a local or remote SQL Server. This enables you to run processes on other machines and work with information across servers, not just *local* databases.

An application program written in Access can also execute stored procedures, providing an optimum solution between the client-side software and SQL Server.

Although an in-depth exploration of stored procedures is beyond the scope of this chapter, it's worthwhile to take a brief look at how to define stored procedures—a process you can actually perform by sending SQL statements to the server from your programs. In the following sections, we consider in slightly more depth how to use stored procedures from your Access applications.

As you saw previously, using stored procedures from the SQL Server Query Analyzer utility is simple. Similarly, invoking a procedure from your application can be accomplished with only a single statement. The following section discusses how your application can call stored procedures from code.

Calling Stored Procedures From Your Application

Before you call stored procedures from the Access and VBA application environments, you should know about a few useful tricks. For starters, when your stored procedures take parameters, you have a couple of different options.

First, you can always provide all parameters in the order in which they're declared. Although this is easy to develop for, consider carefully whether this makes sense in the long run. There will probably be cases in which you want to make a multipurpose stored procedure that calls for more parameters than would be required, on the whole, for any given call. In these cases, you're *expecting* to have some parameters that aren't specified in each call.

You use a test for **NULL** on a parameter to determine whether it was provided. This means you can test directly against **NULL**, or you can use the **IsNull** comparison operator.

On the application side, it can be quite cumbersome to have to specify each value on every call to the stored procedure, even in cases in which the value is **NULL**. In these cases, the calling application can use *named arguments* to pass information to SQL Server and the stored procedure. For example, if your stored procedure allows up to three different arguments—name, address, and phone—you can call the routine as follows:

```
exec usp_routine @name="Lars Klander", @address="home"
```

When you provide the name of the argument being passed, SQL Server can map it to its corresponding parameter. This is typically the best way to pass information to SQL Server, and it also helps make the code more readable, because you can tell which parameters are being passed.

In general, you'll use the ADO **Command** object and its **Execute** method to send commands down the wire to the SQL Server. Code to execute a stored procedure named **usp_routine** might look similar to the following:

```
cmdLocal.CommandText = "exec usp_routine @name=""" & strNameParam & """"
Set rstLocal = cmdLocal.Execute()
```

Note

*Although this technique will work, generally most programmers prefer to set the **adCmdStoredProc** value for the **CommandType** property and append individual parameters to the **Command** object's **Parameters** collection, rather than including the parameters inline in this form.*

Understanding Procedure Resolution And Compilation

The benefit of using a stored procedure for the execution of a set of Transact-SQL statements is that it's compiled the first time that it's run. During compilation, the Transact-SQL statements in the procedure are converted from their original character representation into an executable form. During compilation, any objects that are referenced in procedures are also converted to alternate representations; for example, table names are converted to their object IDs and column names to their column IDs.

An execution plan is also created just as it would be for the execution of even a single Transact-SQL statement. The execution plan contains, for example, the indexes to be used to retrieve rows from tables that are referenced by the procedure. The execution plan is kept in a cache and is used to perform the queries of the procedure each time it's subsequently executed. In general, the procedure will always execute from the cache, unless certain conditions occur that result in recompilation of the procedure. The following section discusses automatic recompilation of procedures.

Automatic Recompilation

Normally, the procedure's execution plan is run from the memory cache of procedures—a process that helps the procedure to execute rapidly. A procedure, however, is automatically recompiled under the following circumstances:

♦ A procedure is always recompiled when SQL Server is started, usually after a reboot of the underlying operating system, and when the procedure is first executed after it has been created.

♦ A procedure's execution plan is also automatically recompiled whenever an index on a table referenced in the procedure is dropped. A new execution plan must be compiled, because the current one references an object, the index, for the retrieval of the rows of a table that doesn't exist. The execution plan must be redone to permit the queries of the procedure to be performed.

♦ Compilation of the execution plan is also reinitialized if the execution plan in the cache is currently in use by another user. A second copy of the execution plan is created for the second user. If the first copy of the execution plan weren't in use, it could have been used rather than a new execution plan being created. When a user finishes executing a procedure, the execution plan is available in the cache for reuse by another user with appropriate permissions (the execution plan will remain in the procedure cache until the cache fills and SQL Server needs the space, the server is stopped, or one of the various **RECOMPILE** methods is used on the procedure in question).

♦ A procedure is also automatically recompiled if the procedure is dropped and re-created. All copies of the execution plan in the cache are removed because the new procedure may be substantially different from the older version, and a new execution plan is necessary.

Note that because SQL Server attempts to optimize stored procedures by caching the most recently used routines, it's still possible that an older execution plan, one previously loaded in cache, may be used in place of the new execution plan.

To prevent this problem, you must drop and re-create the procedure or stop and restart SQL Server to flush the procedure cache and ensure that the new procedure is the only one that will be used when the procedure is executed.

You can also create the procedure using the **WITH RECOMPILE** option so the procedure is automatically recompiled each time it's executed. You should do this if the tables accessed by the queries in a procedure are very dynamic. Dynamic tables have rows added, deleted, and updated frequently, which results in frequent changes to the indexes that are defined for the tables.

Warning

*You can't use the **WITH RECOMPILE** option in a **CREATE PROCEDURE** statement that contains the **FOR REPLICATION** option. You use the **FOR REPLICATION** option to create a procedure that's executed during replication, and SQL Server is incapable of recompiling those stored procedures during every replication activity—not to mention that recompiling would likely have a substantial impact on performance.*

In other cases, you may want to force a recompilation of a procedure when it wouldn't be done automatically. For example, if the statistics used to determine whether an index should be used for a query are updated, or an entire index is created for a table, recompilation isn't automatic, but you will likely want to do so. You can use the **WITH RECOMPILE** clause on the **EXECUTE** statement when you execute the procedure to do a recompilation. The syntax of the **EXECUTE** statement with a recompile clause is:

```
EXECUTE procedure_name AS
   Transact-SQL statement(s)
WITH RECOMPILE
```

If the procedure you're working with uses parameters and these parameters control the functionality of the routine—that is, any variation in the parameters may result in substantial impact to the construction of the resultset—you may want to use the **RECOMPILE** option. If the routine's parameters are the key determinant of the best execution path, it is often beneficial to have the SQL Server determine the execution plan at runtime, rather than determining it one time and maintaining that same (potentially inappropriate) plan in the cache. Then the server will use the plan determined at runtime for all accesses to the stored procedure during that execution, and will compute a new execution plan the next time the program is executed.

Tip

It may be difficult to determine whether a procedure should be created using the **WITH RECOMPILE** *option. If in doubt, you'll probably be better served by not creating the procedure with the* **RECOMPILE** *option. If you create a procedure with the* **RECOMPILE** *option, the procedure is recompiled each time it is executed, and you may waste valuable CPU time to perform these compiles. You can still add the* **WITH RECOMPILE** *clause to force a recompilation when you execute the procedure.*

You can add the **ENCRYPTION** option to a **CREATE PROCEDURE** statement to encrypt the definition of the stored procedure that's added to the system table **syscomments**. You use the **ENCRYPTION** option to prevent other users from displaying the definition of your procedure and learning what objects it references and what Transact-SQL statements it contains.

Warning

Unless you absolutely must encrypt procedures for security reasons, you should leave them unencrypted. When you upgrade your database for a version change or to rebuild it, your procedures can only be re-created if the entries in **syscomments** *aren't encrypted.*

Stored procedures, together with flow-control statements, are two of the biggest benefits of using a server-side database engine. We have already discussed procedures in detail; the following section moves on to a discussion of flow-control statements.

Using Flow-Control Statements

Transact-SQL contains several statements that are used to change the order of execution of statements within a set of statements, such as a stored procedure. The use of such flow-control statements permits you to organize statements in stored procedures to provide the capabilities of a conventional programming language, such as VBA. You may find that some of the retrieval, update, deletion, addition, and manipulation of the rows of database tables can more easily be performed through the use of flow-control statements in objects such as stored procedures.

In general, your analysis should focus on the reduction of network traffic. If the decision making (for the flow control) can effectively be made at the server, meaning that the decision is solely dependent on the data within the database itself, you may be better off placing the decision making at the server. If the decision making requires information from the client (front end), then you're generally better off with the flow control at the front end. As you work more with the client/server environment, you'll become more comfortable with the decision about where to put flow-control code. The most commonly used type of flow-control statement is the **IF...ELSE** combination. The following section discusses this construction.

Using IF...ELSE With SQL Server

You can use the keywords **IF** and **ELSE** to control conditional execution within a batch, such as a stored procedure. The **IF** and **ELSE** keywords enable you to test a condition and execute either the statements that are part of the **IF** branch or the statements that are part of the **ELSE** branch. You define the condition for testing as an expression following the keyword **IF**. The syntax of an **IF...ELSE** statement is as follows:

```
IF expression
    statement
[ELSE]
    [IF expression]
    statement
```

The keyword **EXISTS** is usually followed by a statement within parentheses when used in an **IF** statement. The **EXISTS** statement is evaluated to either **True** or **False**, depending on whether the statement within the parentheses returns one or more rows, or no rows, respectively.

You needn't use an **ELSE** clause as part of an **IF** statement. The simplest form of an **IF** statement is constructed without an **ELSE** clause. In the following example, a **PRINT** statement is used to display a confirmation message that a row exists in a database table. If the row doesn't exist in the table, the message "No entry" is displayed. Unfortunately, the message is also displayed after the verification message is displayed because the code doesn't use the **ELSE** option:

```
IF EXISTS (SELECT * FROM Workers WHERE Badge=1234)
   PRINT 'entry available'
PRINT 'No entry'
```

In the following example, the row isn't found in the table so only the **PRINT** statement that follows the **IF** statement is executed:

```
IF EXISTS (SELECT * FROM Workers WHERE Badge=1235)
   PRINT 'entry available'
PRINT 'No entry'
```

The previous two examples show the problem of using an **IF** statement that doesn't contain an **ELSE** clause. In the examples, it's impossible to prevent the message, "No entry," from appearing. You should add an **ELSE** clause to the **IF** statement to print the "No entry" message if a row isn't found and the condition after the **IF** isn't **True**.

In the following example, the previous examples are rewritten to use **IF** and **ELSE** clauses. If a row that's tested for in the **IF** clause is in the table, only the message "employee present" is displayed. If the row isn't found in the table, only the message "employee not found" is displayed:

```
IF EXISTS (SELECT * FROM employees WHERE name='Bob Smith')
  PRINT 'employee present'
ELSE
  PRINT 'employee not found'
```

> **Warning**
> *Unlike VBA, when used alone, the Transact-SQL **IF** statement can have only one statement associated with it. As a result, there's no need for a keyword, such as **END IF**, to define the end of the **IF** statement. See the next section, "Using BEGIN...END," for information on grouping statements and associating them with an **IF...ELSE** condition.*

In addition to the common **IF...ELSE** construction, you will also frequently use **BEGIN...END** blocks. These blocks allow you to group sets of statements together, and are explained in detail in the next section.

Using BEGIN...END

You use the keywords **BEGIN** and **END** to designate a set of Transact-SQL statements to be executed as a unit. You use the keyword **BEGIN** to define the start of a block of Transact-SQL statements. You use the keyword **END** after the last Transact-SQL statement that's part of the same block of statements. **BEGIN...END** uses the following syntax:

```
BEGIN
  statements
END
```

You often use **BEGIN** and **END** with a conditional statement such as an **IF** statement. **BEGIN** and **END** are used in an **IF** or **ELSE** clause to permit multiple Transact-SQL statements to be executed if the expression following the **IF** or **ELSE** clause is true. As mentioned earlier, without a **BEGIN** and **END** block enclosing multiple statements, only a single Transact-SQL statement can be executed if the expression in the **IF** or **ELSE** clause is true.

The following code shows how to use **BEGIN** and **END** statements with an **IF** statement to define the execution of multiple statements if the condition tested is true. The **IF** statement contains only an **IF** clause; no **ELSE** clause is part of the statement:

```
IF EXISTS (SELECT * FROM employees WHERE badge=1234)
  BEGIN
```

```
      PRINT 'entry available'
      SELECT name,department FROM employees
          WHERE badge=1234
   END
```

This code will display the text "entry available", then output the information associated with **badge 1234**. The following code listing adds an **ELSE** clause to the **IF** statement to display a message if the row isn't found:

```
IF EXISTS (SELECT * FROM employees WHERE department='Sales')
   BEGIN
      PRINT 'row(s) found'
      SELECT name, department FROM employees
          WHERE department='Sales'
   END
ELSE
   PRINT 'No entry'
```

As your procedures become more complex, it is likely that you will need to use looping constructs within them to handle specific types of processing. In general, you can use the **WHILE** keyword to indicate a loop that will iterate until a certain condition is met. The following section explains the use of the **WHILE** keyword.

Using WHILE

You can use the keyword **WHILE** to define a condition that executes one or more Transact-SQL statements when the condition tested evaluates to **True**. The statement that follows the expression of the **WHILE** statement continues to execute as long as the condition tested is true. The syntax of the **WHILE** statement is as follows:

```
WHILE
   boolean_expression
   sql_statement
```

*As with the **IF...ELSE** statements, you can execute only a single SQL statement with the **WHILE** clause. If you need to include more than one statement in the routine, use the **BEGIN...END** construct as described previously.*

In the following code fragment, a **WHILE** statement is used to execute a **SELECT** statement that displays a numeric value until the value reaches a limit of five:

```
DECLARE @x int
SELECT @x=1
```

```
WHILE @x<5
  BEGIN
    PRINT 'x still less than 5'
    SELECT @x=@x+1
  END
```

You define the data type of a variable using a **DECLARE** statement to control the way information is represented in the variable. A variable is always preceded by an *at* sign (@), like a SQL Server parameter. In the example, the value stored in the variable is initialized to one and subsequently incremented. The statements associated with the **WHILE** execute until the variable **x** reaches a value of five.

I'll show you a more meaningful example of the use of a **WHILE** statement after introducing and explaining two additional Transact-SQL keywords—**BREAK** and **CONTINUE**. The next section discusses the use of **BREAK** together with **WHILE**.

Using BREAK

You use the keyword **BREAK** inside a block of Transact-SQL statements that's within a conditional **WHILE** statement to end the execution of the statements. The execution of a **BREAK** results in the first statement following the end of the block to begin executing. The syntax of a **BREAK** clause is as follows:

```
WHILE
  boolean_expression
  sql_statement
BREAK
  sql_statement
```

In the following code fragment, the **BREAK** within the **WHILE** statement causes the statement within the **WHILE** to terminate. The **PRINT** statement executes once because the it is located before the **BREAK**. After the **BREAK** is encountered, the statements in the **WHILE** clause aren't executed again:

```
DECLARE @x int
SELECT @x=1
WHILE @x<5
  BEGIN
    PRINT 'x still less than 5'
    SELECT @x=@x+1
    BREAK
  END
```

In general, a **WHILE** loop will iterate until it encounters either the ending condition or a **BREAK** statement. However, there may be situations within a **WHILE** loop when you want the loop to iterate immediately, rather than executing the remaining code within the loop. In such cases, you can use the **CONTINUE** keyword, explained in the next section.

Using CONTINUE

You use a **CONTINUE** keyword to form a clause within a conditional statement, such as a **WHILE** statement, to explicitly continue the set of statements that are contained within the conditional statement. The syntax of the **CONTINUE** clause is as follows:

```
WHILE
  boolean_expression
  statement
BREAK
  statement
CONTINUE
```

In the following code fragment, a **CONTINUE** is used within a **WHILE** statement to explicitly define that execution of the statements within the **WHILE** statement should continue as long as the condition specified in the expression that follows **WHILE** is **True**. The use of **CONTINUE** in the following example skips the final **PRINT** statement:

```
DECLARE @x int
SELECT @x = 1
WHILE @x < 5
  BEGIN
    PRINT 'x still less than 5'
    SELECT @x = @x + 1
    CONTINUE
    PRINT ''this statement will not execute'
  END
```

Needless to say, you should generally avoid using **BREAK** and **CONTINUE** whenever you can. Not only are they bad programming style, but they also tend to be confusing to anyone who reads your procedures. Instead, you should carefully construct your loops so that your ending conditions are correctly met during the loop's normal execution. However, there will occasionally be times when using either of these statements will be necessary for your programming, so don't discard their use entirely.

More On Using WHILE, BREAK, And CONTINUE

Although the examples earlier in this chapter use **BREAK** and **CONTINUE** alone, you don't typically use either **CONTINUE** or **BREAK** within a **WHILE** statement alone. Both **BREAK** and **CONTINUE** are often used following an **IF** or **ELSE** that is defined within a **WHILE** statement, so an additional condition can be used to break out of the **WHILE** loop. If two or more loops are nested, **BREAK** exits to the next outermost loop.

In the following code, a **BREAK** is used with an **IF** statement, both of which are within a **WHILE** statement. The **BREAK** is used to terminate the statements associated with the **WHILE** if the condition specified by the **IF** statement is **True**. The **IF** condition is **True** if the value of the local variable, **@y**, is **True**:

```
DECLARE @x int
Declare @y tinyint
SELECT @x=1, @y=1
WHILE @x<5
  BEGIN
    PRINT 'x still less than 5'
    SELECT @x=@x+1
    SELECT @y=@y+1
    IF @y=2
      BEGIN
        PRINT 'y is 2 so break out of loop'
        BREAK
      END
  END
PRINT 'out of while loop'
```

In the following code, a **WHILE** statement is used to permit only the rows of a table that match the criteria defined within the expression of the **WHILE** statement to have their values changed:

```
BEGIN tran
  WHILE (SELECT avg(price) FROM titles) < $30
    BEGIN
      SELECT title_id, price
      FROM titles
      WHERE price >$20
      UPDATE titles SET price=price * 2
    END
```

You must be careful when defining the **WHILE** statement and its associated statements. As shown in the following example, if the condition specified with the **WHILE** expression continues to be **True**, the **WHILE** loop executes indefinitely:

```
WHILE EXISTS (SELECT hours_worked FROM pays)
  PRINT 'hours worked is less than 55'
```

If the evaluation of the expression following the **WHILE** returns multiple values, you should use an **EXISTS** instead of any comparison operators.

In addition to the conditional-construct keywords that you have seen in this section, there are also a large number of additional procedure and batch keywords. In the following section, we will discuss the use of some of these keywords.

Using Additional Procedure And Batch Keywords

Several additional keywords can be used within stored procedures or batches of Transact-SQL commands. These additional keywords don't fall into a single descriptive category of similar function. Some of these keywords include **GOTO**, **RETURN**, **RAISERROR**, **WAITFOR**, and **CASE**.

Using GOTO

You use a **GOTO** to perform a transfer from one statement to another statement that contains a user-defined label. A **GOTO** statement used alone is unconditional. The statement that contains the destination label name follows rules for identifiers and is followed by a colon (**:**).

You only use the label name without the colon on the **GOTO** line. The syntax of the **GOTO** statement is as follows:

```
label:
GOTO label
```

The following code fragment shows the use of the **GOTO** statement that transfers control to a statement displaying the word "yes" until the value of a variable reaches a specified value. The **COUNT** was turned off before execution of the statements in the example:

```
DECLARE @COUNT smallint
SELECT @COUNT =1
RESTART:
  PRINT 'yes'
  SELECT @COUNT =@COUNT + 1
  WHILE @COUNT <= 4
    GOTO RESTART
```

As you have seen, a **GOTO** statement transfers execution within the stored procedure. However, when the procedure finishes its execution—as all procedures eventually should—you should explicitly exit the procedure. There may also be times when you need to return a value to the calling program. The **RETURN** statement exits the procedure and lets you return a value, as described in the following section.

Using RETURN

You use the **RETURN** statement to formally exit from a query or procedure and optionally provide a value to the calling routine. A **RETURN** is often used when one procedure is executed from within another. The **RETURN** statement, when used alone, is unconditional, though you can use the **RETURN** within a conditional **IF** or **WHILE** statement. The syntax of the **RETURN** statement is as follows:

```
RETURN integer
```

You can use a **RETURN** statement at any point in a batch or procedure. Any statements that follow the **RETURN** aren't executed. A **RETURN** is similar to a **BREAK** with one difference: A **RETURN**, unlike a **BREAK**, can be used to return an integer value to the procedure that invoked the procedure containing the **RETURN**. Execution of statements continues at the statement following the one that executed the procedure originally.

To understand the use of the **RETURN** statement, you must first understand the action performed by SQL Server when a procedure completes execution. SQL Server always makes an integer value available when a procedure ends. A value of zero indicates that the procedure executed successfully. Negative values from –1 to –99 indicate reasons for the failure of statements within the procedure. These integer values are always returned at the termination of a procedure even if a **RETURN** statement isn't present in a procedure.

You can optionally use an integer value that follows the **RETURN** statement to replace the SQL Server value with your own user-defined value. You should use nonzero integer values so your return status values don't conflict with the SQL Server status values. If no user-defined return value is provided, the SQL Server value is used. If more than one error occurs, the status with the highest absolute value is returned. You can't return a **NULL** value with a **RETURN** statement. Table 12.1 shows several of the return status values that are reserved by SQL Server.

You must provide a local variable that receives the returned status in the **EXECUTE** statement, which invokes the procedure that returns status. The syntax to specify a local variable for the returned status value is the following:

```
EXEC[ute] @return_status=procedure_name
```

You can, therefore, pass in a variable from the ADO **Command** object and use the return value from the stored procedure with the variable to perform client-side processing in the case of a return from a server-side procedure. The most commonly returned value from a procedure, however, is one that you send back in response to an error in processing. In such cases, you should use the **RAISERROR** statement to let the user know of the problem. The following section discusses the **RAISERROR** statement.

Table 12.1   Selected Microsoft SQL Server status values.

Return Value	Meaning
0	Successful execution
−1	Missing object
−2	Data type error
−3	Process was chosen as a deadlock victim
−4	Permission error
−5	Syntax error
−6	Miscellaneous user error
−7	Resource error, such as out of space
−8	Nonfatal internal problem
−9	System limit was reached
−10	Fatal internal inconsistency
−11	Fatal internal inconsistency
−12	Table or index is corrupt
−13	Database is corrupt
−14	Hardware error

Using RAISERROR

You use the **RAISERROR** statement to return a user-specified message in the same form that SQL Server returns errors. **RAISERROR** also sets a system flag to record that an error has occurred. The syntax of the **RAISERROR** statement is as follows:

```
RAISERROR (integer_expression|'text of message',
    severity, state,
    argument1, argument2)
WITH LOG
```

The *integer_expression* is a user-specified error or message number and must be in the range 50,001 to 2,147,483,647. The *integer_expression* is placed in the global variable **@@ERROR**, which stores the last error number returned. An error message can be specified as a string literal or through a local variable. The text of the message can be up to 255 characters long and is used to indicate a user-specified error message. A local variable that contains an error message can be used in place of the text of the message. **RAISERROR** always sets a default severity level of 16 for the returned error message.

You can also add your message text and an associated message number to the system table **sysmessages**. You use the system stored procedure **sp_addmessage** to add a message with a message identification number within the range detailed in the previous paragraph. The syntax of the **sp_addmessage** system procedure is as follows:

```
sp_addmessage message_id, severity,
    'message text', language, {true | false},
    REPLACE
```

*If you enter a user-specified error number that hasn't been added to the **sysmessages** table and don't explicitly specify the message text, you'll receive an error that the message can't be located in the system table, as shown here:*

"RAISERROR could not locate entry for error 99999 in sysmessages"

User-defined error messages generated with a **RAISERROR** statement, but without a number in the **sysmessages** table, return a message identification number of 50,000.

The severity level is used to indicate the degree or extent of the error condition encountered. Although severity levels can be assigned in the range of 1 through 25, you should usually assign your custom message a severity level value from 11 to 16.

Severity levels of 11 through 16 are designed to be assigned through the **sp_addmessages** statement, and you can't assign a severity level from 19 to 25 unless you're logged in as the administrator. Severity levels 17 through 19 are more severe software or hardware errors, which may not permit your subsequent statements to execute correctly.

Severity levels of 20 through 25 are severe errors and won't permit subsequent Transact-SQL statements to execute. System messages that have severity levels over 19 can be problems, such as connection problems between a client system and the database server system or corrupted data in the database.

Microsoft suggests that severe errors (that is, those that have a severity level of 19 or higher) should also notify the database administrator in addition to the user. The database administrator needs to know of these problems because such problems are likely to affect many different users and should be attended to as soon as possible.

To specify an error message, place the desired text (which can be up to 255 characters) within single quotes. The remaining parameters of the **sp_addmessage** procedure are optional. The *language* parameter specifies one of the languages SQL Server was installed with. U.S. English is the default language if the parameter is omitted.

The next parameter, either **true** or **false**, controls whether the system message is automatically written to the Windows NT application event log. Use **true** to have the system message written to the event log. In addition, **true** results in the message being written to the SQL Server error log file.

The last parameter, **REPLACE**, is used to specify that you want to replace an existing user-defined message in the **sysmessages** table with the new entry.

You can use the system-stored procedure **sp_dropmessage** to remove a user-defined message from the system table **sysmessages** when it's no longer needed. The syntax of the **sp_dropmessage** is as follows:

```
sp_dropmessage [message_id [, language | 'all']]
```

You're only required to enter the message number to drop the message. The two additional optional parameters permit you to specify the language from which the message should be dropped. You can use the keyword **ALL** to drop the user-defined message from all languages—a technique you generally want to follow, unless you have a specific reason for generating language-specific errors (by which, I don't mean errors in German or French, but errors specific to the French or German version).

Using WAITFOR

You use a **WAITFOR** statement to specify a time, a time interval, or an event for executing a statement, statement block, stored procedure, or transaction. The syntax of the **WAITFOR** statement is as follows:

```
WAITFOR {DELAY <'time'> | TIME <'time'> | ERROREXIT | PROCESSEXIT |
    MIRROREXIT}
```

The meaning of each of the keywords that follow **WAITFOR** is shown in Table 12.2.

In the following example of a **WAITFOR** statement, a **DELAY** is used to specify that the program pause for 40 seconds before executing the subsequent **SELECT** statement:

```
WAITFOR DELAY '00:00:40'
SELECT * FROM employees
```

In the following code, a **TIME** statement makes the program wait until 3:10:51 P.M. of the current day until the subsequent **SELECT** statement is executed:

```
WAITFOR TIME '15:10:51'
SELECT * FROM employees
```

Earlier in this chapter, you read about the use of the **IF...THEN** construct. As you saw, it allowed you to perform conditional processing within your procedures based on the result of a specific condition. However, you will often need to make conditional processing decisions

Table 12.2   Descriptions of the keywords for the WAITFOR statement.

Keyword	Description
DELAY	Specifies an interval or time to elapse
TIME	A specified time, no date portion, of up to 24 hours
ERROREXIT	Until a process terminates abnormally
PROCESSEXIT	Until a process terminates normally or abnormally
MIRROREXIT	Until a mirrored device fails

based on where a variable falls within a series of values. To meet such requirements, SQL provides the **CASE** keyword, explained in the next section.

Using CASE Expressions

You can use a **CASE** expression to make an execution decision based on multiple options. Using the **CASE** construct, you can create a table that will be used to look up the results you're testing and apply them to determine what action should be taken. The syntax of the **CASE** expression is as follows:

```
CASE expression
WHEN simple expression1|Boolean expression1 THEN expression1
    [[WHEN simple expression2|Boolean expression2 THEN expression2]
    [...]]
    [ELSE expressionN]
END
```

If you use a comparison operator in an expression directly after the **CASE** keyword, the **CASE** expression is called a *searched expression* rather than a *simple* **CASE** expression. You can also use a Boolean operator in a searched **CASE** expression.

In a simple **CASE** expression, the expression directly after the **CASE** keyword always exactly matches a value after the **WHEN** keyword. In the following example, a **CASE** expression is used to return a corresponding set of alternate values for three department values of a table company:

```
SELECT name,division=
CASE department
  WHEN "Sales" THEN "Sales & Marketing"
  WHEN "Field Service" THEN "Support Group"
  WHEN "Logistics" THEN "Parts"
  ELSE "Other department"
END,
badge
FROM company
```

If you don't use an **ELSE** as part of the **CASE** expression, a **NULL** is returned for each nonmatching entry.

You'll recall that a searched **CASE** expression can include comparison operators and the use of **AND** as well as **OR** between each Boolean expression to permit an alternate value to be returned for multiple values of the column of a table. Unlike a simple **CASE** expression, each **WHEN** clause isn't restricted to exact matches of the values contained in the table column.

In the following code fragment, comparison values are used in each **WHEN** clause to specify a range of values that are substituted by a single alternative value:

```
SELECT "Hours Worked" =
CASE
  WHEN hours_worked < 40 THEN "Worked Insufficient Hours"
  WHEN hours_worked = 40 THEN "Worked Sufficient Hours"
  WHEN hours_worked > 60 THEN "Overworked"
  ELSE "Outside Range of Permissible Work"
End
FROM pays
```

Warning

*You must use compatible data types for the replacement expression of the **THEN** clause. If the replacement expression of a **THEN** clause is a data type that's incompatible with the original expression, an error message is returned. For example, a combination of original and replacement data types is compatible if one is a variable-length character data type (**VARCHAR**) with a maximum length equal to the length of a fixed-length character data type (**CHAR**). In addition, if the two data types in the **WHEN** and **THEN** clauses are integer and decimal, the resultant data type returned will be decimal to accommodate the whole and fractional portion of the numeric value.*

You can also use both the **COALESCE** and **NULLIF** functions in a **CASE** expression. You use the **COALESCE** function to return a replacement value for any **NULL** or **NOT NULL** values that are present in, for example, the column of a database table. The syntax of one form of the **COALESCE** function is:

```
COALESCE (expression1, expression2)
```

You can also use a **NULLIF** function with or in place of a **CASE** expression. The **NULLIF** function uses the following syntax:

```
NULLIF (expression1, expression2)
```

Throughout the previous sections, you've studied some of the additional types of Transact-SQL code that you might use within your stored procedures, or call from within your applications, in certain rare situations. In general, I have focused on drawing parallels (where possible) between Transact-SQL and VBA, to simplify your educational process.

Using Triggers

In Chapter 11, you learned about triggers—a special kind of stored procedure. As you learned, triggers *fire* or *execute* whenever a particular event occurs. The following subsections demonstrate the different events that can cause a trigger to execute and should give you some more definitive ideas of what you might have your trigger do when such events occur.

Using INSERT And UPDATE Triggers

INSERT and **UPDATE** triggers are particularly useful because they can enforce referential integrity constraints and ensure that your data is valid before it enters the table. Typically, **INSERT** and **UPDATE** triggers are used to update time stamp columns or to verify that the data on the columns that the trigger is monitoring meets the criteria required. Use **INSERT** and **UPDATE** triggers when the criteria for verification are more complex than a declarative referential integrity constraint can represent.

In the following code, the trigger executes whenever a record is modified or inserted into the **SALES** table. If the order date doesn't fall during the first 15 days of the month, the record is rejected:

```
CREATE TRIGGER Trig_Ins_Sales
ON SALES
FOR INSERT, UPDATE
AS
  /* declare local variables needed */
  DECLARE @nDayOfMonth tinyint

  /* Find the information about the record inserted */
  SELECT @nDayOfMonth = DatePart( Day, I.ORD_DATE )
  FROM SALES S, INSERTED I
  WHERE S.STOR_ID = I.STOR_ID
  AND S.ORD_NUM = I.ORD_NUM
  AND S.TITLE_ID = I.TITLE_ID

  /* Now test rejection criteria and return an error if necessary */
  IF @nDayOfMonth > 15
    BEGIN
      /* Note: Always Rollback BEFORE you invoke the error handler.
      You can never be sure what kind of error processing
      a client may do that may force locks
      to be held for unnecessary amounts of time */
      ROLLBACK TRAN
      RAISERROR ('Orders must be placed before the 15th of the month',
        16, 10 )
    END
```

Tip

*Notice how the previous join refers to the inserted table. SQL Server specially creates this logical table to enable you to reference information in the record you're modifying. By using the alias **I** as shown, you can easily reference the table in the join criteria specified in the **WHERE** clause.*

Notice that the code segment references a new table. If you review the list of tables, you'll notice that the database doesn't include the table. In this case, the inserted table contains a copy of every row that would be added if the transaction were allowed to complete. You use the inserted table's values to feed the information to any comparisons that you want to make to validate the transaction.

The columns in the inserted table exactly match those in the table with which you're working. You can perform comparisons on the columns as in the example, which compares the columns against the sales database to verify that the sales date is valid.

You can also create triggers that can do their work only if a given column is updated. You can use the **IF UPDATE** statement in your trigger to determine whether the trigger processing should continue:

```
IF UPDATE(au_lname) AND (@@rowcount=1)
  BEGIN
    ...
  END
```

In this case, the only time that the code within the segment executes is if the specific column, **au_lname**, is updated. Keep in mind that although a column is being updated, it isn't necessarily being *changed*. Many applications, including most proprietary systems, simply update the entire record if any change is made.

Before taking further action in the trigger, you might find it helpful to compare the new value against the old value (which the inserted table stores) to see whether the value has indeed changed.

In addition to performing update actions with a trigger, you can also use triggers to perform or stop deletions automatically. The following section discusses the use of **DELETE** triggers in more detail.

Using DELETE Triggers

DELETE triggers are typically used for two reasons. The first reason is to prevent deletion of records that will cause data integrity problems if they, indeed, are deleted. An example of such records are those used as foreign keys to other tables.

The second reason for using a **DELETE** trigger is to perform a cascading delete operation that deletes children records of a master record. You might use such a trigger to delete all the order items from a master sales record.

Tip

When you create a trigger, remember that it can affect more than one row. You must consider this possibility in any procedure the trigger runs. Be sure you check the **@@rowcount** *global variable to see exactly what is happening before you begin working with the information.*

*Triggers take into account the sum total of all rows the requested operation affects, so they must be capable of considering the different combinations of information in the table and respond according to what you need. For example, if you issue a **DELETE * FROM Authors** statement, the trigger must accommodate the fact that the statement will delete all records from the **Authors** table.*

As you might have guessed already, triggers play an important role in the server's processing at all times, but can play a particularly important role when working with transactions. The following section discusses the use of rollback triggers with transactions.

Performing Special Transaction Management With ROLLBACK TRIGGERs

If you're working with triggers and transactions, you might want to consider working with a special trigger option, the **ROLLBACK TRIGGER**:

```
ROLLBACK TRIGGER [with raiserror errornumber [message]]
```

The **ROLLBACK TRIGGER** option is, in essence, an abort-all statement. When a rollback is encountered, the trigger's processing stops and the data modification that caused the trigger to execute in the first place is allowed.

When you use the **ROLLBACK TRIGGER** statement, you have the option—even the responsibility—to indicate an error number and optional message. Except in very rare situations, you should use the **RAISERROR** option because it tells the calling routines you've stopped the action from occurring. The **ROLLBACK TRIGGER** statement doesn't stop processing for a batch of updates; instead, the trigger fails only the current item. Therefore, the code you develop to update the database must check the return state of the update to ensure it succeeded.

When the routine returns from the update operation, always check the **@@ERROR** global variable to ensure that the updates happened as planned. In addition to such crucial processing as that performed by **DELETE** and **ROLLBACK** triggers, you can also use triggers to assist you in other areas of database management. A useful tool provided to you by triggers is the ability to construct a trigger that sends email. The following section discusses triggers that send email in detail.

Using Triggers That Send Email

One of the better features of SQL Server is its capability to invoke behavior directly from the operating system. You must predefine such behavior through SQL Server's extended procedures, but they enable you to create incredibly powerful trigger operations. SQL Server is relatively unique in its capability to support features specific to the operating system. SQL Server can offer this support because it runs on Windows NT, which has a very standardized programming interface across all its supported hardware platforms.

Triggers can call any of the extended procedures (**xp_***) available to the server and any external procedures you add to the server with the **sp_addextendedproc** system-level stored procedure. In the following code fragment, the trigger demonstrates how to send email when a record is deleted from the underlying **AUTHORS** table:

```
CREATE TRIGGER Trig_Del_Authors_Mail
ON AUTHORS
FOR DELETE
AS
  /* Declare some variables to store the author's name */
  DECLARE @sLName varchar(40), @sFName varchar(20),
     @sAuthor varchar(60)

  /* Now get the value of the author being removed */
  SELECT @sLName = D.AU_LNAME, @sFName = D.AU_FNAME
     FROM AUTHORS A, DELETED D
     WHERE A.AU_ID = D.AU_ID

  /* Send mail message */
  SELECT @sAuthor = @sLName + ', ' + @sFName
  Exec master.dbo.xp_sendmail @recipient = 'Acquisitions Editor',
    @message = 'deleted ' + @sAuthor
GO
```

Though triggers in and of themselves are very useful, and generally not too complex, you can build layers of triggers to create more complexity in your data validation and to perform a variety of tasks in response to a single event. Such constructs are known as *nested triggers*, and are explained in the next section.

Using Nested Triggers

Triggers become nested when the execution of one trigger modifies another table that includes another trigger, which, therefore, executes.

You can nest triggers up to 16 layers deep. If nested trigger operations aren't desirable, however, you can configure SQL Server to disallow them. To toggle this option, use the nested trigger option in the **sp_configure** system stored procedure.

Tip

*You can check your nesting level at any time by inspecting the value in @@**NestLevel**. The value is from 0 through 16.*

SQL Server can't detect nesting that causes an infinite loop during the creation of a trigger until the situation occurs at execution time. For example, suppose that **TABLE1** includes **TRIG1**, which executes when **TABLE1** is updated. When executed, **TRIG1** causes an update on **TABLE2**. **TABLE2** has a similar trigger, **TRIG2**, that executes when **TABLE2** is updated and causes an update of **TABLE1**. Thus, if a user updates either table, the two triggers continue executing each other indefinitely. On detecting such an occurrence, SQL Server shuts down or cancels the trigger.

If a trigger causes an additional modification of the table from which it executes, the trigger doesn't cause itself to execute recursively. The current version of SQL Server has no support for *reentrant* stored procedures or triggers.

Warning
Triggers and Declarative Referential Integrity (DRI) usually don't work well together. Wherever possible, you should implement either triggers or DRI for integrity constraints, but not both.

Dropping Triggers

You might want to remove triggers from a table or tables for several reasons. You might, for example, be moving into a production environment and want to remove any triggers you put in place to ensure good quality but that were hurting performance. You might also want to drop a trigger simply to replace it with a newer version.

To drop a trigger, use the following syntax:

```
DROP TRIGGER [owner.]trigger_name[,[owner.]trigger_name...]
```

Dropping a trigger isn't necessary if a new trigger is to be created to replace the existing one. When you drop a table, you also drop all its child-related objects, including triggers.

Using Access Data Projects To Manage SQL Server Objects

With the addition of new Access Data Projects, the new Access 2000 supports client/server design at a level never before possible in Access. Access projects let you actually design client/server databases directly against a SQL Server back end and maintain them from within Access. Moreover, the project is essentially a very thin client against the back-end database.

The support within Access for new Data Access Pages (DAPs) makes designing Web pages that work against a SQL Server database easier than ever before. The Access Database window even supports new objects to help you work with SQL Server databases when you create an Access Data Project (ADP).

When you are working with an ADP, the Database window adds support for views, database diagrams, and stored procedures, and removes queries from the accessible objects. It also maintains support for forms, reports, and modules. In the following sections, we will briefly consider these new objects as they relate to ADPs, and in the following couple of chapters we will consider some programming issues that you will commonly encounter with ADPs.

As you have learned previously, *views* allow you to specify exactly how a user will see data. From the Access programmer's perspective, views are very much like query objects. From within the ADP database window, you will work with the resultsets that come from views as if they were ordinary tables. From within the Access 2000 Database window, you will use the Query Designer to build views. This window lets you look at underlying data sets, review the view definition by column, even look at the SQL statement or statements (if you use **UNION** in the definition) that specify the view's contents. Figure 12.1 shows the Access 2000 View Designer.

As you can see from the third pane of the **vwPhonesAndCustomers** designer, views are essentially stored queries—just like query objects in Access.

Stored procedures, on the other hand, are precompiled sequences of Transact-SQL statements. As you saw in Chapter 11, because stored procedures are precompiled, they run much more quickly than straight SQL queries do. Stored procedures have no direct corollary to Access objects, primarily because they are constructed using T-SQL, and may include, in addition to standard SQL statements such as **SELECT**, **INSERT INTO**, and **UPDATE**,

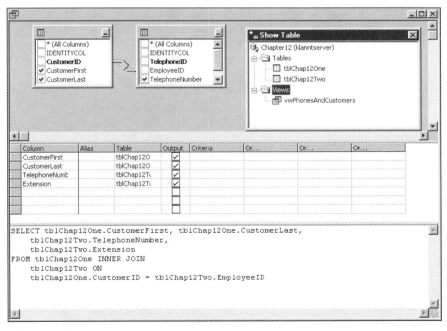

Figure 12.1
The View Designer includes several different panes to simplify view creation.

```
: Stored Procedure                                                    _ □ X
create proc sp_SessionNew @AccountNo int ,@ipAddress varchar(15), @SessionType char(1)
as
declare @i tinyint,
                @SessionId varchar(20),
                @SessionKey varchar(20),
                @PageId varchar(20),
                @seed float
/*seed*/
select @seed = rand(DatePart(ms,GetDate()))
/* Create Unique Session Id */
while 1=1
begin
        select @i=0
        select @SessionId=""
        while @i < 20
        begin
                select @SessionId=ltrim(@SessionId) + char((55*rand())+65)
                select @i=@i+1
        end
        /* Unique? */
        if not exists (select SessionId from session where SessionId =@SessionId)
                break
end
/* Create Session Key; 2 key security */
select @i=0
select @SessionKey=""
while @i < 20
begin
        select @SessionKey=ltrim(@SessionKey) + char((55*rand())+65)
        select @i=@i+1
end
```

Figure 12.2
Stored procedures are named sequences of Transact-SQL statements that are compiled and
maintained on the SQL Server.

T-SQL language constructs such as iterative (**while**) and conditional (**if-then-else**) constructs. Figure 12.2 shows a stored procedure inside the ADP designer.

As you have seen already in this chapter, triggers are complex stored procedures designed to
automatically execute when certain actions are performed against the database. To add
triggers to a table defined inside of an ADP, right-click on the table from the Database
window, and choose Triggers from the resulting pop-up menu. The Triggers dialog box will
appear, from which you can edit or create triggers for the table in question. Whether editing
or creating, you will do so from within the Trigger Designer, which looks substantially similar to the procedure design window, as you can see in Figure 12.3.

As mentioned previously, triggers allow you to ensure data integrity, domain integrity, and
referential integrity within your database in situations where the necessary decisions are too
complex to be resolved with simple constraints. All of these objects can be defined within
ADPs using the guidelines that have been laid out earlier in this chapter.

ADPs are a powerful and useful tool for front-end client/server development; in the event
you want to develop SQL Server applications directly from Access, you can use ADPs. In
addition to all the SQL Server tools discussed earlier in this chapter, you can also use database diagrams to create databases and specify specifics about the database on an SQL Server.

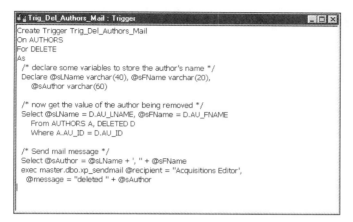

Figure 12.3
The Trigger Designer in Access with a trigger on the **AUTHORS** table displayed.

Using Database Diagrams To Create Databases

You can use database diagrams to create, edit, or delete database objects for SQL Server or MSDE databases while you're directly connected to the database in which those objects are stored. Database diagrams graphically represent tables, the columns they contain, and the relationships between them. We discussed database diagrams in depth in Chapter 9, and rather than revisit the topic here, in the interests of space, you can look to that chapter.

The most important thing to understand about database diagrams is that, for the most part, they are akin to designing database objects from within Access' Relationships window. The most substantial improvement made with diagrams for SQL Server 7 is the ability to generate scripts capable of creating or changing existing objects in the database. The similarities to the Relationships window can be clearly seen in Figure 12.4.

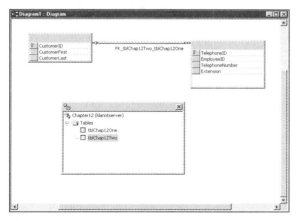

Figure 12.4
Two tables and the relation between them as seen within the database diagram.

Where To Go From Here

Now that you have explored all of the fundamental objects and items that comprise effective SQL Server development, it is time to really focus on using that knowledge to do complex design with Access 2000 and SQL Server. In Chapter 13, you will learn about how to use ADPs with SQL Server and security models and implementations that result from that type of design. In Chapter 14, you will put all of the knowledge discussed in Chapter 13, this chapter, and previous chapters together to create some more complex solutions with SQL Server and Access 2000.

Access Data Projects And Security

To develop a client application that establishes a connection to a data source, you must plan the way in which the connection is made. This includes determining the security mode of the designated data source, and whether it requires a user ID and password. In the context of Access Data Projects (ADPs), what you should focus on is the use of SQL Server security, because the ADP really passes everything back through to the back end and lets it do the processing. In this chapter, I will focus on SQL Server security, and how it works with the ADP client program.

SQL Server Security Modes

As I have already indicated, security is necessary to protect the information contained in the database. When working with SQL Server, you will typically implement one of these primary security options:

♦ *Standard security mode*—Standard security uses SQL Server's own login validation process for all connections. Connections validated by SQL Server are referred to as *nontrusted connections*.

♦ *Integrated security mode*—Integrated security allows SQL Server to use Windows NT authentication mechanisms to validate SQL Server logins for all connections. Connections validated by Windows NT Server and accepted by SQL Server are referred to as *trusted connections*. Only trusted connections are allowed in integrated security mode.

♦ *Mixed*—Mixed security allows SQL Server login requests to be validated by either integrated or standard security methods. Both trusted connections (as used by integrated security) and nontrusted connections (as used by standard security) are supported.

Standard Mode

Standard security mode is the default security mode for SQL Server. Standard mode uses the SQL Server security model for every connection to the database. It supports nontrusted environments, such as the Internet. For example, if you implement a solution that allows users to connect to a SQL Server over the Internet, users will not necessarily first connect to a Windows NT server for authentication. SQL Server will perform its own authentication in this situation. The system administrator or database owner can create user IDs, aliases, user names, and groups for each database on the server. When this mode is in use, the user must enter a user ID and password combination that has been established for the database.

When using standard mode, you can pass security information to a data source in one of the following three ways:

♦ Hard-code all connection information

♦ Prompt the user for some information and hard-code the rest

♦ Prompt the user for all information

Also, standard security provides backward compatibility for older versions of SQL Server. Figure 13.1 shows the steps involved for SQL Server to authenticate a login through standard security.

When a server's login security mode is set to standard, a component's or user's login (which I will generally refer to as "client login" hereafter, and specifically as one or the other when the difference is important) is validated as follows:

1. When a client attempts to log on to the server, SQL Server looks in the **syslogins** table for the client's login ID and password. A client supplies the login ID and password through the **ConnectionString** property of the ADO **Connection** object.

2. If the login ID and password are valid, the client is connected to SQL Server.

3. If the login ID and password are invalid, the client cannot connect to SQL Server, although the client, if a component (and specifically a Microsoft Transaction Server [MTS] component), may be logged on to Windows NT Server with the user account specified in its package's **Identity** property. The Windows NT user account name and password are inconsequential.

Integrated Mode

Integrated security mode allows SQL Server to use Microsoft Windows NT authentication mechanisms to validate users for all connections to the database. You can use integrated security in network environments in which all clients support trusted connections. A trusted connection is one that recognizes users who have been granted system administrator status, have valid Windows NT accounts, or otherwise have access to the database.

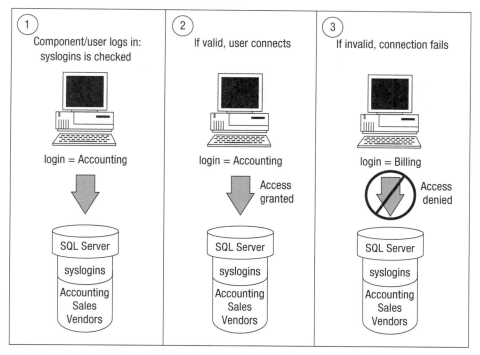

Figure 13.1
The steps that SQL Server performs to authenticate a standard security login.

Integrated security allows applications to take advantage of Windows NT security capabilities, which include encrypted passwords, password aging, domain-wide user accounts, and Windows-based user administration. With integrated security, users maintain a single user ID and password for both Windows NT and SQL Server.

Figure 13.2 shows the steps involved for SQL Server to authenticate a login through integrated security.

When a server's login security mode is set to integrated, a client's login is validated as follows:

1. To access SQL Server, a client first obtains a valid Windows NT user account. MTS components use the Windows NT user account specified in their package's **Identity** property. If the Windows NT user account is in a domain, the user name and password are validated by the domain controller's security accounts database when the MTS package EXE launches. On the other hand, if the account is in a Windows NT workgroup, the user name and password are validated by the local security accounts database.

2. The client connects to SQL Server, and SQL Server looks in the **syslogins** table for a mapping to a SQL Server Login ID. This mapping is created as part of the configuration process. If the mapping exists, the client is logged in to SQL Server with the privileges associated with that login ID. If the mapping does not exist, the client is logged in to SQL Server using the default SQL Server Login ID (usually called **guest**) or, if the

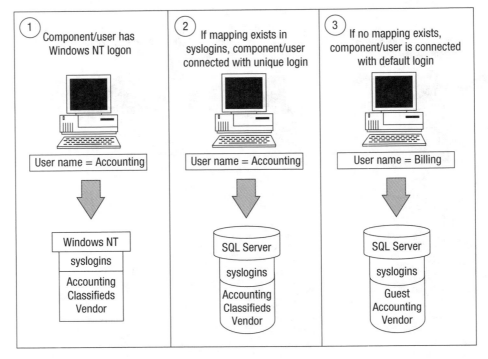

Figure 13.2
The steps that SQL Server performs to authenticate an integrated security login.

client's Windows NT user account has administrative privileges on Window NT, to **sa**. If the mapping does not exist, and there is no default login, the client is denied access to the SQL Server.

3. Once the login process is complete, access to individual SQL Server tables is managed through the permissions granted within the table's parent SQL Server database.

Mixed Security

When you use mixed security, SQL Server validates login requests using either integrated or standard security methods. Both trusted connections (as used by integrated security) and nontrusted connections (as used by standard security) are supported. Mixed security is often useful in network environments that have a mix of clients. For those clients that support trusted connections, Windows NT validates logins. For clients that only support nontrusted connections, SQL Server validates logins.

Figure 13.3 shows the steps involved for SQL Server to authenticate a login through mixed security.

When you set a server's login security mode to mixed, a client's login is validated as follows:

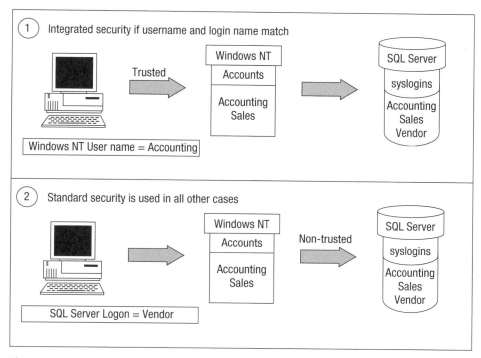

Figure 13.3
The steps that SQL Server performs to authenticate a mixed security login.

1. When a client attempts to log on to the server over a trusted connection, SQL Server examines the login name. If this login name matches the client's network user name, or if the login name is blank or consists of spaces, SQL Server uses the Windows NT integrated login rules (as for integrated security).

2. If the requested login name is any other value, the client must supply the correct SQL Server password, and SQL Server uses its own login validation process (as for standard security). If the login attempt is not over a trusted connection, the client must supply the correct login ID and password to establish the connection, and SQL Server uses its own login validation process (as for standard security).

Microsoft recommends integrated or mixed security for enterprise solutions using Windows NT Server, MTS, and SQL Server. Integrated security makes management of logins easier, because accounts can be administrated from one source in Windows NT. Also, you can avoid coding login IDs and passwords into your components, or placing them in ODBC DSNs. Moreover, Microsoft recommends using application component connections. Although we will not discuss application roles in detail in this book, they are an important security concept to keep in mind for development considerations. Any login changes under standard security would force components to be recompiled, or ODBC DSNs to be tracked down and updated.

Logins, Roles, And Groups

Logins are the core of SQL Server security. A login is an ID and password. A user or component must supply a login to establish a connection with SQL Server. A component supplies its login through the **ConnectionString** property of the ADO **Connection** object. Alternatively, the login can be passed as a **ConnectionString** parameter to the **Open** method of the **Connection** or **Recordset** object. If a component supplies a login ID and password, the component connects using standard security. If the component does not supply a login ID and password, the component connects using integrated security, and its package's identity is used as the login.

If you are connecting through an OLE DB provider, you must notify the provider that you are connecting using integrated security. You do not provide a user ID or password, and you set the **Trusted_Connection** attribute as shown in the following example code:

```
Public Sub OpenTrusted()
   Dim conn as ADODB.Connection
   Set conn = New ADODB.Connection

   conn.Provider = "SQLOLEDB"
   conn.ConnectionString = "Data Source=SQLSERVER;" & _
       "Initial Catalog=Pubs;Trusted_Connection=Yes"
   conn.Open
 ' Error-checking goes here
End Sub
```

The next section looks at the issues involved in the creation of logins, particularly using SQL Server Enterprise Manager.

Adding Login Accounts

To use a database on SQL Server, a user first connects to the server, using a login account. A login account can be:

♦ The user's Windows NT user account or the account of any group of which the user is a member

♦ A SQL Server login account that you create

♦ A default SQL Server login account

Logins are stored in the master database's **syslogins** system table. Understanding the part that logins, roles, and groups play in the administration of security for your database is an often-complex task. Starting off with the default settings that occur with SQL Server—both for each new account and after the initial setup of the server—may help make some of the interactions clearer.

Default Databases

When a login is added to SQL Server, it often is assigned a default database. Assigning a default database to a login account sets the default context for actions that the user takes; it does not give the user access to the database. As with any database, to gain access to the assigned default database, the user must be granted access, be a member of a Windows NT group that has been granted access, or be a member of a SQL Server role that has been granted access. If the default guest user account exists in the database, it can be used to gain access to the assigned default database. If you do not assign a default database, the default database will be the master database.

Default Login Accounts

SQL Server has two default login accounts: **sa** and **BUILTIN\Administrators**:

◆ System administrator (**sa**) is a special SQL Server login that has all rights on the SQL Server and in all databases.

◆ **BUILTIN\Administrators** is provided as the default Windows NT login account for all Windows NT administrators. It has all rights on the SQL Server and in all databases.

Granting A Windows NT Account Access To SQL Server

If a user connects to SQL Server using a Windows NT-authenticated login, that user is represented by his or her own Windows NT user account and the accounts of all Windows NT groups of which he or she is a member. You can use SQL Server Enterprise Manager or the **sp_grantlogin** system stored procedure to allow a Windows NT user or group account to connect to SQL Server. Only system or security administrators (as represented by the server admin and security admin roles) can grant access to Windows NT users or groups.

To grant a Windows NT user or group access to SQL Server using the SQL Server Enterprise Manager, perform the following steps, once for each login you are granting rights to:

1. Expand your server group and then expand your server in SQL Server Enterprise Manager.

2. Expand Security, right-click on Logins, and then click on New Login.

3. Click on Windows NT Authentication.

4. Select the domain where the accounts reside.

5. Enter the Microsoft Windows NT account name to add after the domain name in the Name field.

6. Select whatever database you wish to administer as the default database; leave the default language as is.

7. Click on OK to create the login.

Note

If you receive an error message stating, "The login name has not been granted access to the default database and therefore will not be able to gain access to the default database. Continue?", just click on OK. You will grant database access rights to the login later in this chapter.

Alternatively, as I mentioned a few paragraphs back, you can use system procedures to manage logins—specifically, you can use **sp_grantlogin** to add a Windows NT login to SQL Server. The following example uses the **sp_grantlogin** procedure to add the Windows NT user Jeff as a SQL Server login:

```
sp_grantlogin 'KLSENT\Jeff'
```

The *login* parameter is the name of the Windows NT user or group to be added. The Windows NT user or group must be qualified with a Windows NT domain name (therefore, in the previous example, Jeff is a member of the KLSENT domain). The limit for combined domain and user or group names is 128 characters.

Consider the following facts and guidelines about adding Windows NT logins to SQL Server:

♦ Because SQL Server has a single login for a Windows NT group, no changes to SQL Server are required when membership in a Windows NT group changes. This prevents orphaned objects (objects that are owned by a user who no longer exists in SQL Server), as long as you do not drop the group.

♦ Deleting a Windows NT group or user from the NT domain in User Manager for Domains does not drop that group or user from SQL Server. This prevents orphaned objects (objects whose owners have been deleted from SQL Server).

♦ When you remove Windows NT users or groups, you should first remove them from Windows NT to disallow network access. Then use **sp_changeobjectowner** to change the owner of objects owned by the account you wish to drop. Finally, remove the login from SQL Server.

♦ Add a login account for a Windows NT group account if every member of the group will be connecting to the SQL Server.

♦ Add a login account for an individual Windows NT user account only if the user is not a member of a group that can be granted permission collectively.

♦ Although users log on to SQL Server as members of Windows NT groups, when in integrated or mixed security modes, SQL Server still knows the identities of the users. The **SUSER_SNAME** function returns users' domain and login names when users are members of a Windows NT group.

You can use two other system stored procedures for managing Windows NT login accounts:

♦ **sp_revokelogin**—Removes the login entries for a Windows NT user or group from SQL Server. Note that removed permissions can still be inherited from other groups the user is a member of that maintain those permissions. Permission inheritance will be discussed at length in the following sections.

♦ **sp_denylogin**—Prevents a Windows NT user or group from connecting to SQL Server. Note that denied permissions can't be inherited from elsewhere; the user will still be denied access, whether or not other groups the user is a member of maintain those permissions. Permission inheritance will be discussed at length in the following sections.

Note

*Users can change their own passwords at any time by using the **sp_password** system stored procedure. System administrators can change any user's password using SQL Server Enterprise Manager or by using **sp_password** with **NULL** as the old password.*

Adding A SQL Server Login

You can use SQL Server Enterprise Manager or the **sp_addlogin** system stored procedure to create a SQL Server login. Only system or security administrators can create SQL Server logins. To use SQL Server Enterprise Manager to add SQL Server login accounts, perform the following steps, repeating them once for each login you wish to create:

1. Expand your server group and then expand your server in SQL Server Enterprise Manager.

2. Expand Security, right-click on Logins, and then click on New Login.

3. Enter the name of the new SQL Server login.

4. Click on SQL Server Authentication.

5. Enter the password.

6. Select the database you wish to set as the default database; leave the default language as is.

7. Click on OK to create the login.

Note

As in the previous example, if you receive an error message stating, "The login name has not been granted access to the default database and therefore will not be able to gain access to the default database. Continue?", just click on OK. You will grant access to this database later in this chapter.

Alternatively, as I mentioned a few paragraphs back, you can use the **sp_addlogin** system stored procedure to create a login. The following example creates the login *Shane* with the password of *password*, with a default database set to the Northwind database:

```
sp_addlogin 'Shane' , 'password' , 'Northwind'
```

The **sp_addlogin** system stored procedure adds a record to the **syslogins** table of the master database. After **sp_addlogin** is executed, the user can log on to SQL Server with that account. SQL Server logins and passwords can contain up to 128 characters, including letters, symbols, and digits. However, logins cannot:

- Contain a backslash character (\ ) other than the one required to delimit the domain name of a Windows NT login

- Be a reserved login account—for example, **sa** or **public**—or an existing login account

- Be **NULL** or an empty string (' ')

Granting Access To Databases

After a user is connected to SQL Server, he or she needs to be given access to one or more databases. A user gains access to databases based on user accounts or roles created and managed separately in each database. Although you can create a login for an individual user, normally you create logins for Windows NT groups, allowing all members of the group access to the database.

If a user is connected to SQL Server using a Windows NT-authenticated login, that user is represented by his or her own Windows NT user account as well as the accounts of all Windows NT groups of which he or she is a member. The user can therefore gain access to a database if database access has been granted to any of these accounts.

If a user is connected to SQL Server using a SQL Server-authenticated login, the user is represented by the SQL Server login only. The user can therefore gain access to a database only if database access has been granted to the SQL Server login they are using.

Granting Database Access To Logins

To access a database, a *login* (which can be a Windows NT user or group account that has been granted access to SQL Server, a SQL Server login, or one of the default SQL Server logins) uses either an assigned database user account or one of the default database user accounts. User accounts can be assigned to Windows NT users, Windows NT groups, or SQL Server logins.

To assign a user account to a login, you can use SQL Server Enterprise Manager or execute the **sp_grantdbaccess** system stored procedure. Only database owners and database access administrators can assign a user account to a login. An entry is added to the **sysusers** table in the database to which access is granted.

To grant database access with SQL Server Enterprise Manager, perform the following steps for the logins Jeff and Shane, which were created earlier in this chapter (one is an NT-authenticated account, the other a straight SQL Server account):

1. In SQL Server Enterprise Manager, expand your server.

2. Expand Security, and then click on Logins.

3. In the details pane, right-click on the login to modify, and then click on Properties.

4. On the Database Access tab, check the box next to Northwind (it should already be checked for Shane as a result of the stored procedure on the previous page).

5. Click on OK to close the SQL Server Login Properties dialog box and assign database access to the login.

Alternatively, as I have mentioned, you can grant database access with the **sp_grantdbaccess** system stored procedure. The following examples use the **sp_grantdbaccess** statement to give the logins Jeff and Shane access to the database:

```
sp_grantdbaccess 'Jeff', "Jeff-SQL"
sp_grantdbaccess 'STUDYSQL\Shane'
```

The first parameter (the *login* parameter) is the name of the login for the new account in the database. It can be any Windows NT user, Windows NT group, or SQL Server login. The second parameter (the *name_in_db* parameter) is an optional name or alias for the account in the database.

Tip

*It is possible to use the **sp_grantdbaccess** system stored procedure to grant access to a Windows NT user or group that has not been added as a login. This is not possible in SQL Server Enterprise Manager. Granting access in this way allows a user to connect to the SQL Server using one Windows NT account and then be granted access to a database based on another account. Remember that every user is represented by his or her own Windows NT user account as well as the accounts of all Windows NT groups of which he or she is a member.*

You can take advantage of two other very useful stored procedures for managing database access:

♦ **sp_revokedbaccess**—Removes a security account from the current database

♦ **sp_change_users_login**—Changes the relationship between a SQL Server login and a SQL Server user in the current database

Default User Accounts
Each database within SQL Server also has two default user accounts: **dbo** and **guest**.

♦ *The Database Owner (dbo) Account*—The **sa** login account and members of the System Administrators (**sysadmin**) role are mapped to a special user account inside all databases called **dbo**. Any object that a system administrator creates automatically belongs to **dbo**. The **dbo** user cannot be dropped.

♦ *The Guest User Account*—The **guest** user account allows logins without user accounts access to a database. Logins assume the identity of the **guest** user account when both of the following conditions are met: first, the login has access to SQL Server but does not have access to the database through its own user account; second, the database contains a **guest** user account.

Permissions can be applied to the **guest** user account as if it were any other user account. You can drop and add the **guest** user to any database except the **master** and **tempdb** databases.

By default, the **guest** user account is not given any permissions, but it is a member of the **public** role. You should therefore be careful when assigning permissions to the **public** role; drop the **guest** user account if necessary.

Assigning Logins To Roles

Roles provide a means of assembling users into a single unit to which permissions can be applied. SQL Server provides predefined fixed server and database roles for common administrative functions so that you can easily grant a selection of administrative permissions to a particular user.

You can also create your own database roles to represent work that a class of employees in your organization performs. As employees rotate into certain positions, you simply add them as members of the role; as they rotate out of the positions, remove them from the role. You do not have to grant and revoke permissions repeatedly as employees commence or leave various positions. If the function of a position changes, it is easy to change the permissions for the role and have the changes apply automatically to all members of the role.

Fixed Server Roles

The fixed server roles provided by SQL Server are listed in Table 13.1. Fixed server roles provide groupings of administrative privileges at the server level. They are managed independently of user databases and are stored in the **master..syslogins** system table. It is not possible to add new server roles. Note that the permissions of the **sysadmin** and **securityadmin** fixed server roles span all of the other fixed server roles. The **sysadmin** role is the equivalent of the **sa** login.

Assigning A Login Account To A Fixed Server Role

You can use SQL Server Enterprise Manager or the **sp_addsrvrolemember** system stored procedure to add a login account as a member of a fixed server role. Only members of the fixed server roles can add a login account as a member of a fixed server role. To use SQL Server Enterprise Manager to assign a login to a fixed server role, perform the following steps:

1. Expand your server group, then expand your server.

2. Expand Security, and then click on Server Roles.

3. In the details pane, right-click on the role Security Administrators, and then click on Properties.

Table 13.1   **Fixed server roles that SQL Server provides from the installation.**

Fixed Server Role	Description
sysadmin	Can perform any activity in SQL Server
serveradmin	Can configure serverwide settings
setupadmin	Can install replication and manage extended procedures
securityadmin	Can manage server logins
processadmin	Can manage processes running in SQL Server
dbcreator	Can create and alter databases
diskadmin	Can manage disk files

4. On the General tab, click on Add.

5. Click on the login to add KLSENT\Jeff.

6. Click on OK twice to close the dialog boxes and assign KLSENT\Jeff to the Security Administrators fixed server role.

You can also use the **sp_addsrvrolemember** to assign a login to a fixed server role. The following example adds the login Jeff to the **securityadmin** role:

```
sp_addsrvrolemember 'KLSENT\Jeff', 'securityadmin'
```

When you add a login to a server role, the corresponding row for the login in the **syslogins** table is updated to indicate that the login is a member of the role. The login then has the permissions that are associated with the server role. Consider the following facts about assigning login accounts to fixed server roles:

♦ Fixed server roles cannot be added, modified, or removed.

♦ Any member of a fixed server role can add other login accounts to that role.

♦ You can add a Windows NT user or group to a role, even if the user or group has not yet been added as a login. The user or group will be added as a login automatically when you execute **sp_addsrvrolemember**.

♦ The **sp_addsrvrolemember** system stored procedure cannot be executed within a user-defined transaction.

♦ Use the **sp_dropsrvrolemember** system stored procedure to remove a member from a fixed server role.

Fixed Database Roles

In addition to the fixed server roles detailed in Table 13.1, SQL Server defines a series of fixed database roles. The fixed database roles provided by SQL Server are listed in Table 13.2.

Table 13.2   Fixed database roles defined by the SQL Server engine.

Fixed Database Role	Description
db_owner	Can perform the activities of all database roles, as well as other maintenance and configuration activities in the database
db_accessadmin	Can add or remove Windows NT groups, Windows NT users, and SQL Server users in the database
db_datareader	Can see any data from all user tables in the database
db_datawriter	Can add, change, or delete data from all user tables in the database
db_ddladmin	Can add, modify, or drop objects in the database
db_securityadmin	Can manage roles and members of SQL Server database roles, and can manage statement and object permissions in the database
db_backupoperator	Can back up the database
db_denydatareader	Cannot see any data in the database, but can make schema changes
db_denydatawriter	Cannot change any data in the database

*The permissions of the **db_owner** fixed database role span all of the other fixed database roles.*

Fixed database roles provide groupings of administrative privileges at the database level. Fixed database roles are stored in the **sysusers** system table of each database.

The public Role

The **public** role is a special database role to which every database user belongs. The **public** role performs all of the following operations:

♦ Maintains all default permissions for users in a database

♦ Cannot have users, groups, or roles assigned to it because users, groups, and roles already belong by default

♦ Is contained in every database, including master, msdb, tempdb, model, and all user databases

♦ Cannot be dropped

Without being granted any specific permissions, a user possesses the permissions that are granted to the **public** role and can do any of the following activities in the database:

♦ Execute statements that do not require permissions, such as the **PRINT** statement

♦ View system table information and execute certain system stored procedures to retrieve information from the master database and user databases to which he or she has access

♦ Gain access to any database for which the guest account has been granted access permissions.

*In the pubs and Northwind databases, the **public** role has been granted all permissions. Security is set this way only because these are sample databases; you should never grant all permissions to the **public** role in production databases.*

Assigning A Security Account To A Fixed Database Role

You can use either SQL Server Enterprise Manager or the **sp_addrolemember** system stored procedure to add a security account as a member of a fixed database role. Only members of the **db_owner** role can execute the **sp_addrolemember** system stored procedure. To use SQL Server Enterprise Manager to assign security accounts to a fixed database role, perform the following steps:

1. Expand your server group, and then expand your server.

2. Expand Databases, and then expand the Northwind database.

3. Click on Users.

4. In the details pane, right-click on Shane, and then click on Properties.

5. Under Database Role Membership, click on **db_datareader** and **db_datawriter**. (Make sure the boxes next to the roles are checked.)

6. Click on OK to close the dialog box and add Shane to the **db_datareader** and **db_datawriter** fixed database roles.

7. In the console tree, click on Roles.

8. In the details pane, right-click on the role **db_datareader**, and then click on Properties.

9. Under User, click on Add.

10. Select Jeff to add.

11. Click on OK twice to close the dialog boxes and add Jeff to the **db_datareader** fixed database role.

Alternatively, you can use the **sp_addrolemember** stored procedure to assign security accounts to a fixed database role. You can use the **sp_addrolemember** statement as shown in the following example, which adds the user Jeff to the **db_datareader** role:

```
sp_addrolemember 'Jeff', 'db_datareader'
```

Consider the following facts when you assign security accounts to a fixed database role:

♦ Fixed database roles cannot be added, modified, or removed.

♦ Any member of a fixed database role can add other login accounts to that role.

Use the **sp_droprolemember** system stored procedure to drop a security account from a role.

User-Defined Database Roles

Creating a user-defined database role allows you to create a group of users with a set of common permissions. You add a user-defined role to the database when a group of people needs to perform a specific set of activities in SQL Server and no applicable Windows NT group exists. In general, this happens in one of the following situations:

♦ If you do not have permissions to manage Windows NT user accounts

♦ When you are using mixed mode authentication

For example, a company may form a new Charity Event committee that includes employees from different departments at several different levels. These employees need access to a special project table in the database. A Windows NT group does not exist that includes only these employees, and there is no other reason to create one in Windows NT. You could create a user-defined role, **CharityEvent**, for this project and then add individual Windows NT user accounts to the role. When permissions are applied, the individual user accounts in the role gain access to the project table.

Creating A User-Defined Database Role

You can use SQL Server Enterprise Manager or the **sp_addrole** system stored procedure to create a new database role. An entry is added to the **sysusers** table of the current database for each user-defined role. Only members of the **db_securityadmin** or **db_owner** roles can execute **sp_addrole**. To execute **sp_addrole** to create a user-defined database role, the **Cust_mgmt** role, you would invoke the stored procedure as shown in the following code sample:

```
sp_addrole 'Cust_mgmt'
```

The *owner* parameter must be a user or role in the current database and defaults to **dbo**. Consider the following facts and guidelines when you create a database role:

♦ The **sp_addrole** system stored procedure adds a new SQL Server role to the current database.

♦ When you apply permissions to the role, each member of the role gains the effects of the permission as if the permission were applied directly to the member's own account.

Assigning A Security Account To A User-Defined Database Role

After you add a role, use SQL Server Enterprise Manager or the **sp_addrolemember** system stored procedure to add users or roles as members of the role. Only members of the **db_owner** fixed database role or a role owner can execute **sp_addrolemember** to add a member to a user-defined database role. To use SQL Server Enterprise Manager to create a user-defined database role and assign a security account to the role, perform the following steps:

1. Expand your server group, and then expand your server.
2. Expand Databases, and then expand the NorthwindCS database.
3. Right-click on Roles, and then click on New Database Role.
4. Enter the name of the new role: **Cust_mgmt**.
5. Click on Add to add members to the standard role.
6. Select Jeff and Shane.
7. Click on OK twice to close the dialog boxes and add the new user-defined role and its members.

Alternatively, you can use the **sp_addrolemember** stored procedure, as shown in the following example, which adds Jeff to the **Cust_mgmt** role:

```
sp_addrolemember 'Cust_mgmt', 'Jeff'
```

Consider the following facts when you assign security accounts to a user-defined database role:

♦ When you use the **sp_addrolemember** system stored procedure to add a security account to a role, any permissions applied to the role are applied to the new member.

♦ You can add a SQL Server role as a member of another SQL Server role, but you cannot create recursive roles. Therefore, role A cannot be added as a member of role B if role B is already a member of role A. Furthermore, role A cannot be added as a member of role C if role B is already a member of role A and role C is already a member of role B.

♦ Nesting roles multiple times can decrease system performance.

You can use two additional system stored procedures for managing database roles:

♦ **sp_droprole**—Drops a SQL Server role from the current database

♦ **sp_droprolemember**—Drops a security account from a SQL Server role

SQL Server Object Permissions

Regardless of whether you use standard security or integrated security to connect, SQL Server uses the login to identify the connection. Having a connection does not mean that the component has access to all of the database objects in SQL Server. The component must have permissions to perform any operations on the database. The component's permissions depend on its login.

You map each login to a set of permissions for each database object. The permissions are either enabled or disabled. For example, the login Kim may have **SELECT** permissions on the **Authors** table that allow Kim to perform **SELECT** statements on that table. But Kim may have no **SELECT** privileges on the **Employee** table, meaning she cannot get any data from that table.

You must grant permissions to a login before any components using that login can access databases or the objects inside those databases. The permissions describe the capabilities of each login. They describe what statements a login can issue against database tables, such as **SELECT, INSERT, UPDATE**, or **DELETE**. They also describe whether a login can execute specific stored procedures.

If a login has execute permissions on a stored procedure, then that login may run the stored procedure. The stored procedure runs even if it performs actions for which the login has no permissions. For example, the login Kim may have execute permissions on a stored procedure named **AddCustomer**. Even though Kim does not have **INSERT** permissions on the **Customers** table, the **AddCustomer** stored procedure can successfully execute an **INSERT** statement to add the new customer.

You can provide better control over login capabilities by granting each login only the permissions necessary for the login to execute stored procedures. This forces logins to act within the capabilities of the stored procedures, rather than giving them unnecessary open capabilities on database objects, such as the capability to do any kind of **UPDATE**.

The Three Types Of Permissions

SQL Server offers three types of permissions: statement, object, and implied. Table 13.3 summarizes the SQL Server permissions, grouping them by type, and indicates which database or object the permission applies to.

Statement Permissions

Activities that involve creating a database or items in a database require a class of permissions called *statement permissions*. These permissions give users the privilege of issuing certain Transact-SQL statements. Statement permissions, such as **CREATE DATABASE**, are applied to the statement itself, rather than to a specific item that is defined in the database. Only members of the **sysadmin**, **db_owner**, or **db_securityadmin** role can grant statement permissions.

Object Permissions

Activities that involve working with data or executing procedures require a class of permissions known as *object permissions*. There are four different types of object permissions:

♦ *Table and view permissions*—Object permissions for tables and views control users' abilities to gain access to data using the **SELECT**, **INSERT**, **UPDATE**, and **DELETE** statements against the table or view. Object permissions are therefore called **SELECT**, **INSERT**, **UPDATE**, and **DELETE**. Using a **WHERE** clause in an **UPDATE** statement requires both **SELECT** and **UPDATE** permissions.

Table 13.3   Types, objects, and names of the various SQL Server permissions.

Permission Type	Permission	Applies To
Statement	**CREATE DATABASE**	master database
	CREATE DEFAULT	All databases
	CREATE PROCEDURE	All databases
	CREATE RULE	All databases
	CREATE TABLE	All databases
	CREATE VIEW	All databases
	BACKUP DATABASE	All databases
	BACKUP LOG	All databases
Object	**SELECT**	Tables, views, and columns
	INSERT	Tables and views
	DELETE	Tables and views
	UPDATE	Tables, views, and columns
	REFERENCES (DRI in SQL Server Enterprise Manager)	Tables and columns
	EXECUTE	Stored procedures
Implied	Fixed role	Object owner
	Depends on role	The owned object

♦ *The REFERENCES permission*—Another object permission called **REFERENCES** applies to tables. When a user adds a row to a table or changes data in a table with a **FOREIGN KEY** constraint, SQL Server must validate the data in the table that is referenced in the **FOREIGN KEY** constraint. If the user does not have **SELECT** permissions on the referenced table, the **REFERENCES** permission for the table must be granted to the user. In SQL Server Enterprise Manager, the **REFERENCES** permission is referred to as DRI (Declarative Referential Integrity).

♦ *Column permissions*—**SELECT**, **UPDATE**, and **REFERENCES** permissions can be applied selectively to individual columns. This means that rather than giving a user or role access to an entire table, you can grant access to certain columns of the table only. To work with column permissions, you must use Transact-SQL. SQL Server Enterprise Manager does not allow you to grant, revoke, or deny column permissions.

Tip

I recommend that you use views rather than column permissions. Views are easier to manage and perform better than column permissions.

♦ *Stored procedure permissions*—The **EXECUTE** permission is the only object permission for a stored procedure. This permission allows a user to execute the stored procedure.

Implied Permissions

Members of fixed roles and owners of database objects can perform certain activities apart from those governed by normal statement and object permissions. Permissions to perform these activities are called implied, predefined, or implicit permissions:

♦ *Fixed role permissions*—Fixed roles have implied administrative permissions. For example, a user who is added as a member of the **sysadmin** role automatically inherits full permissions to do or read anything in a SQL Server installation. The **sysadmin** role has permissions that cannot be changed, as well as implied permissions that cannot be applied to other user accounts, such as the ability to configure the SQL Server installation.

♦ *Object owner permissions*—Object owners also have implied permissions that allow them to perform all activities on objects that they own. For example, a user who is a table owner, or a member of a group that is designated as the table owner, can perform any activity that is related to the table. The user can view, add, or delete data, alter the table definition, and control the permissions that allow other users to work with the table.

Tip

*It's usually not a good idea to grant individual user accounts the ability to create objects. It adds a layer of complexity to your security model that is difficult to manage. A better idea is to use the implied permissions of roles such as **db_owner** and **sysadmin** so that all objects are owned by the same role.*

Permission States

Permissions for a user or role can be in one of three states: granted, denied, or revoked. Permissions are stored as entries in the **sysprotects** system table. If a permission is granted or denied, an entry is recorded in the **sysprotects** table. If a permission has not been granted or denied, or if it has been revoked after being granted or denied, there is no entry for that permission in the **sysprotects** system table. Note that a permission is in the revoked state if it has never been granted or denied; in other words, it does not have to be explicitly revoked with the **REVOKE** statement. Table 13.4 summarizes the three states of a permission.

Granted permissions are cumulative—users can perform all of the actions that they have been granted individually or as a result of Windows NT group membership, as well as all of the actions granted to any roles to which they belong. Role hierarchies mean that users can get permissions indirectly by being members of a role that is in turn a member of another role to which permissions have been granted.

The **DENY** statement prevents users from performing actions. It overrides a permission, whether the permission was granted to a user directly or to a role to which the user belongs.

Users have permission to perform an action only if both of the following are true:

♦ They have been granted the permission directly or they belong to a role that has directly or indirectly been granted the permission.

♦ The permission has not been denied to the user directly or to any of the roles of which the user is a member.

Figure 13.4 shows an example of a user who is a member of a Windows NT group (NT group A) and a database role (role C). NT group A is a member of role A, and role C is a member of role B. The figure shows how the user accumulates permissions directly from NT group A and role C and indirectly from role A and role B. Notice that the **DELETE** permission is revoked from role C, but this does not prevent members of role C from getting the **DELETE** permission from role B.

Figure 13.5 shows the same roles, NT group, and user as Figure 13.4. Notice that the **DELETE** permission is denied to role C; this prevents members of role C from getting the permission from role B.

Table 13.4   SQL Server object permissions can be in one of three states.

Permission State	State Of Entry In sysprotects Table	Effect
GRANT	Positive	Can perform action; can be overridden by role membership
DENY	Negative	Cannot perform action; cannot be overridden by role membership
REVOKE	None	Cannot perform action; can be overridden by role membership

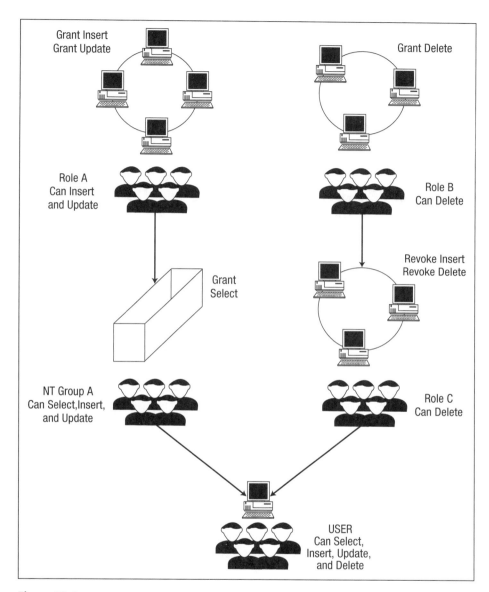

Figure 13.4
How granted and revoked permissions interact.

Granting Permissions

You grant permissions to security accounts to allow them to perform activities or work with data in a database. Consider the following facts when you grant permissions:

♦ You can grant permissions in the current database only.

♦ The right to grant permissions defaults to members of the **sysadmin**, **db_owner**, and **db_securityadmin** roles and to object owners.

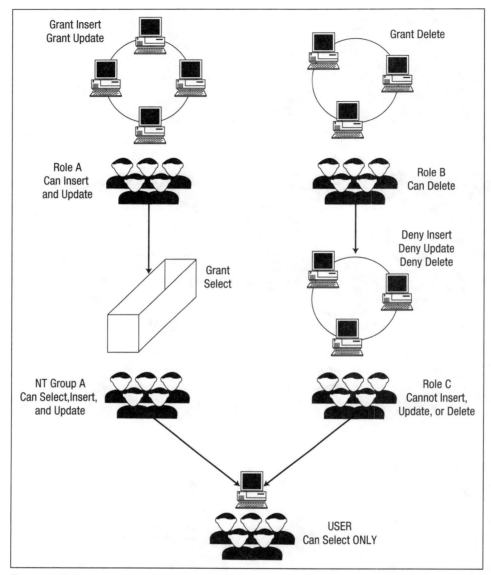

Figure 13.5
How granted and denied permissions interact.

The **CREATE DATABASE** statement permission can be granted only to users and roles in the master database. This is because records are added to system tables in the master database when you create a new database.

Use SQL Server Enterprise Manager or the **GRANT** statement to grant permissions. The syntax for the **GRANT** statement for statement permissions is as follows:

```
GRANT {ALL | statement [,...n]}
TO security_account[,...n]
```

The syntax for the **GRANT** statement for object permissions is as follows:

```
GRANT {ALL [PRIVILEGES] | permission[,...n]}
  {
          [(column[,...n])] ON {table | view}
      | ON {table | view}[(column[,...n])]
      | ON {stored_procedure | extended_procedure}
  }
TO security_account[,...n]
[WITH GRANT OPTION]
[AS {group | role}]
```

When used to assign statement permissions, the **ALL** argument specifies that all statement permissions are granted. When used to assign object permissions, the **ALL** argument specifies that all object permissions that apply to the specified object are granted. Only the system administrator and database owner can use the **ALL** argument.

Note
Windows NT user names must be enclosed in brackets when they are referenced in a statement—for example, [KLSENT\Jeff].

Denying Permissions

You occasionally may want to limit the permissions of a certain user or role by denying permissions to that security account. Denying permissions on a security account does the following:

♦ Negates the permissions that were previously granted to the user or role

♦ Deactivates permissions that are inherited from another role

♦ Ensures that a user or role does not inherit permissions from any other role in the future

Consider the following facts when you deny permissions:

♦ You can deny permissions in the current database only.

♦ Permission to deny permissions defaults to members of the **sysadmin**, **db_owner**, and **db_securityadmin** roles and to object owners.

Use SQL Server Enterprise Manager or the **DENY** statement to deny permissions. The syntax for the **DENY** statement for statement permissions is as follows:

```
DENY {ALL | statement[,...n]}
TO security_account[,...n]
```

The syntax for the **DENY** statement for object permissions is as follows:

```
DENY {ALL [PRIVILEGES] | permission[,...n]}
 {
    [(column[,...n])] ON { table | view}
      |  ON {table | view} [( column[,...n])]
      |  {procedure | extended_procedure}
 }
TO security_account
```

Revoking Granted And Denied Permissions

You can deactivate a granted or denied permission by *revoking* it. Revoking is similar to denying permissions in that both actions remove a granted permission. The difference is that although revoking a permission removes a granted permission, it does not prevent the user or role from inheriting that permission in the future. You can also remove a previously denied permission by revoking the **DENY** statement for the permission.

Consider the following facts when you revoke permissions:

♦ You can revoke permissions in the current database only.

♦ Revoking a permission removes the entries in the **sysprotects** system table that were created by granting and denying the permission.

♦ Permission to revoke permissions defaults to members of the **sysadmin**, **db_owner**, and **db_securityadmin** roles and to object owners.

You can use SQL Server Enterprise Manager or the **REVOKE** statement to remove a previously granted or denied permission. The syntax for the **REVOKE** statement for statement permissions is as follows:

```
REVOKE {ALL | statement[,...n]}
FROM security_account[,...n]
```

The syntax for the **REVOKE** statement for object permissions is as follows:

```
REVOKE [GRANT OPTION FOR]
    {ALL [PRIVILEGES] | permission[,...n]}
 {
    {[(column[,...n])] ON {table | view}
     | {procedure | extended_procedure}
 }
FROM security_account[,...n]
[AS {group | role}]
```

When A Revoke Is Not A Revoke

Because a revoke will remove previously granted or denied permissions, the result of a revoke may be that an account no longer has permissions, or it may be that an account now has permissions. For this reason, you must carefully consider the result of revoking or denying permissions. The following example illustrates this somewhat confusing behavior. Assume that User is a member of role A:

1. Permission is granted to role A—User has permissions based on membership in role A.

2. Permission is denied to User—User has no permissions. The deny for User overrides the grant from role A.

3. Permission is revoked from User—User *has* permissions, because the *denied* permission is revoked and User now goes back to having permission based on membership in role A.

4. Permission is revoked from role A—User has *no* permissions, because the *granted* permission is revoked from the role from which User was getting permissions.

Planning Security

This section looks at creating a plan to allow appropriate user access to resources. It also discusses default logins and roles and their use in this plan. The goals in creating a security plan are as follows:

♦ List all of the items and activities in the database that must be controlled through security.

♦ Identify the individuals and groups in the company.

♦ Cross-reference the two lists to identify which users can see what data and perform what activities in the database.

The next few sections introduce five common considerations that can help you create your security plan.

Determine The Use Of Default Logins

When you're creating a security plan, you need to determine how or whether you will use the **sa** or **BUILTIN\Administrators** logins. The following sections consider each choice and its implications.

The sa Login

Although **sa** is a built-in administrator login, it should not be used routinely. Instead, system administrators should be members of the **sysadmin** fixed server role and should log on with their own logins. The **sa** login cannot be dropped or disabled. Log on as **sa** if you inadvertently remove all members of **sysadmin**.

> *Tip*
>
> *When SQL Server is installed, the **sa** login is not assigned a password. I strongly recommend that you change the password immediately to prevent unauthorized access to SQL Server with the **sa** login.*

The BUILTIN\Administrators Login

The local Windows NT group Administrators is automatically mapped to the SQL Server **BUILTIN\Administrators** login. By default, **BUILTIN\Administrators** is a member of the **sysadmin** role.

If you do not want all Windows NT administrators in your organization to have complete access to your SQL Server, you can remove the **BUILTIN\Administrators** login or remove the login from the **sysadmin** role. You can replace the login and assign permissions to it if you later decide that you do want to use it. Another method of limiting the **BUILTIN\Administrators** login is to remove the Domain Admins global group from the local Administrators group in Windows NT.

Determine public Role Permissions

The **public** role is a special database role to which every database user belongs. It controls the permissions that all users have by default in each database. You should carefully consider which permissions the **public** role will have in each database; by default, the **public** role has no permissions.

Determine The Function Of The guest User Account

The **guest** user account allows a login without a user account to gain access to a database. You should decide whether your databases will have a **guest** account and, if so, what permissions the **guest** account should have. New databases do not automatically have a user called **guest**. If you wish to enable the **guest** user in a database, you must add it to the database using SQL Server Enterprise Manager or **sp_grantdbaccess**. When you add a user called **guest** to a database with SQL Server Enterprise Manager, you do not have to specify a login name, because the **guest** user is a special user not associated with a login. When you add a user called **guest** to a database with **sp_grantdbaccess**, you must specify *guest* as the login name and as the name in the database.

Map Logins To User Accounts And Roles

Before assigning logins to a database, decide whether you will use user accounts or roles to apply permissions. In general, Microsoft and I both recommend the following mappings:

♦ If members of a Windows NT group are the only ones who perform a series of tasks, create a user account for the group and apply permissions to it.

♦ If more than one login will perform a group of tasks, create a role and assign the login to the role.

♦ If a login will perform common administrative tasks, map the login to the appropriate fixed server or database role.

Create Objects With Owner dbo

It is very important to determine which users and roles can create objects in a database. In general, it is recommended that only the **sysadmin**, **db_owner**, and **db_ddladmin** fixed database roles be permitted to create database objects.

It is further recommended that all objects be defined with the **dbo** user specified as the object owner. Defining objects with **dbo** as the owner enables any user in the database to refer to the object without including the owner name. Any object created from the **sysadmin** role has **dbo** as the owner. From any other role, always specify the **dbo** user as the owner name when you create the object; otherwise, the object will be created with your user name as the object owner.

Changing Object Owners

If objects were not created with the **dbo** user as the object owner, you can change the object owner with the **sp_changeobjectowner** system stored procedure, following the prototype shown here:

```
sp_changeobjectowner [@objname =] 'object' ,[@newowner =] 'owner'
```

Consider the following facts about changing database object owners:

♦ Only members of the **db_owner** and **db_ddladmin** fixed database roles and members of the **securityadmin** server role can change database object owners.

♦ Scripts and batch files that included the old owner name in references to the object need to be updated manually. SQL Server cannot perform this update automatically.

Security Best Practices

Needless to say, security can be complex to implement, test, and manage. The following list includes some best practices to help you implement security in your applications:

♦ *Set up SQL Server for integrated (or mixed) security, when possible.* By using integrated or mixed security, you avoid coding login IDs and passwords directly into MTS components or ODBC DSNs. It is a more flexible approach to security, because you can change security credentials by modifying a package's Windows NT user accounts, rather than recompiling the components in the package.

♦ *Use stored procedures for all data access.* This allows you to assign execute permissions on stored procedures for packages rather than having to determine all the different types of permissions each package should have. Also, stored procedures run much faster than submitting SQL statements from the components.

♦ *Stage applications on a Quality Assurance (QA) server before moving them to production.* The QA server should have the same security settings as the production server on which the application will ultimately run. These security settings include NTFS permissions, MTS roles, and SQL Server users. Without such a server, there is a chance that an application that runs fine on a developer's machine will encounter permission problems when put into production. When testing an application on the QA server, be sure to log on as a user that is not a member of the Administrators group.

♦ *Grant end users access to resources through group accounts rather than individual accounts.* The end users of an application should gain access to all resources through membership of a Windows NT group, rather than through granting them direct access to any resource (databases, files, or MTS components). This makes managing end-user security easier, because you can control security at one point, the Windows NT groups, rather than tracking down each resource to which they have been granted access and making changes.

♦ *Create at least one Windows NT group account for each application.* If differing roles in an application require different levels of access to resources, then you should create a Windows NT group for each of these roles, such as Bank Tellers and Bank Managers.

♦ *Create at least one role for each MTS package.* If there are different levels of access, then there must be a role for each type of access, such as Tellers and Managers on the Bank package. Thus, there is a one-to-one relationship between Windows NT groups and roles: Bank Tellers to Tellers, and Bank Managers to Managers.

♦ *Design auditing requirements into your business and database components.* Database auditing does not work as expected under the three-tier security model, because all users access the database through the same user ID (the package's account). To implement logging on your MTS component, use the **GetOriginalCallerName** method. This returns the Windows NT name of the end user, even if the MTS component was called directly by another component. For example, if the **Customer** component keeps a log of all modifications to business data, it can use **GetOriginalCallerName**. The return value is the name of the end user, not the name of an MTS package, which is the direct caller. The call might look like this:

```
Dim strModifiedBy as String
strModifiedBy = GetObjectContext().Security.GetOriginalCallerName()
```

Connecting To A Secure SQL Server

Unless your application hard-codes the user ID and password values, you must prompt the user for these values before connecting to the database. The following example code prompts the user for a user name and password:

```
Sub cmdConnect_Click()
  Dim sUsername As string
  Dim sPassword As string
```

```
Dim cnSQLServer As Connection

Set cnSQLServer = New Connection
sUsername = InputBox("Please enter your user name:")
sPassword = InputBox("Please enter your password:")
With cnSQLServer
  .Provider = "SQLOLEDB"
  .ConnectionString = "User ID=" & sUsername & _
      ";Password=" & sPassword & ";Data Source=SQLSERVER;" & _
      "Initial Catalog=Library"
  .Open
End With
End Sub
```

Where To Go From Here

In this chapter, you learned all about SQL Server security, including integrated, standard, and mixed mode security. You also learned about the importance of logins, users, and roles. Additionally, we discussed permissions—granting, denying, and revoking—in detail, including a consideration of situations in which any of them might be appropriate.

In Chapter 14, we will take the concepts that we have discussed in this and the previous four chapters, and apply our knowledge of the ADP file type and the SQL Server database to solve a relatively complex database problem, including the connections and displays that go with it.

Advanced Programming With Access Data Projects

As I have discussed in previous chapters, Access Data Projects (ADPs) are a key component of Microsoft's long-term strategy with Access 2000. The move away from the Jet engine to SQL Server as the underlying, essential technology is a good one for the future of application design with Access. However, as you have hopefully already learned, substantial differences in programming have been made to both platforms, and an additional layer of complexity is inherent in SQL Server that does not exist with Jet. In this chapter, I will explain how to support some of the most useful Access objects—forms and reports—within your ADPs, while also addressing some of the important techniques you must be able to apply within your development projects to take best advantage of the new SQL Server support.

Reporting And Forms With ADPs

After connecting to one or more remote data sources and filtering, aggregating, or combining them with other sources, you can present your results with Access 2000. Because tables, views, and stored procedures are tightly integrated with forms, reports, and modules, you can easily deliver client/server data in the same way that Access has been serving up file-server data sources since its initial release. Prior Access releases made client/server data available, but they never made true client/server processing so easy. Can ADP files do for client/server data sources what MDB files did for file-server data sources? It depends on your interest and imagination. The upcoming samples might spark some ideas as to where you can use ADP files in your organization.

Sorting, Formatting, And More With Reports

The Query Designer makes it relatively easy to filter, combine, and aggregate data, but it does not offer much in the way of presentation capabilities. Recall that you cannot even sort the records in a view. Reports, on the other hand, have relatively limited processing capabilities, but are great at sorting and formatting data for printers (and even the World Wide Web, if you consider snapshots).

Figure 14.1 shows how to use Access Project views with Access reports so that they complement each other. The report sorts records by **FamID**. It also conditionally formats the color for displaying a row based on the value of **FamID**: Values of less than 6 appear in black, but values of 6 or greater are in red. In addition, the display shows the normal report flourishes, including a title, a bar separating the title column headings from the column entries, and formatting for column headings and the report title that contrasts with the formatting of the body of the report.

Aside from the union query coding for the view, this report requires no programming. After you build your view, you simply set the report's **Record Source** property to the name of the view. Except for the different colors based on **FamID**, all of the report features are default tabular report settings. The new Conditional Formatting command on the Format menu dramatically simplifies the task of conditionally applying colors to the contents of text boxes. In the past, such capabilities required **Format** event procedures. By bringing the view and report together, you can use each to do the task that it performs best. Because reporting is a

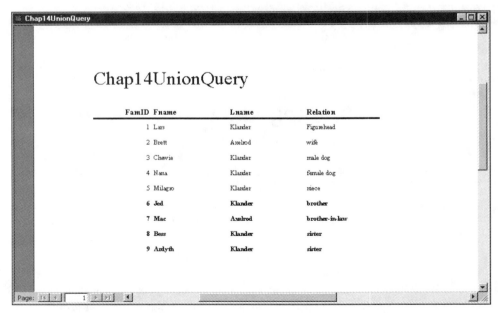

Figure 14.1
A report based on a view called Chap14UnionQuery.

major Access strength, the ADP file's ability to process client/server data sources can dramatically lower the cost of delivering informative, easy-to-read reports throughout an organization.

Adding Hyperlinks

There is no **Hyperlink** data type in SQL Server databases. (Recall that Jet supports this data type as an extension of the **Memo** data type, as discussed previously.) However, you can still insert and follow hyperlinks in forms within Access Projects. There are four steps for doing this:

1. Assign a table column one of these data types: **char, nchar, nvarchar,** or **varchar.** These are fixed and variable-length string data types in Unicode or non-Unicode format.

2. Open a form in Design view and make the table the record source for the form (which you can do from the Properties dialog box, as always with forms in Access).

3. Assign the field with the **string** data type to one of the form fields.

4. Set the field's **IsHyperlink** property to **Yes.** This is a new property in Access 2000 that exists explicitly for hyperlinks on forms in Access Projects.

After setting up the table and form, you can add hyperlinks to the table through the form using the Insert | Hyperlink command, which opens a dialog box for setting or editing the hyperlink's URL and its display text. Once the hyperlinks are formatted, users can follow them to designated Web locations by simply clicking on the entry in a hyperlink field. Their default browser takes them there. Then they can return to Access by clicking on the back arrow. Access 97 introduced this functionality; it is now available for SQL Server and MSDE databases through Access 2000.

Figure 14.2 shows the **LinkSample** Access form in the process of having its hyperlink entry edited. You can browse to the desired Web location so that you do not have to type the URL. In addition, you can use the Text To Display text box to enter text that appears instead of the URL. Notice also that you can use this dialog box to set hyperlinks for files on a local file server or even link to email addresses. The latter option starts the browser workstation's default email package with the name and email address that you specify in the link.

Viewing And Editing Data Using Forms

Access Data Projects offer two **Recordset Type** property settings for working with forms and traditional data sources, such as tables of employees or customers. These settings are unique to ADP files. The traditional MDB files have different **Recordset Type** property settings.

When you design an application that uses forms with data from a SQL Server or MSDE database, your client application always works with a snapshot of the original data on the server. Although the locally available data is a snapshot of the data on the server, you can

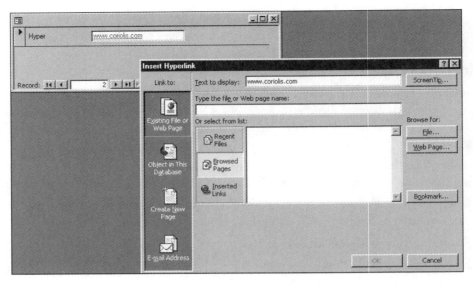

Figure 14.2
You can use the Insert Hyperlink dialog box to enter and edit hyperlinks into a shared client/server database of hyperlinks.

update it on the server. To accommodate this functionality, Access 2000 offers **Updatable Snapshot** and **Snapshot Recordset Type** settings for ADPs. You can set these properties on the Data tab of the form's Property dialog box. You can also manipulate the **Recordset Type** setting using VBA or an Access macro.

When you set a form's **Recordset Type** property to **Updatable Snapshot**, users can change the form's underlying data source as if the file were on a local file server. Using the **Lock** property for individual controls, you can selectively enable editing on a subset of a form's controls. In addition, you can control the type of changes permitted at client workstations. There are separate **Yes/No** settings for **Allow Edits**, **Allow Deletions**, and **Allow Additions** properties. Changes you make from the ADP file propagate to the server. Each user of an ADP should have a separate copy of the ADP file even though each user relates to a common client/server database. Although data changes propagate from the client workstations to the server database, users must choose Records | Refresh to view changes made by others.

Figure 14.3 shows a sample form in an ADP based on data in a remote server. Below the form is an excerpt from the form's property sheet. It exposes the two possible settings for the **Recordset Type** property. Because **Updatable Snapshot** is in effect, users can change the form's underlying record source. In fact, because of the **Yes** settings for **Allow Edits**, **Allow Deletions**, and **Allow Additions**, they can perform all three standard types of database revisions. You can turn off all three capabilities by setting the **Recordset Type** property to **Snapshot**.

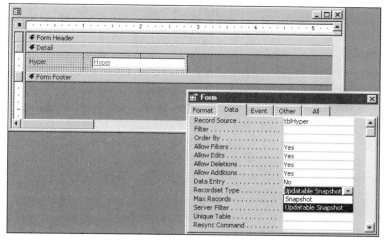

Figure 14.3
You can use forms in Access Projects to modify data on a database server.

The form was prepared using the AutoForm Wizard (with a minor amount of editing). Moving to the next record passes any edits that a user makes to fields back to the server. If the **Recordset Type** setting is **Snapshot**, Access responds that the recordset is not updateable. The button marked with an X lets users abort a lengthy download of many records to a local workstation.

Resynchronizing A Form With Its One-To-Many Data

When the source for a form in an ADP is based on a recordset with a one-to-many relationship between two tables, you can automatically populate all the fields on the one side by setting the foreign key on the many side. This feature is especially convenient when you add new records. For example, if you are designing a form that presents employee and sales data, the one-to-many relationship follows from the fact that each employee can have multiple sales. You simply enter the employee ID for the sales table and commit the record. This action automatically populates all the employee fields on the one side of the underlying record source. Then you enter the sales data on the many side of the record source. You can update the employee information for a previously existing record just as easily.

To enable this feature, your form must use **Updatable Snapshot** as the **Recordset Type** setting. You assign to the **Unique Table** property the table on the many side of the relationship. You must also set the **Resync Command** property to a string representing a SQL statement that enables the resynchronization. You'll learn a trick for quickly constructing this statement in the next several paragraphs.

Figure 14.4 shows the one-to-many Design view for the **vwForResync** view. The top panel shows the one-to-many relationship in the line connecting the **Employees** and **Orders**

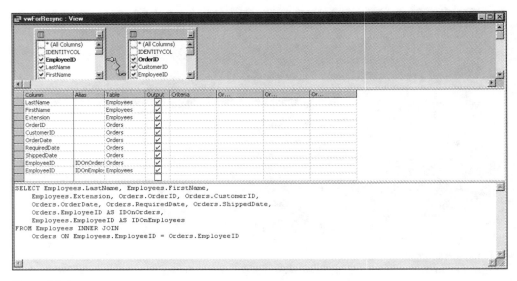

Figure 14.4
This view represents a one-to-many relationship like that used for resynchronization on a form. The SQL statement forms the basis of the **Resync Command** property setting.

tables. Notice that the view links the tables using the primary key in the **Employees** table and the corresponding foreign key (**EmployeeID**) in the **Orders** table. The bottom panel shows the SQL for the view. The form's **Resync Command** property requires a simple modification of this statement.

Figure 14.5 shows a form just after 1 has been entered into the **EmployeeID** text box. The form is a standard AutoForm with some minor editing. Clicking on the record selector brings up data automatically to all the other employee fields on the form. Entering a new value into the **EmployeeID** text box and clicking on the record selector automatically brings up employee data corresponding to the new ID value. That is the benefit of the resynchronization function.

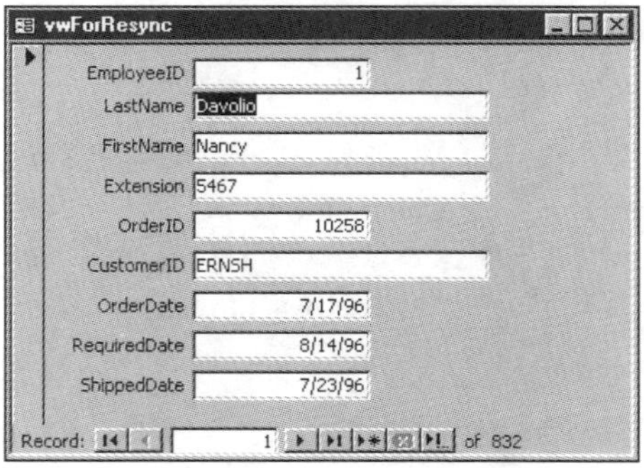

Figure 14.5
A form that demonstrates resynchronization against a remote database.

Figure 14.6 shows the form settings that enable this automatic resynchronization. The **Recordset Type** is **Updatable Snapshot**, and the form's **Unique Table** property points at the *many* side of the underlying recordset—namely, the **Orders** table. The zoomed **Resync Command** setting is exactly the same as the SQL for the underlying form with one extra line: **WHERE Orders.OrderID = ?**. This final step completes the tasks for enabling a form by using the resynchronization function.

Programmatic Issues

One way to extend the capabilities of your ADPs is with SQL. This is particularly true for views and stored procedures. Several of the preceding samples have shown what you can do with SQL. However, you can also put your VBA and ADO knowledge to use. The remaining samples in this chapter show how to apply your expertise in these areas to working with ADPs or even to working with SQL Server and MSDE databases without the convenient user interface of ADPs.

Working With Forms

Although the ADP user interface delivers extraordinary functionality with remote data sources, you can automate and simplify certain processes by developing custom programmatic solutions. We'll look at three areas pertaining to ADPs: opening a form, finding a record, and viewing changes made by other users.

> **Note**
>
> *The database used in this chapter can be generated automatically by running the Chap14-setup.sql script, found on the companion CD-ROM, where you can also locate completed versions of the forms, reports, and so on mentioned throughout this chapter.*

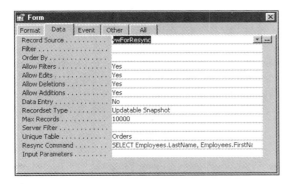

Figure 14.6
The Data tab of the form's property sheet. The Updatable Snapshot and Resync Command settings are necessary for resynchronization.

Opening A Form

When you open a form with the ADP interface, the form populates a local copy of the remote data in the client workstation. This local copy is a snapshot, at that particular point in time, of the remote data for the form. When you open the form programmatically, you must create the local copy of the remote data. One advantage to programmatically opening a form is that you can dynamically assign values to the local cache of the remote data. Your application can do this because the recordset that you assign to the form with VBA over-rides the **Record Source** setting on the form's property sheet.

The following procedure constructs a recordset for a form before opening it:

```
Sub openForm()
Dim rst1 As ADODB.Recordset

'Establish a local recordset and populate it with values;
'can override property sheet settings.
    Set rst1 = New ADODB.Recordset
    rst1.CursorLocation = adUseClient
    rst1.Open "Select * From employees", _
        CurrentProject.Connection, adKeySet, _
        adLockPessimistic
'Optionally run with where clause to demo override effect.
'    "Select * From employees where employeeid>3"

'Open the form.
    DoCmd.openForm "frmemployees2"

'Assign recordset to the open form; can override a
'setting on the property sheet.
    Set Forms("frmemployees2").Recordset = rst1

End Sub
```

It starts by setting a reference to a new recordset instance: It assigns **adUseClient** to the recordset's **CursorLocation** property to establish the location of the form's data. (Recall that the form gets the data from the local cache on the workstation, not from the remote server.) Next, it opens the recordset with a SQL statement that extracts data from the remote source into the local copy. The sample works with the form from Figure 14.6. A commented line shows a SQL statement that can override the form's default record source. After making the local copy of the remote data, the procedure opens the form and assigns the local copy to the form's **Recordset** property. This new property possesses the functional-ity of the **RecordsetClone** property; in addition, changes to the recordset appear on the form automatically—the **RecordsetClone** property provides a read-only copy of a form's recordset. Like the **RecordsetClone** property, a form's **Recordset** property is available only programmatically.

The recordset created for a recordset instance is available only if the form remains open. Closing and reopening the form manually causes the form to revert to the **Record Source** *setting on its property sheet.*

Finding A Record

One common task when you work with data in a form is finding a specific record. The following two procedures accomplish this task. The **locateEmployee** procedure prompts for an employee ID value and passes that value along to the second procedure, **findByID**. The second procedure taps the **FindRecord** method of the **DoCmd** object to search for and position the form at a new record:

```
Sub locateEmployee()

'Ask for employee ID and pass it on to findByID.
    employeeNumber = InputBox("Type the ID for the employee you want", _
        "Client/Server Solutions with Access 2000")
    findById CLng(employeeNumber)

End Sub


Sub findById(eid As Long)
On Error GoTo findByIdTrap

'Set focus to employee ID field and launch find.
    Forms("frmemployees2").EmployeeID.SetFocus
    DoCmd.FindRecord eid

findByIdExit:
'Report mismatch before exiting.
    If Forms("frmemployees2").EmployeeID <> eid Then
        MsgBox "No employee with ID " & eid & ".", _
            vbExclamation, " Client/Server Solutions with Access 2000"
    End If
    Exit Sub

findByIdTrap:
    If Err.Number = 2450 Then
'Open form if it is closed and start find again.
        openForm
        Resume
    Else
```

```
        Debug.Print Err.Number, Err.Description
    End If

End Sub
```

The second procedure detects two potential problems. First, if there is no match, the procedure issues a message to that effect. Second, neither procedure is an event procedure, so they can be invoked from outside the form. If the form is closed, the procedure detects the problem and opens it so that it can try again to find the target record.

Viewing Changes Made By Other Users

Access is inherently a multiuser development environment, and ADPs frequently serve multiuser purposes. Therefore, you need a way to refresh the local cache so that you can view updates, additions, and deletions made by others. The following procedure does this by repopulating the local recordset for the form from the remote data source. Like the preceding samples, this one is based on the form in Figure 14.6:

```
Sub requeryRemoteRestoreID()
Dim int1 As Integer

'Turn off screen updates and save employee ID.
    DoCmd.Echo False
    int1 = Forms("frmemployees2").EmployeeID

'Requery local recordset from the server.
    openForm

'Reposition to employee ID before requery and
'restore screen updating.
    Forms("frmemployees2").EmployeeID.SetFocus
    DoCmd.FindRecord int1
    DoCmd.Echo True

End Sub
```

This procedure refills the local data cache by invoking the **openForm** procedure (which we discussed earlier in the chapter). If the form is already open, the call simply repopulates the cache. Because repopulating a form's recordset automatically makes the first record current, the procedure saves the current record position before repopulating the local cache from the remote data store. After repopulating the cache, the procedure searches through the records to find the preceding current record. This restores the old record position if that record is still available (that is, not deleted). If another user has deleted the former current record, the form displays the first record in the local cache.

Working With Standalone Modules

All the emphasis on ADO throughout this book will serve you well when you develop custom solutions against MSDE and SQL Server data sources. You have seen more than a few samples for dealing with remote data sources. In the following sections, let's revisit some programmatic issues in the context of Access Projects and MSDE.

Opening A Table

The following sample integrates opening a table in a remote data source with writing the results to the Immediate window as a telephone directory. It uses ADO **Connection** and **Recordset** objects to do this:

```
Sub openTableOnRemoteServer()
Dim cnnRemote As ADODB.Connection
Dim rstRemote As ADODB.Recordset

'Open connection to AccCSNwindVariant database
'on SQLSERVER server.
    Set cnnRemote = New ADODB.Connection
    strCnn = "Provider=sqloledb;" & _
        "Data Source=SQLSERVER;" & _
        "Initial Catalog=AccCSNwindVariant;" & _
        "User Id=sa;Password=;"
    cnnRemote.Open strCnn

'Open employee table with a forward-only,
'read-only recordset; this type is OK for a single
'pass through the data.
    Set rstRemote = New ADODB.Recordset
    rstRemote.CursorType = adOpenForwardOnly
    rstRemote.LockType = adLockReadOnly
    rstRemote.Open "employees", cnnRemote, , , adCmdTable

'Print an employee telephone directory.
    Do Until rstRemote.EOF
        Debug.Print rstRemote.Fields("FirstName") & " " & _
            rstRemote.Fields("LastName") & " has extension " & _
            rstRemote.Fields("Extension") & "."
        rstRemote.MoveNext
    Loop

'Close the connection and recover the resource.
    cnnRemote.Close
    Set cnnRemote = Nothing

End Sub
```

The procedure starts by creating a new instance of an ADO **Connection** object. Then it defines a connection string and uses that string to open a connection to the AccCSNwindVariant database on the SQLSERVER server. Next, it opens a Forward-Only, read-only recordset based on the **Employees** table in AccCSNwindVariant. This type of recordset is acceptable for a report that makes a single pass through a recordset. The procedure prints the employee directory in the Immediate window with the help of a **Do** loop for passing through successive records.

The test environment for this chapter has an MSDE server on the local machine named LAPTOP, in addition to the SQL Server database manager on the machine named SQLSERVER. The syntax for referring to local servers is slightly different than the syntax for referring to remote ones. Instead of having to designate a specific server by name, you can simply specify **(local)**. Because my local computer also has the AccCSNwindVariant database installed, no other change in the procedure is necessary. The procedure is identical to the preceding one, with the exception of the one block that appears below. Notice the new server name. In practice, you might want to have users designate their own login account name or have them use a limited one with fewer privileges than sa:

```
'Open connection to AccCSNwindVariant database
'on the local server.
    Set cnnLocal = New ADODB.Connection
    strCnn = "Provider=sqloledb;" & _
        "Data Source=(local);" & _
        "Initial Catalog=AccCSNwindVariant;" & _
        "User Id=sa;Password=;"
    cnnLocal.Open strCnn
```

You can process views by using the same syntax that you use for tables. Simply enclose the view's name in quotes, just like you do for a table. You must still use the **adCmdTable** setting for the **Option** parameter. The companion CD-ROM includes a sample named **openViewOnRemoteServer** that demonstrates this approach.

Opening A Stored Procedure

Stored procedures can return recordsets. Your applications have more flexibility when they provide recordsets using stored procedures instead of tables, because you are not restricted to the tables in the current data source or even exact copies of the tables in the current data source. With stored procedures, you can filter records, compute new values, and aggregate field values across the records in a table.

The following procedure invokes the stored procedure named **Ten Most Expensive Products** and prints the 10 product names and prices in the Immediate window. Because the procedure name includes spaces, it must be in brackets. Notice also that the procedure uses an **Options** argument of **adCmdStoredProc**. This tells the ADO processor to expect a procedure name that contains SQL, not an actual SQL statement. Because the procedure always processes 10 records, the procedure for printing out the records uses a **For** loop that goes from 1 through 10. In other respects, the procedure for printing the return set from a stored procedure is identical to the procedure for printing an entire table:

```
Sub openProcedureOnRemoteServer()
Dim cnnRemoteRemote As ADODB.Connection
Dim rstRemote As ADODB.Recordset
Dim int1 As Integer

'Open connection to AccCSNwindVariant database
'on SQLSERVER server.
    Set cnnRemote = New ADODB.Connection
    strCnn = "Provider=sqloledb;" & _
        "Data Source=SQLSERVER;" & _
        "Initial Catalog=AccCSNwindVariant;" & _
        "User Id=sa;Password=;"
    cnnRemote.Open strCnn

'Open employee table.
    Set rstRemote = New ADODB.Recordset
    rstRemote.CursorType = adOpenForwardOnly
    rstRemote.LockType = adLockReadOnly
    rstRemote.Open "[Ten Most Expensive Products]", _
        cnnRemote, , , adCmdStoredProc

'Print prices for 10 products.
    For int1 = 1 To 10
        Debug.Print rstRemote.Fields(0) & " has a unit price " & _
            "of $" & rstRemote.Fields(1) & "."
        rstRemote.MoveNext
    Next int1

'Close the connection and recover the resource.
    cnnRemote.Close
    Set cnnRemote = Nothing

End Sub
```

Assigning CursorLocation Values

CursorLocation settings can profoundly affect performance, especially as table sources grow to even moderate size. The following sample demonstrates this with a recordset source of just over 19,000 records. It forms this recordset with a view based on the Cartesian product of the **Employees** and **Order Details** tables. The view's name is **vwLargeView**.

The sample opens its recordset source with either **adUseClient** or **adUseServer** as its **CursorLocation** setting. The **adUseServer** setting causes a procedure to progressively move through the records one at a time on the server. The **adUseClient** setting transfers the records to the local workstation so that procedures can access the records from a local workstation without returning to the server for each record.

The first procedure in the sample prompts for an instruction about which **CursorLocation** setting to use. The second procedure prepares a report and prints it in the Immediate window. It prints the cursor location and type as well as the start time, end time, and the duration for the task. You can adapt this general model for testing various combinations of database settings with your own data sources:

```
Sub openRemoteWithCursorLocation()
Dim cnnRemote As ADODB.Connection
Dim rstRemote As ADODB.Recordset
Dim start As Date, done As Date

'Open connection to AccCSNwindVariant database
'on SQLSERVER server.
    strCnn = "Provider=sqloledb;" & _
        "Data Source=SQLSERVER;" & _
        "Initial Catalog=AccCSNwindVariant;" & _
        "User Id=sa;Password=;"
    Set cnnRemote = New ADODB.Connection
    If MsgBox("Use local cursor?", vbYesNo, _
        "Client/Server Solutions With Access 2000") = vbYes Then
        cnnRemote.CursorLocation = adUseClient
    Else
        cnnRemote.CursorLocation = adUseServer
    End If
    cnnRemote.Open strCnn

'Open vwLargeView view; create the view in the remote
'database server before running the procedure.
'The sample uses the Cartesian product of the
'Employees and Order Details tables.
'Notice that the connection setting for CursorType silently
'overrides the recordset property setting.
    Set rstRemote = New ADODB.Recordset
    rstRemote.CursorType = adOpenKeyset
    rstRemote.LockType = adLockOptimistic
    rstRemote.Open "vwLargeView", cnnRemote, , , adCmdTable
    start = Now
    Do Until rstRemote.EOF
      temp = rstRemote.Fields(1)
      rstRemote.MoveNext
```

```
    Loop
    done = Now
    reportResults cnnRemote.CursorLocation, rstRemote.CursorType, _
        start, done
End Sub


Sub reportResults(cloc As Integer, ctype As Integer, _
    startedAt As Date, endedAt As Date)

    Debug.Print "Results for: "
    Select Case cloc
        Case adUseServer
            Debug.Print "       Cursor Location: adUseServer"
        Case adUseClient
            Debug.Print "       Cursor Location: adUseClient"
        Case Else
            Debug.Print "       Faulty Cursor Location setting"
    End Select
    Select Case ctype
        Case adOpenForwardOnly
            Debug.Print "       Cursor Type: adOpenForwardOnly"
        Case adOpenKeyset
            Debug.Print "       Cursor Type: adOpenKeyset"
        Case adOpenDynamic
            Debug.Print "       Cursor Type: adOpenDynamic"
        Case adOpenStatic
            Debug.Print "       Cursor Type: adStatic"
    End Select
    Debug.Print "Start time to nearest second: " & startedAt
    Debug.Print "End time to nearest second: " & endedAt
    Debug.Print "Difference in seconds: " & DateDiff("s", & _
        startedAt, endedAt)
End Sub
```

Figure 14.7 shows the results of running the procedures using an **adUseClient** setting and then an **adUseServer** setting. It took just 1 second to loop through the records with a local cursor, but it took 27 seconds to loop through the records with a server-side cursor. Results can vary depending on a wide range of factors, so it's a good idea to test for other settings and your particular databases.

This sample is instructive for a few reasons. First, the performance outcomes are drastically different. Second, you can see that ADO changes your settings if they conflict. For example, the program sets the cursor type to **adOpenKeyset**, but this setting conflicts with **adUseClient**, so the ADO interpreter silently changes the cursor type setting to **adStatic**. This happens in other contexts as well. Third, this sample presents a simple model that you can readily adapt for exploring database settings in your own custom applications.

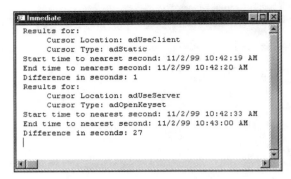

Figure 14.7
Sample output showing the results of processing the same data source with an **adUseClient** or an **adUseServer** setting.

Where To Go From Here

Throughout the previous chapters, we have explored the use of Access 2000 with SQL Server back ends, and the issues that will be new for you as a result of the differences between SQL Server and Access. I have also presented many of the possible ways in which you will implement and use the new Access Data Projects (ADPs) as a tool for working with complex, highly scalable environments.

In Chapter 15, I will move on to the greatest client/server environment of them all—the Internet. I will consider using Access 2000 with the Internet, beginning with some of the common, historical methods of using the product with the Internet, and finishing with a discussion over several chapters on the use of the new Data Access Page (DAP) technology included with Access 2000.

Part IV

The Internet With
Access 2000

Chapter 15

Introduction To Data Access Pages

Key Topics:

- ◆ *Data Access Pages For Web Front Ends*

- ◆ *Using Pivot-Style Controls With DAPs*

- ◆ *Using Office Web Controls With DAPs*

- ◆ *Different DAP Configurations*

- ◆ *Properties Of DAPs*

As you likely already know, a wide variety of means are at your disposal for placing front ends on your databases on the Web or on your corporate intranet. In addition to the many methods discussed elsewhere in this book—such as Active Server Pages (ASPs) and Visual Basic 6 WebObjects—and third-party products such as Cold Fusion or other server products, Access 2000 provides a very convenient method for converting your applications into Web pages that your users can easily access using a simple front end.

Understanding Data Access Pages (DAPs)

The primary tool for HTML-based publishing is called a *Data Access Page (DAP)*. Microsoft has integrated DAPs so closely into the Access Interactive Development Environment (IDE) that they've actually added them onto the Database window. Figure 15.1 shows the new DAP tab added to the Database window for Access 2000.

As you can see, the tab offers you three options for working with DAPs—creating with a wizard, creating from Design view, and editing a currently existing page. In the following sections we'll consider each of these options, as well as the Save As option that you can use to convert forms. We'll also consider some differences between DAPs and forms.

Probably the three most common uses of a DAP are as a vehicle for displaying and editing existing data, as a means for adding new

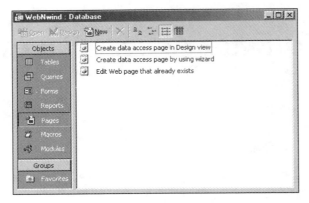

Figure 15.1
The new DAP tab (called Pages) in the Database window.

data, or as a method of displaying output only, using a report-style DAP page. Fortunately, Access provides numerous features that enable you to build DAPs that greatly ease the data-entry process for your users. Access also makes it easy for you to design DAPs that allow your users to view data but not modify it, view and modify data, or add new records only.

Strategies For Creating Data Access Pages

Needless to say, DAPs open up a whole new world of possibilities for database front-end design. Although they aren't necessarily the greatest thing ever, they're useful tools for responding to four specific needs: analyzing data, entering and editing data, making projections, and reviewing data. The following sections discuss how you can use DAPs to perform such tasks.

Analyzing Data

Arguably, the best way to analyze data from a Data Access Page is to use an Office PivotTable list control. The PivotTable control lets you reorganize data in different ways, but it downloads the necessary data only once (unless a change results in a change to recordset organization). The control's ability to provide data rapidly and in an interactive manner makes it very useful in DAP design. You can bind a PivotTable list to data in the database or use data from a Microsoft Excel spreadsheet. You can use the PivotTable list as the only control on a page or use it in combination with other controls. However, keep some important considerations in mind when working with PivotTable list controls:

♦ When using a PivotTable list on an ungrouped page, place the PivotTable list control and other controls in either the body or the data section.

♦ When using a PivotTable list on a grouped page, place the PivotTable list and any other bound controls in the data section.

♦ When using a PivotTable list on a grouped page, make sure the PivotTable list is in the innermost group level.

♦ When using a PivotTable list on a grouped page, if the PivotTable list is the only control in a section, delete or hide the navigation section for the group level that the PivotTable list is in.

♦ Finally, when using a PivotTable list on a grouped page, make sure the **DataPageSize** property in the Sorting And Grouping box is set to 1.

Modifying Or Entering Data

Perhaps the most common implementation of a DAP is as a Web-based form that users can employ to enter, edit, and delete data in the database. Though this type of DAP is very similar to a form, keep some important design points in mind when creating this type of page. Although most of the design rules for forms still hold, remember the following additional considerations:

♦ You can place controls in either the body or in the section. If you aren't binding the page to a data source, you can delete the section.

♦ Create only one group level for the page. The Sorting And Grouping box will list only one group record source. Note that if you do grouping for the page from within the Page Wizard, the wizard will automatically make the page read-only if you place grouping levels on the page.

♦ Make sure the **DataPageSize** property in the Sorting And Grouping box is set to 1.

♦ You should use the Office spreadsheet control (explained later) to perform calculations on the fields in a record. After you perform the calculations, you can either display the calculated values in the spreadsheet control or hide the control and display the calculated values in bound HTML controls.

♦ If you want to edit data from tables that have a one-to-many relationship, create one page that's bound to the table on the one side of the relationship and another page that's bound to the many side. Then you can use the Insert Hyperlink dialog box to create a link between the two pages. To display the data from both pages on a single browser page, you can use an HTML editor to create frames within the browser—specifying the one page as the left frame and the many page as the right frame.

Creating A DAP For Use In Making Projections

You can use the Office chart control to analyze trends, show patterns, and make comparisons on the data in your database. If you need to perform calculations on data, you can provide users with an enabled Office spreadsheet control in which they can do so. If you use a spreadsheet control in this fashion, be sure to keep in mind the following design considerations:

♦ When using an Office spreadsheet control on an ungrouped page, you can place the spreadsheet control and other controls in either the body or in the section. Again, you can delete the section if you don't need it.

♦ When using a spreadsheet control on a grouped page, place the spreadsheet control and other controls bound to fields in the database in the section. You can use a spreadsheet control in any group level.

♦ Make sure the **DataPageSize** property in the Sorting And Grouping box is set to 1 for the section that contains the spreadsheet control.

Using Pages For Data Review

Pages give you a way to let your users interact with large amounts of data across the Internet or a corporate intranet in a selective way. By expanding and collapsing groups of records, users can focus on just the data they want to see. Keep the following points in mind when you create a grouped page and want to make it load faster into Internet Explorer:

♦ Use bound HTML controls instead of text boxes.

♦ Make sure the **ExpandedByDefault** property is set to **No** for all group levels. Users will use the Expand control to expand the information they need.

♦ Make sure the **DataPageSize** property in the Sorting And Grouping box, which determines the number of records displayed in a group on a page, is set to a lower number rather than a higher number or to **All**. The lower the number, the faster the records display.

Describing The Data Access Page's Components

Like Access forms, DAPs contain a few sections, each of which has its own function and behavior. The three sections of an Access DAP are:

♦ *Caption*—The Caption section is used to display information that doesn't change from record to record (such as a page title).

♦ *Group Header*—Unlike forms, the Group Header section of a DAP is the main section—at least for the display of data (rather than the Detail section). It's the section that's used to display the data of the table or query underlying the DAP. As you'll see, the Group Header section can take on many different looks; it's very flexible and robust.

♦ *NavigationSection*—The NavigationSection is used to display navigation information about the record being viewed, and also lets the user perform tasks such as setting filters (unless you disable these features, as discussed later). Command buttons that control the DAP are often placed in the Group Header or NavigationSection of the DAP. An example would be a command button that allows the user to view all the projects associated with a particular client. Controls can also be used to help the user navigate around the records associated with the DAP.

Selecting The Correct Control For The Job

Windows programming in general, and Access programming in particular, isn't limited to just writing code. Your ability to design a user-friendly interface will often determine the success of your application. Access and the Windows programming environment offer a variety of controls; each is appropriate in different situations. The next sections discuss each control that the DAP structure supports, outlining when and how you should use each one.

Labels

Labels are used to display information to your users. Attached labels are automatically added to your DAP as you add other controls such as text boxes, drop-down list boxes, and so on. They can be deleted or modified as necessary. Their default captions are based on the **Caption** property of the field that underlies the control to which they are attached. If nothing has been entered into the **Caption** property of the field, the field name is used for the caption of the label.

The Label tool, found in the toolbox, can be used to add any text to the DAP. Click on the Label tool, and click and drag the label to place it on the DAP. Labels are often used to provide a description of the DAP or to supply instructions to users. You can customize labels by modifying their font, size, color, and so on. They can't be modified by the user at runtime, but they can be modified at runtime using Visual Basic for Applications (VBA) code.

Text Boxes

Text boxes are used to obtain information from the user. *Bound text boxes* display and retrieve field information, whereas *unbound text boxes* gather information from the user that's not related to a specific field in a specific record. For example, an unbound text box can be used to gather information from a user regarding report criteria.

Text boxes are automatically added to a DAP when you click and drag a field from the field list to the DAP and the **Display Control** property for the field is set to **Text Box**. Another way to add a text box to a DAP is to select the Text Box tool from the toolbox, and then click and drag to place the text box on the DAP. This process adds an unbound text box to the DAP. If you want to bind the text box to data, you must set its **Control Source** property.

Combo Boxes

Access offers several easy ways to add a combo box to a DAP. If the **Display Control** property of a field has been set to **Combo Box**, a combo box is automatically added to a DAP when the field is added to the DAP. The combo box automatically knows the source of its data as well as all its other important properties.

If the **Display Control** property of a field hasn't been set to **Combo Box**, the easiest way to add a combo box to a DAP is to use the Control Wizard. The Control Wizard, when selected, helps you to add combo boxes, list boxes, option groups, and subDAPs to your DAPs. Although all the properties set by the Combo Box Wizard can be set manually, using the wizard saves both time and energy. If you want the Combo Box Wizard to be launched when you add a combo box to the DAP, make sure the Control Wizard tool in the toolbox has been pressed (switched on) before you add the combo box. You'll learn more about adding combo boxes to your DAPs later in this chapter.

Combo boxes are extremely powerful controls. Though covering them in much detail is beyond the scope of this book, you'll use and analyze them in several different implementation environments over the course of this book's examples and solutions.

List Boxes

List boxes are very similar to combo boxes, but differ in three major ways:

♦ They consume more screen space.

♦ They let the user select only from the list that's displayed. This means that you can't type new values into a list box (as you can with a combo box).

♦ They can be configured to allow you to select multiple items.

As with a combo box, the **Display Control** property of a field can be set to **List Box**. If the **Display Control** property has been set to **List Box**, a list box is added to the DAP when the field is clicked and dragged from the field list to the DAP.

The List Box Wizard is almost identical to the Combo Box Wizard. After running the List Box Wizard, the list box properties affected by the wizard are the same as the combo box properties.

Checkboxes

Checkboxes are used when you want to limit your user to entering only one of two values. The values entered can be limited to Yes/No, True/False, or On/Off. You can add a checkbox to a DAP in several ways:

♦ Set the **Display Control** property of the underlying field to **Check Box**, and then click and drag the field from the field list to the DAP.

♦ Click on the Check Box tool in the toolbox, and then click and drag a field from the field list to the DAP. This method adds a checkbox to the DAP even if the **Display Control** property of the underlying field isn't a checkbox.

♦ Click on the Check Box tool in the toolbox, and then click and drag to add a checkbox to the DAP. The checkbox you've added is unbound. To bind the checkbox to data, you must set the **Control Source** property of the control.

Option Buttons

You can use option buttons alone or as part of an option group. An option button alone can be used to display a True/False value, but this isn't a standard use (checkboxes are standard for this purpose). As part of an option group, option buttons force the user to select from a mutually exclusive set of options. An example is payment type—credit card, cash, check, and so on.

Toggle Buttons

Like option buttons, toggle buttons can be used alone or as part of an option group. A toggle button by itself can display a True/False value, but this isn't a standard use. Toggle buttons are more commonly used as part of an option group, as discussed in the next section.

Option Groups

Option groups allow the user to select from a mutually exclusive set of options. They can comprise checkboxes, toggle buttons, or option buttons. The most common implementation of an option group is option buttons.

The easiest way to add an option group to a DAP is to use the Option Group Wizard. To ensure that the Option Group Wizard will run, make sure the Control Wizards button in the toolbox is selected. Click on Option Group in the toolbox, then click and drag to add the option group to the DAP. This will launch the Option Group Wizard.

Bound HTML Control

The Bound HTML control is, essentially, a "thin" text box control. You can use it within your DAPs to display information from a record source. In general, HTML controls will load faster through the browser than will text box controls. This is especially helpful in large, banded DAPs. Bound HTML controls are windowless controls, whereas the text boxes used in Internet Explorer are windowed controls. Thus, each text box requires a certain amount of overhead to be drawn on the screen.

If the controls wrap text in a way that you don't like, select the Bound HTML control, open the property sheet to the Format tab, and set the **Overflow** property to **Hidden**.

Note, however, the limitations of Bound HTML controls: You can't use them with updateable fields, and you can't index or filter based on their contents.

Scrolling Text Control

The Scrolling Text control, which the DAP toolbox includes, is actually the Microsoft Marquee ActiveX control. This control lets you place text within a rectangular area on a DAP, which will then scroll around the control based on the properties you specify. You might use this control to provide update information, advertising, or similar marquee-style displays on your DAPs.

Although the control can be bound to a data source, you're probably more likely to set the text the control displays within the Design view. Alternatively, you might use VBScript that you attach to the page to change the control's scrolling value based on actions that the user performs on the page (such as moving the mouse over a specific field, and so on).

Hyperlink And Bound Hyperlink Controls

The Hyperlink control lets you place hyperlinks on your DAPs—a necessary tool for helping users navigate around the DAPs that comprise the Web front end. When you insert a Hyperlink control onto a DAP, Access will display the Insert Hyperlink dialog box, as shown in Figure 15.2.

As you can see, the dialog box lets you insert a hyperlink to an existing file or Web page, to another DAP, or to an email address. It also lets you create a new page and insert a hyperlink to that new page on the current page.

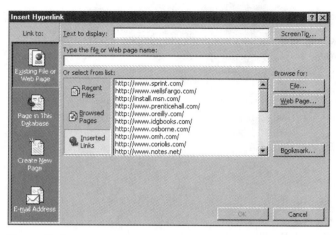

Figure 15.2
The Insert Hyperlink dialog box.

You can also use the Bound Hyperlink control, which lets you specify the hyperlink that appears within the page by binding the control to a **Hyperlink** field in a database. For example, if you have an **Employees** database, you might associate a **Hyperlink** field with each employee, which corresponds to that employee's email address. You can then use a **Bound Hyperlink** field on the DAP to display that email address with the employee information. The user could then click on the email address to send email to the employee in question. As the user navigates the database, moving from employee to employee, the value in the **Bound Hyperlink** field will change to reflect the value stored for each new record.

Other Controls You Can Use With DAPs

In addition to the standard controls detailed in the previous sections, you can use a large number of other controls with DAPs. In fact, you can insert any ActiveX control that supports Web downloading into a DAP. Table 15.1 lists some of these controls and their uses.

Each of the controls listed in Table 15.1 is included with the Access 2000 installation; however, a great number of third-party controls are available that you can also use when designing DAP pages.

Morphing A Control From One Format To Another

When you first build a DAP, you might not always make the best choice for the type of control to display each field on the DAP. Alternatively, you might make what you think is the best choice for the control only to find out later that it wasn't exactly what your user had in mind. Unfortunately, although you can easily convert a control type when working with forms, the DAP designer doesn't let you change the type of a control once it's placed. You must, instead, delete the existing control, and replace it with the new control.

Table 15.1 **Other ActiveX controls that you can use with DAPs.**

Control Name	Description
Expand	When you use grouping levels or other ordering controls in your DAPs, you may want to provide users with the ability to expand the detail information, or hide the detail information and view only summary information. The Expand control lets you do just that.
Hotspot Image	The Hotspot Image control lets you place an image onto a DAP and associate that image with a hyperlink. If the user clicks on the image, the browser will navigate to the hyperlink associated with the image inside the control.
Image	The Image control lets you embed an image onto your DAP page.
Line	The Line control lets you draw lines on your DAP page. You'll generally use this control either for decoration or to clarify the flow of a page for your users.
Movie	The Movie control lets you embed MPG, AVI, QuickTime, and other video files within your DAPs. In general, you'll likely provide additional script on the page that lets the user invoke this control. For example, your **Employees** database might include a link to a movie file that contains an introduction for each employee in the database. Users could then click on a button on the DAP that had VBScript behind it to load and play the movie file within the control.
Office Chart	The Office Chart control lets you display charts and graphs within your DAPs. You can use the properties of the control to specify where the chart obtains its data, the appearance of the chart, and so on.
Office PivotTable	A PivotTable is a table that summarizes, or cross-tabulates, large amounts of data. PivotTables are very interactive because the user can rotate the data, changing the way it's displayed. PivotTables are in widespread use in Excel, and the control lets you display them within your DAP using Access table data. PivotTables are excellent for accessing and viewing data stored in OLAP cubes.
Office Spreadsheet	The Office Spreadsheet control is a thin-client control that lets you display data from Access within a DAP in a spreadsheet-style format.
Record Navigation	The Record Navigation control lets you provide a navigation bar to the user. If you use the Page Wizard to design your DAP, the wizard will always insert the Record Navigation bar at the bottom of the DAP. If you design your DAP from scratch, you'll need to insert this control manually (alternatively, you can design your own record navigation interface).
Rectangle	The Rectangle control lets you draw rectangles onto a form. You'll generally use this control either for decoration or to clarify the flow of a page for your users.

Let's take some time, before discussing all the different types of objects and so on that you can use with your DAPs, to look briefly at the process of creating a new DAP, and some of the steps you will follow during that process.

Creating A New DAP

You can create a new DAP in several ways. The most common is to select the DAP tab of the Database window and click on New. The New Data Access Page dialog box appears, as shown in Figure 15.3.

This dialog box lets you select from the multitude of options available for creating a new DAP. DAPs can be created from scratch using Design view or with the help of six wizards. We'll cover these wizards briefly before moving on to the process of creating a DAP from scratch. Even the most experienced developers employ DAP wizards to complete certain tasks.

Creating A DAP Using The Page Wizard

The easiest way to get started with DAPs is to use the Page Wizard to create your first page. The steps to creating the DAP are as follows:

1. Inside the database window, double-click on the Create A New Data Access Page By Using Wizard option. Access will display the Page Wizard dialog box, as shown in Figure 15.4.

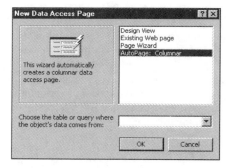

Figure 15.3
The New Data Access Page dialog box.

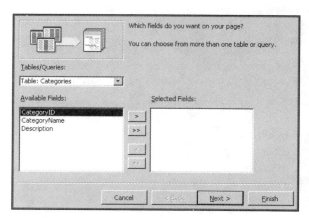

Figure 15.4
The Page Wizard dialog box.

2. Select the table to work from to create the page. Using the Chap15.mdb database, select the **Employees** table. Next, click on the >> button to copy all the fields to the page. Click on Next to move to the next dialog box in the wizard.

3. The next dialog box asks if you want to add any grouping levels to the page (much as the Report Wizard does). In this case, select Group By Title. When you finish, the dialog box will look similar to Figure 15.5.

4. The next dialog box asks you to select sorting levels to use with the DAP. For this example, select **LastName** and **FirstName** as your sorting fields. Click on Next to move to the last dialog box.

5. The last dialog box lets you name the page and open it for viewing or additional design. Click on the Finish button to exit the wizard.

Creating A DAP Using The AutoPage Wizard

The second most common way to create a simple DAP is to use the AutoPage Wizard. The AutoPage Wizard creates a DAP that contains all fields (except fields that store pictures) and records in the underlying table, query, or view. The steps to creating the DAP with the AutoPage Wizard are as follows:

1. Within the Database window, make sure the display is set to Pages. Then, click on the New Page icon at the top of the window. Access will display the New Data Access Page dialog box.

2. Select the AutoPage: Columnar option, then choose the table or query to work from to create the page within the drop-down list. Using the Chap15.mdb database, select the **Employees** table. Next, click on the OK button.

The AutoPage Wizard will generate a simple DAP with all the fields in the underlying table and a navigation bar across the bottom. Figure 15.6 shows the simple page created by the wizard.

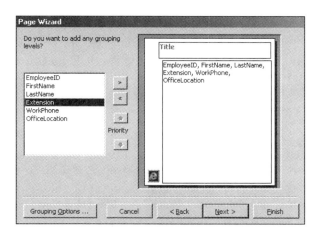

Figure 15.5
The Page Wizard with Group By Title selected.

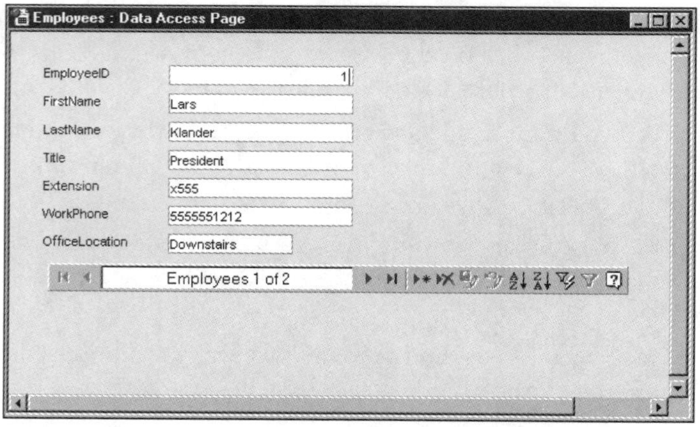

Figure 15.6
The simple page generated by the AutoPage Wizard.

Note that Access applies the default theme to the page. If you haven't set a default theme, it uses the Straight Edge theme. Additionally, when you create a page using the AutoPage Wizard, Access automatically saves the page as an HTML file in the current folder and adds a shortcut to the page in the Database window.

Creating A DAP From Design View

Although the DAP wizards are extremely powerful and useful, in many cases it's better to build a DAP from scratch, especially if you're building a DAP that's not bound to data. To create a DAP without using a wizard, click on the Pages tab, then click on New. The New Data Access Page dialog box appears. Select Design view (the default choice). If your DAP will be bound to data, use the drop-down included in the New Data Access Page dialog to select the table or query that will serve as the foundation for the DAP. Click on OK. The DAP Design window will appear as shown in Figure 15.7.

Once you have created the DAP—by whatever means are most appropriate for your current efforts—you can go ahead and begin adding objects to the DAP and manipulating the objects directly. The next sections discuss how to perform these activities.

Adding Fields To The DAP

Fields can be easily added to a DAP using the Field List window, because the Field List window contains all the fields that are part of the record source for the DAP. For example, in Figure 15.7 the record source of the DAP is **qryAssetsByEmployee**. The fields listed in the Field List window are the fields that are part of the query. The record source for the DAP is the table or query that underlies the DAP. To add fields to a DAP, follow these steps:

1. Make sure the Field List window is visible. If it's not, click on the Field List button on the toolbar.

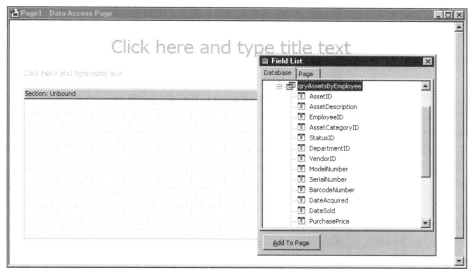

Figure 15.7
The DAP Design window.

2. Locate the field you want to add to the DAP. Click and drag the field from the field list to the location on the DAP where you want the field to appear. The location you select becomes the upper-left corner of the text box. The attached label appears to the left of where you dropped the control.

To add multiple fields to a DAP at the same time, select several fields from the field list. Use the Ctrl key to select multiple noncontiguous fields or the Shift key to select multiple contiguous fields. Click and drag any of the selected fields to the DAP. All selected fields are added to the DAP at once. Although Microsoft has indicated that multiple-field selection functionality will be supported in the release of the Office 2000 product (or perhaps in a service pack for the Office 2000 product), it is *not* supported in the release version of Office 2000.

Manipulating DAP Objects

The easiest way to select a single object on a DAP is to click on it. When the object is selected, you can move it, size it, or change any of its properties. Selecting multiple objects is a bit trickier and can be done in several ways. Different methods are more efficient in different situations. To select multiple objects, you can hold down the Shift key and click on each object that you want to select. Each selected object is surrounded by selection handles, indicating that it's selected.

You can also select objects by lassoing them. To lasso objects, the objects must be located close to one another on the DAP. Place your mouse pointer on a blank area of the DAP (not over any objects), then click and drag. You'll see that a thin line appears around the objects that your mouse pointer is encircling. When you let go, any objects that were anywhere within the lasso, including those that were only partially surrounded, are selected. If you want to deselect any of the selected objects to exclude them from the selection, hold down your Shift key and click on the object you want to deselect. Again, as noted previously, although Microsoft has indicated that multiple-field selection functionality will be supported in the release of the Office 2000 product, it was *not* supported within the beta was used while writing this book—using either the Shift+click method or the lassoing method.

One other useful way to select multiple objects is to use the horizontal and vertical rulers that appear at the edges of the DAP Design window. Click and drag within the ruler. Notice that as you click and drag on the vertical ruler, two horizontal lines appear, indicating which objects will be selected. As you click and drag across the horizontal ruler, two vertical lines appear, indicating the selection area. When you let go of your mouse, any objects that are anywhere within the lines are selected. As with the process of lassoing, to remove any objects from the selection, hold down your Shift key and click on the object you want to deselect.

Moving Things Around On The DAP

To move a control along with its attached label, you don't need to select it first. Place your mouse over the object and click and drag. An outline appears, indicating the new location of the object. When the object reaches the desired position, release the mouse. An attached label automatically moves with its corresponding control.

To move more than one object at a time, you must first select the objects you want to move. Select the objects using any of the methods outlined in the previous section. Place your mouse over any of the selected objects and click and drag. An outline appears, indicating the proposed new position for the objects. Release the mouse when you've reached the desired position.

Sometimes, you want to move a control independent of its attached label, which requires a special technique. If you click on a control, such as a text box, you see that as you move your mouse over the border of the control, a hand appears with five fingers pointing upward. If you click and drag, both the control and the attached label move as a unit. The relationship between them is maintained. Placing your mouse pointer over the larger handle in the upper-left corner of the object makes the mouse pointer appear as a hand with only the index finger pointing upward. If you click and drag here, the control moves independently of its attached label. The relationship between the objects changes.

Aligning Objects To One Another

Access makes it easy to align objects within a DAP. Notice that the attached labels of both the objects are selected. To align any objects (even objects of different types), select Format | Alignment And Sizing. Access displays the Alignment And Sizing toolbar, as shown in Figure 15.8.

Figure 15.8
The Alignment And Sizing toolbar.

You can align the left, right, top, or bottom edges of any objects on a DAP. You can also align the center of each object.

Don't confuse the Alignment And Sizing toolbar with the Align tools on the Formatting toolbar. The Alignment And Sizing toolbar aligns objects one to the other, whereas the Align tools on the Formatting toolbar align the text of an object within its borders.

Using The Snap To Grid Feature

The Snap To Grid feature determines whether the objects snap to the gridlines on the DAP as you move and size them. This feature is located under the Format menu. If you turn this feature off (it's a toggle), objects can be moved and sized without regard for the gridlines.

Most developers leave the Snap To Grid feature on all the time. However, you can use a special trick to temporarily deactivate the feature when needed. To do this, hold down your Ctrl key as you click and drag to move objects. The Snap To Grid setting is then ignored.

DAP Control Sizing Techniques

Just as there are several ways to move objects, there are also several ways to size objects. When an object is selected, each handle (except for the handle in the upper-left corner of the object) can be used to size the object. The handles at the top and bottom of the object allow you to change the height of the object. Those at the left and right of the object allow you to change the width of the object. The handles in the upper-right, lower-right, and lower-left corners of the object allow you to change the width and height of the object simultaneously. To size an object, place your mouse pointer over a sizing handle and click and drag. You can select multiple objects and size them at the same time. Each of the selected objects increases or decreases in size by the same amount. The relative sizes of the objects remain intact.

Access provides several powerful methods of sizing multiple objects, found on the Alignment And Sizing toolbar:

♦ *Size Height*—Sizes the selected objects to the height of the tallest object within the selection.

♦ *Size Width*—Sizes the selected objects to the width of the widest object within the selection.

♦ *Size Height/Width*—Sizes the selected objects to the width of the narrowest object and the height of the shortest object within the selection.

Modifying Object Tab Order

The tab order for the objects on a DAP is determined by the order in which you add the objects to the DAP. This order isn't necessarily appropriate for the user, so it might become necessary to modify the tab order of the objects on the DAP. Unfortunately, unlike forms, DAPs don't have a Tab Order dialog box. Instead, you have to manually set the **TabIndex** property of the controls on the DAP to ensure that they're in the order you desire.

Adding A Combo Box To A DAP

To add a combo box to a DAP, select the Dropdown List tool in the toolbox. Click and drag to place the Dropdown List control on the DAP. The Combo Box Wizard launches. In the first dialog box of the wizard, you're asked whether you want the combo box to look up the values in a table or query or whether you prefer to type the values yourself. You should select the first option if your combo box is going to be used to select the data that's stored in a field. An example would be the state associated with a particular client.

Most developers rarely, if ever, use the second option, which requires that you type the values for the combo box. Populating a combo box this way makes it difficult to maintain. Every time you want to add an entry to the combo box, your application must be modified.

The second step of the Combo Box Wizard lets you select a table or query to populate the combo box. For optimal performance, you should select a query. The third step of the Combo Box Wizard allows you to select the fields that appear in your combo box.

The fourth step of the Combo Box Wizard lets you specify the width of each field in the combo box. Access will recommend that the key column for the table or query be hidden. The idea is that the user will see the meaningful English description while Access worries about storing the appropriate key value into the record.

The fifth and final step of the Combo Box Wizard prompts for the text that becomes the attached label for the combo box. Pressing the Finish button completes the process, building the combo box and filling in all its properties with the appropriate values.

As you can see, working with DAPs is, in many ways, very similar to the Access forms that you are used to manipulating. However, as you have seen, and would expect, there are some differences. Before getting into such issues as pivot tables, it is worthwhile for you to understand the different DAP properties at your disposal.

Understanding And Using DAP Properties

DAPs have many properties that can be used to affect the look and behavior of the DAP. The properties are broken down into three categories—Format, Data, and Other. To view a DAP's properties, you must select the DAP in one of two ways:

◆ Click on the DAP Selector (the blue bar across the top of the DAP designer window).

◆ Select Edit | Select Page (Ctrl+R).

After you select the DAP, you should choose View | Properties to display the DAP's properties (or click on the Properties button on the toolbar). Alternately, you can right-click on the DAP and select the Properties option from the pop-up menu.

Working With The Properties Window

After a DAP has been selected for design work, setting DAP properties (and the properties of any DAP components) is a simple task. Determining what DAP properties to set isn't quite so simple; many people have suggested that DAP design is more of an art than a science, requiring nothing so much as experience to develop quality interfaces. To view the properties for a DAP, click on the Properties button on the toolbar. Access then displays the Properties window.

Notice that the Properties window consists of four tabs: Format, Data, Other, and All. Many developers prefer to view all the DAP's properties at once (in which case you can select the All tab), but a DAP has a total of more than 50 properties. Rather than viewing all the properties at once, try viewing the properties by category.

The Format category includes all the physical attributes of the DAP. These attributes affect the DAP's appearance. An example is the DAP's background color. The Data category includes all the properties that relate to the data to which the DAP is bound. An example is the DAP's underlying record source. The Other category contains a small number of properties that don't fit into either of the other two categories.

Format Properties

The Format properties of a DAP affect its physical appearance. DAPs have 26 Format properties, as detailed in the following list:

- **Background**—The **Background** property lets you specify a file name for a background to use with the page (which might be a corporate logo or a similar graphic).

- **Background Color**—The **Background Color** property lets you set the background color for the DAP. This property always defaults to **#FFFFFF** (white), but can be set to any color in the color table. If you use a background that fills the page, this property has no effect.

- **BackgroundPositionX**—This property lets you specify where to place the background horizontally on the page—at the left side, centered, or at the right side. You can also specify a distance from the left edge of the page as a percentage of the page's total size.

- **BackgroundPositionY**—This property lets you specify where to place the background vertically on the page—at the top, centered, or at the bottom. You can also specify a distance from the top edge of the page as a percentage of the page's total size.

- **BackgroundRepeat**—This property lets you specify whether to repeat the background image (tiling) or simply place one copy on the page. You can control the nature of the repeating as well—multiple copies across, multiple copies down, and so on.

- **BorderColor**—The **BorderColor** property lets you specify the color of the page border.

- **BorderStyle**—The **BorderStyle** property lets you specify the style of the border. The default is **Inset**.

- **BorderWidth**—The **BorderWidth** property lets you specify the size of the border. The default is **Medium**; additional values are **Small** and **Large**.

- **Display**—The **Display** property lets you specify how the page will be displayed. It allows you to select from seven options; whichever option you select will become the default view for the DAP. These options define how the page's contents appear, and are important considerations when using a PivotTable control or other Web component.

- **FgColor**—The **FgColor** property lets you specify the default foreground color for all controls on the sheet. You can override this setting for individual controls by setting the control's **Color** property.

- **FontFamily**—The **FontFamily** property lets you specify what font family to use for the fonts on a DAP. The default is **Tahoma**.

- **FontSize**—The **FontSize** property lets you specify the default font size for the page.

- **FontStyle**—The **FontStyle** property lets you specify additional characteristics about the default font, including whether or not it's italicized, underlined, superscript, subscript, and so on.

- **FontVariant**—The **FontVariant** property lets you specify variant characteristics about the default font. Other than **Normal**, the other option for this property is **Small-Caps**.

- **FontWeight**—The **FontWeight** property lets you specify characteristics about the font's display, including **Bold**, **Bolder**, **Lighter**, and various intensity values. The default is **Normal**.

- **Grid X, Grid Y**—The **Grid X** and **Grid Y** properties can be used to modify the spacing of the horizontal and vertical lines that appear in the DAP when in Design view. By setting these properties, you can affect the precision of the placement of objects on the DAP when the Snap To Grid option is active.

- **Height**—The **Height** property lets you specify the height of the page. The default is **Auto**, which determines the page's height based on its contents.

- **Left**—The **Left** property lets you specify the left-most position of the page. Again, this is generally automatically determined by the page's contents.

- **Overflow**—The **Overflow** property lets you specify how the page will display contents that exceed the size of the containing controls. The default is **Visible**. You can also choose **Hidden** or **Scroll**, which forces the control to scroll data from right to left inside the control.

- **Position**—The **Position** property provides you with further control over how the page appears within the Web browser. If you use frames, Active Server Pages (ASPs), JScript menus, or similar additional objects within the browser, and embed the DAP within them, or when you are inheriting style sheets, you will want to set the position to **Relative**. The default is **Static**.

♦ **TextAlign**—The **TextAlign** property lets you specify the default alignment for text on the page, whether within Label, Text Box, or other controls. You can override this property for each control on the DAP.

♦ **Top**—The **Top** property is used to specify the top of the DAP. This option defaults to **Auto** and generally won't be changed unless you have a specific requirement to do so. You might want to set this property manually when you're inheriting style sheets from elsewhere on the Web site and have display specifics within the style sheet that appears at the top of the page.

♦ **Visibility**—The **Visibility** property specifies whether the page is visible or hidden. It defaults to **Inherit**, which means its visibility will be set by the controlling page that opens the page.

♦ **Width**—The **Width** property is used to specify the width of the DAP. This option is most often set graphically by clicking and dragging to select an appropriate size for the DAP. You might want to set this property manually when you want more than one DAP to be exactly the same size.

♦ **ZIndex**—The **ZIndex** of the page specifies where it will appear when displayed. In general, the **ZIndex** is automatically determined based on what is already open in the application. However, if a page must always appear in front, setting the **ZIndex** will let you force where the computer displays the page.

Data Properties

You'll use the Data properties of a DAP to control the source for the DAP's data, to specify what actions the user can take on the data within the DAP, and to determine how the data within the DAP is locked in a multiuser environment. A DAP contains seven Data properties, which are detailed within the following list:

♦ **ConnectionString**—The **ConnectionString** is the ADO connect string to the data source for the page. It includes such values as the provider name, the nature of the connection, whom the user logs in as, and the actual name of the data source itself. Without a **ConnectionString**, a DAP is treated as unbound.

♦ **Data Entry**—The **Data Entry** property is used to determine whether your users can only add records within a DAP. Set this property to **Yes** if you don't want your users to be able to view or modify existing records but you do want them to be able to add new records.

♦ **DefaultControlType**—Specifies the default control type for the page. Valid values are **Text Box** or **Bound HTML**.

♦ **DisplayAlerts**—Controls whether the page will display database alerts to the user. The default is **True**.

♦ **MaxRecords**—Controls the maximum number of records displayable within a single page. Although not important for data-entry–style pages, this value can be important if you're using DAPs as report pages and returning large sets of records. The default value is **10,000**.

♦ **RecordsetType**—The **RecordsetType** property is used to specify whether the recordset for the DAP is a read-only Snapshot or an updateable Snapshot. DAPs support *only* Snapshot-type recordsets—you can't, for example, set this value to Dynaset.

♦ **UseRemoteProvider**—Lets you specify whether the user should use a provider on the local machine (preferable) or a provider on the remote machine (the database server) to get the data to fill the page.

Other Properties

In addition to the DAP properties detailed in the previous sections, some DAP properties appear only under the Other tab (and under the All tab). These properties control a variety of different features, as shown in the following list of six commonly-used Other properties:

♦ **Title**—The **Title** property specifies the title to display in the browser's window bar when the user accesses the page.

♦ **BaseURL**—The **BaseURL** property specifies the **BaseURL** for the page. This consideration is important if, for example, you place certain types of relative hyperlinks (as opposed to absolute hyperlinks) onto the page. In such cases, the browser will resolve the relative hyperlink from the **BaseURL** value. Using **BaseURL**s often simplifies Web site administration—making it easier to relocate pages without breaking links.

♦ **Dir**—The **Dir** property allows you to specify how the contents of the page are placed within the designer. The default is **Not Set**, which lets you place them as you desire. The other two settings are **Ltr**, which left-justifies all the contents of the page, and **Rtl**, which right-justifies all the contents of the page. Again, you can overload this setting for specific controls with the control's **Dir** property.

♦ **InheritStyleSheets**—The **InheritStyleSheets** property controls whether the page inherits style sheets used on your Web site. This property is particularly important in intranet applications, where most pages on the site share a common style sheet. Telling the page to inherit the style sheet results in the style sheet being applied to the page, just as it would if the page was a standard HTML document.

♦ **LinkColor**—The **LinkColor** property is used to specify the default color for hyperlinks on the page. You'll generally use it in conjunction with the **AlinkColor** and **VlinkColor** properties, which also control the appearance of hyperlinks.

♦ **NodeValue**—This property is not implemented in Access 2000, but is reserved for further development by Microsoft.

Considering The Available Control Properties

Although many different properties are available for DAPs, these properties will be consistent from DAP to DAP. Control properties, on the other hand, will vary significantly, depending on the type of control you're working with. The more common properties are covered in this section. More individualized properties are covered throughout the book as they apply to a specific topic, and you can find more about any property from within the Access online help file.

Format Properties Of A Control

Though control properties differ, Access groups them into the same three categories that it groups DAP properties into: Format, Data, and Other. The first of the property sets is the Format category. The Format category's values will vary. However, most of the Format properties are consistent with the Page Format properties. Some of the most common properties are shown in the following list:

♦ **Left, Top, Width, Height**—These properties are used to set the position and size of the control. They're generally expressed in fractions of an inch.

♦ **BackgroundColor, BackgroundImage, BackgroundPositionX, BackgroundPositionY, BackgroundRepeat**—The Background properties control the background of the control. Their values are consistent with property sets for the page; however, you can specify an individual image as a background for each control on the page.

♦ **Position**—The **Position** property lets you modify how the control is placed on the form. The default is **absolute**; however, if you set specific values for the page's **Top** and **Left** properties, you can set the control's position as being relative to these values.

Data Properties Of A Control

Just as you'll typically affiliate a DAP with a data source—a database that you connect it to with the **ConnectionString** property—you'll typically create sections on that DAP that correspond to specific data sources—such as recordsets. You'll then affiliate the controls on your DAP with specific items within that data source. Generally, each field in the record source will correspond to one control in the DAP's area for that record source. The following list describes the common control data properties to help you format the control's output correctly:

♦ **AlternateDataSource**—This property lets you instruct the control to get data from a source other than the default data source for the section on the page. For example, a combo box might use a query as an alternate record source.

♦ **Control Source**—The **Control Source** property is used to specify the field from the record source that's associated with that particular control. A control source can also be any valid Access expression.

◆ **DataFormatAs**—This property allows you to specify a format string or other format information to control how data in the control (returned from the data source) is displayed within the page.

◆ **Default Value**—The **Default Value** property of a control determines the value that's assigned to new records entered within the DAP. This property can be set within the field properties. A default value set at the field level is automatically inherited into the DAP. The default value set for the control overrides the default value set at the field level.

◆ **TotalType**—The **TotalType** property lets you specify summary information to place within the control. You'll generally use this property when you're creating a report-type DAP.

Other Properties Of A Control

Just as with DAPs, in addition to the Format and Data properties, most controls have other miscellaneous properties, which Access groups together under the Other tab in the Properties window. The following list describes some of the most common properties:

◆ **ID**—Employ the **ID** property to name the control. This name is used when you refer to the control in code. It's also displayed in various drop-down lists that show all the controls on a DAP. It's very important to name your controls, because named controls improve the readability of your code and facilitate the process of working with Access DAPs and other objects (and naming doesn't mean Text1, Text2; it means meaningful names for Access objects).

◆ **Disabled**—Similar to the form control's **Enabled** property, this property lets you specify whether a control is enabled or disabled.

◆ **ReadOnly**—The **ReadOnly** property specifies whether the user can change the value displayed within a bound control. Typically, this property inherits from the data source for the control.

◆ **Tab Index**—The **Tab Index** property is used to set the tab order for the control. Most developers generally set the **Tab Index** property using View | Tab Order, rather than by setting the value directly within the **Tab Index** property of the control.

◆ **Wrap**—When the user reaches the "end" of a control, some controls will automatically "wrap" text to the next line. This property lets you control whether the page inserts a hard return (**Hard** setting) or a soft return (**Soft** setting) when the control wraps the text.

Bound, Unbound, And Calculated Controls

Important differences exist between bound and unbound controls. Unbound controls are used to display information to the user or gather information from the user that isn't going to be stored within your database. Examples of unbound controls include the following:

◆ A label providing instructions to the user

◆ A logo placed on a DAP

♦ A combo or text box placed on a DAP so the user can enter report criteria

♦ A rectangle placed on the DAP to logically group several controls

Bound controls are used to display and modify information stored in a database table. A bound control automatically appears in the DAP specified in its **Display Control** property. The control automatically inherits many of the attributes that were assigned to the field to which the control is bound.

A Calculated control is a special type of control that displays the results of an expression. The data within a Calculated control can't be modified by the user. The control's value automatically changes as the values within its expression are changed. For instance, the Sales Total within an invoice DAP would change as the Price or Quantity of different objects changes.

Adding A PivotTable List Control To A DAP

As you saw earlier in this chapter, the PivotTable list control is one of the most useful controls for interactive page design with Access. It does have its limitations, however; although you can rearrange the layout in a PivotTable list and set properties to affect its look and behavior, you can't ever add, delete, or change the stored values in the control in a DAP.

To add a PivotTable list control to a DAP, you need to perform a pair of steps. Firstly, from the Design view, make sure that the toolbox is displayed. Next, within the toolbox, select the Office PivotTable component. Click on the page and drag until the control is the size you want and until it displays the entire toolbar.

What you do next with the PivotTable depends on what kind of data you want to display within the control. To use the current Access or SQL Server database as the data source for the PivotTable list (that is, the database that the page is bound to), first display the page's Field List dialog box (select View | Field List). Next, drag from the Field List dialog box the table or query for the DAP to use with the PivotTable. Alternatively, you can drag individual fields from a single record source or multiple record sources, one field at a time.

When you create a PivotTable list by dragging fields from the field list, Microsoft Access automatically sets the Data Source control option in the PivotTable properties to MSODSC, an acronym for Microsoft Online Data-Source Control. This predefined system value specifies that Access will use the same data source for the PivotTable list as it does for the page itself.

The steps are a little bit different to use an external data source for the PivotTable list. To use an external data source, perform the following steps:

1. Right-click on the control and select Property Toolbox from the pop-up menu to display the PivotTable Property Toolbox.

2. Within the Property Toolbox, click on the Data Source bar. The Property Toolbox will look similar to Figure 15.9.

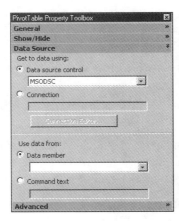

Figure 15.9
The Property Toolbox for the PivotTable control.

3. Next, click on the Connection option. The dialog box will enable the button labeled Connection Editor. Click on the Connection Editor button, and Access will display the Data Link Properties dialog box, as shown in Figure 15.10.

4. Within the Data Link Properties dialog box, click on the Provider tab. The dialog box will display a list of installed OLE DB providers. Select the OLE DB provider you want to use to retrieve the data from the list.

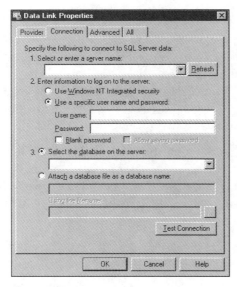

Figure 15.10
The Data Link Properties dialog box.

5. Next, click on the Connection tab, where you will provide the necessary connection information to the data you want to use for the PivotTable list. The connection string will be similar to the ADO connection string you would use to connect to the database. If you need assistance with the dialog box, you can click on the Help button for more information about establishing the connection. You can also click on the Test Connection button to ensure that the program is able to successfully connect to the data source. After you finish the connection, click on OK to exit the dialog box.

Warning

Once you set a connection, you should not move the source database; if you do, you will need to update the connection information in all the DAPs that access that database. Similarly, you should be careful about moving DAP HTML pages, as the database may not be able to locate them either, and could cause your program's execution to halt.

After selecting a connection, choose one of the following options from within the Use Data From section of the PivotTable Property Toolbox:

♦ To use the data from a specific record source within the database, click on the Data Member option button, then select the element you want from the drop-down list.

♦ To use a query or command, such as a SQL statement, to select the data, click on the Command Text option button, then type the query or command in the text box. Make sure your query syntax conforms to the specifications for the external data source.

Finish the PivotTable list by arranging the layout and using the toolbar in the PivotTable list and the PivotTable Property Toolbox to add totals, set properties, and so on until the control looks and behaves the way you want.

You should keep a few important considerations in mind when working with the PivotTable control within your Data Access Pages. These include the following:

♦ To create a PivotTable list that uses data from an Excel worksheet, you have to publish the data to a Web page from Excel. If you then want to turn the exported Web page into a DAP, you need to open it in Access, and then add controls bound to Access or SQL Server database data.

♦ When you have a Web Component control bound to an external data source on the same page with controls bound to an Access database or a SQL Server database, the component control will use a *different data source control* than the rest of the page. This may result in somewhat slower page loading.

♦ When you add a PivotTable list to a grouped page, a PivotTable list appears for each unique group and contains only records for that group. For example, on a page grouped by month with a PivotTable list containing sales information, there will be a PivotTable list for each month, which contains only the sales data for that month.

> **Warning**
> *You can't display the PivotTable for more than one group at a time within a single page.*

Adding An Office Spreadsheet Control To A DAP

As you've learned, you can add a spreadsheet control to a DAP to provide some of the same capabilities you have in a Microsoft Excel worksheet. You can enter values, add formulas, apply filters, and so on. You can enter raw data in the spreadsheet, import data from an external source (a Web page or a text file), or use data from other data sources in your business—including other controls on the same page. To add the Office Spreadsheet control, perform the following steps:

1. Within the toolbox, click on the Office Spreadsheet tool.
2. Click on the DAP, then drag until the control is the size you want.
3. Within the resulting control, enter the data and formulas you want to use or right-click on the control to display the Property Toolbox. Within the Property Toolbox, enter the address from which the control should import the data. You can even tell the control to update the data it displays every time it loads within the page.

You can also use the scripting model for DAPs to direct and manage the performance of the spreadsheet control at runtime.

Scripting With Data Access Pages

As you've seen in previous chapters, most Access objects are exposed to the Visual Basic for Applications (VBA) object model, which lets you apply program control to the user's actions. As you might expect, because they're designed for distribution through a browser, Data Access Pages are a bit different.

DAPs expose their functionality through VBScript, a subset and derivative of the Visual Basic programming language. Like Visual Basic, VBScript is event-oriented; most of your code with DAPs will manipulate VBScript in the background to accomplish responses to events. Moreover, most of the code in VBScript is very similar to VBA code. For example, the following script sequence is evoked whenever the user moves the mouse over the AssetDescription control:

```
<SCRIPT event=onmouseover for=AssetDescription language=vbscript>
<!--
EmployeeID_Label.innerText = "Changed!"
-->
</SCRIPT>
```

As you can see, the event is called **onmouseover** and is the Internet Explorer equivalent to the VB **MouseOver** event. The code within the event changes the caption of the **EmployeeID_Label** control to **"Changed!"** Presumably, there's other code elsewhere (like the **onmouseover** event for the entire page) that changes the caption back to its normal value.

In general, event scripting in DAPs takes the place of event code in Access forms and reports. The next section details how you enter a script that's associated with a given control on a DAP.

Note

As a side note, the scripting environment for Access is based on Microsoft Developer Studio and Visual InterDev. Although there are some changes in appearance from the VBA environment that you're used to, getting comfortable with the scripting environment won't take long.

Calculating A Total On A Grouped DAP

As you've learned, you can use certain fields within your DAPs to represent totals or other summary information. To create a field that calculates a total, perform the following steps:

1. Open the DAP in Design view.

2. Add the controls that are bound to fields you'll use in the expression to the page.

3. Click on the Bound HTML tool in the Toolbox, and draw the control onto the page where you want the control's upper-left corner to be.

4. Display the Properties sheet for the newly placed Bound HTML control.

5. In the **ControlSource** property for the control, enter an alias and an appropriate expression. For example, if you want to compute the salary for an employee and format it as currency, with the two component fields having the names **HourlyWage** and **AnnualHours**, enter the following expression in the **ControlSource** property for the Bound HTML control:

```
Salary: Format(HourlyWage * AnnualHours, "$###,##0.00")
```

If you don't want to display the values in the fields used in the expression when the user views the page, you can hide or delete the controls. To hide the controls, set their **Visibility** property to **Hidden**. If a page is based on a query, you can put the expression in the page's underlying query. If you're going to calculate totals for groups of records, it's easier to use the name of a calculated field.

Note that you should really apply this method only to simple calculations involving straightforward math. If you need to do complex calculations instead, which may or may not use spreadsheet functions, you should probably use the Office Spreadsheet control.

Understanding Themes

A *theme* is a set of unified design elements and color schemes for bullets, fonts, horizontal lines, background images, and other DAP elements. A theme helps you easily create professional and well-designed DAPs. Microsoft provides you with a large number of themes that install with the Access product.

When you apply a theme to a DAP, the following elements are customized in your Data Access Page:

- Body and heading styles
- Background color or graphic
- Table border color
- Horizontal lines
- Bullets
- Hyperlink colors
- Controls

You can apply a theme for the first time, apply a different theme, or remove a theme using Format | Theme. When you select the option, Access displays the Theme dialog box, as shown in Figure 15.11.

You can preview a theme before applying it by selecting it from the list of available themes and viewing the display of sample DAP elements in the Sample Of Theme box. Before applying a theme to the page, you can also select options to apply brighter colors to text and

Figure 15.11
The Theme dialog box from within the DAP designer.

graphics, animate certain theme graphics, and apply a background to your DAP. Theme graphics are animated only when you view the DAP in a Web browser, not while you view the DAP in Microsoft Access.

Tip

If you have Microsoft FrontPage 4, 98, or 2000 installed, you can use the FrontPage themes as well. Additional themes are available from the Microsoft Web site.

Choosing A Default Theme For New DAPs

When you're designing a series of DAPs, particularly for a corporate intranet, you'll generally want to have all the pages display the same background. To set a default theme for your pages, perform the following steps:

1. Open any DAP in Design view.
2. Select Format | Theme. Access will display the Theme dialog box.
3. In the Choose A Theme list, click on the theme that you want to be the new default theme.
4. Click on the Set Default button. Access will set the theme as your new default theme.
5. Within the same dialog box, click on the Yes button and then click on OK to exit the dialog box.

Optimizing Data Access Page Performance

Because Data Access Pages are a relatively new technology, there aren't quite as many known ways to optimize their performance as there are with forms and other Access objects. However, you can use several known optimization techniques to make your DAPs load faster in Page view or in Internet Explorer 5. Although we discussed many of these earlier, they're worth restating and expanding here (in addition to these, typical rules for Web page design apply):

♦ Avoid overlapping controls on a page.

♦ Make sure the **ExpandedByDefault** property in the Sorting And Grouping box is set to **No** for the highest group level. Doing so ensures that the page opens faster because it doesn't need to display all the entries at once. Setting it to **No** for lower group levels will speed up other interactions once the page is opened.

♦ Make sure the **DataPageSize** property in the Sorting And Grouping box is set to a lower number rather than a higher number or to **All**. The lower the number, the faster the records are displayed.

♦ Use Bound HTML controls instead of text boxes to display any data that isn't updateable. Common examples of appropriate places to use Bound HTML controls include autonumber values, values derived from expressions, and hyperlinks. Note, however, that you can't sort or filter the values in a Bound HTML control.

♦ On grouped pages (that is, where the data is read-only), use Bound HTML controls, instead of text boxes, to display data.

♦ On pages used for data entry, set the **DataEntry** property of the page to **True**, so the page opens to a blank record.

♦ On grouped pages that contain records with a one-to-many relationship, group records by table rather than by a field or expression.

♦ On grouped pages based on tables with a one-to-many relationship, bind each section to a table rather than to a query. Access retrieves the records from a table only as it needs to display them on the page. With a query, Access retrieves all the records before it displays any records on the page. Use a query only when you want to limit the data used on the page, calculate aggregate values, or perform a task that's possible only in a query.

This list is by no means exhaustive—it just points out some of the issues to watch for in your design.

Setting Document Properties For The DAP

As part of your optimization process—or at many other points during DAP programming—there may be times when you want to set properties that apply to the entire DAP. To do so is a relatively simple process. First, open the DAP in Design view. Next, select File | Page Properties (you may have to expand the menu). Access displays the Page Properties dialog box, as shown in Figure 15.12.

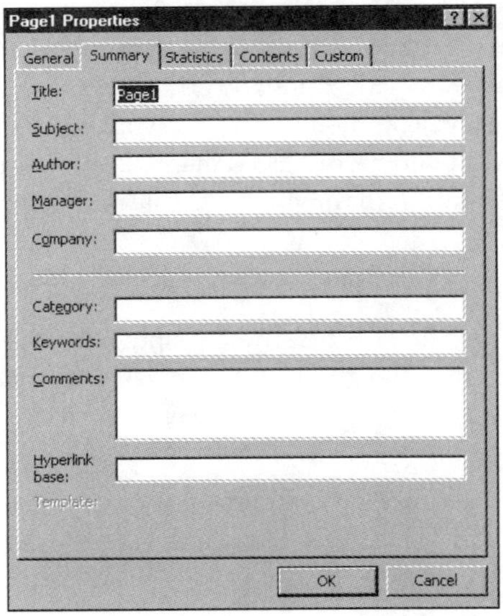

Figure 15.12
The Page Properties dialog box.

The Page Properties dialog box lets you set the following page properties:

♦ *General*—This is the same information that's displayed when you right-click on the name of a file in Windows Explorer, then click on Properties on the shortcut menu. The only difference is that when you view these properties in Access, the Attributes settings are read-only. You can't make changes to this tab.

♦ *Summary*—The information you enter on this tab is added to the **SummaryInfo Document** object in the **Documents** collection. Summary information allows you to better identify a page both from within Access and from other programs, such as the Windows Find Files program. The Hyperlink Base setting on the Summary tab is used to create the base hyperlink path that's appended to the beginning of relative **HyperlinkAddress** property settings. Additionally, information you insert in this tab will appear when you document pages.

♦ *Statistics*—This information includes the date and time the active page was created, the last date and time it was modified, who modified it, the number of times it's been revised, and total editing time. Again, you can't modify the entries on this tab.

♦ *Contents*—This tab displays the page's title and the connection string it uses to connect to its data source. This information is read-only.

♦ *Custom*—The custom properties you enter become properties of the **UserDefined Document** object in the **Documents** collection. The tab provides you with a list of predefined custom properties and also lets you enter your own custom properties. You'll typically use these properties to simplify site management.

Where To Go From Here

Clearly, DAPs provide a powerful solution to many pressing intranet design issues for most businesses, and we have barely scratched their surface in this chapter. In Chapter 16, we will move on to a more specific, programmatically directed discussion of how to use DAPs with Access 2000, including in-depth coverage of using pivot tables, designing effective reports, and more.

In Chapter 17, we will discuss the use of DAPs with SQL Server back ends, and then in the chapters following, we will introduce you to Visual InterDev 6 and how to use it for database programming, together with a basic discussion of Active Server Page (ASP) design issues. We'll also discuss why using ASPs will often be a comparable or better solution to using Data Access Pages, and clarify situations in which DAPs are the only viable, or at least best-considered, solution.

Web Programming With Access 2000

In the previous chapter, I introduced you to Data Access Pages (DAPs), a data-bound HTML technology that you can use to program with Access 2000. In this chapter, I will consider that technology, as well as some traditional approaches that you can use for Web programming with Access. In Chapter 17, I will move on to working with Visual InterDev, Active Server Pages, and a bunch of other Internet-based technologies external to the Access 2000 product that you can nevertheless use to program with Access 2000 or some other back-end database solution. Let's begin with a discussion of some traditional approaches.

Traditional Approaches

The traditional Access Web technologies are particularly appropriate for developing low-volume (around 10,000 visitors per day or fewer) Web and database solutions. Because browsers can be incompatible across manufacturers and versions, traditional approaches are safe and relatively easy to use. Access 2000 offers three such approaches:

♦ Publishing datasheets in HTML, IDC/HTX, and ASP format.

♦ Using HTML forms. Access does not offer a built-in development environment for HTML forms, but you can adapt your old HTML form solutions to OLE DB/ADO (ActiveX Data Objects) technology.

♦ Publishing reports in snapshot format to an FTP folder. This simplifies your ability to provide content in the form of Access reports to users with Netscape browsers.

Publishing Datasheets

You can choose Export from the File menu in the database window to export an Access datasheet, such as a table. This command (which also publishes datasheets behind forms and reports) offers some of the functionality associated with the obsolete Publish To The Web wizard. It publishes datasheets in HTML, IDC/HTX, and ASP formats. The HTML format is static, but easy to edit with standard HTML editors. The latter two formats are dynamic. They use the server to write out HTML content to reflect the most recent results in a datasheet.

The IDC/HTX format targets the first two releases of Microsoft Internet Information Server (IIS), but it also works with more recent releases. The ASP format works only with more recent releases (IIS 3 and higher), but it lets you mix Microsoft Visual Basic Scripting Edition and Microsoft JScript with HTML code. You should not automatically choose one of the dynamic formats. If you have large datasheets or many users, and if the content in a datasheet changes infrequently or if timeliness is not an issue, then the static HTML format might be the best choice, because static pages publish faster.

Publishing In HTML Format

To publish a datasheet in HTML format, select a table, query, form, or report in the database window and then choose Export from the File menu. In the Export dialog box, use the Save In drop-down list box to select a location for the file. If you are publishing to an intranet, this can be a folder at the site. If you are publishing to a remote Web server, you can use any local folder to collect your HTML pages and then transfer the pages to a remote server using the File | Import command in FrontPage 2000. You can also use another transfer technique, such as File Transfer Protocol (FTP).

Figure 16.1 shows the Export dialog box for publishing the datasheet behind the Products form from the NorthwindCS Access database. The Save As Type drop-down list box shows the HTML format. The Save In box designates the folder KLS_Office_2000, the root folder of a local intranet site with the same name. The Autostart checkbox is selected, so the page will appear as soon as it is published. This can cause a browser session to start with the Products datasheet open.

When you click on Save, the HTML Output Options dialog box appears. Here you can specify a template for the page containing the datasheet. If you have a theme set for the default.htm page, you can reference that page containing the theme. Otherwise, you can reference a local file with formatting that you will use at a remote site.

One of the advantages of the HTML format is that you have an HTML table to edit. Figure 16.2 shows the Table Properties dialog box, which shows some of the formatting options, including cell padding, cell spacing, and background color or image. You can also set properties for cells, rows, and columns. You can undo any custom formatting in FrontPage, and you can even select individual columns and rows and selectively delete them.

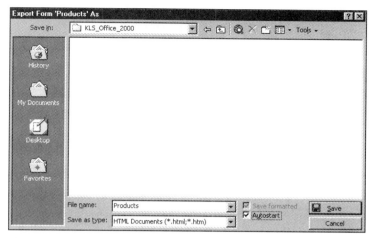

Figure 16.1
The Export dialog box.

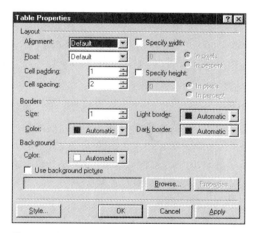

Figure 16.2
After loading your datasheets into FrontPage, you can edit the resulting HTML table.

Publishing In IDC/HTX Format

When you publish a datasheet in either dynamic format, you need an open database connectivity (ODBC) Data Source Name (DSN). The DSN must reside on the Web server along with the database to which it refers. The file DSN approach is, in theory, more flexible because you can send it to the server, but Internet service providers (ISPs) often impose special rules that make them less than straightforward to run. On the other hand, some ISPs manage DSNs as a Web site resource. They routinely issue one or more DSNs for each Web site account with database usage privileges. Therefore, it's often easier to use system, rather than file, DSNs. In any event, system DSNs offer a performance advantage.

After selecting a datasheet source in the database window and choosing File | Export, select Microsoft IIS 1-2 (*.htx;*.idc) in the Save As Type list box. Make other selections as you would for an HTML file. Clicking on Save opens the HTX/IDC Output Options dialog box (shown in Figure 16.3). You can use the Browse button to select a template that formats the page returning the results from the IDC file. To run, the IDC file needs a DSN name on the server. In the Data Source Name text box, enter the name of the DSN that your Webmaster set up for this task. The dialog box also includes user ID and password fields in case the database on the Web server runs with user-level security. (This is very rare, particularly in Internet applications.)

The IDC and HTX files complement one another. The IDC file runs a query against an Access database on the Web server. The HTX file uses HTML extensions to format the return set in HTML for viewing by a browser. Though you can code the HTX file in an HTML extension, it returns pure HTML to the browser so that any browser can read its results. Because the only way that an IDC file can expose its return set is through an HTML file, this format processes datasheets. However, it is not appropriate for processing forms, because the HTML return format does not serve as a good input for most HTML forms.

When you run an IDC/HTX pair from a Web server, browsers reference the IDC file, which must reside in a Web server folder that can run scripts. The IDC file automatically invokes the HTX file, which in turn processes the return set from the IDC file and sends HTML-formatted results back to the browser.

Publishing In ASP Format

Like IDC and HTX files, ASP files require a reference to a DSN. In the Export dialog box, select Microsoft Active Server Pages (*.asp) in the Save As Type list box. In the Microsoft Active Server Pages Output Options dialog box, enter a DSN name. Other fields in the dialog box are optional and depend on your formatting preferences and database security settings. (These fields are optional in the IDC/HTX and HTML dialog boxes as well.)

The ASP format differs from the IDC/HTX format in that there is only one file. This ASP file performs the query and formats the result for the browser. The file runs its query and

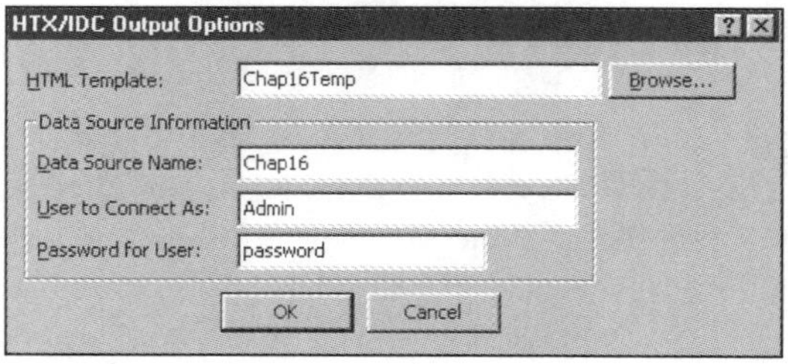

Figure 16.3
The HTX/IDC Output Options dialog box.

creates its HTML on the server, and then the Web server transports the HTML page back to the browser.

The fact that the browser receives pure HTML makes ASP appropriate for many different kinds of browsers. Composing HTML on the fly is the reason why browsers pause when launching an ASP file. Pages with more iterations and field translations require more composing time than those with just a few fields and rows. You should plan your ASP contents so that they deliver sufficient information in a single page without incurring undue processing delays.

Note
We will work extensively with ASP in later chapters, particularly Chapters 18 and 21.

Using HTML Forms

One of the strengths of ASP technology is its support of HTML forms. This is important because all browsers support HTML forms. You can use these forms to gather information from site visitors or return database results in a record layout (as opposed to a datasheet layout). An HTML form consists of one or more controls for displaying or storing information. Typically, the form contains at least one button for submitting the form fields to the Web server. If the form requires a reply, a program on the server can process the form fields and generate a response page.

HTML forms often work like a call-and-response game between a browser and a Web server. The browser user fills in the fields and clicks on the Submit button for the form. When the browser sends the form to the server, it transmits form field values and the name of a program on the server that knows what to do with those field values. This is the *call* part of the game. The Web server sends the form field values to the right processing program on the server. That program can echo the input values, check them for validity, append them to a record source, look up data from a record source, or more. It typically prepares some kind of return page for the browser. This is the *response*. ASP files can serve as both the initial form that accepts the call and the response program that replies to the call.

Figure 16.4 shows a pair of HTML forms that illustrate the call-and-response character of HTML form processing. The top form includes a drop-down list box with the names of employees in the NorthwindCS Access database. A user can select a name, such as Klander, and click on Get Extension to submit the form to the server. This is the *call* action. The Web server takes the input form and passes it to telereturn.asp, which reads the entry in the list box, looks up the telephone number for the employee, and writes a page with the information for the browser. The Web server sends the page back to the browser. This is the *response* action.

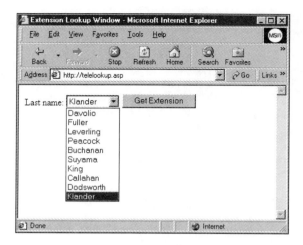

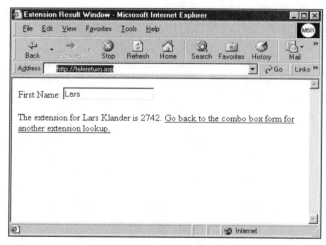

Figure 16.4
The HTML form on the top calls the Web server and invokes the reply page on the bottom.

Access 2000 does not include built-in wizards for building these kinds of pages with HTML forms, but the process is straightforward. The main challenge is learning the syntax for a few HTML form controls and how to intermix HTML and script, such as VBScript, in an ASP file. The code that the top page in Figure 16.4 requires is contained in the telelookup.asp file on the companion CD-ROM. In turn, the bottom page of the figure is contained entirely within the telereturn.asp file, also contained on the companion CD-ROM.

After creating a recordset with information for the employee selected in telelookup.asp, telereturn.asp formats a page. The page contains the employee's first name in an HTML text box, a simple HTML string with the name and extension, and a hyperlink for returning control to telelookup.asp. When the Web server passes this page back to the browser, the call-and-response cycle ends.

Using Hyperlinks

We have previously discussed how to use hyperlinks to navigate around forms in a custom application. This is only a small portion of the functionality that hyperlinks can deliver. You can also navigate to other Access databases, to bookmarks in a Word document, or to intranet and Internet URLs. You can even use hyperlinks to open your email software (such as Microsoft Outlook) with the address of a specific individual and a designated subject.

Types Of Hyperlinks

Hyperlinks can appear as labels, command buttons, and unbound image controls on forms, reports, and data access pages. You can also create bound hyperlinks so that a table can contain a set of hyperlinks. You can assign a unique hyperlink to each record in a table. One obvious use for this is associating a URL with each record entity (for example, companies). After following either a bound or unbound hyperlink, you can use the Back control on the Office Web or browser toolbar to navigate back from a hyperlink target address to Access.

The Hyperlink Data Type

When you use bound hyperlinks, your application specifies the **Hyperlink** data type, which can contain up to four parts, each delimited by the number (#) sign. The display text part appears first if you specify it. This text appears in place of the address to which a hyperlink navigates. For example, instead of a hyperlink showing the address for the Coriolis Web site, it can simply say Coriolis.

The second part is the address—the URL or UNC address for a target file. The address can be absolute or relative. It is common at Web sites to specify hyperlinks relatively—that is, in relation to the base address of the Web site. In Access, a relative address extends from the **Hyperlink Base** setting in an Access file. You can examine this setting by choosing the Database Properties command from the File menu in the database window.

The third part is the subaddress, which names a part of a file to navigate to. The parts you can navigate to vary by Office component. In Access, you can navigate to database objects, such as forms, reports, tables, and queries. You can specify a database object type, such as table, and the name of a specific object, such as **Customers**. You do not have to specify an object type, but if a database contains multiple objects with the same name, Access navigates to them in an arbitrary order. If a hyperlink includes both address and subaddress parts, the link navigates to another file. If the address part is missing, the link navigates to an object in the current database.

The fourth part, a screen tip, is new in Access 2000. This text appears when you rest the cursor over a hyperlink. It can offer a reminder about the purpose of a hyperlink. These tips appear in hyperlinks on pages viewed with Internet Explorer 4 and later. They also appear in Access 2000 custom applications.

Inserting And Editing Hyperlinks

You can type a new hyperlink address, but it is simpler and safer to use the Insert Hyperlink tool or its corresponding menu command. You can invoke the Insert Hyperlink command from any point at which you can add a hyperlink to a document. For example, you can choose Insert Hyperlink from the Design view of a form to add a hyperlink as a label. You can give a command button navigational abilities by clicking on the Build button next to its **Hyperlink Address** or **Hyperlink SubAddress** property. You can assign navigational capabilities to an image in the same way.

All these actions open the Insert Hyperlink dialog box. Figure 16.5 shows this dialog box for creating a label hyperlink on a form. Click on ScreenTip to open a second dialog box that allows you to enter text for the screen tip associated with the hyperlink.

You can click on the E-mail Address button on the Option bar to open the version of the dialog box for email. The dialog box automatically inserts the **mailto:** protocol prefix to invoke a workstation's default email package from a browser. You can also specify the recipient and the subject. Just as you can select from sites previously visited when you assign a hyperlink address, you can also select a previously entered email address and subject. The hyperlink that Figure 16.6 creates displays the phrase *Send Me A Message*. When a user clicks on this phrase, the user's email software opens, with the recipient *lklander@lvcm.com* and with *Chapter 16* as the subject.

After you insert a hyperlink in an application, you can right-click on it and choose Hyperlink from the shortcut menu to see an array of options for processing existing hyperlinks. The Edit Hyperlink command is the most obvious choice for revising a hyperlink. This opens the Edit Hyperlink dialog box, which has the same layout as the Insert Hyperlink dialog box. You can use it to update any of the hyperlink fields. Over time, you might have to fine-tune

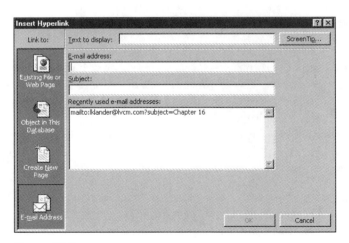

Figure 16.5
The Insert Hyperlink dialog box for a URL.

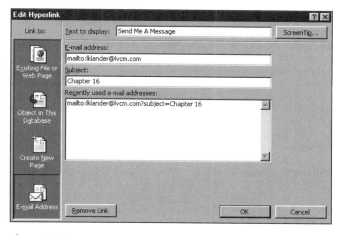

Figure 16.6
The Edit Hyperlink dialog box for an email message.

the display text or the URL for a hyperlink. Similarly, you can add to the recipient list for links that send email so that messages route to more recipients directly.

Hyperlink Samples

One of the most popular pages at many Web sites is the Favorites page, which points to sites that the author finds valuable or interesting. You can insert similar pages in your custom Access solutions. Such sites can include email or Web links to your business and can include site addresses with free or low-cost technical support.

Figure 16.7 shows a Favorite Links page that is an Access form with two labels. Both serve as hyperlinks. The two label hyperlinks open fake email links to myself and The Coriolis Group.

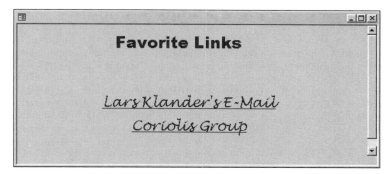

Figure 16.7
A Favorite Links page with two labels that serve as hyperlinks.

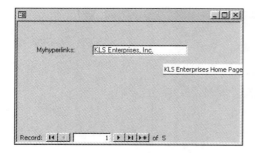

Figure 16.8
The form with a bound hyperlink shows a screen tip for the first hyperlink in the table.

Figure 16.8 shows a form with a bound hyperlink that is based on a table of hyperlinks. The table appears below the form in the figure. The screen tip, KLS Enterprises Home Page, appears for the first hyperlink. The bottom display presents that hyperlink in Edit mode, which exposes the hyperlink parts. Notice that there is display text and an address part, but no subaddress. The hyperlink concludes with the screen tip text.

Revisiting Data Access Pages

As discussed previously, Data Access Pages (DAPs) are data-bound HTML files. In many ways, they look and behave like a cross between a traditional Access report and a form, because you can use them to browse through the records in a data source. The page's database connection enables users to add, update, and delete data. Typically, but not necessarily, the data is from a database object in the current database file. You can use the Sorting And Grouping tool to hierarchically display data—for example, in reports that have multiple, nested bands or group headings. The Pages icon in the database window represents the DAP objects associated with a database. But Access does not store pages in the database; they are separate DHTML files in the file system—for example, in a folder on your intranet server. The **Pages** collection in a database file is a collection of hyperlinks to the DHTML files. You create pages within Access, and users can then open them in Internet Explorer 5 or Access 2000.

Note

If multiple users will launch a page from browsers on different workstations, you might have to revise the Data Source setting in the DHTML file so that it does not reference local drive letters. Use a Uniform Naming Convention (UNC) address instead.

Creating A Data Access Page

Access 2000 contains wizards for basing a new Data Access Page on either a tabular or columnar layout. You can also base a new page on an existing Web page. However, many developers will likely prefer to create a DAP by opening a blank page in Design view and populating it with controls from the Field List dialog box, as shown in Figure 16.9.

To populate a page, you can open the Tables or Queries node to reveal the table names in the active connection. If you see a table from which you want to select values for the page, you can expand the table to view the individual fields. You can then select fields by dragging and dropping them on the page. Alternatively, you can populate a page with all fields in a table by dragging a table name to the page. You can then choose to arrange fields in a columnar or pivot table layout. You can perform the same kind of operations with queries.

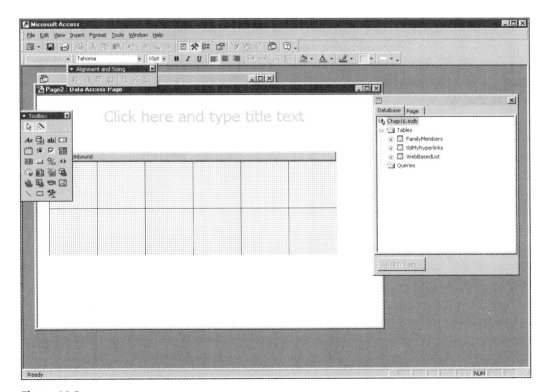

Figure 16.9
You can use the Field List dialog box to populate a blank Data Access Page with controls bound to database fields.

The pivot table report layout (which originated in Excel) is a special kind of tabular layout that facilitates creating interactive, aggregate summaries of the information in a record source. The pivot table promises to become a popular front end for work-ing with multidimensional data cubes. As you spend time working with On-Line Analytical Processing (OLAP) solutions, particularly those that use SQL Server's built-in support for OLAP, you will find yourself using pivot tables extensively as a means of managing complex data sets returned from such data sources.

To change the active connection, right-click on the database connector in the top left corner of the Field List dialog box and choose Connection from the shortcut menu. In the Data Link Properties dialog box that appears, select an OLE DB connection driver and a database consistent with that driver. When you close the dialog box, the Field List dialog box shows the tables and queries from the new database source.

Creating And Using A Simple Columnar Page

Figure 16.10 shows a simple DAP that serves as a form for the **FamilyMembers** table in a database file. Four fields appear on the form. A control below the fields supports navigation and other functions. Clicking on the two navigator buttons on either side of the record indi-cator window moves the current record's position back and forth in the underlying recordset.

The first six buttons to the right of the indicator for the record source and number are as follows, from left to right:

♦ *Next Record button*—Moves to the next record

♦ *Last Record button*—Moves to the last record

♦ *New Record button*—Adds a record

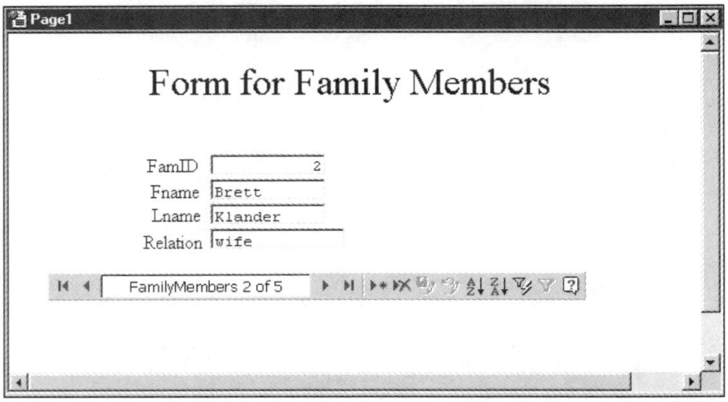

Figure 16.10
This Data Access Page serves as a form. Users can browse, add, delete, edit, sort, and filter records using the navigation control below the fields.

◆ *Delete Record button*—Deletes the current record

◆ *Save Record button*—Saves any changes to the current record

◆ *Undo Record button*—Undoes any unsaved changes to the current record

If you enter a record that you later want to remove, use the Delete button to delete it. You can also edit records by simply typing over them, adding new content, or removing existing content. If you want to preserve your revisions, click on Save Record. Otherwise, click on Undo Record.

The remaining buttons on the navigation control (except the Help button on the far right) are for sorting and filtering:

◆ *Sort Ascending and Sort Descending buttons*—Specify the sort direction. To sort on the values in a field, click in that field for any record, and then click on one of these buttons.

◆ *Filter By Selection button*—Applies a filter based on the current value in a field. Click in the field to choose a value for filtering (for example, the **Lname** field with a value of Klander), and then click on Filter By Selection. The display changes to show only those records that match the previously selected filter value. For example, if you choose Klander for **Lname** in Figure 16.10, the record indicator changes from FamilyMembers 2 of 5 to FamilyMembers 2 of 2.

◆ *Toggle Filter button*—Applies or removes the filter.

All this functionality is available from within Access as well as from a browser on an intranet. Data Access Pages display best and all their features function with Internet Explorer 5. Various degrees of degradation occur with Internet Explorer 4. Users of browsers other than Internet Explorer 5 must obtain ActiveX controls for reading and working with a DAP.

Grouping Records

One powerful feature of Data Access Pages is their ability to group records and conditionally expand a group to show the individual entries within. Figure 16.11 demonstrates this capability. The page shown in the figure groups records from the **FamilyMembers** table by the **Lname** field. All records from the table with the same last name group together. When a user clicks on the gray expand button (it changes from + to -), a second, nested navigation control appears for moving through the records with the same last name. Clicking on the outer navigation control closes the expanded display and moves to the first record with the next last name.

You can show more than a single record on a page. You use the Data Page Size setting in the Sorting And Grouping window to specify how many records to show at a time. This window lets you set the page size independently for the grouping field as well as the fields within a group. You can use the Sorting And Grouping window for DAPs to control whether groups

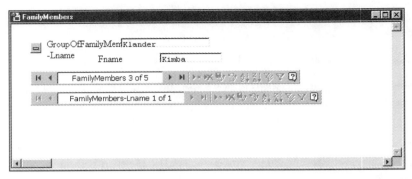

Figure 16.11
You can group and conditionally expand records within groups on Data Access Pages.

have header and footer sections, just like you use the corresponding window for reports. You can use the Group On setting to specify intervals, ranges of values, and prefixes for grouping fields.

Figure 16.12 shows the Design view of the page in Figure 16.11. Notice that it contains two navigation controls. You can assign a grouping function to a field by selecting the field and clicking on the Promote button (the left-pointing arrow) on the Page Design toolbar. When the record source for a page derives from a one-to-many relationship, you can use the Sorting And Grouping tool to group all the fields from the one side of the relationship over the fields on the many side. Access sorts and groups the records by the primary key for the one side of the relationship in this case.

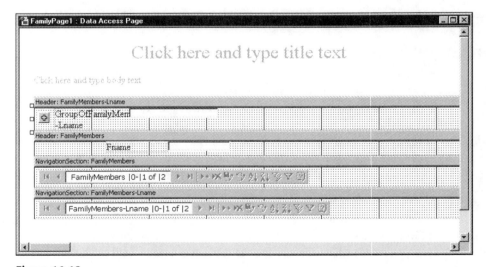

Figure 16.12
In Design view, you can add Expand controls to let users interact with your pages and conditionally expand them to see the records within a group.

Office 2000 Web Components On Data Access Pages

Three Office 2000 Web Components ship with Office 2000 (the Standard, Professional, Premium, and Developer editions): spreadsheet, chart, and PivotTable list components. You can use these to complement and extend the basic database functionality provided by Data Access Pages. If a site has a license that permits intranet distribution, the site administrator can configure browsers under the license to automatically download and configure the Office Web Components the first time they load a page using a component. (For more information on configuring Office Web Components, see the Microsoft Office 2000 Resource Kit.)

An Office Spreadsheet Sample

There are many uses for a spreadsheet component on a Data Access Page. For example, assume that you have controls on a page that show the **CategoryName**, **ProductName**, and **ProductSales** fields for the Sales By Category query from the NorthwindCS database. This query computes sales by product in 1997 for each product. This would be a good page. However, consider Figure 16.13, which goes a little further.

The sample in Figure 16.13 extends the basic query that I postulated in the previous paragraph by projecting sales from 1998 through 2001 and displaying the resulting information in the DAP. First, the component copies the current value of the ProductSales control from

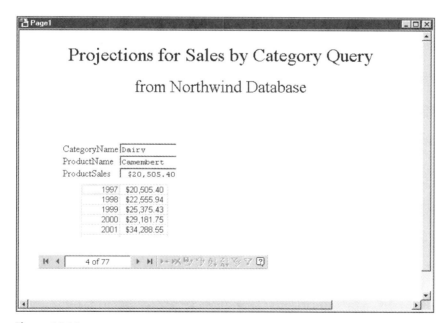

Figure 16.13
The spreadsheet component on this DAP uses sales from the database for 1997 to project sales through 2001.

the page to the spreadsheet. Then it applies a progressive series of growth rates to sales starting with 1997. These rates increase sales from one year to the next. Whereas the growth rates are the same for all products, the actual sales levels vary between products, because the 1997 sales are different for each product. Finally, to protect the formulas from damage, you can lock selected spreadsheets or cells to block users from inadvertently changing them.

You can insert an Office 2000 Spreadsheet Component using the Insert | Office Spreadsheet command and adapt the component for use in your application by right-clicking on it and choosing Property Toolbox. The spreadsheet in Figure 16.14 hides the toolbar, title bar, column headers, and row headers. In addition, the component's horizontal and vertical scrollbar settings are set to False.

The top sales cell in the spreadsheet has a formula that updates with each new record on the DAP: **=document.productsales.value**. The term *document* references a Data Access Page. The term *productsales* references a specific control on the page. Finally, the *value* property references the current value of the control on the DAP. This value changes only if the user moves to a new record in the page's underlying record source.

The sales entries for 1998 through 2001 all evaluate to **#VALUE!** in Design view. This is not an error. It results from the fact that there is no value for 1997 in Design view. Recall from Figure 16.14 that there are legitimate values for these cells in Page view. This results from the formula in the top spreadsheet cell evaluating to the current value of **productsales** on the Data Access Page.

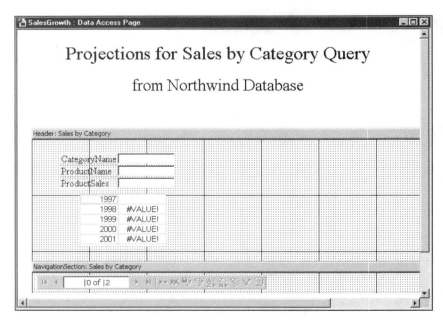

Figure 16.14
The Design view of the DAP from Figure 16.13.

An Office Chart Sample

You can build on the sample discussed in the previous section by adding an Office 2000 Chart Component that charts the values in the spreadsheet. The chart shows a graphical depiction of how sales grow over time for each product. Figure 16.15 shows a product with spreadsheet projections and a graphical depiction. The chart dynamically updates each time the values in the spreadsheet change.

To add a chart to a page, select the area of the page where you want the chart to appear, and then choose Insert | Office Chart. The command starts a wizard that walks you through the process of formatting a chart. You can select a chart type, choose a record source for the chart, and set values to display in the chart. After you finish using the wizard, you can right-click in the chart and choose Property Toolbox to edit your choices or specify other options that were not explicitly presented at setup time.

An Office PivotTable List Sample

The PivotTable list control lets users sort, group, filter, outline, and manipulate data. It can also work with data from more providers than a normal Data Access Page or other Office 2000 Web Components can. Its data sources can include a worksheet, a database, and a multidimensional data cube.

Figure 16.16 shows a PivotTable list control on a DAP that is based on the **Orders** table in the NorthwindCS database. It counts orders by **ShipCountry**, **CustomerID**, and **EmployeeID**.

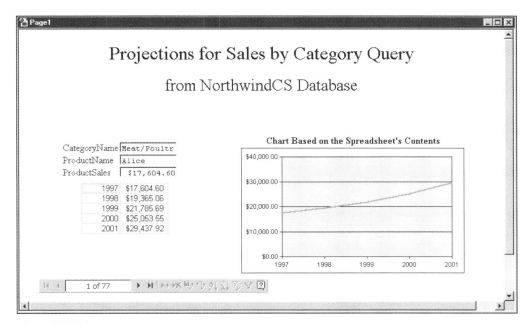

Figure 16.15
The Chart Component on a DAP accepts values from a Spreadsheet Component that changes its sales projections when a user moves off the current record.

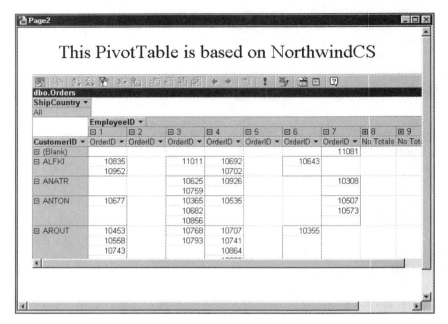

Figure 16.16
A PivotTable list on a DAP that displays data from the NorthwindCS database.

You can click on the Expand control next to the **EmployeeID** and **CustomerID** fields to expand the table within that column or row. In addition, you can selectively show a subset of the table by opening the list of elements comprising all countries, customers, and employees and selecting just one or a few from each set. A toolbox along the top of the PivotTable list presents still more analysis options, such as filtering and sorting.

Programmatic Issues For Data Access Pages

You can program solutions with Data Access Pages at several different levels. DAPs can also serve as hosts for Office Web Components. Both DAPs and Office 2000 Web Components have object models that you can use to develop programmatic solutions. You can also code solutions in VBA or a Web scripting language, such as VBScript.

This section explores solutions based on VBA, the **AllDataAccessPages** collection, and the **DataAccessPage** object. The **AllDataAccessPages** collection works like the **AllForms** and **AllReports** collections. Its members are not database objects, but rather **AccessObject** objects. These objects are available whether or not a DAP is open. The **AllDataAccessPages** collection lets you track the full set of all DAPs associated with a database project. The following short VBA procedure lists all the DAPs in a project and notes whether they are open:

```
Sub listPages()
Dim myPage As AccessObject

  For Each myPage In _
      Application.CurrentProject.AllDataAccessPages
  Debug.Print myPage.Name & IIf(myPage.IsLoaded, _
      " is loaded.", " is not loaded.")
  Next myPage

End Sub
```

The **FullName** property of an **AccessObject** object in the **AllDataAccessPages** collection has a special meaning. Recall that pages are not stored as objects in the database file; they are separate DHTML files. The location of the pages can be anywhere on a LAN. The **FullName** property indicates the path and file name for a Data Access Page. The next procedure lists all the pages in a project and itemizes them by their **Name** and **FullName** properties. The **Name** property value is the shortcut name for the DAP that appears in the database window:

```
Sub whereArePages()
Dim myPage As AccessObject
Dim obj As Object

  Set obj = Application.CurrentProject
  For Each myPage In obj.AllDataAccessPages
      Debug.Print "The link "; myPage.Name & " points at " & _
          myPage.FullName & "."
  Next myPage

End Sub
```

The only method for a **DataAccessPage** object is **ApplyTheme**. You can use this method to automate the application of a Microsoft Office theme to the pages that members of the **AllDataAccessPages** collection point to. This method works properly only if the page is open in design mode. The following two procedures assign a theme to all the DAPs in a project whether or not they are open and whether or not they are open in design mode:

```
Sub callSetTheme()
  'Test with Artsy or Blends.
  'Clear with Blank.

  setTheme "Artsy"
End Sub
```

```
Sub setTheme(ThemeName As String)
  Dim myPage As AccessObject
  Dim obj As Object
  Dim blnCloseit As Boolean
  Dim blnMakePageView As Boolean

  'Loop through all DataAccessPages.
  Set obj = Application.CurrentProject
  For Each myPage In obj.AllDataAccessPages
    'Get Page open in Design view.
    If myPage.IsLoaded = False Then
      DoCmd.OpenDataAccessPage myPage.Name, _
          acDataAccessPageDesign
      blnCloseit = True
    Else
      If DataAccessPages(myPage.Name).CurrentView <> _
          acDataAccessPageDesign Then
        DoCmd.Close acDataAccessPage, myPage.Name
        DoCmd.OpenDataAccessPage myPage.Name, _
            acDataAccessPageDesign
        blnMakePageView = True
      End If
    End If

'Apply Theme.
    DataAccessPages(myPage.Name).ApplyTheme ThemeName
    DoCmd.Save acDataAccessPage, myPage.Name

'If necessary, restore page.
    If blnCloseit = True Then
      DoCmd.Close acDataAccessPage, myPage.Name
      blnCloseit = False
    ElseIf blnMakePageView = True Then
      DoCmd.Close acDataAccessPage, myPage.Name
      DoCmd.OpenDataAccessPage myPage.Name, _
          acDataAccessPageBrowse
    End If
  Next myPage
End Sub
```

As part of their processing, the procedures also restore each DAP to its former open and current view status before applying the theme. If you do not like a theme selection, you can rerun the **callSetTheme** procedure with an argument of **Blank**.

Where To Go From Here

In this chapter, I have gone a little further with the exploration of both some traditional and some newer, nontraditional solutions that you can use when Web programming with Access 2000. We looked (albeit briefly) at traditional solutions like IDC/HTX, and touched on Active Server Pages (ASPs), a concept that I will explore in depth throughout the remainder of the book. I also went a bit deeper into the discussion of Data Access Pages (DAPs).

Although the remainder of the book focuses on the use of ASPs, and the benefits of doing so, exploring the uses of DAPs is an excellent investment—particularly if you are going to design pages that take advantage of the PivotTable capabilities provided by the new Office 2000 Web components.

Part V

The Internet With Other Microsoft Technologies

Microsoft Web-Based Design Techniques

In previous chapters, we have looked extensively at different types of client/server architectures—from very simple architectures, involving only the linking and embedding of data into Access databases, to substantially more complex architectures taking advantage of such important technologies as Data Access Pages (DAPs), which, as we discussed, are intended primarily as an intranet solution. For true Internet solutions, you will generally need to deploy your applications over the World Wide Web. Client/server applications that are deployed as a Web-based application require an architecture that is robust, secure, and scalable, and that can accommodate rapidly changing technologies.

This expanded deployment environment results in any number of issues that you must effectively address to provide viable solutions; unfortunately, the Access Interactive Development Environment (IDE) is not designed for the creation of applications deployed over the Web. Instead, you will have to design HTML pages, as well as other type of pages, that access your existing data sources. One of the options you have in this situation is to use a third-party product, such as Cold Fusion, which lets you manage the data. Another option is to use Microsoft's Internet Information Server (IIS) product for a back end and Visual InterDev as a front-end development tool. In this chapter, as in the rest of this book, we will focus on the Microsoft answer to this technology problem. To that end, we will consider InterDev as our primary development product. To help you understand the model that we will work with throughout this chapter, consider Figure 17.1, which shows the generalized structure of today's common Web-based solutions.

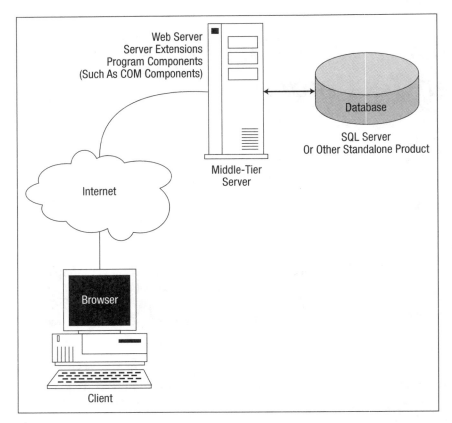

Figure 17.1
The structure of a modern Web-based solution.

Evolution Of The Web

In the mainframe era, the computing model began as a host-based model within which users working at terminals ran programs that resided on the mainframe computer. With the advent of PC workstations and computer networks, the client/server model emerged. In the client/server model, users run programs that reside on their own PCs. These client-side programs, in turn, request information across the network from a server computer. In a two-tier client/server architecture, the client program handles the user interface and user-input validation while the server program processes client requests. The client and server communicate over a network.

One of the best ways to understand the traditional two-tier client/server model and how it applies to the Internet is to consider *Hypertext Transfer Protocol (HTTP)* transactions over the Internet between a client and a server. Because of widespread Internet use, the HTTP model has continued to evolve client/server processing. Within the HTTP-based model, a client (normally a browser) interacts with a server. Typically, the client/server interaction involves client requests to the server to provide specific Web pages. Because Web pages consist of HTML documents, the model is sometimes called the HTTP-HTML client/server model. As you probably know, the World Wide Web is based on this HTTP-based model, as Figure 17.2 shows.

From the user's perspective, the HTTP model is inactive, offering little or no interaction. In short, the user could simply view a Web page's contents without interacting with elements on the page. Therefore, an interactive model was the natural next step for the Web's evolution. The Web gained such interactivity through the use of interactive forms that programmers created with the Common Gateway Interface (CGI), Perl, and other programming languages. Using HTML entries, a Web designer can create a form with which users (via their browser) can interact with the server. When users click their mouse on a form's Submit button, the browser sends the form to the server that, in turn, runs a program (normally written in Perl in the classic CGI model) that processes the form's entries. Depending on the server program's purpose, the program may generate an HTML-based response the server sends back to the browser.

The drawback to CGI-based forms processing is that the server must spawn (create) a new process every time the browser invokes a CGI script. As the number of server processes increases, the server's processing power decreases. Figure 17.3 shows a client/server model that uses CGI.

Several years back (not terribly long after the introduction of Windows 95), Microsoft introduced the Active Platform—a computing model Microsoft designed specifically for the Internet. The Active Desktop and its companion, the Active Server, are functionally symmetric, which means you can use ActiveX controls and scripting on both. In other words, both the client and the server can take advantage of ActiveX controls.

After the introduction of the ActiveX Internet model, the development of Web pages—specifically Web front ends for databases—became much, much easier. Microsoft introduced

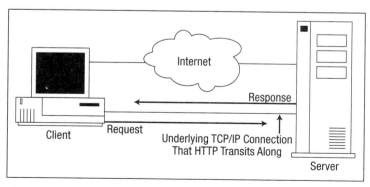

Figure 17.2
The HTTP-based Web model.

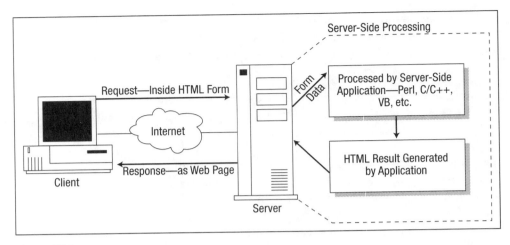

Figure 17.3
A CGI client/server model.

a handful of supporting technologies to go along with the new model, and also upgraded and renamed some existing technologies. The release of new versions of development platforms like Visual Basic has also had important implications. Specifically, early iterations of the ActiveX Internet model required that the server be Windows NT running Internet Information Server (IIS), which would then serve up Web pages that only Internet Explorer (IE) could read. Figure 17.4 shows an abstraction of how the model was constructed.

Many developers pushed back hard against Microsoft on the Active Platform. When you design pages that are meant to be seen by thousands, hundreds of thousands, or millions of viewers, there's no way to control what browser they're using. Developers became forced to develop two sets of Web sites—one that ran on IE and one that ran on other platforms.

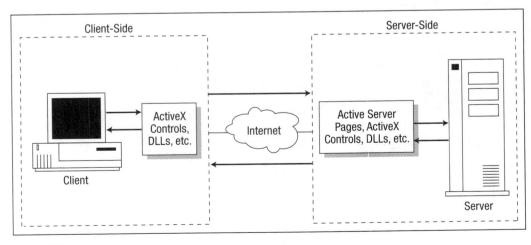

Figure 17.4
The ActiveX Internet model with Microsoft products on both ends.

Needless to say, it was a logistical nightmare. So Microsoft introduced some new server-side technologies that, when used in conjunction with the new HTML 4 standard, simplified the design of browser-independent Web sites. Such technologies included the expansion of the Internet Server API (ISAPI) model and the creation of the new Visual Basic (VB) Web Objects technology. Figure 17.5 shows how these technologies differ from some of the other Active Platform technologies.

There are still specific features—namely ActiveX controls—that you can use within Active Web pages that can make them browser-specific. However, the growth of technologies like persistent client-side Java applets have made this problem less significant—and the power of the server-side tools has gone a long way toward simplifying development.

How has all this changed in the last several years? To understand that, we must look closely at the evolution of browsers and servers since the Web began.

Evolution Of Web Servers

Internet protocols and technologies have advanced rapidly since the World Wide Web's inception in 1993. There have been three distinct generations of Web servers during this time period:

♦ First-generation Web servers delivered mostly static content—HTML pages with embedded graphics, sound files, and other basic features.

♦ Second-generation servers supported dynamic content through server-side extensions, such as CGI and binary server APIs, and database integration.

♦ Third-generation servers support Web-based applications that integrate with other enterprise services, such as transaction support. Optimally, these Web-based applications

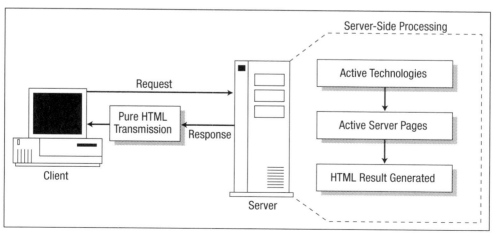

Figure 17.5
New technologies make the Active model more browser-independent.

can be developed in popular programming languages and can make use of the existing object technologies and services for the platform.

Evolution Of Web Browsers

Web browsers have also evolved to support new technologies and capabilities. Three general phases comprise the evolution of Web browsers:

◆ Static content, which primarily consisted of static HTML and embedded media.

◆ Dynamic content, which included scripting and client-side active components such as Java applets, ActiveX controls, and plug-ins.

◆ Integration, which includes XML, Dynamic HTML, and scriptlets. Better integration also occurs between the host user interface and the operating system. For information about newer versions of the HTML specification and the XML meta-language specification, go to the W3C Organization Web site at **www.w3c.org**.

Note

In this chapter, the term Web-based solution describes a generic solution that employs the Web to solve a particular business need. Subsequent chapters focus on the actual Web-based application and the applications that run on it.

Microsoft has a full range of products and technologies for enabling solutions that range from publishing simple Web-based applications to integrating the Web into a comprehensive business solution platform. Almost all Microsoft products and technologies now contain some Internet capability, and can be grouped according to their specific functionality or purpose. Internet functionality spans client and server products, development tools, and content-authoring tools.

Table 17.1 lists some of the main Microsoft Internet-related products and technologies that apply on the client side. In addition to the products that Microsoft provides for the client-side, a substantial number of server-side products are essential to the creation of data-driven Web-based applications, as shown in Table 17.2.

In addition to the server-side and client-side products and technologies detailed in Tables 17.1 and 17.2, Microsoft also provides a variety of development tools, designed for the purpose of simplifying the development of Web- and Windows-based solutions. Table 17.3 details the development tools that we will discuss throughout this book.

Table 17.1   Microsoft client-side products and technologies.

Product	Description
Internet Explorer 4/5	Web, FTP, and Gopher browser with desktop integration features. Add-ons give NetMeeting, NetShow, VRML, and other capabilities.
Outlook Express	Email and Internet news client.
Outlook 98/2000	The client for Microsoft Exchange Server.

Table 17.2 Microsoft server-side products and technologies.

Product	Description
Internet Information Server	Web server integrated into Windows NT Server.
Microsoft BackOffice	Windows NT Server and integrated products: Exchange Server (email), SQL Server (database), Proxy Server (Internet access and firewall), and others.
Windows NT Option Pack	Update to Windows NT Server components, as well as additional components such as Index Server, Certificate Server, Microsoft Transaction Server, and Microsoft Message Queue Server (MSMQ).
Microsoft Office 2000	Office 2000 back-end services provide PivotTable support as well as other Office 2000-specific services.
Microsoft Site Server	Products to help enhance, deploy, and manage Microsoft Web servers. Includes Commerce Server, Content Replication System, Site and Usage Analysis, and more.

Table 17.3 The Microsoft development tools detailed and discussed in various sections of this book.

Product	Description
Visual Studio 6	Integrated development products including Visual Basic, Visual C++, Visual J++, and Visual InterDev. Visual Basic 6 is the premier environment for designing complete, Internet-supporting applications, without the extensive delays common with other programming languages, such as C/C++ or Java. Also, through the Visual Basic for Applications (VBA) subset language, Visual Studio provides extensive customization features for most Microsoft products.
Microsoft Developer Network Library (MSDN)/Site Builder Network	Developer CD-ROM and online reference, newsletter, and online resources for all types of developers, including Web developers.
FrontPage 98/2000	HTML authoring and Web construction product. Includes Image Composer for graphic composition.
Microsoft Office 2000	Integrated package including Microsoft Word, Excel, PowerPoint, and Access. All include HTML export or authoring capabilities. As you have learned previously, Access 2000 includes support for the new Data Access Pages (DAP) technology, which lets you perform pivot table and other types of complex report processing across a corporate intranet—activities that other development products may not support.

Note

In this chapter, we are focusing on the Microsoft development tools and technologies necessary to build and deploy Web solutions. Throughout the next several chapters we will concern ourselves with Visual InterDev 6 because of its usefulness in the creation of data-based Web applications.

Considering The Web-Based Solution Models

Just as you saw in earlier chapters with the discussion of the different types of models that you might want to take advantage of when creating your client/server solution, you can choose from several different types of models when developing a Web-based solution. As you saw in earlier chapters, models are effective for a variety of reasons, but are most useful because they provide proven design methodologies that can save you time and effort. Such design methodologies are particularly important when you are moving from a design environment that you are comfortable with—such as Access 2000 (presumably)—to a Web-based design environment. Although the underlying data storage methods will be similar between the two environments, and although the programming solutions in both environments will share similar characteristics, there will be a marked difference between the two environments during certain parts of the deployment.

To plan an effective Web-based solution, you must first understand several Web-related concepts and processes. You should also be familiar with the different types of application models used in the client/server architecture—particularly because, to this point, we have discussed only one of the different types. We will begin our discussion with a consideration of the services model.

Using The Services Model

When designing your Web-based application, you can use a service-based application model. The term *service-based* means that the functionality of an application is specified as collections of services that meet specific user needs.

A service-based application is typically composed of three categories: *user services*, *business services*, and *data services*. Figure 17.6 shows a basic model of the interactions between these three categories of services.

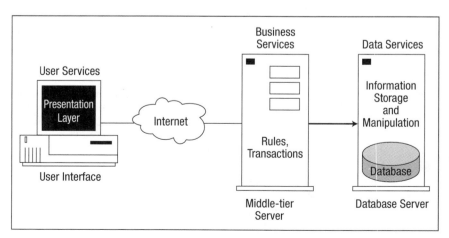

Figure 17.6
The three categories of services that make up a service-based application.

Before moving on to a more complete discussion of this model and its related concepts, it is worthwhile to consider the roles of the three types of services, as discussed in the following list:

♦ *User services*—These provide an application with its user interface. The user of a service can be a person or another service. Therefore, the interface for a service can provide a graphical user interface or a programmatic interface. Typically, user services will be implemented as either Web pages or using some front-end design product, such as Access 2000 or Visual Basic.

♦ *Business services*—These services enforce business rules and handle transactions. Business services may impose constraints or apply transformations to change user input or raw database information into usable business information. Generally, these services will be implemented (within the Microsoft model) as Component Object Model (COM) components, residing on some type of middle-tier server (such as a Windows NT Server running the Microsoft Transaction Server [MTS] service).

♦ *Data services*—These services provide storage and low-level manipulation of data in a database. Examples of data services include create, read, update, and delete, which are used by business services to modify a database. A business service does not need to know where data is located, how it is implemented, or how it is accessed because these tasks are handled by data services. For example, in a SQL Server-based environment, data services are often implemented by stored procedures residing on the server.

Clearly, the service-based application model is substantially more complex—even if you consider only the introduction of this new middle-tier concept—than the simple, two-tier client/server model that we have considered thus far. Let's take a look at the benefits and implications of these differences.

Benefits Of Using The Services Model

After determining what capabilities you need for your Web-based application—or for any other three-tier application, for that matter, a concept that we will consider in more depth in Chapter 20—you can then decide how to implement the application. Using services to define the division of functionality in your Web-based application provides the following benefits:

♦ *Clear and consistent development goals*—By dividing your Web-based application into services, you enable a Web development team to easily envision the direction of development. The functionality of each service, implemented as a component, is clearly defined.

♦ *Isolation of functionality within each service*—The functionality of a specific service is encapsulated, so any error in the implementation of a service can be easily traced to the corresponding component.

♦ *Better manageability of projects*—Because services divide the functionality of your Web-based application into distinct tasks, any changes in the implementation of one service will not introduce changes to another service component.

♦ *Division of labor amongst your team*—Identifying services enables you to determine which member of the Web development team is best suited to build and complete the corresponding component.

Over the past few decades, the architecture of applications, especially large enterprise, mission-critical applications, have evolved from single-tier to two-tier and n-tier designs. The driving force for this change has been the improvement of the performance of applications distributed over complex environments, particularly ensuring that the application's scalability, separation and encapsulation of functionality, maintainability, multiuser support, and ability to be distributed are maximized to the greatest degree possible. This sounds like a relatively simple process, but in reality it isn't: As long as there is scarcity of computing resources (which there *always* will be, at some level), there will always be trade-offs amongst these different areas of performance.

Understanding Service Tiers

Tiers are a logical concept that provide a way to describe how applications can be segmented into services, specifically the three types of services discussed in the previous section—user, business, and data.

The three types of tiers are generally described as user (first), business (second or middle), and data (third) service tiers. The concept of tiers emphasizes the logical segmentation of the services, and is neither about implementing the services nor about the number of physical computers involved in deploying the solution. You should consider three basic types of application models when you're evaluating service tiers—single-tier, two-tier, and n-tier (also commonly called three-tier) applications. The following sections briefly discuss each of these concepts.

Single-Tier Applications

A single-tier application is simply a monolithic, standalone program that runs on the user's computer. It may communicate with a database, but that database resides on the same computer (or perhaps on a mapped network drive). The key point about a single-tier application is that all three services—user, business, and data—are architecturally combined into a single program.

Typically, each installation of a single-tier application is used only by a single person—there is no sharing of data amongst systems, unless done so manually by the user. Figure 17.7 shows the model of a single-tier application.

Two-Tier Client/Server Applications

The simplest type of distributed computing is the two-tier client/server application. In this type of application, the database (and perhaps a portion of the data services) is separated from the user interface and business logic. Typically, the database is placed on a dedicated server.

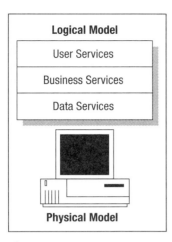

Figure 17.7
The basic implementation model of a single-tier application.

Two-tier client/server applications are the most common type of client/server applications built today. They offer significant benefits over single-tier applications because data processing is centralized and becomes a shared resource among (potentially) many users.

> **Note**
> *There is not necessarily a perfect mapping between the corresponding physical and logical tiers. For example, although business logic is generally placed on a separate application server, some business services such as validation code may map to a client computer, or be partially implemented in stored SQL procedures on the database server. Likewise, data services may be distributed on either the application server or the database server.*

Figure 17.8 shows the common model for a two-tier client/server application.

This model is still popular, and has been common for some time. However, like most things in the computer world, it has evolved somewhat over the last several years—most specifically, because of the continually increasing need to handle Web-based applications and process their requests, without all of the transmissions required to handle a two-tier client/server application style.

In recent years, we have seen a move to the so-called *n-tier*, or three-tier, application. This move has been driven heavily by such industry-wide technologies as Java and CORBA, but is generally implemented in a very specific manner when you standardize on Microsoft products, as discussed in the next section.

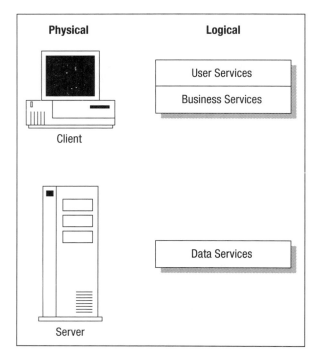

Figure 17.8
The basic implementation model of a two-tier application.

Three-Tier Client/Server Applications

As mentioned in the previous section, over time it has become apparent that the two-tier client/server model is simply not flexible, powerful, scalable, manageable (and any other number of adjectives) enough to handle many larger applications. Maintaining a dialogue between each client workstation and the central database server can result in high network traffic and poor performance. The most common example of this limitation, and the one that anyone who has worked in an office for any length of time can relate to, is what happens when too many users try to gain simultaneous access to a database.

Three-tier client/server applications help address these issues by putting another layer between the users and the database—the application server, also known as the *middle-tier server*. This type of central application service can manage network traffic and database server loads more efficiently.

Typically, the application layer handles most of the business services, and may be implemented on its own server computer, separate from the database. One of the main advantages of a three-tier architecture is the ability to extract the business logic from the user and data tiers and place it in the middle tier, where it is easier to maintain. Figure 17.9 shows a common implementation of the physical components in a three-tier client/server model, and how the services model generally maps to those components.

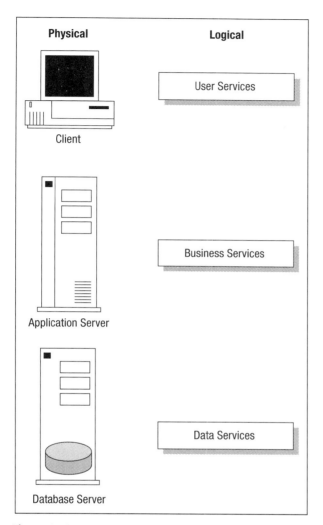

Figure 17.9
The basic implementation model of a three-tier application.

Three-tier applications are also commonly referred to as n-tier applications, because of the fact that any number of intermediate tiers can be inserted between the user layer and the data layer—for example, it is quite common to deploy Microsoft Message Queue Server (MSMQ) on a different machine than the MTS service. Additionally, the layer of indirection between the user and data layers results in the ability to deploy multiple data service providers, and have the access to all of those different providers be completely invisible to the user.

So, by now, you should be able to pretty clearly visualize how each of the application models works. The single-tier model is your Access applications running only on the local machine, the two-tier model is your Access Data Project (ADP) or databases linked using Access applications, and the three-tier model is substantially more complex than even that two-tier model, inserting additional application logic between your front end and your back end. Clearly, the implications for in-network programming are substantial—but what happens when you program for out-of-network, specifically for access over the World Wide Web? In the next section, we will consider the implications of the models that we discussed previously and how that affects Web-based application design.

Web-Based Applications

Web-based applications, by their browser/server nature, are forced to follow either the two- or n-tier model. The application models discussed so far leave a substantial part of the application on the client workstation. Conversely, applications designed for the Web place as little of the application as possible on the client, and keep all the processing centralized on one or more servers. Figure 17.10 shows how services generally map to physical components in a Web-based application.

In the early days of the Web, a single person—the Webmaster—often performed all code writing, authoring, publishing, and administration. However, modern Web development (when the corporate budget allows) is typically performed by a specialized team, which consists of a minimum of three people: a Web developer, a programmer, and an HTML author. Of course, if the budget does not allow, these tasks may all be folded into one or two employees.

In any event, specific sets of responsibilities must be addressed by specific development players. Table 17.4 summarizes each team member's responsibilities and lists the Microsoft-specific

Table 17.4 Responsibilities, tools, and members of the development team.

Team Member	Responsibilities	Primary Tools Used
Web developer	Analyzes and designs Web-based application architecture; creates the code for client-side and server-side scripts necessary for tying together the logic of the Web-based application.	Visual InterDev, Script Wizard
Programmer	Creates and maintains the applications and components used for a Web-based application: COM and MTS components, ActiveX controls, Java programs, stored SQL procedures, and others.	Visual Studio language tools: primarily Visual Basic, Visual C++, and Visual J++; Microsoft Transaction Server (MTS); SQL Server or Access 2000; Microsoft Message Queue Server (MSMQ)
HTML author	Authors Web-based application content; creates HTML files; gathers appropriate graphics and other media.	FrontPage 2000, Office 2000, Image Composer, Liquid Motion

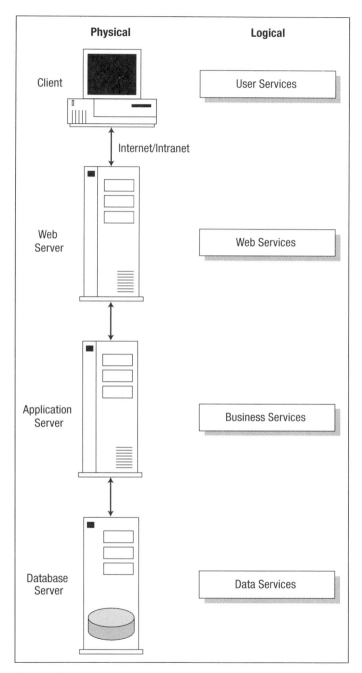

Figure 17.10
How services map to the physical components of a Web-based application.

development tools that they might use (of course, they might use other products as well—for example, the Web developer might use Cold Fusion, in addition to his or her other tools).

Several supporting team members may also play roles in Web-based application development (though, in all honesty, if you have this many members on your team, you should consider yourself *very* lucky). Table 17.5 describes these supporting team members, their responsibilities, and the Microsoft tools they might take advantage of.

Microsoft Visual InterDev contains the tools most team members will use for Web-based application development, enabling team members to collaborate on the development of a Web-based application.

For most businesses, the return on investment (ROI) is a key factor for determining a Web-based application's success. To help manage the total cost of ownership and increase the value of both internal and external Web-based applications, many businesses are implementing so-called Web Life Cycle solutions. The following section considers the Web Life Cycle.

Defining The Web Life Cycle

The Web Life Cycle represents the cycle of events involved in creating, managing, and maintaining a typical business's Web-based application. These events include those detailed in the following list:

♦ Analyzing customer requirements and available technologies

♦ Designing the site architecture and content areas

Table 17.5 Responsibilities and tools of the supporting members of the development team.

Supporting Team Member	Responsibilities	Primary Tools Used
Graphic artist	Designs and creates the graphic and multimedia elements.	Image Composer, Liquid Motion, third-party drawing and graphics editing packages
Test/documentation specialist	Documents the Web-based application for maintenance; tests the content, navigation, and active content.	Visual InterDev, Internet Explorer
Web administrator	Installs the content and maintains server processes.	Windows NT administration tools, Internet Service Manager, Microsoft Site Server
Database administrator	Installs and maintains the database management system (DBMS) and data sources used by the Web solution.	Microsoft SQL Server, Windows NT administration tools

- Developing content, including static HTML, media elements, Active Documents, and links to outside resources; dynamic elements such as client-side and server-side script and server components; and integrated database information
- Staging and deploying new and updated content quickly and securely
- Applying and managing site security
- Managing and troubleshooting the site environment
- Measuring and analyzing site usage
- Incorporating site enhancements that drive business value

Figure 17.11 graphically represents the Web Life Cycle.

Clearly, looking at the development of Web applications in this manner has some substantial implications for Web application developers. Though a substantial number of issues are addressed by this model, arguably the most important is the issue of security. In the next section, we will briefly consider how security applies to Web application design.

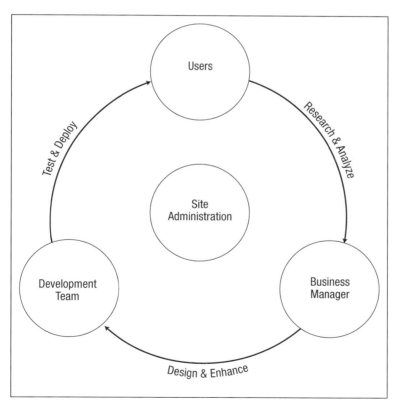

Figure 17.11
The Web application life cycle model.

Security Model And Issues With Web Applications

Ever since the first computers were connected with networks, security has been a major concern of network operating system vendors, developers, and administrators. The high-profile encroachments on any number of systems, particularly U.S. federal government systems, in the last several years, have really brought home to many business leaders the importance of securing networks from outside attack. Implementing a security plan can help protect a computer system and its data from loss, corruption, and unauthorized use.

The Internet has made addressing security concerns even more critical. Now all computers connected to the Internet directly (termed *hosts*) or indirectly though a proxy server are potential victims of security attacks. A complete discussion of security, security models, and related issues is well beyond the scope of this book, but it is worthwhile to take a little time to consider how security should affect the design of your Web application.

Categories Of Security Threats

Security threats can be divided into five broad categories based on the consequences of the attack. Table 17.6 describes each type of security threat, starting with the most serious.

Often a security penetration will consist of a combination of the categories described above. A complete security strategy will include deterrence, protection, detection, and response measures. This book will concentrate on protection measures implemented programmatically or through administrative tools.

Because of the pervasive nature of the Web, security issues when designing for such a deployment can be much more complex than those of a typical file server environment. When

Table 17.6   The five broad categories of security threats.

Security Threat	Description
System modification attacks	Unauthorized or malicious actions that alter computer files or settings. For example, a program that surreptitiously deletes important operating system files.
Invasion of privacy attacks	Unauthorized access to private computer data or monitoring of the computer user's actions. For example, a program that surreptitiously reads the contents of the user's file system and reports this information back to a software vendor.
Denial of service attacks	Overuse or hoarding of a computer's resources, which effectively blocks the user from using that aspect of the computer. For example, Java applets can be created that lock up browsers, forcing the user to close the browser.
Misdirection attacks	Any purposely misleading information presented to the user. For example, a program can mimic system dialogs to try to mislead the user into performing unnecessary actions.
Antagonistic attacks	Any purposefully annoying but essentially harmless action. For example, changing the user's desktop color settings in an unauthorized manner.

planning a Web-based application, you must consider various aspects of Web technology and develop a security plan based on specific scenarios. As a general rule, you must consider—at a bare minimum—the following aspects of a Web-based application and the resulting security implications:

♦ *Client issues*—Generally, the client's main concern is that the browser or the downloaded dynamic content does not endanger the user. Client compatibility is also an important security concern, especially in a heterogeneous client environment such as the Web. For example, although basic (plain text) authentication is not as secure as the Windows NT Server Challenge-Response (NT/CR) mechanism, the former is supported by all commercial Internet browsers, whereas NT/CR is currently supported only by Internet Explorer.

♦ *Server issues*—For the server, the most important security concerns are to determine who can access your Web-based application, what files a user can access, and what type of access rights—read, write, or execute—the user has to each.

♦ *Shared issues*—Secure communications and user identity are critically important for both client and server. Certain security issues and technologies apply differently to internal (trusted) users versus external (inherently nontrusted). In fact, a whole class of products—Internet proxies and firewalls—was created to bridge the different concerns of these two types of access.

Figure 17.12 depicts the architecture of a Web-based application and highlights important security issues.

When designing a Web-based solution using Microsoft tools, you can implement security using existing security features of both server and client products. Microsoft client and server security technologies comprise an extensible security model upon which you can

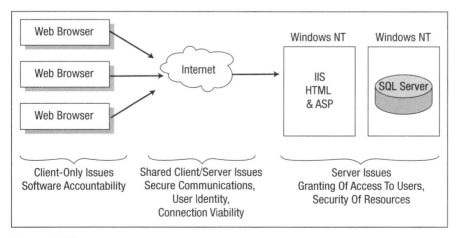

Figure 17.12
Areas where security is crucial in your Web-based applications.

build your solution. The following sections discuss some of these security considerations at both the client- and server-side of the model.

Microsoft Client Solutions

Microsoft Internet Explorer relies on a number of security technologies to protect the client from malicious attacks. The following list details some of the most important of these technologies:

♦ The Internet Options dialog box in Internet Explorer allows the user to set the security level for Java applets, ActiveX controls, cookies, scripts, Certificate Authorities (CAs), and other entities. These options can be set during installation by using the Internet Explorer Administrator's Kit (IEAK). Using Internet Security Zones, security restrictions can be specified for the following Internet zones: Local, Trusted, Internet, Restricted.

♦ Microsoft Java Virtual Machine (JVM) protects the user against nontrusted applets by running them in a secure process space called a *sandbox*.

♦ The ActiveX scripting architecture of Internet Explorer allows only safe (a complex distinction, to be sure, and one that the architecture makes based on a variety of different considerations) embedded scripts to be executed from within a Web page.

♦ Authenticode allows trusted code to be downloaded, optionally installed, and run on the client's computer. Authenticode uses digital signatures and certificate authorities to identify the author and assure the authenticity of a component.

Clearly, Internet Explorer provides some valuable tools for ensuring the safe, controlled access of content. Most other browser products—namely Netscape Communicator—support similar levels of assurance, though Communicator makes no direct allowance for ActiveX control downloading, and Communicator uses a similar, but competing, digital signature technology to Authenticode.

As a developer, security at the client side is important—but watching out for your company's interests will almost always be your number one priority. To that end, let's take a look at some of the security solutions that Microsoft provides for the server side of your environment.

Microsoft Server Solutions

Every Microsoft server product has built-in access security that is integrated with Windows NT Server's Access Control Security. This model satisfies the following two requirements:

♦ *Verification of user identity (authentication)*—All users must have a Windows NT account to log on to the network. An account consists of a unique account name and password. This is called the NT Challenge/Response logon protocol. The User Manager tool is used to set users, groups, and rights.

♦ *Controlled access to resources (authorization)*—Each user or group of users is given access rights to the computer's resources. Windows NT Explorer is used to set access rights to files and folders.

Although there are any number of variations on this model—different rules apply to SQL Server, MTS, IIS, and other server products—the underlying requirements of the model are always met by any BackOffice product, and should form the foundation of your server-side security model.

As noted in the "Categories Of Security Threats" section, some security threats are shared— they apply equally to both server and client. For such shared threats, it is necessary to find shared solutions, as described in the following section.

Shared Solutions

Both the client and server can utilize Windows NT Server's Access Control Security to provide secure communications and user authentication. In addition, Microsoft Internet products support the Windows NT security model and extend it in the following ways:

♦ Internet Information Server (IIS) also allows anonymous and basic text logon of Internet users. The Internet Service Manager tool can be used to set security options for this Web server. IIS is, for many developers, the tool of choice when developing over Windows NT, for many reasons, not just that it comes with the operating system.

♦ Microsoft Certificate Server enables the creation of certificates that can be used for identifying Internet users, establishing private communications, and signing code components. For many Web designers, the use of Certificate Server for designing secure applications has become an important part of the development process—both on the corporate intranet and for the outside Internet.

♦ IIS and Internet Explorer support the Secure Sockets Layer (SSL) 3.0, Private Communications Technology (PCT) 1.0, and Secure Electronic Transaction (SET) protocols for private point-to-point communication.

Introducing Visual InterDev

Microsoft Visual InterDev 6 is for developers who are designing, building, testing, debugging, deploying, and managing component-based, data-intensive Web applications. Most developers will use Visual InterDev to create the following:

♦ Data-driven Web applications using data sources supported by Open Database Connectivity (ODBC) or OLE DB

♦ Broad-reaching Web pages using HTML and script in Web applications that take advantage of the latest advances in browser technology

♦ Integrated solutions that can include applets or COM components created in Microsoft Visual Basic, Visual C++, Visual J++, and Visual FoxPro

Visual InterDev provides a robust development environment with a scripting object model, design-time controls, and an extensible toolbox for rapid design, testing, and debugging. In the following sections, we will digress a bit, to consider the techniques you will commonly apply to develop a Web application from within Visual InterDev, and introduce you briefly to working with InterDev IDE, based on the presumption that it is somewhat unfamiliar to you. In the event it *is* familiar to you, you can certainly skip this section and move ahead to the section entitled "Using Layouts."

The first step in developing a Web application is to create a new Web project. We will discuss this in the next section.

Starting A Web Project

The Web Project Wizard walks you through four steps that create a new project for you and set default properties for the project. The Web Project Wizard helps you complete the tasks listed in Table 17.7.

When a team builds a Web-based application, files can be hosted in three different locations:

♦ *Test Web server*—When a Web development process begins, a team member creates a project in Visual InterDev on a test Web server. This is where the master files for a site are hosted until the site is fully developed and tested.

♦ *Team development computers*—Team members edit files on their local development computers and save them to the Web-based application test server. When a master file is available on the test server (no one has a working copy of the master), any team member can retrieve and edit a copy of the master file.

♦ *Production Web server*—Once the files for the Web-based application are finished, the Web team publishes the files to a secure Web server. This ensures that files are not arbitrarily changed. The team can also provide the appropriate security on the production Web server so that no malicious tampering can occur.

Now that you have seen some of the basic issues that surround the creation of a Web application, it is worthwhile to consider what file types will make up Web applications that you create with Visual InterDev. Unlike creating applications with Access—where you generally have only a single file, or at most a single file and some VBA or HTML files—Visual InterDev Web applications use a wide variety of file types, specifically designed to address the different issues involved in creating a Web site. Let's look at the different file types.

Table 17.7   Tasks performable from the Web Project Wizard.

Task	Description
Start a new project	Creates the project and sets its default values.
Open an existing project	Takes you directly to the list of Visual Studio projects that exist on the developer's workstation.
Open one of the most recently used existing projects	Takes you directly to the Visual InterDev solutions that exist on the developer's workstation.

Starting Other Types Of Projects

You can also use the wizard to start other types of related Visual Studio projects, such as:

- *Start a database project*—Lets you create a new database project and allows direct manipulation of the database objects and data.

- *Create a distribution unit*—Automates the process of creating any one of three types of distribution files. Here you can create cabinet files, self-extracting setup files, and Zip files.

- *Create a utility project*—Creates a project to be used as a container for files that you want to build, such as a master project for several subprojects, or a list of custom build rules.

- *Create a Visual Studio Analyzer project*—Creates a project that contains performance data from all the components and systems.

You may occasionally find that you want to create these types of projects—most notably database projects—but we will not consider them in this book.

Web Application File Types

Web applications are composed of a number of different files. Table 17.8 lists those that are commonly used. Each file type is described in further detail later in this chapter.

In addition to using a variety of different file types, InterDev uses a series of child directories to help organize the placement of those files, as it is presumed that there may be many of them. The Web Project Wizard creates the folders detailed in Table 17.9 for a new Web project.

Table 17.8   File types that comprise the Web application.

File Type	Description
Global.asa	Each project might contain a single Global.asa file. This file is not absolutely required for ASP applications, but is included by default in InterDev-generated projects. Each project may not, however, have more than a single Global.asa file. This Active Server Application file contains global data and scripts for the Web application—global variables, database connections, and initialization and cleanup code.
.asp	Active Server Page files, which contain static text as well as data-bound controls that display data from a database.
.css	Cascading style sheet files, which contain information on customizing page element appearance.
.gif, .jpg, .jpeg, .bmp	Graphics files of various types that can be displayed in a Web application.
.htm or .html	HTML pages, which can contain forms and controls, static text, images, and links to other pages.
.sln	Solution files, which contain references to project, page, and other files that compose a Web application.
.vip	Project definition files, which contain Visual InterDev-specific information about the project.

Table 17.9   Folders automatically created by Visual InterDev when creating a new Web application.

Folder Name	Description
<root>	Named after the project; contains the default home page and the top-level pages for the site.
_Layouts	Contains the template HTML files for your selected layout, if you chose to apply a layout to the project.
_Private	Contains miscellaneous internal project files.
_ScriptLibrary	Contains the source for script objects used by Visual InterDev controls.
_Themes	Contains the bitmaps and the cascading style sheets for a selected theme, if you chose to apply a layout to the project.
Images	Created empty, this folder contains bitmaps added to the site's HTML pages.

By default, the Web Project Wizard creates two pages in the root directory: Search.htm (the Web-based application search page) and Global.asa (the Active Server Page application-wide script file). Additionally, InterDev will add all additional page files that you create into the root directory, although you can change this default performance at runtime.

Once you have created your Web application, you must do something with it—like an Access ADP file, the Visual InterDev project does not really contain anything until you add items to the project. When you add components to the project, you will often want to edit those components, even control how they integrate with the rest of the components within the project. Understanding the different editing modes that InterDev supports is therefore important, so you will learn about them in the next section.

InterDev's Editing Modes

The files for your Web application reside in two places: in the project directory on your computer and in the virtual directory on the master Web server. When you are working in your project, you are working on the local files. The way in which your changes are made to the version on the master Web server depends on which of two project modes you are working in—local mode or master mode.

In *local mode*, changes made to the files are not immediately saved to the master Web server. The new versions are sent to the master Web server when you explicitly request that the master Web server be updated. In *master mode*, changes are saved to the local version and the master version at the same time.

Tip

When you import an existing page into your project, Visual InterDev adds the page to the master Web server and locks it. To edit the page, you must first request a working copy.

Whichever mode you choose, you must add some components to the Web site to make it work. In the next section, we will consider the Web Project Wizard, and what it can help you to accomplish with InterDev.

Generating Components Of The Web Application

To create a new project, you typically use the New Project dialog box to specify a new project and then launch the Web Project Wizard to generate a set of starter Web directories and pages.

The Web Project Wizard features four steps, each with its own dialog box. The following list outlines the choices presented in each of these dialog boxes:

♦ Create a new project, a process that includes entering a project name and location. Next, specify a server and development mode, which includes entering the name of the server that you will be using, specifying whether or not you want to connect to that server using the Secure Sockets Layer, and selecting the mode in which you want to work. As detailed in the previous section, master mode updates the master Web application automatically, whereas local mode lets you control when updates are made.

♦ Specify the name for your Web application, including choices that let you create a new application with the same name as that of the project, connect to an existing Web application on the server to which you connected in the first step, enable or disable site searching, and more.

♦ Apply navigation control layout to your project, including specifying the location for navigation bars on the pages you will create.

♦ Apply a visual look and feel to your project, including specifying default backgrounds, headings, and list styles to the pages that you create.

The easiest way to design a Web-based application is to create a *site diagram*. A site diagram is a graphical tool that lets you design the hierarchical relationships among pages in a site. Let's take a look at how to use site diagrams.

How A Site Diagram Works

In a site diagram, you create hierarchical relationships among pages by grouping them into *trees*. A tree contains one or more parent pages and one or more child pages. Each Web application can have multiple site diagrams, and each site diagram can have multiple trees.

To create parent, child, and sibling relationships, you drop pages beside or beneath one another in a site diagram. Use the dashed link lines to aid you in creating relationships. Site diagrams use layouts to create and maintain the links between pages. To add a site diagram to a project, perform the following steps:

1. From the Project menu, click on Add Web Item.

2. Click on Site Diagram.

3. Assign a name to the diagram in the Name text box and click on Open.

When you create a site diagram, a home page with a file name of default.htm is automatically created for the site and placed at the top of the diagram. To create the rest of the site, you add either HTML pages or Active Server Pages (ASPs) to the site diagram. When all of the content of the Web page is static, you should use HTML pages. When some or all of the Web page content is dynamic, you should use ASPs. To add a Web page to a site diagram, and therefore to the Web site itself, perform the following steps:

1. Place the cursor anywhere on the site diagram and right-click.

2. From the pop-up menu, select the type of page that you want to add: a new HTML page, a new ASP page, an existing page, or another home page.

3. Use the drag-and-drop feature to create the hierarchical relationship among the pages in the site.

4. Apply the appropriate layouts for the pages at the various levels of the site.

Warning

You can convert an ASP page to an HTML page by changing the extension, but you cannot convert an HTML page to an ASP page.

Before you begin using site diagrams in any depth, you should understand what layouts are and how they are related to site diagrams. In this next section, you will learn about layouts.

Using Layouts

Layouts define how the navigation controls of a site are arranged on a page. They depend upon setting parent, children, and sibling relationships among pages on a site. Layouts make use of different combinations of regions on a page. Figure 17.13 shows the five possible regions of the page that can be controlled by a layout.

For the most part, layouts make use of the top, left, and bottom portions of a page. Visual InterDev creates these regions by using HTML tables, and each layout is based on a unique HTML template. The template contains the source text for the layout. When the layout is applied to the page, Visual InterDev inserts header and footer information into the page.

Changing Layouts

You can specify a layout for a site when you create the project. You can also change layouts for individual pages while creating the site diagram. In addition, you can change the layout and theme for a page at any time during the development process. To change the theme

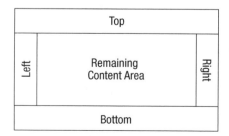

Figure 17.13
The possible regions of the page that you can control with layouts.

and/or the layout for a page, select the page and then, from the Edit menu (or the context menu), choose the Apply Theme And Layout command.

You can use the layout templates available in Visual InterDev, but you can also create a custom layout template by modifying an existing template and saving it with a new name to the _Layouts directory.

Cascading style sheets (CSSs) let you define a set of styles that override the browser's standard HTML styles. For example, you can use a CSS to set a specific font style, face, and color attribute for all **<H1>** tags. Cascading style sheets also let you adjust layout and formatting—for example, line spacing, justification, and border properties—for HTML elements and the entire document. This lets you give your pages a unique and consistent design. In the next section, we will look at the ways in which you can implement style sheets within your application.

*While a complete discussion of style sheets is well beyond the scope of this book, Visual InterDev Help does offer substantial suggestions on their use, and the W3C Organization includes the specification for the style sheets standard on their Web site at **www.w3c.org**.*

Implementing Style Sheets

You can implement style sheets in three ways within your Web application. Each of these three methods will be appropriate in different situations. The following list itemizes each of the possible choices you have:

◆ *Linked*—Style definitions are stored in a document that is separate from the HTML pages to which it applies. A single style sheet can be linked to many different HTML pages. The CD-ROM that comes with this book contains the samples linkable.htm and linked.css, which show how this works.

◆ *Embedded*—Style definitions are stored in the header section within an HTML document. The style definition applies to all instances of that style within that HTML page. The CD-ROM contains a sample called embed.htm, which shows how this works.

◆ *Inline*—Style definitions, created for individual elements within an HTML page, are added as properties to the elements to which they apply. The CD-ROM contains a sample file called inline.htm, which shows how this works.

Of these three choices, linked CSS allows for the highest degree of reuse and site consistency. If you use all three methods listed above, the inline styles take precedence over the embedded **<STYLE>** block, which in turn overrides the linked styles. To link a style sheet to a page, perform the following steps:

1. Create a new CSS file for the style (or use an existing one). Typically, these files have an extension of .css. Visual InterDev contains a CSS Editor that allows you to create and modify CSS files. Figure 17.14 shows an example of a CSS file loaded in the CSS Editor.

2. Apply the style sheet to a page by adding a **<LINK>** tag in the HTML document heading section (between the **<HEAD>** and **</HEAD>** tags). You can do this by manually inserting a statement such as the following into your page:

```
<LINK REL="stylesheet" TYPE="text/css" HREF="Access2000CS/linkable.css">
```

In Visual InterDev, you can also simply drag the name of the style sheet from the Project Explorer and drop it within the head tags of the HTML or ASP whose styles you want to set.

Understanding Themes

Themes are composed of sets of graphics and one or more cascading style sheets that control styles, font, and graphics. Themes provide your pages with a consistent look and feel.

You can set a default theme for an entire project so that each page you create in that project will have the same theme applied. Even with a default theme for a project, you can override the default on particular files where you might want to apply a different theme or no theme at all. Themes offer two advantages:

♦ They provide your pages with a consistent look and feel.

♦ You can change themes without changing content.

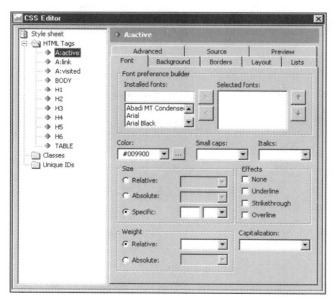

Figure 17.14
An example of a CSS file loaded in the CSS Editor.

Figure 17.15 shows two copies of an Internet Explorer window, each of which contains the same content rendered with two different themes.

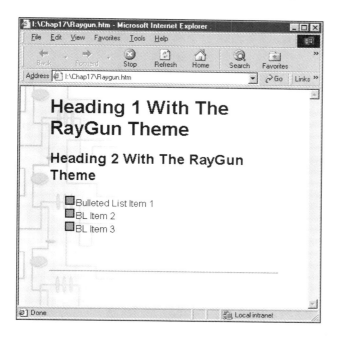

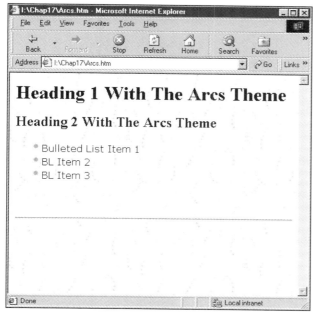

Figure 17.15
Changing application appearance with effective use of themes.

Now that you have learned the basics of working with Visual InterDev, and considered some of the issues to keep in mind when creating Web applications, it is time to go ahead and use Visual InterDev to create some sample content. In the next section, we'll walk through the steps you need to follow to create HTML pages in InterDev. We will consider Active Server Pages creation a little later on.

Creating HTML Pages With InterDev

In this section, you will learn how to create simple HTML pages with InterDev, and how to set global attributes, such as background color, for individual pages. You will also learn how to add text, graphics, and hyperlinks to a page, as well as how to use tables and frames to arrange items on a page.

Note

The goal for this section is to show you how to hand-code some of the typical HTML tags. Larger sites will use style sheets, themes, and layouts to handle layout and formatting issues. Furthermore, this section is not intended to teach you how to use HTML—you should read one of the many excellent books on HTML design available on the market today if you need guidance of this type.

We will begin by discussing how you can control the basic appearance of your Web pages, then move on to consider how you can add constituent components to each individual page while you design.

Setting Page Properties

Just as with an Access Form or a Data Access Page (DAP), each HTML page has properties that you can set in the HTML Editor. These properties affect the appearance of the page and provide information about the scripting language and model to use with the page. To display the property page for an HTML page, perform the following steps:

1. Double-click on the file name in the Project Explorer window.

2. Click on the Source tab at the bottom of the HTML Editor window.

3. Place the cursor on the page and right-click.

4. Select Properties from the pop-up menu.

The Property Pages dialog box contains two tabs—General and Color And Margins. On these tabs, you can set many of the common visual properties for your pages. On the General tab, you can set:

♦ *Background image*—The image that appears on a page behind the contents of the HTML page

♦ *Page title*—A descriptive word or phrase that appears in a browser's title bar when the page is displayed

♦ *Default Scripting Language*—Default client and server scripting language used if not specifically overridden by the code author

The General tab also has advanced settings to determine the behavior of ASP script and Design-Time Controls (DTCs).

Some of the settings for the Color And Margins tab include:

♦ *Background color*—The color that appears behind the contents of the page

♦ *Link text color*—Default color for link text

♦ *Page margins*—Default settings for the top, bottom, left, and right margins for the page

♦ *Text font color*—Default color of the text font used on the page

Now that you have seen how to set important page properties from within the HTML editor, let's consider how you can add text and graphics to an HTML page.

Working With The HTML Editor

The HTML editor makes it easy for you to add text and graphics to an HTML page. To format text portions for a page, you use the HTML toolbar. To design the look and feel of the individual page, you use the Design toolbar. Both these toolbars appear at the top of the InterDev window, and can be hidden, sized, moved, and so on, as necessary.

Warning

These two toolbars are enabled only for Design view.

The following sections take a closer look at the process of adding text and graphics to a single page.

Adding Text To A Single Static Page

You use the HTML editor to apply formatting to an HTML page in the same way that you apply formatting to an Office 2000 document, such as Word 2000. For example, you can cut and paste text or use the drag-and-drop feature to move text to a new location. To change font and paragraph properties, you use the HTML toolbar or the HTML menu.

Some of the available formatting options that let you govern how text appears on the page include the following:

♦ Changing the style of a paragraph to make it centered or aligned right

♦ Changing the text font to make it bold, italic, or underlined

♦ Changing text to a bulleted or numbered list

Managing text is simple—but, then, it usually is. Managing images is also simple, from within InterDev—an improvement over the previous version that may catch you by surprise. The next section discusses the steps involved in effective management of images within a single page.

Adding Images To A Single Static Page

Images make a Web-based application look interesting. In fact, for the majority of your users, images will be a crucial part of making your site *look* and *feel* effective. The HTML editor that comes with Visual InterDev includes a library of clip art for commonly used buttons, icons, and backgrounds. You can also buy third-party clip art, have your graphic artist create custom art, and so on. To insert an image into a static Web page, perform the following steps:

1. Add the image to the images folder.

2. Open the page where you want to insert the image.

3. Drag the image file from Project Explorer onto the page.

4. To set properties for the image, such as alternate text, alignment, and size, right-click on the image, and then click on Properties to display the Property Pages dialog box.

Note

Many users turn off image display to download Web pages faster. Therefore, you should always provide alternate text for images on your Web pages.

Adding HTML Tables To A Page

One of the most common elements in any HTML page—as you saw earlier in the discussion about layouts—is an HTML table. Tables can contain any valid HTML text, images, forms, controls, or other tables. With the HTML editor, you can create a table with the Insert Table dialog box. To create a table within Visual InterDev, perform the following steps:

1. Click on the location where you want the table to appear on the page.

2. On the Table menu, click on Insert Table.

3. In the Insert Table dialog box, select the number of rows and columns, an alignment for the table, and a border size for the table. Furthermore, if you want the table to use a specific percentage of the page, or if you want it to be a fixed pixel size, modify the Width setting in the Table Attributes option group.

After you have inserted a table, you can customize it using the Table menu. To change the properties for individual table cells, right-click on the cell, and then click on Properties. The following list describes some of the cell properties you can set:

♦ *Background color*—Sets the background color of the cell

♦ *Cell alignment*—Sets vertical and horizontal alignment of cell content

♦ *Rows spanned*—Sets the cell to span down more than one row

♦ *Columns spanned*—Sets the cell to span across more than one column

Types Of Graphics Formats Allowed On Web Pages

As you may or may not be aware, there are limitations imposed by the W3C specification on what types of images you can embed within your pages. In fact, only two different graphics formats are commonly used in Web pages and specified as such by the W3C (although such types as TIFs and PNGs have achieved substantial popularity in recent years):

- *Graphics Interchange Format (.gif)*—A GIF file is an encoded and compressed file for images of up to 8 bits of color.
- *Joint Photographic Expert Group (.jpeg)*—A JPEG file is an encoded and compressed file for images of up to 24 bits of color.

It is important to note, however, that Web pages can also embed other graphic format files, such as Windows BMP files, but such formats are not supported on all platforms. You should make sure to carefully evaluate your image embedding decisions before deploying a site accessible from the Internet.

Understanding how Visual InterDev builds and uses tables is important because tables are the primary tool for constructing multicolumn layouts on Web pages. Another primary tool that is essential to successful Web applications—in fact, a tool that is essential to the Web itself—is the use of hyperlinks.

Using Hyperlinks From InterDev

HTML lets you link text or images to another document. The browser highlights these elements to indicate that they are hyperlinks. You add hyperlinks from pages in your current project to a page either on an intranet or on the Web. To create a hyperlink with the HTML Editor, perform the following steps:

1. Select the text that will identify the hyperlink.
2. On the HTML menu, click on Link, or click on the Hyperlink button on the toolbar.
3. In the Hyperlink dialog box, specify the relative or absolute URL to which you want to link and click on OK.

For example, to create a hyperlink to the page Checkout_books.asp in your current Web project, select the content on the page that will be the link text, click on the Link button, and then type "Checkout_books.asp" in the URL box.

The single hyperlink-related tag for HTML is **<A>**, which stands for *anchor*. The following example code shows the HTML that the HTML editor adds to a Web page when you create a hyperlink:

```
<A HREF="Checkout_books.asp">Go to the Checkout Counter!</A>
```

In this example, the syntax makes the text "Go to the Checkout Counter!" a relative hyperlink to the page Checkout_books.asp, which is located in the same folder.

Using Frames With Your Web Pages

Historically, one of the most common design elements that you would encounter on Web pages were frames. Frames are not as popular today—in no small part because of the extra "real estate" that all those different scroll bars consumed. However, frames may still be a sensible choice in some situations. Web pages that use frames include two main elements:

♦ *Main frame HTML file*—This file contains the tags necessary to implement each frame on a page, along with references to the HTML files for each frame. The file does not contain a **<BODY>** tag.

♦ *Source HTML files*—Each frame on a page contains its own source HTML file.

Given this structure, creating a Web page or pages that will use frames requires the creation of a series of files. To create an HTML page with frames, perform the following steps:

1. Create one source HTML file for each frame on a Web page. These source files can contain any HTML tags, though you should try to make sure that the appearance of the files is relatively consistent with the other frame files.

2. Create a new HTML file that contains **<HTML>** and **<HEAD>** tags, but not a **<BODY>** tag. This is the main frame file that users open with a Web browser.

3. In the area of the document that typically contains the **<BODY>** tag, add a **<FRAMESET>** tag for each group of frames.

4. For each frame on a page, add a **<FRAME>** tag, and set the **SRC** (source) attribute to the name of the HTML file that you want to appear in the frame.

The following example code creates two vertical frames, and fills them with cell_1.htm and cell_2.htm in the left and right frames, respectively:

```
<FRAMESET COLS="*, 2*">
   <FRAME SRC="cell_1.htm">
   <FRAME SRC="cell_2.htm">
</FRAMESET>
```

Note that the use of the **"*, 2*"** specification in the **<FRAMESET>** tag results in a left frame that is half as wide as the right frame, because they are treated as relative size attributes—basically stating that the first frame is one-third of the available space, and the right frame is two-thirds of the available space. Figure 17.16 shows what you will see in the browser if you use these **<FRAMESET>** tags and the two files they specify; the frameset.htm example on the companion CD-ROM does just that.

The **<FRAMESET>** tag defines the location, size, and orientation of frames on an HTML page. This tag has two attributes: **ROWS** and **COLS**. You can create a frameset with either rows or columns. The **ROWS** attribute defines horizontal frames. It is followed by a comma-delimited list of the sizes for each frame on the page. The following example code defines a page with two horizontal frames:

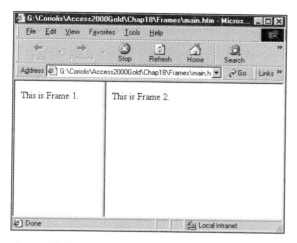

Figure 17.16
The appearance of a simple page that uses frames.

Browsers That Do Not Support Frames

Not all browsers support the frames feature in HTML 3/4. As a consideration to users of these browsers, you can supply alternate HTML by placing it in the **<NOFRAMES>** tag of the main frame HTML file.

The **<NOFRAMES>** tag appears after the **<FRAMESET>** tag, as shown in the following example code:

```
<HTML>
<FRAMESET COLS="*, 2*">
   <FRAME SRC="cell_1.htm">
   <FRAME SRC="cell_2.htm">
</FRAMESET>

<NOFRAMES>
<BODY>
  ...Page Code...
</BODY>
</NOFRAMES>
</HTML>
```

It is important to recognize that although this was an important issue even only a couple years ago, very few browsers in use nowadays do not support frames. However, just to be safe, you should nevertheless design your pages to allow for those few users whose browsers do *not* use frames—although, in most cases, the extent of your allowance will often be a statement such as "this page supports frames, your browser doesn't, get a browser that supports frames."

```
<HTML>
<FRAMESET ROWS="100, *">

</FRAMESET>
</HTML>
```

You can specify actual pixel sizes, percentages, or relative sizes. In the following example code, the first frame is 120 pixels, the third frame is 20 percent of the total height, and the second frame occupies the remainder of the height:

```
<FRAMESET ROWS="120, *, 20%">
```

As you saw previously, you can create vertical frames by using the **COLS** attribute. You specify the frame in the same way as the **ROWS** attribute.

Clearly, navigating through frames requires you to address some minor issues to handle the differences in the way the pages appear. In the next section, you will learn how to manage target frames for hyperlinks.

Target Frames

When a user clicks on a hyperlink in a frame, the link loads in the target frame. When you create a hyperlink, you can change the default target frame where a link should be loaded by using the **TARGET** attribute of the **<A>** tag. Let's consider exactly how this works.

If you specify the **TARGET** as **"frame_name"**, you set the link to load the specified page into a named frame. In the **<FRAMES>** tag of the main frame page, this is the **NAME** attribute of the frame you want to load. In the following sample code, the sample.htm page will be loaded into the target frame named **"frame1"**:

```
<A TARGET="frame1" HREF="sample.htm">
```

If you specify the **TARGET** as **"_blank"**, you set the link to load into a new blank window. The window is not named. The following sample code shows how you will implement such performance:

```
<A TARGET="_blank" HREF="sample.htm">
```

If you specify the **TARGET** as **"_parent"**, you set the link to load into the parent window of the window in which the link is located. The following sample code loads sample.htm into the parent of the current window (this is a common way to eliminate frames):

```
<A TARGET="_parent" HREF="sample.htm">
```

If you specify the **TARGET** as **"_self"**, you set the link to load into the same window in which the link was clicked. This is the default performance—meaning that you do not have to specify such performance, unless you have changed the default somewhere else in the page. The following sample code loads the sample.htm page into the frame in which the page containing the hyperlink is currently displayed:

```
<A TARGET="_self" HREF="sample.htm">
```

If you specify the **TARGET** as **"_top"**, you set the link to load into the entire window. This is also a common way to eliminate frames, as shown here:

```
<A TARGET="_top" HREF="sample.htm">
```

You can also specify that the target frame for loading all hyperlinks on a page should be in the same location. To set this location, you use the **<BASE>** tag with the **TARGET** attribute. In the following example code, the **<BASE>** tag specifies that all links should be loaded in the body of a window:

```
<BASE TARGET="_top">
```

Note
With the HTML editor, you set the target frame in which a link should be loaded by using the Hyperlink dialog box. To set the base target frame for all hyperlinks on a page, you use the Property Pages dialog box.

Controlling the appearance of content within your Web pages—as you have probably guessed already—is a little more complex than doing so with Access or other interface products, because of the way in which HTML pages are parsed. Two of the most powerful tags at your disposal for controlling the appearance of items on your HTML pages are **<DIV>** and **<SPAN>**, discussed in the next section.

Using <DIV>s And <SPAN>s

<DIV> (short for Division) and **<SPAN>** are HTML tags that group elements of an HTML page when you want to perform an action on all of them. You use these tools to apply style or absolute positioning information.

Both **<DIV>**s and **<SPAN>**s are used to group HTML elements together, typically so that an action can be uniformly applied—for example, a cascading style sheet or dynamic HTML operation. In other words, both **<DIV>**s and **<SPAN>**s act as containers for other elements.

The difference between these two tags is that an implicit line break is inserted after the closing **<DIV>** tag—meaning that only items that are not meant to appear within the same horizontal space as other items should be surrounded by **<DIV>** tags. To create a **<DIV>** in your page, perform the following steps:

1. Switch to Design view.
2. Select the portion of the HTML document that you want to include in the **DIV**.
3. From the HTML menu, choose DIV.
4. In the Insert DIV dialog box, choose a positioning option, either Absolute or Inline.

The steps to create a **<SPAN>** are similar; perform the following steps:

1. Switch to Design view.
2. Select the portion of the HTML document that you want to include in the **SPAN**.
3. From the HTML menu, choose SPAN.

The divspan.htm file, contained on the companion CD-ROM, shows a little more about how these two useful tags work.

But enough about formatting the appearance of your Web pages. Our focus is on building front ends against database back ends—a topic we will get to in depth in the next chapter. However, before getting into server-side scripting—the majority of the topic of Chapter 19—it is worthwhile to discuss the classic method of receiving input from a user and sending it to the server: the HTML form.

Working With HTML Forms

One way to obtain information from a user and send it to a Web server is to use an HTML form. An HTML form contains standard HTML controls, which are also referred to as *intrinsic controls*. These controls are supported by all Web browsers. Standard controls include text boxes, command buttons, radio buttons, and drop-down list boxes. In the following sections, you will learn how to add standard HTML controls and forms to an HTML page.

Standard HTML controls reside within forms on an HTML page. On a form, controls are also known as *form fields*. The following illustration shows an HTML form that contains standard HTML controls. To view each type of control on the form, click on the control. Figure 17.17 shows an example of an HTML form within a Web browser.

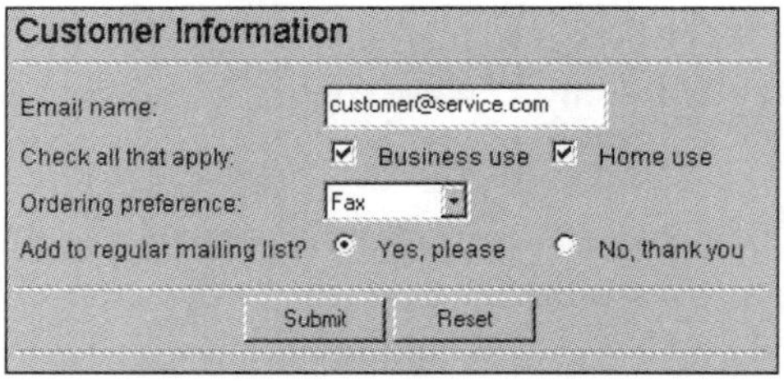

Figure 17.17
The HTML form within a Web browser.

Note

Internet Explorer does not require standard HTML controls to be contained on forms, but other browsers do. Therefore, you should always place standard HTML controls on forms.

Adding intrinsic controls to your HTML forms is a straightforward process. The following list contains the name of each of the controls that are available on the HTML toolbox:

♦ Button

♦ Checkbox

♦ Drop-down list box

♦ File field

♦ Form

♦ List box

♦ Option button

♦ Password

♦ Reset button

♦ Submit button

♦ Text area

♦ Text box

Note

The HTML tab also contains entries for the following HTML elements: horizontal rule, line break, paragraph break, and space.

To add an intrinsic control to an HTML form, perform the following steps:

1. From the HTML tab of the Toolbox, drag the control to its desired position on the page.

2. To set properties for each control, click on the control and edit its properties in the Properties window.

3. When you use the HTML editor to add standard controls to an HTML document, you must also add a form control. The following example code shows how to create a form that contains a text box, two checkboxes, and two buttons:

```
<FORM METHOD=POST>
    Email name: <INPUT NAME="txtEditBox" VALUE="My Name"><P>
    Check all that apply:
    <INPUT TYPE="CHECKBOX" NAME="chkBusinessUse"> Business use
    <INPUT TYPE="CHECKBOX" NAME="chkHomeUse"> Home use<P>
    <INPUT TYPE=SUBMIT VALUE="Submit">
    <INPUT TYPE=RESET VALUE="Reset">
</FORM>
```

Forms can contain any HTML elements except other forms. You can add more than one HTML form to a document; however, forms cannot be nested. HTML forms package the names and values of each control, and then send them to the location specified by the **ACTION** attribute. The location can be a CGI application, an ISAPI application, or an Active Server Page.

In the following example code, the form will send information to the file events.asp:

```
<FORM ACTION=events.asp METHOD=POST>
```

In HTML, the **ACTION** attribute is referred to as a *form handler*. To set a handler for a form, right-click in the form to see the Form Properties dialog box. Once you have designed the basics of the form, you need to configure it to send information to the server.

Sending Control Values To A Server

To send values of a control to the Web server, place a Submit button on the form. Only controls with the **NAME** attribute will be sent to the server.

Note

As mentioned previously, Internet Explorer does not require that all standard controls be placed on forms. However, if you want to send the information from controls to the server, you must use a form.

Only standard HTML controls are submitted with a form. To submit the value of an ActiveX control or Java applet with a form, set the **VALUE** attribute of a standard HTML control to the appropriate property of the ActiveX control or Java applet.

Typically, you use hidden controls to submit values of ActiveX controls or Java applets with a form. You create a hidden control in the form, and then add client-side script to the **OnSubmit** event procedure for the form.

In the **OnSubmit** event procedure of the form, you set the **VALUE** attribute of the hidden control to an appropriate property of the ActiveX control or Java applet. A hidden control is a standard HTML control, so the value of the control will be submitted with the other HTML controls on the form. Most major Web browsers currently support one or both of the two scripting languages: VBScript and ECMAScript (also known as JScript in the Microsoft implementation, and JavaScript in the Netscape implementation). Choosing a scripting language is a very important part of your Web application's development.

Choosing A Scripting Language

When choosing a scripting language, you must consider the following two critical issues:

♦ *Browser compatibility*—Web browsers must include a scripting interpreter for the language you choose. Internet Explorer 4 and later has interpreters for VBScript, JScript, and JavaScript. Netscape Navigator provides an interpreter for JavaScript. As a rule, you should always use ECMAScript within your client-side script code.

♦ *Programmer familiarity*—Choose a scripting language that is similar to a language you know. If you have Visual Basic experience, you can quickly learn VBScript. If you have Java or C experience, JScript and JavaScript will be more familiar to you.

Note

Netscape Navigator does not natively support VBScript, but you can acquire a plug-in from Netscape and NCompass Labs.

You can place script code anywhere on a Web page, but to simplify code maintenance, place all of your code within the same **<SCRIPT>** section. You can insert the **<SCRIPT>** tag in either the **<BODY>** or **<HEAD>** section of the HTML page.

Note

*Browsers that do not support scripting code will display the code as text in a Web page. To prevent browsers from displaying code, add comment tags (**<!--** and **-->**) around the script code.*

Where To Go From Here

In this chapter, you learned about the basics of working with Visual InterDev, designing Web applications, choosing an application model, and more. In Chapter 19, we will move on to a discussion of Active Server Pages with database back ends; in other words, we will work more with VBScript and the use of ADO to connect to data sources.

Many of the issues described in this chapter may seem a bit odd to you, if you haven't worked with HTML in the past. It may be worthwhile for you to pick up a book (such as The Coriolis Group's *Dynamic HTML Black Book*) to help you learn more about HTML, Dynamic HTML, and the issues surrounding effective front-end presentation of your information over the Web.

Chapter 18

Using Active Server Pages For Client/Server

As you saw in Chapter 17, the power of the Web as a database front end really becomes apparent when you use Visual InterDev as your tool for designing the front end and accessing the data. We looked at InterDev in general and briefly considered VBScript as the language you will commonly use when designing with InterDev. I also noted that VBScript can execute at one of two places—at the client or at the server. In fact, for best compatibility, you will often use ECMAScript (also known as JavaScript or JScript) at the client side, and VBScript on the server side. We will consider this concept in more detail in Chapter 20; for now, we will focus on the creation of server-side objects using VBScript. Such objects are known as *Active Server Pages (ASPs)*, and we will consider their use throughout this chapter.

Defining Active Server Pages

Under Internet Information Server (IIS) 4, an *application* is any collection of files in a directory whose properties can be set and that can run in a separate process space. ASP applications are just one type of application that can run under IIS 4.

This chapter explains what ASP applications are and describes their main features; it also moves on to a discussion of common uses for ASP applications and some consideration of how they will integrate into the entirety of your client/server model. ASP applications, for the most part, are like conventional standalone applications—the big difference, of course, is that they are designed to be executed over the Web.

For example, ASP applications can retain user information between sessions, or uses, of the application. These types of applications can also retain information while the user moves from one page to another. ASP applications have two important features that are common (in some form) to all ASP applications—a starting-point directory and global data. In the following sections, we will consider the importance of each of these elements in turn.

A Starting-Point Directory

When you create an application (that is, an ASP application that is running on Windows NT and IIS 4), you will use the IIS Internet Service Manager (a plug-in to the Microsoft Management Console [MMC]) to designate the application's starting-point directory for your Web site. All files and directories under the starting-point directory in your Web site are considered part of the application until another starting-point directory is found.

Therefore, you end up using directory boundaries to define the scope of an application. You can have more than one application per Web site, but each application must be configured differently. Visual InterDev handles all of these tasks for you when you create a new Web project. IIS natively supports several different types of applications, including ASPs, Internet Server Application Programming Interface (ISAPI), Common Gateway Interface (CGI), Internet Database Connector (IDC), and Server-Side Include (SSI) applications.

Note
Under IIS 4, Web applications are handled like Visual Basic applications—that is, you can unload them in the same way that you unload Visual Basic applications. You can also set your application to run in a process space separate from IIS.

Although the directory tree that contains the application defines its scope, you can still have global data within the context of the application itself. This information is maintained within a special file contained in the application's directory structure, as discussed in the next section.

Global Data With Active Server Applications

ASP applications declare global data in the global.asa file. This optional file is processed by the Web server and can be used to make data available to all pages in the application. The server processes the global.asa file automatically whenever the following actions occur:

♦ The application starts or ends.

♦ Individual users start and stop browser sessions that access the application's ASP pages.

This second point is a critical one—it makes the distinction between actually stopping and starting the application (which will likely occur only very rarely, such as when the server needs to be rebooted) and stopping and starting a given connection to the application—a logical concept that ASP considers a "session." We will look more at sessions in a moment.

In general, you will use a global.asa file to handle situations within your application that apply to either one of these overriding concepts—either an application's lifetime, or a session's lifetime. Specifically, in a global.asa file, you can, and generally will, do any of the following:

♦ Initialize application or session variables

♦ Declare Component Object Model (COM) components with application or session scope

♦ Perform other operations that pertain to the application as a whole

An application does not start until a user requests an ASP file in the starting-point directory. However, once started, the application will continue to run until it is no longer being accessed by any users, other applications, connections to data sources, and so on, at which point it will automatically unload itself. Connections to data sources are a particularly important concept in ASP applications—that is, for the most part, the whole reason why you write ASP applications—to access data.

If you intend for your Web application to use data in an Open Database Connectivity (ODBC) database, you connect to the database by adding a data connection to your Web application. Visual InterDev generates script within the global.asa file to save all of the information for connecting to the database in application variables. We will look at data connections in more detail later in this chapter.

Understanding How HTTP And ASP Work Together

As you have seen in previous chapters, Web applications use Hypertext Transfer Protocol (HTTP) to implement communication between the browser and the server. When a user requests a page, the browser creates an HTTP request message and sends it to the server. In response, the server creates an HTTP response message that is returned to the Web browser. The response message contains an HTML document. You saw the fundamentals of the HTTP session in Chapter 17. However, because of the role that Active Server Pages play in the whole process, it is worth taking a brief additional look at the process itself.

An HTTP Session

Figure 18.1 shows an HTTP session and the process that occurs when a user opens an HTML document on a Web server.

The following steps describe the HTTP session process:

1. The browser initiates a TCP/IP connection to the server.

2. The browser packages a request for an HTML document from the server into an HTTP request message, and then sends the message to the server by using a TCP/IP connection. The first line of the message contains the HTTP request method. For a simple page request, the **GET** method is used.

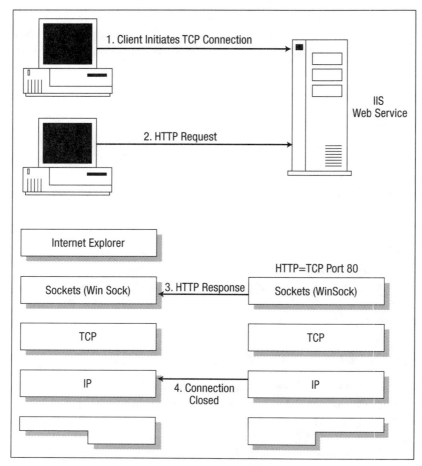

Figure 18.1
The steps that comprise the HTTP session.

3. The server receives the HTTP request and processes it based on the request method contained in the request line.

4. The server then sends back an HTTP response message. Part of the response message is a status line that contains code indicating whether the attempt to satisfy the HTTP request was successful.

5. When the Web browser receives the HTTP response message, the TCP/IP connection is closed, and the HTTP session terminates.

If the requested HTML document contains embedded objects, such as graphic images, the browser makes subsequent requests for each embedded object. For example, if a page contains three GIF images, a background sound, and an ActiveX control, six separate HTTP sessions are required to retrieve the entire page—five for the embedded objects and one for the page itself.

Note

If both the Web browser and Web server support HTTP Keep-Alive packets and retransmissions, connections are maintained even after a connection's initial request is completed. The connection is active and available for subsequent requests. Keep-Alives avoid the substantial cost of establishing and terminating connections. Keep-Alives are supported by Internet Information Server 1.0 (and later), Internet Explorer 2.0 (and later), and Netscape Navigator 2.0 (and later).

The .asp extension for ASP files tells the Web server that the page contains server script that it should process before returning the page to the browser. The main difference between ASPs and HTML pages is the location where the script is run. A special type of HTML page—known as Dynamic HTML, or client script—is run on the client, in the browser, after the page is sent from the server. ASP, or server script, is run on the server before the page is sent to the browser. The Web server processes the script and generates the HTML pages that are returned to the Web browser.

Now that you have seen some of the fundamentals of how an ASP application works, and what the differences are between an ASP application and a standard HTML-based application, let's take a look at how to code ASPs.

Coding Active Server Pages

Server script and client script look very similar because they both use the same languages (presuming you are using VBScript at the client side). The main difference is in how script blocks are specified. You can indicate server script three different ways when writing ASP files. The first manner is the so-called "preferred syntax," and is substantially more formal than the other two. You will most frequently use it when writing larger blocks of script language to run on the server. The implementation looks similar to the following:

```
<SCRIPT LANGUAGE=VBSCRIPT RUNAT=SERVER>
    server-side script goes here
</SCRIPT>
```

In the previous configuration, you explicitly specify not only that the script is server-side, but also what language to use. Alternatively, you can use the following nomenclature, which you will most often encounter with inline scripting. It uses the default script language for the page or project, and is often more difficult to read, but is easier to type. You implement such server-side script as shown here:

```
<% server-side script goes here, on multiple lines %>
```

Finally, you may occasionally need to do some inline scripting that returns only the value of an expression, as shown in the following example:

```
<%= server-side script yielding a result goes here %>
```

In contrast, the following two snippets of sample code contain server and client script that add date and time information to a page. The main difference is that the server script tells users the time and date at the server, whereas the client script tells users the time and date at their computers. The server-side script looks similar to the following:

```
<HTML>
<BODY>
<H3>Welcome to Visual InterDev Programming And Access Client/Server</H3>
The time at the server is <%=Time()%><BR>
The date is <%=Date()%>.
</BODY>
</HTML>
```

On the other hand, the client-side VBScript code looks similar to the following:

```
<HTML>
<BODY>
<H3>Welcome to Visual InterDev Programming and Access Client/Server</H3>
The time at your computer is
<SCRIPT LANGUAGE=VBScript>
Document.Write time()
</SCRIPT>
.<BR>
The date is
<SCRIPT LANGUAGE=VBScript>
Document.Write date()
</SCRIPT>.
</BODY>
</HTML>
```

As you can see, the differences between the two are not particularly substantial, though you do use a significantly different nomenclature to refer to the fact that the **date** and **time** are both simply yielding a result for output to the client.

Note

*The two periods appear on their own, immediately following the closing <**SCRIPT**> tags, because HTML does not insert carriage returns unless instructed to. The periods will print right after the time and date in the previous example.*

Now that you have had the most basic of introductions to the difference between client-side and server-side script, let's talk briefly about processing directives before moving on to the built-in objects that ASP supports.

ASP Processing Directives

You can use @ processing directives in your scripts to send information to IIS about how to process ASP files. For example, the following script uses the **@LANGUAGE** processing directive to set the scripting language to VBScript:

```
<%@LANGUAGE=VBScript
  Dim SampleVar
  Application("SampleVar") = This is my variable
  Response.Write(SampleVar)
%>
```

The following five @ processing directives are supported by ASP in IIS 4:

◆ **@CODEPAGE**

◆ **@ENABLESESSIONSTATE**

◆ **@LANGUAGE**

◆ **@LCID**

◆ **@TRANSACTION**

Because script in ASP pages runs on the server, it has access to a number of objects available on the server. Table 18.1 describes these objects.

With Active Server Pages and the built-in objects that they support (that is, without even creating objects of your own), you can perform any of the following tasks:

◆ Retrieve information passed from the browser to the server using the **Request** object

◆ Send output to the browser using the **Response** object

◆ Store information for a specific user using the **Session** object

◆ Share information among all users of your application using the **Application** object

◆ Work with the properties and methods of components on the server using the **Server** object

Table 18.1   Built-in objects supported by ASP.

Object	Description
Request	Retrieves the values that the browser passes to the server during an HTTP request.
Response	Controls what information is sent to a browser in the HTTP response message.
Session	Used to manage and store information about a particular user session.
Application	Used to manage and store information about the Web application.
Server	Provides access to resources that reside on a server.
ObjectContext	Used to commit or abort a transaction managed by Microsoft Transaction Server (MTS) for ASPs that run in a transaction.

Using The Script Outline Window For Server Script

You can use Script Outline to develop server-side script for your ASP applications. As you will see in Chapter 20, you can also use Script Outline to develop client script. In its initial state, the tree view of Script Outline displays the nodes described in Table 18.2.

Figure 18.2 shows how the Script Outline window might appear for a sample page in Source view.

Working with the Script Outline is a relatively straightforward process. In the next several subsections, we will consider some of the most common tasks that you can perform with the Script Outline window.

Table 18.2   The nodes displayed by the Script Outline application.

Node	Description
Client Objects & Events	The elements that support client script or have client script attached to them with a list of events for the elements.
Client Scripts	The client script for the page with each function or subroutine defined within the script block.
Server Objects & Events	The elements that support server script or have server script attached to them with a list of events for the elements.
Server Scripts	The server script for the page with each function or subroutine defined within the script block.

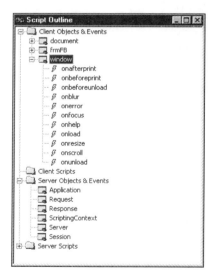

Figure 18.2
The Script Outline window displays code storage nodes.

Using The Script Outline Window

Script Outline automatically generates code stubs for procedures and events you specify, using either VBScript or JavaScript, depending on your default scripting language settings. To set the default language for a project, perform the following steps:

1. Right-click on the project file in the Project Explorer window and click on Properties.

2. Click on the Editor Defaults tab.

3. Select the default language from the Server drop-down list box in the Default script language option group.

Instead of creating a script block manually, you can let Script Outline create a script template for you. To add a server script block to a page, right-click on the location where you want the script block, and select Script Block | Server from the pop-up menu.

The real power of Active Server Pages and Visual InterDev, however, comes in the addition of components to a page, and then the writing of script specifically associated with those components. In the next section, we will look at the steps you must take to add objects to your pages and then write the appropriate VBScript to handle those objects.

Adding Objects And Writing Script For Them

When you add design-time and server components to a page in your project, the HTML editor adds the ID for the object and all the events associated with the object to Script Outline. To add a Textbox design-time control to a project, click on the Design-Time Controls tab in the Toolbox and move the Textbox control to an appropriate location on the page. The HTML editor will add the ID for the text box to Script Outline under Server Objects And Events. The editor will also add header and footer information to the page for handling data from the control.

Note

Design-time controls can be targeted for client or server script, which determines the node in which they will appear. I will cover this issue in more detail when we discuss data environment placement later in this chapter.

Inevitably, whenever you do any work with ASPs (or any other type of programming, as you are well aware), you must do some debugging. ASP provides a special problem, however, because the pages to debug must nevertheless run remotely, on the Web server. In the next section, we will look at what you must do to enable your applications for debugging.

Debugging ASP Pages

Before you can debug script in ASPs, you must first enable debugging. Furthermore, to debug scripts in ASP, you must be running IIS version 4 or later. To enable script debugging in ASPs, perform the following steps:

1. In the Project Explorer window, right-click on the project and click on Properties to display the Property Pages dialog box.

2. Click on the Launch tab.

3. Under Server Script, make sure Automatically Enable ASP Server-Side Debugging On Launch and Automatically Enable ASP Client-Side Debugging On Launch are checked.

When these options are set, Visual InterDev checks to see that the server is correctly configured for debugging. This check process includes:

♦ Setting the IIS application to run in its own memory space

♦ Enabling the IIS application's debugging options

♦ Setting up a Microsoft Transaction Server package to allow you to attach the debugger to the Web application

Warning

All of these steps are crucial for a Visual InterDev debugging session to start correctly. If any of them fails, Visual InterDev will be unable to debug server-side script. Moreover, the errors that can cause these types of failures can be tough to trace—for example, if you are logging into the IIS server as the anonymous Web user, you will often be unable to debug because you don't have sufficient rights. Should you encounter problems when starting a debugging session, you will want to carefully evaluate many of these related issues.

When you quit your debugging session, Visual InterDev restores the server debugging settings and out-of-process settings to their previous values. You can set breakpoints in server script, client script, or both. If you set breakpoints in both, the debugger will stop at the server script breakpoints first. When you continue to run and the page is sent to the browser, the debugger will then stop at breakpoints in the client script.

Handling runtime errors in server script requires many of the same tools that you use for client script. The most important tools are the **On Error Resume Next** statement and the **Err** object.

Further Considering HTTP Communication

Communication between Web browsers, or clients, and servers via HTTP consists of two actions:

♦ A request by a browser for a page

♦ A response by the server with that page

The request from the browser can come in one of two forms:

♦ A request to simply retrieve a page

♦ A request with information to be used on the page before the page is returned to the browser

To handle this exchange of data, HTTP request and response messages have two parts: a header and a body. Figure 18.3 shows these two parts.

The header contains one or more header fields (described in Table 18.3). The body contains information sent by the browser or the server. For example, when a browser requests a page from a server, only header information is necessary. When a browser requests a page and form data is included in the request, both the header and the body are used. Responses from servers typically use both header and body information.

Table 18.3   The different header field types and their corresponding messages.

Header Field	Message Type	Description
Content-Type	Request and Response	The media type contained in the body.
Date	Request and Response	The date and time the message was generated.
Expires	Response	The date and time the content should be considered obsolete.
From	Request	The Internet email address of the user running the browser.
If-Modified-Since	Request	Used with the **GET** request method to return a page only if it has been modified after the specified date.
Location	Response	The absolute URL of the page.
Refer	Request	The URL initiating the request.
User-Agent	Request	Information about the client software initiating the request.

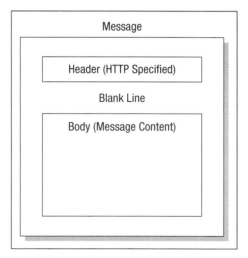

Figure 18.3
The parts of HTTP messages.

HTTP Request Messages

Each HTTP message contains an element that uniquely identifies it. For an HTTP request message, this identifier is the method line (also referred to as the *method field*). A request method line has the following basic syntax:

```
HTTP-method    resource-identifier    HTTP/version
```

The method will be either **GET** or **POST**, the resource identifier corresponds to the requested file, and the HTTP/version is the version number of the HTTP protocol being used in the request. For example, a request to view the URL **http://www.klsenterprises.com/ default.htm** will use this method line:

```
GET default.htm HTTP/1.0
```

Note

The domain name for the resource identifier is unnecessary because the HTTP request message created a TCP/IP communication session prior to establishing a connection with the server.

There are two crucially important types of HTTP methods. The **GET** method, which is the default, retrieves a specified page. With the **GET** method, any information will be appended to the HTTP request for a page and sent in the message header. The size of the information sent with the **GET** method is limited to 1,024 characters.

The **POST** method, on the other hand, sends data to a page. With the **POST** method, any data is sent in the body of the HTTP request message.

Just as there are request messages, the HTTP specification allows for response messages as well—messages whose job it is to let the requestor know that the request has been received, or to send data to the requestor.

HTTP Response Messages

The header of a response message is composed of a status line and any additional response header fields. The body section, if present in any given message, is preceded by a blank line. The **Request** object provides access to any information that is passed to the Web server from the browser.

The **Request** object contains five collections that you can use to extract information from an HTTP request. Table 18.4 lists and describes these five collections.

Clearly, the **Request** object is capable of supporting more than a little bit of processing complexity. Using the **Request** object, however, is nevertheless a simple process.

Table 18.4   The five collections supported by the ASP Request object.

Collection	Description
ClientCertificate	The values of the certification fields in the HTTP request.
Cookies	The values of cookies sent in the HTTP request.
Form	The values of form elements posted to the body of the HTTP request message by the form's **POST** method.
QueryString	The values of variables in the HTTP query string, specifically the values following the question mark (?) in an HTTP request.
ServerVariables	The values of predetermined Web server environment variables.

Each collection of the **Request** object contains variables that you use to retrieve information from an HTTP request. In the following example code, the **SERVER_NAME** variable of the **ServerVariables** collection retrieves the name of the Web server:

```
Request.ServerVariables("SERVER_NAME")
```

You can use the values of these variables to return information to the user. For example, in the following sample code, the name of the Web server is used to create a hyperlink to an HTML document on the same server:

```
<A HREF="http://<%= Request.ServerVariables("SERVER_NAME")%>
/ExamplePage.asp">Link to the Example Page</A>
```

You use the **QueryString** collection of the **Request** object to extract information from the header of an HTTP request message. For example, when a user submits a form with the **GET** method, or appends parameters to a URL request, you use the **QueryString** collection to read the submitted information.

The values you read from the request are the parameters that appear after the question mark (?). For example, suppose the user clicks on the Submit button of the form shown in Figure 18.4.

As a result, the following HTTP request is made:

```
http://name_age.asp?name=Lars&age=30&spouse=Brett
```

You can loop through all of the values in a query string to extract information passed by the user. The following example code loops through all of the values in an HTTP request:

```
<%For Each Item In Request.QueryString
    'Display the Item
Next %>
```

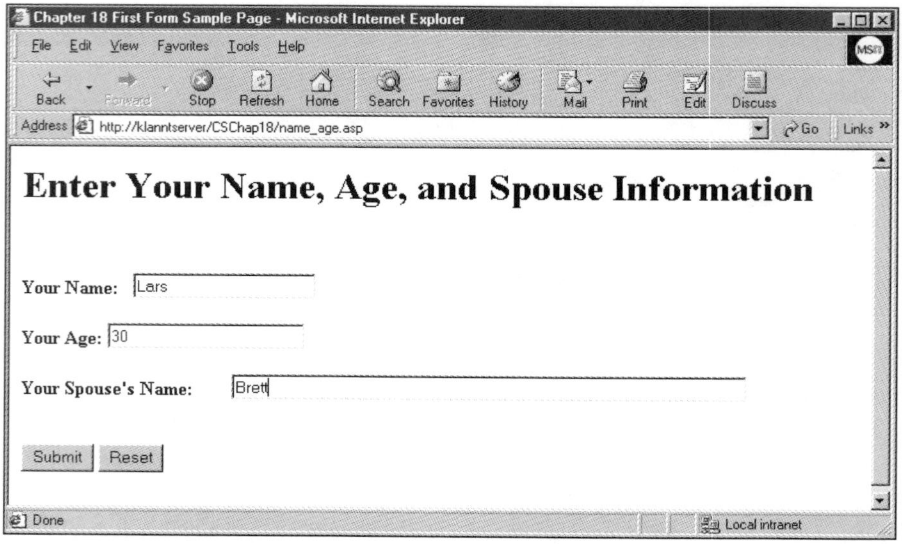

Figure 18.4
Sample form with a Submit button.

If more than one value is submitted with the same value name (which can occur with a multiselect list box on a form), you can use the index of the **QueryString** collection variable to access the individual values. The following example code shows how to access the first and second values of a variable called **phone_nums** in the **QueryString** collection:

```
Request.QueryString("phone_nums")(0)
Request.QueryString("phone_nums")(1)
```

You use the **Form** collection of the **Request** object to extract information from the body of an HTTP request message. The **Form** collection contains the values of each standard HTML control that has a **NAME** attribute. When a user submits a form with the **POST** method, you can read the values of the controls by using the **Form** collection. For example, a user completes and submits a form with the following HTML:

```
<FORM ACTION="submit.asp" METHOD=POST>
Name: <INPUT TYPE=TEXT NAME="name"><P>
Favorite Color: <SELECT MULTIPLE NAME="color">
                    <OPTION>Red
                    <OPTION>Green
                    <OPTION>Blue
                </SELECT><P>
<INPUT TYPE=SUBMIT NAME="cmdSubmit" VALUE="Submit">
</FORM>
```

You can read the submitted information by using the following script in the submit.asp file:

```
Request.Form("name")
Request.Form("color")
```

You can also loop through all of the values on a form to extract information passed by the user. The following example code loops through all of the standard HTML controls in an HTTP request:

```
<% For Each Item in Request.Form
    'Display Item
Next %>
```

If more than one value is submitted for a control on a form with the same value (which can occur with a multiselect list box), you can use the index of the **Form** collection variable to access the individual values. The following example code shows how to access the first and second pet type values selected in the **pet_type** list box:

```
Request.Form("pet_type")(0)
Request.Form("pet_type")(1)
```

Clearly, parsing the passed information is, by itself, not at all difficult. However, when you start posting values into a form, it becomes a bit more complex—a consideration I will address in the next section.

Posting Values To A Form

With Active Server Pages, you can define a form that posts its input values back to the ASP file that contains the form. To do this, you break the ASP file into two parts—one part that displays the form and a second part that responds to the submitted form.

To determine whether a request for an Active Server Page has resulted from the form being submitted, you test to see if the HTML controls contain values. If the controls do not contain values, the user has not yet submitted the form. Therefore you need to display a blank form that the user can complete and submit. The following example code displays a blank form:

```
<% If IsEmpty (Request.Form("txtName")) Then
    ' Display form
Else
    ' Form was submitted
End If %>
```

The **Response** object enables you to control the information sent to a user by the HTTP response message. So, to make this a little clearer, let's consider the **Response** object a bit more.

Properties And Methods Of The Response Object

The **Response** object provides properties and methods that you can use when sending information to the user. Table 18.5 describes some of the most commonly used properties and methods of the **Response** object.

The **Response** object also contains the **Cookies** collection, which you can use to specify the values of cookies. We will discuss cookies in greater detail later in this chapter.

You use the following syntax for the properties and methods of the **Response** object:

```
Response.property|method
```

In the following example code, the **Expires** property of the **Response** object is set to 0. This indicates that the content of the response message returned to the user will expire immediately:

```
<% Response.Expires = 0 %>
```

If the user refreshes the page, the browser will not read it from its cache, but will need to request it again from the Web server. You use the **Write** method of the **Response** object to send information to a user from within the server-side script delimiters.

Table 18.5   Commonly used properties and methods of the Response object.

Property	Description
Buffer	Indicates whether a response is buffered.
Expires	Specifies the length of time before a page cached on a browser expires. If the user returns to the same page before it expires, the cached version is displayed.
ExpiresAbsolute	Specifies the date and time at which a page cached on a browser will expire.
IsClientConnected	Indicates if the client has disconnected from the server since the last **Response.Write**.
Status	Specifies the value of the status line returned by the server. Status values are defined in the HTTP specification.
Clear	Clears any buffered response.
End	Stops the processing of a Web page and returns whatever information has been processed thus far.
Flush	Sends buffered output immediately.
Redirect	Sends a redirect message to the user, causing the response message to try to connect to a different URL.
Write	Writes a variable to the current HTTP output as a string.

Write Method Syntax

The **Write** method adds text to the HTTP response message, as shown in the following example code:

```
Response.Write variant
```

The variant can be any data type (including characters, strings, and integers) that is supported by your default scripting language. The variant cannot contain the character combination %>, which is used to denote the end of a script statement. Instead, you can use the escape sequence %\>, which the Web server will translate when it processes the script.

Warning
If VBScript is your default scripting language, don't use a variable longer than 1,022 characters.

The following example code uses the **Write** method within a loop to display the values of each standard HTML control on a form that is sent in an HTTP request:

```
<%For Each Item In Request.Form
    Response.Write Item
Next %>
```

In the following example code, an HTML tag is added to a Web page that the Active Server Page code is constructing on the fly:

```
<% Response.Write "<TABLE WIDTH = 100%\>" %>
```

As mentioned previously, the string returned by the **Write** method cannot contain the characters %> in an HTML tag, so the escape sequence %\> is used instead within this code.

Buffering Data

To prevent the Web server from sending the HTTP response to the user until all server-side script on the current Active Server Page has been processed, you can buffer the content of the response message.

Note
*Waiting for the server to finish processing all server-side script may cause a lengthy delay. To send pieces of the response to the user, you can use the **Flush** method of the **Response** object throughout your code.*

Setting The Buffer Property

To enable buffering, you set the **Buffer** property to **True**, as shown in the following example code:

```
Response.Buffer = True
```

Tip

*You cannot set the **Buffer** property after the server has sent output to the user. For this reason, you should set the **Buffer** property in the first line of the ASP file.*

Handling Errors With Buffering

If an error occurs during processing, you can use the **Redirect** method of the **Response** object, with buffering enabled. First, you clear the buffer with the **Clear** method, and then you use the **Redirect** method. When an error occurs, the following example code will clear the buffer and redirect the user to an error page:

```
Response.Buffer = True
On Error Resume Next
'code that may cause an unrecoverable error,
'such as failing to open a data connection

If Err.number <> 0 Then
    Response.Clear
    Response.Redirect "error.htm"
End If
```

Instead of sending content from the response message to the user, you can use the **Redirect** method, as discussed in the next section, to redirect the user to another URL.

Redirect Method Syntax

When you use the **Redirect** method of the **Response** object, you provide the URL to navigate to as an argument to the method:

```
Response.Redirect URL
```

The URL specifies the absolute or relative location to which the browser is redirected.

Note

*If you use the **Redirect** method after information has already been sent to the user, an error message will be generated—which is one of the reasons why you will generally buffer output transmissions.*

The following example code uses the **Redirect** method to display a page in high or low resolution, depending on each user's screen resolution:

```
<%
If Request.ServerVariables("HTTP_UA_PIXELS") = "640x480" Then
    Response.Redirect "lo_res.htm"
Else
    Response.Redirect "hi_res.htm"
End If
%>
```

Note

In addition to doing redirects programmatically with ASP, an IIS 4 administrator can also change settings through Internet Service Manager to redirect requests for files in a directory to other files or programs.

Now that you understand some of the objects and means at your disposal for sending and receiving communications to and from your users, let's move on to considering the issues surrounding statefulness within your applications, and why state is such a crucial concept when developing ASP applications.

Understanding The Importance Of State

ASP enables you to maintain state in a Web application. *State* is the ability to retain user information in a Web application. You can maintain three types of state data for a Web application—two types on the server, and one at the client:

♦ *Application state*—Information is available to all users of a Web application; this information is maintained at the server.

♦ *Session state*—Information is available only to a user of a specific session; this information is maintained at the server.

♦ *Cookies*—These allow you to maintain state on a user's computer.

In the next several sections, you will learn how to maintain state in a Web application— both at the server and at the client. I will begin with a discussion of the **Application** object, and how you can use it within your ASP applications.

Using The Application Object

You can use the **Application** object to share information among all users of a Web application. For example, you might store the total number of visitors to a Web site in an application-level variable.

An **Application** object is created when the user of the application requests an ASP file from the starting-point directory of the ASP application. It is destroyed when the application is unloaded.

Using Application Variables

In the example code below, **HelloVar** is a variable that contains a string. **FirstObj** is a component instance. To assign a component instance to an application variable, you use the VBScript **Set** statement, as shown in the following code fragment:

```
<% Application("HelloVar") = "Hello"
Set Application("FirstObj") =
    Server.CreateObject("FirstComponent") %>
```

Locking And Unlocking the Application Object

All users share the same **Application** object, so it is possible that two users might attempt to modify the object simultaneously. The **Lock** and **Unlock** methods of the **Application** object prevent this possibility.

To reduce the inconvenience of a user not being able to access the **Application** object when it is necessary, try to minimize how often you use the **Lock** method, as well as the amount of time you leave it active after invocation. The following example code shows how to use the **Lock** and **Unlock** methods when changing the value of a hit counter used in a Web application:

```
<%
Application.Lock
Application("NumVisits") = Application("NumVisits") + 1
Application.Unlock
%>
This application has been visited
<%= Application("NumVisits") %> times.
```

Notice that the **Application** object needs to be locked only while it is being modified. You use the **Session** object to store information that is needed for a particular user session. Variables stored in the **Session** object will not be discarded when the user navigates between pages in the Web application. Instead, these variables will persist for the entire user session.

Understanding Session Objects

The Web server automatically creates a **Session** object when a session starts. When the session expires or is abandoned, the Web server destroys the **Session** object. A session can begin in any one of three ways:

♦ A new user requests a URL that identifies an ASP file in an application, and the global.asa file for that application includes a **Session_OnStart** procedure.

♦ A user stores a value in the **Session** object.

◆ A user requests an ASP file in an application, and the application's global.asa file uses the **<OBJECT>** tag to instantiate an object with session scope. Chapter 19, which discusses using COM components in more detail, addresses this issue.

A session automatically ends if a user has not requested or refreshed a page in an application for a specified period of time. This value is 20 minutes by default. You can change the default for an application by setting the **Session Timeout** property on the Application Options tab of the Application Configuration property sheet in Internet Service Manager. Set this value according to the requirements of your Web application and the memory capacity of your server. For example, if you expect that users browsing your Web application will linger on each page for only a few minutes, then you may want to significantly reduce the session time-out value from the default. A long session time-out period can result in too many open sessions, which can strain your server's memory resources.

If, for a specific session, you want to set a time-out interval that is shorter than the default application time-out interval, you can also set the **Timeout** property of the **Session** object. For example, the following script sets a time-out interval of five minutes:

```
<%  Session.Timeout = 5  %>
```

You can also set the time-out interval to be greater than the default value, the value determined by the **Session Timeout** property. Further, you can explicitly end a session with the **Abandon** method of the **Session** object. For example, you can provide a Quit button on a form with the **ACTION** parameter set to the URL of an ASP file that contains the following command:

```
<% Session.Abandon %>
```

A session starts the first time a user requests an ASP file. When the session starts, the Web application generates a session ID, which is stored as a cookie that is sent back to the browser.

Disabling Cookies

If a user selects Disable All Cookie Use on the Advanced tab of the Internet Options dialog box of Internet Explorer, the session ID cookies cannot be created for that user. Session state can be disabled through the Internet Service Manager and through the following ASP processing directive:

```
<%@ ENABLESESSIONSSTATE=True|False %>
```

Session Object Syntax

The **Session** object has two properties and one method that use the following syntax:

```
Session.property|method
```

The **SessionID** property is used within your ASP applications to determine the session identification of a user. The **Timeout** property is used to set the amount of time that needs to elapse before the server can shut down an unused session. Finally, you will use the **Abandon** method to destroy a **Session** object and release its resources.

Using The Session Object

The **Session** object enables you to create values that store information about a user. For example, you can use the following code to create and store a user's nickname and hometown values:

```
<% Session("nickname") = "Chewie"
Session("hometown") = "Las Vegas"%>
```

The following example code shows how to use the information stored in the **Session** object:

```
Hello <%= Session("nickname") %>.<BR>
How is the weather in <%= Session("hometown") %>?<BR>
```

Considering Events

Application and **Session** objects both have **On_Start** and **On_End** events. The following sections discuss the differences in implementation between the two event sets.

Application Object Events

The **Application** object has two events: **Application_OnStart** and **Application_OnEnd**. You can add script to these events in the global.asa file. Any script you add to the **Application_OnStart** event will run when the application starts. Conversely, any script you add to the **Application_OnEnd** event will run when the application ends.

The following example code shows how to add the **Application_OnStart** event to the global.asa file:

```
<SCRIPT LANGUAGE=VBScript RUNAT=Server>
Sub Application_OnStart
    'Your Code Here
End Sub
</SCRIPT>
```

Session Object Events

Similar to the **Application** object, the **Session** object has the **Session_OnStart** and **Session_OnEnd** events. Any script you add to the **Session_OnStart** event will run when a user without an existing session requests an ASP file from your application. Any script you add to the **Session_OnEnd** event will run when a user session ends. You can use the

Session_OnStart event to direct users to a page that logs on to your site, regardless of which ASP file they request from your Web application.

Understanding Cookies

Cookies are a mechanism by which state can be maintained in a file on the user's computer. For example, user preferences or other personalized information that should be saved between sessions would be stored in cookies. A cookie file is typically stored in a folder named Cookies.

A cookie is like a token for a specific page that a Web server sends to a user. The user sends the cookie back to the server during each subsequent visit to that page or to a number of pages. Cookies enable information to be associated with a user. You can set and get the values of cookies by using the **Cookies** collection.

When the Web server returns an HTTP response to a user, the response message may also include a cookie. The cookie includes a description of the saved range of URLs for which that cookie is valid. A cookie is introduced to the user by including a Set-Cookie header as part of an HTTP response. Any HTTP requests made by the user included in that range will provide a transmittal of the current value of the cookie from the user back to the server.

Creating Cookies From ASP

To set the value of cookies that your Web server sends to a user, you use the **Cookies** collection of the **Response** object. If the cookie does not already exist, the **Response.Cookies** collection will automatically create a new cookie on the user's computer. The following example code creates a cookie with the city set to Las Vegas:

```
<% Response.Cookies("city")="Las Vegas" %>
```

If you want the cookie to apply to all of the pages in your Web application, you will set the **Path** attribute of the cookie to **"/"**, as shown in the following code fragment:

```
Response.Cookies("city").Path = "/"
```

The cookie will then be sent by the browser during each request for a page in your Web application. You can set other attributes for cookies, such as a cookie's expiration date, as shown in the following fragment:

```
Response.Cookies("Type").Expires = "December 31, 1999"
```

Using Cookies

The browser sends cookies to the appropriate pages in your Web application. To read the value of a cookie, you use the **Cookies** collection of the **Request** object. For example, if the

HTTP request sends a cookie with the city set to Las Vegas, then the following example code will retrieve the value of Las Vegas:

```
<%= Request.Cookies("city") %>
```

Using COM Components

You can run COM components (formerly known as *Automation servers*) on a Web server in response to a user request. These components enable you to extend the functionality of an Active Server Page with any resource, such as a database, located on the Web server. In the following sections, you will learn (briefly) how to use COM components in your Web application. You will address the topic more rigorously in Chapter 19.

Before we can do anything exciting with COM components, you must understand how to use them from within your ASP applications. To use a server component, you first need to understand how to create an instance of a component, or an object. There are two ways to create an object. You can use either the **<OBJECT>** tag, or the **Server.CreateObject** syntax. In the next two sections, we shall consider each of these possibilities in turn.

Using The <OBJECT> Tag

You can use the **<OBJECT>** tag to create a component that runs on the Web server. To use the **<OBJECT>** tag, you set the **RUNAT** attribute to **Server**. You can set the scope of the component by setting the **SCOPE** attribute to **Application** or **Session**. If you do not set the **SCOPE** attribute, the component will have page scope, meaning it can only be referenced on the current page. To specify the type of component to be created, you can use either its registered name, **PROGID**, or its registered number, **CLASSID**.

To understand this better, consider the following example code, in which the registered name (**PROGID**) is used to create a session-scope instance of the fictitious component:

```
<OBJECT RUNAT=Server SCOPE=Session
    ID=SampleComp PROGID="MS.SampleComponent">
</OBJECT>
```

In the following example code, the registered number (**CLASSID**) method is used to create an application-scope instance of **SampleComponent**:

```
<OBJECT RUNAT=Server SCOPE=Application
    ID=SampleComp CLASSID="Clsid:00000293-
    0000-0010-8000-00AA006D2EA4"></OBJECT>
```

When you use the **<OBJECT>** tag to declare a session-scope or application-scope instance of a component, the variable you assign to the component is stored in the session or application namespace. You do not need to use the **Session** or **Application** object to access the instance of the component.

The following example code opens the instance of **SampleComponent** that has been de-clared in the previous example code:

```
<%= SampleComp.GetSomething("some.txt") %>
```

Note

*When you drag a component from the Server Objects tab of the Toolbox, Visual InterDev adds an <**OBJECT**> tag for the component to your ASP. It does not set the **SCOPE** attribute in the tag, so components created this way will have page scope.*

Using The CreateObject Method

You can also use the **CreateObject** method of the **Server** object to create an instance of a component. The following example code creates a reference to the Browser Capabilities component using its **PROGID**:

```
<% Set bc = Server.CreateObject("MSWC.BrowserType") %>
```

To help you create Web applications, IIS 4 provides a large number of COM components that are available on the Server Objects tab of the Toolbox. Table 18.6 describes several of these server objects.

COM components enable you to package and reuse common functions, such as accessing a database and writing information to text files in an ASP application. You can access the components installed on a Web server by using an ASP file with the **CreateObject** method of the **Server** object.

Table 18.6   Some of the most common server objects available for your use.

Server Objects	Description
ADO Command, ADO Connection, and ADO Recordset	ActiveX Data Objects (ADO) that access information stored in a database or other tabular data structures.
Ad Rotator	Automatically rotates advertisements displayed on a Web page, according to a specified schedule.
Browser Capabilities	Determines the capabilities, type, and version of a user's browser.
CDONTS NewMail and CDONTS Session	Collaboration Data Objects for NTS.
Content Linking	Creates a table of contents for Web pages, and links them sequentially, like pages in a book.
File Access	Uses the **FileSystemObject** object to retrieve and modify information stored in a text file on the server.

One of the most commonly used components is the Browser Capabilities component. This useful tool enables you to determine the capabilities of the user's browser.

How The Browser Capabilities Component Works

The Browser Capabilities component compares the browser type and version number provided in the header of the HTTP request to entries contained in the Browscap.ini file stored on the Web server. By default, the Browscap.ini file is found in the Windows\Winnt\ System32\inetsrv folder.

If a match is found, the component uses the capabilities for that particular browser. If a match is not found, the component uses default capabilities in the Browscap.ini file.

Customizing The Browscap.ini File

You can declare property definitions for multiple browsers in the Browscap.ini file. You can also set default values that will be used when a browser that is not listed in the Browscap.ini file makes an HTTP request.

For each browser definition, you provide an HTTP User Agent header, along with the properties and values you want to associate with that header. For information about the format of an HTTP User Agent header, go to the HTTP Specification Web site at **www.w3c.org.**

Using The Browser Capabilities Component

You check values of properties of the Browser Capabilities component to present Web content in a format that is appropriate for a specific browser. Table 18.7 describes some possible properties of the Browser Capabilities component.

In the following example code, the Browser Capabilities component is used to determine whether a browser supports ActiveX controls. If it does, an HTTP response that contains ActiveX controls will be sent:

```
<% Set objBrowser = Server.CreateObject("MSWC.BrowserType")
If objBrowser.ActiveXControls = "True" Then
    'Insert ActiveX Control here
Else
    'Handle Without Control
End If %>
```

You can use another component, File Access, in your Web application to create and read from any text file stored on the Web server. With text files, you can store the state of your Web application when the Web server shuts down.

Table 18.7   Possible properties of the Browser Capabilities component.

Property	Description
ActiveXControls	Specifies whether the browser supports ActiveX controls.
Backgroundsounds	Specifies whether the browser supports background sounds.
Beta	Specifies whether the browser is beta software.
Browser	Specifies the name of the browser.
cdf	Specifies whether the browser supports the Channel Definition Format for Webcasting.
Cookies	Specifies whether the browser supports cookies.
Frames	Specifies whether the browser supports frames.
Javaapplets	Specifies whether the browser supports Java applets.
Javascript	Specifies whether the browser supports JScript.
Platform	Specifies the platform on which the browser runs.
Tables	Specifies whether the browser supports tables.
VBscript	Specifies whether the browser supports VBScript.
Version	Specifies the version number of the browser.

Creating And Opening Text Files

The File Access component contains the **FileSystemObject** object, which you use to open or create a text file. To open a text file, create a **TextStream** object by using the **OpenTextFile** method of the **FileSystemObject** object.

To create a text file, create a **TextStream** object by using the **CreateTextFile** method of the **FileSystemObject** object. The following example code creates a **TextStream** object and opens a text file:

```
' Creates a FileSystem Object
Set fsVisitors = Server.CreateObject("Scripting.FileSystemObject")
' Creates a TextStream Object and opens a text file
Set fileVisitors = fsVisitors.CreateTextFile("c:\visitors.txt", True)
```

If a text file already exists, the **CreateTextFile** method will overwrite the existing file if the overwrite argument is equal to true.

Note

The companion CD-ROM includes a complete example of how to implement ***FileSystem*** *and* ***TestStream*** *objects.*

After you have created a **TextStream** object with either the **CreateTextFile** or **OpenTextFile** method, you can use the **ReadLine** and **WriteLine** methods of the **TextStream** object to read and write text.

The following example code sets an **Application** object value equal to the value read from a text file with the **ReadLine** method:

```
Application("visitors") = fileVisitors.ReadLine
```

Using Page Objects

A **Page** object is an ASP that contains server script that you use in your application. The functions or subroutines on the page can become methods for the **Page** object. Using design-time controls and the scripting object model in Visual InterDev allows you to create and script a Web page using standard object-oriented techniques. You can specify any ASP as a **Page** object. To do so, you use the PageObject design-time control.

A **Page** object is an ASP that contains server script that you use in your application. The functions or subroutines on the page can become methods for the **Page** object. **Page** objects also allow you to create properties, which maintain state over multiple round trips to the server. **Page** objects enable the following activities:

♦ Simplified navigation

♦ An easy way to execute specific script on another page

♦ A means of maintaining state information

♦ A way to execute server script from a page displayed in the browser

Unfortunately, **Page** objects are a bit more complex to create than some other Visual InterDev objects are. To specify a page as an object, perform the following steps:

1. Create or open an ASP file in the HTML editor.

2. Enable the scripting object model for the page. To do so, right-click anywhere in the page away from an object or control, choose Properties, and then choose the General tab.

3. In the General tab, under ASP settings, choose Enable Scripting Object Model. The HTML editor adds the scripting object model framework to the page in **<META>** tags. You should not alter the content of these tags.

4. At this point, you should make sure that you have set options to view controls graphically. From the View menu, choose View Controls Graphically. To set this option as the default, use the HTML node of the Options dialog box.

5. From the Design-Time Controls tab of the Toolbox, drag a PageObject control onto your page. You can drag the control anywhere on the page, although it must be inside the framework of the scripting object model blocks.

6. In the Name box on the PageObject control, type a name for the **Page** object. This will be the name that you can use to reference the object in script.

The name you give your **Page** object is registered in your Web project so that it is available to any other page. Even if you move the page to another location, its **Page** object name remains the same. Once you have added a PageObject control to an ASP, you can define methods and properties for the page.

Defining Page Object Methods

Page objects can define two types of methods: **Navigate** and **Execute**. **Navigate** methods are called by a client page to load the ASP and run a procedure on the page. A common use for **Navigate** methods is to process a form. **Execute** methods are called by a client page to run a procedure on the ASP, without leaving the current page. A common use for **Execute** methods is to validate a user-entered value by looking it up in a database.

All **Page** objects have a default navigate method called **Show**, which displays the contents of the page. To define your own method for a **Page** object, perform the following steps:

1. If the page does not already have one, add a PageObject control to the page and give the control a name.

2. Write the procedures in a script block that has the attribute **RUNAT=SERVER**. Procedures can take any number of parameters, but all are passed by value.

> **Note**
>
> *Parameters are converted to strings when you call a **Page** object method so that they can be successfully passed across the Web. In your **Page** object scripts, you should convert parameter values to the appropriate data type as required.*

3. Right-click on the PageObject control, and then choose Properties to display the Property Pages dialog box.

4. Determine whether the method will be available via navigation or execution. Then in the list under either Navigate methods or Execute methods, find the first blank line. From the drop-down list box, select the procedure that you want to define as a method for the **Page** object.

Calling Page Object Methods

As mentioned in the previous section, **Page** objects support **Navigate** methods and **Execute** methods. Each method is called according to the following general syntax:

```
pageObject.navigate.methodName(parameters)
pageObject.execute.methodName(parameters)
```

However, there are additional considerations for calling **Execute** methods, which can be called in one of two ways:

♦ *Synchronously*—Your script calls the remote procedure and waits for it to return. This is useful if you need the results of the remote procedure before you proceed.

♦ *Asynchronously*—Your script makes the call to a remote script, and then continues processing. The page remains available to users. Asynchronous calls are useful in Web applications because a remote procedure can take a long time while the request goes to the server and back.

When you call an **Execute** method either synchronously or asynchronously, it will not return a single value as you might expect. Instead, it returns a **call** object, which is an object that contains return and status information about the method that you called.

The most commonly used property of the **call** object is **return_value**. It contains the single value calculated or looked up by the method. Other **call** object properties allow you to retrieve more information about the state of the method call.

Defining Page Object Properties

Page object properties have *lifetime* and *visibility* features, as described in Table 18.8.

Defining properties for **Page** objects occurs much as you might expect it to. To define a property for a **Page** object, perform the following steps:

1. If the page does not already have one, add a PageObject control to the page and give the control a name.

2. Right-click on the PageObject control, choose Properties to display the Property Pages dialog box, and then click on the Properties tab.

3. In the Name column, find the first blank line, and then enter the name of the property you want to create.

4. Select the characteristics for the new property from the Lifetime, Client, and Server columns.

To make properties accessible to your scripts, **Page** objects implement **get** and **set** methods. For example, if you define a property called **Color**, you can read its value using the **getColor** method and set it using the **setColor** method.

Table 18.8   Features and characteristics of the properties of Page objects.

Feature	Settings	Description
Lifetime	Application	Available to any page of your application. Application values use application variables to store values.
	Page	Available to scripts anywhere on the page until you navigate to another page.
	Session	Available to any page in your application for the current session. Session values use session variables to store values.
Visibility	Client	There are three possible visibility settings at the client: None, Read, and Read/Write
	Server	There are two possible visibility settings at the server: None and Read/Write

To access the methods or properties of another **Page** object, you must first create a reference to that page on the current page. To reference another **Page** object from the current page, perform the following steps:

1. If the page does not already have one, add a PageObject control to the page and give the control a name. If your scripting target is **Server**, the scripting object model must be enabled for the page.

2. Right-click on the PageObject control, choose Properties to display the Property Pages dialog box, and then choose the References tab.

3. In the Name column, click on the three-dot button to display the Create URL dialog box.

4. Select the ASP file that you want to reference as a **Page** object. Enter options for how to call the **Page** object, and then click on OK.

Accessing Page Object Properties

As we just mentioned, when you define a property for a **Page** object, the scripting object model creates a **get** method and a **set** method that you use to access the property. For example, if you have defined a property called **UserName**, you can read the value of the property using the method **getUserName**, and set it using **setUserName**, as shown in the following example:

```
newUser = PageObj1.Navigate.getUserName()
PageObj1.Navigate.setUserName(txtUserName.Value)
```

When working with properties, you need to be aware of their lifetimes. For example, if you have defined the property's lifetime as "page," you can get and set its value only until you leave the page and display another one. (Calling the same page again to execute a method retains property values scoped to the page.) However, after you navigate to another page, the property is reset.

Tip

You can call methods and use properties on the current page using the default **Page** *object name of* ***thisPage***.

Security Issues With Active Server Pages

In Chapter 17, we discussed briefly some of the important issues for you to consider in terms of security for your Web applications. I gave a brief overview of some of the issues you need to keep in mind when developing Web applications, and some of the traps to watch out for. However, that overview was just that—an overview. In the next several sections, you will learn about the specifics of security issues as they relate to ASPs. You can apply four levels of security through ASP applications:

♦ ASP application security supported through Visual InterDev

♦ IIS-level security

♦ Operating system file-level security

♦ SQL database-level security

I will begin with a brief security overview of ASP application security, and then move on to Web application security specifics.

Brief Security Overview

The main Web security issues that you need to address with any Web application—no matter what the underlying platform is—are authenticating user identity and controlling user access to files and resources. Table 18.9 identifies some of the specifics surrounding these two broad security issues, suggested locations for their control, their purpose, and the options available for managing them.

In the following sections, I will focus on addressing all of these issues, except the determination of a SQL Server security model—a discussion covered in some detail in Chapter 14. Let's begin with user authentication.

Determining And Enforcing User Rights

Every Web application on a Web server has permission settings that identify authorized users and specify their privileges. These settings are specified from the Settings tab of the Permissions dialog box. By default, a new Web application inherits the same permissions as the root Web server. You can customize these permissions, and then control the permissions for individual users and groups.

Table 18.9 Considerations for security implementation.

Issue	Location	Purpose	Security Option
User authentication	Web server	Identify the user requesting files in a Web application.	Basic Authentication, Anonymous Logon, or Windows NT Challenge/ Response
File permissions	Web server	Control access to files in the application.	Read, write, script, and execute permissions for files and folders
File permissions	Web application	Control access to files in the application.	FrontPage Server Extensions
File permissions	Operating system	Control access to files in the application.	Access Control Lists in NTFS
Database permissions	Database	Control access to objects in the database.	SQL Server Standard Security, Integrated Security, or Mixed

To set unique permissions for a Web application, perform the following steps:

1. In the Project Explorer window, select the project for which you want to set permissions.

2. Select Project | Web Project | Web Permissions.

3. On the Settings tab, select Use Unique Permissions For This Web Application. This specifies that the current Web application does not inherit its permissions setting from the root Web application.

4. Choose Apply.

You can also limit browse access to the Web application from this dialog box by clicking on the Only Registered Users Have Browse Access option on the bottom of the Users tab in the Permissions dialog box.

In Microsoft Visual InterDev, you can set one of three levels of user permissions:

♦ *Browse*—Lets the user view pages at both design-time and runtime

♦ *Author*—Lets the user view and modify pages at design-time only

♦ *Administer*—Lets the user view and modify pages at both design-time and runtime

Note

To set Web application security in Windows NT, the Web application files must be stored on a disk using the NTFS file system, not FAT.

You use the Internet Service Manager to set the access permissions on the virtual directories of your Web site. As you have learned previously, the Internet Service Manager is a snap-in component of the Microsoft Management Console (MMC).

There are five possible levels of permission that you can grant for a virtual directory. The following list describes the differences among these settings:

♦ *Read*—Enables Web clients to read or download files stored in a home directory or a virtual directory. Give Read access permission only to directories containing information to publish (HTML files, for example). Disable Read permission for directories containing CGI applications and ISAPI DLLs to prevent clients from downloading the application files.

♦ *Write*—Enables Web clients to upload files to the enabled directory, or to change the content in a write-enabled file.

♦ *Script*—Enables applications mapped to a script engine to run in this directory without having Execute permission set. Use Script application permission for directories that contain ASP scripts, Internet Database Connector (IDC) scripts, or other scripts. Script permission is safer than Execute permission because you can limit the applications that can be run in the directory.

♦ *Execute*—Enables any application to run in this directory, including applications mapped to script engines as well as DLL and EXE files.

♦ *None*—Does not allow any programs or scripts to run in this directory.

If the directory is on a Windows NT File System (NTFS) drive, the NTFS settings for the directory must match these settings. If the settings do not match, the most restrictive settings take effect. For example, if you give a directory Write permission in this property sheet, but give a particular user group only Read access permissions in NTFS, those users cannot write files to the directory because the Read permission is more restrictive. To set access permissions on virtual directories, perform the following steps:

1. Select Start | Programs | Windows NT 4.0 Option Pack | Microsoft Internet Information Server | Internet Service Manager. Windows NT will run the Microsoft Management Console.

2. Click on Properties.

3. Click on the Home Directory tab.

4. Set the appropriate access permissions for the virtual directory.

Windows NT requires assigned user accounts and passwords. If you want to allow everybody to access your Web server, you must either provide a valid Windows NT account for every user or allow anonymous logon.

Using Anonymous Logon

Anonymous logon allows users to access your Web server without providing a user ID and password. When an IIS Web server receives an anonymous request, it maps the user to a special anonymous logon account, referred to as the Internet Guest account. The user receives the access rights that have been granted to this account. To enable anonymous logon, perform the following steps:

1. Select Start | Programs | Windows NT 4.0 Option Pack | Microsoft Internet Information Server | Internet Service Manager. Windows NT will run the Microsoft Management Console.

2. Within the virtual root, right-click on Default Web Site.

3. Click on Properties.

4. Select the Directory Security tab.

5. Click on Edit in the Anonymous Access And Authentication Control group box.

6. Click on the Allow Anonymous Access checkbox.

Setting The Account Used For Anonymous Access

When you install IIS, it creates an account named **IUSR_*computername***. For example, if the computer name is "marketing," the account name will be **IUSR_marketing**. By default, this account is used for anonymous Internet logons.

IIS adds the **IUSR_***computername* account to the Guests group, and the account therefore receives any permissions assigned to that group. You should review the settings for the Guests group to ensure that they are appropriate for the **IUSR_***computername* account. To change the account name and/or password used for anonymous logon, perform the following steps:

1. Select Start | Programs | Windows NT 4.0 Option Pack | Microsoft Internet Information Server | Internet Service Manager. Windows NT will run the Microsoft Management Console.

2. Within the virtual root, right-click on Default Web Site.

3. Click on Properties.

4. Select the Directory Security tab.

5. Click on Edit in the Anonymous Access And Authentication Control group box.

6. Click on the Allow Anonymous Access checkbox and disable the Basic Authentication and Windows NT Challenge/Response options.

7. Click on Edit.

8. Disable the Enable Automatic Password Synchronization option.

9. Set the Username and Password text boxes to the values that you want.

10. Select OK to exit each of the dialog boxes.

Disabling Anonymous Logon

If you prevent anonymous logon, each request made to your Web server must include a valid Windows NT logon ID and password. To obtain this information, the browser will prompt the user for an account name and password. To prevent anonymous logon, perform the following steps:

1. From the Microsoft Management Console, under the virtual root, right-click on Default Web Site.

2. Click on Properties.

3. Select the Directory Security tab.

4. Click on Edit in the Anonymous Access And Authentication Control group box.

5. Disable Allow Anonymous Access.

6. Enable Basic Authentication, Windows NT Challenge/Response, or both.

7. Select OK to exit each of the dialog boxes.

Authentication Methods

You can specify how the logon information is sent from the Web browser to the Web server by setting the authentication method. In the next several sections, we will discuss the authentication methods you can choose from when using IIS.

Basic Authentication

If you select Basic Authentication, the username and password are sent from the Web browser to the Web server as plain text. This method is useful because it is generally supported by all Web browsers.

Windows NT Challenge/Response

Windows NT Challenge/Response authentication (often called NTLM authentication) is the most secure form of authentication available when using Windows NT, because the username and password are not sent across the network. Instead, the Windows Security Provider interface is used to provide an encrypted challenge/response handshake mechanism that is functionally unbreakable. This method of authentication is supported by Internet Explorer version 4 and later.

Note

For obvious reasons, this type of authentication is really only practical on an intranet.

Using Both Basic Authentication And Windows NT Challenge/Response

If you select both Basic Authentication and Windows NT Challenge/Response authentication, Windows NT Challenge/Response will be used if the user's browser supports such authentication. Otherwise, IIS will use Basic Authentication.

If you select all three methods of authentication (Anonymous, Basic, and Windows NT Challenge/Response), every request to a Web page will attempt to access the page as anonymous. If the request fails, the user will be prompted for a login ID and the request will be attempted again.

File Permissions For The Web

You should place your Web pages and data files on an NTFS partition. When you use an NTFS partition, you can set permissions for users or groups of users on individual files and folders. To set permissions on files and folders on an NTFS partition, perform the following steps:

1. Start Windows NT Explorer.
2. Right-click on the file or directory for which you want to set permissions.
3. Click on Properties.
4. Select the Sharing tab.
5. Enable Shared As and give the folder or directory a Share Name.
6. Click on Permissions.
7. Add or remove users and specify the type of access allowed for each user.

You can use a combination of IIS settings, NTFS permissions, and server script to protect your Web pages. For example, if you want to allow all users to access most of your Web site, but restrict a few pages to certain users, you can configure your Web site as follows:

1. In Internet Service Manager, enable Allow Anonymous, Basic Authentication, and Windows NT Challenge/Response.

2. For the pages you want to restrict, use Windows NTFS file permissions to remove the Anonymous account **IUSR_*computername*** from the access list, and then add the users for whom you want to allow access.

After setting these options, when a user requests a Web page, the user is logged on as anonymous and IIS attempts to access the Web page. If access is denied, the user will then be prompted for a login ID and password. Only users who provide a valid login ID and password will be able to access the restricted page.

Data Access From Active Server Pages

Data access in Visual InterDev is very easy—in fact, it is similarly easy to performing advanced data access from Access 2000. Within InterDev, you simply add controls to a page, connect a source for data to your project, and connect the data to the controls. The following list outlines the steps for displaying data from a database in an ASP:

1. Add an object to your project to hold information about the connection to the database. This object is known as a *data connection*.

2. Next, connect to the database by creating a data source name. You can create a data source name to identify a database from within InterDev or by using the Win32 ODBC driver manager.

3. Add an object to your project to hold information about what data to retrieve. This object is known as a *data command*.

4. Next, in your ASP, add a control that will connect the data in the database to the data-bound controls on the form. This control is called a *Recordset control*.

5. Add a data-bound control to display data from the database. Depending on what you are trying to display, you can use any of the different data-bound controls on the Toolbox.

6. Set the properties of the data-bound control so it displays the data. To do this, you use the properties sheet of the data-bound control.

7. Add a RecordsetNavbar control, which lets users scroll the displayed data.

The steps outlined here assume that the structure of the database is finished before you begin. However, if you want to design or manipulate the tables in a database, you can use the Database Designer.

Features of the Visual Database Tools that allow you to alter the structure of a database are available only in the Enterprise Edition of Visual InterDev.

Considering The Data Environment

The data environment is the focal point and repository for storing and reusing data connections and data commands in a Visual InterDev project. (If you are an experienced VB6 programmer, you will recognize the data environment in Visual InterDev—it works in exactly the same way as VB6.)

A data environment holds the information required to access data in a database. It contains one or more data connections. Each data connection can contain one or more data commands that represent a method for querying or modifying a database.

The first time you add a data connection to your project, Visual InterDev creates a DataEnvironment folder as a subfolder of the global.asa file. It is located here because data connection information is stored in application-level variables in global.asa and can be used by multiple ASPs. Figure 18.5 shows you the location of the data environment within a project.

As part of creating a data connection, you need to add the name of a source for data. A data source name (DSN) stores information about how to connect to a specific data provider. These data source names are identical to those you learned how to create in Chapter 2 using the ODBC Data Source administrator applet.

Types Of Data Source Names

There are two different types of DSNs: machine DSNs and file DSNs. A machine DSN stores information for a database in the system registry. A file DSN is a text file that contains connection information for a database. This file is saved on your computer. A file DSN is used when the production version of the database is not on the local computer,

Figure 18.5
The Project View, displaying the data environment within a project.

whereas a machine DSN is used when the production version of the database *is* on the local computer.

Setting Up A Data Source Name

You can add a DSN to a project when adding a data connection. You do this from the Select Data Source dialog box. The following steps outline the process for creating a new DSN when adding a data connection:

1. Start the process of creating a new data source by clicking on New in the Select Data Source dialog box.

2. Set the driver for the data source by choosing Select The Database Driver Name in the Create A New Data Source dialog box.

3. Locate the data source that you want to connect to your project by browsing available data source locations and selecting the appropriate name. This creates a file with the extension .dsn.

As part of the process of creating a new data source to a SQL server, you are given two options for verifying the authenticity of a user login ID. If you select the Integrated Security option, it means you are using Windows NT authentication for validating access to the SQL Server—which means the server uses the network login ID of the user to grant rights in the database. In turn, the user is given guest account privileges on the database server based on the user's Windows NT login ID. If you support anonymous logins, the user will end up with the guest rights on the SQL Server (defined by the **public** role).

If you select the Standard Security option, it means you are using SQL Server authentication—meaning that access is granted to the server by checking the login ID and password entered by the user. In turn, the user is given specific account privileges on the database server based on the user's SQL Server login ID and password.

Standard Vs. Integrated Security

When a Web user requests an Active Server Page that connects to a Microsoft SQL Server database on a separate computer running Windows NT, the user is first logged on to the computer running Windows NT, and then logged on to the SQL Server. Figure 18.6 shows the logon process from a Web browser to a SQL Server.

The following steps outline the logon process that occurs when a user requests an Active Server Page that connects to a SQL Server database:

1. If the Web server allows anonymous logon, the user is mapped to the anonymous account.

2. The ASP file runs script to connect to a SQL Server database.

3. For the ASP file to connect to the SQL Server database, the user is first logged on to the Windows NT-based computer where SQL Server is installed.

4. Finally, the user is logged on to the SQL Server itself.

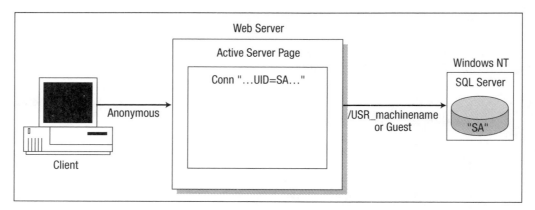

Figure 18.6
Logging into the SQL Server from the Web.

Using Data Connections

To access data in a database for use on an ASP, you need to add a data connection to your Visual InterDev project (alternatively, as you will learn later, you can simply use ADOs to connect; the data connection allows you to simplify the process using IDE objects). A data connection tells the project how to access the database, and usually contains information about:

♦ The type of database to be accessed (for example, Microsoft SQL Server) and the server name (if appropriate)

♦ The name of the database (for example, pubs)

♦ A username

♦ A password

Note

*A data connection corresponds directly to an ADO **Connection** object. In fact, if you look in the global.asa file after attaching a data connection to the project, you will find a **Connection** object that contains all the values you set for the data connection.*

You can add as many data connections to a project as you need. For example, if your application requires access to two different databases, you would add two data connections.

When you create a data connection, Visual InterDev reads connection information from a DSN on your computer. In addition, Visual InterDev creates a Data View window through which you can view and select data from a database. To add a data connection to your project, perform the following steps:

1. On the Project menu, click on Add Data Connection.

2. Add the name of a data source.

3. Set the Connection Name and Connection String properties for the connection.

Authentication Specifics From InterDev

Visual InterDev 6 offers a new feature that lets you easily test database access during development. You can quickly switch between design-time and runtime authentication from the Authentication tab on the Connection Properties dialog box.

When specifying design-time authentication, you choose the type of security for your authorization. For maximum security, you can choose to be prompted for a password each time you connect to the database. For less stringent security, you can choose not to be prompted. In this case, Visual InterDev encrypts your password and stores it in the project.

When you specify runtime authentication, you do not have this choice. You cannot prompt users for a password, because the prompting would occur on the Web server. Therefore, you must include the password with the username. The password is encrypted and stored in the project so it can be passed to the database each time a user connects to the database when the application is running.

Note

You can also add a data connection or a data command to your project by right-clicking on the Data Environment listing within the Project Explorer window and using the pop-up menu.

Understanding Data Commands

A data command contains information about accessing a particular database object. For example, a data command might query the **authors** table of the **pubs** database so that you can display the contents of that table in a Web page. A data command can run a SQL statement or a stored procedure. Figure 18.7 shows the Properties dialog box for the **authors** data command.

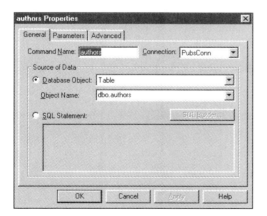

Figure 18.7
A simple data command that returns all the rows in the **authors** table.

There are four ways to create a data command, as discussed briefly in the following list:

♦ You can move a database object from the Data View window to the data environment. This will automatically create a data command in the data environment.

♦ You can create a data command using the Data Command dialog box and selecting a database object.

♦ You can create a data command using the Data Command dialog box and typing in a SQL statement.

♦ You can create a data command using the Data Command dialog box and clicking on SQL Builder. This invokes the Query Designer.

Note

When you move a data command onto an HTML page or Active Server Page, Visual InterDev will automatically add a Recordset control to the page.

Query Designer—that is, quite possibly, a new one for you. Let's take a look at the Query Designer window.

Using The Query Designer

The Microsoft Query Designer is a graphical tool for creating SQL commands. You can create complex, multitable queries by dropping tables into your query, setting options, and entering values.

Query Designer is aware of the differences between databases such as Microsoft SQL Server and Oracle, so it can generate and recognize database-specific SQL commands.

Queries created in Query Designer can both return data using SQL **SELECT** commands and create queries that update, add, or delete records in a database, using **UPDATE**, **IN-SERT**, and **DELETE**.

The Query Designer consists of four panes, described in the following list:

♦ *Diagram pane*—Displays the input sources—the tables or views—that you are querying

♦ *Grid pane*—Displays your specific query options, including which data column to display, what rows to select, and how to group rows

♦ *SQL pane*—Displays the SQL statement for the current query

♦ *Results pane*—Displays the results of the most recently executed query

To open and use the Query Designer from within Visual InterDev, perform the following steps:

1. Right-click on the Command object.

2. Click on Properties.

3. Select SQL Statement.

4. Click on SQL Builder.

5. From the Data View window, drop the table or tables that you want to include in the query into the Diagram pane.

Now that you have a command created—that is, you have incoming data for the page—you must add components to the page to display that data. Such is the job of data-bound controls.

Working With Data-Bound Controls

Data-bound controls are user interface elements, such as labels, text boxes, and option groups, that can display the contents of a database. They are connected, or bound, to the database through a Recordset control.

Data-bound controls are located on the Design-Time Controls tab on the Toolbox. To add a control to an ASP, click and drag the control name onto the page. For purposes of our discussion, data-bound controls can be divided into two generalized categories—data display controls and data manipulation controls. Data display controls include labels, text boxes, and list boxes. You should be familiar with these types of data-bound controls.

Data manipulation controls include Recordset, RecordsetNavBar, and other controls. These controls are analogous to controls that you have likely used inside your Access projects, and definitely when designing Data Access Pages (DAPs), as discussed in earlier chapters; however, their implementations are slightly different with Visual InterDev.

How Do Design-Time Controls Work?

A design-time control is a user interface element that you use to create application functionality. When you set the properties of a design-time control it generates script that executes at runtime. For example, when you need to get text information from a user, you place a design-time text box control on the form to receive the data.

At design time, these controls act just like controls that you put on a form in Access 2000. You set their properties to specify their appearance and behavior. However, when you change a property, you also change the script that executes when the page runs.

Data Manipulation Controls

The following list describes the different types of data manipulation controls and their uses:

♦ *Recordset*—A data source for data-bound design-time controls. The Recordset control connects controls on an ASP with fields in the tables of a database. Recordset controls do not appear on an ASP.

♦ *RecordsetNavBar*—Creates a set of forward and backward buttons that lets users navigate the data being displayed on an ASP.

♦ *FormManager*—Creates sets of event-driven forms, such as a data-entry form with Browse, Edit, and Insert modes.

Data-bound controls in Visual InterDev are a special form of a design-time control (DTC) that support data binding. You bind fields in a database to the control by setting the control's design-time properties.

Advantage Of Using Design-Time Controls

The key advantage to using design-time controls is their flexibility in targeting—you do not need to write one script for client-side processing and another for server-side processing. For example, if you want your Web application to run on many different browsers, you target the server as the platform, and all of the generated code will run on the server. However, if you want your Web application to take advantage of Internet Explorer's client-side data binding capability, you can generate script that will run on the client.

Connecting The ASP To The Database

In the following sections, you will learn how to connect the fields in a database to the data-bound controls on an ASP. You will also learn about a number of Recordset control features and practice adding a data command, a data-bound grid control, and a Recordset control to your project.

The Recordset Control

The key to data access in ASPs is the Recordset control. The Recordset control does not appear as a part of the user interface. Instead, it connects items in a database to data-bound controls on an ASP. The Recordset control, as part of its existence, specifies the following information that is used by the data-bound controls on the ASP:

♦ A **Data Connection** object, which you must have previously defined, and then (generally) built a **Command** object from.

♦ A database object within that connection or a SQL statement querying the database. This object may be a **Command** object, or may be some other command executed against the connection.

♦ Other properties that determine how data is read from and written to a database, such as cursor type and cursor location.

Adding A Recordset Control To A Page

There are a number of ways to add a Recordset control to an ASP. The Microsoft-recommended method is to drag a **Data Command** object onto a page. Visual InterDev automatically creates the control and binds it to the DE, or **Data Environment**, object. However, you can bind a Recordset control to:

- A **Data Command** object
- A stored procedure
- A table
- A view

You can also manually add the Recordset control from the Toolbox. Figure 18.8 shows an example of a Recordset control on an ASP.

Recordset Control Properties

Recordset controls have a number of properties that you can manipulate. The following list describes some of the important choices. All of them are found on the Advanced tab of the Recordset Property dialog box. The items in the list are in alphabetical order, rather than order of use:

- *Cache Size*—Sets the size of the cache that will be used for the recordset. Default setting is 100K.
- *Command Timeout Duration*—Sets the amount of time, in seconds, that is allotted for a command to execute before processing is stopped and the timeout message is returned from the database.
- *Cursor Location*—Sets the location for the cursor, either client-side or server-side. The default setting is client-side cursor.
- *Cursor Type*—Sets the type of cursor that will be used to view and manipulate the data. Default setting is 3 - Static. You were introduced to cursors in Chapter 6, and will learn more about cursor types in Chapter 21.
- *Lock Type*—Sets the type of record locking that takes place when several users try to access records simultaneously. The default setting is 3 - Optimistic. You will learn more about lock types in Chapter 21.

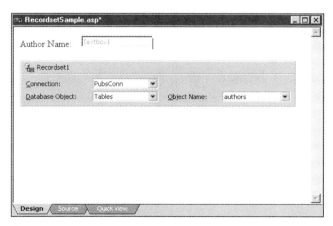

Figure 18.8
The Recordset control specifies connection information.

◆ *Maximum Records To Display*—Sets the maximum number of records that will be displayed in the browser.

In addition to these specific properties of the recordset, it is also important to determine where in the connection—either at the client- or server-side—the Recordset control will be constructed.

Specifying The Recordset Control's Visibility

When setting the properties for a Recordset control, you can specify either the server-side (Server ASP) or client-side (IE 4 DHTML) scripting platform. You can change the setting at any time, and Visual InterDev will automatically generate the appropriate code to populate the recordset and its related data-bound controls. Generally, you have two types of targeting options. If you are targeting non-Microsoft browsers, which is the standard Internet construction, you will build the recordset at the server and use ActiveX Data Objects (ADO) as your underlying technology. On the other hand, if you are targeting Microsoft browsers only, and intend to reduce the number of round trips to the server, you should construct the recordset at the client and use the Remote Data Service (RDS) as your underlying technology.

Note
For more information on ADO with InterDev and RDS, see Chapter 21.

It is import to recognize, by the way, that when you change the scripting platform for the Recordset control, all the controls that are bound to it automatically inherit the scripting platform.

Recordset Cache Properties

As you saw in the previous section, you can specify the visibility of the Recordset control from the Implementation tab of its properties. From the Implementation tab, you can also set how much of the recordset is maintained in memory and which record appears when the recordset is opened. Figure 18.9 shows the Implementation tab of the **Recordset** object's Properties dialog box.

Limiting The Information Displayed On The Page

To make an ASP more user-friendly, you will want to limit the number of records displayed on the page. You can do this in one of two ways:

◆ If you are displaying data from a database in individual data-bound controls, use the RecordsetNavBar control.

◆ If you are displaying data from a database in a grid control, use the settings on the Navigation tab of the Property Pages dialog box for the grid.

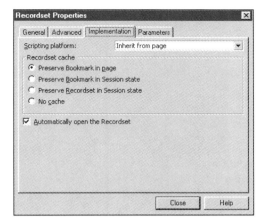

Figure 18.9
You can set visibility and cache properties from the Implementation tab.

The RecordsetNavBar control is located on the Design-Time Controls tab of the Toolbox. You add it to your page as you would any other design-time control, but you need to add it after you have placed all the controls that it will be handling. To use the RecordsetNavBar control on an ASP, perform the following steps:

1. Add the design-time controls that will contain data from the database to your ASP.

2. Add the RecordsetNavBar control to the page below the controls that it will be using.

3. On the General tab of the RecordsetNavBar Property Pages dialog box, set the **Recordset** data property to the name of the appropriate recordset.

4. Check to see that the **Recordset** data properties for each of the data-bound controls on the page are set to the appropriate values.

Scripting Object Model

In this chapter, you have added design-time controls to a page and implicitly used Visual InterDev scripting objects. In the following sections, you will learn how to use a scripting object programmatically.

Script objects are part of the scripting object model, which defines a set of objects with events, properties, and methods that you use to create Web applications. When you add a design-time control to your Web application and set its properties, you are actually creating and manipulating script objects.

Visual InterDev provides you with the following script objects:

♦ **Button**

♦ **Checkbox**

♦ **Grid**

- Label
- Listbox
- OptionGroup
- PageObject
- Recordset
- RecordsetNavbar
- Textbox

Each of these script objects has specific properties, methods, and events. However, the **OnChange** event is common to all of these objects. Each of these script objects also has a common method—the **Advise** method. With the **Advise** method, you can extend the set of events available to an object by "advising" for an event, or registering the object to be notified when the event occurs. After you have advised for an event, you can write event handlers for that event for that object as you would for any other event.

Using Script Objects

The following example code shows how to use some methods and properties of the **Listbox** and **Recordset** script objects:

```
Sub Listbox1_OnChange()
    ' make the current record be the class the user selected
    Recordset1.moveAbsolute(Listbox1.selectedIndex+1)
End Sub
```

Script objects provide the following advantages:

- Browser and platform independence
- Data binding
- Simplified page navigation
- Remote scripting

Enabling The Scripting Object Model

Before you can use the scripting object model, you must enable it so that it can construct the scripting object model framework for the page.

Note

Visual InterDev design-time controls require the scripting object model. If you add a design-time control to a page that does not already have the scripting object model enabled, Visual InterDev prompts you to enable it.

To enable the scripting object model for a page, perform the following steps:

1. Right-click anywhere in the page away from an object or control, choose Properties, and then choose the General tab.

2. Under ASP Settings, choose Enable Scripting Object Model. The HTML editor adds the scripting object model framework to the page in **<META>** tags. You should not alter the content of these tags.

Note
Script objects are available only in Visual InterDev.

FormManager is a design-time control that facilitates the creation of data input forms. You add the controls that you need, and FormManager generates the script that enables and disables the buttons, and updates or cancels changes to the recordset. All you need to do is set values for methods and properties for the controls on the form. FormManager handles most of the other operations. When you use FormManager, instead of writing script, you specify modes that handle property settings for controls and events on the page. To create an input form using FormManager, perform the following steps:

1. Create the data entry ASP form in a project.

2. Add a **Data Connection** object to the project, along with a data source name.

3. Create a Recordset control.

4. Leave the **Lock Type** on the default 3 - Optimistic or any setting other than read-only.

5. Add data-bound controls that will display the fields in the database and make sure that the **Recordset** property points to the recordset that you added earlier.

6. If you use separate data-bound controls to display the contents of the database, add a RecordsetNavBar control, and set the **Recordset** property to the recordset that you added earlier.

7. Add the command buttons—such as add, delete, or save—that will implement the different modes that your page will have.

8. Add a FormManager control at the bottom of your page.

To specify the modes that your page will use, follow these steps:

1. Identify each mode and specify the property settings and methods for the control while the mode is active.

2. Specify the transition events between the modes that trigger specific actions.

3. Add the actions that occur after the transition event is triggered but before the transition is complete.

Note

To validate user input, you will need to develop and call separate validation functions.

Where To Go From Here

In this chapter, you learned the basics of Active Server Page design—you learned how to work with VBScript, and how to manage the ASP built-in objects to effectively communicate over the Web. You also learned how to use your own custom-made components—namely, COM components—within your ASPs. Finally, you saw how to take advantage of the built-in InterDev Data Environment to add database support to your applications, and learned about the different steps you must perform to take advantage of recordsets in the information you display to your users.

In the next several chapters, you will take the knowledge that you acquired in this chapter and apply it to some more in-depth development models with InterDev and related technologies. In Chapter 19, you will develop a simple COM component, and then see how it integrates with your Active Server Pages, accessing a back-end database (in this case, SQL Server) on the ASP's behalf. In Chapter 20, you will look in more depth at the data access specifics of working with ADO and Active Server Pages.

Creating Middle-Tier COM Components With Visual Basic 6

In Chapters 17 and 18, I talked about the principles behind creating effective Web-based client/server applications. We focused on models, and the importance of VBScript in programming Active Server Pages (ASPs). If you recall, however, one of the most important concepts that I detailed is the separation between the presentation, business, and data *layers* of a multitiered environment. I have detailed parts of the business layer in previous chapters, and have spent most of this book on the data layer. In later chapters, we will look briefly at the presentation layer, at least inasmuch as it relates to Web design.

However, I have indicated, but not really spent much time with, the most important piece for the business layer. In this chapter, we will look at how using Component Object Model (COM) components developed in Visual Basic lets you perform more complex business processes, by increasing the feature richness of your application.

More Closely Evaluating The Business Layer

Evaluating the business layer fully requires the definition of three key topics—*business rules*, *business processes*, and *business objects*. Each of these components—whether logical or actually implemented—forms a key piece of the business layer's existence. In the next several sections, we'll take a look at each of these topics.

Understanding Business Rules

A business rule is an algorithm that determines how information is processed. For example, if a credit card number is entered into a form, one business rule may check the credit card number for the limit available in that account. If the available credit limit exceeds the transaction, credit will be granted and the transaction will proceed. On the other hand, if the available credit does not exceed the transaction amount, the business rule may require that the credit approver evaluate exactly *how much* the transaction exceeds the available credit, and may approve the transaction if it exceeds the limit by only a few dollars. In addition, depending on the company's business policies, if the transaction *does* exceed their prespecified limit, the company might charge a $25 fee for exceeding their credit limit.

Each of these individual decisions is the implementation of a business rule; ensuring that the $25 fee is assessed when certain conditions occur is the responsibility of the entire business process, discussed in the next section.

Combining Tasks To Accomplish Business Processes

A *business process* is a sequence of related tasks that produces a specific response to a user's request. For example, when a user submits an order form to purchase a product from an online catalog, a transaction is executed. This is a business process.

Other examples of business processes include activities such as opening a new bank account, retrieving customer information, or retrieving benefit options for a specific employee. For each of these examples, a business process acts on a business rule.

Business processes are commonly represented as middle-tier objects—commonly referred to as *business services*. By using this approach, you can represent and implement business processes in an object-oriented environment as you plan your Web site. Furthermore, business services can be implemented as COM components and encapsulate a set of business processes.

Using Business Objects

Using an object-oriented model to create business processes offers several advantages, as summarized in the following list:

♦ *Simplification of complex processes*—You can simplify a complex business process by breaking its individual parts into smaller pieces, or objects. Conceptually, you can think of each part of the process as a specific object, where an object performs a specific function of the process.

♦ *Natural modeling techniques*—Because object-oriented methodology reflects a natural way of looking at real-world objects and processes, components are often easier to analyze, design, and develop with object-oriented techniques. Furthermore, such objects tend to be more maintainable and reusable once they are developed.

♦ *Encapsulation*—Each business object encapsulates the data and functionality needed to accomplish its task. A business object exposes only those methods needed by other business objects. By encapsulating only specific data and functionality in each object, business objects are self-contained and isolated from changes made to other objects.

There are many different ways to create business objects—for example, many modern-day Unix solutions use the CORBA standard to build their objects. However, I have discussed Microsoft products and techniques throughout this book, and now is no exception—the recommended method for creating objects to run over Windows networks is to create them as COM components.

Implementing Business Objects As COM Components

A COM component is a unit of code that provides a specific, predefined functionality. By breaking your code into components, you can decide later how to most effectively distribute your application. Most programmers working in modern-day, multitier environments agree that the appropriate way of designing such environments is by using components. In the Microsoft universe, the best way to create such components is by adhering to the COM standard.

COM components offer several benefits:

♦ They provide a standard method of creating reusable, higher-level components.

♦ They can be created with and used from a variety of programming languages such as Visual Basic, Visual J++, and C++. COM guarantees interoperability regardless of the language used to implement the components.

♦ Scriptlets can also be modified to create COM components (more specifically, ActiveX controls).

♦ COM components work with Microsoft Transaction Server (MTS)—specifically, you can use MTS as a wrapper for enforcing transaction integrity and allowing for substantial scalability of your components.

♦ COM components can be installed and used on both the server and the client. However, because they run machine-dependent code, use on the client requires a rather homogenous client environment, which is not generally the case on a Web site. Nonetheless, COM components can be effectively used on servers running Win32 operating systems, as well as on Macintosh systems and certain types of Unix systems.

This brief summary barely touches on the benefits of modular development in general, and COM development in specific. However, any number of great books are available on COM development; in this book, I discuss it only as a useful supporting technology for Web site design. The concept work is really not necessary because of how I am treating COM for our purposes, so let's jump right into COM component design.

Tip

Though you can use the Office 2000 Developer edition with the COM component management add-in to trick Office 2000 into letting you develop COM components from the VBA Interactive Development Environment (IDE), it is generally simpler—and more useful—to use the Visual Basic development environment directly. However, when developing COM add-ins whose purpose will be to manage communications between multiple Office 2000 applications, Microsoft does recommend the use of the new add-in manager.

Creating COM Components In Visual Basic

You have several different techniques that you can choose from when creating COM components in Visual Basic, but I will presume in this chapter that you are going to use your components with MTS—although you may design them outside of MTS, I will presume that the components may eventually be deployed to the MTS platform. Because of the capabilities of MTS, one of its specifications regarding component design is that the COM components you implement in MTS must be implemented as dynamic-link libraries (DLLs). Therefore, I will work with the ActiveX DLL project in Visual Basic 6. The following sections discuss how to create and implement such a project, and what to watch out for in its design.

Additionally, you will learn how to add class modules to your ActiveX DLL project whose job it is to define objects that encapsulate the internal functionality of a COM component. You will also learn how to expose methods from objects to make the COM components interoperable with other components and applications.

A Brief Discussion Of COM DLLs Vs. COM EXEs

As I suggested earlier in this chapter, Visual Basic provides you with several different ways of creating COM objects. Generally, with Visual Basic, you can build and run either in-process or out-of-process components. You will implement in-process components as ActiveX DLLs. Out-of-process components are implemented as ActiveX EXEs. Table 19.1 lists the advantages and disadvantages of using in-process and out-of-process components.

Table 19.1 A short comparison of in-process versus out-of-process objects.

Type Of Component	Advantages	Disadvantages
In-process DLL	Faster access to objects	Less fault-tolerant; if the DLL fails, the entire executable fails.
Out-of-process EXE	Fault-tolerant; if the EXE fails, other processes in the system will not fail. Can be retained in memory as independent process.	Slower because of marshaling.

Tip

For more information about the differences between in-process and out-of-process components, search for "How Marshaling Affects ActiveX Component Performance" in Visual Basic Books Online.

MTS Constraints For Components

As I mentioned earlier in this chapter, Microsoft Transaction Server (MTS) places certain restraints and requirements on COM components that run under it. Components that you intend to run under MTS must meet the following constraints:

♦ Components must be compiled as an ActiveX DLL (that is, an in-process COM component).

♦ Each component must provide a type library that describes its interfaces.

♦ The components must be self-registering.

Fortunately, Visual Basic satisfies the last two options automatically when building COM components.

Choosing From The Project Templates

When you create a new project in Visual Basic, you first choose a template. To create a COM component, you choose either the ActiveX EXE or the ActiveX DLL template in the New Project dialog box. Selecting either type of template sets a number of default values that are important for creating code components. Figure 19.1 shows the standard Visual Basic templates within the New Project dialog box.

As mentioned previously, we will focus on ActiveX DLLs in this chapter. However, when you create a new ActiveX DLL or ActiveX EXE project, you also set properties that affect how your component runs. Let's consider those project properties, as detailed in the following section.

Figure 19.1
The templates you can choose from when creating a new VB project.

Understanding COM Component Project Properties

You set properties for a project by clicking on <*projectname*> Properties on the Project menu. Then, you click on the General tab of the Project Properties sheet to select the options you want. Table 19.2 describes the options you typically set for a new ActiveX DLL or ActiveX EXE project.

Understanding Class Modules

Visual Basic provides a type of module called a *class module*. Each class module defines one type of object. A class module represents a logical object in your component. In an application, you can have several class modules. At runtime, you create an object by creating an instance of a class. A class is a template for an object. An object is an instance of a class.

For example, you can create an **Employee** class that has properties such as **LastName** and **FirstName**, and a method such as **Hire**. Class modules, as used in Visual Basic, are functionally identical to class modules that you implement in Access from the VBA IDE. The

Table 19.2   Project properties you will manipulate for COM objects.

Option	Description
Project type	Provides the four template options: Standard EXE, ActiveX EXE, ActiveX DLL, and ActiveX Control. When you create a new ActiveX DLL or ActiveX EXE project, Visual Basic automatically sets the Project Type property. The project type determines how other project options can be set. For example, options on the Component tab are not available when the project type is set to Standard EXE.
Startup object	Sets which form or **Sub Main** procedure in the current project runs first. For most ActiveX EXEs and ActiveX DLLs, you set the Startup Object field to (None). If you want initialization code to run when the component is loaded, set the Startup Object property to **Sub Main**. If you want initialization code to run when an instance of a class is created, use the **Class_Initialize** event.
Project name	Specifies the component name to which the client application refers.
Project description	Enables you to enter a brief description of the COM component, along with the objects it provides. The contents of this field appear in the References dialog box when you select references for other Visual Basic projects. The text also appears in the Description pane at the bottom of the Object Browser.
Unattended execution	Specifies whether the component will run without user interaction. Unattended components do not have a user interface. Any runtime functions, such as messages that normally result in user interaction, are written to an event log. If this box is checked, the project will be built to use the apartment-threading model. Using this model will make your objects run more efficiently.
Threading model	The threading model list box is only activated for ActiveX DLL and ActiveX Control projects. The only options are single-threaded and apartment-threaded.

only difference for the purposes of this chapter's discussion is that the class modules each represent separate types of objects with the in-process COM component.

Adding A Class Module To A Project

When you create a new ActiveX DLL project by choosing the ActiveX DLL template in the New Project dialog box, Visual Basic creates a project with one class module. You can add new class modules by clicking on Add Class Module on the Visual Basic Project menu. You can then add methods, properties, and events to the class.

To create an instance of a class in the project that defines the class, you use the **Dim** and **Set** statements. This example code creates an instance of the **Customer** class:

```
Dim objCustomer As Customer
Set objCustomer = New Customer
```

You can also use the more compact syntax **Dim ObjCustomer As New Customer** instead of using the **Set** statement. However, issues can arise with instancing objects in either of these fashions when using MTS, so be careful about how you construct your code. In fact, as I will discuss later in this chapter, when constructing statements with MTS, you should use the Visual Basic **CreateObject** method, rather than the **New** statement.

Once you have created an object, you can use methods and properties of the object. This example code invokes the **Add** method of the **Customer** object:

```
objCustomer.Add "Brett", "Lawyer", 32
```

To determine the behavior of a component, you set properties for each class module in the component. The **Name** and **Instancing** properties provide classes with information about components, which client applications use to instantiate objects.

Naming The Class

To create a name for the class, set the **Name** property in the Properties window. This name will be used by the client application to create an instance of an object.

For example, the following code creates an instance of a class named **DataClass**, which is defined in the project named **DataProject**:

```
Dim objSample As Object
Set objSample = CreateObject ("DataProject.DataClass")
```

The class name is combined with the name of the component to produce a fully qualified class name, also referred to as a *programmatic ID* or *ProgID*. In the previous example code, the fully qualified class name of the **DataClass** class is **DataProject.DataClass**.

Instancing Property

The **Instancing** property determines whether applications outside of the Visual Basic project that defines the class can create new instances of the class, and if so, how those instances are created. The available **Instancing** property settings are different for ActiveX EXE and ActiveX DLL projects in Visual Basic. Figure 19.2 shows the **Instancing** property settings for a class module within an ActiveX DLL project.

When you create a business object, set the **Instancing** property to **MultiUse**. Table 19.3 describes each of the **Instancing** property settings.

For classes to be useful, they must contain methods that implement the functionality that your application requires of your component, such as business services. For every class module you create, Visual Basic automatically supplies two built-in event handlers called **Initialize** and **Terminate** (also known as event procedures) for which you can supply handler methods. You must add other general methods manually.

> **Warning**
> *Keep in mind that these methods you create will be the interfaces of the COM components running as part of the IIS server process. As a general rule, server processes should not have a user interface (UI). Therefore, if you do not implement user interfaces within your components (which you should not), you must not call Windows GUI interface methods, like **MsgBox**, in the methods you create.*

Working With Initialize And Terminate Event Handlers

To add code to a class module event, you open a Visual Basic code window for the class, and then click on Class in the Object drop-down list box.

Figure 19.2
The Properties dialog box for a class module.

Table 19.3   Different settings for the Instancing property.

Setting	Description
Private	Other applications are not allowed access to type library information about the class and cannot create instances of it. **Private** objects are used only within the project that defines the class.
PublicNotCreatable	Other applications can use objects of this class only if the component creates the objects first. Other applications cannot use the **CreateObject** method or the **New** operator to create objects of this class. Set the **Instancing** property to this value when you want to create dependent objects.
MultiUse	Multiple clients can use the same instance of the component. If multiple clients create objects from the component, the same instance of the component is used for all clients.
GlobalMultiUse	Similar to **MultiUse**, except that properties and methods of the class can be invoked as though they were global functions. It is not necessary to create an explicit instance of a class, because one will automatically be created.

Initialize Event

The **Initialize** event occurs when an instance of a class is created, but before any properties have been set. You use the **Initialize** event handler to initialize any data used by the class, as shown in the following example code:

```
Private Sub Class_Initialize()
  'All methods in this class use a global Log object
  'to record each method call
  Set objLog = New Log

  objLog.Write "Object Initialized"
End Sub
```

In general, you will almost always put some initialization code within this event. In many cases, for example, your component could be talking to a database server on another machine, in which case you might want to create a new connection to the database every time a new instance of the class is created.

By the same token, you will often want to perform certain clean-up processing whenever you release an instance of the class. You will do such processing within the **Terminate** event, as detailed in the next section.

Terminate Event

The **Terminate** event occurs when an object variable goes out of scope or is set to **Nothing**. You use the **Terminate** event handler to save information, unload forms, and perform tasks that you want to occur only when the class terminates, as shown in the following example code:

```
Private Sub Class_Terminate()
    objLog.Write "Object Terminated"
    Set objLog = Nothing
End Sub
```

Needless to say, creating robust initialization and termination events can mean the difference between a well-behaved component (one that sets itself up and then cleans up after itself when finished) and a poorly designed component. Close attention to these two events is important.

General Methods Within Your Classes

To add methods to an object, you create public **Sub** or **Function** procedures within the class module for that object. The public **Sub** and **Function** procedures will be exposed as methods for the object. Obviously, deciding whether to use a **Sub** or **Function** procedure depends on the goals you are trying to achieve with the method—whether it returns one or more values, is meant to be interpreted within a complex statement, and so on.

Note
*You must add the **Public** keyword before **Sub** or **Function** to make the procedure available to other objects and applications. Otherwise, the procedure is private and can be accessed only from the object.*

To create a method for an object, you can either type the procedure heading directly in the code window, or click on Add Procedure on the Tools menu and complete the dialog box. The following example code creates a method that accepts a number and then returns the number squared:

```
Public Function SquareIt (Num As Integer) As Integer
  SquareIt = Num * Num
End Function
```

To view the properties and methods you have defined for an object, you can use the Object Browser. Once you finish defining methods and properties, you can test the COM component to ensure that it works correctly.

Testing COM Components

You can use Visual Basic to test a COM component before using the component on a Web server. To test an ActiveX DLL project, you create another project within the same instance of Visual Basic. To test an ActiveX EXE project, you must run a second copy of the Visual Basic development environment, because this type of component runs in a separate process.

To understand how this works, in the following steps you will create a project group in Visual Basic and use a Standard EXE project to test the **NumberProcessing** component, which is implemented in the Chap19DLL.vbp project contained in the Chapter 19 directory on the companion CD-ROM. To try this testing procedure, perform the following steps:

1. From within Visual Basic, open the Chap19DLL.vbp project, contained in the Chapter 19 directory on the CD. Visual Basic will open the project, including the single class module that it contains.

2. On the File menu, click on Add Project, and in the New tab, double-click on Standard.EXE. This will add a new project to the Project Group window.

3. To make the new Standard.EXE project the start-up project for your application, right-click on the new project, and then select Set As Start Up from the pop-up menu. Whenever you run the component, your new project will start first.

4. In the new project, add a reference to the Chap19DLL project by clicking on Project | References | Chap19DLL. You now have the necessary pieces in place to take advantage of the DLL. However, to effectively test the DLL, you must add code to invoke the **Square** method that the DLL exposes.

5. To add code to call a method, you should first add a user interface element to the form to invoke the method. To that end, add a command button to the form.

6. In the **Click** event for the command button, add the following code to create an instance of the class defined in the ActiveX DLL:

```
Dim objChap19DLL As Object
Set objChap19DLL = New Chap19DLL.Square
```

7. Still within the **Click** event, call the **SquareIt** method to test the component, as shown in the following example code:

```
Print objChap19DLL.SquareIt(5)
```

Clearly, this is a very simple component—therefore a very simple testing procedure is all that is necessary. However, just to make sure that you have a handle on how the whole thing works, let's do a little debugging. To watch the execution stream with the object, perform the following steps:

1. Place the cursor in the following line of code:

```
Print objChap19DLL.SquareIt(5)
```

2. On the Debug menu, select the Toggle Breakpoint option. The line of code is highlighted in red to indicate that it is a breakpoint and that the code will suspend execution when the program reaches this line. Now, to see how it works, you will want to trace the source code of the method.

3. On the Run menu, select the Start option. VB will execute the project.

4. Click on the command button on the form. The program will stop its execution at the highlighted line of code.

5. On the Debug menu, select the Step Into option. The program will step directly into the **SquareIt** function as it is called (you can also use the toolbar or the F8 key).

6. Hold the mouse over the variables in the code to see the values that are currently in the variables (you can also set watches to accomplish this task). When you enter the object, the current value of **SquareIt** is 0. As you continue stepping into the code, the value of **SquareIt** changes to 25.

7. Click on the Continue button to continue execution, and then click on the command button on the form. The program prints the value 25 to the form.

Testing COM components is, in many ways, very similar to testing normal applications. One tip: Make sure that you have the IDE set to Break In Class Module for most application debugging that uses class modules. However, there are some differences. You should read some articles on the testing and debugging process—in Books Online, third-party magazines, and so on—for more information about testing COM components.

Using The Business Component In The Web Site

Having created a business component, you can work with it in a variety of scenarios to enhance a Web site's functionality. In this section, you will learn how to call COM components from a Web page and how to include them directly in a Microsoft Visual InterDev project. In addition, you will learn how to register a component and how to set version compatibility options from within Visual Basic.

Registering A Component

Before you can use a COM component, it must be registered. Registration ensures that a component is recognized by the Windows operating system. This process creates entries in the Windows registration database. There are three ways to register an in-process (DLL) component:

♦ *Build the DLL*—On the development computer, Visual Basic automatically registers the component as part of a successful build process.

♦ *Run Regsvr32.exe*—Regsvr32 is a utility that registers a DLL. Pass the DLL file name as an argument to the Regsvr32 utility, as shown in the following code:

```
Regsvr312.exe mydll.dll
```

◆ *Create a setup program*—When you run the setup program, the component is registered.

When a component is no longer needed, it can be unregistered. Unregistering components is a process comparably easy to registering them. You have two mechanisms to choose from when unregistering components:

◆ To remove a DLL entry from the Registry, run Regsvr32.exe, including the **/u** option and the name of the DLL file, as shown in the following code (this technique works with DLLs built on the computer as well):

```
Regsvr32.exe /u mydll.dll
```

◆ If the component was installed by a setup program, you should be able to uninstall it by using the Add/Remove Programs applet in the Control Panel.

Registering A Server Component From Visual InterDev

If a component in your Web application is designed to run on the server, you must make sure it is registered on the production server. In a Microsoft Visual InterDev Web project, you can designate a component to be registered as a server component. When you use the Copy Web Application feature in Visual InterDev, your component will be automatically registered on the server. To mark a server component for registration, perform the following steps:

1. In Project Explorer, add the component to your Web project.

2. Select the component you want to register on the server.

3. In the Properties grid, select Custom.

4. In the Component Installation tab of the Custom property page, select Register On Server, and then click on OK.

You can deploy COM components as part of your Web project directly from Project Explorer in Microsoft Visual InterDev 6. This enables you to distribute an integrated solution that includes files created using other Visual Studio tools. For example, you can integrate an ActiveX DLL file (a COM component) that you created with Visual Basic directly into your Visual InterDev project. If a component is designed to run on the server, you must specify that the component be registered on the server.

Note

The deployment of a Web application with components requires Microsoft FrontPage Server Extensions on the production server. The FrontPage server extensions install automatically with the Windows NT Option Pack, or they can be downloaded for other platforms from the Microsoft Web site.

To deploy a Web application with components, perform the following steps from within Visual InterDev:

1. In Project Explorer, select the project that points to the Web application you want to deploy.

2. Select Project | Web Project | Copy Web Application.

3. In the Copy Project dialog box, choose the copy of the application you want to deploy.

Note

If you work on a team, you typically deploy the master version, because it includes the updated files from the team members.

4. In the Server Name box, enter the name of the Web server you want to use.

5. In the Web Project box, enter the name you want the users to type for the URL.

6. Select Register Server Components and click on OK.

Visual InterDev adds a new application to the destination Web server and copies the files in the Web application to that new folder. The name you specified in the Copy Web Application dialog box becomes part of the application's URL. You can now test the application on the production server.

Creating COM Component Instances From Active Server Pages (ASPs)

In an Active Server Page, you can create an instance of a COM component by using the **CreateObject** method. Once you have created an instance of a component, you can access its properties and methods. The following example code shows how to use the **CreateObject** method, and then output the return value of a method to an HTML response:

```
<% Set bc = Server.CreateObject ("MyServer.MyObject") %>
<% Response.Write bc.method( ) %>
```

When you build your COM component, you should specify that all parameters be passed using **ByVal**. This is the most efficient way to pass a parameter to a COM component.

Warning

*If you pass parameters into COM components using **ByRef**, you must convert each parameter into the data type that the method expects. This is because Visual Basic Scripting Edition (VBScript) uses variants for all variable types. If you call a method of a COM component that does not accept parameters of type **Variant**, then you must explicitly convert the arguments to the correct type.*

The following example code shows how to call the **SquareIt** method on the **Math** object (implemented within the Chap19 directory). It also shows how to convert the argument to an **Integer** data type and print the result to an HTML response (note the explicit conversion of the passed-in value to type **Integer** to ensure compliance with COM parameter rules):

```
<% Set mathobj = Server.CreateObject ("Math.Object") %>
<%= mathobj.SquareIt (cint(5)) %>
```

Note

*Once you have created a COM component by using the **CreateObject** method, its corresponding DLL will remain loaded in memory by IIS until it stops running. If you are testing the DLL, you will not be able to recompile until the DLL is freed from memory. To force IIS to free the DLL, stop and restart the Web service in the Internet Service Manager.*

Working With COM Components Inside Web Applications

As you have learned, you can run COM components (formerly known as Automation Servers) on a Web server—whether as part of the Web application's normal processing or in direct response to a user request. These components enable you to extend the functionality of an Active Server Page with any resource, such as a database, located on the Web server. In the following sections, I will focus again on using COM components, and explain some of the specifics involved in using COM components in your Web application.

Using Server-Side COM Components

To use a server component, you first need to understand how to create an instance of a component, or an object. There are two ways to create an object. You can use:

♦ The HTML-defined **<OBJECT>** tag

♦ The VBScript **Server.CreateObject** syntax

The following sections briefly discuss each technique.

Using The <OBJECT> Tag

You can use the **<OBJECT>** tag to create a component that runs on the Web server. To use the **<OBJECT>** tag, you set the **RUNAT** attribute to **Server**. You can set the scope of the component by setting the **SCOPE** attribute to **Application** or **Session**. If you do not set the **SCOPE** attribute, the component will have page scope, meaning it can only be referenced on the current page. To specify the type of component to be created, you can use either its registered name (**PROGID**), or its registered number (**CLASSID**).

In the following example code, the registered name (**PROGID**) is used to create a session-scope instance of the fictitious component:

```
<OBJECT RUNAT=Server
        SCOPE=Session ID=SampleComp
        PROGID="Coriolis.SampleComponent">
</OBJECT>
```

In the following example code, the registered number (**CLASSID**) method is used to create an application-scope instance of **SampleComponent**:

```
<OBJECT RUNAT=Server
        SCOPE=Application ID=SampleComp
        CLASSID="Clsid:00000293-0000-0010-8000-00AA006D2EA4"></OBJECT>
<!-- More code here  -->
```

When you use the **<OBJECT>** tag to declare a session-scope or application-scope instance of a component, the variable you assign to the component is stored in the session or application namespace. You do not need to use the **Session** or **Application** object to access the instance of the component.

The following example code opens the instance of **SampleComponent** that has been declared in the previous example code:

```
<%= SampleComp.GetSomething("some.txt") %>
```

Note
*When you drag a component from the Server Objects tab of the Toolbox, Visual InterDev adds an **<OBJECT>** tag for the component to your ASP page. It does not set the **SCOPE** attribute in the tag, so components created this way will have page scope.*

Using The CreateObject Method

You can also use the **CreateObject** method of the **Server** object to create an instance of a component. The following example code creates a reference to the Browser Capabilities component using its PROGID:

```
<% Set bc = Server.CreateObject("MSWC.BrowserType") %>
```

To help you create Web applications, Internet Information Server (IIS) 4 provides a large number of COM components that are available on the Server Objects tab of the Toolbox. Table 19.4 describes several of these server objects.

Table 19.4   Server objects implemented by Microsoft's Internet Information Server (IIS).

Server Objects	Description
ADO Command, ADO Connection, and ADO Recordset	ActiveX Data Objects (ADO) that access information stored in a database or other tabular data structures.
Ad Rotator	Automatically rotates advertisements displayed on a Web page, according to a specified schedule.
Browser Capabilities	Determines the capabilities, type, and version of a user's browser.
CDONTS NewMail and CDONTS Session	Collaboration Data Objects for NTS.
Content Linking	Creates a table of contents for Web pages, and links them sequentially, like pages in a book.
File Access	Uses the **FileSystemObject** object to retrieve and modify information stored in a text file on the server.

COM components enable you to package and reuse common functions, such as accessing a database and writing information to text files in an ASP application. You can access the components installed on a Web server by using an ASP file with the **CreateObject** method of the **Server** object.

Remote Business Objects

In Chapter 21, you will learn about how the Remote Data Service (RDS) of ActiveX Data Objects (ADO) allows a client to create instances of remote business objects. Though you haven't learned about the *reasons* for doing this yet, this seems the most appropriate place to talk about how to do it; you will learn about the reasons in Chapter 21.

Creating An Instance Of A Remote Business Object

To create an instance of a remote business object, you insert the **RDS.DataSpace** object into an HTML document and then call the **CreateObject** method of the **RDS.DataSpace** object. **CreateObject** creates an instance of the business object on a Web server. In the case of an out-of-process component, it creates a proxy on the client to marshal method calls to the object. **CreateObject** returns an object reference, which you use to invoke methods of the business object.

The syntax of the **CreateObject** method is as follows:

```
RDS.DataSpace.CreateObject ProgID, ServerName
```

In the prototype, **ProgID** corresponds to the fully qualified name of the object, or the globally unique CLASSID of the object. The **ServerName** parameter qualifies to the machine name of the remote server on which the object resides. The following example code uses the **CreateObject** function to create an instance of the **Library.Member** business object using DCOM. Then it invokes the **Add** method of the object to add a new member to the library's member list:

```
set objEnroll = ADS1.CreateObject("Library.Member","SQLSERVER")
objEnroll.Add (Session("memberID"),Session("memberName"))
```

Client Vs. Server

There are several reasons for creating an instance of a business object by using the **RDS.DataSpace** object on the client rather than by using an Active Server Page on the server. **RDS.DataSpace** provides the following advantages over using ASP at the server:

♦ The ability to call multiple business objects from a single Web page without retrieving new pages. This permits more flexibility in the design of a Web page. Active Server Pages can also call multiple business objects; however, they can only get information from a submitted HTML form, which is more limiting.

♦ The ability to use the **RDS.DataSpace** object to retrieve the data and cache it on the client.

This improves performance by reducing the load on the server, and is especially useful if business objects return a large amount of data. However, you should use an Active Server Page instead of **RDS.DataSpace** in the following situations:

♦ When business objects must perform secure transactions. In such cases, using the **RDS.DataSpace** object would expose the code of the business objects by creating them on a Web page, where it could be misused. When the code is placed in server-side script in an Active Server Page, it will never be returned to a client.

♦ When the client cannot run ActiveX controls. If the client is of an unknown type—that is, not necessarily Internet Explorer—then you should use Active Server Pages (ASPs) to protect against browser conflicts.

A Little More On How COM Components Work

When you compile a project, Visual Basic creates a unique class identifier (CLSID), a unique interface identifier (IID), and a unique type library ID. Applications invoking and managing your component will require these identifiers to create and use objects. If these identifiers change in a new version of a component, existing applications will not be able to use the new version.

Type Library IDs

A COM component stores its data type information and object characteristics, including descriptions of methods and properties, in a type library. When a COM component is registered with Microsoft Windows, an entry is created under HKEY_CLASSES_ROOT\TypeLib in the Registry, associating a globally unique identifier (GUID) with its type library data. By providing access to an object's type library through a unique type library ID, a client can manipulate the methods and properties of the object.

Version Compatibility

Version compatibility is very important when you're building components for use in a distributed environment. When you compile an ActiveX EXE or ActiveX DLL project, its classes expose methods that clients will use. If at some point you change a class in a component by deleting or changing the signature of a property or method, that component will no longer work with old clients. When you next compile the component, a new type library ID will be created, which will be incompatible with existing versions of the component used by clients.

Visual Basic provides three options to help control version compatibility. To set the version compatibility, click on Project | Project Properties. In the Project Properties sheet, click on the Component tab and set the Version Compatibility option. Figure 19.3 shows the Component tab of the Project Properties dialog box.

If you make any change to the component (for example, if you delete a property) that is incompatible with the version on your Web server specified in the Project Compatibility field, Visual Basic displays a warning message and generates a new type library ID.

There are three options for version compatibility, as detailed in Table 19.5.

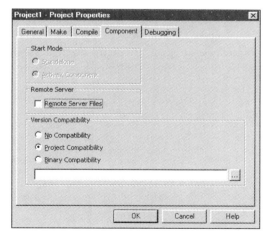

Figure 19.3
The Component tab of the Project Properties dialog box.

Table 19.5   The different version compatibility settings.

Option	Description
No Compatibility	Each time you compile the component, the type library ID, CLSIDs, and IIDs are re-created. Because none of these identifiers match the ones existing clients are using, backward-compatibility is not possible.
Project Compatibility	Each time you compile the component, the CLSIDs and IIDs are re-created, but the type library remains constant. This is useful for test projects so you can maintain references to the component project. However, each compilation is not backward-compatible with existing clients. This is the default setting for a component.
Binary Compatibility	Each time you compile the component, Visual Basic keeps the type library ID, CLSIDs, and IIDs the same. This maintains backward-compatibility with existing clients. However, if you attempt to delete a method from a class, or change a method's name or parameter types, Visual Basic will warn you that your changes will make the new version incompatible with previously compiled applications. If you ignore the warning, Visual Basic will create new CLSIDs and IIDs for the component, breaking its backward-compatibility.

Where To Go From Here

In this chapter, you saw the basics of how to implement COM components from within Visual Basic for use with your Web applications. We also saw how to implement COM components from within ASP code, and considered some situations where you might want to implement them slightly differently than others.

In Chapter 20, we will examine Dynamic HTML and the Document Object Model (DOM). Then, in Chapter 21, we'll look at the use of ActiveX Data Objects with Active Server Pages more closely, and we will consider cases where you can easily implement ADO within your Web applications and discuss the benefits that such implementations will provide to you.

Chapter 20

Using The Dynamic Client

Needless to say, if you haven't figured it out already, programming for Web distribution—whether using a server-side technology such as Active Server Pages (ASPs) or a client-side scripting technology such as ECMAScript or VBScript—is a pretty complex animal in and of itself. In this chapter, I will delve further into a consideration of some of the options at your disposal with client-side programming, focusing on the development of Dynamic HTML scripts with the VBScript programming language. In the next chapter, we will continue our exploration with a visit to server-side VBScript, keeping in mind the types of database support and powerful processing you can accomplish with server-side script. Let's begin with a discussion of Dynamic HTML.

Understanding Dynamic HTML

Dynamic HTML (DHTML) is built on top of HTML. That is, DHTML includes all the elements that make up a traditional Web page. However, with DHTML, all of those elements are now programmable objects. You can assign each element an ID and then use scripting to alter them after the page has been downloaded.

Dynamic HTML allows you to dynamically control the look and content of a Web page. There are four basic types of features that you can manipulate dynamically: *dynamic styles*, which allow you to change element styles on a page; *dynamic positioning*, which lets you change the position of an element on the page; *dynamic content*, which adds new text or HTML content to a page during viewing; and *data binding*, which binds elements to records in a database. We will consider the first three in this chapter.

For example, adding two functions, an **ID** for the **<H1>** tag, and calls to the two functions lets you dynamically change the color of the text in the following code example whenever the user moves the cursor over that text:

```
<HTML>
<SCRIPT LANGUAGE="VBScript">
<!--
Sub ChangeColor()
  header.style.color = "red"
End Sub

Sub ChangeBack()
  header.style.color = "black"
End Sub
-->
</SCRIPT>
<BODY>
<H1 ID="header" onmouseover="ChangeColor()"
  onmouseout="ChangeBack()">Chapter 20 ColorChange!</H1>
</BODY>
</HTML>
```

Note

*When you add the **ID** attribute to the **<H1>** tag and assign it the value "header," you are creating a programmable object whose properties can then be manipulated in script.*

Both Microsoft and Netscape have worked closely with the W3C to create a standard for DHTML. Both models propose the following items: a Document Object Model (DOM); a way to control elements on the page using scripting; multimedia controls for animations and other effects; and a way to bind data to an HTML page. The primary differences are in the extent of the object model and the scripting language to be used.

Note

The Internet Explorer 4 implementation of DHTML is platform-independent, which means that it will run on any platform that supports Internet Explorer 4, including Macintosh and Unix. However, it is not browser-independent, meaning that there will be minor variations in the implementation of DHTML in other browsers versus what you see in this chapter. For an excellent resource on programming for different browser types, refer to Dynamic HTML Black Book, *from Coriolis, 1998.*

The DOM proposed by Microsoft is both browser and language independent. Figure 20.1 shows you the structure of the Microsoft DOM.

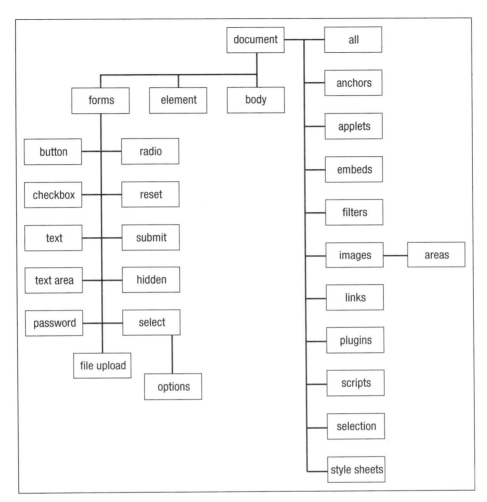

Figure 20.1
The structure of the Microsoft Document Object Model.

Working With DHTML And The DOM

DHTML enables data binding and multimedia effects. We'll cover data binding later in this chapter, whereas multimedia effects are well beyond the scope of what we are trying to accomplish in this book. *Scripting* is the primary tool that enables dynamic pages. However, scripting is more than just a language; in fact, it combines three elements—a language, an object model, and event handling. In this section, you will learn about three scripting languages available for most current browsers: VBScript, JScript, and JavaScript. You will also learn about the DOM.

Choosing A Scripting Language

When choosing a scripting language, consider the following two issues:

♦ *Browser compatibility*—Web browsers must include a scripting interpreter for the language you choose. Internet Explorer 4 and later has interpreters for VBScript, JScript, and JavaScript. Netscape Navigator provides an interpreter for JavaScript (and, as you will see, for JScript by extension), though you can download an interpreter for VBScript over Navigator.

♦ *Programmer familiarity*—Choose a scripting language that is similar to a language you know. If you have Visual Basic experience, you can quickly learn VBScript. If you have Java or C/C++ experience, JScript and JavaScript will be more familiar to you.

VBScript, then, is a subset of Microsoft Visual Basic for Applications (VBA). VBScript lets you create variables and constants, use conditional logic, and create procedures in a fashion very similar to VBA. JScript and JavaScript, on the other hand, are, respectively, the Microsoft and Netscape implementations of the ECMAScript standard. Both languages are fully compliant with the ECMAScript standard, and therefore are generally better choices for the development of client-side code.

> **Note**
> *Netscape Navigator does not natively support VBScript, but you can acquire a plug-in from Netscape by going to **www.ncompasslabs.com**.*

Differences Between VBScript And JScript

The following examples show the difference between two procedures/functions—one written in VBScript, and one written in ECMAScript (called JScript in Internet Explorer, and JavaScript in Netscape Navigator). The code in both procedures displays a message box. Because it should look more familiar by this point in the book, let's look first at the VBScript example:

```
<SCRIPT LANGUAGE=VBScript>
<!--Sub SayHello()
    MsgBox "Hello, world!"
End Sub-->
</SCRIPT>
```

As you can see, the code is nearly identical to much of the VB and VBA code that you have written over the course of this book. The script wrappers are also standard: The first code line indicates that the procedure code is written in VBScript, and then the `<!--`tag (which browsers will interpret as a comment tag) at the beginning of the second line of the example tells the browser that if it doesn't understand VBScript, it should ignore everything else it encounters until the `-->` at the end of the code example. The JScript example looks quite similar, though there are some differences in language construction and the way the interpreter reads it, as you can see here:

```
<SCRIPT LANGUAGE=JScript>
<!--function SayHello()
{
  alert ("Hello, world!");
}
//--></SCRIPT>
```

The long and short of it all: Use ECMAScript for client-side scripting anywhere you cannot be sure what type of browser will execute the code. All the major browsers understand ECMAScript, so you are guaranteed relatively successful interpretation of the code. We will not discuss ECMAScript in any detail in this book—plenty of excellent JavaScript books are available in the marketplace.

Tip

Browsers that do not support scripting code will display the code as text in a Web page. To prevent browsers from displaying code, add comment tags (<!-- and -->) around the script code.

You can place script code anywhere on a Web page—in either the **<BODY>** or **<HEAD>** sections of the HTML page—but to simplify code maintenance, place all of your code within the same **<SCRIPT>** section.

Understanding JavaScript

JavaScript was created by Netscape Communications Corporation (now partially a division of America Online and partially a division of Sun Microsystems, as the result of a three-way purchase agreement in 1998). Netscape Navigator 4 and later provides a JavaScript interpreter. JavaScript differs from VBScript in a number of important ways:

- All procedures are declared as functions.
- Statements are semi-colon terminated.
- **Var** statements are used to declare variables.
- Braces are used to group statements together.

Note, however, that both JavaScript and Internet Explorer's JScript are implementations of the ECMAScript standard. Functionally, very few differences exist between the two—the most notable differences coming in the object model of the underlying browser program.

Using The Script Outline Window

The Script Outline window in Visual InterDev displays the objects that are available to your document and the scripts on the page when you are working in Source view. In Script Outline, you can:

♦ Display a tree view of all elements on your page that have their **ID** or **NAME** attributes set.

♦ Display events for each element.

◆ Navigate quickly to any script in the page.

◆ Quickly create new handlers for events on the page.

In its initial state, the tree view of Script Outline displays the nodes described in Table 20.1.

Script Outline generates either VBScript or JavaScript, depending on the default scripting language settings you have chosen.

Tip

To set the default language for a project, right-click on the project file in Project Explorer and click on Properties. In the dialog box, click on the Editor Defaults tab. Within the Default Script Language Option group, select the default language from the Client drop-down list box.

If Script Outline is not open when you open a window, you can open it manually. To do so, select View | Other Windows | Script Outline.

Creating Script Blocks

Instead of creating a script block manually, you can let Script Outline create a script template for you. To add a client script block to a page from within Script Outline:

1. Place the cursor at the location for the script block.

2. Right-click at the cursor and select Script Block from the pop-up menu.

3. Select Client from the second pop-up menu. Visual InterDev will automatically generate the block on your behalf.

Adding Objects And Writing Script For Them

When you add HTML, design-time, and ActiveX controls to a page in your project, the HTML editor adds the ID for the object and all the events associated with the object to Script Outline. For example, to add a Textbox control and an event procedure to a project, perform the following steps:

1. Click on the HTML tab in the Toolbox.

Table 20.1   Nodes displayed in the Script Outline window by default.

Node	Description
Client objects and events	The elements that support client script or have client script attached to them with a list of events for the element.
Client scripts	The client script for the page with each function or subroutine defined within the script block.
Server objects and events	The elements that support server script or have server script attached to them with a list of events for the element.
Server scripts	The server script for the page with each function or subroutine defined within the script block.

2. Drag the Textbox control to an appropriate location on the page. The HTML Editor will add the ID for the control to Script Outline under Client Objects And Events.

3. Open the Text1 node to display the events associated with the control.

4. Double-click on the event procedure that you want to implement. The HTML editor adds a template for the event procedure to the top of the page. It also adds an item for the script under the Client Scripts node.

Note

Targeting design-time controls for client or server script determines the node in which they will appear. You will learn more about this issue in Chapter 22.

Debugging Script Blocks

Script debugging is closely integrated into Visual InterDev 6 and Internet Explorer 4. This debugging functionality allows Web developers to browse, debug, and edit HTM and ASP files. The debugger works with ECMAScript, VBScript, and other scripting languages. All scripting languages can reference the Internet Explorer scripting object model to interact with Web documents, the browser, and the current window.

If you are writing client script in an HTML page, debugging is enabled automatically. Enabling debugging in Active Server Pages (ASPs) requires some more work—you have to install certain additional utilities from the option pack. Chapter 18 detailed the techniques involved in setting up server-side debugging with ASP.

There are generally four different techniques you can use to start script debugging:

◆ *In response to an error on a page*—If the browser or server encounters a syntax or runtime error in a script, it displays a message that offers you the opportunity to start the debugger at the line where the error occurred.

◆ *From Microsoft Internet Explorer*—Choose Script Debugger from the View menu in Internet Explorer, and then Open or Break At Next Statement. Script Debugger starts, and then opens the current HTML source file. This starts the Visual InterDev debugger.

◆ *From Visual InterDev*—From the Debug menu, click on Start.

◆ *In a script*—When writing a script, include a Stop statement (VBScript) or a Debugger statement (JScript) in a script. When script execution reaches that line, the Visual InterDev debugger will start.

Figure 20.2 shows the debugger in Break mode—you will note that it looks remarkably similar to the VBA debugger in Break mode.

Some of the features of the Visual InterDev debugger include the following:

◆ *Breakpoints*—You can set breakpoints anywhere in your code. In Break mode, you can single-step through the code. An Immediate window will display the value of variables.

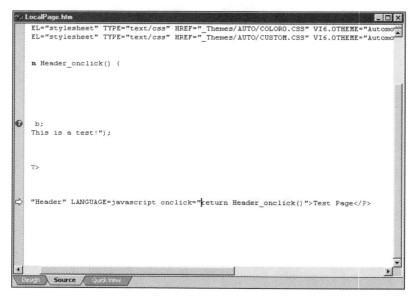

Figure 20.2
The Visual InterDev debugger when executing in Break mode.

- ◆ *Call Stack*—A Call Stack window displays which procedures have been invoked.
- ◆ *Syntax coloring*—The HTML and script syntax is displayed with different colors to help you read and debug your script.

Note
The debugger opens a copy of a Web page in a temporary Internet cache. Any edits you make while running the debugger apply only to the cached Web page. To correct an error permanently, you must edit the source file on the Web server.

Error Handling In Web Applications

To create a robust Web application, you should anticipate possible script errors and include error-handling code in your Web pages. The error-handling code in your application should attempt to resolve the error or return an appropriate message to the user. On the whole, your strongest partner in error-handling operations is the **On Error** statement, which is constructed much as it is in VBA. The **On Error** statement enables an error-handling routine and specifies the location of the routine within a procedure. The **On Error** statement syntax can have any of the forms described in the Table 20.2.

Table 20.2   The On Error subset supported by VBScript.

Statement	Description
On Error Resume Next	Specifies that when a runtime error occurs, control will go to the statement immediately following the statement where the error occurred, and execution will continue. Use this form rather than **On Error Go To** when accessing objects.
On Error GoTo 0	Disables any enabled error handler in the current procedure.
On Error GoTo *line*	Enables the error-handling routine that starts at the line specified in the required ***line*** argument. The specified line must be in the same procedure as the **On Error** statement; otherwise, a compile-time error occurs.

Note

*VBScript does not support the **On Error GoTo label** statement, and you cannot write an error handler that is called automatically when an error occurs. Therefore, you must implement inline error handling to check for an error after each statement that can cause an error.*

Handling Errors With The Err Object

When an error does occur, Internet Explorer stores the error information in the **Err** object. To detect runtime errors, check the **Number** property of the **Err** object after each statement that might cause an error. If **Number** is zero, an error has not occurred; if it is not zero, an error has occurred. To retrieve information about the error, check the **Description** property of the **Err** object.

When an error occurs, the **Err** object will contain the error information until another error occurs. If a statement runs successfully, the **Err** object will not be cleared. Therefore, after an error occurs, you should clear the error by invoking the **Clear** method of the **Err** object.

The following code, then, shows generally how you would handle errors resulting from program execution using the **Err** object:

```
Sub cmdSubmit_OnClick
  On Error Resume Next
  'Statement that might cause an error
  If Err <> 0 Then
    Msgbox "An error occurred. " & Err.Description
    Err.Clear
  End if
  'Statement that might cause an error
  If Err <> 0 Then
    Msgbox "An error occurred. " & Err.Description
    Err.Clear
  End if
End Sub
```

To test your own error-handling code, you can purposely cause an error by using the **Raise** method of the **Err** object. VBScript does not use all available numbers for its errors. If you want to generate your own errors, begin a numbering scheme with 65535 and work your way down (unlike Visual Basic, VBScript does not support the **vbObjectError** constant). For example, you might raise a site-specific error with the following code:

```
Err.Raise 65000
```

Working With Objects

To use objects, you must first create the object, and then identify it by setting its **ID** or **NAME** attribute. You can set an **ID** attribute for any object, but the **NAME** attribute applies only to standard HTML controls and Java applets. You use the **ID** or **NAME** attribute to create event procedures and to access an object's properties and methods. The syntax for assigning names varies slightly for different types of objects. Table 20.3 lists the standard objects that you can use on a Web page and describes how you identify each in code.

> **Note**
>
> *If an element has both an **ID** and **NAME** attribute set, then VBScript event handlers must use the **NAME** attribute. Also, you must use the **NAME** attribute for standard HTML controls to implement forms.*

Accessing Properties And Invoking Methods

To access the value of a property in VBScript, you use syntax identical to normal VBA references. In other words, the code looks similar to the following:

```
Object.Property = Value
```

To retrieve the values of properties, you use the following similarly constructed syntax:

```
Value = Object.Property
```

Table 20.3   Standard Web page objects and the necessary tagging for their use.

Object Type	ID	Name	Example
Standard HTML objects	Y	N	**<H1 ID="chap20H1">**
Standard HTML controls	Y	Y	**<INPUT TYPE="BUTTON" NAME="btnChap20Button">**
ActiveX controls	Y	N	**<OBJECT CLASSID="clsid:99B42120-6EC7-11CF-A6C7-00AA00A47DD2" ID=lblOccupation>**
Java applets	Y	Y	**<APPLET CODE=Outline.class NAME=outline HEIGHT=150 WIDTH=200> </APPLET>**

Thus, the following example sets the value of **shiptime** equal to the **Value** property of the **ShipDate** object:

```
shiptime = ShipDate.Value
```

As you might expect, you invoke methods in script by using the following syntax:

```
[Call] Object.Method
```

The following example code, then, calls the **Today** method of the **ShipDate** object:

```
Call ShipDate.Today()
```

In VBScript, you are not required to use the **Call** keyword when calling a procedure. However, if you use the **Call** keyword to call a procedure that requires arguments, the argument list must be enclosed in parentheses. If you omit the **Call** keyword, you also must omit the parentheses around the argument list.

Working With Object Models

Object models are composed of two different types of entities—objects and collections of objects. For example, a window can contain one or more frames. A document can contain one or more images or forms. A collection is a feature of DHTML and object-oriented programming in general that makes it easy to organize and access similar objects.

The **Document** object, for example, contains a number of collections, including anchors, frames, forms, links, and scripts. There are two methods for accessing members of a collection—you can use either the index of the collection member, or its name.

For example, in the following code, the first line accesses the second member of the **images** collection using the index 1. The second line accesses the member of the **images** collection that is named **myimage**.

```
document.images(1)
document.images("myimage")
```

Note

Collections in Dynamic HTML are zero-based—unlike some collections in Visual Basic, which may be one-based. However, this zero-based model is consistent with the way C/C++ programmers (and, by extension, Java and JavaScript programmers) would implement the collection, and so the designers of VBScript were a bit more rigorous in ensuring that VBScript collections are all zero-based.

Every collection in Dynamic HTML has two properties: the **Length** property, which contains the number of elements in the collection, and the **Item** property, with which you can retrieve an element or a collection of elements from the current collection.

Working With The Document Object Model

The DOM exposes several important browser objects and collections that you will access on a regular basis. In this section, you will learn how to use four common browser objects: the **Window** object, the **Navigator** object, the **Frames** collection, and the **Location** object. Figure 20.3 depicts the browser object hierarchy.

Importance Of The Window Object

The **Window** object represents the browser window that contains the HTML document the user is viewing. It is the top-level object in the object model hierarchy. You can use methods and properties of the **Window** object to modify the appearance of a window and retrieve information about the browser. The **Window** object has several subobjects and collections as properties, including the **Navigator** object, the **Frames** collection, and the **Location** object.

Using The OnLoad Event

The **Window** object has an **OnLoad** event that is called to initialize a page when the browser has finished loading the page. The object also has an **OnUnLoad** event that is called when the page has been unloaded. When an HTML page loads, the **OnLoad** event of the **Window** object will run. To use this event, you can either create a subprocedure named **Window_OnLoad** or add the **OnLoad** attribute to the **<BODY>** tag.

In the following example code, the **Window_OnLoad** event procedure initializes a form by calling the **Initialize_ShipForm** subprocedure:

```
Sub Window_OnLoad()
  Initialize_ShipForm
End Sub
```

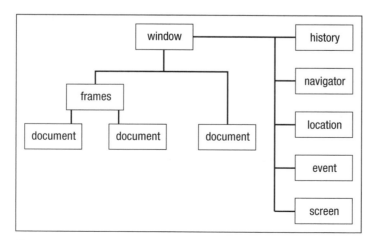

Figure 20.3
The browser object hierarchy that you will work with.

Alternatively, you can use code more similar to the following example, which sets the **OnLoad** attribute of the **<BODY>** tag to call the **Initialize_ShipForm** procedure when the page loads:

```
<BODY LANGUAGE=VBScript OnLoad = Initialize_ShipForm()>
```

Note that this example has parentheses after the procedure name, whereas the previous implementation does not. This difference is simply the result of varying implementations— the first is VBScript, whereas the second is defined by the HTML specification.

Displaying And Retrieving Information

To display and retrieve information from a user, you use the **Alert** and **Prompt** methods of the **Window** object. The **Alert** method displays a message; the **Prompt** method prompts a user for input.

The following example code prompts the user for a name with the **Prompt** method, and displays the name to the user with the **Alert** method:

```
<SCRIPT Language=VBSCRIPT>
Sub Window_OnLoad()
  strName = Window.Prompt ( "Enter your name")
  Window.Alert "Hello " & strName
End Sub
</SCRIPT>
```

Using The Navigator Object

The **Navigator** object contains information about the browser application being used to view the HTML document. It includes the browser name and version number. You can use the **Navigator** object to detect the browser and use other objects in the object model to load an alternate document that was specifically authored for the browser. Different browsers have different capabilities, so by using this object you can ensure that the user gets the appropriate content. Table 20.4 describes the properties of the **Navigator** object that expose the browser name and version.

Table 20.4   Properties of the Navigator object used for obtaining browser information.

Property	Description
appCodeName	Mozilla, for both Internet Explorer and Netscape Navigator.
appName	Either Internet Explorer or Netscape Navigator.
appVersion	Version number for the browser.
userAgent	Contains the HTTP user-agent string that was specified in the HTTP request. It is a concatenation of the **appCodeName** and **appVersion** properties.

The following example code illustrates using the **Navigator** object to display the name and version of the browser:

```
<HTML>
<HEAD><TITLE>Displaying information from the navigator object</TITLE>
<SCRIPT LANGUAGE="VBScript">
Sub DisplayBrowserVer()
  Dim strName, strVersion

  strName = window.navigator.appName
  strVersion = window.navigator.appVersion

  Alert("The browser is " & strName & _
      ", version " & strVersion)
End Sub
</SCRIPT>
</HEAD>
<BODY onload="DisplayBrowserVer()">
</BODY>
</HTML>
```

Working With The Frames Collection

The **Frames** object represents a collection of frames in a window. Each frame is also a **Window** object with its own properties, including a **Document** property that returns a **Document** object.

The scope of scripting code is at the frame level of a document. If you want to write script in one frame to access an object in another frame, you must navigate the object model to retrieve the parent window, and then use the **Frames** collection to retrieve the frame you want to access.

To access a different frame with script, refer to the **Frames** collection of the parent window of the current frame by using one of these syntax methods:

```
Parent.Frames("FrameName")
Parent.FrameName
```

Using The Location Object

The **Location** object represents the URL of the current document. To load another document, you change the properties of the **Location** object. You have several different techniques at your disposal for manipulating which document to display, but using the **Location** object is the best client-side technique.

Navigating Programmatically

To load another document, you set the **HRef** property of the **Location** object. The following example code would load the default document from the Coriolis Web site:

```
Location.HRef = "http://www.coriolis.com/"
```

Running Script From A Hyperlink

You can define a hyperlink as an object, and then create an event procedure for the hyperlink that performs some logic and, depending on the result, loads another document. To define a hyperlink as an object with events, you set the **HREF** and **ID** attributes of the hyperlink.

If you set the **HREF** attribute to a URL, the script will run and then display the new document. If you set **HREF** to "", the script will run, but will not display a new document. The following example code, then, assigns the identifier **JumpNext** to the hyperlinked text and implements a procedure to perform the appropriate processing:

```
<A HREF="" ID="JumpNext">Next Page</A>

<SCRIPT LANGUAGE=VBSCRIPT>
Sub JumpNext_OnClick()
  If Navigator.appName = "Microsoft Internet Explorer" Then
    Location.HRef = "IE-SpecificPage1.htm"
  Else
    Location.HRef = "OtherPage1.htm"
  End If
End Sub
</SCRIPT>
```

In the **OnClick** event procedure, the script determines which browser is viewing the page, and then goes to the location for another document on a Web site. The primary reason for creating an event procedure for a hyperlink is to perform more than one action, such as changing a document in multiple frames, in response to one user event.

Note

Note that, if you are not running Internet Explorer or Navigator with the VBScript plug-in, this code wouldn't run at all, and the user wouldn't navigate anywhere after clicking on the hyperlink.

Figure 20.4, for example, shows a document with three frames. The hyperlink in the links frame has an event procedure that changes the documents contained in all three frames.

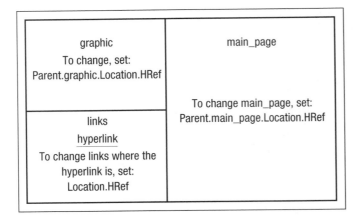

Figure 20.4
An example of an appropriate situation where hyperlink management is useful.

The following example code shows how this particular hyperlink event procedure might be written to accomplish this task:

```
'Change the source of the frame the hyperlink is in
Location.HRef = "Page1.htm"

'Change the source of the frame named "main_page"
Parent.main_page.Location.HRef = "Page2.htm"

'Change the source of the frame named "graphic"
Parent.graphic.Location.HRef = "Page3.htm"
```

Using The Document Container's Event Object

In the following sections, you will learn about the **Event** object. You will also learn how to write event procedures, and how to use event bubbling to make your scripts more compact and efficient.

Events and event handling form the basis of Dynamic HTML. *Events* are notifications that an action has taken place. For example, a notification occurs when the user clicks on a Submit button or rolls the mouse pointer over an element on a Web page.

Dynamic HTML provides the mechanism for capturing and handling these events. With the introduction of Internet Explorer 4, the **Window** object now contains an **Event** object, which provides your Web application with detailed information about a user's actions.

To create interactive Web applications using Dynamic HTML as your key technology, you should understand the following terms:

♦ *Event binding*—The association of a script with a notification from a document or from an element in a document

♦ *Event object*—Exposes the information related to an event to the script

♦ *Standard user events*—Mouse, keyboard, focus, and help events that are available on almost every element in a document

These concepts should all be familiar to you from your work with VBA.

Properties Of The Event Object

The **Event** object is a language-independent mechanism for accessing information related to an event, and for controlling whether the event bubbles and the default action for the event occurs. The **Event** object is a property of the **Window** object and exposes the properties listed in Table 20.5.

The following example code shows you how to use the **srcElement** property to determine where an event occurred:

```
<HTML>
<BODY>
<SCRIPT FOR="document" EVENT="onmousedown()" LANGUAGE="VBScript">
  msgbox "The click event happened in the " &
      window.event.srcElement.tagName & " element."
</SCRIPT>

</BODY>
</HTML>
```

Handling Standard User Mouse Events

Dynamic HTML exposes events for tracking the different states of the mouse, including moving over and off of page elements. The following list describes three of the most common mouse events:

♦ **onclick**—The left mouse button or the default button was clicked.

♦ **onmouseover**—The mouse pointer entered the scope of an element on the page.

♦ **onmouseout**—The mouse pointer exited the scope of an element on the page.

Table 20.5   Properties of the Event object.

Property	Description
srcElement	What element originated the event sequence.
cancelBubble	Whether to cancel event bubbling. By setting **cancelBubble** to **False**, you prevent the parent element from receiving the event.
returnValue	The default action for the event. By setting **returnValue** to **False**, you prevent the default action for that event.

There are other mouse events, but these are the crucial ones. You will see code that responds to each of these events in later sections of this chapter. Each mouse event will fire for each named object on the page. After creating and naming the objects on a Web page, you create event procedures and bind them to elements on the page.

Binding Events To Scripts

There are four methods for binding an event to a script. Three of them work in both VBScript and JScript, whereas the fourth only works with VBScript. The method that you choose depends upon which language you use and what you want to accomplish. You can create an event procedure for an object in four different ways:

♦ Create a separate **<SCRIPT>** block for the event procedure.

♦ Assign the event procedure in an HTML tag for the object.

♦ Include the script in the HTML tag that defines the object.

♦ Name a procedure **ObjectName_Event**.

I will consider each of the possibilities in turn in the following sections.

Create A Separate <SCRIPT> Block

You can create a separate **<SCRIPT>** block that contains script that runs for a specific event of a control. The following code, for example, contains script that will run when the **Click** event of the **Calendar1** control occurs:

```
<SCRIPT LANGUAGE="VBScript" FOR="Calendar1" EVENT="Click()">
  ' code goes here.
</SCRIPT>
```

You can use this method in either ECMAScript or VBScript to create event procedures for ActiveX controls and standard HTML controls.

Assign The Event Procedure When Creating The Object

In the HTML tag that creates an object, you can specify an event name and the procedure to be invoked when that event occurs. Your code must contain a **<SCRIPT>** block that includes the procedure declaration before the HTML tag that defines the object.

This method is useful if you want events from different objects to invoke the same procedure. You can use this method to assign event procedures for standard HTML controls. In the following example code, the **ProcessOrder** procedure is called when the user clicks on the option button:

```
<SCRIPT LANGUAGE=VBScript>
Sub ProcessOrder ()
  ' code goes here.
```

```
End Sub
</SCRIPT>
<INPUT TYPE=RADIO NAME=RadioGroup onClick="ProcessOrder">
```

As with the previously described method, this method is also supported by both VBScript and ECMAScript.

Include Script In The HTML Tag

In the HTML tag that creates the object, you can specify an event name and the script to run when that event occurs. You can use this method to assign event procedures for standard HTML controls. To see how this works, consider the following example, which displays the message "Hello World" when a user clicks on the Hello button:

```
<INPUT LANGUAGE="VBScript" TYPE=button VALUE="hello"
    onClick="Msgbox &quot;Hello World&quot;">
```

This method is also supported by both ECMAScript and VBScript.

Name The Procedure ObjectName_Event

If you name a procedure **ObjectName_Event**, the procedure will run automatically when the event for the object occurs. This naming convention is the same as the convention used to define event procedures in Visual Basic. This method is supported by VBScript only.

In the following example code, the procedure runs when the user clicks on Button1:

```
Sub Button1_OnClick ()
  ' code goes here.
End Sub
```

Understanding Event Bubbling

When an event occurs, it fires first on the source element and then on the parent of the source element. It continues to fire on successive parent elements until it has reached the top element, the document.

For example, when the user clicks on a button on a Web page, the **OnClick** event is first fired on the button itself, then on the form that contains the button, then the document, and so on. Figure 20.5 shows how an event bubbles through the browser object hierarchy.

Event bubbling is useful and important for many reasons. Among the most important are the following:

♦ Event bubbling allows multiple common actions to be handled centrally.

♦ Event bubbling reduces the amount of overall code in the Web page.

♦ Event bubbling reduces the number of code changes necessitated by changes in the document.

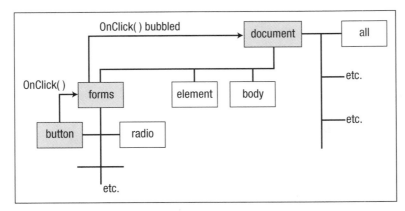

Figure 20.5
Tracing the event up through the hierarchy.

You will see event bubbling in some of the more complex code in this chapter. However, let's first consider a brief example, using HTML **<SPAN>** tags. In this example code, when the user moves the mouse pointer over the text "This Chapter 20 example uses span", a dialog box appears with the text "SpantheFirst". When the user moves the mouse over the second span, which contains the text "This continuing Chapter 20 example ALSO uses spans", another dialog box appears with the text "SonofSpan":

```
<HTML>
<BODY>
  <SPAN ID=SpantheFirst STYLE="background-color: red" LANGUAGE=vbscript
      OnClick="Alert('You clicked ' &  window.event.srcElement.id)">
    This Chapter 20 example uses span
    <SPAN ID=SonofSpan STYLE="background-color: blue">
      This continuing Chapter 20 example ALSO uses spans
    </SPAN>
  </SPAN>
</BODY>
</HTML>
```

The **OnClick** event for the **SonofSpan** element is handled even though it does not have an event handler. The **OnClick** event from the **SonofSpan** element bubbles up to its parent element, which is the **SpantheFirst** element. **SpantheFirst** does have an event handler registered for the **OnClick** event, so it fires.

Every time an event is fired, a special property of the **Window** object is created. This special property contains the **Event** object. The **Event** object contains context information about the event that just fired, including mouse location, keyboard status, and most importantly, the source element of the event.

*Set the **cancelBubble** property of the **Event** object to **True** when you want to prevent
an event from bubbling to the element's parent.*

Manipulating Objects In The DOM

Objects exposed by the Document Object Model provide all of the functionality that DHTML
exploits. In the following sections, you will learn more about scripting, object models, and
event handling. I will focus on two specific areas—writing script to handle routine page-
level issues, and adding dynamic features to interactive pages.

Using Element Objects

Every HTML tag and its attributes in a document are represented in the object model as an
element object. An element object exposes methods and properties that enable you to get
information about and change the attributes of the corresponding element.

You do not refer to an element object through the object model directly, but indirectly
through document collections. For more information on document collections, see "Using
Document Collections," later in this chapter.

Most element properties have the same name and take the same values as the corresponding attributes. Some properties do not correspond to element attributes. These properties
typically give additional information about the element that is not available through attributes. Table 20.6 lists the commonly used properties of element objects.

The following example code illustrates how the **className** property of an element object
can be used in a procedure:

```
Sub DoClick()
  If (window.event.srcElement.className = "parent") Or
     (window.event.srcElement.className = "image") Then
    ExpandCollapse
  End If
  window.event.cancelBubble = True
End Sub
```

Table 20.6   Common properties of most element objects.

Property	Purpose
ID	Gets the string identifying the element.
tagName	Gets the name of the HTML tag of the element.
className	Sets and gets the style sheet class name of the element.
style	Subobject used to set and get styles associated with the element.
children	Gets the collection of child elements in the element hierarchy.
parentElement	Gets the parent element in the element hierarchy.

You can use three of these properties to identify elements in code: **tagName**, **ID**, and **className**. For example, when you want your code to apply to a particular element, you should use the **ID** property to reference that single element. On the other hand, when you want your code to apply to all the elements of the same type, use the **tagName** property to reference all the elements of that single type. Finally, when you want your code to apply to a set of elements with the same style sheet class name, use the **className** property to reference that set or any other set that you define.

Using Document Collections

The DOM contains several collections that enable finding and adding different types of elements in an HTML document. Three important document collections are the **all**, **children**, and **styleSheets** collections. You can access individual element objects within collections with their index, name, or ID.

Using The all Collection

The **all** collection represents all of the elements in the document in the order that they appear in the HTML source code. It can also include elements not in the document, comments, and unknown or invalid tags. The reason for including these other elements is to give you accurate information about the document. The **all** collection is automatically updated to reflect any changes in the document such as when elements and their contents are added or removed.

The following example code uses the **all** collection to display a list of all the tags in the document:

```
<HTML>
<HEAD><TITLE>Displaying the all collection</TITLE>
<SCRIPT LANGUAGE="VBScript">
Sub ShowElements()
  Dim i, tagNames
  tagNames = ""
  For i = 0 To document.all.length-1
    tagNames = tagNames & document.all(i).tagName & " "
  Next
  Alert("This document contains: " + tagNames)
End Sub
</SCRIPT>
</HEAD>
<BODY onload="ShowElements()">
<!-- A comment -->
<P>This document has an <ZZZ>unknown</ZZZ> and an invalid</B> tag.
</BODY>
</HTML>
```

Using The children Collection

The **children** collection contains all the elements directly contained by a parent element. For example, examine the following example code:

```
<DIV ID=parentDiv>
<IMG SRC="images/blue.gif">
<DIV ID=childDiv>
<A HREF="home.htm">General Information</A>
</DIV>
</DIV>
```

The **children** collection for the **<DIV>** tag with the **ID parentDiv** will contain the image and the **<DIV>** tag with the **ID childDiv**. The **children** collection for **childDiv** will contain the hyperlink.

Using The styleSheets Collection

The **styleSheets** collection contains all the style sheet objects corresponding to each instance of a **<LINK>** or **<STYLE>** element in the document. The following example code uses the **styleSheets** collection to add a style sheet to a document:

```
Sub AddStyleSheet(strUrl)
  ' pass URL for .css file
  ' containing the style sheet
  document.styleSheets(0).addImport(strUrl)
End Sub
```

Working With Dynamic Styles

DHTML offers Web designers the ability to alter the style for elements dynamically, in response to interaction with the user. For example, you might change the font family or font color of an item when the cursor is over it to show users their immediate choices. This approach is often found in tables of contents.

Using static HTML, you would need to download a new page to change the size of the font, which means a trip to the server. With DHTML, you can change font size without having to reload the page.

There are a number of reasons to dynamically change the styles for elements on a page, including wanting to make the page visually interesting, wanting to provide feedback to users as they interact with the page, and wanting to provide visual customizing to users who might not otherwise be able to use the page.

Note

To create dynamic styles, you need to be familiar with using cascading style sheets (CSS) and defining styles for a Web page.

Process For Adding Changeable Styles

Changing styles on a Web page entails completing three processes. First, you must change the elements in an HTML document. To most easily accomplish this task, you generally define two styles with class names and attributes. Next, you write code to dynamically change a section of text. Typically, you accomplish this in a three-step process:

1. Create an object with the **ID** attribute.
2. Add a style class name to the section using the **CLASS** attribute.
3. Add a script function name to the event attribute for the section.

Finally, you might want to create a style-changing function. To do so, create a separate script function that changes the style to one of those defined in the style tags.

Changing Styles Using The Style Object

You can change styles using the **Style** object for the element. Each CSS style is a property of the **Style** object for the element. The following example code shows how to change an element's style inline:

```
<H1 ID=Chap20StyleSample OnClick="this.Style.color=blue">
    This text will change to blue when clicked
</H1>
```

Dynamic Positioning

Dynamic positioning enables you to change the placement of elements in the document. The **Positioning** attributes set for an element determine how it is affected by changes in the flow of the document, such as when the user resizes the browser window, or when content is added or removed. Table 20.7 details the concepts involved with dynamic positioning.

The differences among these concepts are based on the following facts about DHTML:

♦ A document has a default flow in which elements are consecutively placed on the page, with the spacing depending on the type of element and the content of the element.

♦ Elements can contain other elements (that is, be parents of other elements). If an element is not contained by another element, its default parent is the **<BODY>** tag.

♦ Absolute positioning takes the element out of the default flow, and allows you to specify exact x-, y-coordinates relative to the parent of the element.

♦ Relative positioning leaves the element in the default flow, but allows you to specify exact x-, y-coordinates relative to the previous element in the document flow.

♦ When using absolute positioning and two or more elements occupy the same x-, y-position in the document, their z-order determines which is displayed on top of the other.

Table 20.7   The five governing concepts of dynamic positioning.

Concept	Description
Absolute positioning	The x- and y-coordinates for the element are relative to the parent element, regardless of the position of any other elements.
Relative positioning	The x- and y-coordinates for the element are relative to the preceding element in the document.
z-index	The z-index affects how elements positioned in the same place in the document are displayed. Positive z-index values are positioned above a negative (or lesser) z-index value. Two elements with the same z-index value are stacked according to the order in which they appear in the HTML source code.
Visibility	Setting the **Visibility** property to **hidden** means that an element has a reserved space on the document but its contents are not visible on screen. Setting visibility to **visible** means that an element appears in the document.
Display	Setting the **Display** attribute to **none** means that an element does not appear in the document, and no space is reserved for it on screen. The element is completely removed from the flow of the document.

Dynamic Content

Dynamic content enables you to add or remove text or HTML content in an HTML document, without having to reload the page from the server. The Web browser will automatically reflow the document when you add or remove content.

The process for adding dynamic content is the same as for adding dynamic styles. Specifically, to add dynamic content to an element, perform the following steps:

1. Add an **ID** attribute.

2. Add event attributes and assign them function names.

3. Add script for each of the functions and assign the additional content to the **ID** attribute.

4. Use the appropriate text or HTML property to add the content.

You add content using two different kinds of properties—text properties and HTML properties (described in Table 20.8). Text properties insert text, including HTML tags, as text. For example, the browser will read **<H3>** as the string "**H3**", not as the HTML tag to render the following text as an H3. In contrast, the browser will read any tags within the HTML properties with the correct format.

In addition, two methods—**insertAdjacentText** and **insertAdjacentHTML**—let you manipulate text or HTML content. The **insertAdjacentText** and **insertAdjacentHTML** methods take two parameters—**where** and **text**. Table 20.9 describes the values for the parameter **where**—note that these parameters are all case sensitive.

Table 20.8 Dynamic content properties you can use to manage content text.

Text Properties	HTML Properties
innerText	innerHTML
outerText	outerHTML

Table 20.9 The values for the insert methods' where parameter.

Parameter	Description
BeforeBegin	Inserts the text immediately before the element.
AfterBegin	Inserts the text after the start of the element, but before all other content in the element.
BeforeEnd	Inserts the text immediately before the end of the element, but after all other content in the element.
AfterEnd	Inserts the text immediately after the end of the element.

Creating A Dynamic Outline

You can create a dynamic outline using DHTML. A dynamic outline is a list of items that you add to or remove from. You can also expand and collapse items in the outline at any time using parent items and child items. The companion CD-ROM includes an example dynamic outline in the Chap20\Dynamic directory.

Building An Outline Using Parent And Child Items

A parent item is associated with a graphic and a name and can contain zero or more child items. A parent item consists of a **<DIV>** element and contains an **<IMG>** element and another **<DIV>** element. The inner **<DIV>** is a container for all the child items for the parent. This nesting structure makes it easier to insert child items and control the appearance of all the child items for a parent as a group.

The **<DIV>** for the parent item also has an **ID**. The **ID** uniquely identifies the parent and makes it easy to locate it within the document. It also allows you to add new child items to a specific parent at any time. The following example code illustrates the HTML structure of a parent item:

```
<DIV ID=Id CLASS="parent">
<IMG CLASS="image" SRC="images/blue.gif" ALT="*"
    ALIGN=MIDDLE BORDER=0 WIDTH=11 HEIGHT=11>Parent Name
<DIV CLASS="child">
</DIV>
</DIV>
```

In this example, a child item is a hyperlink that is inserted within its parent, and has the following HTML structure:

```
<A HREF="Url" CLASS="link">Child Name</A><BR>
```

Making The Outline Expand And Contract

In addition to adding and removing items, the dynamic outline supports expanding and collapsing items. The following example code is a VBScript procedure that expands and collapses all of the child items for a parent:

```
Sub ExpandCollapse()
  Dim objElement
  Dim objTargetDiv
  Dim imgIcon

  Set objElement = window.event.srcElement

  ' did the user click the image or the parent name?
  If objElement.className = "parent" Then
    Set objTargetDiv = objElement.children(1)
    Set imgIcon = objElement.children(0)
  Else
    Set objTargetDiv = objElement.parentElement.children(1)
    Set imgIcon = objElement
  End If

  ' if the parent has children, expand or collapse them
  If objTargetDiv.children.length > 0 Then
    If objTargetDiv.style.display = "none" Then
      objTargetDiv.style.display = ""
      imgIcon.src = "images/red.gif"
    Else
      objTargetDiv.style.display = "none"
      imgIcon.src = "images/blue.gif"
    End If
  End If
End Sub
```

This procedure expands or collapses all the child items by checking the class name of the element the user has clicked on. It first checks to see if the user clicked on the image or name of a parent item. It does this so it can get the element object for the inner **<DIV>** of the parent (which contains all its child items) and the element object for the image associated with the parent.

If the parent does have child items, it expands or collapses them and changes the image associated with the parent depending on the current state. If the child items are currently expanded, it sets their style to **display:none** to hide them, and changes the image to a blue triangle. If the child items are currently collapsed, it sets their style to **display:""** to make them visible, and changes the image to a red triangle.

Before moving on to advanced server-side design in the next chapter, it is worthwhile to briefly consider one last Dynamic HTML technique that you can take advantage of—scriptlets.

Working With Scriptlets

Scriptlets allow Web page authors to create reusable components with script, without having to harness the full power of C, C++, or other control-building environments. Microsoft Scripting Components (scriptlets) provide you with a way to create reusable controls and components. You create scriptlets using a scripting language such as ECMAScript or VBScript.

A scriptlet is a complete Web-ready HTM file, but includes information that allows you to work with it as a control—you can get and set its properties, call its methods, and so on.

Advantages Of Using Scriptlets

Scriptlets are small, text-based, scripting files that provide powerful tools, including:

♦ *Reusability*—Scriptlets allow Web page authors to create reusable user interface components without having to use C, C++, or other control-building environments.

♦ *Accessibility*—Scriptlets allow developers using Visual Basic, Visual InterDev, and other development environments that support controls to make use of features built into Web pages.

♦ *Ease of use*—Scriptlets are substantially easier to create and maintain than full HTML documents are.

♦ *Efficiency*—Because scriptlets only contain script code necessary to accomplish their purpose, scriptlets are small and efficient.

For example, with scriptlets you can accomplish any of the following tasks:

♦ Use the graphical and hypertext capabilities of Web pages as a visually rich interface for an application (such as a calendar control that you can display in a Web page) in Visual Basic or in another environment.

♦ Create components that incorporate business rules that you can call from a Web server, a browser, or any other type of application.

♦ Use them as prototype controls that you intend to write in other environments. Because writing a scriptlet is quick and easy, you can test ideas. When you have completed your design, you can reimplement the control in another environment, such as C++, Visual Basic, or J++, if you want greater performance or a different means of packaging your control.

Types Of Scriptlets

There are two kinds of scriptlets—DHTML scriptlets and server scriptlets. DHTML scriptlets are used in the browser, whereas server scriptlets are used in external applications or on a Web server. DHTML scriptlets typically display a user interface, whereas server scriptlets do not.

By default, the browser exposes standard methods and properties to scriptlets. Scriptlets expose standard properties, methods, and events to the browser.

Using Standard Methods And Properties

Table 20.10 describes some of the methods and properties the browser exposes that scriptlets can take advantage of.

Scriptlets, for their part, expose a couple of properties of their own, including the **Event** property, which provides state information about a standard DHTML event passed from the scriptlet to the browser window. Additionally, scriptlets provide the **readyState** property, which returns information about the load state of the scriptlet from the browser.

Exposing Custom Methods And Properties

You can expose any number of properties and methods in VBScript by using the keywords described in Table 20.11.

The following example code creates a property function that imports the style sheet from a URL and makes it the style sheet for the current document:

```
Sub Public_Put_StyleSheet(strUrl)
    document.stylesheets(0).addImport(strUrl)
End Sub
```

Table 20.10   Methods and properties exposed by the browser to the scriptlets.

Properties And Methods	Description	Syntax
Frozen property	Indicates whether the browser window containing the scriptlet is ready to handle events.	**boolean = Window.external.Frozen**
bubbleEvent method	Sends event notification from the scriptlet to the browser window when a standard event has occurred.	**Window.external.bubbleEvent()**
raiseEvent method	Passes a custom event notification from the scriptlet to the browser window.	**Window.external.raiseEvent (eventName, eventObject)**
setContextMenu method	Constructs a context menu that is displayed when a user right-clicks on a scriptlet in the browser window.	**Window.external. setContextMenu (menuDefinition)**

Table 20.11 **Exposing custom properties and methods from scriptlets with the VBScript equivalent of property functions.**

Scenario	Solution
To create a read/write property	Declare a variable scoped at the page level, and assign it the prefix **public_**.
To create a readable property function	Define a function with the prefix **public_get_**.
To create a writable property function	Define a function with the prefix **public_put_**.
To create a method	Define a function with the prefix **public_**.

Exposing Events From Scriptlets

When you use a DHTML scriptlet in your Web page, you can be notified about events that occur in the scriptlet. A scriptlet can expose two types of events: standard DHTML events, such as the **onclick** event and the **onkeypress** event, and custom events, which are events that you define or that are not provided as standard events. For example, a scriptlet can fire an event when a property value changes. You can expose custom events in either DHTML or server events.

Handling Standard Events

A DHTML scriptlet can expose the following standard DHTML events:

♦ onclick

♦ ondblclick

♦ onkeydown

♦ onkeypress

♦ onkeyup

♦ onmousemove

♦ onmousedown

♦ onmouseup

Standard events are triggered for the scriptlet container object. Use a custom event to pinpoint which control in the scriptlet triggered the event. To work with standard events in the host application, you must write handlers in two places: one in the scriptlet to send the event, and another in the host application to capture the event.

To pass a standard DHTML event from a scriptlet, perform the following steps:

1. Attach an event handler script to the event that you want to pass.

2. Within the event handler script, call the **bubbleEvent** method to send the event to the host application.

3. Check the scriptlet's **frozen** property to be sure that the container object is ready to handle events.

For example, you might write code similar to the following, which shows how you can pass a text box's **ONKEYUP** event to the host application:

```
<INPUT TYPE=text ONKEYUP="passKeyUp" NAME="t1" VALUE="">

<SCRIPT LANGUAGE="VBScript">
Sub passKeyUp
   // script statements here if required
    window.external.bubbleEvent
   // further script statements here if required
End Sub
</SCRIPT>
```

Creating And Handling Custom Events

Although the standard, built-in events are powerful, you may occasionally want to expose custom events from your scriptlets. Custom events allow you to perform any of the following actions:

♦ Notify the hosting page about nonstandard changes in the scriptlet, such as when the value of a property changes.

♦ Send more detail about a standard event that occurred—for example, which of several buttons in the scriptlet was clicked.

♦ Notify the host page about DHTML events that are not among the standard events handled by the **bubbleEvent** method.

As with standard DHTML events, you must send the event from the scriptlet and capture the event in the host page. To send a custom event in the scriptlet to the host page, first check the scriptlet's **frozen** property to make sure that the host page is ready to handle events. Next, call the scriptlet's **raiseEvent** method. On the side of the host page, make sure that you create an event handler for the **onscriptletevent** event.

For example, the following code shows how you can send a custom event called **onbgcolorchange** whenever the scriptlet's **backgroundColor** property is reset:

```
<SCRIPT LANGUAGE="VBScript">
Sub public_put_backgroundColor(value)

   window.document.bgColor = value
   window.external.raiseEvent "event_onbgcolorchange",window.document
End Sub
</SCRIPT>
```

You should be struck (I hope) by the similarities between the property definition actions with a scriptlet and the way you define properties within VBA classes. On the host page's side of the equation, the following example code (in VBScript) shows how you can determine what control triggered an event:

```
Sub MyScriptlet_onscriptletevent(txtTitle, eventData)
    objName = eventData.srcElement.ID
    MsgBox "The event " & txtTitle & " occurred in " & objName
End Sub
```

Using Your DHTML Scriptlets

After you have created a DHTML scriptlet, you can use it in your applications. Using DHTML scriptlets is similar to using other controls and components.

If you are working with a Web page, you can use the **<OBJECT>** tag to reference the scriptlet. You can add a scriptlet to the Microsoft Visual InterDev Toolbox to simplify its use. To do so, from within the Project Explorer, right-click on the scriptlet's HTM file, and then choose Mark As Scriptlet.

An **<OBJECT>** tag containing a pointer to that scriptlet is added to the Scriptlet tab of the Toolbox. (If this is the first scriptlet in the Toolbox, the Scriptlet tab is created.) You can then drag the scriptlet from the Toolbox onto another page and automatically create the **<OBJECT>** tag necessary to implement the scriptlet.

Note

*When you add a scriptlet to the Toolbox, it includes the scriptlet's absolute URL. After you drag a scriptlet onto your page, you might need to modify the **<OBJECT>** tag's **URL** property in the Properties window or in Source view to make the link relative.*

Alternatively, you can create an **<OBJECT>** tag yourself that references the scriptlet. To do so, you would create an **<OBJECT>** tag with the following syntax, substituting the scriptlet's URL and name for url/scriptletName:

```
<OBJECT ID="Chap20Scriptlet" TYPE="text/x-scriptlet" WIDTH=300 HEIGHT=200>
    <PARAM NAME="url" VALUE="url/scriptletName">
</OBJECT>
```

After creating an instance of the DHTML scriptlet, you can write scripts for it as you would for any other control. The object you are using to work with properties and methods is the scriptlet host page; the exact properties and methods you can use are defined by the scriptlet identified in the container's **URL** property.

Before getting a scriptlet's properties or calling its methods, you must be sure that the scriptlet has been fully loaded. For details, see the container object's **onreadystatechange** event and **readyState** property, and the scriptlet's **frozen** property.

Where To Go From Here

As you can see, scripting the client-side of the two-way browser communication process comes with its own issues. However, effective management of client-side code can result in powerful, robust, and interactive applications that provide the user with a very rich software experience.

In the next two chapters, we will pursue that "rich experience" a little further. In Chapter 21, we will explore the techniques that you can use to add full data connectivity to your Active Server Pages. In the final chapter, we will consider the use of some Visual Basic applications to accomplish many of the tasks using InterDev discussed throughout the previous chapters.

Server-Side Data Support Techniques

As you learned in Chapters 18 and 20, adding powerful client- and server-side scripting to your Web applications from inside Visual InterDev is a relatively simple and straightforward process, although it can be tedious at times. The information we have covered so far will no doubt be invaluable for the design of many sites; however, as you well know, this book is focused on data-driven programming. Luckily, the real power of Active Server Pages (ASPs) really comes out when you start creating data-driven code with server-side VBScript. In this chapter, we will focus on that topic. Additionally, toward the end of the chapter we will briefly digress into a discussion of some client-side data access techniques. These tend to be browser-dependent, so for the most part, we will stay away from them.

Adding Data Support To Your Server-Side Pages

In this chapter, we will focus on how to create Web pages that retrieve and update information in a database by using ActiveX Data Objects (ADO). We will also look at the Remote Data Service (RDS), a superset of the ADO designed for client-side data access. Let's begin with ADO.

ActiveX Data Objects

As you well know, ADO comprises the application-level programming interface that allows you to write applications that access data from OLE DB data sources, including ODBC data sources. It is based on automation. When using ADO with Active Server

Pages, all data access and manipulation is done on the server. Though ADO has some slight implementation differences in ASP than it does in the VBA programming you have been doing thus far, it is generally the same in construction and implementation.

Remote Data Service

The Remote Data Service (RDS) allows you to access data on a server and manipulate it on the client, reducing the number of round trips to the server. RDS extends ADO by adding substantial client-side data support to the object model.

Both ADO and RDS are collections of Component Object Model (COM) objects. They are installed with the Windows NT Option Pack as part of Microsoft Data Access Components.

Note

If you haven't figured it out yet, using RDS requires that you run Internet Explorer at the client—making it a less-than-optimal solution for Internet applications. Moreover, you can generally accomplish the majority of tasks from the server side with great efficiency using ADO in your ASP pages. However, we will look briefly at the use of RDS, and how it can speed intranet solution performance.

Microsoft Data Access Components

The Microsoft Data Access Components (MDACs) are the key technologies that enable Universal Data Access. MDAC 1.5 includes the latest versions of the following components:

♦ ActiveX Data Objects (which includes Remote Data Service)

♦ OLE DB Provider for ODBC

♦ ODBC Driver Manager

♦ Updated ODBC drivers for Microsoft SQL Server, Microsoft Access, and Oracle

The client components of MDAC ship with Internet Explorer 4 (and later). The server components ship with the Windows NT Option Pack (or can be installed from the Visual Studio BackOffice installer).

Understanding Microsoft Universal Data Access (UDA)

Microsoft Universal Data Access is a platform for developing multitier enterprise applications that access diverse relational or nonrelational data sources across intranets or the Internet. UDA consists of a collection of software components that interact with each other using a common set of system-level interfaces defined by OLE DB.

As you have learned in previous chapters, OLE DB is a Microsoft system-level programming interface to diverse data sources. OLE DB specifies a set of Microsoft COM interfaces that contain database management system services. These interfaces enable you to create software components that implement the UDA platform.

UDA components consist of:

- Data providers, which contain and expose data
- Consumers, which use data
- Services, which process and transform data

The structure of the Universal Data Access platform, then, looks very similar to Figure 21.1.

Universal Data Access is supported by two related data access technologies—ActiveX Data Objects and the Remote Data Service.

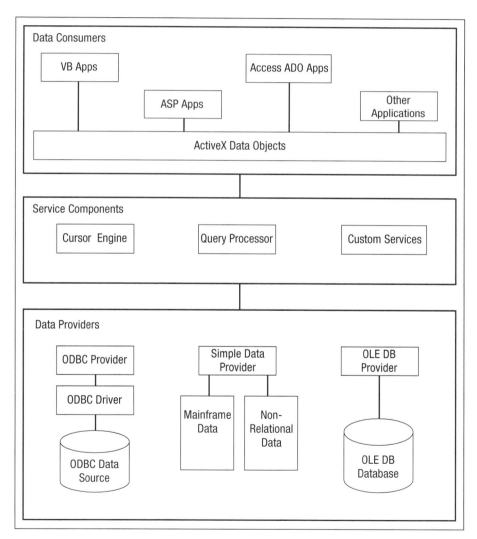

Figure 21.1
An illustration of the Universal Data Access platform and how it is constructed.

Using ActiveX Data Objects (ADO) From Active Server Pages (ASPs)

Now that we have covered all of the supporting issues, let's look at using ADO in the manner it was intended—as a direct database connector from your server-side scripting. Over the next several sections, we will look at topics we covered previously in extensive depth while discussing VBA programming—including working with connections, navigating records, and so on.

Establishing A Database Connection

A **Connection** object represents an open connection to a data source or OLE DB provider. You can use the **Connection** object to run commands or queries on the data source. When a recordset is retrieved from the database, it is stored in a **Recordset** object.

Opening A Connection

To define the connection, you set properties for the **Connection** object. The following steps describe how to create an ADO connection with a data source:

1. Create a **Connection** object by calling the **Server** object's **CreateObject** method and passing it the **ADODB.Connection** parameter.

2. Set the **ConnectionTimeout** property of the **Connection** object. **ConnectionTimeout** determines, in seconds, how long the object will wait before timing out when connecting to a data source.

3. Set, in seconds, the **CommandTimeout** property of the **Command** object. **CommandTimeout** determines, in seconds, how long the object will wait for the results of a command or query.

4. Use the **Open** method to connect to the data source.

The syntax for the **Open** method is as follows:

```
connection.Open ConnectionString, User, Password
```

The parameters to the **Open** method work exactly like I described the same parameter set in Chapter 5. Just as with the ADODB library, after the **Open** method succeeds in connecting to the data source, you can run queries. The following example code, then, creates a **Connection** object, and opens a connection to the library data source (note that the connection object is a variant, as are all variables in VBScript):

```
Set conn = Server.CreateObject("ADODB.Connection")
conn.ConnectionTimeout = 10
conn.CommandTimeout = 20
conn.Open "DSN=library;DATABASE=library", "SA", ""
```

The following methods are important features of the **Connection** object (whether running over ASP or in VBA):

♦ The **Execute** method runs a SQL query.

♦ The **BeginTrans** method initiates a transaction between the client and the database.

♦ The **CommitTrans** method ensures a transaction will occur.

♦ The **RollbackTrans** method returns a database to its original state if the transaction fails.

Using Connection Information

Rather than using literal values for the **Connection** object properties, you can—and generally should—use application variables. When you use Visual InterDev to add a data connection to a Web project, it adds script to the Global.asa file that stores information about the connection in application variables. You can access these application variables from code in an ASP file.

The advantage to using application variables when creating a connection is that you can change the value of the variables in the Global.asa file, and the new values will be used by any of your ASP files that refer to the variables. If you change the properties of a data connection in Visual InterDev, it modifies the script in the Global.asa file to set the variables to the new values.

The following example code shows how you can use application variables to create a connection:

```
Set conn = Server.CreateObject("ADODB.Connection")
conn.ConnectionTimeout = Application("library_ConnectionTimeout")
conn.CommandTimeout = Application("library_CommandTimeout")
conn.Open Application("library_ConnectionString"), _
    Application("library_RuntimeUserName"), _
    Application("library_RuntimePassword")
```

Closing A Connection

When you have finished working with the database, you use the **Close** method of the **Connection** object to free any associated system resources. Using the **Close** method does not remove the object from memory. To completely remove an object from memory, you set the object variable to **Nothing**.

The following example code closes a data connection and sets the object variable to **Nothing**:

```
conn.Close
Set conn = Nothing
```

Connection Pooling

Web database applications that frequently establish and terminate database connections can reduce database server performance. IIS supports efficient connection management by using the connection-pooling feature of ODBC and the Microsoft Transaction Server (MTS) Transaction engine.

Connection pooling maintains open database connections and manages connection sharing across different user requests to maximize performance. On each connection request, the connection pool first determines whether an idle connection exists in the pool. If so, the connection pool returns that connection instead of making a new connection to the database.

If you want your ODBC driver to participate in connection pooling, you must set the driver's CPTimeout property in the Windows Registry. The CPTimeout property determines the length of time that a connection remains in the connection pool. If the connection remains in the pool longer than the duration set by CPTimeout, the connection is closed and removed from the pool.

You can selectively set the CPTimeout property to enable connection pooling for a specific ODBC database driver by creating a Registry key with the following settings:

```
\HKEY_LOCAL_MACHINE\SOFTWARE\ODBC\ODBCINST.INI\driver-name\CPTimeout
    = timeout (REG_SZ, units are in seconds)
```

Note

By default, IIS activates connection pooling for SQL Server by setting CPTimeout to 60 seconds.

Retrieving Records

To retrieve records from a database, you create a **Recordset** object. You use properties and methods of the **Recordset** object to manipulate the data in the recordset. This section shows you how to create a recordset. It also discusses four different kinds of cursors.

Creating A Recordset Using CreateObject

To create a **Recordset** object using the **CreateObject** function, you must first define a **Recordset** object variable by passing **ADODB.Recordset** as an argument to **CreateObject**. Then you call the **Open** method of the **Recordset** object.

Just as with VBA-based ADO, the **Open** method uses the following syntax:

```
recordset.Open Source, ActiveConnection, CursorType, LockType, Options
```

> **Note**
> You can include a file named adovbs.inc in your Active Server Pages that use ADO. The file enables you to use VBScript constants for ADO option parameters, so you do not need to remember the numeric value for the option. The file is installed in the \Program Files\Common Files\system\ado folder of the Web server by the Windows NT Option Pack Setup program.

The following example code uses the **CreateObject** function to define a **Recordset** object variable and then uses the **Open** method to create the **Recordset** object. The example passes a connection string when invoking the **Open** method of the **Recordset** object:

```
Const adOpenKeyset = 1
Const adLockOptimistic = 3

Set rs = Server.CreateObject ("ADODB.Recordset")
rs.Open "Select * from members", "DSN=library;UID=SA;PWD=", _
    adOpenKeyset, adLockOptimistic
```

When you pass a connection string to the **Open** method of the **Recordset** object, a connection will be created. However, a separate connection is opened for each recordset you create using this method.

If you want to share a connection with multiple recordsets, create the **Connection** object first, and then pass the **Connection** object variable, rather than a literal string, when invoking the **Open** method of a **Recordset** object. The following code provides an example:

```
Set conn = Server.CreateObject ("ADODB.Connection")
conn.Open "DSN=library;DATABASE=library", "SA", ""

Set rs = Server.CreateObject ("ADODB.Recordset")
rs.Open "Select * from members", conn, _
    adOpenKeyset, adLockOptimistic
```

Creating A Recordset Using The Execute Method

There are two other ways to create a recordset. You can either use the **Execute** method on a **Connection** object, or use the **Execute** method on a **Command** object. We have discussed both techniques in previous chapters; we will revisit using the **Execute** method of a **Command** object from the ASP perspective later in this chapter.

Cursor Types

When you open a recordset, it contains a cursor, which points to the current record. When you call a navigation method such as **MoveNext**, you move the cursor. When you create a recordset, you can specify which type of cursor to create. Each cursor type supports different functions. To determine your cursor type, identify the features you need and which cursor types your database provider includes. Table 21.1 describes the features of the different cursor types.

Table 21.1   A brief description of cursors with the ADO library used for Internet development.

Cursor Type	Cursor Features
Forward-only	Lets users move forward through read-only data.
Static	Lets users move back and forth through read-only data.
Keyset	Lets users move back and forth through read/write data and see modifications and deletions made by other users.
Dynamic	Lets users move back and forth through read/write data and see additions, modifications, and deletions made by other users.

Note

Just as with VB, Forward-only cursors are the fastest cursors, but they include only one view of the data.

In any recordset, there is one current record (unless the recordset is empty). To change the current record, you use one of the **Move** methods of the **Recordset** object. The **BOF** (beginning of file) or **EOF** (end of file) property is **True** if you are at the beginning or the end of the recordset, respectively. If there are no records in a recordset, both the **BOF** and **EOF** properties are **True**. As you move through a recordset, check the value of the **BOF** and **EOF** properties to determine when you reach the end of the recordset.

The following example code moves through all the records in a recordset:

```
Do Until rs.EOF
  ' while not at end of recordset,
  ' move to the next record
  rs.MoveNext
Loop
```

To retrieve data from a field in the current record, use the **Fields** collection and specify the name of the field, as in the following example code:

```
customer = rs.Fields("First_Name")
```

You can also use the **Fields** collection to loop through all fields in the current record. The following example code displays all fields from the current record:

```
For i = 0 to rs.Fields.Count -1
  Response.Write rs.fields(i)
Next
```

To add, modify, and delete records from a recordset, you can use methods of the **Recordset** object.

Although the following sections discuss recordset manipulation by methods of the Recordset object, just as I described with VB manipulation across a remote deployment, it will often be better to use SQL DML commands instead. That decision usually rests in part on how close the two systems (the Web server and the SQL Server) are to each other, whether there is a firewall between the systems, and so on.

Adding Records

To add a record to a database, use the **AddNew** method of the **Recordset** object, set values for the record, and then use the **Update** method to save the record. The following example code retrieves values from the **Request** object in an ASP file and adds a new record to the **Majors** table, assuming that the table is encapsulated within the **rsMajors** recordset and the user or Active Server Page has the appropriate level of permissions to add new records to the table:

```
rsMajors.AddNew
  rsMajors("MajorID")= Request("MajorID")
  rsMajors("Description")= Request("Description")
rsMajors.Update
```

If you invoke the **AddNew** method and then move from the current record, or if you invoke another **AddNew** method before calling **Update**, ADO automatically updates the record. To cancel an update, you must call the **CancelUpdate** method.

Updating Records

To change the values of the current record, set the appropriate fields and then use the **Update** method to save the changes.

The following example code changes the **Description** field of the current record in the **rsMajors** recordset to the string value of "Science", and saves the changes:

```
rsMajors("Description") = "Science"
rsMajors.Update
```

*If you have opened the recordset with a lock type of **adLockBatchOptimistic**, you must call the **UpdateBatch** method to save changes.*

Deleting Records

To delete the current record, use the **Delete** method of the **Recordset** object. After you delete a record, invoke a **Move** method to move to the next record. Otherwise, the current record pointer points to an empty record.

The following example code deletes the current record in the **rsStudents** recordset:

```
rsStudents.Delete
rsStudents.MoveNext
```

Executing A Command

You do not need to create a **Recordset** object to open a database and query it. You can use a **Command** object and execute a SQL **INSERT**, **UPDATE**, or **DELETE** statement to add or modify records. Using a SQL statement is more efficient than creating a recordset and using recordset methods.

The collections, methods, and properties of the **Command** object vary, depending on the database provider. However, they are relatively consistent.

Creating A Command Object

To create a **Command** object, you pass **ADODB.Command** as an argument to the **CreateObject** function. To create a **Command** object, perform the following steps:

1. Call **CreateObject** and pass it the **ADODB.Command** parameter.
2. Set the **CommandText** property equal to the text that you want to have executed.
3. Set, in seconds, the **CommandTimeOut** property of the **Command** object. The **CommandTimeOut** property determines how long the object will wait for the results of a command.
4. Make the **Command** object the active connection for the data source.
5. Call the **Execute** method to run the command.

The following example code retrieves a value from the **Request** object in an ASP file, creates a **Command** object, sets properties for the command, and then runs it (this code would generally be found within a server-side script block in the ASP):

```
frmClassID = Request("classID")
Set cmd = Server.CreateObject("ADODB.Command")
cmd.CommandText = "exec ClassList " & frmClassID
cmd.CommandTimeOut = 30
cmd.ActiveConnection = conn ' use existing Connection object
cmd.Execute
```

The syntax for the **Execute** method is as follows:

```
command.Execute RecordsAffected, Parameters, Options
```

Note

*If you do not explicitly state a value for the **Options** parameter, it will default to 8 - adCmdUnknown, and try each option type one at a time against the command until it finds one that will run. This will slow execution time. Specify the option if you know it, so the command will execute immediately.*

The following example code runs a SQL command that changes a member's last name (presuming that the **frmmemberid** variable has somehow been initialized to a value corresponding with one of the expected values in the table's primary key field). The code then displays the number of records affected by the update:

```
sql= "UPDATE Members SET Last_Name= " & _
    "'" & frmNewName &"'" & _
    " WHERE MemberID = " & frmmemberid
cmd.CommandText = sql
cmd.Execute iRecordsAffected, , adCmdText

Response.Write "Number of Records updated = " & iRecordsAffected
```

To execute a SQL command that returns a recordset, save the return value from the **Execute** method in a **Recordset** object variable. This example code runs the stored procedure **CommandText**, which returns a recordset:

```
cmd.CommandText = "Exec BookList " & frmBookID
Set rs = cmd.Execute
```

Note

*Recordsets created from the **cmd.Execute** method will have a Forward-only cursor, and will be read-only. If you need a different cursor type or write access, create a **Recordset** object independently and specify the cursor type in the **Open** method.*

Running Stored Procedures With Parameters

To run a stored procedure that accepts parameters, you can create a **Parameter** object for each parameter, and then append the **Parameter** object to the **Parameters** collection of the **Command** object. To create a **Parameter** object, you invoke the **CreateParameter** method of the **Command** object.

The syntax of the **CreateParameter** method is as follows:

```
command.CreateParameter Name, Type, Direction, Size, Value
```

Note

*You can pass parameters by assigning values to the **Parameters** collection without using **CreateParameter**. However, the disadvantage to this method is that each assignment causes the **Command** object to query the data source for the type of the parameter.*

Using **CreateParameter** to create parameters explicitly, and then appending the **Parameter** objects to the **Command** object, requires a few more lines of code, but will avoid extra network trips to the database. The following code creates some parameters and calls a stored procedure called **GetStudentGPA** that computes a student's GPA, passing in the **StudentID** value as an input parameter, and receiving the **GPA** value as an output parameter:

```
cmd.CommandText = "GetStudentGPA"
cmd.CommandType = adCmdStoredProc
set parm = cmd.CreateParameter("StudentID",adInteger,adParamInput,4,1)
cmd.Parameters.Append parm
set parm = cmd.CreateParameter("GPA",adSingle,adParamOutput,4)
cmd.Parameters.Append parm
cmd.Execute
response.write cmd.Parameters("GPA")
```

If a stored procedure returns an output parameter and a recordset, you must read the output parameters before accessing the recordset. Once you access the recordset, the output parameters can no longer be read.

Handling Errors

When you create Web applications that access a database, you should anticipate possible database errors and include error-handling code in your script. For general information on how to write error-handling code in VBScript, refer back to Chapter 20.

Error-Handling Strategy

The best strategy for handling errors is to provide code that attempts to correct the error. For example, if a database connection fails to open, you can write code that connects to a back-up database. If this works, the user doesn't need to know that an error has occurred.

You can also try to prevent errors. For example, if you have a form in which the user enters a date range, you can place validation code on the form to verify the dates before the form is submitted.

If an error cannot be corrected or prevented, you can return an informative message to the user. One way to supply a message is to redirect the user to another Web page that will display the message.

To redirect the user to another Web page, you call the **Redirect** method of the **Response** object. However, **Redirect** works only if it has been placed in the server script before the <**HTML**> tag is read. By placing all of the server script before the <**HTML**> tag, you can trap errors and display a different Web page if necessary. The following code traps errors, and then redirects the user to a custom-built error page that displays information about the cause of the errors:

```
'This code is placed before the <HTML> tag
'Run code to perform work here
If err.number <> 0 Then
  session("ErrorTitle") = "Error Title to be Displayed"
  session("ErrorText") = "Description of Error" \
  'Redirect to custom error page that will display the session variables
  response.redirect "error.asp"
End If
```

The Errors Collection

The **Connection** object provides an **Errors** collection that contains information on database errors. To determine whether an error occurred, you can use the **Err** object provided by VBScript or the **Errors** collection.

The advantage of using the **Errors** collection is that if multiple errors occur during a single database operation, all of the errors will be stored in the collection. The **Err** object contains information only on the last error returned.

Performance Considerations For ADO

As I have mentioned earlier in several places in this chapter, effective management of your ADO objects, together with the way you invoke code against the objects, will make your applications perform substantially more effectively. The following sections describe some issues to consider when using ADO in your applications.

Use SQL Commands Instead Of A Recordset

When you create an ADO **Recordset** object, the recordset is created on the server. This is referred to as a *server-side cursor*. It is an expensive operation because it consumes server system resources.

To update a database, you can use SQL commands instead of creating a recordset and using methods of the **Recordset** object. For example, to insert a record into a table, you can execute a SQL **INSERT** command rather than creating a recordset and using the **AddNew** and **Update** methods. When you use the SQL **INSERT** command, no recordset is created.

Manage Recordset Size For Efficiency

If the records returned from a query can be displayed on one Web page, you can write server-side script that creates a recordset, scrolls through the recordset, returns all the data as HTML text, and then closes the recordset. In this case, you can set the cursor type for the recordset to Forward-only. This is the fastest type of cursor.

If the records returned from a query do not fit on one Web page, you can provide command buttons on the Web page for the user to request another page of records. To do this, you have several choices:

- When you create the initial recordset, you can store the **Recordset** object in a session variable. When the user requests a new page of records, you use the stored **Recordset** object to retrieve the next set of records. Storing a **Recordset** object consumes server resources. Therefore, this approach may not be practical if your Web site has many concurrent users.

- Another approach is to save only the number of the current record in a session variable. In this case, you create a recordset, return one page of records, save the number of the last record returned, and then close the recordset. When the user requests the next page of records, you query the database again, use the saved recordset number to return the next page of records, and then close the recordset again. This approach reduces data server resources, because no recordsets are kept open during a session.

- A third alternative is to use RDS instead of ADO. RDS stores a recordset on the client workstation rather than on the server.

Place Data Updates In Business Objects

The best approach to working with data updates is to place the update code in business objects rather than directly in ASP files. The ASP file can then create an instance of the business object and invoke methods to perform an update. You can use ADO in Visual Basic to implement business objects. There are several reasons to place code for data updates in business objects, including the following:

- You can create multiple business objects, each one responsible for a discrete task. Breaking an application into discrete components simplifies maintenance and testing.

- Business logic should be isolated from the user interface, which is provided by the ASP file. Business logic determines how a database can be modified based on rules of the business. For example, a university may have a rule that a student who has a grade point average below 2.0 cannot enroll in any new classes. When you write code to add a record to an enrollment table, you must ensure that the student meets the required grade point average. By placing this logic in a business object, you isolate the code. If the business rule changes, you modify the business object rather than redesign the ASP file.

- A business object can be invoked by many types of clients, such as ASP files and Visual Basic or Visual C++ applications. If you have a general business object that updates a database, many applications can use the object. Code in ASP files works only with browser clients.

- If a business object fails, the error is isolated. It will not cause the entire Web server to fail.

Working With RDS For Client-Side Data Support

As I have mentioned previously, RDS is a set of components that you can use to build Web applications for accessing ODBC-compliant databases. RDS binds the data from a recordset to data-aware HTML elements or ActiveX controls on a Web page.

To use RDS, you work with COM components, HTML, and client-side script. You add the **RDS.DataControl** object to an HTML document, and set properties to indicate the data to retrieve. You then set attributes on HTML elements to bind them to the **RDS.DataControl** object.

You can also write client-side script to request a new set of records or submit changes to the database at runtime.

RDS Component Overview

The components of RDS are divided into client-side components and server-side components. RDS client-side components run in an HTML document to provide dynamic data to the user. These components are not visible in the HTML document. Instead, they provide data from a recordset in data-bound ActiveX controls that are visible. The following list describes the RDS client components:

◆ **RDS.DataControl**—The **RDS.DataControl** object runs queries and makes the resulting recordsets available to the data-bound controls on an HTML document. You set properties for the object to identify the Web server, data source, and SQL statement to retrieve records.

◆ **RDS.DataSpace**—The **RDS.DataSpace** object creates instances of business objects that reside on a Web server. You can write client-side script to use these objects to invoke instances of your own custom business objects on the Web server.

◆ **ADOR.Recordset**—The **RDS.DataSpace** object creates an **ADOR.Recordset** object when it retrieves records. This type of recordset object is similar to the ADO **Recordset** object, but does not include all of the same features. Because it includes fewer features, it is smaller and can download quickly.

On the server-side, the most important component of RDS is the **RDSServer.DataFactory** object. The **RDSServer.DataFactory** object is a business object that has been implemented as a COM server component. This is the default object used by the **RDS.DataControl** object to run queries.

The following list outlines the sequence of events that occurs when RDS displays a recordset:

1. The user submits a query on an HTML document.

2. The client-side script assigns the query to the **RDS.DataControl** object and calls the **Refresh** method.

3. The **RDS.DataControl** object submits the query by using HTTP to the Web server.

4. RDS routes the query to the **RDSServer.DataFactory** object, which runs the query against the data source.

5. The resulting recordset is sent back to the **RDS.DataControl** object by using HTTP.

6. The data-bound controls on the HTML document display records from the recordset.

7. The recordset is cached on the client side.

8. When a user moves through the recordset, the controls display the data without making another trip to the Web server.

Binding Data To An Element

Data binding is based on a component architecture that consists of four major pieces:

♦ Data source objects, which provide the data to a page

♦ Data consumers, which are data-consuming HTML elements that display data

♦ Binding agents, which ensure that both provider and consumer are synchronized

♦ The table repetition agent, which works with tabular data consumers to provide a data set

Internet Explorer 4 supports data binding and the use of data source objects. RDS is simply one more data source object.

Data Source Objects

To bind data to the elements of an HTML page in Internet Explorer 4, a data source object (DSO) must be present on that page. A DSO implements an open specification that allows the DSO developer to determine the following:

♦ How the data is transmitted to the page. A DSO can use any transport protocol it chooses. This might be a standard Internet protocol such as HTTP or simple file I/O.

♦ Whether the transmission occurs synchronously or asynchronously. Asynchronous transmission is preferred, as it provides the most immediate interactivity to the user.

♦ How the data set is specified. A DSO might require an ODBC connection string and a SQL statement, or it might accept a simple URL.

♦ How the data is manipulated through scripts. Because a DSO maintains data on the client, it also manages how the data is sorted and filtered.

♦ Whether updates are allowed.

Data Consumers

Data consumers are elements on the HTML page capable of rendering data supplied by a DSO. Elements include many of those intrinsic to HTML, as well as custom objects implemented as Java applets or ActiveX controls. Internet Explorer 4 supports HTML extensions to allow authors to bind an element to a specific column of data in a data set exposed by a DSO. Applets and ActiveX controls support additional binding semantics.

Binding Agents

Binding agents perform the following two functions:

♦ When a page is first loaded, the binding agent finds the DSOs and the data consumers among those elements on the page.

♦ The binding agent also maintains the synchronization of the data that flows between all DSOs and data consumers. For example, when the DSO receives more data from its source, the binding agent transmits the new data to the consumers. Conversely, when a user updates a data bound element on the page, the binding agent notifies the DSO.

The repetition agents work with tabular data consumers (such as the HTML **<TABLE>** element) to repeat the entire data set supplied by a DSO.

> **Note**
> *Individual elements in the table are synchronized through interaction with the binding agent.*

Using A Data Source Object

To use the **RDS.DataControl** object in your page:

1. Insert the data source object onto a page using the **<OBJECT>** tag.

2. Set the **DATASRC** attribute/property of the HTML element to which you want to bind data equal to the **ID** of the data source object you inserted.

3. Set the **DATAFLD** attribute/property equal to the column of the data source from which you want data.

Inserting The RDS.DataControl Object

The **RDS.DataControl** object functions like a recordset in ADO. It provides data to data-bound elements, like a text box control, on an HTML page in a Web application. The **RDS.DataControl** object runs queries and makes the resulting recordset available to data-bound elements on an HTML page. You bind data from the **RDS.DataControl** to data-aware controls by setting attributes of the elements.

To use **RDS.DataControl** in your Web application, you add the ActiveX control to your Web page. To add **RDS.DataControl** to your page so that you can script it from within your applications, you must first add the following object tag anywhere on the page (preferably, however, before the bound objects, for clarity):

```
<OBJECT classid="clsid:BD96C556-65A3-11D0-983A-00C04FC29E33"
    ID=Chap21DataSource Width=1 Height=1>
    <PARAM NAME="SERVER" VALUE="http://AccessCS.Coriolis.com">
    <PARAM NAME="CONNECT" VALUE="dsn=Chap21Sample">
</OBJECT>
```

Make sure that you set the ID attribute of the control, replacing the **ID=Chap21DataSource** line in the sample code with an appropriate name for the control inside of your application.

Setting Attributes

Table 21.2 describes the attributes you set for the **RDS.DataControl** object.

Using the **RDS.DataControl** object after you have inserted it into a page is a relatively simple process. To use it, simply perform the following steps:

1. Add the appropriate HTML controls to your HTML document.
2. Set the **DATASRC** attribute to the **ID** of the **RDS.DataControl** and place a pound symbol (#) in front of it. For example:

```
<TABLE DATASRC=#Chap21DataSource>
```

3. Set the **DATAFLD** attribute of the HTML control to a field in the **DATASRC**:

```
<TD DATAFLD=Name>
```

You can add client-side script to your HTML document to change properties of the **RDS.DataControl** object and submit a new query to the Web server at runtime.

Sending A New Query

To send a new query to RDS, you modify the **SQL** property of the **RDS.DataControl** object and use the **Refresh** method to run the query. A new set of records will be retrieved and the data-bound controls will be updated automatically with the new data.

The following example code sets the **SQL** property of the **RDS.DataControl** object based on input from a user, then queries the database again:

```
Sub cmdFind_OnClick
  Chap21DataSource.SQL = "exec classlist " & "'" & txtid.value & "'"
  Chap21DataSource.Refresh
End Sub
```

Changing The Current Record

The **RDS.DataControl** object uses a recordset that always specifies a current record. The current record is displayed in the data-bound controls. To change the current record, you run script that uses one of the move methods of the **RDS.DataControl** object. The data-bound controls display the new current record. Because the recordset is cached on the client

Table 21.2   The attributes you set for the RDS.DataControl object.

Attribute	Description
SQL	Specifies the SQL statement to retrieve records.
CONNECT	Specifies the data source name, user ID, and password.
SERVER	If you are using HTTP, the value of this attribute is the name of the Web server computer.

workstation, a user can browse a large recordset without sending additional requests to the Web server for new data.

The following example code moves the current record forward one record:

```
Sub cmdMoveNext_OnClick
  Chap21DataSource.MoveNext
End Sub
```

Tip

*For some ActiveX controls, you must set a property on the control to enable editing, in addition to the manner in which you construct the recordset. For example, you must set the **AllowUpdate** and **AllowAddNew** properties of the data-bound Grid control to allow the user to edit or add data in the control.*

Changing Data

Data-bound controls enable the user to visually edit, add, or delete records. All changes made by the user are stored locally until the user explicitly submits or cancels the update.

Note

*To enable the user to change data on data-bound controls, you must add the **For Browse** statement to the end of the query. Currently, only SQL Server supports this statement—though, presumably, if Active Server Pages continue to be a dominant technology, and RDS becomes more prevalent, other database products will add support for this statement.*

To submit changes, invoke the **SubmitChanges** method of the **RDS.DataControl** object. To cancel changes, invoke the **CancelUpdate** method. The following example code shows how an Update button and a Cancel button can be used to submit or cancel changes to a recordset:

```
Sub Update_OnClick
  Chap21DataSource.SubmitChanges
End Sub
```

```
Sub Cancel_OnClick
  Chap21DataSource.CancelUpdate
End Sub
```

Using The RDSServer.DataFactory Object

In most cases, you will not need to use the **RDSServer.DataFactory** object directly. When you use the **RDS.DataControl** object, it invokes the **RDSServer.DataFactory** object for you. However, when you use the **RDS.DataControl** object to create a recordset, you cannot write script that reads the data in the recordset programmatically. If you need to read the data in a recordset programmatically, you can use **RDS.DataSpace** and **RDSServer.DataFactory** objects to create the recordset.

You will need to programmatically read data in a recordset if you want to display the data from the recordset in controls that are not data-aware. In this case, you must write script to read the recordset and then set the value of the controls. To create a recordset using the **RDSServer.DataFactory** object, perform the following steps:

1. Insert the **RDS.DataSpace** control on your HTML document.

2. Create an instance of the **RDSServer.DataFactory** object by invoking the **CreateRecordset** method of the **RDS.DataSpace** object.

3. Create a recordset by invoking the **Query** method of the **RDSServer.DataFactory** object.

4. Assign data from the current record to HTML text box controls.

The following example code creates an **RDSServer.DataFactory** object, queries the library database for a list of all cardholders, and then assigns the first and last names from the current record to HTML controls (in this example, **ADS1** is an **RDSServer** variable):

```
set ADF = ADS1.CreateObject("AdvancedDataFactory","http://SQLServer")
set RdsRS = ADF.Query("DSN=Chap21Data;UID=sa;PWD=;", _
    "select * from members")
txtFirstName.value = RdsRS.fields("First_Name")
txtLastName.value = RdsRS.fields("Last_Name")
```

If you also want to display the data from the recordset in data-aware controls, you can insert the **RDS.DataControl** object in your HTML document and add the data-aware controls. Then, you set the **Recordset** property of the **RDS.DataControl** object to the recordset object returned by **RDSServer.DataFactory**. The following example code sets the **Recordset** property of **RDS.DataControl** to the recordset variable **RdsRS**:

```
Chap21DataSource.Recordset = RdsRS
```

Some data-bound controls enable users to scroll through records. Depending on the purpose of your HTML document, you may want to update other controls in response to a user moving through the recordset. You can set the **Bookmark** property of a **Recordset** object to reposition the current record.

The following example code shows a data-bound list box that displays a list of student IDs. When a user selects a student ID in the list box, the script sets the **Bookmark** property of the recordset to the selected item from the list box and updates the HTML text boxes:

```
Sub DBList_Click()
  RdsRS.BookMark = DBList.selecteditem
  txtFirstName.value = RdsRS.fields("First_Name")
```

```
        txtLastName.value = RdsRS.fields("Last_Name")
End Sub
```

Performance Considerations With RDS

Clearly, if you can (and want to) standardize on RDS, you can create very efficient Web applications. The following sections summarize some of the advantages of using RDS to design and build applications that enable data retrieval and updates on your Web site.

Data Retrieval

RDS is ideal for retrieving and displaying records from both small and large recordsets. RDS caches records on the user's computer, which enables the user to browse all of the records in a recordset without having to retrieve additional HTML documents from the Web server.

Data Updates

Your Web site will be easier to maintain and will serve a larger number of users if you isolate the data updates in business objects instead of placing the data update code directly in HTML documents. You use a tool such as Visual Basic or Visual C++ to create business objects. In the business object, you define methods that update the database. From an HTML document, you can use the **RDS.DataSpace** object to create an instance of your custom business objects and then invoke methods of the object.

Where To Go From Here

In Chapter 22, we will look at some of the techniques at your disposal for using Visual Basic projects for creating Web-based applications. As you will see, the root of these techniques ends up being Visual Basic code that works against the same scripting models I showed to you in this chapter and Chapter 20. You will implement these COM-based applications in a manner designed to achieve the same goals as those you have accomplished using server- and client-side VBScript in the last couple of chapters. However, you may find that these types of solutions end up being slightly faster in larger environments.

Chapter 22

Web-Based Solutions With Visual Basic 6

Key Topics:

- *Building Active Documents As Front Ends*

- *Using DHTML COM Components For Fast Client-Side Processing*

- *Using IIS COM Components For Fast Server-Side Processing*

W ith Visual Basic, you can create Web-based applications that perform their processing on the server, and are accessible from Web browsers on any platform. You can combine the low overhead costs and other benefits of deploying an application over the Internet with the efficiency and security of Component Object Model (COM) components. Although I have spent a substantial amount of time discussing the ways in which you can integrate VB-developed COM components with your Visual InterDev-developed Active Server Page (ASP) code, Visual Basic actually provides you with a set of different techniques and object constructions that you can take advantage of to perform advanced Web programming.

Some of these changes are improvements that came about with the release of Visual Basic 6—most notably, the DHTML and IIS project types. Their goals are relatively straightforward: DHTML projects result in COM components that are designed to be executed at the client (that is, downloaded from the server and run locally), whereas IIS projects are Internet Server Application Programming Interface (ISAPI) dynamic-link libraries (DLLs). Specifically, as you saw in Chapter 19, IIS projects are COM components designed to run at the server. Finally, Active documents are a special kind of COM component designed to run within a *container* application. In their initial release, Microsoft was pitching Active documents as being able to run within several different kinds of containers, but it has really only implemented them as objects inside of Internet Explorer. In the next several sections, we will consider Active documents first, as they are the simplest of the technologies and the easiest, in many ways, to use.

Using Active Documents

You can use Visual Basic to create applications that run within an Internet browser window. These applications are called *Active documents*. In the following sections, you will learn about Active documents and Active document containers. You will learn how to implement Active documents in Visual Basic, and how to use Visual Basic to determine the container application and persist data in an Active document.

Active documents, essentially, are Visual Basic-developed COM components that implement a special set of interfaces that allow the applications to be hosted inside of an Internet browser window—specifically, an Internet Explorer browser window. Active documents can also be hosted in the Office Binder and other container applications that support OLE document objects; however, for our purposes, I will discuss them solely from the perspective of Internet design.

Advantages Of Active Documents

There are many reasons why you might want to create your Internet or intranet application as an Active document. Table 22.1 summarizes some of the benefits of using Active documents rather than other available technologies.

Creating an Active document is similar to creating any other kind of application in Visual Basic. The primary differences are that you use a **UserDocument** object instead of a form for the user interface, and you test your application in its container application.

To create a simple Active document in Visual Basic, perform the following steps:

1. Design the features and appearance of your document, and determine the properties, methods, and events it will provide.

2. Create a new Visual Basic project using either the ActiveX Document DLL or the ActiveX Document EXE project template. Create a DLL file if you want to create an in-process component. Create an EXE file if you want to create an out-of-process component. You learned about differences between these two component types in Chapter 19.

3. Add controls and code to the **UserDocument** object to implement the user interface of your document, and write code to implement its properties, methods, and events.

4. Compile your document to create a VBD file, and test it with all potential target applications.

Working With The UserDocument Designer

In Visual Basic, you create an Active document by adding controls and code to a **UserDocument** object in an Active document designer. The **UserDocument** object is the foundation for all Active documents.

Table 22.1   A brief summary of the benefits of using Active documents for Web design.

Advantage	Description
Widely available container	Active documents enable a generic, widely available container application to host a variety of different document types. This allows users to work with information in any number of formats through common browser functionality.
Visual Basic knowledge	If you are a Visual Basic programmer, you already have the knowledge to create a solution. You do not have to learn HTML to create an application for the Internet.
Visual Basic programming environment	The full development environment is available to you, including the Visual Basic code window, debugger, and compiler.
Execution on a local computer	Active document technology enables computationally intensive processing to take place locally, and reduces the processing and load on a network.
Immediate visual feedback	Unlike coding in HTML, creating an Active document in Visual Basic provides immediate visual feedback about the layout of the elements in your application. Moreover, the elements that you create inside of the Active document will have an appearance similar to that which you are likely used to—a Visual Basic application's interface.

The **UserDocument** object is similar in functionality to the **UserControl** object (an object that Visual Basic programmers use to create their own custom ActiveX controls). Like the **UserControl** object, the **UserDocument** object can raise events, and can support properties and methods. Though **UserControl** objects can have substantial benefit for Web developers—most notably in the creation of ActiveX controls that you can then embed inside Web pages—they don't have quite as broad a set of uses as **UserDocument**s.

The **UserDocument** object also implements interfaces that enable it to be hosted within a document container. Figure 22.1 shows a new Active document project viewed in the Visual Basic Project Explorer.

This project contains a user document, which is the default Visual Basic **UserDocument** object included in a new Active document project. You can add additional documents to a

Figure 22.1
An Active document project viewed in the Visual Basic Project Explorer.

project by selecting Project | Add User Document. When the Add User Document dialog box appears, click on User Document, and then click on Open.

Working with the **UserDocument** object is similar to working with a form. For example, you place controls on the **UserDocument** object to create the visual appearance of an Active document.

You can always start a new Active document project, but you may have a form you want to migrate to an Active document. Visual Basic provides the ActiveX Document Migration Wizard to automate the process. To use the ActiveX Document Migration Wizard, perform the following steps:

1. Open the project that contains the form you want to convert.
2. On the Add-Ins menu, click on Add-In Manager.
3. In the list of available add-ins, select VB 6 Active Doc Migration Wizard.
4. Under Load Behavior, select the Loaded/Unloaded checkbox to add the wizard to your project, and then click on OK.
5. On the Add-Ins menu, click on ActiveX Document Migration Wizard.
6. Follow the directions until the wizard has finished its task.

The wizard asks you to identify the form that you want to convert and to make a few choices, such as whether to remove the original form after conversion. It then performs the tasks described Table 22.2.

There are some situations unique to Active documents that you may want to handle in your code. For example, a user may attempt to open your document in a container other than the one you intended. You can write code that determines the container and responds appropriately for that container.

Table 22.2 Steps performed by the ActiveX Document Migration Wizard when converting a form to an Active document.

Form Element	Action Taken
Properties	Form properties are copied to a new **UserDocument** object.
Controls	All controls are copied from the form to the **UserDocument** object. Their names are retained.
Valid code	All code behind the form is copied to the **UserDocument** object.
Invalid code	Code that doesn't apply in the Active document situation (such as code to show, hide, load, and unload forms) is commented out by the wizard.
Project file	The project type is switched to ActiveX Document DLL or ActiveX Document EXE, depending on the option you chose in the wizard.
Event handlers	Event handlers are copied to the **UserDocument** object, with "Form" replaced by "UserDocument" where appropriate. For example, **Form_Click** becomes **UserDocument_Click**. In cases where there is no exact counterpart in the **UserDocument** object, the event handler is copied to the General section of the code window, leaving the original procedure name intact.

Another common requirement for Active documents is the ability to store data associated with the page so that it is available the next time it is opened. In Visual Basic, you can use the **PropertyBag** object to persist data in an Active document.

Determining The Container Application

To determine the container of an Active document, you use the **TypeName** statement with the **Parent** property of the **UserDocument** object, as shown in the following example code:

```
Dim strContainer As String
strContainer = TypeName(UserDocument.Parent)
```

The process of connecting an Active document to its container, or assigning it a site in the container, is called *siting*. When an Active document is sited on its container, the **Show** event occurs. You can use this event to determine the container being used. When a document is sited, the container properties become available.

The string value returned by the **Parent** property in Internet Explorer is **IWebBrowserApp**. The following sample code checks to see whether **IWebBrowserApp** is the string value returned by the **Parent** property of the **UserDocument** object:

```
Private Sub UserDocument_Show()
  Dim strContainer As String
  strContainer = TypeName(UserDocument.Parent)

  If strContainer = "IWebBrowserApp" Then
    MsgBox "Confirmation: This document  " & _
        "works with Internet Explorer " & _
        "3.0 or later."
  Else
    MsgBox "Sorry, please open this "& _
        "document with Internet Explorer "& _
        "3.0 or later."
  End If
End Sub
```

If **IWebBrowserApp** is true, the code lets you know that you are running version 3.0 or later of Internet Explorer—which is, as you know, required for the execution of Active documents.

Persisting Data In An Active Document

Users often navigate away from an Active document in Internet Explorer or another container, and then navigate back to it. They expect not to lose data or settings on that page, so you must ensure that property values are preserved for your Active document. You can do this by writing code that uses the **PropertyBag** object to persist data for that document.

Saving Property Values

You save property values in the **WriteProperties** event of the **UserDocument** object. This event is raised whenever the **PropertyChanged** method is invoked in your code. The **WriteProperty** method takes three arguments: a string indicating the property to save, a value for the property, and a default value.

Tip

Before saving the property value, the default value is compared with the property value. If they are the same, the property value doesn't have to be saved, because default values will be set automatically when the document is reopened. This keeps the data file from being cluttered with default entries unnecessarily.

The following example code shows how to save current property values by notifying the container that a property has changed, and then saving the value with the **WriteProperty** method of the **PropertyBag** object:

```
Private Sub txtEmpName_Change()
  'Notify container that Employee Name property has changed

  PropertyChanged "EmployeeName"
End Sub


Private Sub UserDocument_WriteProperties(PropBag As PropertyBag)
  PropBag.WriteProperty "EmployeeName", txtEmpName.Text, "No Name"
  PropBag.WriteProperty "EmployeeNumber", txtEmpNum.Text, "000"
End Sub
```

As you can see, each invocation of **WriteProperty** saves a separate value into the **PropertyBag**. When you use properties within your applications, you will always persist properties in this manner. You will find that you use properties in your VB applications with surprising regularity—but as a rule, you will almost always use them with Active documents and ActiveX controls.

Reading Property Values

You retrieve property values in the **ReadProperties** event of the **UserDocument** object. This event is raised when the document is opened in its container. The **ReadProperty** method takes two arguments: a string designating the property name and a default value. If a property value has been saved, the **ReadProperty** method returns the value. If a property value has not been saved, the method returns the default value.

The following example code shows how to use the **ReadProperty** method to return the saved value of the **EmployeeName** and **EmployeeNumber** properties:

```
Private Sub UserDocument_ReadProperties(PropBag As PropertyBag)
  txtName.Text = PropBag.ReadProperty("EmployeeName", "No Name")
```

```
    txtNum.Text = PropBag.ReadProperty("EmployeeNumber", "000")
End Sub
```

Library Checkout Application

In the interests of space, and because the creation of Active documents is a bit off of the topic of this book, I have not placed the entirety of an Active document application inside this chapter. Instead, I have placed a heavily commented Active document application on the companion CD-ROM, inside the Chap22\ActiveD directory.

This application, which should be installed on your IIS server, uses a Data Source Name (DSN) called **SQLLibraryDB**. You should create a DSN with the same name on your IIS server, which points to the **library** database on the SQL Server in your environment.

This (simple) library application lets you add new members over the Internet, as well as view current status of a member's account—what books are checked out, reserved, and so on—and finally re-serve additional books for the member. The code within the application walks you through most of the steps necessary for the creation of the application.

Using DHTML Components

With Visual Basic, you can create Web-based applications that perform their processing on the Web client, and combine the efficiency and security of COM components with the power of Dynamic HTML (DHTML).

DHTML is a technology built into Internet Explorer 4 that defines an object model for HTML pages. You can use DHTML to programmatically respond to events and modify elements on an HTML page at any time, not just while downloading or refreshing the page. Client-side Web applications created in Visual Basic are called *DHTML applications*. In the following sections, you will learn how to use Visual Basic to develop DHTML applications.

> **Tip**
>
> *Obviously, DHTML applications are usable only with Internet Explorer—and, therefore, are generally appropriate solutions only when used in an intranet environment, where you can ensure that all the clients who will be accessing the page wrapping the component are using Internet Explorer.*

Reasons For Using DHTML

If you want to create a Web-based application that performs its processing on the Web client, you can develop a DHTML application in Visual Basic. A DHTML application consists of one or more HTML pages and a COM component that interacts with the page(s). The HTML page(s) act as the user interface for the application, and the COM component contains the functionality for the application. Figure 22.2 shows the parts of a DHTML application, and indicates where the processing for the application occurs.

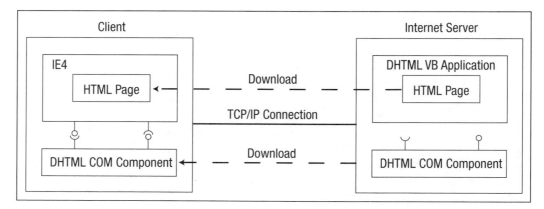

Figure 22.2
The DHTML application's components and execution locations.

Using the DHTML Page designer, you can create a Web-based application as easily as you create a form-based application. Although the user interface for the application is an HTML page, you can create the page using visual tools instead of HTML tags. You also have access to the standard Visual Basic editing features and debugging tools to write and test the COM component used by your DHTML application.

The DHTML Page designer exposes the DHTML object model to you so that you can change the content and format of the HTML page as the user views the page. The DHTML object model is pretty large, and well beyond the scope of our current endeavor—but the Visual Basic help file will provide you with extensive information on the topic.

A DHTML application can run in Internet Explorer 4 or any other container that supports DHTML, such as a custom application built using the **WebBrowser** control. The processing associated with a DHTML application occurs on the Web client, although the application can make calls to a server. To create a DHTML application in Visual Basic, perform the following steps:

1. Create a new project in Visual Basic using the DHTML Application project template. Your project will contain a DHTML Page designer and a code module by default.

2. Create an HTML page or use an existing HTML page as the user interface for your application. There is a one-to-one relationship between DHTML Page designers and HTML pages in Visual Basic. If you want to use more than one HTML page in your application, add more DHTML Page designers to your project by selecting Project | Add DHTML Page.

3. Assign a unique identifier to each element of the HTML page that you want to access programmatically.

4. Write code to add functionality to your application.

5. Test and debug your application as you would any other Visual Basic application. When you start your DHTML application from Visual Basic, it will run in Internet Explorer, but you will still debug your code in the Visual Basic IDE.

6. Compile your application, and use the Package And Deployment Wizard to package the DLL and supporting files for distribution.

When you develop a DHTML application, you use the DHTML Page designer during design time to create and modify an HTML page that acts as your user interface. You must assign a unique identifier to each element of the HTML page that you want to modify or manipulate as an object in your code.

Using The DHTML Page Designer

The DHTML Page designer is a design-time tool in Visual Basic that enables you to quickly create and modify an HTML page that acts as the user interface in your DHTML application. The DHTML Page designer contains two panels. The panel on the right is where you edit the text on your HTML page and add controls to it, just as you would a form. The Treeview panel on the left displays an outline of the object model for the HTML page as it is created. Figure 22.3 shows the DHTML Page designer with the Treeview panel on the left and the HTML page on the right.

Working With HTML Pages

You can create a new HTML page as your user interface, or you can import an HTML page that was created in an external editor. To import an existing HTML page into a DHTML Page designer, perform the following steps:

1. Select the DHTML Page designer, and then click on the DHTML Page Designer Properties toolbar button.

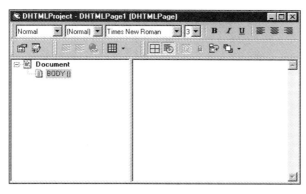

Figure 22.3
The DHTML Page designer while designing the COM component.

2. In the Properties dialog box, on the General tab, click on Save HTML In An External File, and then click on Open. The Open dialog box appears.

3. Select the HTML file you want to import, and then click on Open.

4. In the Properties dialog box, click on OK.

The HTML file you imported is displayed in the right panel of the designer, and its object model is displayed in the left panel.

Note

*Before you can write code to the elements on your HTML page, you need to specify a value for the **Id** property in the Properties window for each element you want to treat as an object in your code.*

Figure 22.4 shows a command button selected in the DHTML Page designer. Its Properties window is open, displaying the **Id** value for that button. Notice the **Id** is also displayed in the left panel of the designer as part of the object model hierarchy.

Once you have created the user interface for your DHTML application and specified **Id** values for the elements that you want to work with programmatically, you can write code to add functionality to your application.

Using DHTML Objects

The DHTML Page designer represents the elements of your HTML page in a hierarchy in the left panel of the designer. Each element in the hierarchy is a DHTML object. Although you will learn how to use a few specific objects in this chapter, as I mentioned earlier in this

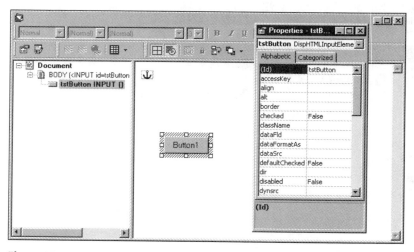

Figure 22.4
Working with the properties of an HTML page within the DHTML Page designer.

chapter, discussing the Dynamic HTML object model in its entirety is beyond the scope of this book.

Any element of the HTML page that has an **Id** value is displayed in bold text in the left panel of the designer. You can double-click on the bold text in the left panel, or double-click on the object itself in the right panel of the designer to display the code window associated with that object. Then you can write code for the object just as you would write code for a control on a form.

Manipulating HTML Pages At Runtime

Using Dynamic HTML, you can manipulate the style and content of HTML pages at any time during runtime of your DHTML application.

A common operation in DHTML applications is to dynamically change the text on an HTML page. To do this, use the **InnerText** property of the paragraph tag. The following example code sets the contents of the **idStudentName** paragraph to "Robert Klander":

```
idStudentName.innerText = "Robert Klander"
```

Testing And Debugging DHTML Applications

You can test and debug your DHTML application using the same powerful debugging tools that you are accustomed to using in Visual Basic. When you run your application from the Visual Basic environment, the HTML page that acts as the user interface is opened in Internet Explorer. However, you will still debug your code using the Visual Basic Integrated Development Environment (IDE).

Saving The HTML Files Associated With A DHTML Application

When you compile your application, Visual Basic generates a DLL file and saves the HTML files associated with your application. You can save HTML files as part of the Visual Basic project or as external files. You may want to save HTML files as external files if you have imported them from an existing Web site project. To choose how to save an HTML file from the DHTML application, perform the following steps:

1. Select the DHTML Page designer, and then click on the DHTML Page Designer Properties toolbar button.

2. In the Properties dialog box, on the General tab, choose Save HTML As Part Of The VB Project, and then click on OK. Alternatively (depending on how you want to save the pages), in the Properties dialog box, on the General tab, choose Save HTML In An External File, and then click on OK.

Deploying A DHTML Application

You can use the Visual Basic Package And Deployment Wizard to prepare your DHTML application for distribution. The wizard compresses the COM component and supporting

---

DHTML-Based Library Checkout Application

In the interests of space, and because the creation of DHTML components is a bit off of the topic of this book, I have not placed the entirety of a DHTML application inside this chapter. Instead, I have placed a heavily commented DHTML application on the companion CD-ROM, inside the Chap22\DHTML directory.

This application, which should be installed on your IIS server, uses a DSN called **SQLLibraryDB**. You should create a DSN with the same name on your IIS server, which points to the **library** database on the SQL Server in your environment. Note that, when the user accesses the HTML page that causes the COM component to be downloaded, the COM component will come to the local computer—but the DSN will not; instead, it will remain at the server.

Just like the Active document application, the simple DHTML library application lets you add new members over the Internet, as well as view the current status of a member's account—what books are checked out, reserved, and so on—and finally reserve additional books for the member. The code within the application walks you through most of the steps necessary for the creation of the application.

HTML files that make up the DHTML application into a CAB file. It also provides you the opportunity to mark each page in your application as safe. The Package And Deployment Wizard can also copy the CAB file and other supporting files for your application to either a Web site or a folder for distribution to your users.

Creating Internet Information Server (IIS) Applications

Server-side Web applications created in Visual Basic are called Internet Information Server (IIS) applications. In the following sections, you will learn how to use Visual Basic to develop IIS applications.

If you want to create a Web-based application that performs its processing on the Internet server, you can develop an IIS application in Visual Basic. IIS applications, like DHTML applications, are implemented as COM components, though IIS applications also include an additional ASP file, and do not get copied from the server to client. An IIS application consists of a COM component and a simple ASP file. The COM component contains the functionality for the application; the ASP file exists only to instantiate the COM component on the Internet server. Just like DHTML applications, the IIS application will end up instantiating one or more HTML files that it uses to communicate with the client and, therefore, the end user.

Figure 22.5 shows the parts of an IIS application, and indicates where the processing for the application occurs.

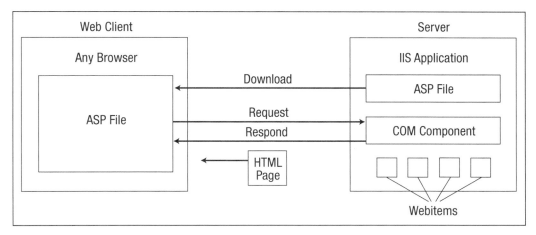

Figure 22.5
The basic architecture of the IIS application and its components.

The biggest benefit of using IIS applications, rather than DHTML applications, should already be evident to you, without any further discussion: The IIS application can effectively run in any browser product, because of the nature of the code that it yields up. This, of course, is a substantial benefit over the DHTML application, which is a COM object that must attach to the Internet Explorer application on the client side. The downside of IIS applications, when compared to DHTML applications, is that the client must go back to the server to request changes, just as it would with a regular HTML page. However, as we've seen in earlier chapters, the benefits of ASP outweigh client-side scripting for accessing data. As was discussed, in general, the benefits of placing all of the data-access logic at the server side substantially outweigh the detriments of doing so, except when the client is connecting over a prohibitively slow connection.

Using The WebClass Designer To Build IIS Applications

Using the WebClass designer, you can create a dynamic Web-based application without relying on script in an ASP file. Instead, you use the Active Server Page object model in your COM component to respond to events sent to you by the client browser (which are, in turn, generated by actions that the remote user takes inside the client browser).

The user interface for an IIS application consists of one or more HTML pages. You can either create HTML pages in an external editor and import them into your project, or you can write code in your COM component to dynamically return content to the Web client. You use the standard Visual Basic editing features and debugging tools to write and test your COM component. The bootstrap ASP file used by your application is generated for you at compile time.

Creating IIS applications is not substantially different than creating any other type of COM object from inside Visual Basic. To create an IIS application in Visual Basic, perform the following steps:

1. Create a new project in Visual Basic using the IIS Application Project template. The project contains a WebClass designer and a code module by default. A reference is automatically set to the Microsoft Active Server Page Object Library (if you inadvertently remove this reference, the application will not execute correctly, so I strongly suggest that you leave it alone).

Warning

To use the IIS Application Project template, you must have Internet Information Server or Personal Web Server installed on your computer. You can obtain either of these services by installing the NT Option Pack that is included on the Visual Basic CD.

2. Create custom webitems to represent each page in your application, or import existing HTML pages as webitems. You will learn more about webitems later in this chapter.

3. Define the functionality of your application by adding code to the webitems and the **Start** event of your webclass.

4. Test and debug your application as you would any other Visual Basic application. When you start your IIS application from Visual Basic, it will run in Internet Explorer, but you will still debug your code in the Visual Basic IDE.

5. Compile your application, and use the Package And Deployment Wizard to package the DLL and supporting files for distribution.

When you develop an IIS application in Visual Basic, you use a WebClass designer to define the COM component. A single *webclass* represents the entire Web application, which can contain multiple pages. Each page in the application is represented by a *webitem*. You can either create custom webitems using the WebClass designer, or you can import existing HTML pages to use as webitems.

Using The WebClass Designer

The WebClass designer is a design-time tool in Visual Basic that enables you to quickly create and modify the webitems that represent the pages in your application. The WebClass designer contains two panels. The Treeview panel on the left displays the webitems that make up the webclass. The Details panel on the right displays information about the currently selected item in the Treeview panel. Figure 22.6 shows the WebClass designer in Visual Basic.

Adding Webitems To A Webclass

To add pages to your application, you add webitems to your webclass. Each webitem represents one page in your application. You can either create custom webitems or import existing HTML pages to use as webitems. To create a custom webitem, perform the following steps:

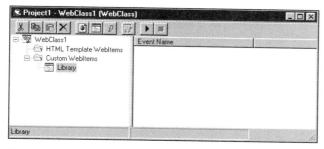

Figure 22.6
The WebClass designer, which looks very similar to the DHTML Page designer.

1. On the WebClass toolbar, click on the Add Custom WebItem toolbar button. A new webitem appears at the end of the list of custom webitems in the Treeview panel of the WebClass designer.

2. Type the name for the new webitem.

Alternatively, as mentioned previously, you can choose to create your webitems by importing existing HTML pages into your IIS application project. To import an existing HTML page as a webitem, perform the following steps:

1. On the WebClass toolbar, click on the Add HTML Template WebItem toolbar button. The Add HTML Template dialog box appears.

2. Select the HTML page you want to add as a webitem, and click on Open. A new webitem appears at the end of the list of HTML template webitems in the Treeview panel of the WebClass designer. In the Details panel, the tags in the HTML page are listed as objects you can use in your code.

3. Type the name for the new webitem.

So, as you have seen so far, a webclass is a Visual Basic COM component that sends information to a Web browser from an Internet server. You use the built-in events of the webclass and the Active Server Page object model to respond to Web browser requests. Webitems in your webclass also have events, properties, and methods that you can use to define the functionality of your application. You can also add custom events to webitems. In the next section, we will look at some of the different techniques at your disposal for communication with the browser from your webitems.

Sending Information To The Web Browser

You use the Active Server Page object model in your COM component to communicate with the Web browser. In custom webitems, you use the **Write** method of the **Response** object to write string information to the Web browser. The following example code writes a heading to the Web browser:

```
Response.Write "<H1>Access 2000 Client/Server Solutions
    IIS Component</H1>"
```

Note

*This **Response** object works in a fashion identical to that which you learned in Chapters 17 and 18 regarding the use of VBScript to generate return information from an Active Server Page.*

In HTML template webitems, you use the **WriteTemplate** method of the webitem to write the entire contents of the webitem to the Web browser. The following example code writes the contents of the webitem named **Welcome** to the Web browser:

```
Welcome.WriteTemplate
```

Warning

*The **WriteTemplate** method does not fire the **Respond** event for the associated webitem. Microsoft recommends that you call the **WriteTemplate** method only from within the **Respond** event of the webitem and that the **Respond** event be triggered by setting the **NextItem** property.*

Using The Start Event Of A Webclass

A webclass has several built-in events, including **Initialize**, **Start**, and **Terminate**. The **Start** event fires when the ASP file associated with the IIS application creates an instance of the webclass on the Web server.

Default code in the **Start** event uses the **Response** object to write out HTML in response to the Web client's request. The following listing shows the default code that VB automatically inserts into the **Start** event:

```
Private Sub WebClass_Start()
  Dim sQuote As String
  sQuote = Chr$(34)
  'Write a reply to the user
  With Response
    .Write "<HTML>"
    .Write "<body>"
    .Write "<h1><font face=" & sQuote & "Arial" & sQuote & _
        ">WebClass1's Starting Page</font></h1>"
    .Write "<p>This response was created in the Start event of WebClass1.</p>"
    .Write "</body>"
    .Write "</html>"
  End With
End Sub
```

You can add code to the **Start** event of your webclass to write directly to the Web browser or to navigate to the first webitem in your application. In the next section, you will look at techniques for navigating between webitems, and you will also see an example of this initialization technique.

Navigating Between Webitems In A Webclass

You use the **NextItem** property of the webclass to navigate between webitems in your application. When you navigate to a webitem using **NextItem**, a **Respond** event is fired for that webitem. You write code in the **Respond** event to display the next page to the user.

You may also want to provide a hyperlink in one webitem that jumps to another webitem in your webclass. To do this, you need a Uniform Resource Locator (URL) for that webitem, but you won't know the value of the hyperlink at design time. Use the **URLFor** function to generate a hyperlink that points to another webitem at runtime.

So, then, the following sample code uses the **NextItem** property of a webclass, the **Respond** event of a webitem, and the **URLFor** function to enable navigation between webitems:

```
Private Sub WebClass_Start()
  Set NextItem = Welcome
End Sub


Private Sub Welcome_Respond()
  With Response
    .Write "<HTML>"
    .Write "<BODY>"
    .Write "<H1>Welcome to The SQL Server PUBS Database</H1>"
    .Write "<BR>"
    .Write "<A HREF=" & WebClass.URLFor(PubList) & _
        ">Click here to see the list of Publishers in the Database.</A>"
    .Write "<BR>"
    .Write "<A HREF=" & WebClass.URLFor(Welcome) & ">Home Page</A>"
    .Write "</BODY>"
    .Write "</HTML>"
  End With
End Sub
```

Clearly, using the existing events inside of your webitems is a crucial part of their effective implementation. However, you will generally find that you also want to implement custom events within your webitems. The following section discusses exactly how to go about implementing those events.

Using Custom Events In A Webitem

You can pass an event argument with the **URLFor** function to specify a custom event that the webitem can handle. When a specific event argument is passed by the **URLFor** function, it is handled by a built-in event in the webitem called **UserEvent**.

IIS Library Checkout Application

Guess what! Because of space limitations, even though IIS applications are arguably right on point for this book, I have nevertheless not placed the entirety of the ISS version of the Library checkout application inside this chapter. Instead, I have placed a heavily commented IIS application on the companion CD-ROM, inside the Chap22\IIS directory.

This application, which should be installed on your IIS server, and uses a DSN called **SQLLibraryDB**. You should create a DSN with the same name on your IIS server, which points to the **library** database on the SQL Server in your environment. Note that, when the user accesses the HTML page that references the COM component, neither the component itself nor the DSN will be downloaded to the local computer. Instead, both will execute remotely, at the server.

Just like the Active document application and the DHTML library application, the IIS application lets you add new members over the Internet, as well as view current status of a member's account—what books are checked out, reserved, and so on—and finally reserve additional books for the member. The code within the application walks you through most of the steps necessary for the creation of the application.

Custom events that you add to a webitem do not have to be declared. You just need to add code to the **UserEvent** event to handle the custom event arguments you expect to use. Anything that you can manipulate in the **UserEvent** code can be passed as an event name, even dynamically created information such as the key to a record in a database.

The following example code raises a custom event named **CurrentStatus** for the webitem named **MemberInfo**:

```
Response.Write
    "<A HREF=" & WebClass.URLFor(MemberInfo, "CurrentStatus") & ">
    Click here to get this Member's Current Status</A>"
```

As I mentioned previously, you can test and debug your IIS application using the same debugging tools that you always use in Visual Basic. When you run your application from the Visual Basic environment, the HTML pages that act as the user interface are opened in Internet Explorer. However, you will still debug your code using the Visual Basic Integrated Development Environment (IDE). You will only stop using the VB IDE when it comes time to deploy the application, as discussed briefly in the following section.

Deploying An IIS Application

When you compile your application, Visual Basic generates a DLL file and a simple ASP file that instantiates your COM component on the Internet server. You can use the Package And Deployment Wizard to package your application for distribution. The wizard compresses the COM component and any supporting files into a CAB file, and provides you the opportunity to mark the component as safe. Files that are not marked as safe and not digitally signed will likely not be opened by the consumer.

You can use the same wizard to deploy your CAB file and ASP file to a server on a network or to a folder.

Where To Go From Here

Throughout this book, we have discussed many of the different alternatives available to you for client/server development. I have shown you the basics, as well as more advanced techniques that you can take advantage of to achieve the best possible performance with your distributed applications.

Where do you go from here? Go out and take the examples, samples, and educational code that I have provided to you, and make it work in your environment. Make it work at home. Install the local version of SQL Server, and start building yourself some substantial, impressive applications.

But always remember the design principles that I have discussed throughout this book. Remember that reducing round trips is always important, but maintaining data integrity is even more important. To keep yourself from becoming frustrated, remember that there are often a half dozen different ways to accomplish any task in programming. And remember that code that works fine, and seems appropriate to you today, may be the first code you change when you have a chance to take advantage of a new technology—computer programmers are notorious tinkerers, after all. But no matter what you do, make sure that you have fun with it, and build exciting things.

Part VI

Appendixes

Appendix A
DAO And ADO Reference

DAOs and collections, and ADO objects and collections, provide a framework for using code to create and manipulate components of your database system. Objects and collections have properties that describe the characteristics of database components and methods that you use to manipulate them. Together these objects and collections form a hierarchical model of your database structure, which you can control programmatically.

Objects and collections provide different types of containment relations: Objects contain zero or more collections, all of different types; collections contain zero or more objects, all of the same type. Although objects and collections are similar entities, the distinction differentiates the two types of relations.

In Table A.1, the type of collection in the first column contains the type of object in the second column. The third column describes what each type of object represents.

As Chapters 6 and later discuss in some detail, the object model for ActiveX Data Objects (ADO) programming differs substantially from that for the DAO model. Table A.2 details the objects that make up the ADO object model.

Collections are used a bit differently in ADO than they are in DAO. Table A.3 details the four collections that you will use with ADO, and their parent objects.

Table A.1 DAO collections, objects, and descriptions.

Collection	Object	Description
Connections	**Connection**	Information about a connection to an ODBC data source (ODBCDirect workspaces only)
Containers	**Container**	Storage for information about a predefined object type (Microsoft Jet workspaces only)
Databases	**Database**	An open database
None	**DBEngine**	The Microsoft Jet database engine
Documents	**Document**	Information about a saved, predefined object (Microsoft Jet workspaces only)
Errors	**Error**	Information about any errors associated with this object
Fields	**Field**	A column that is part of a table, query, index, relation, or recordset
Groups	**Group**	A group of user accounts (Microsoft Jet workspaces only)
Indexes	**Index**	Predefined ordering and uniqueness of values in a table (Microsoft Jet workspaces only)
Parameters	**Parameter**	A parameter for a parameter query
Properties	**Property**	A built-in or user-defined property
QueryDefs	**QueryDef**	A saved query definition
Recordsets	**Recordset**	The records in a base table or query
Relations	**Relation**	A relationship between fields in tables and queries (Microsoft Jet workspaces only)
TableDefs	**TableDef**	A saved table definition (Microsoft Jet workspaces only)
Users	**User**	A user account (Microsoft Jet workspaces only)
Workspaces	**Workspace**	A session of the Microsoft Jet database engine

Table A.2 Summary of the objects within the ADO object model.

Object	Description
Command	Embodies a SQL statement
Connection	Enables exchange of data
Error	Embodies an error on a connection
Field	Embodies a column of a **Recordset** object
Parameter	Embodies a parameter of a SQL statement
Property	Embodies a characteristic of an ADO object
Recordset	Enables navigation and manipulation of data

Table A.3 Summary of ADO collections and parent objects.

Object	Collection	Description
Connection	**Errors**	All the **Error** objects created in response to a single failure on a connection
Command	**Parameters**	All the **Parameter** objects associated with a **Command** object
Recordset, Command	**Fields**	All the **Field** objects associated with a **Recordset** or **Command** object
Connection, Command, Recordset, Field	**Properties**	All the **Property** objects associated with a **Connection**, **Command**, **Recordset**, or **Field** object

Appendix B

ANSI SQL Vs. Jet SQL Data Types

T able B.1 lists ANSI SQL data types and the equivalent Microsoft Jet database engine SQL data types, and their valid synonyms.

It's important to note that the ANSI SQL **BIT** data type does not correspond to the Microsoft Jet SQL **BIT** data type, but rather corresponds to the **BINARY** data type. There is no ANSI SQL equivalent for the Microsoft Jet SQL **BIT** data type. Additionally, the **VALUE** reserved word does not represent a data type defined by the Microsoft Jet database engine.

Table B.1   ANSI data types, Jet data types, and supported synonyms.

ANSI SQL Data Type	Microsoft Jet SQL Data Type	Synonym
BIT, BIT VARYING	**BINARY** (See Notes)	**VARBINARY**
Not supported	**BIT** (See notes)	**BOOLEAN, LOGICAL, LOGICAL1, YESNO**
Not supported	**BYTE**	**INTEGER1**
Not supported	**COUNTER**	**AUTOINCREMENT**
Not supported	**CURRENCY**	**MONEY**
DATE, TIME, TIMESTAMP	**DATETIME**	**DATE, TIME, TIMESTAMP**
Not supported	**GUID**	none
DECIMAL	Not supported	none
REAL	**SINGLE**	**FLOAT4, IEEESINGLE, REAL**
DOUBLE PRECISION, FLOAT	**DOUBLE**	**FLOAT, FLOAT8, IEEEDOUBLE, NUMBER, NUMERIC**
SMALLINT	**SHORT**	**INTEGER2, SMALLINT**
INTEGER	**LONG**	**INT, INTEGER, INTEGER4**
INTERVAL	Not supported	none
Not supported	**LONGBINARY**	**GENERAL, OLEOBJECT**
Not supported	**LONGTEXT**	**LONGCHAR, MEMO, NOTE**
CHARACTER, CHARACTER VARYING	**TEXT**	**ALPHANUMERIC, CHAR, CHARACTER, STRING, VARCHAR**
Not supported	**VALUE**	none

Web Sites And Support Resources For Access, VBA, And Office 2000

This appendix provides you with a variety of resources to supplement the knowledge you've acquired from this book. Refer to it when you need additional information and/or guidance, or when you simply have something you believe is worth sharing with the Access programming community.

Access Developer Web Sites

www.microsoft.com/Accessdev/

www.access-developer.com

members.xoom.com/AccessFreak/

VBA Developer Web Sites

msdn.microsoft.com/vbasic/

www.pinpub.com/vbd/

www.summsoft.com/vba/

Office 2000 Developer Web Sites

www.microsoft.com/officedev/ode/ode2k.htm

Access Developer Magazines

www.informant.com/icgmags.asp

www.informant.com/mod/

www.advisor.com/wHome.nsf/wPages/AVmain/

www.zdjournals.com/ima/index.htm

Access User Groups

www.yahoo.com/computers_and_Internet/Software/Databases/Access/User_Groups/

Access And VBA Third-Party Products

www.fmsinc.com/products/index3.html

www.wdn.com/ems/access.htm

Access Training Programs

www.takethelead.fullerton.edu/CertProg/MicroAcc.htm

it-training.ucdavis.edu/references/access.html

Access Newsgroups

microsoft.public.access.gettingstarted

microsoft.public.access.tablesdbdesign

microsoft.public.access.queries

microsoft.public.access.forms

microsoft.public.access.formscoding

microsoft.public.access.reports

microsoft.public.access.macros

microsoft.public.access.modulesdaovba

microsoft.public.access.commandbarsui

microsoft.public.access.odbcclientsvr

microsoft.public.access.externaldata

microsoft.public.access.interopoledde

microsoft.public.access.multiuser

microsoft.public.access.replication

microsoft.public.access.security

microsoft.public.access.setupconfig

microsoft.public.access.conversion

microsoft.public.access.activexcontrol

microsoft.public.access.devtoolkits

microsoft.public.access.3rdpartyusrgrp

VBA Newsgroups

microsoft.public.access.devtoolkits

microsoft.public.access.formscoding

microsoft.public.access.macros

microsoft.public.access.queries

microsoft.public.officedev

microsoft.public.vb.ole.automation

microsoft.public.vb.database.dao

microsoft.public.vb.database.odbc

microsoft.public.vb.database.rdo

microsoft.public.word.word97vba

Index

X

Z

What's On The CD-ROM

The *Access 2000 Client/Server Solutions* companion CD-ROM contains elements specifically selected to enhance the usefulness of this book, including:

♦ *Access-native databases*—Databases designed using the Access 2000 product's native Jet engine.

♦ *SQL Server-compliant databases*—Databases designed using new features in Access 2000 to include complete support for SQL Server 7 constructions, including detailed instructions on how to attach prebuilt SQL Server databases to your system.

♦ *Source code*—Ready-to-run versions of all the code and databases contained in the book.

♦ *Ready-to-run script files*—SQL Server script (.sql) files that you can use to create your own copies of the databases contained in the book, including detailed explanations of how the various scripting components work to yield the resulting database design.

♦ *Web development examples*—Sample programs taking advantage of Web technologies such as Dynamic HTML, Active Server Pages, and Visual Basic Active Documents, heavily commented, and not reprinted in the book.

♦ *Installation program*—A complete installation program to place the files on the CD-ROM onto your hard drive, ready for you to use and modify for your own implementations.

♦ *Database modeling and design demos*—Several demo versions of popular tools for database design and modeling, with complete installation and use instructions.

♦ *Knowledge management, OLAP, and data mining/display demos*—Several demo versions of data mining and management tools, ready for installation and use.

System Requirements

Software

♦ Your operating system must be Windows 95, 98, NT 4, or 2000.

♦ Access 2000 and Internet Explorer 5 are required to complete the programs in this book. In addition, you may require the Office 2000 Premium Edition, a network installation of SQL Server 7, and/or a network installation of Oracle8 to complete some of the examples in the book. (The software is not provided on this CD-ROM.)

♦ Additionally, for projects in later sections of the book, Visual Basic 6, Visual InterDev 6, or both may be needed. (The software is not provided on this CD-ROM.)

Hardware

♦ An Intel (or equivalent) Pentium 100MHz processor is the minimum platform required; an Intel (or equivalent) Pentium II 200MHz processor is recommended.

♦ 32MB of RAM is the minimum requirement, though 64MB is recommended.

♦ Office 2000 requires approximately 200MB of disk storage space for a full install, and the databases and supporting code on the CD-ROM require approximately 40MB of disk storage space. Visual Basic or other Visual Studio components, SQL Server, Personal Web Services (PWS) or Internet Information Server (IIS), and Oracle may require as much as 1.2GB or more of disk storage space for a full install.